P9-CFB-422

GUIDE TO THE National Parks OF THE United States

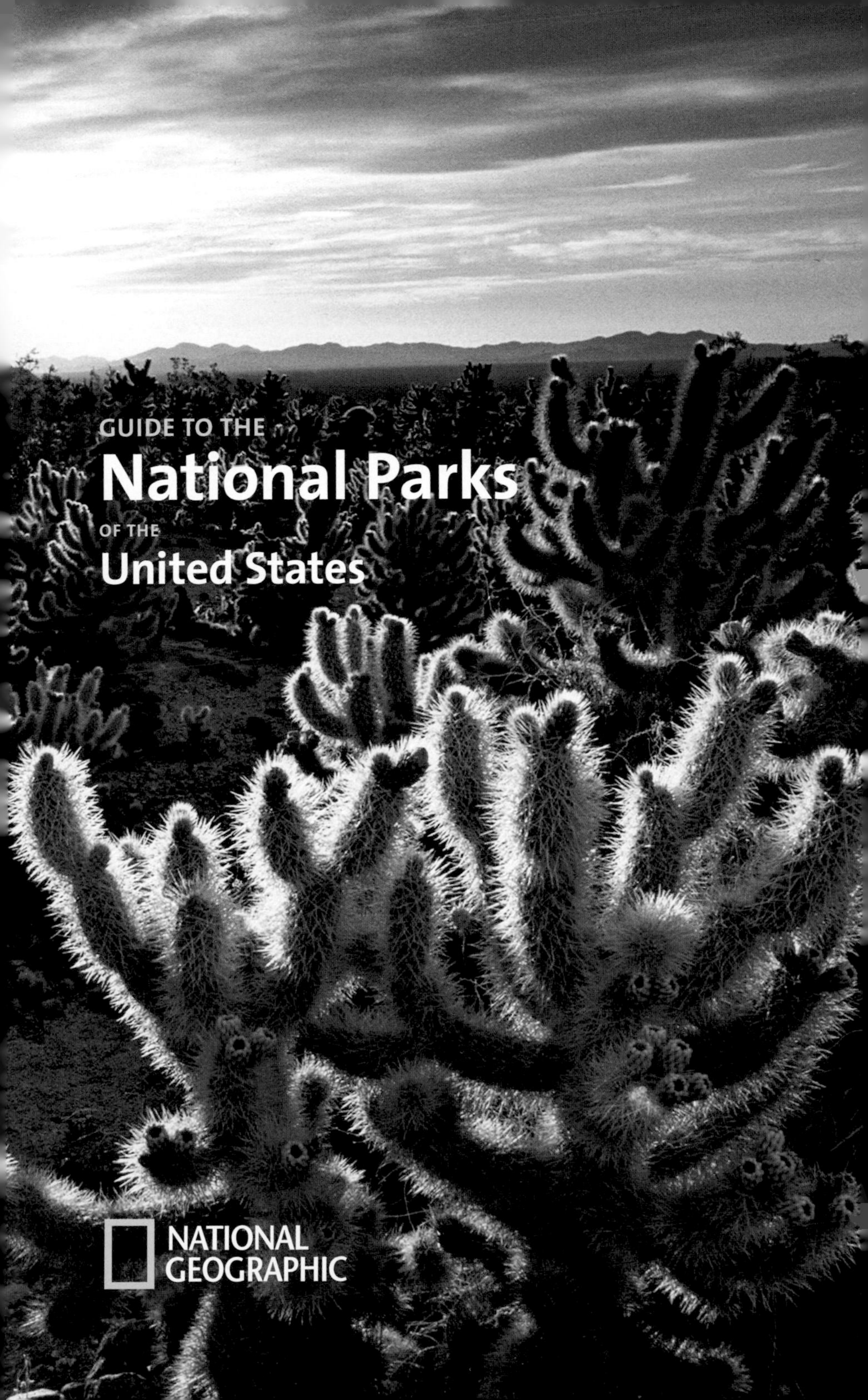
GUIDE TO THE
National Parks
OF THE
United States
NATIONAL
GEOGRAPHIC

CONTENTS

Cover: Colorado River, Grand Canyon NP
pp. 2-3: Jumping chollas, Joshua Tree NP
Opposite: Merced River, Yosemite NP

Sunset over Pine Glades Lake, Everglades NP

THE GIFT OF THE PARKS

One of the things that distinguishes this guidebook is its conscience—its attention to the welfare of the parks it describes. As you read, you will find the travel information interspersed with news of some threat to a park, or the history of a threat that lost out. National parks have been battlegrounds of the conservation movement, and the battles continue.

But even the battles can offer inspiration and instruction, and both the parks and the ideals by which we manage them evolve continually. Indeed, it has been said that the establishment of a park is only the beginning; that if we do it right, we never stop establishing that park, because we never stop learning about it, and about ourselves.

There was a time when Congress set up national parks to protect a few specific things: the wildlife here, the geysers there, the scenery over there. Other parts of the park got less attention, or were even mistreated. Well into the 1930s managers killed predators in some parks to protect the "good" animals. In the early days of Yosemite National Park, woodpeckers were shot if their tapping disturbed the sleep of hotel guests. Yellowstone allowed com-

mercial fishing until well after 1900.

Only as the science of ecology matured, and we began to realize that everything in the park was interrelated, did our view change. Slowly, we realized that what we had was not best measured in acres of meadow and that a park is not a zoo.

Instead, we seek to save the whole thing, the whole creeping, flying, grazing, preying, photosynthesizing, eroding, raining, erupting, evolving scene. Call it wildness, or naturalness, or an ecosystem, or whatever you like, it is this entangled collection of processes that we must save.

That means many things, some of which haven't been easy to hear. It means that people like me, who love to fish, have to leave enough trout in the streams to feed the otters, pelicans, bears, and other wild fishermen. It means we don't pick flowers, or collect rocks, removing them from their place in the natural system. It means we stop feeding wildlife, and let the animals find their own way, in balance with their environment.

In short, it means a revolution in the way we appreciate nature. We as a nation have decided that here, in these precious, rare places, we shall give nature a little more room to make its choices. If that means we must be prepared to watch a bear half a mile away through binoculars rather than watch it eating aluminum foil right outside the car window, so be it; everybody knew all along which was best for the bear. If that means we must respect the role naturally caused fire has played in regenerating forests for thousands of years, so be it.

Anyone who reads the papers knows that this doesn't always work smoothly. Nature isn't much for respecting our rules. Bears have a way of reminding us we're not always in charge. And, as Yellowstone showed us in 1988, fires can get a lot bigger than anybody expected. Nobody said this was going to be easy. But the more we try, the more we learn.

And so these great parks, which enchant us with their beauty and restore us with their peace, have yet another gift to give. They are laboratories of ideas, offering profound lessons in the natural way of things, and in what that way can mean to the human soul. The lessons don't always come easily, but they're always worth the trip.

Paul Schullery
Yellowstone National Park

Mother and cub, Denali NP

USING THE GUIDE

Each of the 58 scenic parks offers you fun, adventure, and—usually—enthralling splendor. What you experience will depend on where you go and what you do. But exploring an unknown land is best done with a guide, a companion who has tested the trail and learned the lore.

Our coverage of each park begins with a portrait of its natural wonders, ecological setting, history, and, often, its struggles against man and alien species. You'll see why a single step off a trail can harm fragile plants, and why visitors are detoured from certain areas that shelter wildlife. The parks are not just for people; they conserve ecosystems. Thirteen parks have been designated United Nations World Heritage sites for their outstanding scenic and cultural wonders; 22 have international biosphere reserve status, signaling the distinctive natural qualities.

Before starting off on your park exploration, use this *Guide* to preview the parks you may want to visit. You'll notice that each park introduction is followed by the following three how-and-when sections:

How to Get There

You may be able to include more than one park in your trip. The regional chapter maps show the connecting highways. Base your itinerary not so much on mileage as on time, remembering that parks do not lie alongside interstates; park roads are usually rugged—and, in summer, crowded.

When to Go

Instead of going to a popular park in midsummer, avoid peak crowds by scheduling the trip for June or late August and timing your arrival early on a weekday. In many parks, fall is glorious, and autumn vistas coincide with a relative scarcity of visitors. Spring brings wildflowers to many parks and with winter comes snow-swept beauty, summoning cross-country skiers, snowshoe hikers, and ice skaters. Although parks are generally open year-round, off-season visitor facilities may be limited. Consult this heading for each park.

How to Visit

Don't rush through a park. Give yourself time to savor the beauty. Incredibly, the average time the typical visitor spends in a park is half a day. Often, that blur of time flashes past a windshield. No matter how long you decide to stay, spend at least part of that time in the park, not your car. Each park's **How to Visit** section recommends a plan for visits of one-half, one, two, or more days. *Guide* writers devised the plans and trekked every tour, but don't be afraid to explore on your own. And don't neglect the **Excursions** at the end of many park entries; they take you to other natural areas nearby.

Other features of the *Guide:*

Maps

The park maps and regional maps were prepared as an aid in planning your trip. For more detail on trails and other facilities inside a park, contact the Park Service, call the park, or visit www.nps.gov. Always use a road map when traveling.

The maps note specially designated areas within park borders: *Wilderness Areas* are managed to retain their primeval quality. Roads, buildings, and vehicles are not allowed in them. *National Preserves* may allow hunting. For a list of abbreviations see p. 479.

Information & Activities

This section, which follows each park entry, offers detailed visitor information. Call or write the park, or visit the park's website (www.nps.gov) for further details. Brochures are usually available free of charge from the parks. For a small fee you can buy a copy of the "National Park System Map and Guide" by contacting Consumer Information Center at 888-8783256 or by visiting www.pueblo.gsa.gov

Entrance Fees. The entrance fees listed in this book reflect fees at press time. In addition to daily or weekly fees, most parks also offer a yearly fee, with unlimited entries.

For $50 you can buy a National Parks Pass, which is good for a year and admits all occupants of a private vehicle to all national parks. The pass does not cover parking fees where applicable. For an additional $15 you can purchase a Golden Eagle sticker to affix to the pass for unlimited admission to U.S. Fish and Wildlife Service, U.S. Forest Service, and Bureau of Land Management sites.

People over 62 can obtain a lifetime Golden Age Passport for $10, and blind and disabled people are entitled to a lifetime Golden Access Passport for free, both of which admit all occupants of a private vehicle to all national parks and other federal sites and a discount on usage fees. These are available from any federal area that charges entrance fees.

For further information on buying park passes, call (888) 467-2757 or visit www.national parks.org.

Pets. Generally they're not allowed on trails, in buildings, or in the backcountry. Elsewhere, they must be leashed. Specific rules are noted.

Facilities for Disabled. This section of the *Guide* explains which parts of each park, including visitor centers and trails, are accessible to visitors with disabilities.

Special Advisories. • Do not take chances. People are killed or badly injured every year in thel parks. Most casualties are caused by recklessness or failure to heed warnings.
• Stay away from wild animals. Do not feed them or try to touch them — not even raccoons or chipmunks (which can transmit diseases). Try not to surprise a bear and do not let one approach. If one does, scare it off by yelling, clapping your hands, or banging pots. Store all your food in bear-proof containers (often available

at parks); keep food out of sight in your vehicle, with windows closed and doors locked. Or suspend it at least 15 feet above ground, and 10 feet out from a post or tree trunk.

• Guard your health. If you are not fit, don't overtax yourself. Boil water that doesn't come from a park's drinking-water tap. Chemical treatment of water will not kill *Giardia,* a protozoan that causes severe diarrhea; it lurks even in crystal clear streams. Heed park warnings about hypothermia and Lyme disease. In western parks, take precautions to prevent Hantavirus pulmonary syndrome, a potentially fatal airborne virus transmitted by deer mice.

• Expect RV detours. Check road regulations as you enter a park. Along some stretches of road you will not be able to maneuver large vehicles.

Campgrounds. The National Parks Reservation System (NPRS)(800-365-2267 or http://reservations.nps.gov) handles reservations for camp-

grounds at the following parks: Acadia, Channel Islands, Death Valley, Everglades, Grand Canyon, Great Smoky Mountains, Joshua Tree, Katmai, Mammoth Cave, Mount Rainier, Rocky Mountain, Olympic, Sequoia & Kings Canyon, Shenandoah, Waterton-Glacier, and Zion. Check early for the reservation schedules.

The National Recreation Reservation Service (www.reserveUSA) accepts reservations for Arches, Big Bend, Black Canyon of the Gunnison, Bryce, Lassen, North and Cascades.

Hotels, Motels, & Inns. The *Guide* lists accommodations as a service to its readers. The lists are by no means comprehensive, and listing does not imply endorsement by the National Geographic Society. The information can change without notice. Many parks keep lists of lodgings in their areas, which they will provide on request. You can also contact local chambers of commerce and tourist offices for suggestions.

1 EPC

THE EAST

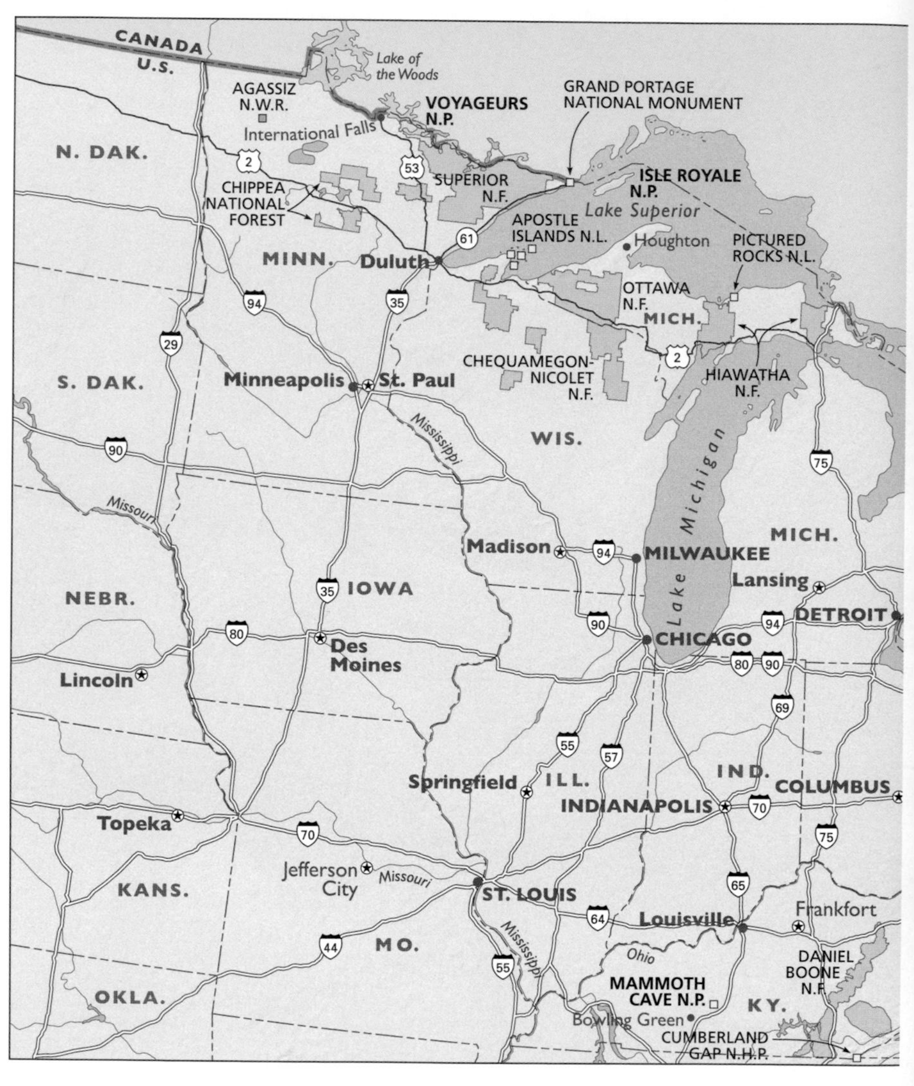

THE EAST

Not until well into the 20th century, long after the idea of preserving the West's grand vistas had taken hold, did park planners turn their attention to the more subtle beauties of eastern scenery. The threats to nature from expanding cities and, after World War I, the surge in automobile travel and highway building boosted the movement to create eastern parks. Between 1919 and 1926, Congress authorized the

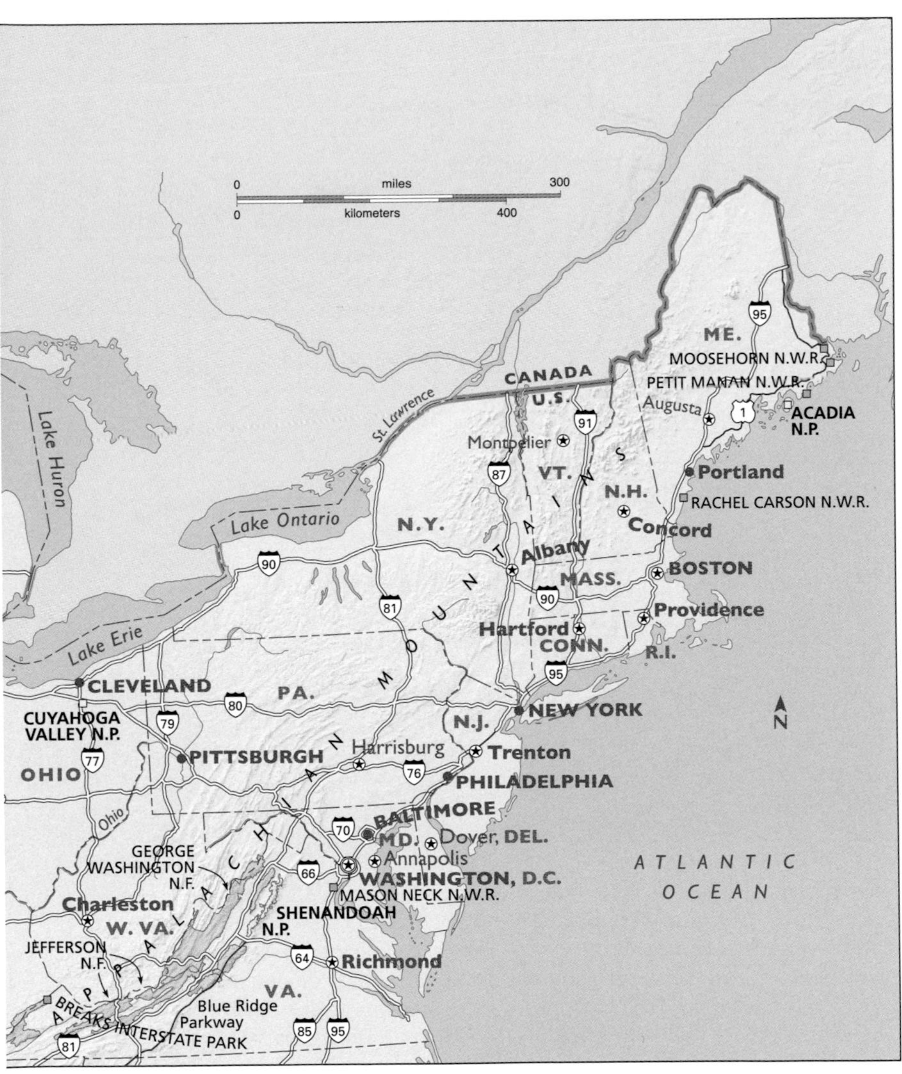

first three in the crumpled belt of the Appalachian Mountains. Today these parks—Acadia, Great Smoky Mountains, and Shenandoah—rank among the most visited in the nation.

Acadia protects the plants and animals that inhabit the mountains, islands, sea, and tide pools along a stretch of wild New England coast. The hardwood forests and flowering meadows of Shenandoah, on land

Americans' love for the automobile led to the demand for highways to drive and helped spur the creation of national parks in the East. In 1935 the Blue Ridge Parkway was begun as a public works project. It became part of the Park Service the following year. The parkway receiving the most recreational use, the Blue Ridge links Shenandoah's Skyline Drive to Great Smoky Mountains National Park. Together, the drives create a spectacular 574-mile stretch of ridgetop road punctuated by wayside exhibits and trails.

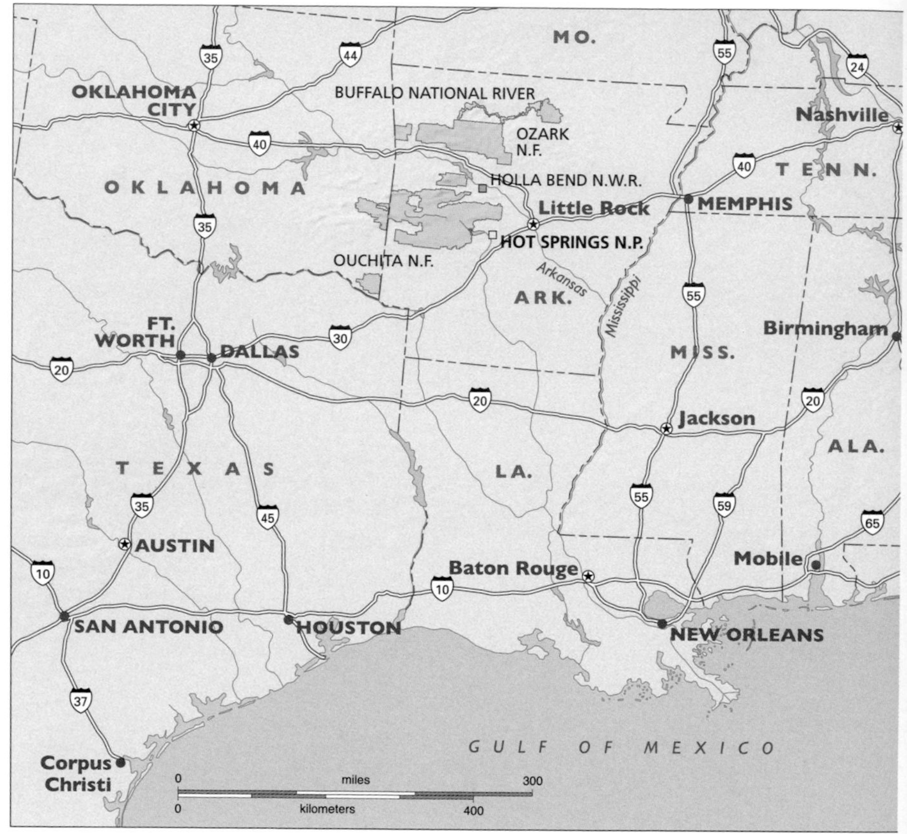

that had been logged, farmed, and grazed for 250 years, are studies in nature's power of recuperation. Great Smoky preserves large stands of virgin forest on 6,000-foot slopes and shelters more than a hundred species of trees.

Since the 1920s, Congress has moved to safeguard other distinctive eastern biomes. Inside Mammoth Cave lies the world's longest known cave network, with more than 350 miles of mapped passages. Isle Royale on the U.S.-Canada border encompasses an entire island ecosystem. In and around its lakes, thick forest, and fjordlike coast live wolves and moose, their prey.

Not far away, scores of lakes and streams lace the forests of Voyageurs National Park, named for the French-Canadian fur traders who for 100 years paddled these waters.

Other kinds of waters inspired the creation of diminutive Hot Springs National Park. Most of the 47 hot springs lead into the plumbing of this former resort town's bathhouses.

Underwater wilderness awaits visitors to Florida's Biscayne National Park, home of the northernmost living coral reef in the continental United States. West of Biscayne lies Everglades National Park, established in 1947 less to preserve scenery than to safeguard the unique ecosystem created by a slow-moving river, inches deep and some 50 miles wide. Itself

In the 1960s the National Park Service set a goal to create a park as a "vignette of primitive America" in every major natural community in the country. The newer parks of the East—Cuyahoga Valley, Biscayne, Voyageurs, Congaree, and Dry Tortugas—have expanded the diversity of the region's parks.

endangered by the diversion of water to the towns and agribusinesses of South Florida, Everglades provides habitat for an enormous variety of wildlife.

About 70 miles west of Key West, on a 7-mile-long archipelago rich with birds and marine creatures, Dry Tortugas National Park maintains an abandoned 19th-century brick fortress, the largest from that century in America. And far to the southeast, Virgin Islands National Park protects much of St. John, where hillsides thick with bay, mango, and trumpet trees slope to crescent beaches rimmed by coral reefs.

Otter Cliff, one of the highest coastal headlands north of Rio de Janiero

ACADIA

MAINE

ESTABLISHED FEBRUARY 26, 1919

47,633 acres

Sea and mountain meet at Acadia, where, as one presumably ambidextrous visitor wrote, "you can fish with one hand and sample blueberries from a wind-stunted bush with the other." Most of the park is on Mount Desert Island, a patchwork of parkland, private property, and seaside villages that seasonally fill with what residents call "the summer people." Other bits are scattered on smaller islands and a peninsula.

Mount Desert Island once was continental mainland, a mountainous granite ridge on the edge of the ocean. Some 20,000 years ago, towering glacial ice sheets—sometimes a mile thick—flowed over the mountains, rounding their tops, cutting passes, gouging out lake beds, and widening valleys. As the glaciers melted, the sea rose, flooding valleys and drowning the coast. The pre-glacier ridge was transformed into today's lake-studded, mountainous island, which thrusts from the Atlantic like a lobster's claw.

Samuel de Champlain, who explored the coast in 1604, named the island L'Isle des Monts Déserts, sometimes translated as "the island of barren mountains." From his ship he probably could not see the mountains' forested slopes. The summer people rediscovered Mount Desert in the mid-19th century, built mansions they called "cottages," anchored their yachts in rock-girt harbors, and cherished the wild. To preserve it, they donated the nucleus land for the park, the first east of the Mississippi. The original name, Lafayette National Park, was changed in 1929.

Dependent on donated land since its inception, the park took what it could get, skirting around private property and growing piece by piece. Acadia's real estate was so patchy that not until 1986 did Congress set its official boundaries.

One of the smaller national parks, Acadia is one of the most visited—by almost two and one-half million people a year. Heavy traffic can produce a phenomenon unknown to Mount Desert's first summer people: gridlock. The Island Explorer shuttle bus has helped alleviate the problem.

How to Get There

From Ellsworth, 28 miles southeast of Bangor, follow Me. 3 south for 18 miles to Mount Desert Island, where most of the park is located; the visitor center is 3 miles north of Bar Harbor. Another section lies southeast of Ellsworth, on the Schoodic Peninsula, a 1-hour drive from Bar Harbor. To get to the park's islands, see **The Islands** p. 24. Airports: Bangor and Bar Harbor.

When to Go

Year-round, but main visitor center is open from mid-April through October. Expect heavy traffic in July and August. Spectacular foliage also attracts crowds around the end of September. Snow and ice close most park roads from December through April, but parts of the park are open for cross-country skiing.

How to Visit

Allow at least a day for **Mount Desert Island,** with a drive on the 20-mile **Park Loop Road** and the road to the summit of **Cadillac Mountain.** If fog comes, enjoy its gift: a softening of sights and sounds. On a second day, enjoy an uncrowded view of the rocky coast of Maine by visiting the **Schoodic Peninsula.** If you have more time, take your pick of one of the trails or smaller islands.

MOUNT DESERT ISLAND

60 miles; at least a full day

To get the most from a tour of Mount Desert Island on the Park Loop Road in summer, get up very early. (On clear days, traffic is heaviest between 10 a.m. and 3 p.m.) The day before, check the time of sunrise in a local newspaper or at the visitor center. About 30 minutes before dawn, take coffee and a blanket and drive from the visitor center to 1,530-foot **Cadillac Mountain.** The 3.5-mile mountain road switchbacks up to a parking area.

From there walk to the **Summit Trail,** find an east-facing niche in the rocks, and settle in on the highest east coast mountain north of Brazil. Here is one of the places where dawn first touches the continental United States. After enjoying the sunrise, hunt for blueberries along the trails radiating from the summit. The blueberry season runs from late July through August.

On the way down, stop at one of the eastern overlooks for a view of **Frenchman Bay,** a vast, island-dotted seascape; its name takes note of the role of the French in the area's history. (Another way to see the bay is on a 2-hour sea cruise; check schedules at the Municipal Pier in Bar Harbor or in the park's publication, "Beaver Log.")

Return to the loop road and turn right. Less than a half mile farther, bear right again (here the road becomes one-way), and continue south

Bass Harbor Head lighthouse at dusk

toward the ocean. Two worthwhile stops you'll soon approach are the **Sieur de Monts Spring Nature Center** (June–Oct.) and the **Wild Gardens of Acadia,** both of which showcase the habitats of Mount Desert Island.

Farther along the road, pass up **Sand Beach** for now. You may want to return to the beach later for sunbathing or a very brisk swim (the summer water temperature remains between 50°F and 55°F).

Not quite a mile farther, a sign marks **Thunder Hole.** Park on the right and walk down the concrete steps to the cleft in the rocks, named for the roars produced when air, trapped and squeezed by incoming surf, explodes out of a cavern. A stop here may disappoint you, for you'll probably hear the thunder only at half tide with a rising sea, or during a storm. Other times, you may hear only gurgles and sloshes.

Continue to the 110-foot **Otter Cliff.** Park, cross the road, and walk the shore path to **Otter Point.** Numerous brightly colored lobster buoys bob offshore. Linger here to savor the essence of the Maine coast: rocks, gulls, the tang of salt air. At **Hunters Head** the loop road turns away from the sea and soon becomes two-way as you head back to where you started. You'll pass **Jordan Pond,** one of many glacier-carved ponds on the island.

Your drive has taken you around the eastern side of the island. To explore the western side, you must drive out of park property and back in again. Continue north on the loop road, cross the bridge, and bear right to get on Me. 233. Head west to Me. 198, then head south on Me. 102 toward Southwest Harbor. Continue south. On your left, though obscured, is **Somes Sound,** the only fjord on the U.S. Atlantic coast. On your right is **Echo Lake,** a swimming spot with a small beach.

Me. 102 passes through Southwest Harbor. Beyond, near Manset, bear left on Me. 102A, which leads into a large patch of park property. You can picnic at **Seawall,** then stretch your legs on the nearby 1.25-mile **Ship Harbor Nature Trail,** which gives a lesson in how a forest shore is knit to the tidal sea.

A short detour off Me. 102A takes you to **Bass Harbor Head,** site of a 19th-century lighthouse. Take Me. 102A through **Bass Harbor** and bear left on Me. 102 toward Tremont. Continue north for 7 miles to a tract of park called **Pretty Marsh,** a beautiful picnic spot. A short, worn path leads to the rock-strewn shore. Continue on Me. 102 and retrace your route from Somesville to the visitor center.

CARRIAGE ROADS & HIKES

In 1917 John D. Rockefeller, Jr., a summer resident of Mount Desert Island, launched the building of a 57-mile network of broken stone roads for horse-drawn carriages. Convinced that the newfangled automobile would destroy the tranquillity of the island, he banned it from the carriage roads. The roads were graced by 17 hand-built granite bridges, each a unique work of art. Rockefeller later donated most of the road network, along with 11,000 acres of his land, to the park. The carriage roads, still not open to cars, are a treasure prized by hikers,

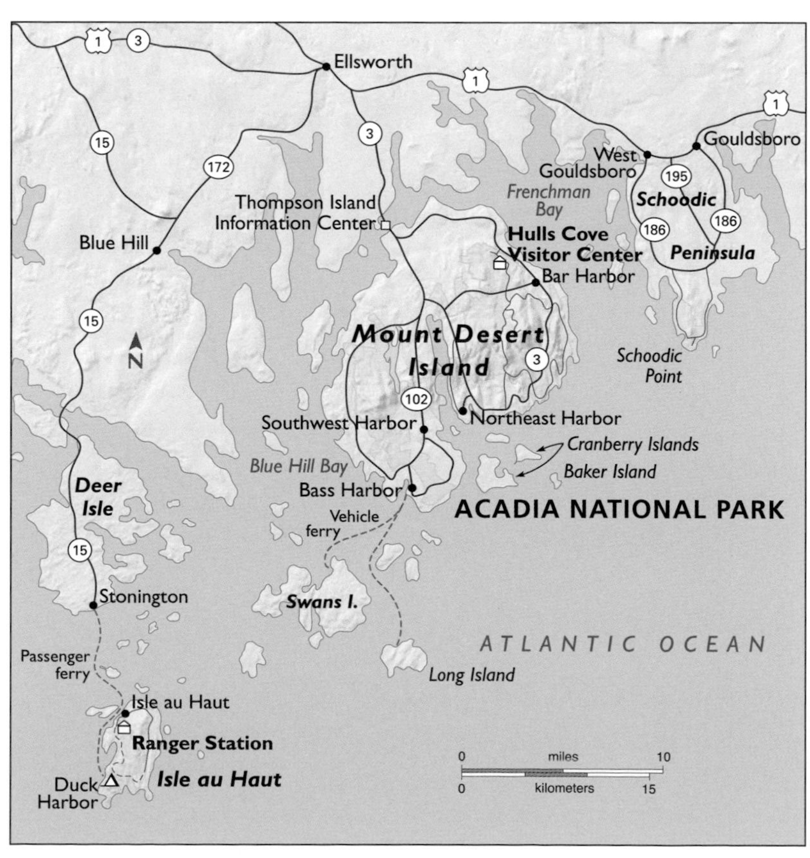

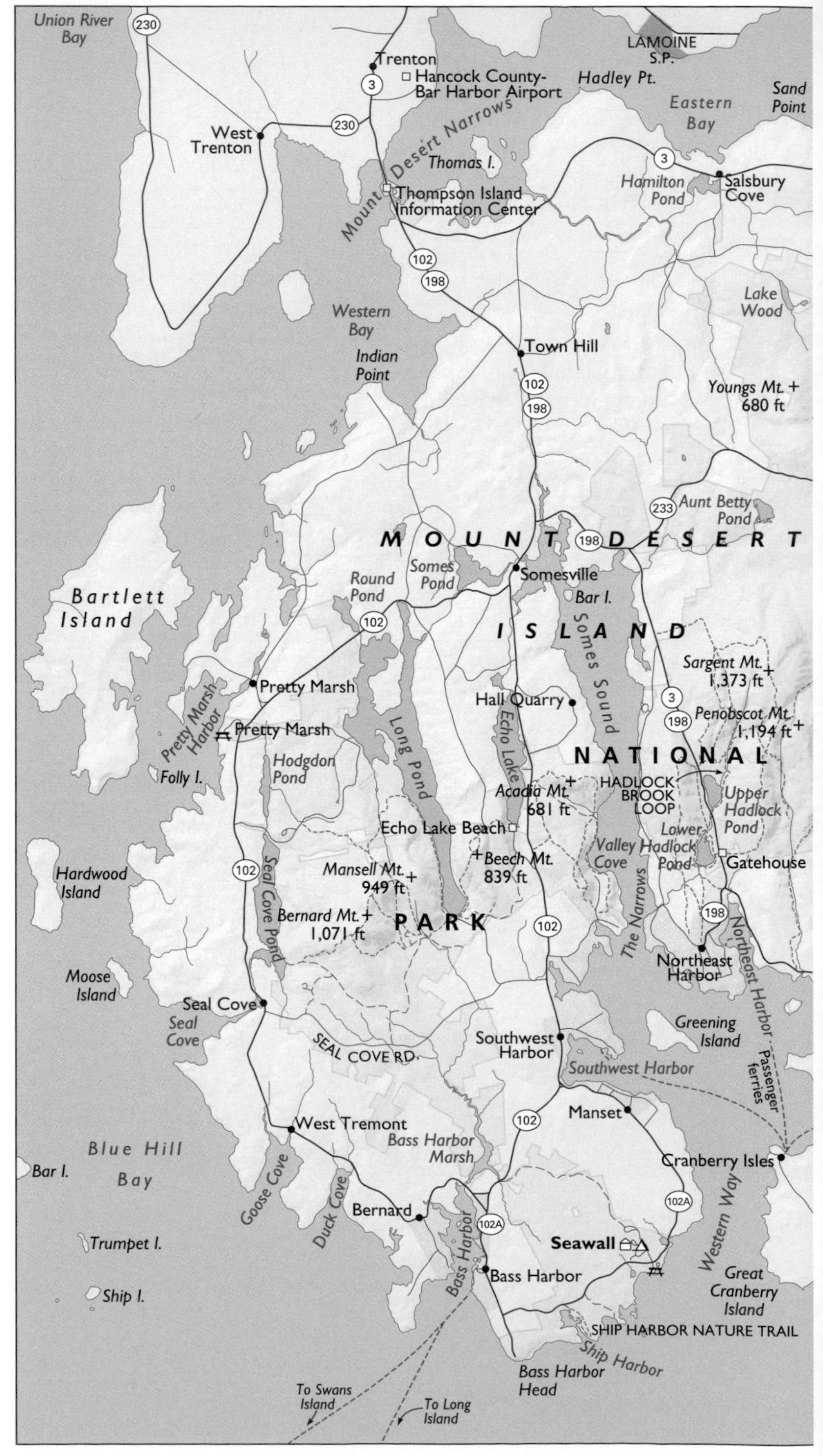

Union River Bay
Trenton
Hancock County-Bar Harbor Airport
LAMOINE S.P.
Hadley Pt.
Eastern Bay
Sand Point
West Trenton
Mount Desert Narrows
Thomas I.
Hamilton Pond
Salsbury Cove
Thompson Island Information Center
Western Bay
Lake Wood
Town Hill
Indian Point
Youngs Mt. 680 ft
Aunt Betty Pond
MOUNT DESERT ISLAND
Somes Pond
Somesville
Round Pond
Bar I.
Bartlett Island
Somes Sound
Sargent Mt. 1,373 ft
Pretty Marsh
Hall Quarry
Pretty Marsh Harbor
Penobscot Mt. 1,194 ft
Long Pond
Echo Lake
ACADIA NATIONAL PARK
Hodgdon Pond
Folly I.
Acadia Mt. 681 ft
HADLOCK BROOK LOOP
Upper Hadlock Pond
Echo Lake Beach
Lower Hadlock Pond
Valley Cove
Gatehouse
Hardwood Island
Seal Cove Pond
Mansell Mt. 949 ft
Beech Mt. 839 ft
Bernard Mt. 1,071 ft
The Narrows
Northeast Harbor
Moose Island
Seal Cove
Greening Island
Southwest Harbor
SEAL COVE RD.
Passenger ferries
Manset
West Tremont
Bass Harbor Marsh
Blue Hill Bay
Bar I.
Cranberry Isles
Goose Cove
Duck Cove
Bernard
Western Way
Seawall
Trumpet I.
Bass Harbor
Great Cranberry Island
Ship I.
SHIP HARBOR NATURE TRAIL
Ship Harbor
Bass Harbor Head
To Swans Island
To Long Island

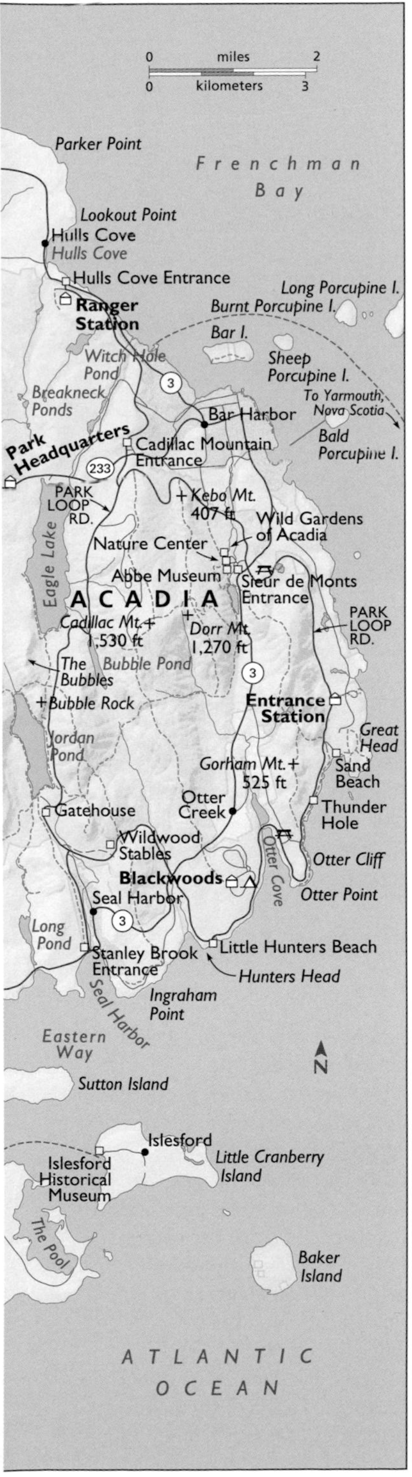

bikers, horseback riders, cross-country skiers, and anyone seeking a respite from the incessant hum of the internal combustion engine.

To introduce yourself to the carriage roads, try the 4-mile **Hadlock Brook Loop.** Park at the Me. 198 (Parkman Mountain) parking area just north of **Upper Hadlock Pond** and walk to the trailhead. Take the left fork east toward **Hemlock Bridge,** a gem of hand-hewn stone. Follow the rising road to another handsome span, **Waterfall Bridge,** site of a 40-foot cascade. (You can turn around here, cutting your hike to about 2 miles round-trip.) Cross the bridge and walk south for a mile to one of the network's well-marked intersections. Turn right at intersection 19 and right again at intersection 18 and continue along the pond. Watch for loons—and listen for their haunting call. The road crosses **Hadlock Brook Bridge** and loops back to the trailhead.

The park has more than 120 miles of hiking trails, which range from easy strolls along the ocean or around ponds to steep climbs up Cadillac and other mountains. For a jaunt into history try the **Gorge Path,** which, like several other trails, has stone steps to ease your way up slopes. The steps, flat stones imbedded in rising ground, were built by turn-of-the-20th-century summer people who wanted to rough it, but not too much. The path begins at a parking spot on the Park Loop Road, near 407-foot **Kebo Mountain,** and leads to a wooded trail. Cairns mark the trail when it follows a rocky, brook-washed ravine. About a mile into the woods is an intersection. Depending upon your time and stamina, you can turn and retrace your steps or push on to Cadillac or **Dorr Mountain,** each a steep hike of more than 1.5 miles.

Morning fog over rowboats and fishing boats in Seal Harbor

SCHOODIC PENINSULA

100 miles; a half day

The 45-mile drive around Frenchman Bay to the park's only mainland portion, the Schoodic Peninsula, provides several scenic views of Mount Desert Island. Starting from Bar Harbor, take Me. 3 to US 1, south of Ellsworth, and head east to West Gouldsboro. Go south via Me. 186 to Winter Harbor, then follow signs to the park entrance. From there, drive or bike the 6-mile one-way road to **Schoodic Point.** The massive granite rocks here are laced by black diabase dikes, the product of magma that welled up into cracks. Schoodic's displays of thundering surf usually top those of Mount Desert Island. And the audiences are much smaller; the peninsula does not draw crowds the way Mount Desert does.

A trail system explores the western section of the point, running through wetland and forest with spurs to the ocean. The longest is the **Anvil Trail,** which begins at the Blueberry Hill parking lot and climbs about 440 feet for views of Little Moose Island and Frenchman Bay. In this wilderness, keep a lookout for moose, white-tailed deer, rabbits, porcupines, and raccoons.

THE ISLANDS

a full day each

Fragments of Acadia are on islands. Two worth visiting are Isle au Haut, about half of which is park property, and Little Cranberry Island, home to the Islesford Historical Museum. Both islands are served all year by mail boats and by seasonal tour boats. Get boat schedules from the visitor center or from the boat operators.

The trip to **Isle au Haut,** or "high island," named by Samuel de Champlain, begins at Stonington, at the tip of Deer Isle, about 40 miles from Ellsworth. To make the boat on time from Mount Desert Island, allot at least 2 hours for the drive and for finding a rare legal parking place near the harbor. Bring lunch. The mail boat takes passengers on a first-come, first-served basis. The 45-minute voyage ends at the Town Landing. In summer, the boat also stops at **Duck Harbor,** a park campsite and trailhead.

For a fine hike, get off at the Town Landing and turn right. A short distance down the road is a ranger station. Here begins the 4-mile **Duck Harbor Trail,** which takes you through upland forest, along the shore, and past blueberry brambles (picking and eating allowed) to Duck Harbor. Spend the day here wandering the area's trails, enjoying woods-and-water scenery, and watching for ospreys and bald eagles. Catch the late afternoon boat back.

The 2.5-mile boat ride from Northeast Harbor to **Little Cranberry Island** takes about 20 minutes in good weather; you can also catch a boat at Southwest Harbor, on the opposite side of Somes Sound.

The tiny island, with rocky shores, spruce trees, and quiet country lanes, boasts 70 year-round residents, many of whom can trace their ancestry back to the 18th century. As your boat nears the picturesque village of **Islesford,** winding among bobbing lobster boats in the protected harbor, you'll spot two buildings of note: the gabled, wooden **Blue Duck Ships's Store** and, directly behind, the **Islesford Historical Museum,** housed in a brick Georgian Revival building. Both structures are part of Acadia National Park. They contain turn-of-the-20th-century ship models, navigation aids, dolls and toys, photographs, tools, and other relics that tell the story of the Cranberry Isles—a cluster of five islands—and their seafaring people.

Another option for getting out on the water is to take an **Islesford Historical Cruise** (207-276-5352. Fare, reservations required), a ranger-led boat tour focusing on island history and making stops at Sutton Island and Little Cranberry Island. Meet at the municipal pier in Northeast Harbor.

View of the Porcupines in Frenchman Bay, from Cadillac Mountain

INFORMATION & ACTIVITIES

HEADQUARTERS
P.O. Box 177, Bar Harbor, ME 04609.
Phone (207) 288-3338.
www.nps.gov/acad

SEASONS & ACCESSIBILITY
Open all year. In winter visitor facilities close and much of the Park Loop Road is unplowed. For recorded weather information call (207) 667-8910. For boats to Isle au Haut call (207) 367-5193; for mail boat ferry call (207) 244-3576.

VISITOR & INFORMATION CENTERS
Visitor center on Me. 3 just south of Hulls Cove, open daily mid-April through October. **Thompson Island Information Center** on Me. 3, just before crossing onto Mount Desert Island. Open May to mid-Sept. Off season, information at **headquarters** 2.5 miles west of Bar Harbor on Me. 233.

ENTRANCE FEE
June 23–Oct. 12: $20 per vehicle for 7-day pass; May–mid-June & mid-Oct.–late Oct., $10 per vehicle for 7-day pass.

PETS
Permitted on leashes except on swimming beaches, in public buildings, on a few hiking trails, and at Isle au Haut campsite.

FACILITIES FOR DISABLED
Visitor center, some restrooms, and carriage roads are wheelchair accessible. Wildwood Stables has two carriages designed to hold wheelchairs. Free guidebook available.

THINGS TO DO
Free ranger-led activities: nature walks, photography workshops, stargazing, films, slide shows. Also available, bus tours—call (207) 288-3327 for National Park tours or (207) 288-9899 for Oli's Trolley—bay and island cruises, carriage rides, auto tape tour, hiking, bicycling, swimming, fishing, cross-country skiing, snowshoeing, ice-skating and ice fishing, and snowmobiling.

SPECIAL ADVISORIES
- Be careful on ledges and rocks along shore; algae are slippery.
- In spring and fall, watch out for strong storm waves.

OVERNIGHT BACKPACKING
Not allowed.

CAMPGROUNDS
Blackwoods open all year; reserve through NPRS (see p. 10)—required May–Oct.; other times first come, first served. Fee $20 per night. **Seawall** open late May–Sept.; first come, first served. Fees $14–$20 per night. Showers outside park. Tent and RV sites; no hookups. **Duck Harbor** on Isle au Haut open mid-May–mid-Oct.; reservations required (207) 288-3338. Fee $25 per night.

HOTELS, MOTELS, & INNS
(unless otherwise noted, rates are for 2 persons in a double room, high season)

In Bar Harbor, ME 04609:
Bar Harbor Inn Newport Dr. (800) 248-3351 or (207) 288-3351. 153 units. $199-$369. Pool, rest.
Bayview 111 Eden St. (800) 356-3585 or (207) 288-5861. 33 units. $145-$460. Pool. Mid-May to mid-Oct.
Cleftstone Manor 92 Eden St. (207) 288-4951. 17 units. $100-$225. Mid-April–late Oct.
Cromwell Harbor Motel 359 Main St. (207) 288-3201. 26 units. $95-$150.
Wonder View Inn & Suites 50 Eden St. (888) 439-8439 or (207) 288-3358. 79 units. $139-$199. Pool, rest. May–Nov.
In Northeast Harbor, ME 04662:
Asticou Inn Me. 3/198. (800) 258-3373 or (207) 276-3344. 47 units. $95-$325, 2 meals. Pool, rest. Mid-May–mid-Oct.
Kimball Terrace Inn 10 Huntington Rd. (800) 454-6225 or (207) 276-3383. 72 units. $75-$150. Pool, rest.
In Southwest Harbor, ME 04679:
Moorings Inn Shore Rd., Manset. (800) 596-5523 or (207) 244-5523. 22 units, some kitchens; 4 cottages. $105-$165. Mid-May–mid-Oct. Boat rental.

For additional accommodations, call the Chambers of Commerce of Bar Harbor (207) 288-5103, Northeast Harbor (207) 276-5040, or Southwest Harbor (207) 244-9264.

EXCURSIONS

MOOSEHORN NATIONAL WILDLIFE REFUGE

CALAIS, MAINE

At dawn and dusk in spring, the male American woodcock soars into the air to begin his mating ritual. The refuge's two units along the Atlantic flyway protect the essential habitat of the bird as well as other waterfowl and forest wildlife species. 24,409 acres. Hiking, boating, bicycling, fishing, hunting, winter sports. Open all year, dawn to dusk. Headquarters at the Baring Unit, off US 1, about 75 miles from Acadia NP. (207) 454-7161.

PETIT MANAN NATIONAL WILDLIFE REFUGE COMPLEX

STEUBEN, MAINE

Migrating waterfowl and shorebirds take rest on Petit Manan Peninsula and more than 40 offshore islands. The peninsula's two hiking trails lead visitors through spruce-fir forests, blueberry barrens, and along the rugged rocky coastline. Petit Manan Island features one of the largest seabird nesting colonies in Maine and a 123-foot lighthouse (closed April–Aug.). 7,300 acres. Hiking trails. Peninsula open all year, dawn to dusk. Accessible from US 1 in Steuben, about 35 miles from Schoodic Unit of Acadia NP. (207) 546-2124.

RACHEL CARSON NATIONAL WILDLIFE REFUGE

WELLS, MAINE

Stretching along Maine's coast from Kittery to Cape Elizabeth, this refuge's ten units protect the fragile and dynamic world of the tidal estuary. The unit at Wells contains the 1-mile-long self-guided Carson Trail. Breeding and migrating shorebirds, wading birds, waterfowl, and raptors also featured. 5,200 acres. Hiking, canoeing, hunting, scenic drives, cross-country skiing. Picnic areas, handicapped access. Open all year, dawn to dusk. Headquarters at Wells, on Me. 9, off US 1, about 160 miles from Acadia NP. (207) 646-9226.

School of baitfish fleeing a predator

BISCAYNE

FLORIDA
ESTABLISHED JUNE 28, 1980
172,924 acres

Biscayne, a seascape in watercolor, offers vistas ashore and beneath the sea. Standing on the park's narrow shore, you look out upon a bay that is tranquil on the surface and teeming with life below. Aboard a glass-bottom boat or, better yet, on a snorkeling tour, you look down and see some of that life—dazzlingly colored fish, fantastically shaped corals, gently waving fronds of sea grass.

Biscayne is an underwater wilderness. Only five percent of the park is land—about 40 small barrier coral reef islands and a mangrove shoreline, the longest such undeveloped shore on Florida's east coast. Park wildlife musters under water in the form of minuscule, unusual, or rarely seen animals. The most extensive life-form is a community known as the coral reef—colonies of tiny polyps that secrete limestone and live within ever growing rocky crannies. The coral reefs at Biscayne are part of the only living ones in the continental United States.

The park reprieved a living system condemned to die under the pressure of progress. The threat came in the 1960s, when developers were making plans to build resorts and subdivisions on Florida's northern keys, from Key Biscayne to Key Largo. Conservationists campaigned to preserve Biscayne Bay; it became a national monument in 1968. When Biscayne National Park was established, boundaries were expanded to encompass several more of the bay's keys and reefs.

Biscayne embraces a complex ecosystem that extends from the mangrove shoreline to the Gulf Stream. Besides the mangrove coast and living reef, the ecosystem includes two other biological realms found on the small islands and the shallow bay's marine nursery. The realms are interwoven, and each sustains still other webs of life.

Guarding all this are the northernmost Florida Keys, ancient exposed coral reefs that keep ocean waves from battering the bay. Thus shielded, the bay offers sanctuary to the life within it and beauty to those who come to look beneath the surface.

How to Get There

From Miami, take Florida's Turnpike (Fla. 821) south to Speedway Boulevard, and turn left (south). Continue 4 miles on Speedway Boulevard to North Canal Drive and turn left (east). Follow Canal Drive another 4 miles to the park entrance. From Homestead (about 9 miles), take s.w. 328th Street (N. Canal Dr.) to the park entrance at Convoy Point. Airport: Miami.

When to Go

Year-round. The best time to visit the park's islands is from mid-December to mid-April, subtropical Florida's dry season. In summer, you face the perils of mosquitoes and fast-moving thunderstorms, but seas are generally the calmest—making it ideal for snorkeling and diving. Hurricanes are occasional.

How to Visit

Unless you have your own boat, plan to see Biscayne on a concessioner-run cruise. You can look underwater on a **reef cruise** aboard a glass-bottom boat or swim the shallow waters on a snorkeling cruise. There are also scuba cruises to the outer reef for qualified divers. You should make reservations in advance. Cruises may be canceled if there are too few passengers or the weather is inclement. Although this is a water park, a walk around the mangrove shore will give you a chance to examine the coastal edges of the bay's ecosystem. The Dante Fascell Visitor Center offers a museum, audiovisual programs, and ranger talks.

REEF CRUISE

a half day

Sign up for a cruise well ahead (see **Information & Activities** p. 34 for details). Schedules vary by season. At **Convoy Point,** the glass-bottom boat's home port and site of **Dante Fascell Visitor Center,** you can get an orientation to the bay's unique flora and fauna before setting out. A cruise for boaters or snorkelers takes about 3 hours. Cruises for scuba divers last longer and cost more.

Brain coral

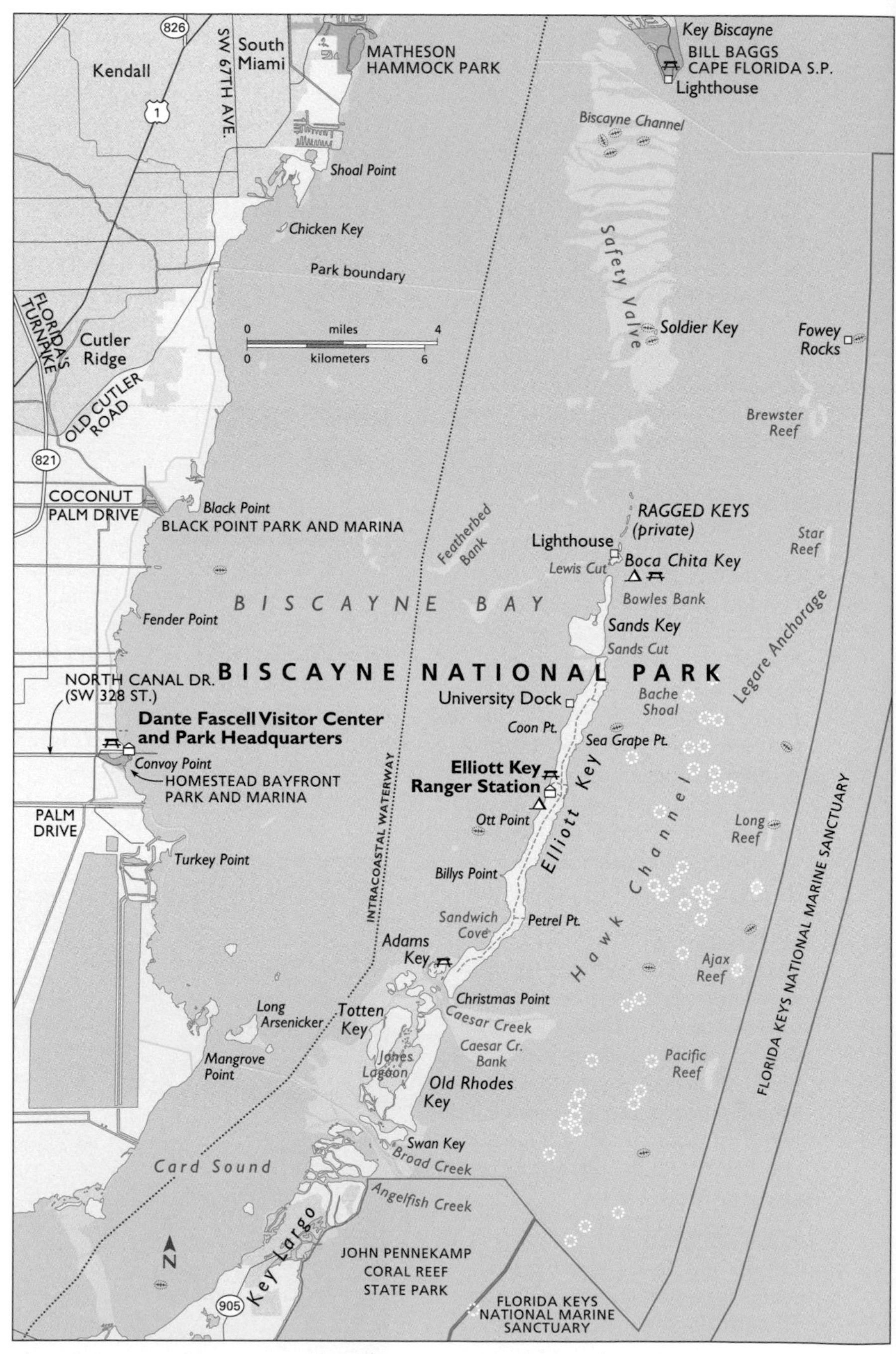

Key Biscayne
BILL BAGGS CAPE FLORIDA S.P.
Lighthouse
Kendall
South Miami
SW 67TH AVE.
MATHESON HAMMOCK PARK
Biscayne Channel
Shoal Point
Chicken Key
Safety Valve
Park boundary
miles
kilometers
Soldier Key
Fowey Rocks
FLORIDA'S TURNPIKE
Cutler Ridge
OLD CUTLER ROAD
Brewster Reef
COCONUT PALM DRIVE
Black Point
BLACK POINT PARK AND MARINA
Featherbed Bank
RAGGED KEYS (private)
Lighthouse
Lewis Cut
Boca Chita Key
Star Reef
Bowles Bank
B I S C A Y N E B A Y
Fender Point
Sands Key
Sands Cut
Legare Anchorage
NORTH CANAL DR. (SW 328 ST.)
B I S C A Y N E N A T I O N A L P A R K
University Dock
Bache Shoal
Dante Fascell Visitor Center and Park Headquarters
Coon Pt.
Sea Grape Pt.
Convoy Point
HOMESTEAD BAYFRONT PARK AND MARINA
Elliott Key Ranger Station
Elliott Key
INTRACOASTAL WATERWAY
PALM DRIVE
Ott Point
Long Reef
Turkey Point
Billys Point
Hawk Channel
FLORIDA KEYS NATIONAL MARINE SANCTUARY
Sandwich Cove
Petrel Pt.
Adams Key
Ajax Reef
Christmas Point
Long Arsenicker
Totten Key
Caesar Creek
Caesar Cr. Bank
Mangrove Point
Jones Lagoon
Old Rhodes Key
Pacific Reef
Swan Key
Broad Creek
Card Sound
Angelfish Creek
Key Largo
JOHN PENNEKAMP CORAL REEF STATE PARK
FLORIDA KEYS NATIONAL MARINE SANCTUARY

Mangrove shoreline on Elliott Key

The center of the boat's deck is a rectangular viewing chamber. Rows of broad, angled windows make up its floor. Passengers line rails around the chamber and peer down at the constantly changing, green-tinted scene.

As the boat crosses the bay, a park ranger prepares the audience by passing out pieces of hard coral and previewing the sights that will be seen in the reefs. A ruffled seabed and waving strands of turtle grass pass under the windows. Vast beds of turtle grass and water only 4 to 10 feet deep make Biscayne Bay a nursery for a host of young marine animals, including shrimp, spiny lobsters, sponges, and crabs. You can see some of these animals through the windows. More than 325 types of fish swim in park waters. You may also see large, graceful sea turtles.

If you walk to the outer edge of the deck, you can watch boats skimming the bay and brown pelicans flapping by. When they spot fish, they dive headfirst into the sea to scoop them up in their huge bills. Among the many other birds you will see are cormorants and herons.

Through the bay runs the Intracoastal Waterway, marked by posts whose signs bear numbers keyed to navigational charts. In one short, shallow stretch near the waterway natural grass beds rise near the surface and are visible at low tide. Bonefish, prized by sportfishermen for their speed and strength, inhabit the grass beds.

The boat slips through the keys toward the reefs beyond. Once it arrives at its destination, the boat lingers for the floor show: the multicolored flash of a passing parrotfish, the sinuous glide of an angelfish, the little jungles of coral. Slowly the boat moves to another vantage point, and a new seabed show begins to roll by. Giant brain coral and mountainous star coral dominate the reefs, many so high that the glass bottom of the boat seems close enough to graze

Florida manatee

them. Sea fans and other soft corals ripple in the calm, clear water. The ranger helps viewers identify the vibrantly colored fish flitting around the massive coral formations. Before reaching the outer reefs the boat turns for home.

The cruise passes through **Caesar Creek,** named for Black Caesar, a legendary pirate said to have lurked here in the 1700s. More than 50 shipwrecks have been cataloged within park boundaries. Federal law protects them from salvagers or souvenir collectors. Visitors who have made the trip in their own boats can also dock at Adams Key for a picnic and walk on a nature trail.

Elliott Key has primitive campsites, restrooms, a nature trail, a swimming area, a ranger station, and what conservationists label a "road scar"—a bulldozer's legacy and a reminder of how close devastation came to these keys. To the north is **Boca Chita Key,** which has a boat dock, primitive campsites, and restrooms, but no drinking water. The lighthouse is only ornamental.

MANGROVE SHORE

0.25 mile; at least an hour

If you have little time, no boat, but some curiosity, walk the shore around **Convoy Point,** a fine place for a picnic. If you have more time, inquire about renting a canoe or kayak to explore mangrove tidal creeks.

The mangroves are critical to this marine environment. They stabilize the shore, trapping their own fallen leaves and other organic material in the tangles of their stiltlike roots. The trees attract many birds—including, on rare occasions, the peregrine falcon and bald eagle, two of the more than a dozen endangered animal species monitored by park scientists. Barnacles, fish, and other sea creatures cluster at the trees' half-submerged roots. The decaying mangrove leaves, rich in protein, provide food to the tiny animals at the bottom of a food chain that ends with the fisherman who eats the gray snapper he caught in the bay.

The mangroves also filter damaging pollutants from the freshwater runoff into the bay. Whether you walk or paddle a boat, watch carefully for the bay animals that find food and refuge in the mangrove waterways. On a winter's day the creatures may include the manatee, a huge, grass-chewing "cow of the sea"; they can reach 10 to 12 feet long and weigh up to 1,800 pounds. The scene keeps changing as each outgoing tide carries its bounty of nutrients out to sea and each incoming tide brings in new inhabitants for the sheltering mangroves.

Clockwise from top: Yellow snapper and soft coral; filefish on soft coral; Nassau grouper; porcupine fish; queen angelfish

INFORMATION & ACTIVITIES

HEADQUARTERS
9700 s.w. 328th St., Homestead, FL 33033. Phone (305) 230-1144. www.nps.gov/bisc

SEASONS & ACCESSIBILITY
Open all year. Keys (islands) can be reached by boat only. Private concessioners operate daily, though underbooked cruises may be canceled in the off-season. Private boats allowed; boat docks available on Elliott, Adams, and Boca Chita Keys ($15 overnight docking fee at Elliot and Boca Chita).

VISITOR & BOAT INFORMATION
Dante Fascell Visitor Center open daily all year. For park information, call (305) 230-7275.
For information and reservations for concessioner-run glass-bottom boat, snorkeling, scuba diving, island and canoe trips, call (305) 230-1100. Rentals available. Tours leave from Convoy Point.

ENTRANCE FEES
None. $15 overnight docking fee for private boats at Elliott and Boca Chita Keys (free campsite included). Fees charged by concessioner for boat trips.

PETS
Allowed on leashes (6-ft. maximum length) in the developed areas of Convoy Point and Elliott Key. Not permitted on boat tours.

FACILITIES FOR DISABLED
Dante Fascell Visitor Center is fully accessible, as are restrooms at Elliott Key and Boca Chita Key. Concessioner boat tours accessible with assistance.

THINGS TO DO
Ranger-led activities: glass-bottom boat tours, canoe trips, island nature tours, interpretive exhibits. Also available: swimming, snorkeling, scuba diving, water skiing, boating, canoe rentals, fishing, lobstering, hiking, bird-watching. Special events: Family Fun Fests, lecture series. Offered seasonally; call for details.

SPECIAL ADVISORIES
• Do not touch coral or other living things on the reef. They are easily damaged; they can also inflict deep cuts and cause serious infections.
• Mosquitoes and other insects can be a problem on the islands, particularly from April to December; carry plenty of repellent.

CAMPGROUNDS
Two boat-in campgrounds, both with 14-day limit. **Elliott Key** and **Boca Chita Key** open all year, first come, first served. Water at Elliott Key only. Tent sites only. $10 fee per site per night (no boats); one campsite is free with overnight docking ($15). Group campground at Elliott Key. Fees $25 per site per night.

HOTELS, MOTELS, & INNS
(unless otherwise noted, rates are for 2 persons in a double room, high season)

In Florida City, FL 33034:
Best Western 411 S. Krome Ave. (305) 246-5100 or (800) 528-1234. 114 units. $135. AC, pool.
Comfort Inn 333 S.E. 1st Ave./US 1. (305) 248-4009. 123 units. $79-$169. AC, pool.
Coral Roc Motel 1100 N. Krome Ave. (305) 247-4010. 16 units, 4 with kitchenettes. $36-$159. AC, pool.
Hampton Inn 124 E. Palm Dr. (305) 247-8833 or (800) 426-7866. 123 units. $102. AC, pool, breakfast incl.
Knights Inn 1223 N.E. 1st Ave./US 1. (305) 247-6621. 48 units, 6 with kitchenettes. $79-$169. AC, pool.

In Homestead, FL 33030:
Days Inn 51 S. Homestead Blvd. (305) 245-1260. 100 units. $109. AC, pool, restaurant.
Everglades Motel 605 S. Krome Ave. (305) 247-4117. 14 units. $59. AC, pool.

For additional accommodations, write or call the Homestead/Florida City Chamber of Commerce, 43 N. Krome Ave., Homestead, FL 33030. (305) 247-2332.

EXCURSIONS

JOHN PENNEKAMP CORAL REEF STATE PARK

KEY LARGO, FLORIDA

In the world's first undersea park, a living coral reef may be viewed through a diver's mask or a glass-bottom boat. 63,085 acres. Visitor center, 47 campsites, trails, boating, boat ramps, fishing, picnic areas, water sports, handicapped access. Open all year during daylight. Off US 1 in Key Largo, about 40 miles from Biscayne NP and 35 from Everglades NP. (305) 451-1202.

NATIONAL KEY DEER REFUGE

BIG PINE KEY, FLORIDA

The Key deer—a diminutive subspecies of the white-tailed deer—struggle to survive in this mangrove and pine-palm habitat. It's illegal to feed them. 9,150 acres. Hiking and wildlife observation. Open all year, dawn to dusk. Off US 1 on Big Pine Key, about 150 miles south of Biscayne NP. (305) 872-0774.

GREAT WHITE HERON NATIONAL WILDLIFE REFUGE

BIG PINE KEY, FLORIDA

Dedicated to the protection of the great white heron, this site partly overlaps the National Key Deer Refuge. These mangrove islands also shelter ibis, white-crowned pigeon, and the roseate spoonbill. 192,584 acres. No camping or other facilities. Access by boat only. No pets allowed. Open all year, dawn to dusk. Information at National Key Deer Refuge; see above.

Boardwalk Loop Trail

CONGAREE

CENTRAL SOUTH CAROLINA
ESTABLISHED 2003
22,200 acres

Say the word "swamp," and the first image that probably comes to mind is of a wet, sticky, mosquito-infested mire that few people would want to visit. Such an image certainly might have kept some visitors away from Congaree Swamp National Monument, a 22,000-acre forest in South Carolina.

Yet, after the monument gained national park status in November 2003—and dropped the unappealing "s" word from its name—the number of visitors each month increased significantly.

Technically speaking, Congaree is not a swamp, because it does not contain standing water throughout most of the year. The newest national park is actually a floodplain forest that floods about ten times a year. Spreading northeast from the meandering Congaree River, the land is the largest contiguous tract of old-growth bottomland hardwoods in the United States.

Push back the ghostly Spanish moss that drips from the bald cypresses, and you enter a lush backcountry inhabited by bobcats, wild boars, and playful river otters. Yellow-bellied sapsuckers drill holes into trees one day and return the next to feast on the sap that has filled the holes. The rapid-fire series of knocks you hear is from one of the many woodpeckers found in the park, also hard at work boring holes into trees.

At night in the fall and spring, rangers lead visitors on an "owl prowl," so they can hear the eerie calls of barred owls and see the glowing fungi that grows on the cypresses. According to local legends, the cypress tree's trademark "knees"—small, knobby wood growths that rise around the trunk's base—are really wood elves who come to life at night to dance through the forest.

Congaree was named for the Native American tribe that lived here centuries ago. They were decimated in the 18th century, victims of a smallpox epidemic that came over with European settlers.

Toward the end of the next century, the country's burgeoning lumber industry moved south, with an eye on Congaree's giant hardwood trees. However, because of the remoteness of the area and the lack of navigable waterways many of the old giants were saved from the ax.

Conservationists worked hard to save the rest. In 1976, Congress rewarded their efforts by setting Congaree aside as a national monument. Since its establishment, the park has been designated as a national natural landmark, a globally important bird area, and an international biosphere reserve.

How to Get There

From Columbia, 20 miles southeast on I-77 to exit 5 (Bluff Road or S.C. 48). Follow the Congaree National Park direction signs to the park.

When to Go

Year-round. Spring and fall are the most pleasant seasons. Boaters find easier paddling after a rain in late winter and early spring.

How to Visit

Allow a full or half day. From the visitor center, take the **Low** and **High Boardwalk Trails** (2.4 miles total). Then do the **Weston Lake Loop Trail** (4.4 miles) around the oxbow lake. Birders like the 11.7-mile **Kingsnake Trail** into a remote part of the park.

BOARDWALK TRAIL

2.4 miles; 2 hours

In this woodland, giant loblolly pines and hardwoods rise to a canopy higher than in the Amazon rain forest. Loblolly pines rise up more than 160 feet to reach the sunlight, and some majestic old bald cypresses measure more than 25 feet in circumference, their leafy crowns shuttering the world below into a landscape of liquid echoes in shades of brown and green.

Congaree is home to some of the country's tallest trees, some state and/or national champions. The tallest water hickory is 143 feet tall, and the park's tallest loblolly

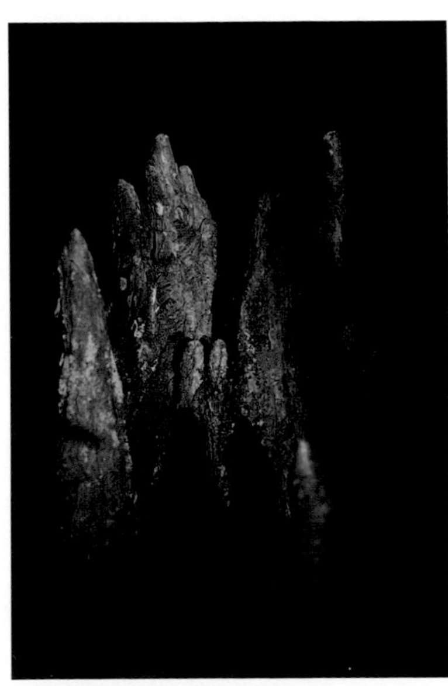

Bald cypress knees

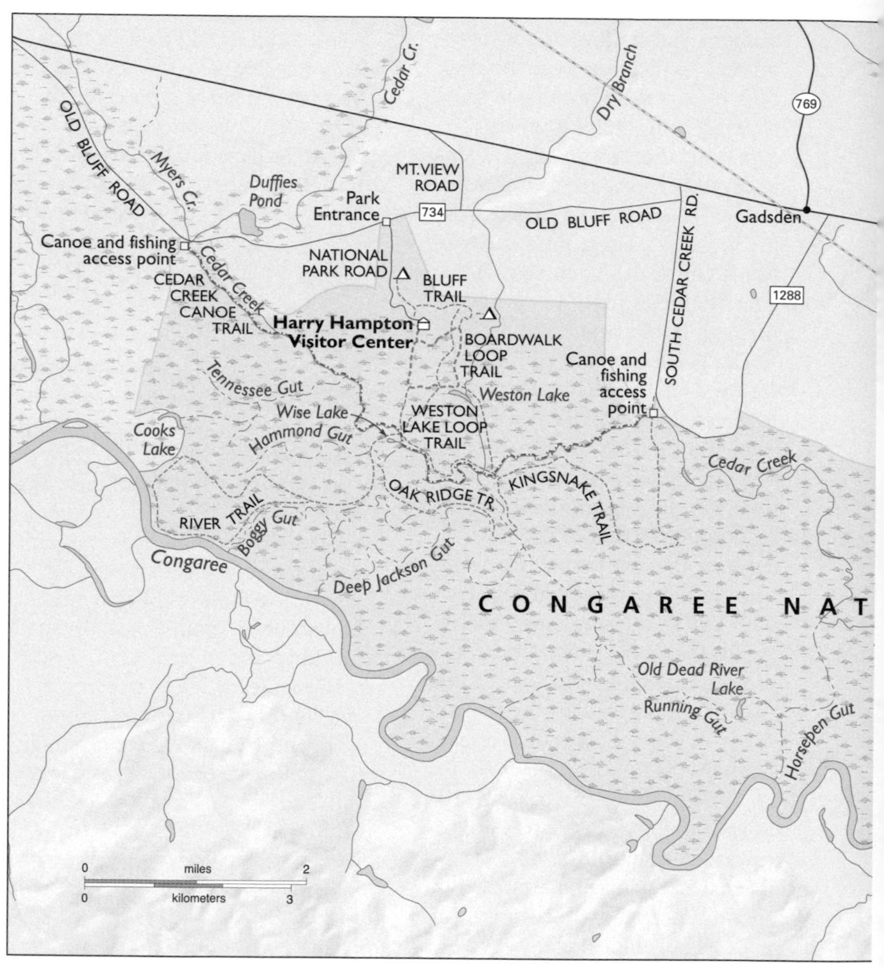

pine reaches 167 feet, as high as a 17-story building.

Logging began in swamps across the Southeast in the 1880s, and soon thereafter it focused on the old-growth bald cypress. During the next two decades all the stands within easy reach were cut, and South Carolina's floodplain forests suffered a drastic reduction. However, along the Congaree a lack of accessible waterways needed to remove the timber helped save the irreplaceable tract.

Fierce winds from Hurricane Hugo in 1989 put a dent in the old-growth forest, toppling some of the national and state champion trees harbored here. The storm also opened up holes in the dense canopy, clearing the way for fresh growth. Dead trees, meanwhile, became homes for various birds, bats, reptiles, insects, and fungi.

About ten times a year, the floodplain is inundated, usually following dam releases and heavy rains from upstate. Sloughs and guts (narrow creeks) overflow, carrying nutrients that enrich the soil. Shallow-rooted

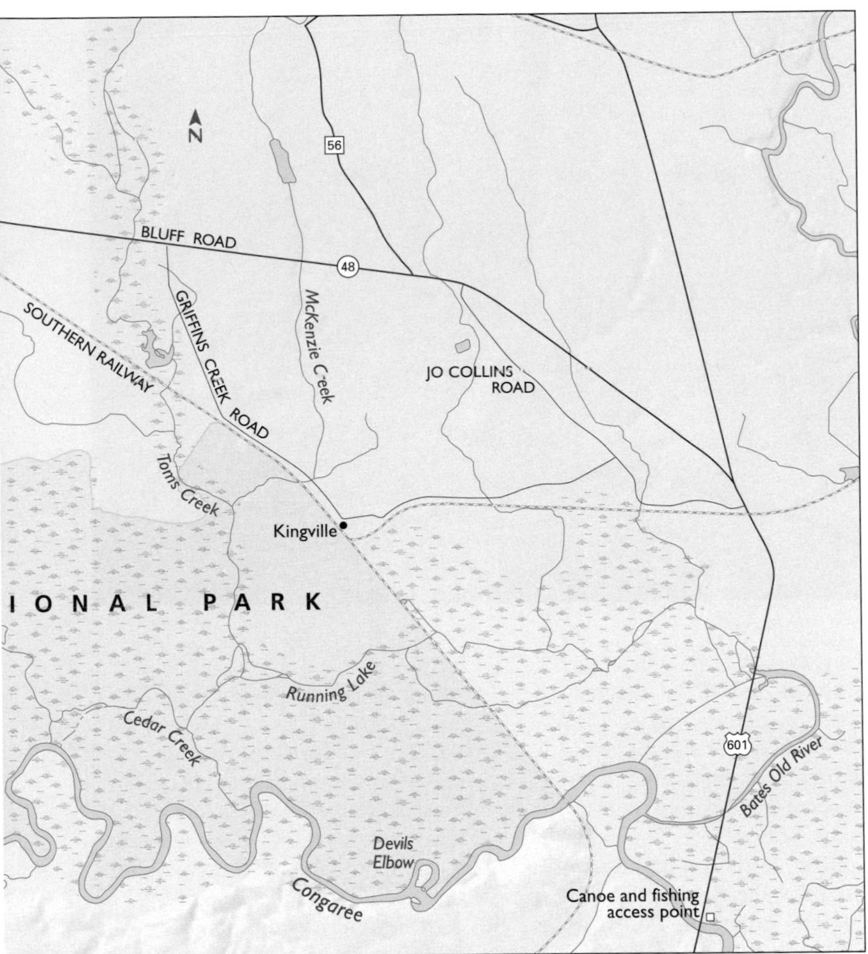

hardwoods occasionally fall, but cypress trees with far-reaching roots and supportive knees as tall as seven feet rarely topple. Animals seek higher ground, and some even find refuge on floating logs.

On a topographical map you will see very few contour lines within the park's boundaries; the elevation dips only about 20 feet from the west side to the east, so excess water can slosh all over the floodplain. Yet even that slight, seemingly insignificant change of elevation produces dramatically different biological communities: At the higher, drier levels of the park live sweet gums, cherrybark oaks, and hollies, whereas cypresses, water tupelos, and water ashes thrive at the lower, wetter levels.

Pick up the **Boardwalk Loop Trail** at the visitor center where trail maps, information, and suggestions for other hikes are available. As you gradually enter the floodplain forest, the vegetation changes from upland pines and hardwoods to the old-growth loblolly pines and mixed hardwoods of the swamp.

During floods, the water level

Cypress trees in summer

can rise as high as the elevated boardwalk, or even higher. Thick vines of muscadine grapes and climbing hydrangeas hug the trunks of ancient trees, adding to the primordial atmosphere. The hairy vines belong to poison ivy, and it's worth noting that these vines and dormant stems can irritate the skin as much as the leaves.

Farther along, tupelos and cypresses grow in standing brown water, stained by the tannin of decayed vegetation. A light rainfall is an especially evocative time for a walk through here—raindrops ping the reflective water, a gauzy mist blankets the forest primeval, and the birdsong seems to come from far away in time. Back in these shady depths you almost expect to find creatures from another age.

Continue down the boardwalk toward picturesque **Weston Lake.** Dwarf palmettos just off the walk lend a tropical accent to the surroundings. The riddled trunks of sweet gums and other trees bear the marks of woodpeckers. All eight varieties of woodpeckers—red-bellied, red-cockaded, red-headed, pileated, downy, hairy, yellow-bellied sapsucker, and yellow-shafted flicker—found in the South inhabit Congaree.

In summer, hummingbirds zoom for the showy orange flowers of the trumpet vine, while sparrows dart about for berries and seeds. Fallen logs lie moldering in puddles of wet vegetation. Small-scale communities are built upon the pits and mounds of overturned trees.

River otters can occasionally be seen frolicking in Weston Lake, and red-bellied turtles line up on floating logs. The small oxbow lake, measuring 25 feet deep, was once a bend in the Congaree River; thousands of years ago, the river changed course—leaving the bend as a lake—and now flows 2 miles away. Near here stand dwarf forests of gnarled cypress knees; the farther you walk around to the east, the more old-growth cypress you encounter.

The boardwalk then takes you through a forest of tupelos, hollies, loblolly pines, and, above all, cypresses. Touch the rippling bell-bottom trunks of the older cypresses; their mossy surface feels like velvet. Extend the Boardwalk Loop by taking the 4.4-mile **Weston Lake Loop Trail,** which follows a cypress-tupelo slough down to Cedar Creek. In this largest of the park's creeks, you have the best chance of spotting herons and otters.

MORE TRAILS IN THE PARK

a half to full day

For a longer outing, the **Oak Ridge Trail,** accessible off the Weston Lake Loop Trail, pushes farther south into the old-growth forest and makes for a 6.6-mile round-trip hike from the visitor center. If you want to walk to the river and back, plan to spend most of the day on a trek starting with the boardwalk, then taking the western sections of the Weston Lake Loop and Oak Ridge Trails; the 10-mile **River Trail** takes you the rest of the way.

The 11.7-mile out-and-back **Kingsnake Trail** offers further opportunities for wildlife watching—especially birds—and secluded exploration in the park's little-visited eastern section. The trailhead is off the Cedar Creek parking area.

The **Cedar Creek canoe trail** within Congaree slips through sunless channels of brown water haunted by reclusive birds and other animals. The stillness of the place will make you feel you've entered another world. Once a month, the park staff offers a guided trip into these mysterious parts and provides canoes for participants. Otherwise, plan to rent a canoe from one of the many outfitters in nearby Columbia.

North American river otter

INFORMATION & ACTIVITIES

HEADQUARTERS
100 National Park Road, Hopkins, SC 29061. Phone (803) 776-4396. www.nps.gov/cosw

SEASONS & ACCESSIBILITY
Open all year. Call after heavy rains to see if park is flooded or for current foot trail and canoe trail conditions.

VISITOR & INFORMATION CENTERS
Open daily year-round. Located off S.C. 48, 1.2 miles beyond park entrance on National Park Road.

ENTRANCE FEE
There is no fee to enter the park.

PETS
Pets must be on leashes and are not allowed on the boardwalks.

FACILITIES FOR DISABLED
Visitor center, restrooms, picnic shelter, and primitive campgrounds are wheelchair accessible. So is the 2.4-mile Boardwalk Loop trail.

THINGS TO DO
Free naturalist-led activities: nature walks and canoe tours. Environmental education and nature study. Hiking, fishing (S.C. state license required), primitive camping, bird-watching, picnicking, canoeing, kayaking (bring your own boat, rentals are not available in the park). Canoes can be rented or trips can be arranged through Adventure Carolina Canoeing & Camping (1107 State St., Cayce, SC 29033. 803-796-4505) and River Runner Outdoor Center (905 Gervais St., Columbia, SC 29201. 803-771-0353).

SPECIAL ADVISORIES
• Carry plenty of water as there is no potable water outside developed areas. If you drink surface water, first chemically purify it.
• Check weather conditions and water levels before leaving on a cone or kayak trip.
• Take a detailed map when kayaking or canoeing.
• Mosquitoes can be brutal carry plenty of repellent.
• There are poisonous snakes in the park; give all snakes a wide pass.

OVERNIGHT BACKPACKING
Permit required; available free from visitor centers. Campsites must be at least 100 feet away from roads, trails, lakes, and flowing water.

CAMPGROUNDS
Two primitive campgrounds and backcountry camping with 14-day limits year-round. Free permits required; available at the visitor center no more than one day in advance. After-hours primitive campsite can accommodate groups. Portable toilets, fire rings, grills, and picnic tables. The Bluff primitive campsite also can accommodate groups; fire rings, grills, and picnic tables in open field. No open fires permitted in backcountry camping.

HOTELS, MOTELS, & INNS
(unless otherwise noted, rates are for 2 persons in a double room, high season)

In Columbia, SC:
Comfort Inn & Suites Fort Jackson Maingate 7337 Garners Ferry Rd., 29209. (803) 695-5555. 67 units. $89-$109. AC, pool.
Fort Jackson Inn–Econo Lodge 4486 Fort Jackson Blvd., 29209. (803) 738-0510. 40 units. $50. AC.
Holiday Inn Express Columbia–Fort Jackson 7251 Garner's Ferry Rd., 29209. (803) 695-1111. 66 units. $67-$97. AC, pool, pets allowed.
Clarion Town House Hotel 1615 Gervais St., 29201. (803) 771-8711 or 800-277-8711. 163 units. $89. AC, pool, restaurant.
Claussen's Inn 2003 Greene St., 29205. (803) 765-0440. 29 units. $145. AC.

For other accommodations, contact the Columbia Metropolitan Convention & Visitors Bureau, (800) 264-4884 or (803) 545-0000.

EXCURSIONS

CAROLINA SANDHILLS NATIONAL WILDLIFE REFUGE

McBEE, SOUTH CAROLINA

Lying between the Piedmont Plateau and the Atlantic Coastal Plain, Carolina Sandhills is home to towering 100-foot longleaf pines. These pines provide homes to the largest population of red-cockaded woodpeckers in the country. The refuge offers a 9-mile auto trail, 3 marked hiking trails, 20 fishing ponds, and a wooden 15-foot observation tower. More than 750 plant species, 190 bird species, 42 species of mammals, 41 types of reptiles, and 25 different amphibians reside within the refuge. 45,348 acres. Open all year; best months April through May and September through October. Approximately 75 miles NE of Congaree NP off US 1 north of McBee. (843) 335-8401.

SANTEE NATIONAL WILDLIFE REFUGE

SUMMERTON, SOUTH CAROLINA

Located to the north of Lake Marion, this refuge provides a haven for nesting and migratory birds. The bald eagle, peregrine falcon, and wood stork are among the 300 species recorded here. It is also a delight for fishing enthusiasts. Opportunities abound to see deer, alligator, bobcat, turkey, and coyote. No camping is permitted to protect the resident and migratory birds. Pine Island is available only to foot traffic. Wildlife drive and hiking trails. 15,095 acres. Open all year. Approximately 50 miles SE of Congaree NP. (804) 478-2217

White-tailed deer grazing under a giant red oak

CUYAHOGA VALLEY

OHIO

ESTABLISHED OCTOBER 11, 2000

33,000 acres

If there is one word that typifies Cuyahoga Valley, it might well be "surprise." To begin, many people are surprised by the simple fact that a national park exists in northeastern Ohio, between the sprawling cities of Cleveland and Akron. In fact, it hasn't existed for long: Cuyahoga Valley was given national park status only in 2000.

Visitors find more surprises: Secluded trails through rugged gorges that seem far removed from civilization; vistas of tree-covered hills where the urban world is out of sight; marshes where beaver, herons, and wood ducks thrive.

Crisscrossed by roads and freeways, encompassing towns, private attractions, and city parks, Cuyahoga Valley is hardly comparable to the vast western wilderness parks—a circumstance that leads to even more surprises. Visitors can ride a scenic railroad, hear a symphony concert, attend an art exhibit, play golf, or, in winter, zoom down snowy ski slopes.

The park's history is as unique as its potpourri of natural and man-made attractions. In the 1960s, local citizens and public officials became concerned that commercial and residential development was threatening the scenic Cuyahoga River Valley, with its villages, quiet byways, and forests. In 1974, Congress passed a bill creating a National Recreation Area, administered by the National Park Service. The park began acquiring private land within the designated 33,000 acres, as well as working out cooperative agreements with developments already in place, such as Cleveland and Summit County metropolitan park districts and Blossom Music Center, the summer home of the Cleveland Orchestra. Eventually, confusion about the meaning of "recreation area" led supporters to call for full national park status.

Today, Cuyahoga Valley NP serves the metropolitan area in a multitude of ways. Residents jog, ride bicycles, or picnic in the park; local children ride sleds down its hills in winter; nature-lovers love its pockets of wild greenery, home to dozens of species of birds and wildflowers; fans of the arts watch Shakespeare and musicals at Kent State University's Porthouse Theatre. Cuyahoga Valley may not fit everyone's idea of a national park, but that doesn't tarnish the appeal of its many rewards.

How To Get There

From Cleveland, take I-77 10 miles south; from Akron, go 5 miles north on I-77 or Ohio 8; from the east or west, I-80 bisects the park, as does I-271. Airports: Cleveland or Akron.

When to Go

Year-round. Weekends can be crowded along the Towpath Trail from spring through fall, and especially in summer. Many activities are curtailed in winter, but downhill skiing, cross-country skiing, snowshoeing, and sledding are popular. Spring wildflowers and fall foliage make these especially colorful and appealing seasons.

How To Visit

Stop at the **Canal Visitor Center** for an overview of canal and valley history and information on park activities; ask about ranger-led tours and special events. Walk or bicycle a portion of the **Towpath Trail** before driving east to take in the beauty of **Tinkers Creek Gorge.** Then head south to see **Brandywine Falls,** continuing to the towns of **Boston** and **Peninsula** for museums and exhibits. Walk some of the scenic trails south of the Happy Days Visitor Center, especially in the area called **The Ledges.**

CANAL TOWPATH TRAIL

2 hours to a half-day or more

A few decades ago, the notoriously polluted **Cuyahoga River** seemed an odd choice to be at the heart of a national park. The Cuyahoga (an American Indian word meaning "crooked") is far cleaner today, after extensive rehabilitation efforts. Though park personnel still don't recommend swimming or boating, the river corridor serves as a thread of life running 22 miles through the center of the park, home to a surprising diversity of wildlife.

During the 1820s, a canal constructed parallel to the river opened up commercial boat traffic between Lake Erie and the Ohio River, fostering economic growth in the Cuyahoga Valley and the nation. Made obsolete by railroads, the Ohio & Erie Canal has long been abandoned—but the adjacent towpath, where mules once trudged towing boats, has been converted into one of the area's most popular hiking and bicycling trails. Running nearly 20 miles through the park (and extending both north into Cleveland and south into Akron), the **Ohio & Erie Canal Towpath Trail** is in many ways the heart of recreational activity in Cuyahoga Valley. Passing through forests, meadows, and wetlands, the fully accessible trail invites

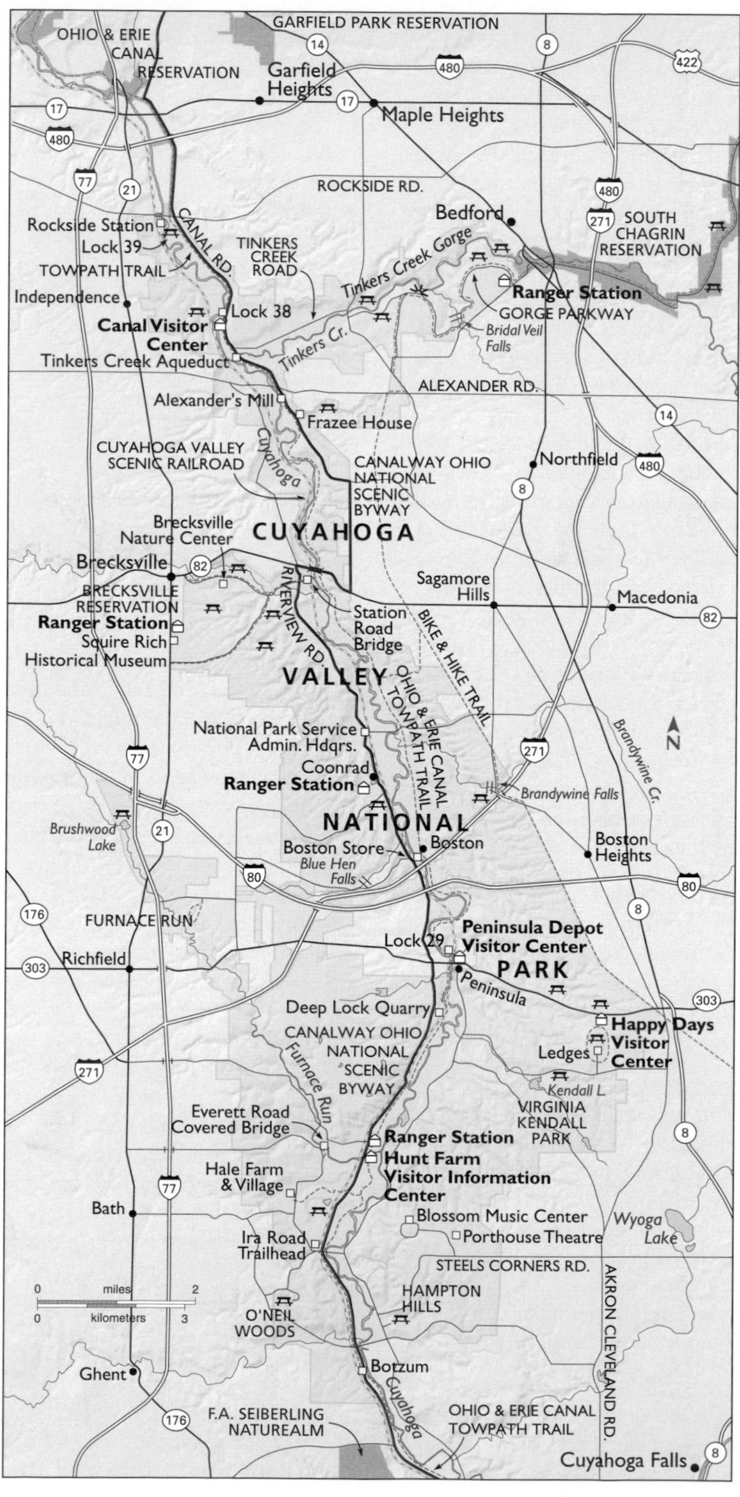

GARFIELD PARK RESERVATION
OHIO & ERIE CANAL RESERVATION
Garfield Heights
Maple Heights
ROCKSIDE RD.
Bedford
SOUTH CHAGRIN RESERVATION
Rockside Station
Lock 39
TOWPATH TRAIL
CANAL RD.
TINKERS CREEK ROAD
Tinkers Creek Gorge
Ranger Station
GORGE PARKWAY
Bridal Veil Falls
Independence
Lock 38
Canal Visitor Center
Tinkers Cr.
Tinkers Creek Aqueduct
ALEXANDER RD.
Alexander's Mill
Frazee House
CUYAHOGA VALLEY SCENIC RAILROAD
Cuyahoga
CANALWAY OHIO NATIONAL SCENIC BYWAY
Northfield
Brecksville Nature Center
CUYAHOGA
Brecksville
BRECKSVILLE RESERVATION
Ranger Station
Squire Rich Historical Museum
RIVERVIEW RD.
Station Road Bridge
Sagamore Hills
Macedonia
BIKE & HIKE TRAIL
VALLEY
OHIO & ERIE CANAL TOWPATH TRAIL
National Park Service Admin. Hdqrs.
Coonrad
Ranger Station
Brandywine Falls
Brandywine Cr.
N
NATIONAL
Brushwood Lake
Boston Store
Boston
Blue Hen Falls
Boston Heights
FURNACE RUN
Lock 29
Peninsula Depot Visitor Center
PARK
Richfield
Peninsula
Deep Lock Quarry
Happy Days Visitor Center
CANALWAY OHIO NATIONAL SCENIC BYWAY
Furnace Run
Ledges
Kendall L.
VIRGINIA KENDALL PARK
Everett Road Covered Bridge
Ranger Station
Hunt Farm Visitor Information Center
Hale Farm & Village
Bath
Blossom Music Center
Porthouse Theatre
Wyoga Lake
Ira Road Trailhead
STEELS CORNERS RD.
0 miles 2
0 kilometers 3
HAMPTON HILLS
O'NEIL WOODS
AKRON CLEVELAND RD.
Botzum
Ghent
Cuyahoga
F.A. SEIBERLING NATUREALM
OHIO & ERIE CANAL TOWPATH TRAIL
Cuyahoga Falls

casual walking and serious fitness running or biking.

At the **Canal Visitor Center,** an 1820s canal house off Canal Road, you can watch a video and inspect historical displays. Just outside is **Lock 38,** the canal's last operational lock within the park, one of a series that allowed boats to negotiate 395 feet of elevation change as they traveled from Lake Erie to Akron, and vice versa. Costumed rangers and volunteers demonstrate the lock's function on summer and fall weekends.

As you explore the Towpath Trail (and the rest of the Cuyahoga Valley), consider taking advantage of the **Cuyahoga Valley Scenic Railroad.** It parallels the river on its route from Akron to Independence, making seven stops within the park. Some trips allow hikers and bikers to follow the Towpath Trail as far as they wish, then board the train and return to their starting point. Themed rail trips are offered throughout the year.

Drive east along Tinkers Creek Road and Gorge Parkway into beautiful **Tinkers Creek Gorge,** a national natural landmark. An overlook along the parkway presents a fine view of the wooded valley and the creek, 200 feet below. Farther east is the parking lot for **Bridal Veil Falls,** where a short walk into a steep-sided valley brings you to a pretty spot where a tributary of **Tinkers Creek** drops over a series of sandstone ledges—one of nearly 70 waterfalls in the gorge. Here, as at scattered other spots in the park, the shaded ravine is home to hemlocks, beeches, maples, oaks, and birches, creating an environment reminiscent of more northerly hardwood forests. The paths that meander through the gorge make up part of 186 miles of trails in the Cuyahoga Valley, allowing short strolls just off paved roads and day-long loop hikes that can take in a variety of habitats and landscapes.

A 19th-century barn

BRANDYWINE FALLS & THE LEDGES

a full day or more

Perhaps the park's most-visited natural feature, **Brandywine Falls** cascades over a staircase-like series of sandstone-covered shelves in the eastern part of the park, reached by a walkway to viewing platforms, one high and another lower, at streamside. The falls' winter aspect can be just as striking as that of spring's high water, with flows and icicles creating a white curtain of columns and swirls. Not quite so grand, but also exquisite and always less crowded, **Blue Hen Falls** is just minutes away on the west side of the Cuyahoga River, in an intimate valley forested in maple and beech.

Be sure to stop at the 1836 **Boston Store,** in the nearby village of Boston. You'll enjoy a fascinating exhibit on the design and building of the boats that plied the Ohio & Erie Canal during its heyday as a thriving commercial corridor. Just south, the town of **Peninsula** produced boats in its workshops that were widely regarded as the best on the canal. Today, Peninsula is a charming village of shops, cafés,

Fall hiking on the Ohio & Erie Canal Towpath Trail

and art galleries, as well as a bike-rental facility for those who'd like to ride on the adjacent Towpath Trail.

A must-see site can be found southeast of Peninsula, on Kendall Park Road. The main trail at the **Ledges** arcs around a small plateau, beneath dramatically eroded bluffs of 320-million-year-old sandstone conglomerate. The evocative setting of tall trees, ferns, and mosses makes this a hike to be taken slowly, enjoying the chattering of red squirrels and the scolding calls of chickadees. On the east side of the Ledges, venture into the tight passageways of **Ice Box Cave;** on the west, the **Ledges Overlook** is a fine spot for sunset views over wooded ridges rolling away to the horizon.

Check the park schedule during your visit for activities at the **Happy Days Visitor Center,** on Ohio 303. The center hosts concerts, dances, lectures, and children's activities. Thanks to the park's artist-in-residence program and to active local groups, you may run across a painter or folksinger as you walk the Towpath Trail or visit other sites in the park at any time during the warm months.

Ask nearby residents about favorite stretches of the Towpath Trail and you'll get a different answer from nearly everyone. For nature-lovers, though, the section just north of the **Ira Road Trailhead** ranks at the top. You'll find an extensive marsh created by beaver, which returned to the Cuyahoga Valley in the late 1970s after an absence of 100 years. Great blue herons, rose-breasted grosbeaks, red-winged blackbirds, belted kingfishers, and prothonotary warblers are just a few of the wetlands' denizens, along with muskrat and white-tailed deer (best seen at dawn or dusk, as are beavers).

Moving from natural to human history: **Hale Farm & Village,** on Oak Hill Road in the southwestern part of the park, near Bath, is a living-history museum open May through October.

INFORMATION & ACTIVITIES

HEADQUARTERS
Cuyahoga Valley NP, 15610 Vaughn Rd., Brecksville, OH 44141. (216) 524-1497. www.nps.gov/cuva

SEASONS & ACCESSIBILITY
Open all year for individual activities and scheduled events.

VISITOR & INFORMATION CENTERS
Canal Visitor Center, Canal and Hillside Roads, Valley View, open year-round. (216) 524-1497. **Happy Days Visitor Center,** 500 W. Streetsboro, Peninsula, offers information on concerts and special events. Open year-round; hours vary seasonally. **Hunt Farm Visitor Information Center,** along Towpath Trail, open year-round, hours vary seasonally. **Peninsula Depot Visitor Center** serves as a welcome center for the park; hours coincide with train schedule. Closed late Dec. to mid-Feb.

ENTRANCE FEE
Free to enter park. Some concerts, events, and programs charge fees.

PETS
Permitted on leashes.

FACILITIES FOR DISABLED
Many trails, visitor centers, historic properties, and activities accessible. The crushed limestone of the 20-mile Canal Towpath Trail is fully accessible. Contact park for detailed information.

THINGS TO DO
Park personnel and volunteers lead tours and nature walks, while cultural events abound spring through fall at venues such as the Blossom Music Center, (330) 920-8040; and the Porthouse Theatre, (330) 929-4416. Summer activities: picnicking, golfing, walking, fishing, bicycling, horseback riding (no horse rentals inside the park). Winter activities: sledding, cross-country skiing, snowshoeing. For an easy way to explore the park take the **Cuyahoga Valley Scenic Railroad,** (800) 468-4070.

CAMPGROUNDS
No campgrounds exist within park and backcountry camping is not permitted. Contact the visitor bureaus listed below for a list of private campgrounds in the area.

HOTELS, MOTELS, & INNS
(unless otherwise noted, rates are for 2 persons in a double room, high season)

INSIDE THE PARK:

Inn at Brandywine Falls 8230 Brandywine Rd., Sagamore Hills, OH 44067. (330) 467-1812. 3 rooms, 3 suites. $119-$298. AC, breakfast incl.

Stanford Hostel 6093 Stanford Rd., Peninsula, OH 44264. (330) 467-8711. 30 beds. Separate dorms for men, women. $16. $3 bedding rental fee.

For accommodations contact Akron/Summit Convention & Visitors Bureau, (800) 245-4254, www.visitakron-summit.org; or Convention & Visitors Bureau of Greater Cleveland, (800) 321-1001, www.travelcleveland.com.

Re-creating life in a typical mid-19th-century Cuyahoga Valley community, the centerpiece is the 1826 farm of the pioneer Hale family. Other historic buildings have been relocated here to reproduce an early village, where costumed interpreters spin thread, weave cloth, make baskets and candles, blow glass, shape iron in a blacksmith shop, and tell stories. A short drive north, the **Everett Road Covered Bridge** is a re-creation of an 1870s structure that was destroyed in a 1975 flood.

Civilization, in the form of highways, suburbs, and commercial development, is never far away in Cuyahoga Valley NP. But perhaps that is the point: A variety of natural beauty and attractions can endure in an urban setting, and can so reward those who take time to explore.

Bird's-eye view of Fort Jefferson

DRY TORTUGAS

FLORIDA
ESTABLISHED OCTOBER 26, 1992
64,700 acres

In the Gulf of Mexico, about 70 nautical miles west of Key West, Florida, a 7-mile-long archipelago of seven low-lying islands forms the centerpiece of Dry Tortugas National Park. A bird and marine life sanctuary, it harbors some of the healthiest coral reefs remaining off North American shores. Towering incongruously in the midst of this subtropical Eden is Fort Jefferson, a relic of 19th-century military strategy.

Barely 40 acres of the park's 100 square miles are above water. Three easterly keys are little more than spits of white coral sand. A stone's throw from the visitor center in Fort Jefferson, Bush Key is home to a tangle of bay cedar, sea grape, mangrove, sea oats, and prickly pear cactus that reflect the original "desert island" character of the islands. The chain ends about 3 miles west with 30-acre Loggerhead Key, where a lighthouse completed in 1858 still flashes a beacon to mariners.

Spanish explorer Juan Ponce de León, the first European to describe the Florida peninsula, dropped anchor here in 1513. He found pellucid waters teeming with green, hawksbill, leatherback, and loggerhead turtles, and so named the islands *las tortugas,* which means "the turtles." For the next three centuries, pirates relied on the turtles for meat and eggs; they also raided the sandy nests of roosting sooty and noddy terns, over 100,000 of which descend on Bush Key every year between March and September. By 1825, when the islands' first lighthouse began to alert sailors of surrounding reefs and shoals—a grave for more than 200 ships wrecked here since the 1600s—nautical charts warned that the Tortugas were "dry," because of the lack of fresh water.

In 1846, U.S. Army strategists were concerned that hostile nations could disrupt shipping lanes in the Gulf of Mexico. As a result, they decided to build a 450-gun, 2,000-man fort on Garden Key. The intimidating bulk of the 50-foot-high, three-level hexagon, whose 2,000 archways run half a mile around, spared it from ever having to fire a shot in anger. A Union prison for Civil War deserters, it also held physician Samuel Mudd, who was convicted of conspiracy in Abraham Lincoln's murder after he (unknowingly, he claimed) set the broken leg of fugitive assassin John Wilkes Booth. He served four years before being released.

Unfinished after nearly 30 years of intermittent construction, the "Gibraltar of the Gulf" succumbed in 1874 to several factors: yellow fever, hurricane damage, and the new rifled cannon, which rendered its 8-foot-thick walls obsolete. Revived in 1898 as a Navy coaling station—the battleship *Maine* steamed from here to its infamous destiny in Havana's harbor 90 miles south—the fort was permanently abandoned in 1907. In 1935 President Franklin D. Roosevelt signed the papers naming the site a national monument.

How to Get There

Access to Dry Tortugas is by boat or seaplane. Yankee Fleet and Sunny Days run regular boat service. For Yankee Fleet, call (800) 634-0939 or (305) 294-7009; for Sunny Days, call (800) 236-7937 or (305) 292-6100. For names of authorized air taxis and charter boats, call park headquarters. Boat passage from Key West takes about 3 hours; by air, 40 minutes. Private boaters should refer to NOAA Chart #11434 ("Sombrero Key To Dry Tortugas") and Chart #11438 ("Dry Tortugas").

When to Go

Year-round. Temperatures range from the mid-80s to the low 50s. Moderate weather prevails in April and May, when visitation is at its peak. Winter is often windy with rough seas. The tropical storm or "hurricane" season lasts from June through November, when temperatures and humidity are highest.

How to Visit

A day trip by boat or floatplane permits an unhurried visit to **Garden Key** including a self-guided walking tour of **Fort Jefferson,** a stroll around the fort's marine life-rich seawall, swimming, and snorkeling. If **Bush Key** is open to visitors and you can spare an hour, consider swimming the narrow channel to experience a true "desert island" environment. Or use the new land bridge.

GARDEN KEY & FORT JEFFERSON

70 miles from Key West; a full day

When you arrive, check dockside announcement boards for naturalist-led activities. The **visitor center** is just inside the fort entrance. A Florida National Parks and Monuments

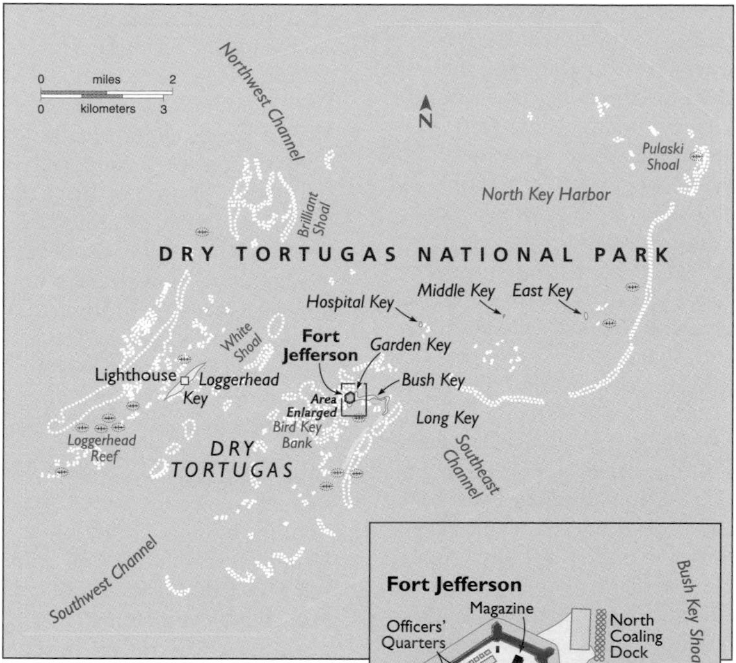

0 miles 2
0 kilometers 3
N
Northwest Channel
Pulaski Shoal
North Key Harbor
Brilliant Shoal
DRY TORTUGAS NATIONAL PARK
Middle Key
East Key
Hospital Key
White Shoal
Fort Jefferson
Garden Key
Lighthouse
Loggerhead Key
Bush Key
Area Enlarged
Bird Key Bank
Long Key
Loggerhead Reef
DRY TORTUGAS
Southeast Channel
Southwest Channel

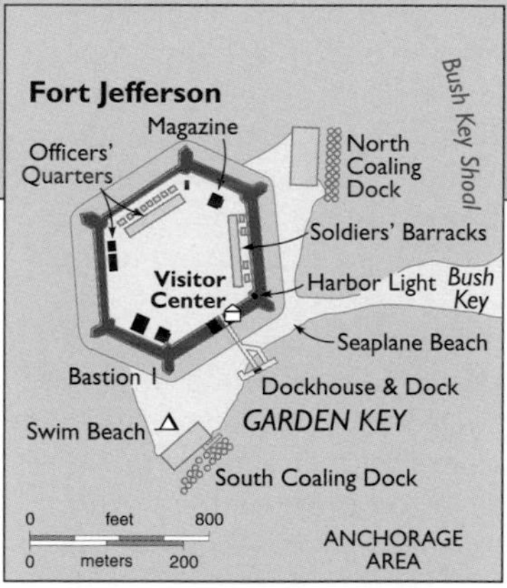

Fort Jefferson
Magazine
Officers' Quarters
North Coaling Dock
Bush Key Shoal
Soldiers' Barracks
Visitor Center
Harbor Light
Bush Key
Seaplane Beach
Bastion
Dockhouse & Dock
Swim Beach
GARDEN KEY
South Coaling Dock
0 feet 800
0 meters 200
ANCHORAGE AREA

Association bookstore has posted hours. View the self-operated video orientation program, then take a self-guided tour of **Fort Jefferson**'s massive architecture and parklike parade ground. Granite spiral staircases lead to open-air gun emplacements atop the fort, where visitors will find splendid 360-degree views—excellent vantage points for binocular-aided bird-watching. (Early on, the population of terns, cormorants, gulls, boobies, plovers, pelicans, peregrine falcons, and twin-tailed frigate birds caught the attention of naturalists like John James Audubon, who sailed here from Key West in 1832 to study them.) Visit the **Garden Key harbor light,** and stroll the grassy parapet, where huge coastal guns are on display.

Stroll along the fort's 0.6-mile-long **seawall** and moat, a sheltered habitat favored by queen conch, yellow stingray, gray snapper, sea

Sunlit archways of Fort Jefferson

INFORMATION & ACTIVITIES

HEADQUARTERS

Dry Tortugas NP headquarters is located at Everglades NP, 40001 State Rd. 9336, Homestead, FL 33034. Phone (305) 242-7700. www.nps.gov/drto

SEASONS & ACCESSIBILITY

Open all year. Visitation peaks in spring, when advance boat or plane reservations are advised. Only Garden Key offers overnight stays (in campgrounds). Loggerhead and Bush Keys available for day use only. Bush Key is closed from March to September during nesting season.

VISITOR & INFORMATION CENTERS

Visitor center open daily all year.

ENTRANCE FEE

$5 per person.

PETS

Permitted only in the campground and must be leashed at all times.

FACILITIES FOR DISABLED

Dock, visitor center, ground level of fort, and Fort Jefferson campground are accessible.

THINGS TO DO

Occasional ranger-led activities. Self-guided walking tours of Fort Jefferson. Also, swimming, snorkeling, wreck diving, underwater photography, bird-watching, sportfishing, camping, stargazing.

SPECIAL ADVISORIES

- Plan to bring all water, food, fuel, and supplies. There is no fresh water available for campers, and no showers for rinsing after swimming.
- Private boats must anchor offshore in designated areas. There are no public boat moorings or slips.
- No public telephone service to the Tortugas.

CAMPGROUNDS

Camping is permitted only on Garden Key, which has 10 primitive sites available. First come, first served. 14-day limit. Fees are $3 per person per night. Groups of ten or more must obtain a special permit in advance from park headquarters. Write for reservations at P.O. Box 6208, Key West, FL 33041; allow 30 days for processing.

HOTELS, MOTELS, & INNS

(unless otherwise noted, rates are for 2 persons in a double room, high season)

In Key West, FL 33040:

Best Western Key Ambassador Resort Inn 3755 S. Roosevelt Blvd. (800) 432-4315 or (305) 296-3500. 101 units. $159-$209. AC.

Duval House 815 Duval St. (305) 294-1666. 29 units, 2 with kitchens. $165-$310. AC.

The Marquesa Hotel 600 Fleming St. (305) 292-1919. 27 units. $285-$430. AC, pool, restaurant.

Westwinds 914 Eaton St. (800) 788-4150 or (305) 296-4440. 26 units, 7 kitchenettes. $165. AC.

For other area accommodations, contact the Key West Chamber of Commerce, 402 Wall St., Key West, FL 33040. (800) 527-8539 or (305) 294-2587.

stars, and other creatures. Outside the wall, a superb snorkeling area—chest deep and decorated with sea fans, brain coral, and turtle grass—teems with many of the 442 species of fish identified in this protected marine sanctuary. (The visitor center has a limited number of goggles, snorkels, and flippers available for loan.)

If you can enlist a companion for mutual safety, consider swimming from the campground's bathing beach along the wall, where fish tend to congregate. Watch for barracuda, which though seldom aggressive are territorial and should be given wide berth.

Sunrise over mangroves in Florida Bay

EVERGLADES

FLORIDA
ESTABLISHED DECEMBER 6, 1947
1,507,850 acres

A short parade of visitors follows a ranger on an Everglades nature walk. For more than an hour she has shown them the living wonders around them—butterflies and snails, alligators and fish, and bird after bird. Near the end of the walk, she gathers the visitors around her. She points to a string of nine white ibis coursing a cloudless sky.

"Imagine seeing ibis in the 1930s," she says. "That would have been a flight of about 90 birds. We are seeing only about 10 percent of the wading birds that were here then. When you get home, write your congressmen and tell them we have to save Everglades." Though park staff may not lobby Congress, in this threatened national park, lobbying happens on nature walks and appears in official literature.

The park is at the southern tip of the everglades, a hundred-mile-long subtropical wilderness of saw-grass prairie, junglelike hammock, and mangrove swamp, that originally ran from Lake Okeechobee to Florida Bay. Water, essential to the survival of this ecosystem, once flowed south from the lake unhindered. But as the buildup of southern Florida has intensified, canals, levees, and dikes have increasingly diverted the water to land developments and agribusinesses. Vast irrigated farmlands have spread to the park's gates. The waning of the ibis carries a warning: Watery habitats in the park are shrinking because not enough water is getting to Everglades.

The park's special mission inspires the crusade to save it. Unlike early parks established to protect scenery, Everglades was created to preserve a portion of this vast ecosystem as a wildlife habitat. The park's unique mix of tropical and temperate plants and animals—including more than 700 plant and 300 bird species, as well as the endangered manatee, crocodile, and Florida panther—has prompted UNESCO to grant it international biosphere reserve status as well as World Heritage site designation.

Everglades environmentalists and crusaders urge the purchase of privately owned wetlands east and north of the park. This would further protect the ecosystem and give the park a larger claim to the water that Everglades shares with its thirsty neighbors.

The diverse life of Everglades National Park, from algae to alligators, depends upon a rhythm of abundance and drought. In the wet season, a river inches deep and miles wide flows, almost invisibly, to the Gulf of Mexico. In the dry season, the park rests, awaiting the water's return. The plants and animals are a part of this rhythm. When humans change it, they put Everglades life at risk.

How to Get There

South from Miami, take US 1—Florida's Turnpike to Florida City, then go west on Fla. 9336 (Palm Dr.) to the Ernest F. Coe Visitor Center, about 50 miles from Miami. West from Miami, take US 41 (the Tamiami Trail) to Shark Valley Visitor Center. From Naples, head east on US 41 to Fla. 29, then south to Everglades City. Airports: Miami and Naples.

When to Go

Everglades has two seasons: dry (mid-December through mid-April) and wet (the rest of the year). The park schedules most of its activities in the dry season; hot, humid weather and clouds of mosquitoes make park visitors extremely uncomfortable during the wet season.

How to Visit

If you can stay only a day for a drive-in visit, get out of your car and learn about Everglades ecology by taking self-guided walks at road turnoffs on the drive from the **Ernest F. Coe Visitor Center** to Flamingo. For a longer stay, pick either **Flamingo** or **Everglades City** as your base and time your travels to the schedules of concession boat tours. In wet or dry season, only a boat or canoe gives you access to the backcountry. Because of mosquitoes, the dry season is best for canoeing. (Near park entrances you'll see signs advertising airboat rides; airboats, which can disturb wildlife and tear up saw grass, are not licensed to operate in the park.)

ROYAL PALM TO FLAMINGO

76 miles round-trip; a full day

The main park road connects the main entrance, southwest of Florida City, with Flamingo on Florida Bay. Make the drive an exploration, not a dash. Stops at the suggested sites can be made on the way to or from Flamingo, depending upon when you want to board a concession tour boat there. Check on that day's

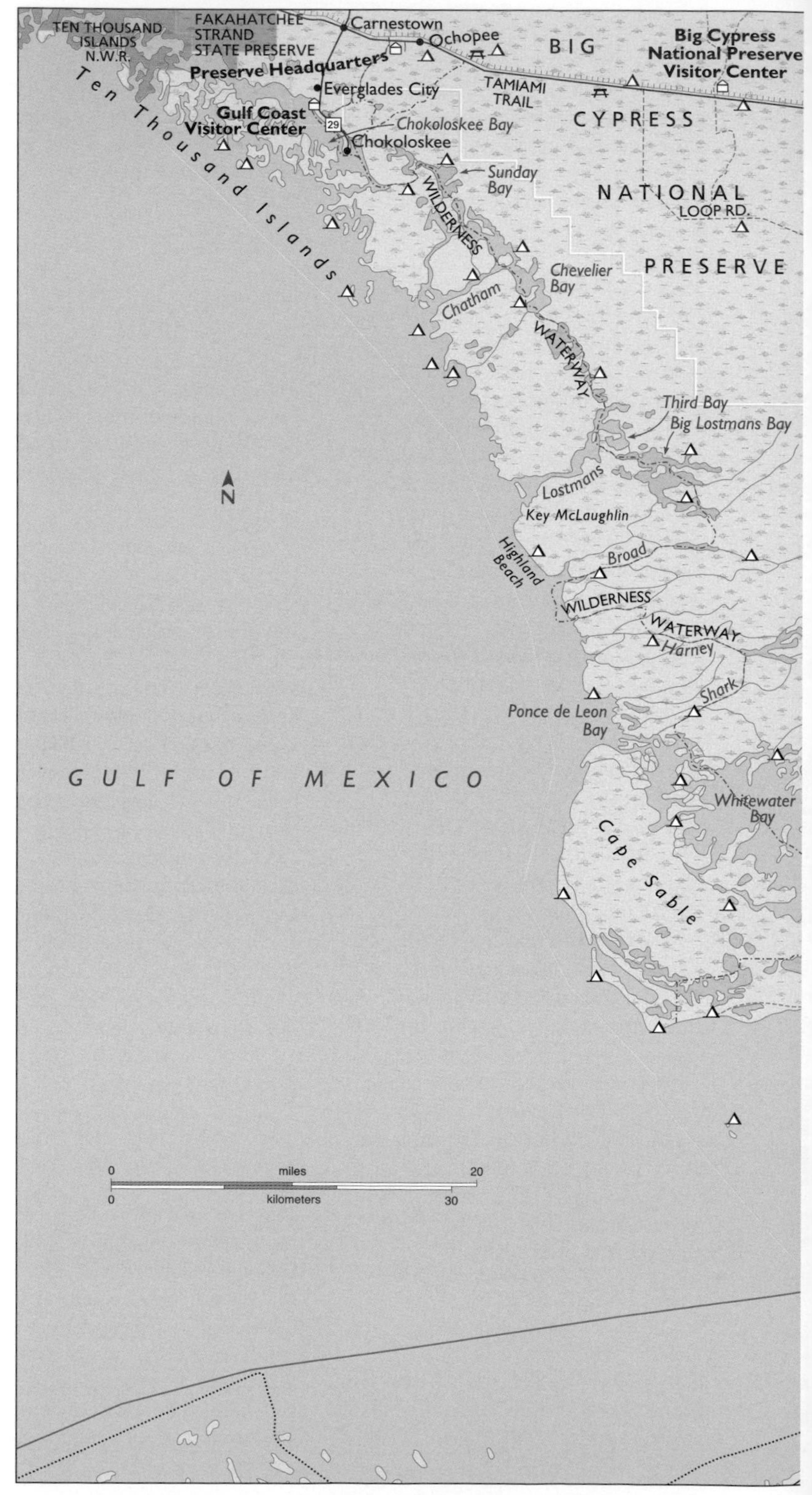

TEN THOUSAND ISLANDS N.W.R.
FAKAHATCHEE STRAND STATE PRESERVE
Carnestown
Ochopee
BIG CYPRESS NATIONAL PRESERVE
Big Cypress National Preserve Visitor Center
Preserve Headquarters
Everglades City
TAMIAMI TRAIL
Gulf Coast Visitor Center
29
Chokoloskee Bay
Chokoloskee
Ten Thousand Islands
Sunday Bay
LOOP RD.
WILDERNESS
Chevelier Bay
Chatham
WATERWAY
Third Bay
Big Lostmans Bay
Lostmans
Key McLaughlin
Highland Beach
Broad
WILDERNESS
WATERWAY
Harney
Shark
Ponce de Leon Bay
Whitewater Bay
Cape Sable
GULF OF MEXICO
N
0
miles
20
0
kilometers
30

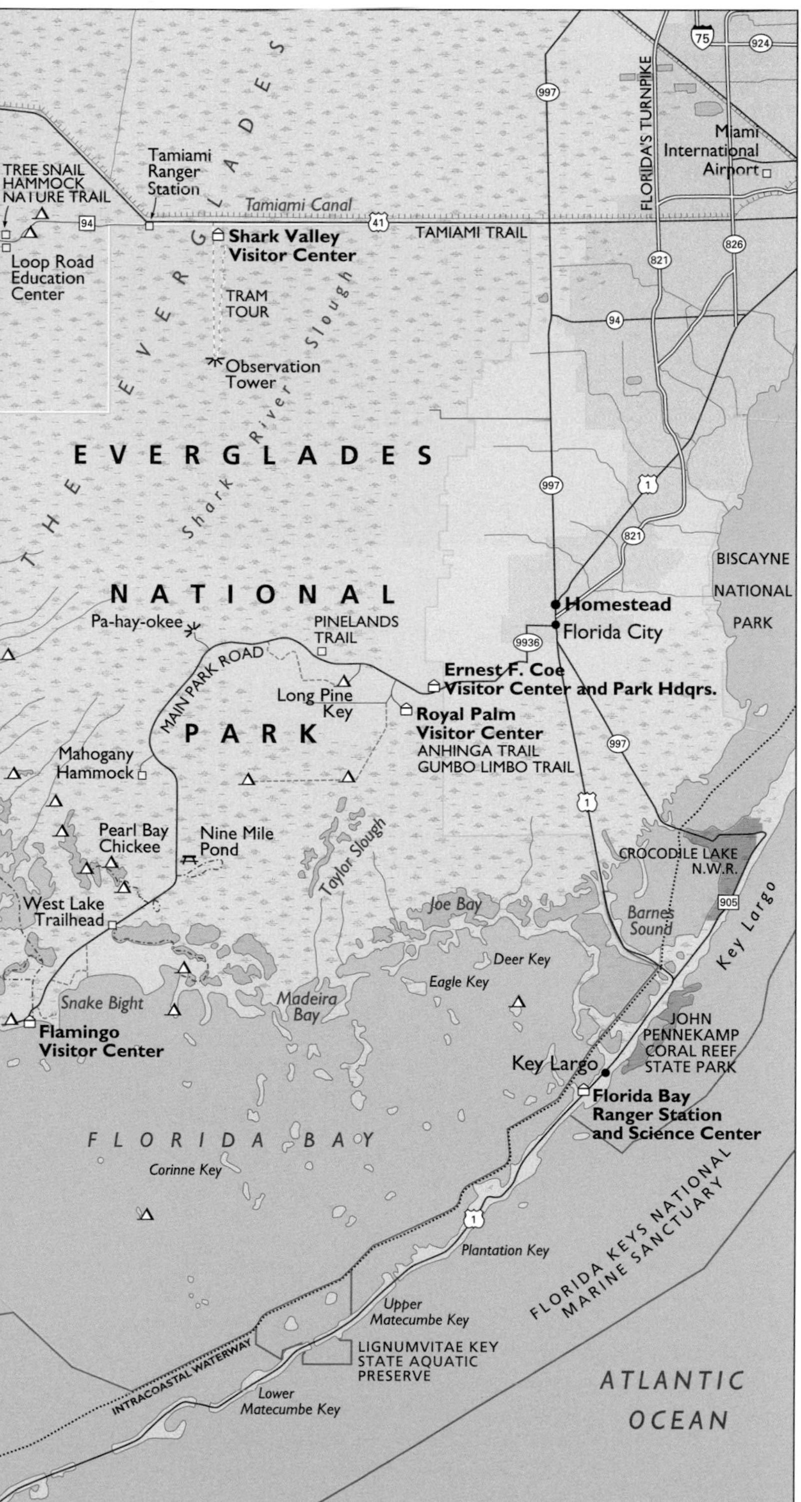

EVERGLADES NATIONAL PARK
THE EVERGLADES
TREE SNAIL HAMMOCK NATURE TRAIL
Tamiami Ranger Station
Tamiami Canal
Shark Valley Visitor Center
TAMIAMI TRAIL
Loop Road Education Center
TRAM TOUR
Shark River Slough
Observation Tower
FLORIDA'S TURNPIKE
Miami International Airport
Pa-hay-okee
PINELANDS TRAIL
MAIN PARK ROAD
Long Pine Key
Ernest F. Coe Visitor Center and Park Hdqrs.
Royal Palm Visitor Center
ANHINGA TRAIL
GUMBO LIMBO TRAIL
Homestead
Florida City
BISCAYNE NATIONAL PARK
Mahogany Hammock
Pearl Bay Chickee
Nine Mile Pond
Taylor Slough
West Lake Trailhead
Joe Bay
CROCODILE LAKE N.W.R.
Barnes Sound
Key Largo
Deer Key
Eagle Key
Snake Bight
Madeira Bay
Flamingo Visitor Center
JOHN PENNEKAMP CORAL REEF STATE PARK
Key Largo
Florida Bay Ranger Station and Science Center
FLORIDA BAY
Corinne Key
Plantation Key
FLORIDA KEYS NATIONAL MARINE SANCTUARY
Upper Matecumbe Key
LIGNUMVITAE KEY STATE AQUATIC PRESERVE
INTRACOASTAL WATERWAY
Lower Matecumbe Key
ATLANTIC OCEAN
75
924
997
41
94
821
826
1
9936
905

Slash pines at sunrise near Mahogany Hammock

cruises by calling the concessioner (see **Information & Activities** p. 62).

At the **Ernest F. Coe Visitor Center,** get oriented to this complex park. A short film stresses environmental threats to the park and alerts you to the subtle, imperiled beauty you will be seeing. Check the center's daily posted schedule for ranger-led walks and talks at the Royal Palm Visitor Center, just ahead, and for that day's cruises at Flamingo, 38 miles away. Time your road travel each way by adjusting to the day's schedules.

Egrets, herons, and other species dot the saw grass and roadside trees. On the road, use a passenger as a bird spotter; simultaneous driving and bird-watching can be dangerous. At 4 miles, turn off to the **Royal Palm Visitor Center.** There are two trails here to stroll.

You can walk the half-mile **Anhinga Trail** on your own, but if you join a ranger-led group you'll have a better chance of spotting wildlife. The boardwalk trail skirts a shallow, freshwater slough (pronounced slew) home to some 18 different grasses and flowering plants. You almost certainly will see alligators and some fascinating birds, including the long-necked, long-beaked fish-spearer for which the trail is named.

The ranger adds lore to what you see: That beautiful zebra butterfly tastes terrible; a predatory bird never tries for second helpings. Those white egg sacs on that branch will hatch apple snails, the prime food of the endangered snail kite. That slim, long-snouted fish gliding through the clear water is a gar; in the dry season it can survive in a mudhole because a primitive lung allows it to breathe air. That alligator loosens the muck in water-filled solution holes and sweeps it away with its tail; in the dry season the gator-made oasis keeps fish, frogs, snails, and birds alive—as long as they are wary of the major resident. In Everglades, unusual adaptations and delicate balances sustain the park's astonishing variety of animals and plants.

The other trail here is the half-mile **Gumbo Limbo Trail,** named for a tree whose peeling red bark gives it another name: tourist tree. The trail takes you to a hammock, an elevated island of tropical hardwood—including gumbo limbos and some magnificent examples of strangler figs—in a sea of saw grass. The slight elevation keeps the ground drier, permitting the hardwoods to flourish and creating a shaded habitat for many creatures, from snakes to deer, foxes, and raccoon.

Watch for "solution holes," limestone depressions that hold moisture and become miniature ecosystems in the dry season. Filled with organic material and seeded by winds or bird droppings, some solution holes evolve into hammocks.

Back on the road, visit the roadside exhibits. Stop-and-walk lessons begin on the 0.75-mile **Pinelands Trail,** 7 miles along the road. Slash pines grow on high ground—5 to 7 feet above sea level—so pinelands were wiped out to develop Miami and other towns. What you see here are remnants of the pines that once covered southeastern Florida. The flowers growing here are the perky tickseed and the ruellia with its purple blooms.

Driving toward Flamingo, you can stop and take a short boardwalk stroll that leads you to **Pinnacle Rock,** a sample of the porous limestone that is South Florida's bedrock. At 12 miles, stop again to see dwarf cypresses, trees stunted by shallow soil.

Half a mile farther is an overlook called **Pa-hay-okee,** or "grassy waters," the Indian name for the Everglades. A boardwalk takes you to a shaded observation stage where you can look out on a seemingly endless prairie of grassy waters. At 19.5 miles is **Mahogany Hammock,** where a boardwalk leads to the largest living mahogany tree in the United States.

If you want to picnic, there are fine spots at **Paurotis Pond** (at 24.5 miles), **Nine Mile Pond** (at 26.5 miles), and **West Lake** (at 30.5 miles).

At **Flamingo,** which offers the only in-park accommodations, sign up for a boat tour in the marina ticket office near the visitor center. While you are waiting, take the self-guided, half-mile walk around the waterfront to see **Florida Bay**, a marine nursery protected by the park. Roseate spoonbills, raccoons,

Paddling on a channel into Florida Bay

black bears, and manatees are just some of the out-of-water critters often spotted here.

The 2-hour backcountry cruise begins in the marina and enters **Buttonwood Canal,** built in 1957. Among the spidery roots of the three species of mangrove you will see along the waterway, watch for shy crocodiles, which sometimes sun on the banks of the canal. The cruise crosses **Coot Bay** and enters **Whitewater Bay,** where backcountry canoeists camp on chickees, tent-size platforms raised on poles. Don't expect to see flamingos; they rarely appear at their namesake town.

SHARK VALLEY TO EVERGLADES CITY

49 miles one way; a full day

The **Tamiami Trail** (US 41) forms part of the park's northeastern border. Near the eastern park entrance, stop at the **Shark Valley Visitor Center.** Here is a 15-mile loop road accessible only on foot, on bike, or, year-round, on a 2-hour, narrated tour aboard an open-sided concessioner tram.

You will not see sharks. The valley gets its name from the **Shark River;** sharks gather at its mouth in the Gulf of Mexico. But you will see alligator trails leading to hammocks in the saw grass—and you will almost certainly see alligators and wading birds. A pathway leads to a 65-foot tower looking down on the vista that became a name: glades that seem to go on forever. It's a marvelous place to spot turtles, alligators, and wading birds. Look for red-shouldered hawks, snail kites, northern harriers, and rare short-tailed hawks over the marsh.

Return to US 41, which veers northward into the 2,400-square-mile **Big Cypress National Preserve,** part of the Everglades ecosystem. Most of the water flowing into the park comes through four floodgates that you can see north of the highway along the park boundary.

At Fla. 29, turn south for Everglades City. Follow the highway through the town to the waterfront. Sign up for one of the regularly scheduled, round-trip, narrated concessioner boat tours (or you can explore by boat or kayak on your own).

The **Ten Thousand Island** trip explores mangrove islands in the Gulf of Mexico. On the way to and from the islands, protected sea mammals—sleek bottlenose dolphins and lumbering manatees—often pop up to look at the boat. You can usually see ospreys, pelicans, and cormorants. From a distance, the islands look like a solid stretch of low-lying green land. Close up, you see a labyrinth of thousands of waterways.

There are far fewer than 10,000 islands, but the number is unknown and ever changing. Islands form from the buildup of leaves and other organic material among the stilt-rooted mangroves. As an island grows, storms and tidal forces may break it into fragments, which continue to grow and spread. The islands, ranging in size from a couple of trees to several hundred acres, provide shelter and food for many creatures in the gulf web of life.

The boat crosses **Chokoloskee Bay,** which shares its name with an island of shells, 15 feet high and 147 acres, built by Native Americans long before the first white men appeared here. The bay is the northern end of the 99-mile Everglades City-to-Flamingo **Wilderness Waterway,** a system of backcountry canoe trails through the estuarine fringes of the park.

Clockwise from top left: raccoon hiding in mangrove roots; tree frog; bull thistle in Shark Valley; alligator in marsh; snail kite in search of food

INFORMATION & ACTIVITIES

HEADQUARTERS
40001 State Rd. 9446, Homestead, FL 33034. Phone (305) 242-7700. www.nps.gov/ever

SEASONS & ACCESSIBILITY
Open all year; some facilities and services limited or unavailable during off-season, May to mid-December.

VISITOR & INFORMATION CENTERS
Ernest F. Coe Visitor Center on Fla. 9336 at park entrance. **Royal Palm Visitor Center** off main park road a few miles inside park entrance. **Flamingo Visitor Center** on main park road at Florida Bay; may close temporarily off-season. **Shark Valley Visitor Center** at north end of park on US 41. **Gulf Coast Visitor Center** at Everglades City on Fla. 29 at northwest entrance.

ENTRANCE FEES
$10 per car per week. $5 per person biking or walking in.

PETS
Pets must be on leashes and are allowed in the campgrounds only.

FACILITIES FOR DISABLED
All visitor centers, campgrounds, restrooms, and tram tours are accessible. Several trails are at least partly accessible. In the backcountry, Pearl Bay Chickee is accessible.

THINGS TO DO
Free naturalist-led activities: nature walks and talks, hikes, exhibits, seasonal evening programs. Also, tram tours; sight-seeing boats; canoe, kayak, houseboat, motorboat, and bicycle rentals; fishing (need license); crabbing; shrimping (ask about regulations). In winter and on holidays, call to reserve space on guided tours and activities.

Rentals and boat tours in Flamingo: (239) 695-3101 ext. 355. Tram tour at Shark Valley: (305) 221-8455. Boat tours and rentals at Everglades City: (239) 695-2591, or (800) 445-7724 in Florida.

SPECIAL ADVISORIES
- You'll need insect repellent year-round, but especially April to December.
- Swimming not advised; alligators, crocodiles, and snakes live in ponds; sharks and barracuda, in saltwater areas.

WILDERNESS CAMPING
Permits required, $10 per permit and $2 per person; obtainable in person, no more than 24 hours before trip, at Flamingo or Everglades City. Fees collected mid-Nov. through April only. No reservations; first come, first served; limits on number of people and length of stay.

CAMPGROUNDS
Two campgrounds, 14-day limit Nov. to May; otherwise 30-day limit. $14 per site collected Nov. through May only. **Flamingo** and **Long Pine Key** open all year. Reservations available mid-Dec. to April; reserve through NPRS (see p. 10); rest of year, first come, first served. Tent and RV sites; no hookups. Three group campgrounds; reservations suggested. Food services limited April to Dec.

HOTELS, MOTELS, & INNS
(unless otherwise noted, rates are for 2 persons in a double room, high season)

<u>*INSIDE THE PARK:*</u>

Flamingo Lodge (end of main park road) 1 Flamingo Lodge Hwy. (800) 600-3813 or (239) 695-3101. 98 units. Lodge rooms $95; cottages with kitchens $135. AC, pool.

<u>*OUTSIDE THE PARK:*</u>

<u>*In Florida City, FL 33034:*</u>

Comfort Inn 333 S.E. 1st Ave./US 1. (305) 248-4009. 124 units. $59-$250. AC, pool.

Coral Roc Motel 1100 N. Krome Ave. (305) 247-4010. 16 units, 4 kitchenettes. $36-$89. AC, pool.

Knights Inn 1223 N.E. 1st Ave./US 1. (305) 247-6621. 49 units, 6 kitchenettes. $79-$169. AC, pool.

<u>*In Homestead, FL 33030:*</u>

Days Inn 51 S. Homestead Blvd. (305) 245-1260. 111 units. $60. AC, pool, rest.

Everglades Motel 605 S. Krome Ave. (305) 247-4117. 14 units. $68. AC, pool.

For other lodgings, contact the Homestead/Florida City Chamber of Commerce, 43 N. Krome Ave., Homestead, FL 33030. (305) 247-2332.

EXCURSIONS

BIG CYPRESS NATIONAL PRESERVE

OCHOPEE, FLORIDA

Dispensing life-giving fresh water to the Everglades and coastal estuaries, this preserve contains marshes, cypress stands, prairies, hardwood hammocks, pinelands, and mangrove forests, along with wading birds and alligators. The endangered Florida panther and black bears roam the area. 729,000 acres. Hiking, birding, fishing, canoeing, off-road vehicles, scenic drives. Six campgrounds, picnic areas. On US 41 (Tamiami Trail); adjoins Everglades NP. (239) 695-4111.

CORKSCREW SWAMP SANCTUARY

NAPLES, FLORIDA

A 2.25-mile-long boardwalk takes visitors on a self-guided tour through this Audubon Society site featuring the country's largest stand of virgin bald cypress forest and varied wildlife, including alligators. 11,000 acres. Hiking and picnic areas. Open all year. Off Fla. 846, about 50 miles northwest of Everglades NP. (239) 348-9151.

J. N. "DING" DARLING NATIONAL WILDLIFE REFUGE

SANIBEL, FLORIDA

Migratory songbirds and a large population of roseate spoonbills feature among the 230 bird species on this island refuge named for Pulitzer Prize-winning political cartoonist and refuge system pioneer Jay Norwood Darling. 6,400 acres. Hiking, canoeing, bicycling, fishing, scenic drive. Open all year, dawn to dusk (closed on Fridays). Visitor center off US 41, about 75 miles northwest of Everglades NP. (239) 472-1100.

Mist-shrouded autumn view from Clingmans Dome

GREAT SMOKY MOUNTAINS

NORTH CAROLINA & TENNESSEE
ESTABLISHED JUNE 15, 1934
521,490 acres

The fact invariably stated about Great Smoky is this: It is the nation's busiest park, drawing more than nine million visitors a year, twice the number of any other national park. Most of the millions see the park from a mountain-skimming scenic highway that, on a typical weekend day during the summer, draws 60,000 people, bumper-to-bumper.

Luckily, there is plenty of park, thinly laced by 384 miles of mountain roads. You can pull off the road, park the car, and stroll one of Great Smoky's many Quiet Walkways, quarter-mile paths into what the signs call a "little bit of the world as it once was." Eight hundred miles of hiking trails, from a half mile to 70 miles long, also give you that world. Relatively few visitors walk the trails; most prefer to stay in their cars.

The park, which covers 800 square miles of mountainous terrain, preserves the world's best examples of deciduous forest and a matchless variety of plants and animals. Because it contains so many types of eastern forest vegetation—much of it old growth—the park has been designated an international biosphere reserve.

The Smoky Mountains are among the oldest on earth. Ice Age glaciers stopped their southward journey just short of these mountains, which became a junction of southern and northern flora. Rhododendron and mountain laurel thrust from the weathered rocks. Amid the woodland and craggy peaks bloom more than 1,600 species of flowering plants, some found only here. Shrubs take over in places, creating tree-free zones called heath balds, laurel slicks (because of the shiny leaves), or just plain hells (because they are so hard to get through).

The tangle of brush and trees forms a close-packed array of air-breathing leaves. The water and hydrocarbons exuded by the leaves produce the filmy "smoke" that gives the mountains their name. Air pollution in recent years has added microscopic sulfate particles to the haze, cutting visibility back about 60 percent since the 1950s. The pollution has also affected the park's red spruce stand—the southern Appalachians' largest. And insects are destroying the Fraser fir, the spruce's high-altitude companion.

The park also preserves the humble churches, cabins, farmhouses, and barns of the mountain people who began settling here in the late 1700s. Most people left, when the park was founded; but some chose to stay and live out their lives here.

How to Get There

From Knoxville, Tenn. (about 25 miles away), take I-40 to Tenn. 66, then US 441 to Gatlinburg entrance. From Asheville, N.C. (about 40 miles away), take I-40 west to US 19, then US 441, to park's southern entrance near Cherokee, N.C. For a scenic, low-speed approach, take the 469-mile Blue Ridge Parkway that connects Virginia's Shenandoah National Park with Great Smoky. Airports: Knoxville and Asheville.

When to Go

Year-round. In summer and in fall (when spectacular foliage draws huge crowds), time your visit to midweek, and arrive early. Visitor centers open year-round.

How to Visit

On a 1-day visit, take the **Newfound Gap Road** to **Clingmans Dome** and get the best overview of the park by seeing it from the highest point. The best second-day activity is the **Cades Cove loop road,** a chance to drive or cycle through pioneer history. For a longer stay, focus on the self-guided nature trails and drives, which get you away from the crowds and show you the flora and fauna.

NEWFOUND GAP ROAD TO CLINGMANS DOME

40 to 45 miles; a half to full day

Newfound **Gap Road,** which begins at 1,200 feet and ascends to 5,048 feet, connects the park's major visitor centers, **Sugarlands** (near Gatlinburg, Tenn.) and **Oconaluftee** (near Cherokee, N.C). The road, passing from lowland hardwood timber to high-altitude spruce-fir forests, gives you a vertical trip that is ecologically equivalent to a journey from Georgia to Canada. Be prepared for rain on almost any day. A clear day below can be a day of mist and fog on high. From Sugarlands (for an Oconaluftee start, reverse the order below), stop after 5 miles at **Chimneys,** a

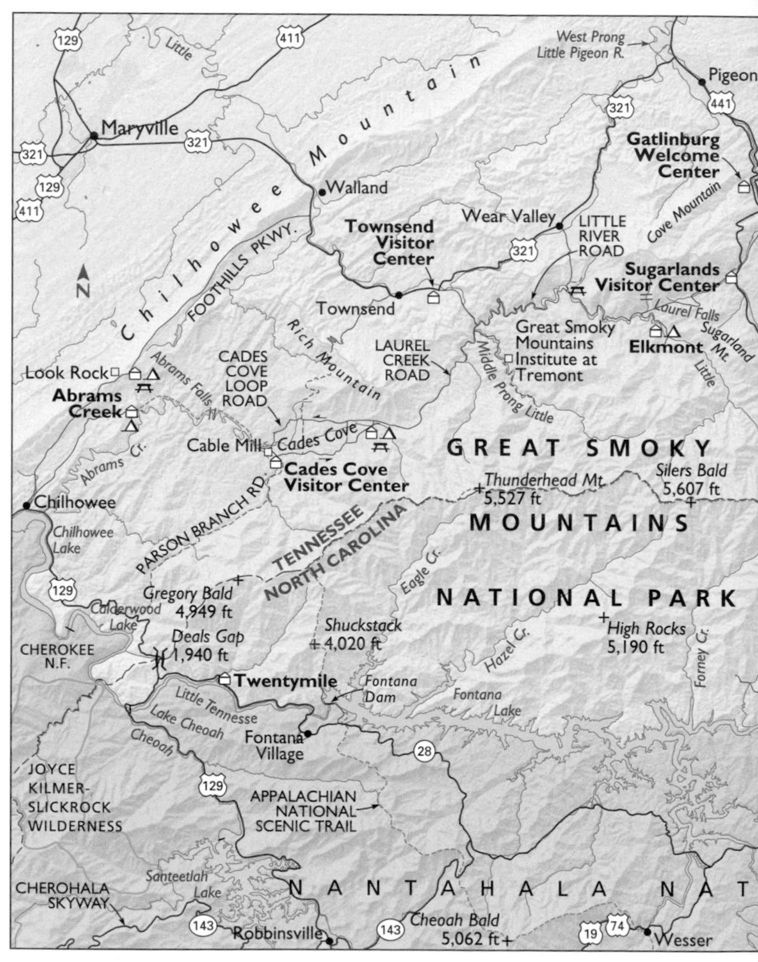

fine picnic spot. Stretch your legs on the 0.75-mile self-guided **Cove Hardwood Nature Trail.** Then return to the car for a short drive to the **Chimney Tops Overlooks,** which offer views of the double summits the Cherokee called Duniskwal-guni ("forked antlers").

Here you can extend your stop with a hike on the steep, 4-mile round-trip **Chimney Tops Trail** through an old-growth forest and up 1,335 feet to the sheer cliffs named the Chimneys. Depending on your time and stamina, you can also get out of the car and hike at the next overlook, where a trailhead leads to a steep climb to **Alum Cave Bluffs,** site of a 19th-century commercial alum mine and reputedly a source of saltpeter for Civil War gunpowder. The trail begins with an easy 1.3-mile trail along a tree-bordered creek to **Arch Rock,** a tunnel made by eons of erosion. The trees include towering 200-year-old eastern hemlocks. This is a magnificent spot for a spring wildflower hike serenaded by the songs of nesting warblers. You can return to your car

or continue on a steep 0.9-mile ascent to the bluffs.

Back in the car, continue on to **Newfound Gap** (5,048 feet), through which runs the Tennessee–North Carolina state line and a long leg of the Appalachian Trail. From the overlook here, on a clear day, you can see **Mount LeConte** (6,593 feet) and your next stop, **Clingmans Dome.** The 7-mile Clingmans Dome Road veers sharply off here and winds through a spruce-fir forest to a parking lot.

There begins a steep half-mile trail ending at a spiral ramp. It leads to a lookout tower at the top of the 6,643-foot dome, the highest point in the park, where you get either a panoramic view or a sense of floating on a sea of churning clouds. From here retrace the route to Sugarlands or, depending on time and destination, continue on to Oconaluftee Visitor Center. The **Mountain Farm Museum,** a cluster of farm buildings gathered from their original locations within the park, stands adjacent to the visitor center. Pioneer-costumed park employees, playing farmstead roles, give demonstrations spring through October. (Between May and October, at **Mingus Mill,** a miller explains how cornmeal and flour would have been produced on an ingenious water-run turbine.)

CADES COVE LOOP ROAD

11 miles; at least a half day

Follow Little River and Laurel Creek Roads for 25 miles from Sugarlands Visitor Center to the Cades Cove loop road. **Cades Cove** traces its history to 1819, when, under a treaty with the Cherokee Indians, settlers cleared the broad, high valley. By 1850 more than 680 people were living there. They left behind structures that evolved into an open-air museum whose galleries are sites along the paved, 11-mile one-way loop road. Official sites are well marked. But you may find yourself making unofficial stops to admire the quietude, to watch white-tailed deer bounding across the valley, or to see black bears feed on acorns or wild grapes.

The first stop is **John Oliver Place,** site 3. The small cabin was built with split-wood shingles and hand-hewn logs. Stand on the porch and look down the long, green-carpeted valley that drew the family to this place, the edge of the American world in 1826. **Primitive Baptist Church,** site 4, is skipped by some visitors because it lies on a two-way dirt road off the loop road. Don't miss it. The plain white-frame church, organized in 1827, guards a small graveyard. Time has made many stones nameless, but the past still can be read on them. The church shut down during the Civil War because, a letter says, "we was Union people and the Rebels was too strong here in Cades Cove."

Mountain laurel along one of the Pigeon River prongs

Methodist Church, site 5, had a door for men and another for women and children. During services, the separation was enforced in the pews by a barrier.

Just past the church is **Hyatt Lane,** an old road out of Cades Cove and today a shortcut that slices off a big piece of the tour. Stay on the loop road and continue to **Missionary Baptist Church,** site 7, formed in 1839 by expelled members of the Primitive Baptist Church. Because the congregation split between Union and Confederacy sympathizers, this church also closed during the Civil War.

Continue on the road, past **Rich Mountain Road,** site 8. Save this for another day. The gravel road, laid over an Indian trail, goes up **Rich Mountain** and provides a spectacular backward glance at Cades Cove before exiting the park. Also requiring more time is the **Cooper Road Trail,** site 9, a onetime wagon road that is now a 13-mile hiking trail ending outside the park.

Ahead on the right is a short, two-way road to the next stops, **Abrams Falls,** site 10, and **Elijah Oliver Place,** site 11. If you take this offshoot, you come to a parking lot and a choice: a 2-hour, 2.5-mile hike up to stunning Abrams Falls, or a half-mile hike to another rustic farmstead owned by early settler Elijah Oliver. The latter features a smokehouse, springhouse, and corn crib.

Continue your drive along the loop road to the next offshoot, which leads to **John Cable Mill,** site 12, where corn was ground into meal. Here, the **Cades Cove Visitor Center** displays artifacts and pictures depicting life in Cades Cove that help visitors connect intellectually and emotionally with the people who called this serene valley their home. Now leave the center and wander about,

Hikers explore one of Great Smoky's trails *(top)*
White-tailed buck leaping over a fence *(bottom)*

reliving the life that centered on the old mill.

Other buildings—a blacksmith shop, a large cantilever barn, a smokehouse—were imported from elsewhere in the park. Check at the visitor center for schedules of farm-life demonstrations; they include the making of sorghum molasses: a horse-powered mill squeezes juice from the stalks, which is then boiled down in an open-air vat.

Just beyond the Cable Mill area is **Parson Branch Road,** which can take you out of the park—and the 21st century. The narrow winding one-way dirt road (sometimes closed by weather; check with the park) was carved out of wilderness about 1838. The 8-mile trip to US 129 can take an hour. If prudence keeps you on the loop road, your next stop will be **Tipton Place,** site 17. Built by Hamp Tipton shortly after the Civil War, it

Black bear climbing down from a cherry tree after an all-night gorge

later became the home of a blacksmith, who put up his shop nearby.

Drive on to the last stop, **Carter Shields Cabin,** site 18. Log cabins like this would be succeeded by board houses, which arrived with lumbering in the early 1900s.

HIKES & DRIVES

Self-guided nature trails begin with an honor system document rack. You drop in 50 cents and pluck out a leaflet keyed to numbered stops. **Balsam Mountain Trail** is the easiest climbing trail in the park, a 1.5-mile loop from Balsam Mountain Campground. The trail gives you a short lesson in the identification of trees and, especially in spring, wildflowers. **Laurel Falls Trail** is paved. The 2.5-mile round-trip trail, which starts on Little River Road near Elkmont, winds through thickets of mountain laurel and rhododendron to one of the park's many waterfalls.

For a longer stay in the park, try some of the more rugged trails. The most rewarding hike is to **Mount LeConte,** at 6,593 feet the park's third highest peak. The shortest (though steepest) way up is via the **Alum Cave Trail,** which starts at Newfound Gap Road (see Newfound Gap Road tour, p. 65). Here begins a steep 5-mile climb to the summit of LeConte. At one point the trail skirts a cliff face so sheer that hikers must grasp a cable to make their way up.

For the motorist, there are also self-guided nature trails using roads. The **Roaring Fork Motor Nature Trail,** 4 miles from Gatlinburg off Cherokee Orchard Road, is a 5-mile curvy, one-way road with a well-warranted 10 mph speed limit. About a mile before the trail begins, you will see the **Noah "Bud" Ogle Place** on your right. A 0.75-mile path takes you around the remains of a farm—a mill, a barn, and the historic Ogle family house.

At the Roaring Fork trail, avail yourself of the self-guiding booklet that suggests scenic stops. The road climbs a hill that provides, on clear days, a splendid view of **Sugarland** and **Cove Mountains.** Along the roadside is an old-growth hemlock forest. Here and there, moldering chestnut logs are poignant reminders of the blight that struck down the onetime forest king.

INFORMATION & ACTIVITIES

HEADQUARTERS

107 Park Headquarters Rd., Gatlinburg, TN 37738. Phone (865) 436-1200. www.nps.gov/grsm

SEASONS & ACCESSIBILITY

Open all year. The road to Clingmans Dome and some unpaved roads closed in winter.

VISITOR & INFORMATION CENTERS

Sugarlands, on US 441 south of the Gatlinburg, Tenn., entrance; **Oconaluftee,** on US 441 north of Cherokee, N.C., entrance; **Cades Cove Visitor Center,** near Townsend, Tenn., entrance; enter off US 321, east of Townsend. All open daily. Call park headquarters for information.

FACILITIES FOR DISABLED

Visitor centers and restrooms are wheelchair accessible. The Sugarlands Valley Nature Trail (a quarter mile south of the Sugarlands Visitor Center) was custom built for visitors with visual or mobility impairments. Laurel Falls Trail is paved but steep; negotiable with assistance only. Free brochure.

THINGS TO DO

Free naturalist-led activities: nature walks (day and evening), children's and campfire programs, pioneer exhibits and demonstrations, slide talks. Also, annual festivals, auto tape tour, hiking, bicycling, fishing (permit needed), horseback riding (several stables in park).

OVERNIGHT BACKPACKING

Permit required; free from visitor centers and ranger stations. Camping only permitted in designated sites. You can reserve rationed sites and shelters up to 30 days in advance; call (865) 436-1231.

CAMPGROUNDS

Ten campgrounds, most with a 7-day limit mid-May through October; other times 14-day limit. Cades Cove and Smokemont open all year; **Elkmont** open April through October. Reservations required mid-May through October; available through NPRS (see p. 10). Other campgrounds open mid-March through October, first come, first served. Fees $12-$20 per night. No showers. Tent and RV sites; no hookups. Seven group campgrounds; reservations required; contact park headquarters.

HOTELS, MOTELS, & INNS

(unless otherwise noted, rates are for 2 persons in a double room, high season)

INSIDE THE PARK:

LeConte Lodge (atop Mount LeConte; access by hiking trail) 250 Apple Valley Rd., Sevierville, TN 37862. (865) 429-5704. 10 cabins, no electricity, shared bathrooms. $86, includes 2 meals. Late March–late Nov.

OUTSIDE THE PARK:

In Bryson City, NC 28713:

Hemlock Inn (on Galbraith Creek Rd., off US 19) P.O. Box 2350. (828) 488-2885. 25 units, $169-$230, includes 2 meals. Restaurant.

In Cherokee, NC 28719:

Best Western Great Smokies Inn US 441 and Acquoni Rd., P.O. Box 1809. (800) 528-1234 or (828) 497-2020. 152 units. $89. AC, pool, restaurant.

Holiday Inn Cherokee US 19S, P.O. Box 1929. (828) 497-9181. 154 units. $99-$130. AC, pool, restaurant.

In Fontana Dam, NC 28733:

Historic Fontana Village Resort N.C. 28, P.O. Box 68. (800) 849-2258 or (828) 498-2211. 90 rooms, $89; 120 cottages with kitchens, $59-$229. AC, pool, rest.

In Gatlinburg, TN 37738:

Buckhorn Inn 2140 Tudor Mountain Rd. (865) 436-4668. 9 rooms, 7 cottages, 3 guest houses. $115-$250. AC, restaurant.

Gillette Motel 235 Historic Nature Trail, P.O. Box 231. (800) 437-0815 or (865) 436-5601. 80 units. $85. AC, pool.

Holiday Inn of Gatlinburg 520 Historic Nature Trail, P.O. Box 1130. (800) 435-9201 in Tenn. or (865) 436-9201. 400 units. $89-$122. AC, pool, restaurant.

Park Vista Hotel 705 Cherokee Orchard Rd., P.O. Box 30. (800) 421-7275 or (865) 436-9211. 312 units. $90-$170. AC, pool, restaurant.

For other accommodations in Gatlinburg, call the Chamber of Commerce at (800) 822-1998 or (865) 436-4178.

EXCURSIONS

PISGAH NATIONAL FOREST
ASHEVILLE, NORTH CAROLINA

The Blue Ridge Parkway traverses this mountainous forest of mixed hardwoods, azaleas, and rhododendrons, rocky gorges, and delicate waterfalls. Stunning in spring and fall. Contains three wilderness areas and Mount Mitchell, the highest peak east of the Mississippi. 506,296 acres. 447 campsites, picnic areas. Hiking, fishing, horseback riding, hunting, scenic drives, swimming. Open all year; most campsites open spring to late fall. Visitor center on US 276, about 50 miles from Great Smoky Mountains NP. (828) 257-4200.

NANTAHALA NATIONAL FOREST
ASHEVILLE, NORTH CAROLINA

The hardwood-covered mountains here contain deep, narrow valleys, canyons, and waterfalls. Noted for azaleas, rhododendrons. Contains three wilderness areas. 531,055 acres. Hiking, boating, fishing, horseback riding, hunting, scenic drives. 395 campsites, boat ramps, picnic areas, handicapped access. Open all year; most campsites open spring to late fall. Adjoins Great Smoky Mountains NP on the south. (828) 257-4200.

BREAKS INTERSTATE PARK
BREAKS, VIRGINIA

Russell Fork cuts through the Pine Mountains here, creating Breaks Canyon, the "Grand Canyon of the South." Features class VI white water. Two rhododendron species provide long blooming season, mid-May through June; fall leaves peak mid-Oct. Gospel music festival Labor Day weekend. 4,600 acres. Hiking, boating, fishing, scenic drives, swimming. 138 campsites, cottages and motel units, visitor center, food service, boat ramp, picnic areas, handicapped access. Open all year; most facilities available April to mid-December. On Va. 80, about 190 miles from Great Smoky Mountains NP. (276) 865-4413.

BIG SOUTH FORK NATIONAL RIVER & RECREATION AREA

ONEIDA, TENNESSEE

The Big South Fork of the Cumberland River bisects the Cumberland Plateau, yielding white water as well as calm stretches, sandstone cliffs, waterfalls, and natural arches. 120,000 acres, part in Kentucky. Hiking, horseback riding, boating, fishing, swimming, hunting. 235 campsites, boat ramp, picnic areas. Open all year. Off US 27, about 100 miles northwest of Great Smoky Mountains NP. (423) 286-7275.

CHEROKEE NATIONAL FOREST

CLEVELAND, TENNESSEE

This rugged mountain backcountry is densely wooded with mixed pines and hardwoods, azaleas, mountain laurels. 640,000 acres. Hiking, boating, fishing, hunting, scenic drives, swimming. 29 campgrounds, boat ramp, 30 picnic sites. Open all year; most campgrounds open May through October. Adjoins Great Smoky Mountains NP on northeast and southwest. (423) 476-9700.

CHATTAHOOCHEE NATIONAL FOREST

GAINESVILLE, GEORGIA

This hardwood forest encompasses a mix of terrain—lakes, streams, valleys, mountains, and piedmont plateau. Contains ten wilderness areas and a stretch of the Chattooga Wild and Scenic River with Tallullah Gorge. Also, Brasstown Bald, the state's highest mountain at 4,784 feet. 750,000 acres. Hiking, sailing, fishing, hunting, scenic drives, swimming. More than 25 campgrounds, boat ramp, picnic areas, handicapped access. Open all year; campsites open May through September. On US 129, about 95 miles from Great Smoky Mountains NP. (770) 297-3000.

View west from Hot Springs Mountain Tower

HOT SPRINGS

ARKANSAS
ESTABLISHED MARCH 4, 1921
5,550 acres

Most national parks cover hundreds of thousands of acres, are far from city streets, and keep natural resources away from commercial users ... but not Hot Springs. This smallest of national parks borders a city that has made an industry out of tapping and dispensing the park's major resource: mineral-rich waters of hot springs.

The heart of this peculiar park is Central Avenue, the main street of Hot Springs, Arkansas. Rising above Central Avenue is Hot Springs Mountain, from which the waters flow. The mountain's lower western side once was coated with tufa, a milky-colored, porous rock formed of minerals deposited from the hot springs' constant cascade.

When Hot Springs prospered as a health spa in the mid-19th century, promoters covered, piped, and diverted the springs into Central Avenue bathhouses. They also prettified the slope by covering it with tons of dirt and planting grass and shrubs. "Ever since then," a longtime Hot Springs resident says, "it's been afflicted by eastern landscape architects who can't stand the sight of rocks."

The park calls itself the "oldest area in the national park system" because in 1832, 40 years before Yellowstone became the first national park, President Andrew Jackson set aside the hot springs as a special reservation. The federal land became a national park in 1921. By then Hot Springs had long been famous as a spa where people "took the waters," seeking relief from bunions, rheumatism, and other afflictions.

The park preserves the springs' "recharge zone," slopes where rain and snow soak into the ground, and the "discharge zone," which contains 47 springs belonging to the park. Each day about 850,000 gallons of water—at 143°F—flow from the springs into a complex piping and reservoir system. This supplies water to commercial baths and to park-maintained "jug fountains," where people flock daily to fill containers with the odorless, fresh-tasting, chemical-free water.

How to Get There

From Little Rock, about 55 miles west on I-30, US 70, and Ark. 7; from the south, Ark. 7; from the west, US 70 or US 270. Airport: Little Rock.

When to Go

Year-round. Summers are hot and July is crowded. Try the late fall, when mountains around Hot Springs produce spectacular foliage. Winter is usually short and mild; four-petaled bluets, the first of many wildflowers, appear in February.

Springs flowing over Tufa Terrace

How to Visit

Walk **Central Avenue's Bathhouse Row,** then continue north to explore on the genteel trails of an urban hillside. To see the rugged side of the park, hike the woodland trails of **Gulpha Gorge.**

BATHHOUSE ROW

4 city blocks; 2 hours

In the early years of this century, elegant buildings lined a stretch of **Central Avenue** dubbed Bathhouse Row. In later years, as medical science's faith in hot springs faded, so did the bathhouses. But you can still enjoy the mystique of taking the waters. First visit the **Hot Springs National Park Visitor Center** (in the former Fordyce Bathhouse), a restored "temple of health and beauty" adorned with stained-glass windows and statuary. In rooms full of gleaming plumbing and luxurious tubs, you walk through a **museum** of the ritual, which in its full form involved three weeks of daily baths and massage. The **Buckstaff** is the Row's only bathhouse still offering a traditional bath. (Some hotels also have baths; ask for information at the visitor center.)

HOT SPRINGS

a half mile; 2 hours

At the corner of Central Avenue and Fountain Street look for **DeSoto Rock,** a huge boulder that commemorates both the Indians who named this "place of the hot waters" and the explorer Hernando de Soto. According to legend, he and his party bathed in the waters in 1541, beginning a tourist tradition. Visit the hot spring pool next to DeSoto Rock. Here you can see and touch the

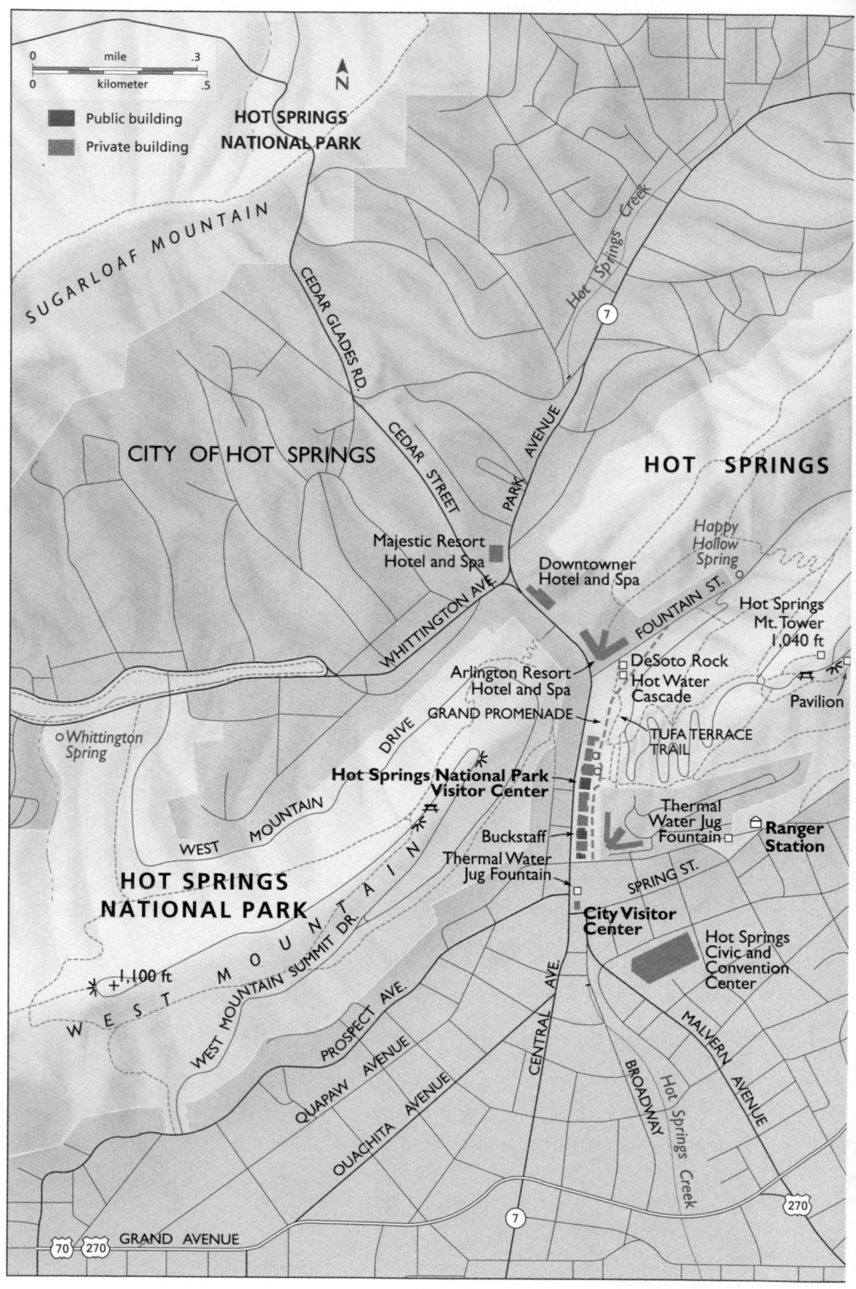

water. It is hot! Next head up the trail adjacent to the **Hot Water Cascade,** created in 1982. The water flowing here began its journey as long as 4,000 years ago when it fell as rain and seeped through fractures. Heated deep in the Earth, the water returns through the faults in the rock of the mountain in a year or two, hardly enough time to cool off.

The tufa created by the cascade's splashing waters builds up at a rate of

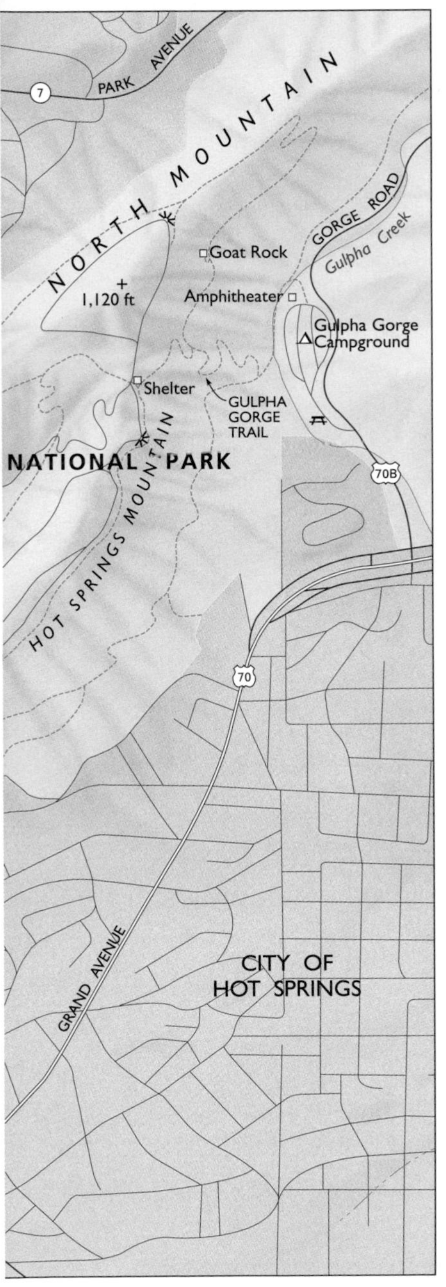

an eighth of an inch a year. The rare brilliant blue-green algae is one of 30 plant species that can survive in the hot waters. So can ostracods, a crustacean about the size of a sand grain found in some of the other springs.

The **Tufa Terrace Trail,** near the Hot Water Cascade, takes you by many concealed springs. To get there, cross the **Grand Promenade,** a landscaped brick walkway that runs behind the bathhouses.

The springs are sealed off—and thus kept sterile—by locked green bunkers that jut out of the lawns carpeting the slope. When some of the hillside springs were open, men and women discreetly took turns soaking their feet at one of them; at another, people cooked eggs. To see more water bubbling out of the earth, follow the trail to **Open Springs** behind the Maurice Bathhouse. The two springs flow into a collecting pool, where you can safely touch the water.

Go up the stairs and finish your trek on the **Grand Promenade.** The walkway, which took 30 years to build and landscape, serves as a pleasant transition between the formal architecture of the bathhouses and the trails of the wooded hillside.

GULPHA GORGE

1.6 miles round-trip; 2 hours

To find the more traditional terrain of a national park, leave **Hot Springs** on Ark. 7 heading north and turn right onto US 70B for Gulpha Gorge Campground, about 3 miles from downtown Hot Springs. Near the amphitheater pick up the **Gulpha Gorge Trail,** which crosses **Gulpha Creek** and courses a woodland rich in dogwood and redbud; in spring and early summer wildflowers flank the trail. In less than a mile the trail intersects with another up to **Goat Rock,** a fine overlook for viewing the mountains. In nearby quarries, Indians once mined novaculite for making arrowheads and spearpoints; under the name Arkansas Stone it is used today as a whetstone.

INFORMATION & ACTIVITIES

HEADQUARTERS
P.O. Box 1860, Hot Springs, AR 71902. Phone (501) 624-3383 ext. 620. www.nps.gov/hosp

SEASONS & ACCESSIBILITY
Open all year. Bathing facilities open generally Monday through Saturday, most Sundays, all year.

VISITOR & INFORMATION CENTERS
Hot Springs National Park Visitor Center, in the middle of Bathhouse Row. Open daily. For information call (501) 624-3383 ext. 640.

ENTRANCE FEE
None, but fees for thermal baths.

PETS
Not allowed in buildings; otherwise permitted on leashes.

FACILITIES FOR DISABLED
Visitor center is fully accessible; the Hot Springs Discovery Tour and the Bathhouse Row Tours are partially accessible.

THINGS TO DO
Free naturalist-led activities: hikes and bathhouse tours. Also: audiovisual and interpretive exhibits, hiking, horseback riding (no stables in park); six bathing facilities offering thermal baths, whirlpools, steam cabinets, hot packs, massages.

SPECIAL ADVISORY
• Bathing in thermal waters not recommended for people with certain ailments; consult your doctor if in doubt.

CAMPING
One campground, **Gulpha Gorge,** with 14-day limit. Open all year on first-come, first-served basis. Fees $10 per night. No showers. Tent and RV sites; no hookups.

HOTELS, MOTELS, & INNS
(unless otherwise noted, rates are for 2 persons in a double room, high season)

In Hot Springs, AR:

1890 Williams House Bed & Breakfast Inn 420 Quapaw Ave., 71901 (800) 756-4635 or (501) 624-4275. 7 units. $99-$189, incl. breakfast. AC.

Arlington Resort Hotel & Spa 239 Central Ave., 71901 (800) 643-1502. 481 units. $98-$295. ac, 2 pools, 3 rest.

Austin Hotel 305 Malvern Ave., 71901 (501) 623-6600. 200 units. $90. AC, pool, rest.

Buena Vista Resort 201 Aberina St., 71913. (800) 255-9030 or (501) 525-1321. 50 units with kitchenettes. $115. AC, pool.

Lake Hamilton Resort 2803 Albert Pike, 71914. (501) 767-8606. 94 units. $94-$109. AC, pool, rest. (on weekends).

Sun Bay Resort 4810 Central Ave., 71913. (800) 468-0055 or (501) 525-4691. 109 condos. $119-$219. AC, 3 pools, rest.

For additional accommodations, write or call the Hot Springs Convention & Visitors Bureau, P.O. Box 6000, Hot Springs, AR 71902. (800) 543-2284 or (501) 321-2277.

EXCURSIONS

OUACHITA NATIONAL FOREST
HOT SPRINGS, ARKANSAS

This pine-hardwood forest features lakes, springs, waterfalls, and the Ouachita River. Contains six wilderness areas. 1.8 million acres, part in Oklahoma. Hiking, boating, fishing, horseback riding, hunting, water sports. 24 campgrounds, picnic areas, handicapped access. Open all year. Entrance on US 270, about 10 miles west of Hot Springs NP. (501) 321-5202.

HOLLA BEND NATIONAL WILDLIFE REFUGE
DARDANELLE, ARKANSAS

Wintering bald eagles and immense flocks of migratory waterfowl share this site along the Arkansas River. 7,055 acres. Hiking, boating, fishing, hunting, scenic drives. Boat ramp. Open all year, dawn to dusk. Off Ark. 154, about 60 miles from Hot Springs NP. (479) 229-4300.

OZARK NATIONAL FOREST
RUSSELLVILLE, ARKANSAS

Oak, hickory, and pine cover the high Ozark mountain bluffs. Many streams and lakes offer excellent fishing. Features Blanchard Springs Caverns and five wilderness areas. 1.2 million acres. Hiking, boating, fishing, hunting, horseback riding, scenic drives, water sports. 359 campsites, 9 cabins, boat ramp, picnic areas, handicapped access. Open all year, including some of the campsites. Information in Russellville on US 64, 80 miles north of Hot Springs NP. (479) 968-2354.

BUFFALO NATIONAL RIVER
HARRISON, ARKANSAS

This park preserves 135 miles of the Buffalo River and adjacent lands. White water on upper river, calmer stretches on lower. 95,700 acres. Boating, fishing, hunting, swimming. 14 campgrounds, restaurant, picnic areas. Open all year, including most campsites. Headquarters at Harrison off Ark. 7, about 170 miles from Hot Springs NP. (870) 741-5443.

Fog over lake at sunrise

ISLE ROYALE

MICHIGAN
ESTABLISHED APRIL 3, 1940
571,790 acres

Out of the vastness of Lake Superior rises an island known more for its immigrant wolves and moose than for its splendors as a park. But the people who discover Isle Royale treat this isolated realm like no other park: Isle Royale visitors typically stay there 3.5 days, while the average visit to a national park is about 4 hours.

Most people get to the 45-mile-long island aboard a commercial or Park Service boat. As soon as they touch land in this wilderness park, they are on their own. They must pack in what they need and carry out their refuse.

This is rough, untamed country. Waterways may be fogbound and trails muddy. Blackflies and mosquitoes may descend upon hikers in swarms. And, because campsites cannot be reserved, a backpacker is never certain where the day's trek may end.

"It's not like deciding to drive into Yellowstone, see Old Faithful, and drive out," a ranger says. In an entire year Isle Royale gets fewer people than Yellowstone sees in a day.

Everyone who lands on Isle Royale—even day-trippers—must stop near dockside to hear a ranger talk about low-impact hiking and camping. For example, water must be boiled for 2 minutes or filtered;

chemical purifiers will not wipe out tapeworm cysts.

Human hikers share trails with wolves and moose. They are descendants of the mainlanders that made Isle Royale an unexpected ark—moose presumably by swimming to it in the early 1900s; wolves likely by walking across the frozen lake between 1945 and 1950. Scientists have been studying the interplay of predator and prey since 1958.

On the trails, all you can expect to see are the animals' tracks and droppings, although quietly grazing moose do surprise hikers, particularly in swamps or dense forest. On beaver ponds you may spot the rippling Vs of the ponds' creators. At campsites watch for foxes looking for a hand-out. Remember: Feeding the animals is illegal. It is not healthy for them and increases the likelihood that they will scavenge for people's food and damage equipment.

How to Get There

Make reservations well in advance for passenger boats from Houghton or Copper Harbor, Michigan, or Grand Portage, Minnesota. The port you pick will determine the length of your visit. Interpretive programs are held aboard the *Ranger III* between Houghton and Isle Royale. For information about boats and charter seaplane service, see **Information & Activities** p. 85. Isle Royale is 56 miles from the Michigan mainland, 18 miles from Minnesota's shore, 2 hours or 22 miles from Grand Portage. Airports: Houghton, Michigan and Duluth, Minnesota.

When to Go

Late June to September; park closes from November to mid-April. Mosquitoes, blackflies, gnats are most pesky in June and July. Summer can be cool (40°F at night). Blueberries and thimbleberries ripen in late July and August.

How to Visit

Although 1-day visits are feasible at **Rock Harbor** or **Windigo,** you need a longer stay to appreciate the wild beauty of Isle Royale. A 1-day visitor must sandwich a couple of hours of sight-seeing between boat arrival and departure. Voyages take 3 to 6.5 hours, depending on the starting point. The best way to see the park is to backpack to campsites strung along the park's 165 miles of trails. Noncampers who plan well ahead can reserve lodgings at Rock Harbor and explore on tour boats and on foot.

WINDIGO

a full day

Take the *Wenonah,* a concessioner passenger boat that makes the trip from Grand Portage, Minnesota, in 3 hours—the shortest from any port serving Isle Royale. On the way into fjordlike **Washington Harbor,** watch for the buoy marking the resting place of the *America,* a 183-foot lake steamer that went down in 1928; the wreck rests at a sharp angle, its ghostly bow about 2 feet below the surface. Scuba divers, with permits, frequently prowl this and the other nine major wrecks around Isle Royale.

As soon as you land, check at the ranger station for the next **Windigo Nature Walk,** a 1-hour ramble around this western entrance to the park that explores many of the area's natural and cultural resources.

If you miss the ranger-guided walk, try the **Windigo Nature Trail,** a 1.25-mile loop that shows the power that Lake Superior exerts on an island molded by fire and ice. You'll learn how the island was born: As

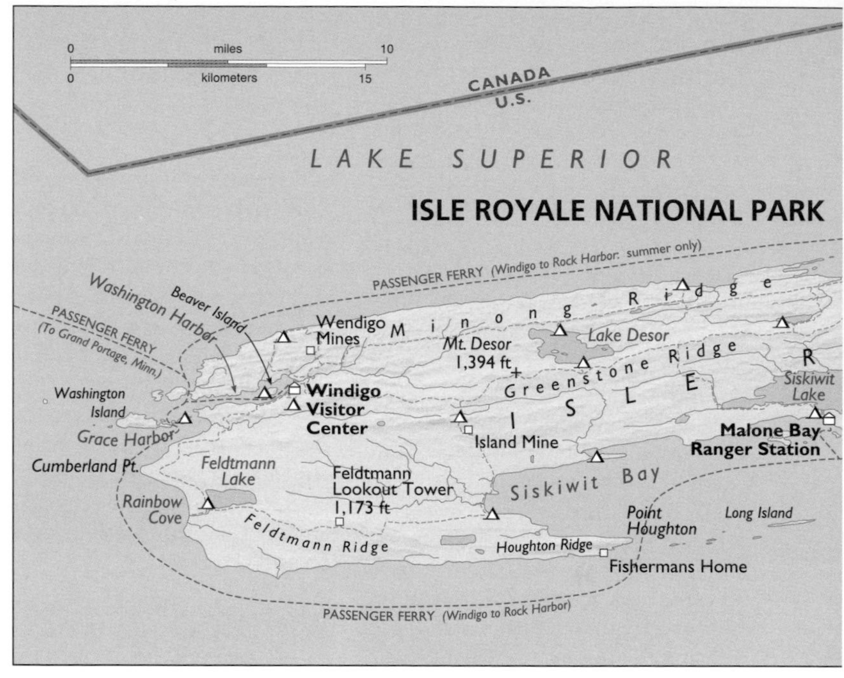

glacial ice retreated some 10,000 years ago, Isle Royale rose above what would become Lake Superior. Gouges in the barren rocks became lakes. Early migrants—lichens, mosses, bird borne seeds—drifted into cracks and crannies, beginning the long work of building soil. Animals also found their way onto Isle Royale, and an ecosystem emerged. It still evolves, with some animals appearing, as did the wolves and moose, and some animals disappearing, as did caribou and coyotes. Be sure to take the short side trip to the fenced-in **Moose Exclosure,** which shows how differently a forest grows when moose don't munch on it. Your stay—about 2.5 hours—will depend on your boat's schedule. So you may have time to stroll westward a while along the **Feldtmann Lake Trail.** This shoreline stretch gives you a view of **Beaver Island** and the harbor's forested northern shore.

ROCK HARBOR

1 or more days

A 1-day visit to Rock Harbor, the park's eastern gateway, can be tight. The voyage aboard *Isle Royale Queen IV* from Copper Harbor takes about 3 hours. You have 4 hours to explore the Rock Harbor area.

If you can stay longer and aren't a backpacker, Rock Harbor offers many relatively easy sojourns. But make advance reservations at the Rock Harbor Lodge (see **Information & Activities** p. 85).

Begin with a walk along **Stoll Trail,** a 4-mile loop that starts at Rock Harbor Lodge and winds through forest and plank-pathed bog. After about half a mile, you'll come to an area where Indians once chipped away, stone on stone, at shallow mining pits to extract outcrops of copper. Unmarked, these pits are hard to detect. Mining here began around

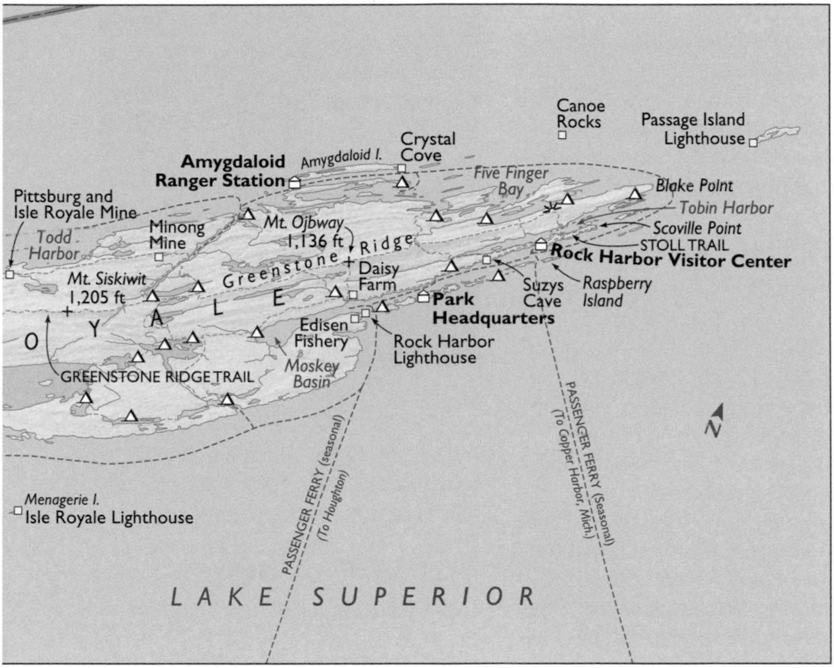

2500 B.C. and continued for at least 1,500 years. The copper, traded along the upper Mississippi Valley, was formed into fishhooks, knives, and awls. More than a thousand mining pits have been found on Isle Royale.

Continue another 1.5 miles, mostly along a rocky shore, to craggy **Scoville Point,** a fine spot for viewing some of the roughly 200 rocky islets that form the Isle Royale archipelago. On the way back you can switch to a branch trail that clings to the forested shore of **Tobin Harbor.** As the trail nears the lodge, you can see traces of **Smithwick Mine,** one of many relics of 19th-century mining ventures.

For a small round-trip fee you can take a shuttle boat from Rock Harbor across a half mile of usually calm water to **Raspberry Island,** where a 1-mile trail introduces you to a boreal forest—white spruce, balsam fir, paper birch, aspen—and a bog. You'll also see a pit dug in 1848 in a vain search for copper. Bring a picnic.

Another boat *(fee)* takes you on a half-day, guided tour into history. The first stop is **Edisen Fishery,** which belonged to the late Pete Edisen, one of the last commercial fishermen on the island. The Park Service has restored his jumble of moss-chinked log cabins and shacks made of odds and ends. Here park employees demonstrate mid-20th-century fishing techniques for visitors, and their catch occasionally makes it to Rock Harbor Lodge. A short trail leads to the **Rock Harbor Lighthouse,** which

Bull moose feeding on water plants

contains a maritime exhibit. Erected in 1855 to guide ore ships, the lighthouse closed in 1859 when the mines shut down; it reopened between 1874 and 1879 during a second mining venture.

INTO THE BACKCOUNTRY

3 to 5 days

To savor Isle Royale's isolated grandeur you must venture into the island's great beyond. Plan your 3- or 5-day stay around passenger boat arrivals and departures.

A sample 5-day itinerary: Arrive at Rock Harbor on Monday aboard the *Isle Royale Queen IV* and hike southwest along the **Rock Harbor Trail** that courses forest, bog, and slanted rocks and roots. At not quite 2 miles, look for a sign to **Suzys Cave,** about 80 yards up a side trail. The cave is an unusual, water-carved arch. At 3 miles is Three Mile Campground. Stay here and head out next morning on the 4.5-mile shore trail to **Daisy Farm;** in this spot daisies have flourished where vegetables never would.

You can camp here for 3 days and start back early Friday to meet the returning *Queen*. Or split the hike into 2 days by spending Thursday night at Three Mile Campground.

While at Daisy Farm, climb Mount Ojibway Trail, a moderate 1.75-mile ascent up the 1,136-foot mountain, which is topped by a lookout tower. You're welcome to climb as far as the cabin, which houses a solar-powered, air-monitoring station. The Park Service runs a network of such monitors to check on air quality in 65 national park areas. From the tower take the Greenstone Ridge Trail, which runs about 40 miles along the backbone of the island. About 1.5 miles west of the

Gray wolf

tower look for the wooden post marking the **Daisy Farm Trail,** which winds back to the campground.

THE WOLVES OF ISLE ROYALE

Visitors to Isle Royale probably will never see a gray wolf. Wolves live in packs as social animals, but avoid people. Only the dominant male and female—the alpha pair—mate and produce young. Others help protect and feed the pups born each spring.

Hundreds of thousands of wolves once roamed North America. But early settlers killed or drove away most of them. Today North America has only about 60,000 gray wolves, principally in Canada and Alaska.

When the first wolves arrived on Isle Royale, between 1945 and 1950, presumably by crossing frozen Lake Superior, they found a growing moose herd with no natural predators. The wolves hunted the old, the young, and the sickly. Both species prospered, the wolves increasing to 50 in 4 packs.

By 1980 the smaller moose herd provided few easy targets, and the wolf population began to fall. As moose rose, the wolves' decline mysteriously continued. The relationship has been in sync in recent years, but remains in a fluctuating state.

INFORMATION & ACTIVITIES

HEADQUARTERS
800 East Lakeshore Dr., Houghton, MI 49931. Phone (906) 482-0984. www.nps.gov/isro

SEASONS & ACCESSIBILITY
Open mid-April through October, reached by boat or seaplane only; full services available mid-June through August. $4 per day fee. Weather and rough waters may delay departures; allow extra time. Mainland headquarters open year-round.

BOAT & SEAPLANE INFORMATION
Reservations required (one to two months in advance). Contact the park for boat schedule from **Houghton** to Rock Harbor. (The Park Service's boat, *Ranger III,* will transport boats 20 feet and under between those points.)

For boats from **Copper Harbor** to Rock Harbor, contact Royale Line, Box 24, Copper Harbor, MI 49918; (906) 289-4437.

For boats from **Grand Portage** to Windigo and Rock Harbor, contact GPIR Transport Lines, 1507 N. 1st St., Superior, WI 54880; (715) 392-2100.

For seaplane information, contact Seaplane Royale Air Service Inc., P.O. Box 15184, Duluth, MN 55815; (877) 359-4753 or (218) 721-0405.

VISITOR & INFORMATION CENTERS
Windigo Visitor Center at west end of island, **Rock Harbor Visitor Center** at east end. Both open daily in season. Phone park headquarters for information.

PETS
Not allowed on boats or within park boundaries, which extend 4.5 miles into Lake Superior.

FACILITIES FOR DISABLED
Park headquarters at Houghton, Rock Harbor Lodge, both visitor centers, and a campsite at Daisy Farm are wheelchair accessible. Boats to island require assistance.

THINGS TO DO
Free naturalist-led nature walks and evening programs. Canoe tour; lighthouse, copper mine, and Edisen Fishery tours; and films. Also, boating (motorized crafts permitted on Lake Superior only), canoeing (rentals at Windigo and Rock Harbor; permit required), kayaking, hiking, scuba diving, fishing (license required for Lake Superior only), boat cruises to the outer islands.

SPECIAL ADVISORIES
• Expect sudden squalls and rough seas on Lake Superior. Do not try to take boats under 20 feet across it. Have the park service transport small boats; see above.

CAMPING
Thirty-six backcountry camping areas; 1- to 5-day limit. Camping allowed mid-April through Oct. First come, first served. No fees but permit required (from visitor centers). Group camping (reservations required) at 17 areas; contact park headquarters for information.

HOTELS, MOTELS, & INNS
(unless otherwise noted, rates are for 2 persons in a double room, high season)

INSIDE THE PARK:

Rock Harbor Lodge P.O. Box 605, Houghton, MI 49931. (906) 337-4993. From Oct. to April write c/o P.O. Box 207, Mammoth Cave, KY 42259. (270) 773-2191. 60 lodge rooms. $170-$319 with meals. 20 cabins with kitchenettes $165-$207. Rest. Mid-June–mid-Sept.

OUTSIDE THE PARK:

In Copper Harbor, MI 49918:

Bella Vista Motel P.O. Box 26. (906) 289-4213. 30 units. $48-$65. May–Oct.

Keweenaw Mountain Lodge US 41. (906) 289-4403. 42 units. $90. Cottages $124. Rest. May–mid-Oct.

Lake Fanny Hooe Resort & Campground 505 2nd St. (off US 41) (800) 426-4451. 17 units. $69-$90. Year-round. 64 campsites. $24-$34. Mid-May–mid-Oct.

In Grand Portage, MN 55605:

Grand Portage Lodge & Casino US 61 and Marina Rd. (800) 543-1384 or (218) 475-2401. 100 units. $75. Pool, rest.

In Houghton, MI 49931:

Best Western-Franklin Square Inn 820 Shelden Ave. (888) 487-1700 or (906) 487-1700. 104 units. $104. AC, pool, rest.

EXCURSIONS

GRAND PORTAGE NATIONAL MONUMENT
GRAND PORTAGE, MINNESOTA

In the 18th and 19th centuries, voyageurs paddling for the North West Company converged at this central supply depot. Tour the reconstructed stockade, great hall, kitchen, and canoe warehouse. Open late May to early Oct. The Grand Portage Trail, open all year, follows the nearly 9-mile route used by voyageurs to avoid the rapids and falls of the Pigeon River. 710 acres. Hiking, historic exhibits, cross-country skiing, snowshoeing. Handicapped access. Off US 61, about 22 miles from Isle Royale NP by boat to Grand Portage. (218) 387-2788.

CHEQUAMEGON-NICOLET NATIONAL FOREST
PARK FALLS, WISCONSIN

Chequamegon (Sho-WAH-ma-gon) means "place of shallow water." Laced with many lakes, streams, and a river, Wisconsin's only national, Chequamegon-Nicolet, is a lush medley of spruce, maple, aspen, and pine. 1.5 million acres. Bird-watching, boating, hunting, scenic drives, nature study, photography, cross-country skiing, snowshoeing. Campgrounds, picnic areas. Open all year. Headquarters on Wisc. 13, 220 miles from Isle Royale NP. (715) 762-2461.

HIAWATHA NATIONAL FOREST
ESCANABA, MICHIGAN

This mixed evergreen-and-hardwood forest dotted with lakes descends to the shores of Lake Superior, Lake Michigan, and Lake Huron. Six wilderness areas and parts of the North Country National Scenic Trail. 860,000 acres. Boating, fishing, horseback riding, hunting, scenic drives, winter sports. 25 campgrounds, handicapped access. Open all year; most campsites open mid-May to mid-September. Information at Rapid River, Escanaba, Munising, and other locations. More than 300 miles from Isle Royale NP (via ferry). (906) 786-4062.

APOSTLE ISLANDS NATIONAL LAKESHORE

BAYFIELD, WISCONSIN

This national lakeshore encompasses 21 of the 22 remote, densely forested Apostle Islands and 12 miles of mainland shoreline. Access to islands by boat; commercial and charter boats, charter fishing trips available. 42,160 land acres. Hiking, boating, fishing, winter sports, water sports, sea kayaking. 65 campsites (permits required), picnic areas, handicapped access. Open all year, including campsites. Visitor center in Bayfield near Wisc. 13, about 250 miles from Isle Royale NP (via ferry). (715) 779-3397.

PICTURED ROCKS NATIONAL LAKESHORE

MUNISING, MICHIGAN

Sandstone cliffs sculptured by nature into formations resembling castles and palisades give this first national lakeshore (1966) its name. The site also features extensive dunes and banks, sand beaches, forests, inland lakes, streams, and waterfalls. 71,400 acres. Hiking, boating, backpacking, fishing, hunting, winter sports, water sports. 66 campsites, picnic areas, handicapped access. Open all year; campsites open mid-May to October. Visitor center at Munising on Mich. 28, about 335 miles from Isle Royale NP (via ferry). (906) 387-3700 or 2607.

OTTAWA NATIONAL FOREST

IRONWOOD, MICHIGAN

Lakes, streams, rivers, and waterfalls abound in this ski-country forest. Also features three wilderness areas, Black River Harbor Recreation Area, and the North Country National Scenic Trail. Nearly one million acres. Hiking, mountain biking, canoeing, kayaking, fishing, hunting, winter sports. 22 campgrounds, boat ramp, picnic areas, handicapped access. Open all year; campsites May to December. Visitor center in Watersmeet on US 2, about 140 miles from Isle Royale NP (via ferry). (906) 932-1330.

Torch tossing—no longer done—to demonstrate 19th-century way of lighting caves

MAMMOTH CAVE

KENTUCKY
ESTABLISHED JULY 1, 1941
52,830 acres

Under a swath of Kentucky hills and hollows is a limestone labyrinth that became the heartland of a national park. The surface of Mammoth Cave National Park encompasses about 80 square miles. No one knows how big the underside is. More than 365 miles of the five-level cave system have been mapped, and new caves are continually being discovered. Two layers of stone underlie Mammoth's hilly woodlands.

A sandstone and shale cap, as thick as 50 feet in places, acts as an umbrella over limestone ridges. The umbrella leaks at places called sinkholes, from which surface water makes its way underground, eroding the limestone into a honeycomb of caverns.

Mammoth, the world's longest known cave system, a United Nations World Heritage site and the core area of an international biosphere reserve, still is as "grand, gloomy, and peculiar" as it was when Stephen Bishop, a young slave and early guide, described it. By a flickering lard-oil lamp he found and mapped some of Mammoth's passages. Bishop died in 1857. His grave, like his life, is part of Mammoth; it lies in the Old Guide's Cemetery near the entrance.

Most visitors see the eerie beauty of the caverns on some of the 10 miles of passages available for tours. Rangers dispense geological lore and tell tales about real and imagined happenings 200 or 300 feet down. The tours are hikes inside the Earth; uphill stretches can be hard going for some visitors. Few seem frightened; people terrified by darkness or tight spots naturally avoid caves. Rangers say they rarely have problems guiding the 500,000 men, women, and children who venture below yearly.

Mammoth does not glamorize the underworld with garish lighting. You never forget that you are deep in the Earth. And nowhere else can you get a better lesson in the totality of darkness and the miracle of light. Usually on a tour a ranger gathers everyone and, after a warning, switches off the lights. The darkness is sudden, absolute. Then the ranger lights a match and the tiny dot of light magically spreads, illuminating a circle of astonished faces.

How to Get There

Mammoth Cave, 9 miles northwest of I-65, is nearly equidistant (about 85 miles) between Louisville, Kentucky, and Nashville, Tennessee. From the south, take the exit at Park City and head northwest on Ky. 255 to the park; from the north, take the exit at Cave City and head northwest on Ky. 70 to the park. Don't be misled by signs proclaiming commercial "mammoth" caves. Airports: Nashville, Tenn. and Louisville, Ky.

When to Go

Year-round. Underground, all days are about the same; temperatures in interior passages fluctuate from the mid-50s to the low 60s. Summer brings the most people, and frequent tours are offered. Though there are fewer tours the rest of the year, they are less crowded.

How to Visit

The tours vary greatly; pick ones to fit your time and stamina. All require you to purchase a ticket. Reservations are strongly advised in summer, on holidays, and on spring and fall weekends. For a half-day visit, you might take the **Historic Tour,** which combines geology with Mammoth's rich history, or the **Introduction to Caving Tour.** If you plan to stay longer, consider the fairly strenuous **Grand Avenue Tour** (there are three steep hills, each nearly 90 feet high). To enjoy the caves safely and comfortably, wear shoes with nonskid soles and take a jacket. Complete your underground trips with a river trip or a walk on the **River Styx Spring Trail.**

The least arduous cave tour (0.25 mile, 75 minutes) is the **Travertine Tour.** A modified version of the **Frozen Niagara Tour,** it has only 18 steps each way (plus an optional 49) and is designed for visitors who want a short and easy trip. The toughest challenge is the 5-mile, 6-hour, belly-crawling **Wild Cave Tour,** offered daily in summer and weekends year-round. By reservation.

HISTORIC TOUR

2 miles; 2 hours

You leave daylight and walk into dimly lit gloom at the **Historic Entrance,** discovered by pioneers in the 1790s and by Indians thousands of years before. Near the entrance, at the **Rotunda,** 140 feet down, are relics of the cave's use as a nitrate mine. Slaves hauled in logs, built leaching vats, and filled them with cave dirt. Water, poured into the vats, trickled into a trough as brine. Two pipelines of hollowed-out logs carried water in and brine out. The residue, nitrate crystals, was used to make gunpowder, some of which found its way into the War of 1812.

Broadway, an underground avenue, leads to a spot called **Methodist Church,** where services may have been conducted in the 1800s. Farther on, **Booth's Amphitheater** recalls the visit of actor Edwin Booth. Here, Edwin, brother of assassin John Wilkes Booth, recited Hamlet's famous soliloquy.

The **Bottomless Pit** looked that way to early visitors; it's 105 feet deep; looking up, you see its dome 38 feet above. (The top of a shaft is a dome, the bottom a pit.) On your way back toward the entrance you pass through **Fat Man's Misery,** a passage polished smooth by generations of squirming spelunkers. You emerge into **Great Relief Hall,** a large chamber where you are able to stand upright. Then back on the trail for the final spectacles: **Mammoth Dome**—192 feet from floor to ceiling—carved by water dripping through a sinkhole, and the **Ruins of Karnak,** a cluster of gleaming limestone pillars that look like an Egyptian temple.

INTRODUCTION TO CAVING TOUR

1 mile; about 3 hours

Cave exploring, otherwise known as "spelunking," can be fun and challenging. Led by park rangers, the Introduction to Caving Tour gives

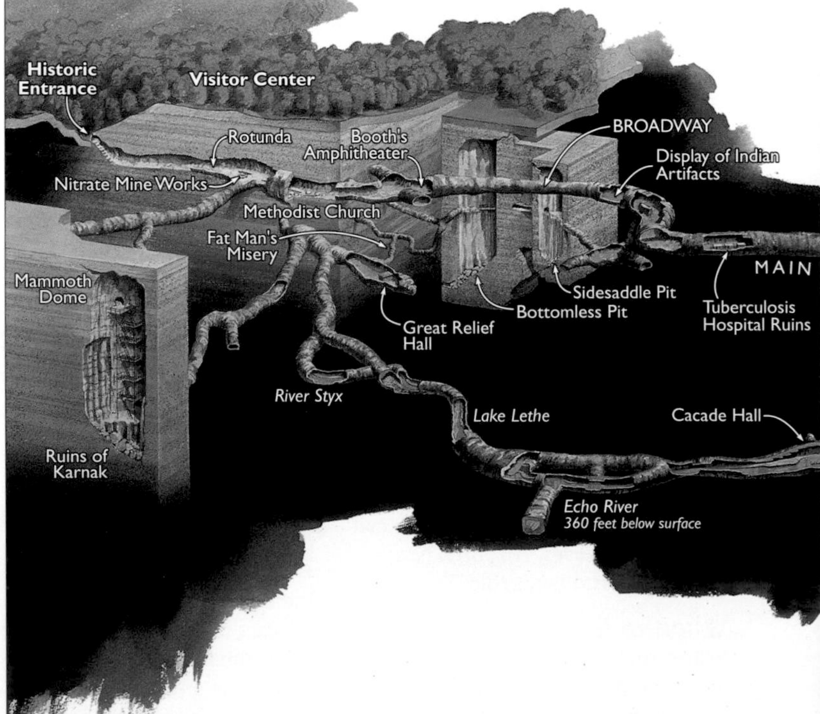

Eyeless, colorless cave amphipod

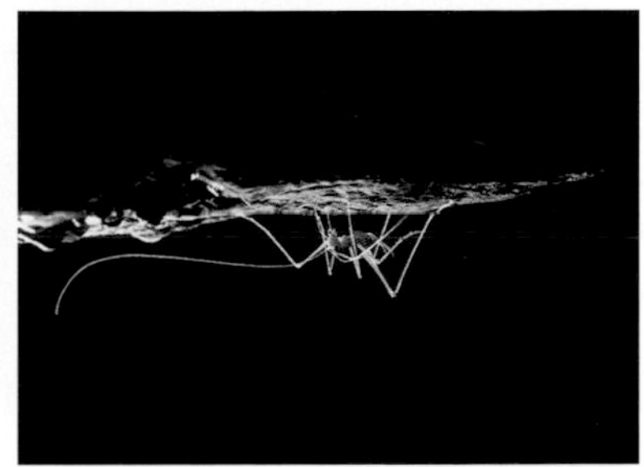

Cave cricket on a Mammoth ceiling

visitors 10 and up some first-hand experience in underground exploration. Offered daily in summer and on weekends in spring and fall, this trip involves hands-and-knees crawling, climbing, stooping, and even canyon-walking, with feet on different ledges and nothing but air in between. Straying from traditional walking paths, you will visit the twisting, convoluted canyons and crawls of **Fox Avenue,** emerging at **Frozen Niagara.** Along the way rangers will explain the geologic processes that result in the varied subterranean spaces. You will also learn the basic rules of safe caving, including what to do if you get lost.

Helmets and lights are provided. Participants should bring knee pads *(no Rollerblade type or hard plastic knee pads allowed)*. Long pants and

Cave formations in the Frozen Niagara area

boots required and gloves recommended. restrooms not available. Youths 10 to 15 must be accompanied by an adult.

GRAND AVENUE TOUR

4 miles; 4.5 hours

The tour (likely to be very crowded in summer) begins with a 5- to 10-minute bus ride from the visitor center to the **Carmichael Entrance,** a concrete bunker and stairway that leads down to **Cleaveland Avenue,** a long tubular chamber tunneled out by a river. Its walls sparkle with flowery patches of gypsum. The white mineral crystallizes below the surface of the limestone from seeping moisture, then bursts out in blossomlike designs (it takes a thousand years for one cubic inch of gypsum to form) that are fascinating.

About a mile beyond is the **Snowball Room,** where the tour stops for lunch. (Food service here is limited to sandwiches, candy, and drinks.) The snowball-like features on the roof, once a dull gray, have been cleaned of much of the black fungus that grows on cave formations.

Another river canyon, **Boone Avenue,** takes you 300 feet into the Earth along a passage so narrow you can touch both walls. The tour ends at **Frozen Niagara,** a massive cascade of flowstone—the legacy of mineral-laden water that seeped here, vanished, and left behind the shimmering stalactites and stalagmites. Such formations build up at the rate of about a cubic inch every 200 years.

BOAT TRIPS & HIKES

To explore the **Green River,** which winds 24 miles through the park, you can buy tickets at the visitor center for a 1-hour scenic boat cruise on *Miss Green River II.* Or you can walk the **River Styx Spring Trail,** which leads to the river. The trail, which begins near the Historic Entrance to Mammoth, shows the interplay between surface features and the cave's underworld. At **River Styx Spring** the water emerges from the cave and flows into the Green River. Farther along the shore, you see **Cave Island,** formed of waterborne logs and silt.

Most of the park's 70 miles of trails are in the backcountry across the Green River. Since within the park, there are no bridges over the river, you can drive onto the Green River Ferry at a crossing southwest of the visitor center, or go to Houchins Ferry at the western edge of the park. Ferries have carried people and their vehicles across the river since the 1800s. While at the Green River ferry landing, try the short **Echo River Spring Trail** that leads past a series of pools formed when the underground river emerges from the caves.

Head north on **Green River Ferry Road** to Maple Spring Group Campground. A gravel road there leads to **Good Spring Church,** founded in 1842. From here you can walk 10 miles on a trail that winds through forests slowly reclaiming land once cleared for farming and logging.

Before leaving the park, make one last stop at **Sloan's Crossing Pond** where a depression in the sandstone has collected enough water to create a tiny ecosystem.

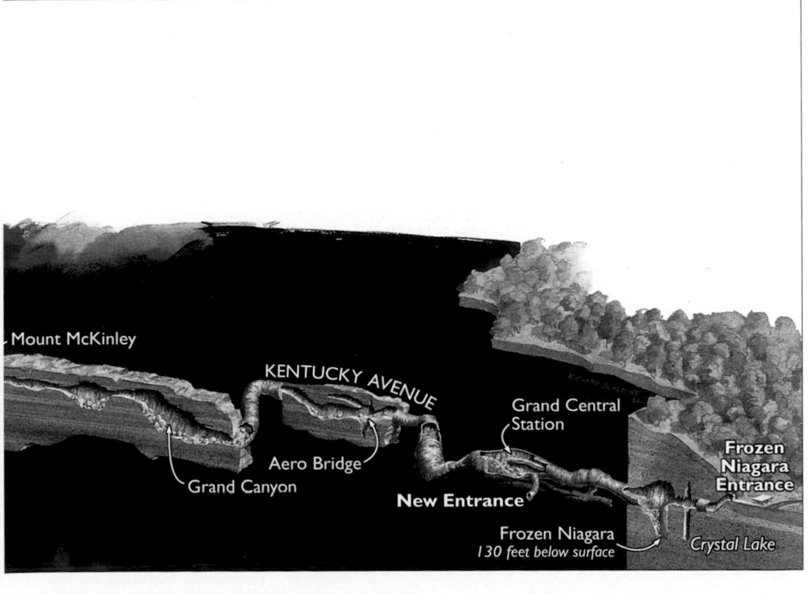

INFORMATION & ACTIVITIES

HEADQUARTERS
P.O. Box 7, Mammoth Cave, KY 42259. Phone (270) 758-2180. www.nps.gov/maca

SEASONS & ACCESSIBILITY
Open all year. Visitors must join a tour to view the caves; tours led daily.

VISITOR & INFORMATION CENTERS
Visitor center open daily. If space is available, you can buy tickets there on the day for all tours except for Wild Cave, for which advance reservations are essential. Tours sell out quickly—especially in summer, on holidays, and on spring and fall weekends—so buy tickets in advance through the NPRS (see p. 10) or online at http://reservations.nps.gov. For more information on ranger-led activities, call (270) 758-2328.

ENTRANCE FEE
None. Fees required for tours, $4-$23 for adults and youths; free for children under 6. Higher fees for special tours; the Wild Cave Tour is $45 per person.

PETS
Permitted on leashes except in caves and visitor center. Kennel facilities through the Mammoth Cave Hotel (see below).

FACILITIES FOR DISABLED
Visitor center, some sites at Headquarters Campground, and restrooms are accessible. The 0.5-mile Pond Walk, 0.25-mile Heritage Trail, and 0.1-mile Sand Cave Trail are fully accessible.

THINGS TO DO
Naturalist-led activities: cave tours, (12 in summer, 5 the rest of the year), children's exploration program, nature walks, evening programs. Nature trails, fishing (no license required), horseback riding, Green River boat trip, bicycling, occasional special events.

SPECIAL ADVISORY
• Cave tours are strenuous; talk with a park staff before selecting one if you have difficulty walking or trouble with your heart or lungs.

• Wear sturdy shoes and take a jacket.

OVERNIGHT BACKPACKING
Permits required. They are free and available at the visitor center.

CAMPGROUNDS
Three campgrounds, all with a 14-day limit. Fees: $12-$30 per night. Tent and RV sites at **Headquarters;** no hookups; showers nearby for a fee; open March through November. Tents only at **Maple Spring Group Campgrounds,** open March through November; and at **Houchins Ferry,** open all year, first come, first served. Use the NPRS (see p. 10) to reserve at Headquarters and Maple Spring. Food services in park.

HOTELS, MOTELS, & INNS
(unless otherwise noted, rates are for 2 persons in a double room, high season)

INSIDE THE PARK:

Mammoth Cave Hotel Mammoth Cave, KY 42259. (270) 758-2225. 92 units. $68-$75; cottages $59. AC, rest.

OUTSIDE THE PARK:

In Cave City, KY 42127:

Best Western Kentucky Inn 1009 Doyle Ave. (800) 528-1234 or (270) 773-3161. 50 units. $55-$75, incl. breakfast. AC, pool.

Days Inn Cave City 822 Mammoth Cave St. (800) 329-7466 or (270) 773-2151. 110 units. $66. AC, pool.

Knights Inn 1006A Doyle Rd. (800) 321-4245 or (270) 773-2181. 100 units. $80. AC, pool, restaurant.

Quality Inn 102 Gardner Ln. (800) 228-5151 or (270) 773-3101. 105 units. $69. AC, pool.

In Park City, KY 42160:

Park Mammoth Resort (I-65 and US 31W) P.O. Box 307. (270) 749-4101. 92 units. $66. AC, pool, restaurant.

In Bowling Green, KY 42104:

Bowling Green Bed & Breakfast 3313 Savannah Dr. (270) 781-3861. 3 rooms. $60, incl. breakfast. AC.

New's Inn 3160 Scottsville Rd. (270) 781-3460. 48 units. $44-$65. AC, pool.

For additional accommodations, call the Chambers of Commerce of Cave City (270) 773-5159 and Bowling Green (270) 781-3200.

EXCURSIONS

DANIEL BOONE NATIONAL FOREST

WINCHESTER, KENTUCKY

Daniel Boone, impressed by vast forest and abundant wildlife, called this land Eden. The 269-mile Sheltowee Trace National Recreation Trail, linking many of the forest's recreation sites, memorializes Boone's Indian name, Sheltowee, or "Big Turtle." Geologic wonders include more than 100 sandstone arches and 3,400 miles of cliff, carved by 70 million years of wind and water. The forest contains two wilderness areas and five wildlife management areas. More than 700,000 acres. Hiking, boating, fishing, hunting, off-road vehicle routes, scenic drives, water sports, horseback riding. Approximately 1,000 campsites, boat ramps, marinas, picnic areas, handicapped access. Open all year; most campsites open April through November. Information at Supervisor's Office, Winchester, Kentucky, about 125 miles from Mammoth Cave NP. (859) 745-3100.

CUMBERLAND GAP NATIONAL HISTORICAL PARK

MIDDLESBORO, KENTUCKY

Indian hunters breached the great wall of the Appalachians long before westering pioneers "discovered" the gap in the mid-18th century. In 1775 Daniel Boone and his band of men forged the Wilderness Trail into Kentucky, opening the West to its first wave of expansion. More than 60 miles of hiking trails lead visitors to the Pinnacle Overlook, White Rocks, Sand Cave, and to the Hensley Settlement atop Brush Mountain—an early 20th-century effort at self-sufficient living. 20,281 acres, part in Virginia and Tennessee. Hiking, scenic drives, cave tours. 160 campsites, picnic areas, handicapped access. Open all year, including campsites. Visitor center at Middlesboro on US 25E, about 190 miles from Mammoth Cave NP. (606) 248-2817.

A babbling brook in Shenandoah National Park

SHENANDOAH

VIRGINIA
ESTABLISHED DECEMBER 26, 1935
197,411 acres

Skyline Drive, which runs for 105 miles along the crest of the Blue Ridge mountains, is flanked by a rumpled panorama of forests and mountains. To many who travel the drive, the highway itself is a park, complete with numerous deer-sightings along the way. But the cars are passing the real Shenandoah. More than 500 miles of trails can be reached from Skyline Drive, and the Appalachian Trail roughly parallels it for nearly its entire length.

The long, narrow park flows outward, upward, and downward from the highway that splits it. The drive, following ridge trails walked by Indians and early settlers, transports visitors to a park built on a frontier that lingered into modern times.

Unlike most national parks, Shenandoah is a place where settlers lived for over a century. To create the park, Virginia state officials acquired 1,088 privately owned tracts and donated the land to the nation. Never before had a large, populated expanse of private land been converted into a national park. And never before had planners made a park of land so used by humans.

In the decade before the park opened, some 465 families moved or were moved from their cabins and resettled outside the proposed park boundaries. A few mountaineers, though, lived out their lives in the park and were buried in the secluded graveyards of Shenandoah's vanished settlements.

Much of Shenandoah consisted of farmland and second- or third-growth forests logged since the early 1700s. Today the marks of lumbering, grazing, and farming have mostly disappeared, as forests have slowly come back.

Spring arrives first in the park valleys and then moves upward. Walking up a valley trail, a visitor can follow spring's path and see, in a single day, a variety of flowers that bloom elsewhere over a span of weeks.

How to Get There

From Washington, D.C. (about 70 miles away), take I-66 west to US 340, then head south to the park's Front Royal (North) Entrance. From Charlottesville, take I-64 to the Rockfish Gap (South) Entrance. From the west, take US 211 through Luray to the Thornton Gap (Middle) Entrance or head east on US 33 to the Swift Run Gap Entrance. Airports: Dulles International, near Washington, D.C. and Charlottesville, Va.

When to Go

Of the nearly 1,600,000 people who visit the park each year, 400,000 go in October to see the foliage. To avoid fall traffic jams, arrive early (preferably on a weekday), park at an overlook, and walk a trail. Snowstorms sometimes close Skyline Drive, the park's north-south highway. Facilities close in winter. Campgrounds fill on summer weekends, but day-trippers still have plenty of park. Wildflowers bloom from early spring to late fall.

How to Visit

On a day's drive-in visit, whatever entrance you use, get out and walk a trail. Even if you venture only a few hundred feet from an overlook, you will see a different Shenandoah beyond the scenic drive. For a longer stay, make a base at one place, such as **Big Meadows** or **Skyland,** and explore from there.

SKYLINE DRIVE FROM FRONT ROYAL TO BIG MEADOWS

51 miles; a full day

Not quite 5 miles south of the **Front Royal Entrance Station** is the **Dickey Ridge Visitor Center,** where exhibits introduce you to the park and its facilities along Skyline Drive. To walk a path of mountain life, cross the drive at the visitor center and start the self-guided, 1.2-mile **Fox Hollow Trail,** named for the family that first settled this hollow, as tenant farmers, in 1837. Their houses have disappeared, but you can see relics of their toil: large, well-stacked piles of rock cleared from farmland. Other stones—rough and dimly lettered—jut from the family graveyard.

Along the drive, stop at overlooks for views of the **Shenandoah Valley** and the peaks looming above it. The views are magnificent (except when pollution levels or fog mar visibility). At many overlooks there are signposts for well-marked trails. Daubs of paint on trees identify the trails: white, the **Appalachian Trail;** blue, a park hiking trail; yellow, a horse trail (hiking also allowed).

At Mathews Arm Campground, 22 miles from Front Royal, the easily accessible 1.7-mile **Traces Trail** takes you through an oak forest back to the time of the earliest white settlers. The traces are faint: an old road, trees, tumbling stone walls.

For a more rugged hike into the past, stop at the parking area past

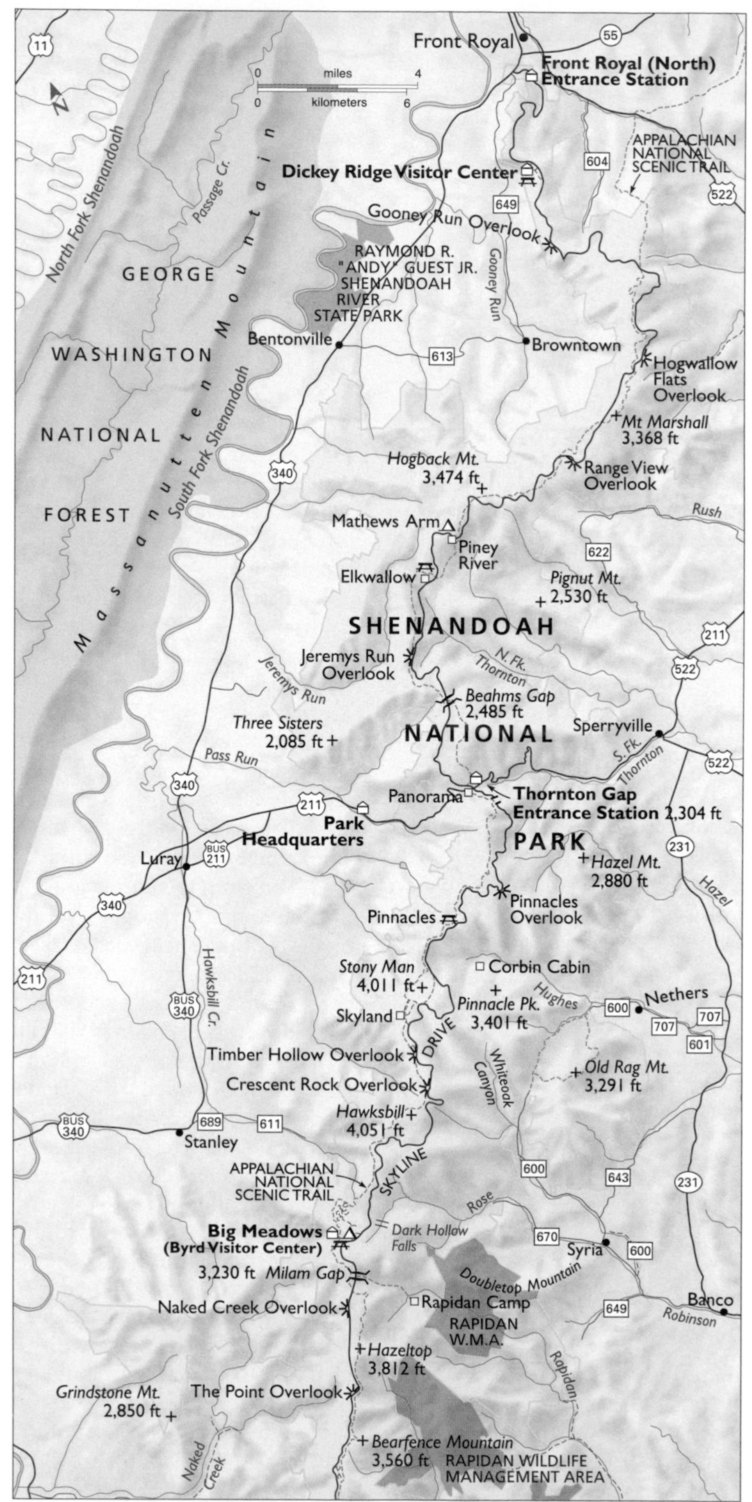
Front Royal
Front Royal (North) Entrance Station
0 miles 4
0 kilometers 6
APPALACHIAN NATIONAL SCENIC TRAIL
Dickey Ridge Visitor Center
Gooney Run Overlook
RAYMOND R. "ANDY" GUEST JR. SHENANDOAH RIVER STATE PARK
Gooney Run
North Fork Shenandoah
Passage Cr.
Massanutten Mountain
GEORGE WASHINGTON NATIONAL FOREST
Bentonville
Browntown
Hogwallow Flats Overlook
Mt Marshall 3,368 ft
South Fork Shenandoah
Hogback Mt. 3,474 ft
Range View Overlook
Mathews Arm
Piney River
Rush
Elkwallow
Pignut Mt. 2,530 ft
SHENANDOAH NATIONAL PARK
Jeremys Run Overlook
Jeremys Run
N. Fk. Thornton
Beahms Gap 2,485 ft
Three Sisters 2,085 ft
Sperryville
Pass Run
S. Fk. Thornton
Panorama
Thornton Gap Entrance Station 2,304 ft
Park Headquarters
Luray
Hazel Mt. 2,880 ft
Hazel
Pinnacles Overlook
Pinnacles
Stony Man 4,011 ft
Corbin Cabin
Hawksbill Cr.
Pinnacle Pk. 3,401 ft
Hughes
Nethers
Skyland
Timber Hollow Overlook
Crescent Rock Overlook
Whiteoak Canyon
Old Rag Mt. 3,291 ft
Hawksbill 4,051 ft
Stanley
SKYLINE DRIVE
APPALACHIAN NATIONAL SCENIC TRAIL
Rose
Big Meadows (Byrd Visitor Center)
Dark Hollow Falls
Syria
3,230 ft Milam Gap
Doubletop Mountain
Naked Creek Overlook
Rapidan Camp
Banco
Robinson
RAPIDAN W.M.A.
Hazeltop 3,812 ft
Rapidan
Grindstone Mt. 2,850 ft
The Point Overlook
Bearfence Mountain 3,560 ft
RAPIDAN WILDLIFE MANAGEMENT AREA
Naked Creek
11
55
604
522
649
613
340
622
211
BUS 211
BUS 340
689
611
600
707
601
231
643
670

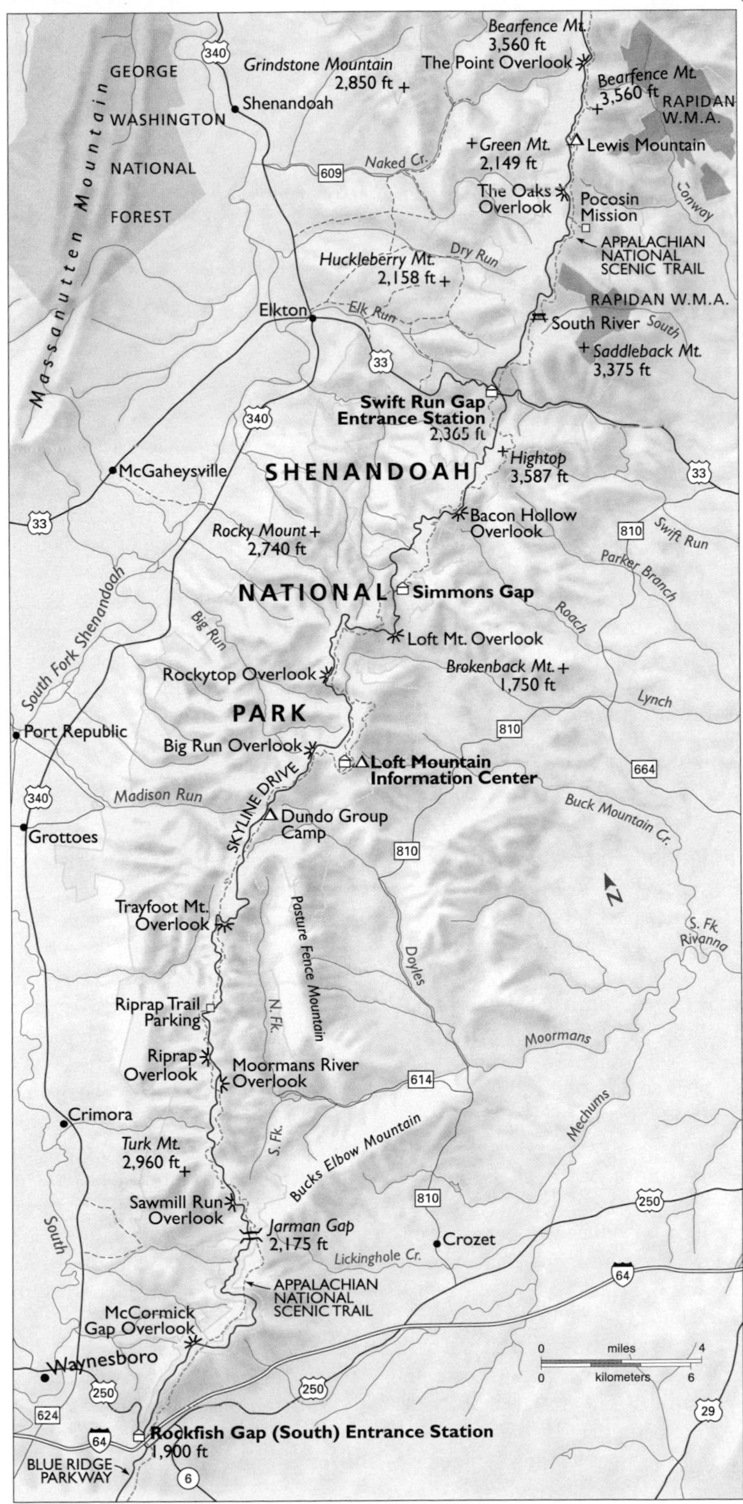
Bearfence Mt.
3,560 ft
The Point Overlook
Grindstone Mountain
2,850 ft
GEORGE
WASHINGTON
NATIONAL
FOREST
Massanutten Mountain
Shenandoah
Bearfence Mt.
3,560 ft
RAPIDAN
W.M.A.
Green Mt.
2,149 ft
Lewis Mountain
Naked Cr.
The Oaks
Overlook
Pocosin
Mission
Conway
APPALACHIAN
NATIONAL
SCENIC TRAIL
Huckleberry Mt.
2,158 ft
Dry Run
RAPIDAN W.M.A.
Elkton
Elk Run
South River
South
Saddleback Mt.
3,375 ft
Swift Run Gap
Entrance Station
2,365 ft
Hightop
3,587 ft
McGaheysville
SHENANDOAH
Bacon Hollow
Overlook
Swift Run
Rocky Mount
2,740 ft
Parker Branch
NATIONAL
Simmons Gap
Roach
South Fork Shenandoah
Big Run
Loft Mt. Overlook
Rockytop Overlook
Brokenback Mt.
1,750 ft
Lynch
PARK
Port Republic
Big Run Overlook
Loft Mountain
Information Center
Madison Run
SKYLINE DRIVE
Buck Mountain Cr.
Dundo Group
Camp
Grottoes
N
Trayfoot Mt.
Overlook
Pasture Fence Mountain
Doyles
S. Fk.
Rivanna
Riprap Trail
Parking
N. Fk.
Moormans
Riprap
Overlook
Moormans River
Overlook
Crimora
S. Fk.
Mechums
Bucks Elbow Mountain
Turk Mt.
2,960 ft
Sawmill Run
Overlook
South
Jarman Gap
2,175 ft
Crozet
Lickinghole Cr.
APPALACHIAN
NATIONAL
SCENIC TRAIL
McCormick
Gap Overlook
Waynesboro
0
miles
4
0
kilometers
6
Rockfish Gap (South) Entrance Station
1,900 ft
BLUE RIDGE
PARKWAY
340
609
33
810
664
614
250
64
624
29
6

Corbin Cabin, relic of a mountaineer past

milepost 37 and take the **Corbin Cabin Cutoff Trail.** The steep trip (1.5 miles each way) ends at **Corbin Cabin,** a typical mountain residence. In 1909 George Corbin cut and hewed logs and, with the help of neighbors, built this cabin. The Corbin family, like many others, lived on what they grew or made, including brandy from peaches and apples. The Potomac Appalachian Trail Club maintains the cabin for rent to members and the public, one of six rustic cabins scattered through the park's backcountry.

Skyland (near milepost 42) dates from the 1890s. The resort, which includes guest rooms, dining room, and cabins, is open from April through November. The 1.6-mile **Stony Man Nature Trail** begins near the parking area and, climbing about 340 feet, reaches the cliffs of **Stony Man**'s summit (4,011 feet, second highest point in the park). From an outcrop on the cliffs you get a sweeping view. The trail loops back around to the start.

The **Limberlost Trail** (near milepost 43), a gently winding walkway of crushed green stone, passes through the remains of old-growth hemlocks before crossing over Whiteoak Canyon Run on a wooden bridge. The 1.3-mile trail is wheelchair accessible with numerous benches located at intervals for hikers to rest and contemplate their surroundings.

Stop at **Crescent Rock Overlook** (near milepost 44) for a look at **Hawksbill Mountain,** at 4,051 feet the highest point in park. Then, 6 miles farther, stop at the parking area for the **Dark Hollow Falls Trail,** a 1.4-mile round-trip to a waterfall, the shortest route to any falls in the park. The steep trail takes you past clusters of ferns, mosses, and liverworts. Split-log benches offer a rest en route.

Big Meadows (milepost 51) has trails, a campground, a lodge, facilities for visitors, and the **Byrd Visitor Center,** where changing exhibits tell the stories of the park.

Today the defoliated trees you see attest to the presence of a natural phenomenon—the hemlock woolly adelgid—among other pests and diseases. Since 1988 the park has lost 80 percent of its hemlock stands due to this pest. But, unlike the chestnut blight early in the 20th century, the woolly adelgid will not wipe out an entire species. Healthy trees will renew the forest in future decades.

You can end your day at Big Meadows with a wildflower walk through the gently undulating meadowlands that give the area its name. On the way, you may startle a deer or two (or even a black bear!).

RAPIDAN CAMP TO ROCKFISH GAP

54 miles; a full day

Park at the west side of Skyline Drive at **Milam Gap** (mile 52.8). Cross the drive to a trail marker to begin the 4-mile round-trip to Rapidan Camp (formerly Camp Hoover). You walk a short distance on the Appalachian Trail, then turn left onto the **Mill Prong Trail,** which passes through a wooded tract, descends to a small waterfall, crosses three streams, and meets a road. Turn right and continue toward the cabins of **Rapidan Camp,** a national historic landmark. The camp satisfied President Herbert Hoover's three requirements for a hideaway: It had to be within 100 miles of Washington, have a trout stream, and be high enough to discourage mosquitoes. The President and First Lady used the camp as a summer White House in 1931. The Brown House, President Hoover's cabin, has been restored to its 1931 appearance and includes some furnishings. It can be visited during the summer and fall on tours from the Byrd Visitor Center. The Prime Minister's Cabin (currently being renovated), also part of Rapidan Camp, can be explored individually.

Scarlet tanager

An 0.8-mile, 1.5-hour hike to **Bearfence Mountain** starts at mile 56.4 before the Lewis Mountain Campground. It demands some scrambling over rocks but finally rewards with a spectacular 360-degree view. The easy 2-mile round-trip to the **Pocosin Mission,** which starts past milepost 59, takes you to the ruins of a missionary church and graveyard.

The **Swift Run Gap** Entrance (near milepost 65) is an old Blue Ridge crossing now paved by US 33. In May, wildflower seekers climb the nearby **Hightop Summit Trail** (3 miles round-trip) to see wildflowers.

Loft Mountain (near milepost 79), with campground and information center, is a southern base for exploring the park. Near a service complex along Skyline Drive, look for the trailhead to the **Frazier Discovery Trail,** a 1.3-mile loop that demonstrates how pasture is evolving back into forest. After the demise of the chestnut trees, other trees and shrubs began repopulating the land. You can see it happening here, and from a rocky vantage point on the trail you can also see it happening on a grand scale throughout the park. Two summit viewpoints offer views to the west, over the Shenandoah Valley to undulating peaks beyond.

At **Rockfish Gap,** near the **Rockfish Entrance Station,** a bison path evolved into a colonial road, and later a modern highway. Here, at the park's southern end, begins the **Blue Ridge Parkway,** a National Park Service highway that connects Shenandoah and Great Smoky Mountains NPS.

INFORMATION & ACTIVITIES

HEADQUARTERS
3655 US 211E, Luray, VA 22835. Phone (540) 999-3500. www.nps.gov/shen

SEASONS & ACCESSIBILITY
Open all year. For recorded information call (540) 999-3500. Skyline Drive may close temporarily during heavy snow or hazardous ice conditions. For weather and road information, call (540) 999-3500.

VISITOR & INFORMATION CENTERS
Dickey Ridge Visitor Center, near North Entrance, open daily late March through November. **Byrd Visitor Center** at Big Meadows, near center of park, open daily late March through November. Opening and closing dates vary each year.

ENTRANCE FEE
$10 per car allows 7-day access.

PETS
Must be kept on leash; not allowed on posted trails or in park buildings.

FACILITIES FOR DISABLED
Visitor centers, amphitheaters, picnic areas, and campgrounds are accessible to wheelchairs. restrooms, lodges, and restaurants are also accessible. The Limberlost Trail is handicapped accessible.

THINGS TO DO
Free ranger-led activities: interpretive walks, talks, evening programs (summer through fall only). Also available, fishing, horseback riding, hiking on some 500 miles of trails.

SPECIAL ADVISORIES
• Rocks around waterfalls are very slippery and dangerous.
• Pull off the road completely when stopping for a view.
• Do not feed or chase wildlife.

OVERNIGHT BACKPACKING
Permits required and available free of charge from headquarters, visitor centers, and entrance stations.

CAMPGROUNDS
Five campgrounds, all with 14-day limit. **Mathews Arm, Lewis Mountain,** and **Loft Mountain** open mid-May through Oct., first come, first served. **Big Meadows** open late March through Nov. Reservations recommended from Memorial Day weekend through October, available through the NPRS (see p. 10); other times, first come, first served. Fee $16-$19 per night. Tent and RV sites; no hookups. Camp stores and restaurants near the campground. **Dundo Group Campground,** open April through Nov. $32 a night, reservations required. Call NPRS (see p. 10). Showers and laundry (except at Mathews Arm and Dundo).

HOTELS, MOTELS, & INNS
(unless otherwise noted, rates are for 2 persons in a double room, high season)

INSIDE THE PARK:
P.O. Box 727, Luray, VA 22835. (800) 999-4714 or (540) 743-5108.
Big Meadows Lodge (mile 51.3) Lodge rooms $68-$129; cabins $85-$93; suites $127-$156. Restaurant. Late Apr.–Oct.
Lewis Mountain Cabin (mile 57.6) Hiker's cabin $25. Ten cabins with outdoor grills. $71-$116. Mid-May–Oct.
Skyland Lodge (miles 41.7 and 42.5) 177 units. Lodge units $85-$135; suites $119-$184; cabins $62-$91. Restaurant. Early Apr.–Nov.

OUTSIDE THE PARK:
In Front Royal, VA 22630:
Quality Inn 10 Commerce Ave. (540) 635-3161. 107 units. $75-$85. AC, pool.
Woodward House on Manor Grade Bed & Breakfast 413 S. Royal Ave. (800) 635-7011 or (540) 635-7010. 7 rooms, 2 cottages. $95-$185, incl. breakfast. AC.
In Sperryville, VA 22740:
Conyers House Inn and Stable 3131 Slate Mills Rd. (540) 987-8025. 7 units. $150-$300, includes breakfast. AC, restaurant.
In Stanley, VA 22851:
Jordan Hollow Farm Inn 326 Hawksbill Park Rd. (888) 418-7000 or (540) 778-2285. 14 rooms. $190-$250. AC, restaurant. no children.
In Waynesboro, VA 22980:
The Inn at Afton I-64 at US 250. (800) 860-8559 or (540) 942-5201. 118 units. $83-$91. AC, pool, restaurant.

EXCURSIONS

GEORGE WASHINGTON NATIONAL FOREST

HARRISONBURG AND ROANOKE, VIRGINIA

Administratively combined with the Jefferson National Forest in 1995, the George Washington National Forest flanks the Shenandoah Valley, rich in Civil War history. Excellent fishing and fall color. Contains six wilderness areas and 62 miles of Appalachian Trail. 1,065,232 acres in three sections, part in West Virginia. Boating, fishing, hiking, horseback riding, hunting, water sports. 807 campsites, food services, boat ramp, picnic areas, handicapped access. Open all year, including many campsites. Visitor center at Massanutten on US 211, about 8 miles from Shenandoah NP. (540) 265-5100.

JEFFERSON NATIONAL FOREST

HARRISONBURG AND ROANOKE, VIRGINIA

Some 272 miles of the Appalachian Trail traverse mountains blanketed in hardwood, pine, and rhododendron. Streams and waterfalls abound. Contains 11 wilderness areas and Mount Rogers National Recreation Area. 723,300 acres, part in West Virginia and Kentucky. Hiking, boating, fishing, horseback riding, hunting, water sports. 670 campsites, picnic areas, boat ramp, handicapped access. Open all year, including some campsites. Information at USFS Roanoke headquarters, about 65 miles south of Shenandoah NP, via Blue Ridge Parkway. (540) 265-5100.

MASON NECK NATIONAL WILDLIFE REFUGE

LORTON, VIRGINIA

Dedicated to the protection of the bald eagle, this refuge lies on the Potomac River, near Washington, D.C. Hardwood forest and marsh combine to form ideal habitat for the eagles and for numerous other wildlife species such as great blue herons, wood ducks, beaver, and deer. 2,277 acres. Hiking, bird-watching. Open all year. On Va. 242, about 75 miles from Shenandoah NP. (703) 490-4979.

Trunk Bay, renowned for its beauty

VIRGIN ISLANDS

UNITED STATES VIRGIN ISLANDS
ESTABLISHED AUGUST 2, 1956
12,909 acres

High green hills dropping down to enchanting turquoise bays, white powdery beaches, coral reefs, and ruins that evoke an era of sugar and a tragic period of slavery all find protection on St. John, one of about a hundred specks of Caribbean land known as the Virgin Islands.

Despite its small size—19 square miles—St. John's wide range of rainfall and exposure give it surprising variety. More than 800 subtropical plant species grow in areas from moist, high-elevation forests to desertlike terrain to mangrove swamps, among them mangoes, soursops, turpentine trees, wild tamarind, century plants, and sea grapes. Around the island live the fringing coral reefs—beautiful, complex, and exceedingly fragile communities of plants and animals, which St. John's famous beaches depend upon.

In 1493 Columbus sighted the large assemblage of islands and cays and named it after St. Ursula's legendary 11,000 virgins. Since then, Spain, France, Holland, England, Denmark, and the United States have controlled various islands at different times. The Danes began colonization in the 17th century, and in 1717 planters arrived on St. John. By mid-century 88 plantations had been established there; slaves stripped the steep hillsides of virgin growth and cultivated the cane. By the time the Danes abolished slavery in 1848, the sugar industry was doomed. A fallow, century-long period known as the "subsistence era" followed.

Fearful that the Germans might capture the islands during World War I, the United States bought St. John, St. Croix, St. Thomas, and about 50 smaller islands from Denmark for $25,000,000. In 1956 conservationist Laurance S. Rockefeller donated more than 5,000 acres for a national park on St. John; in 1962 the park acquired 5,650 undersea acres off the northern and southern coasts. Today, though its boundary includes three-quarters of St. John, the national park owns only slightly more than half the island. Of increasing concern is the escalating pace of development on private inholdings inside its borders. It also feels pressure from the numerous cruise ships that disgorge large numbers of visitors at once, badly straining park resources. Some of the park's trails may be closed for maintenance work; ask at the visitor center.

When to Go

Year-round. High season is mid-December to mid-April.

How to Get There

By plane to Charlotte Amalie, St. Thomas, then taxi or bus to Red Hook, then ferry across Pillsbury Sound to Cruz Bay, a 20-minute ride. Or, try to catch one of the less frequently scheduled ferries from Charlotte Amalie—the boat takes 45 minutes, but the dock is much nearer the airport.

How to Visit

If you have only 1 day, drive the **North Shore Road** as far as the **Annaberg Sugar Mill Ruins,** taking time to stretch your legs along some seaside trails—and perhaps do a little snorkeling. Return via **Centerline Road,** stopping at the ruins of **Catherineberg Sugar Mill.** On a second day, consider hiking the **Reef Bay Trail,** explore the island's **East End,** visit **Saltpond Bay,** and walk to **Ram Head.** With more time, sign up for some of the excellent ranger-led tours and activities.

If you're driving yourself, be prepared for steep, often potholed roads with blind curves, and *stay on the left.* The speed limit is 20 mph. An alternative is to hire a taxi and guide.

NORTH SHORE ROAD-CENTERLINE ROAD LOOP

15 miles; 3 hours to a full day

Begin your visit with a stop at the park visitor center in **Cruz Bay** to pick up a map and a trail brochure, and to find out what ranger-led activities are scheduled. Head north out of town along the **North Shore Road** (Route 20). This road is in good condition but very steep in places. Near the top of the hill, pull off at the overlook for a bird's-eye view of the picturesque town and harbor, the many small adjacent islands, and the big island of **St. Thomas** across the sound. For an even better view of **St. John's West End,** climb **Caneel Hill;** the 0.8-mile, moderately strenuous trail begins a short distance ahead on the right, across the road from the Park Service sign. (Or save this hike for sunset, when it's cooler and the view from the hill-top spectacular.)

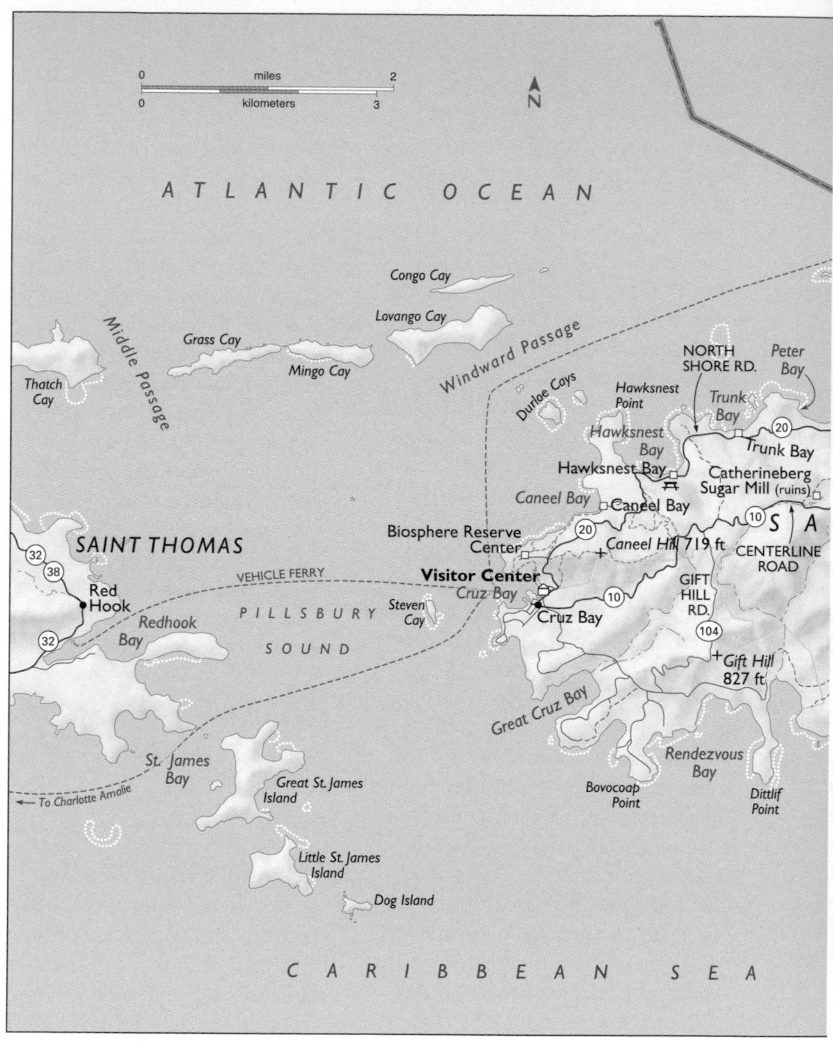

Stop at the next overlook a half mile farther along the road for a view of **Caneel Bay** and, to the northeast, the big island of **Jost van Dyke,** one of the British Virgins. Since the 1930s the site of a famous resort, Caneel Bay was a sugar plantation for most of the 18th and 19th centuries. Its name, both Dutch and Danish for "cinnamon," comes from the cinnamony leaves of the bay tree, a member of the myrtle family. (From the 1860s to the 1930s, oil from the leaves was used to make St. John Bay Rum cologne.)

The entrance to the Caneel Bay resort is down the hill on the left, past road marker 1.5. The land belongs to the park but is leased to the resort, once owned by the Rockefellers. To get a look at its lovely beaches and bays—and palm-studded grounds flowered with bougainvillea and pink oleander—walk the mostly level **Turtle Point Trail** around **Hawks-nest Point,** which takes about an hour. The resort management asks only that you register as a day guest at the front desk; ask there for directions to the trailhead.

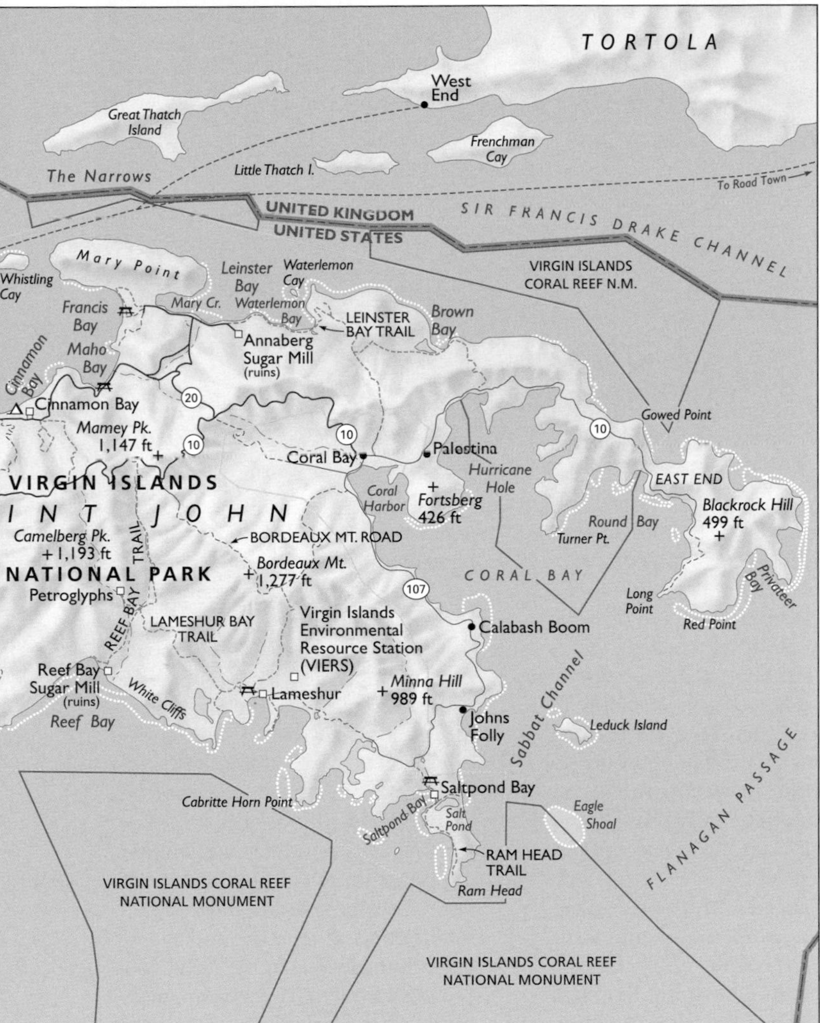

From Caneel Bay the road climbs steeply and descends to **Hawksnest Beach,** where you can swim, snorkel, and picnic. Visitors tend to bypass this beach, but locals flock here on weekends. Exhibits describe the damage being done to the island's fragile reefs by pollutants, swimmers, snorkelers, and the anchors of careless boaters—and strongly urge you not to touch, stand, or sit on the coral.

One of the Caribbean's premier vistas awaits you a mile farther up the road. From the overlook, **Trunk Bay** with its lush palm-fringed crescent beach and dozens of bobbing sailboats lies before you. Off a point in the middle distance is **Whistling Cay,** where in the 19th century a customs shed stopped boats plying the passage between the Danish and British Virgins. Trunk Bay's beauty draws many visitors, especially on days when cruise ships are in. The park has set up an underwater nature trail for snorkelers here; some 16 plaques identify the reef's plants and animals. If you're a serious snorkeler, however, you

Snorkelers bobbing toward a coral reef off Caneel Bay resort

might want to skip this reef for a less traveled one farther along.

Beyond Trunk Bay's entrance be prepared for the road to sharply steepen. Near the top of the hill is the multimillion-dollar development at **Peter Bay,** a private inholding that has been a model for preventing the sediment runoff that other developments have allowed. Park officials and environmentalists say that runoff damages the reefs and sea grass beds.

At **Cinnamon Bay** (road marker 4.5) are a campground and, across the road, the ruins of the Danish (first Dutch) Cinnamon Bay sugar factory, one of the island's oldest. Plaques along the 1-mile trail tell you its history and point out native trees such as bay, lime, teyer palm, and calabash, which produces a gourdlike fruit that's carved into bowls. If you're lucky enough to be there for a tour led by one of the Virgin Islanders on the park staff, you'll learn some colorful local lore as well.

Continue down the road a half mile to yet another stunning, sweeping view—**Maho Bay, Francis Bay,** where sea turtles come to feed, and **Mary Point.** You'll see diving pelicans and frigate birds, which, to avoid water-logging their own enormous wings, harass other seabirds for food. The red roofs visible in the trees belong to a house built in 1952 by an American eccentric named Ethel McCully, who swam ashore from a boat and stayed. Since no paved roads or automobiles existed on St. John then, donkeys hauled the materials from Cruz Bay—a 4-hour trip.

Down the hill, the road flattens, passing a stretch of beach on the left. Continue on for a mile to the road's end and then turn right toward **Annaberg.** On the right, you'll see a thick mangrove swamp, one of many on the island. Its large, tangled roots help protect the shoreline and provide a breeding ground for fish.

On the left, about 100 yards from the turnoff, look for the marker identifying one of the toxic manchineel trees common to the Caribbean; Columbus called their green fruit "death apples." Do not stand under this tree in the rain: Runoff can raise painful blisters on your skin.

Just ahead is **Mary Creek** with a view of Mary Point. An important marine community inhabits the shallow reefs and sea grass beds of the creek, site of a weekly naturalist-led seashore walk. If you wade out *(be sure to wear something on your feet)*, you can find brilliantly colored conchs, spiny black sea urchins, and brittle stars that regenerate their tentacles. Coral rocks host many tiny animals. Pick up and examine the rocks, but put them back as you found them.

From here consider an easy walk along the 0.8-mile **Leinster Bay Trail,** which follows the seashore east to **Waterlemon Bay** and some of the best snorkeling in the park. You can swim and snorkel off the sandy beach at the trail's end. Better yet if you have the stamina, walk out to the point and swim across the narrow channel to snorkel around little **Waterlemon Cay.**

Back at the Leinster Bay trailhead, park in the small lot and walk up the hill to the partially restored ruins of the **Annaberg Sugar Mill.** A quarter-mile self-guided walk introduces you to the slave quarters, windmill, horse mill, oven, cistern, and factory that for much of two centuries produced raw sugar, molasses, and rum for Denmark. Native stone, ballast brick, and coral went into building the thick walls.

From the overlook you can see a number of other Virgin Islands across the narrows, including **Tortola,** largest of the British Virgins, and the dinosaur shape of Britain's **Great Thatch** on the left. In winter, humpback whales sometimes cruise by. Annaberg slaves reportedly tried to swim to Great Thatch after the British freed their slaves in 1833, 15 years ahead of the Danes. Before leaving the overlook, treat yourself to the scent of a frangipani blossom from the nearby tree.

To return to Cruz Bay, drive the more level Centerline Road (Route 10), watching out for blind curves. Slow speeds should pose no hardship, however: The views of the island's East End are truly spectacular. If you have time, look for the Catherineberg Road on the right after driving about 3 miles. A short way up this road are the ruins of the area's 18th-century Catherineberg Sugar Mill. The outer shell of the windmill has been restored, and there are 4-foot stone walls, handsome archways, a massive stone pillar, and some original beams to see.

EAST END: CORAL BAY & SALTPOND BAY

26 miles round-trip; at least a half day

Take Centerline Road (Route 10) out of Cruz Bay, stopping after nearly 3 miles at the Catherineberg Sugar Mill (see above), if you haven't already been there. About a half mile farther is the **Konge Vey Overlook,** where a wayside exhibit points out Jost van Dyke, Great Thatch, and other islands and bays to the north.

The popular **Reef Bay Trail** begins after another 1.25 miles. It descends into a steep v-shaped valley through moist, subtropical forest to dry forest to acacia scrub near the coast. Ruins of sugar estates can be seen along its 2.5 miles and nearby are some mysterious petroglyphs. Walk this trail at least partway to experience the lush forest or, even better, save it for the ranger-led trip ($15), when a boat meets you at the coast and spares you the hike back up.

Back in your car, continue on to the overlook near **Mamey Peak** for a lovely view of Coral Bay and the island's East End. The name of the bay comes not from the island's abundant coral but from an 18th-century Dutch corral *(kraal)* here. The Danes established their first plantations at this end of the island, among them the vast Estate Carolina,

INFORMATION & ACTIVITIES

HEADQUARTERS

1300 Cruz Bay Creek, St. John, USVI 00830. Phone (340) 776-6201. www.nps.gov/viis

SEASONS & ACCESSIBILITY

Open all year. Access by boat. Climate does not vary much during the year, though summers can be hot. Hurricane season here runs typically from June through November.

VISITOR & INFORMATION CENTERS

Cruz Bay Visitor Center, at west end of St. John, open daily all year. Call (340) 776-6201.

ENTRANCE FEE

There is no entrance fee for the park. However, there is a user fee to enter Trunk Bay: $4 for adults; children 16 and under admitted free. $10 annual fee.

PETS

Not allowed on public beaches, in picnic areas, or in campgrounds. Permitted elsewhere on leashes.

FACILITIES FOR DISABLED

Some ferries to St. John are accessible to wheelchairs, with assistance. The visitor center, several Cinnamon Bay campsites, and restrooms there and at Trunk Bay and Hawksnest Bay are also accessible.

THINGS TO DO

Free naturalist-led activities: interpretive talks and exhibits, nature and history walks, hikes, snorkel tours, cultural demonstrations, evening programs. Also available, self-guided nature and underwater trails, swimming, snorkeling, boating, fishing (no license needed),

once the property of the king. They built a fort—called **Fort Frederik**—on **Fortsberg** on the bay's eastern shore. In 1733 a bloody slave uprising began here, reputedly the first in the New World. It would have succeeded—1,087 of the island's 1,295 inhabitants were slaves—had the French not sailed in to quell it.

Continue on Route 10 as it winds eastward outside the park to the village of **Coral Bay,** about 2 miles away. You may well see a mongoose scuttering across the road. Introduced a century ago to kill rats, the mongoose has multiplied explosively, to the detriment of some native island fauna. At Coral Bay, stop to see the handsome pink-roofed **Emmaus Church,** built by Moravian missionaries in the 1780s. If you continued on, you'd be rewarded with magnificent views of **Hurricane Hole, Round Bay,** and the British Virgins. But for now backtrack a short distance and turn left at the intersection of Route 107. Drive 4 miles along the coast to the trailhead for **Saltpond Bay** and a wilder part of the island.

About a fifth of a mile beyond the parking area, the horseshoe bay is fringed by a wide, sandy beach, gently lapped by transparent waters. Continue around the beach and onto the rocky 0.9-mile **Ram Head Trail** that winds up a promontory and down the other side. There a blue pebbly beach and an arid environment await you. Plants include several kinds of cactuses and the century plant, which takes 15 to 20 years to bloom, then dies.

Continue to the crest of the hill for a grand Caribbean view. Watch your footing and hold onto any children you've brought on this windswept point 200 feet above the sea. Here at **Ram Head** you'll be standing on rock that emerged some 108 million years ago, the oldest land on St. John.

windsurfing, bird-watching, photography workshops, archaeology digs, occasional historic bus tours.

OVERNIGHT BACKPACKING

Not allowed in park.

CAMPGROUNDS

One park campground, **Cinnamon Bay;** 14-day limit December to mid-May; other times 21-day limit. Open all year. Reservations recommended; contact Cinnamon Bay Campground, P.O. Box 720, Cruz Bay, St. John, USVI 00831. (800) 539-9998 or (340) 776-6330. Nightly for 2 persons: $27 for bare sites; $80 for tents; $110-$140 for cottages. Cold showers. Food services. Also, **Maho Bay;** reservations, Maho Bay Camp, 17-A E. 73rd St., New York, NY 10021. (800) 392-9004 or (212) 472-9453. 114 equipped tent-cottages, central baths. $110 per night December through April; $75 per night May through November. Reserve early for December to May.

HOTELS, MOTELS, & INNS

(unless otherwise noted, rates are for 2 persons in a double room, high season)

On St. John, USVI 00831:

Caneel Bay P.O. Box 720, Cruz Bay. (800) 928-8889 or (340) 776-6111. 166 units. $450-$1,175. Pool, restaurants.

Gallows Point Suite Resort P.O. Box 58. (800) 323-7229 or (340) 776-6434. 60 units, kitchens. $435-$575. Pool, restaurant.

St. John Inn P.O. Box 37. (800) 666-7688 or (340) 693-8688. 11 units, some kitchens. $140-$200.

Westin Resort St. John P.O. Box 8310. (340) 693-8000. 349 units. $429-$1,659. AC, 3 pools, restaurants.

EXCURSIONS

BUCK ISLAND REEF NATIONAL MONUMENT

ST. CROIX, U.S. VIRGIN ISLANDS

A coral reef nearly encircles this small island, 1 mile north of St. Croix. A marked underwater trail guides snorkelers or passengers of glass-bottom boats through the exquisite reef ecosystem. Breathtaking views of St. Croix and the reef can be had from the top of Buck Island's hiking trail. 176 land acres; 18,839 undersea acres. Trail, picnic areas, water sports. Open all year (daytime only). Access by charter boat from Christianster, St. Croix (charter operators supply snorkeling equipment). (340) 773-1460.

Forested islands of Rainy Lake; Canada in the background

VOYAGEURS

MINNESOTA
ESTABLISHED APRIL 8, 1975
218,054 acres

From the air, the forest areas of Voyageurs look like green pieces of a jigsaw puzzle scattered on a huge mirror. A North Woods realm of more than 30 lakes and more than 900 islands, Voyageurs spans a watery stretch of the U.S.-Canada border.

A third of this national park's area is water, most of it in four large lakes—Rainy, Kabetogama, Namakan, and Sand Point—linked by narrow waterways. Smaller lakes gleam in the forests and bogs of Voyageurs' terra firma, which consists of small islands, a strip of mainland shore, and the Kabetogama Peninsula, a long, bay-fringed landmass.

The splendors of this 55-mile-long park can be reached primarily only by water. Motorboats *(banned in the adjacent Boundary Waters Canoe Area Wilderness)* churn the lakes. Canoes and kayaks glide the narrow waterways. Fishermen sit at the rails of houseboats, hoping to hook walleye, smallmouth bass, and northern pike. Nearly every lake is haunted by the cry of the loon. And probably in no other national park in the lower 48 states is there a better chance to see bald eagles on the nest and on the wing or hear wolves howl at night.

The park is named for French Canadian voyageurs who paddled birchbark canoes for fur trading companies in the late 18th and early 19th centuries. The voyageurs were famous for stamina—paddling up to 16 hours a day—and roisterous songs. Their canoe route between Canada's northwest and Montreal is cited as part of the U.S.-Canada border in the treaty that ended the American Revolution.

In a boat in the labyrinth of waterways and islands, you can unwittingly cross this border. Be sure to take along a high-quality map that includes navigational markers to tell you where you are.

How to Get There

From Duluth, drive north about 110 miles on US 53. For Crane Lake, turn east at Orr and drive 28 miles on County Roads 23 and 24. For Ash River, stay on US 53 for 25 more miles, turn right at the Ash River Trail sign, and continue for 10 miles. For Kabetogama Lake Visitor Center, stay on US 53 for 3 more miles, turn right onto County Road 122, and drive to the lakeshore. For Rainy Lake, stay on US 53 to International Falls, then head east for 12 miles on Minn. 11 to the park's entrance road, following highway information signs; turn right to go to the visitor center. Airports: Duluth and International Falls, Minnesota; and Fort Frances, Ontario.

When to Go

Year-round, but most accessible from spring through early fall. Water travel is curtailed by freeze-up in late fall and ice break-up in early spring. Winter opens the park to cross-country skiing, snowshoeing, snowmobiling, and ice fishing. And the 7 mile ice road at Rainy Lake provides a unique entry into the park: You drive your car on the ice to places that in other seasons you can reach only by boat or floatplane.

How to Visit

The only way to the heart of this park is by water. **Kabetogama Lake, International Falls, Crane Lake,** and **Ash River** are resort communities that, though not within the park, serve as entrances. Begin your trip planning by choosing an entrance; each of them is widely spaced and offers a different experience. You can make motel or lodge reservations at one of the area's resorts or motels listed in the park's newspaper, the *Rendezvous,* or in the **Information & Activities** section on

Modern voyageurs on Kabetogama Lake

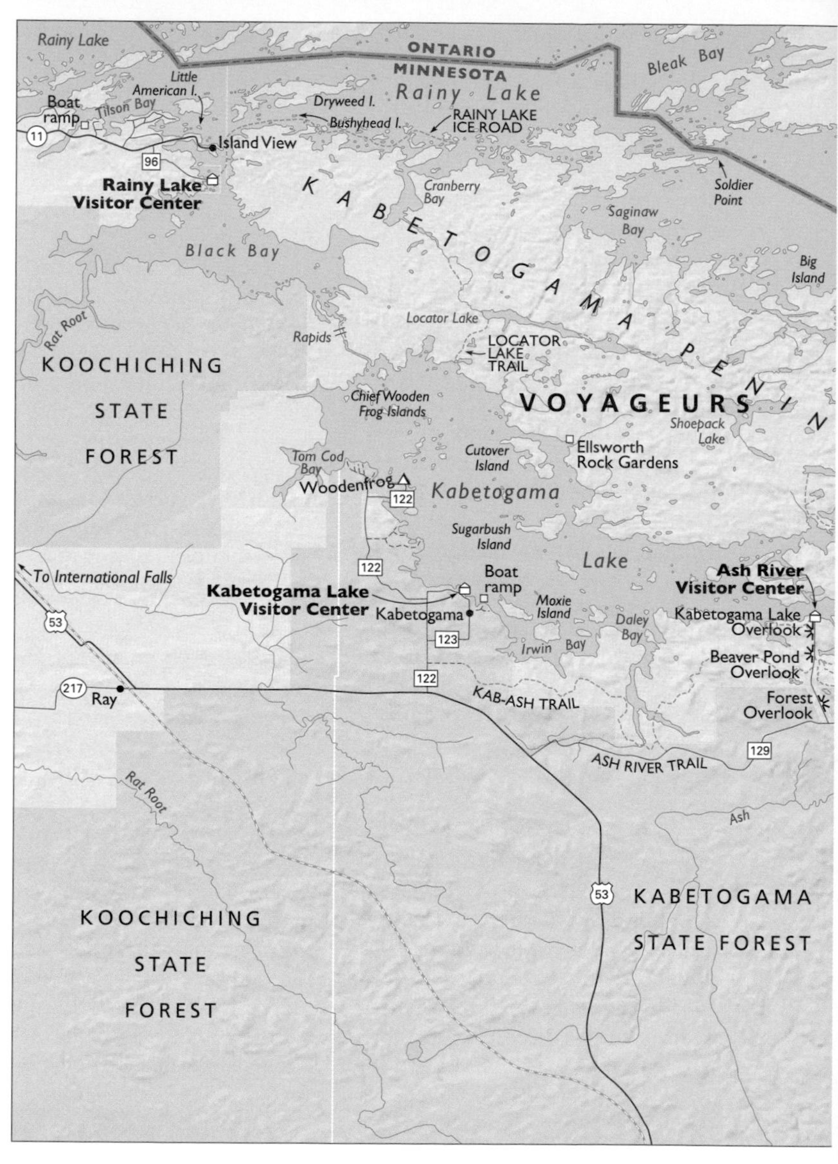

p. 118. You can also stay in a car campground and use the resort as a base for park activities, including fishing and wildlife watching, or rent a houseboat or camp out by boat. Guides, canoes, houseboats, and motorboats are for hire. If you are sufficiently experienced, you can also tow in your own craft.

Sight-seeing boats, with park naturalists aboard, also operate out of visitor centers. Even if you have your own boat, you may want to take a commercial cruise and rely on experienced navigators; the lakes are broad with submerged rocks in shallow areas, and they are sometimes brushed by stiff winds, testing even the most experienced boater.

If your time is limited, Kabetogama Lake is a good place for exploring and understanding the park.

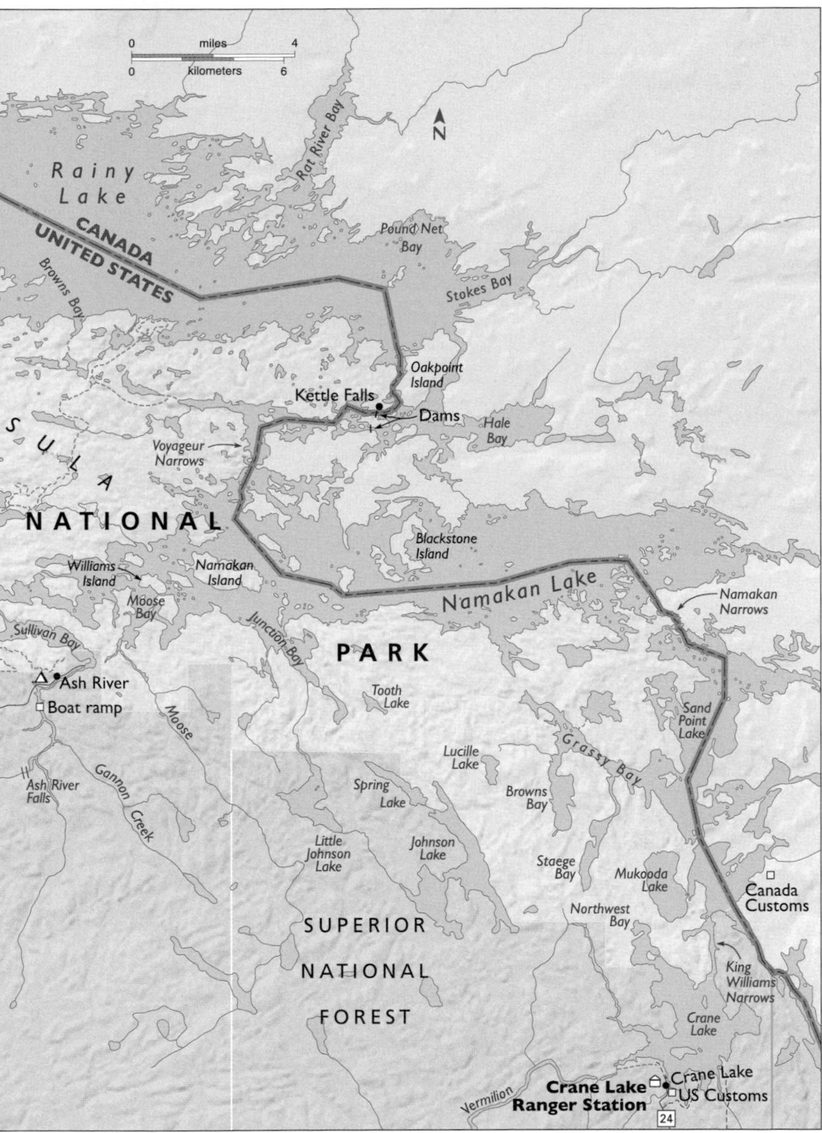

KABETOGAMA LAKE

at least a full day

At the **Kabetogama Lake Visitor Center,** learn about boat tours, guided canoe trips, or children's programs. Or, rent one of the park's cached canoes at Locator Lake by reserving it and picking up the key at the visitor center. If you do this, you must get to the Locator Lake trailhead on your own, with a guide, or in a rented boat. You leave the boat at the trailhead for a 2-mile hike along a spruce bog and past a beaver pond, dam, and lodge. The trail climbs to a ridge and drops to the lakeshore. There you launch your reserved cached canoe and paddle around the lake, watching for muskrat, bald eagles, loons, and blue-winged teal. Another exciting way to explore the park is on

A skein of bur reed edging Browns Bay, on Rainy Lake

an all-day guided cruise to **Kettle Falls.** For details see **Crane Lake & Ash River,** below. The 21-mile **Kabetogama to Ash River Trail** travels through the park and state forest lands; three trailheads, all car-accessible, offer a variety of opportunities.

RAINY LAKE

at least a full day

Although this lake is large—60 miles long, 12 miles wide—you can safely explore it in your own or a rented motorboat, houseboat, or canoe. At the **Rainy Lake Visitor Center** get weather and navigation information and take a self-guided waterborne excursion. About 1.5 miles northwest is **Little American Island,** where the discovery of gold set off a short-lived gold rush a hundred years ago. A short interpretive trail on the island gives a view to the past. About 2 miles east is **Bushyhead Island,** where a mine shaft is carved into the rock.

Lacking your own boat, you can still explore. The park offers naturalist led tour boat trips from the visitor center, as well as free trips aboard a 26-foot reproduction of a voyageurs canoe, guided trips aboard contemporary canoes, and programs for children.

Trails near Rainy Lake Visitor Center: The 2-mile **Oberholtzer Trail** travels through a variety of habitats. The short, water-accessible **Black Bay Beaver Pond Trail** takes visitors to an active beaver pond habitat.

CRANE LAKE & ASH RIVER

at least 1 to 2 days each

Near the Ash River resort area is a visitor center where you can launch your boat, get information about camping, set off on hikes (see below), and obtain charts for navigating the lakes. If you're new to the lakes, *don't fail to use charts.*

For a good exploratory voyage, go to **Kettle Falls,** a waterways hub used by Native Americans, voyageurs, loggers, fishermen, and, during Prohibition, bootleggers smuggling liquor from Canada.

From Crane Lake you travel north through **King Williams Narrows,** across **Sand Point Lake,** and through **Namakan Narrows,** then west across **Namakan Lake** along the U.S.-Canada border, which veers northward here.

From Ash River you go the length of **Sullivan Bay** to the river mouth, then weave through a string of islands into **Moose Bay.** For a scenic trip, pass through the channel on the south side of **Williams Island** (site of a primitive campsite) into **Hoist Bay,** named for the hoisting of logs that were loaded onto a train. You can see pilings that supported a train track, which ran from the middle of the bay to a white-pine sawmill on the mainland. Head north toward **Namakan Island,** site of other campsites, and go around the island's western side.

Both courses take you to the southern end of **Voyageur Narrows.** Pass through the narrows, then head east along the border through **Squirrel Narrows** to Kettle Falls. Near the dock, a dam serves a regional system regulating water flow for electric power. At the dock is a gravel road, a portage trail. Walk the road for about a quarter mile to a white clapboard building with a long front porch—the **Kettle Falls Hotel.** Built in 1910, the hotel welcomed lumberjacks and their money; it still hosts guests—those who make their reservations well ahead.

Another way to get to Kettle Falls is to take a cruise boat. Trips are run several times a week out of the visitor center at Kabetogama Lake. The all-day trip is timed for you to eat lunch or dinner at the hotel before the return voyage.

Trails near Ash River Visitor Center: Three short trails—the **Voyageurs Forest, Beaver Pond,** and **Kabetogama Lake Overlook**—leave from pull-offs on the road to the visitor center. The 2-mile **Blind Ash Bay Trail,** from the visitor center to the mouth of Blind Ash Bay, wends along rock cliffs through pine forest.

Showy lady's slipper *(top)*
American white pelican *(bottom)*

INFORMATION & ACTIVITIES

HEADQUARTERS
3131 US 53, International Falls, MN 56649. Phone (218) 283-9821. www.nps.gov/voya

SEASONS & ACCESSIBILITY
Open all year. Travel within it is by boat, floatplane, and foot in summer; snowmobile, snowshoes, cross-country skis, and ski-plane in winter. Limited access during lake freeze-up (mid-Nov. to mid-Dec.) and break up (April). In winter, weather permitting, an ice road on Rainy Lake connects the visitor center to Cranberry Bay, 7 miles into the park.

VISITOR & INFORMATION CENTERS
Rainy Lake, on Minn. 11 at northwest edge of park; call (218) 286-5258. **Kabetogama Lake,** on County Road 123 at southwest edge of lake, open late May through September; call (218) 875-2111. **Ash River,** on southeast edge of Kabetogama Lake, open late May through September. Call (218) 374-3221. Days vary at all locations; call ahead.

ENTRANCE FEE
None.

PETS
Permitted on leashes in developed areas and at tent, houseboat, and day-use sites on major lakes. Not allowed on park trails, in backcountry, or on interior lakes.

FACILITIES FOR DISABLED
Kabetogama Lake, Rainy Lake, and Ash River Visitor Centers are wheelchair accessible, as is the Kettle Falls Hotel, guided boat trips, and a campsite; call Kabetogama Lake for reservations. Fact sheet available.

THINGS TO DO
Free naturalist-led activities: nature walks, canoe trips (reserve at visitor centers), children's programs, films, exhibits, winter programs. Also, hiking, canoeing and rowboating (boats on Interior Lakes Program $10 a day), boat touring, fishing and ice fishing (guides available, ask park for list; license required), swimming, water-skiing, snowmobiling, cross-country skiing, snowshoeing.

SPECIAL ADVISORY
• Practice safe boating: Use navigational maps; be aware of weather conditions; make sure your boat is well equipped; do not overload it.

CAMPING & HOUSEBOATING
All park sites reached by water. 214 lake country boat-in campsites, 14-day limit. Open all year (may be inaccessible during fall freeze-up and spring thaw); first come, first served. Free permit required for overnights, available at visitor centers and boat launches. No showers. Sites designated for tent camps or houseboats. Also, two small campgrounds. In winter, access mainly by snowmobile, cross-country skis, or snowshoes. Private campgrounds with tent and RV sites near park. Request "Camping, Houseboating, and Day-Use" brochure for planning.

HOTELS, MOTELS, & INNS
(unless otherwise noted, rates are for 2 persons in a double room, high season)

INSIDE THE PARK:
Kettle Falls Hotel (15 miles by water from the Ash River Trail) 10502 Gamma Road, Ray, MN 56669. (888) 534-6835. 12 hotel rooms. $70 double; lodge and suites nearby, some with kitchens, $160-$190.
OUTSIDE THE PARK:
In International Falls, MN 56649:
Holiday Inn 1500 US 71. (800) 331-4443 or (218) 283-8000. 126 units. $80-$130. AC, pool, restaurant.
Island View Lodge (on Rainy Lake) 1817 Hwy. 11E. (800) 777-7856 or (218) 286-3511. 9 rooms $83-$98; 14 cabins with kitchens, $155. AC, restaurant.
In Kabetogama, MN 56669:
Voyageur Park Lodge 10436 Waltz Rd. (800) 331-5694 or (218) 875-2131). 11 cabins with kitchens (summer only), $588-$1,200 per week.

For a listing of accommodations, call Kabetogama Tourism Bureau (800) 524-9085; Crane Lake Visitor & Tourism Bureau (800) 362-7405; International Falls Area Convention & Visitors Bureau (800) 325-5766; Ash River Commercial Club (800) 950-2061.

EXCURSIONS

SUPERIOR NATIONAL FOREST
DULUTH, MINNESOTA

Here the northern lights preside over stands of pine, spruce, fir, alder, and birch, and loons bob on the more than 1,000 portage-linked lakes of the Boundary Waters Canoe Area Wilderness (permit req.). Reservations essential. 2.2 million acres. Hiking, boating, fishing, winter sports, water sports, scenic drives. Campsites, food services, boat ramp, picnic areas. Open all year. La Croix Visitor Center west of Cook on US 53 about 15 miles from Orr, Minn., the southern gateway to Voyageurs NP. (218) 626-4300.

CHIPPEWA NATIONAL FOREST
CASS LAKE, MINNESOTA

This lake-country forest boasts one of the largest breeding bald eagle populations outside Alaska and offers a variety of water-based recreation, including the chance to explore the Mississippi's headwaters by canoe. More than 660,000 acres. Hiking, boating, fishing, scenic drives, historic sites with summer interpretive programs, winter sports, hunting. 23 campgrounds, picnic areas, boat ramps, handicapped access. Open all year; campsites generally open mid-May to mid-Sept. Information at Cass Lake on US 2, about 85 miles from Voyageurs NP. (218) 335-8600.

AGASSIZ NATIONAL WILDLIFE REFUGE
MIDDLE RIVER, MINNESOTA

More than 285 species of migratory and resident birds share this wetlands refuge with about 50 moose and a resident pack of eastern gray wolves—one of the few such packs in any national refuge outside Alaska. 61,500 acres. Hiking, hunting, scenic drives, bird-watching. Handicapped access. Open all year (Lost Bay Habitat Dr. and Maakstad Hiking Trail open May–Oct.). Headquarters on Marshall County Rd. 7, 11 miles east of Holt, 185 miles from Voyageurs NP. (218) 449-4115.

THE SOUTHWEST

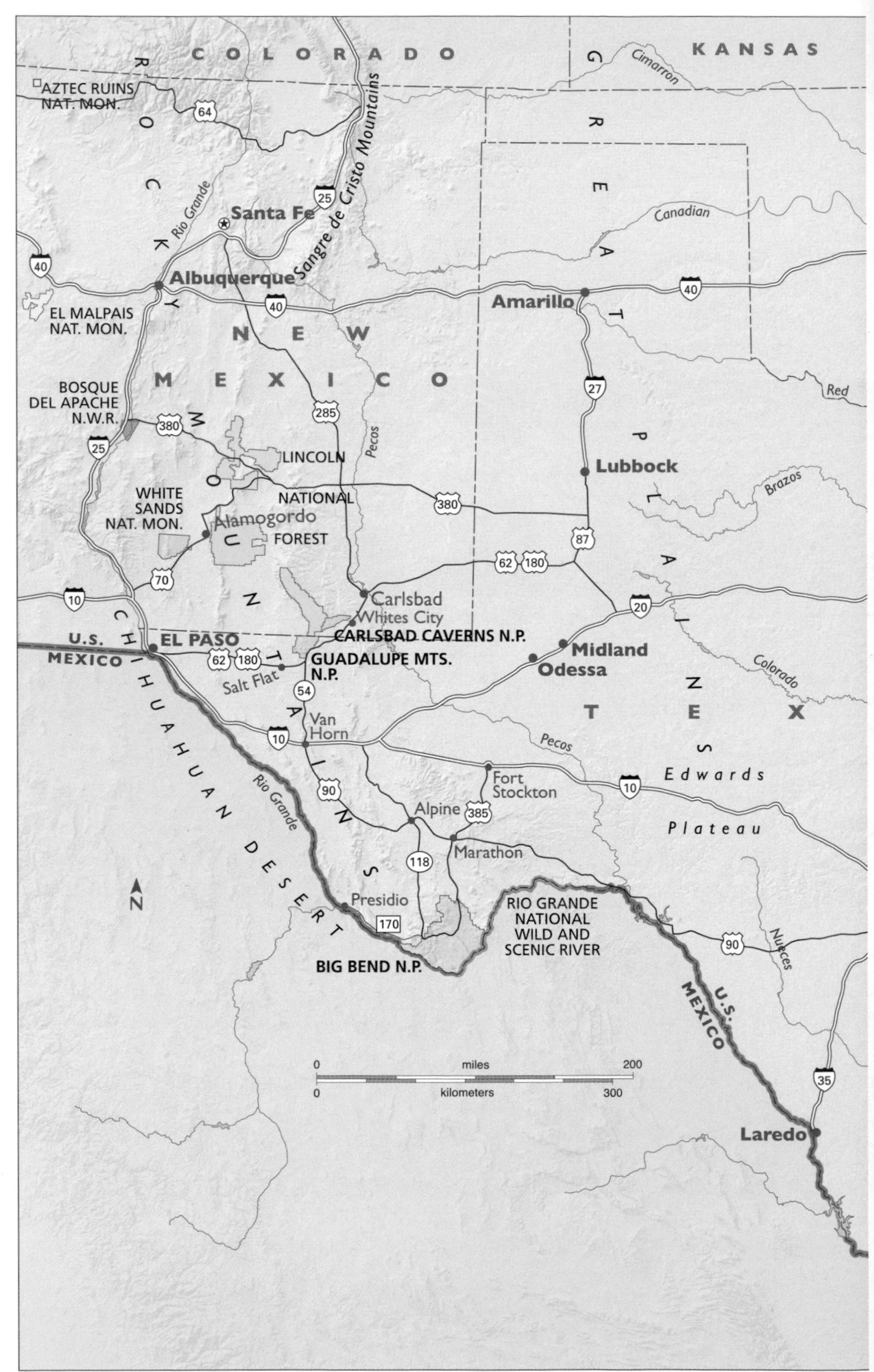
COLORADO
KANSAS
ROCKY MOUNTAINS
GREAT PLAINS
AZTEC RUINS NAT. MON.
Sangre de Cristo Mountains
Cimarron
Rio Grande
Santa Fe
Canadian
Albuquerque
Amarillo
EL MALPAIS NAT. MON.
NEW MEXICO
BOSQUE DEL APACHE N.W.R.
Red
Pecos
LINCOLN
NATIONAL
FOREST
Lubbock
Brazos
WHITE SANDS NAT. MON.
Alamogordo
Carlsbad
Whites City
CARLSBAD CAVERNS N.P.
U.S.
MEXICO
EL PASO
GUADALUPE MTS. N.P.
Salt Flat
Midland
Odessa
Colorado
TEXAS
CHIHUAHUAN DESERT
Van Horn
Pecos
Fort Stockton
Edwards
Plateau
Rio Grande
Alpine
Marathon
Presidio
RIO GRANDE NATIONAL WILD AND SCENIC RIVER
BIG BEND N.P.
Nueces
U.S.
MEXICO
N
0 miles 200
0 kilometers 300
Laredo

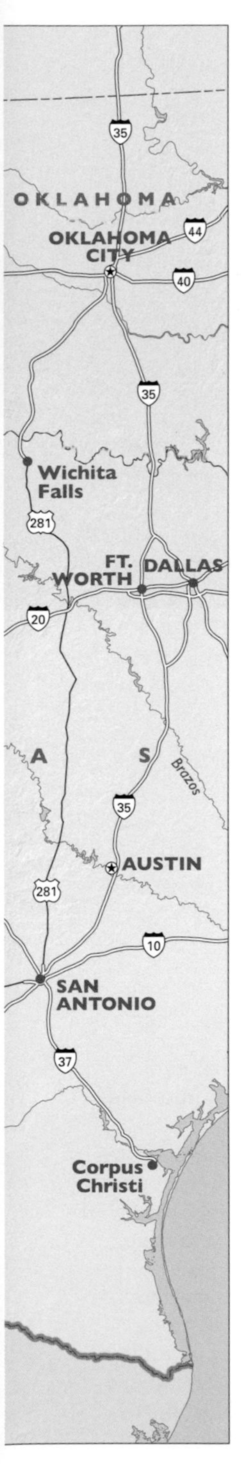

THE SOUTHWEST

The national parks of the Southwest, all set in the Chihuahuan Desert, offer scenery ranging from underground caves to high and rugged mountain peaks. Sparse vegetation opens the spectacular vistas up to visitors without their having to go above tree line.

Water sculptured these landscapes. A reef from an ancient sea forms the 50-mile-long Guadalupe mountain chain. The seeping of water over millions of years created the cool, dark world of Carlsbad Caverns. Rivers etched out the dramatic canyons of Big Bend, and flash floods still tumble boulders from the steep Chisos mountaintops, continuing to rearrange the scenery.

The vagaries of yearly precipitation also determine whether the visitor beholds a land of blossoms—Texas bluebonnets, brilliant red and orange cactus flowers, heavy stalks of white yucca blooms—or, more often, a parched terrain dominated by creosote bush, prickly pear, and dagger-sharp lechuguilla. Where water flows year-round, oases produce gardens that resound with birdsong.

Visitors to the Southwest parks have a chance to view wildlife as diverse as multicolored lizards and snakes, the elusive mountain lion, deer, hundreds of species of birds, and, in Big Bend, pig look-alikes called javelinas. Paleontologists have found fossils of many other creatures, including giant crocodiles and the Big Bend pterosaur, the largest animal ever to fly.

Hikers may take their own trip back in time by climbing up to the pine-fir forests that cloak the cooler, moister mountaintops in the Guadalupes and Big Bend. This type of forest probably covered the region at the end of the last Ice Age, when early peoples hunted camels, mammoths, and four-horned antelope.

Carlsbad Caverns and Guadalupe Mountains National Parks are linked by the Lincoln National Forest; proposals have been made to unite the three areas into one large park encompassing the Guadalupe range. Base yourself at Carlsbad or, even closer, in Whites City to visit these areas. Allow a day to drive the 250 miles from Guadalupe to Big Bend.

Agave on the South Rim

BIG BEND

TEXAS
ESTABLISHED JUNE 12, 1944
801,163 acres

As the Rio Grande winds south along the Texas-Mexico border, it suddenly veers northward in a great horseshoe curve before continuing its journey. Inside the horseshoe lies the region of Texas known as the Big Bend; Big Bend National Park flanks the river at the southerly tip of the curve. A wild and surprising land, the park remains remote enough that only the dedicated reach it.

Chihuahuan Desert vegetation—bunchgrasses, creosote bushes, cactuses, lechuguillas, yuccas, sotols, and more—covers most of the terrain. But the Rio Grande and its lush floodplains and steep, narrow canyons form almost a park of their own. So do the Chisos Mountains; up to 20 degrees cooler than the desert floor, they harbor pine, juniper, and oak, as well as deer, mountain lions, bears, and other wildlife. A heavy rain transforms the desert: Normally dry creek beds roar with water, and seeds long dormant burst into fields of wildflowers.

The rocks of Big Bend are a complex lot. Two seas, one after another, flowed and subsided in the region hundreds of millions of years ago, leaving thick deposits of limestone and shale. The present mountains, except the Chisos, uplifted along with the Rockies, roughly 75 million years ago. Around the same time, a 40-mile-wide trough—most of the present-day park—sank along fault lines, leaving the cliffs of Santa Elena Canyon to the west and the Sierra del Carmen to the east rising 1,500 feet above the desert floor. In the center, volcanic activity spewed layer upon layer of ash into the air and squeezed molten rock up through the ground to form the Chisos Mountains some 35 million years ago. Molten rock also cooled and hardened underground later to be exposed by erosion.

Big Bend's topographic variety supports a remarkable diversity of life, including 1,200 plant species—some found nowhere else in the world. More species of birds—more than 450—have been counted here than in any other u.s. national park.

People have passed through this terrain for at least 10,000 years. The human pageant in historical times has included Apache, Spanish conquistadores, Comanche, U.S. soldiers, miners, ranchers and farmers, Mexican revolutionaries, and international outlaws and bandits.

How to Get There

From Marathon US 385 leads south to the north entrance to the park; Tex. 118 from Alpine leads south to the west entrance; Ranch Road 170, from Presidio, joins Tex. 118 shortly before the west entrance. Nearest airports: El Paso (325 miles) and Midland-Odessa (230 miles).

When to Go

Year-round, though fall and winter may be the best seasons. Deciduous leaves turn color in the mountains in autumn; winters are mild. Summer temperatures in the desert can exceed 110°F; the Chisos Mountains remain cooler. If enough rain falls, the desert blooms stunningly in early spring, and again in late summer. Bird-watching is good all year, but especially in March, April, and May.

How to Visit

Allow several days, especially if you plan to hike. Explore the **Chisos Mountains Basin** and the **Ross Maxwell Scenic Drive**, engineered to take you past many of the park's geological and scenic highlights. Ideally, devote the better part of a day to each area. With extra time on the second afternoon, or on a third day, drive out to **Rio Grande Village** and the **Boquillas Canyon Overlook** to experience the river environment and enjoy views of the Sierra del Carmen, particularly spectacular at sunset. On your way in or out, view the landscape and exhibits along the road between **Panther Junction** and **Persimmon Gap**. For an extended visit, try more of the many rewarding hikes, drive some dirt roads, and consider a leisurely float trip along the Rio Grande through one of the park's three major canyons.

Rocks at entrance to Santa Elena Canyon

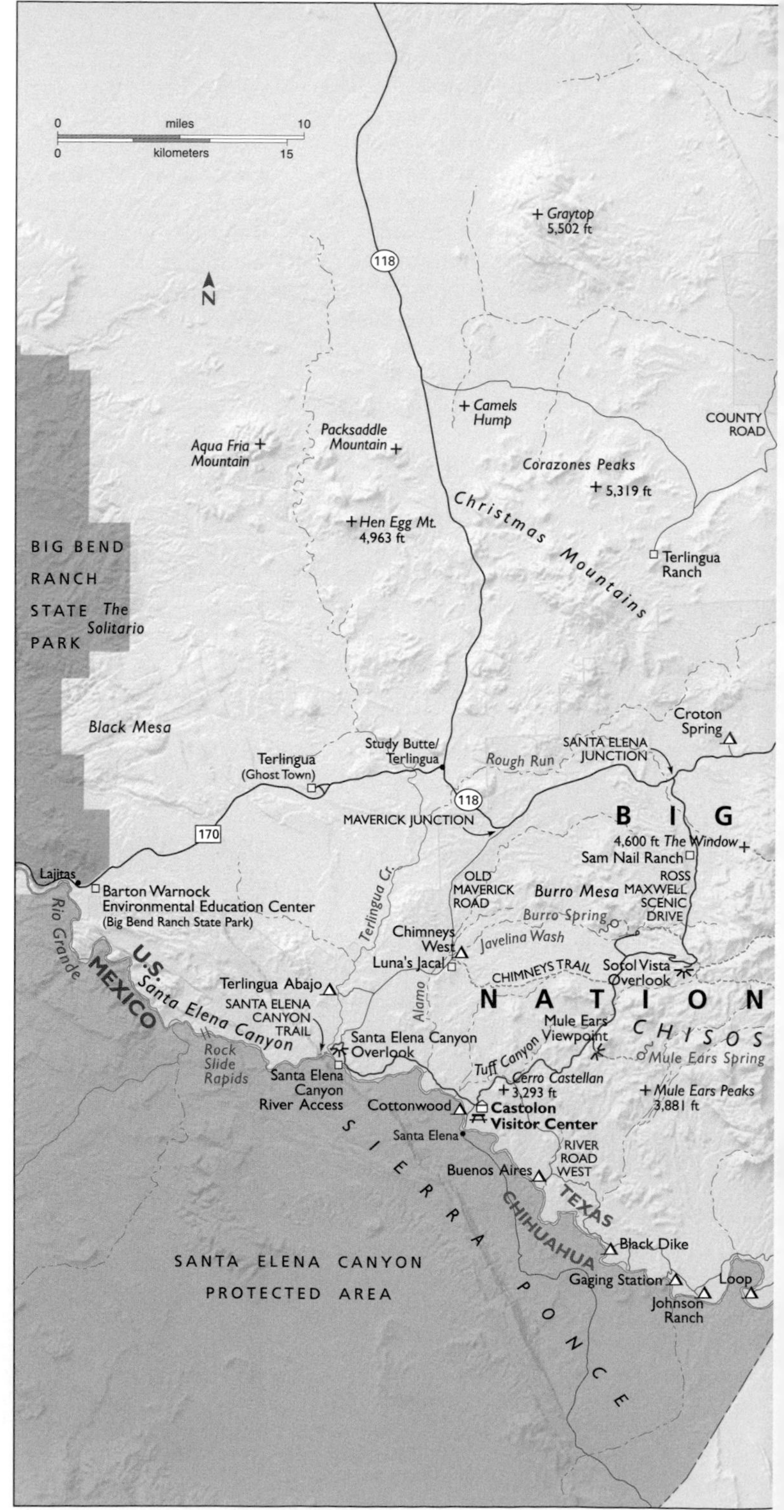

0 miles 10
0 kilometers 15
N
Graytop 5,502 ft
118
Camels Hump
COUNTY ROAD
Packsaddle Mountain
Aqua Fria Mountain
Corazones Peaks
5,319 ft
Christmas Mountains
Hen Egg Mt. 4,963 ft
Terlingua Ranch
BIG BEND RANCH STATE PARK
The Solitario
Black Mesa
Croton Spring
Study Butte/ Terlingua
SANTA ELENA JUNCTION
Rough Run
Terlingua (Ghost Town)
MAVERICK JUNCTION
BIG
4,600 ft The Window
Sam Nail Ranch
170
Lajitas
Barton Warnock Environmental Education Center (Big Bend Ranch State Park)
OLD MAVERICK ROAD
Burro Mesa
ROSS MAXWELL SCENIC DRIVE
Terlingua Cr.
Burro Spring
Rio Grande
Chimneys West
Javelina Wash
Luna's Jacal
CHIMNEYS TRAIL
Sotol Vista Overlook
MEXICO
U.S.
Terlingua Abajo
NATION
Santa Elena Canyon
SANTA ELENA CANYON TRAIL
Alamo
Mule Ears Viewpoint
CHISOS
Santa Elena Canyon Overlook
Tuff Canyon
Mule Ears Spring
Rock Slide Rapids
Santa Elena Canyon River Access
Cerro Castellan 3,293 ft
Mule Ears Peaks 3,881 ft
Cottonwood
Castolon Visitor Center
Santa Elena
RIVER ROAD WEST
Buenos Aires
SIERRA PONCE
CHIHUAHUA
TEXAS
Black Dike
SANTA ELENA CANYON PROTECTED AREA
Gaging Station
Loop
Johnson Ranch

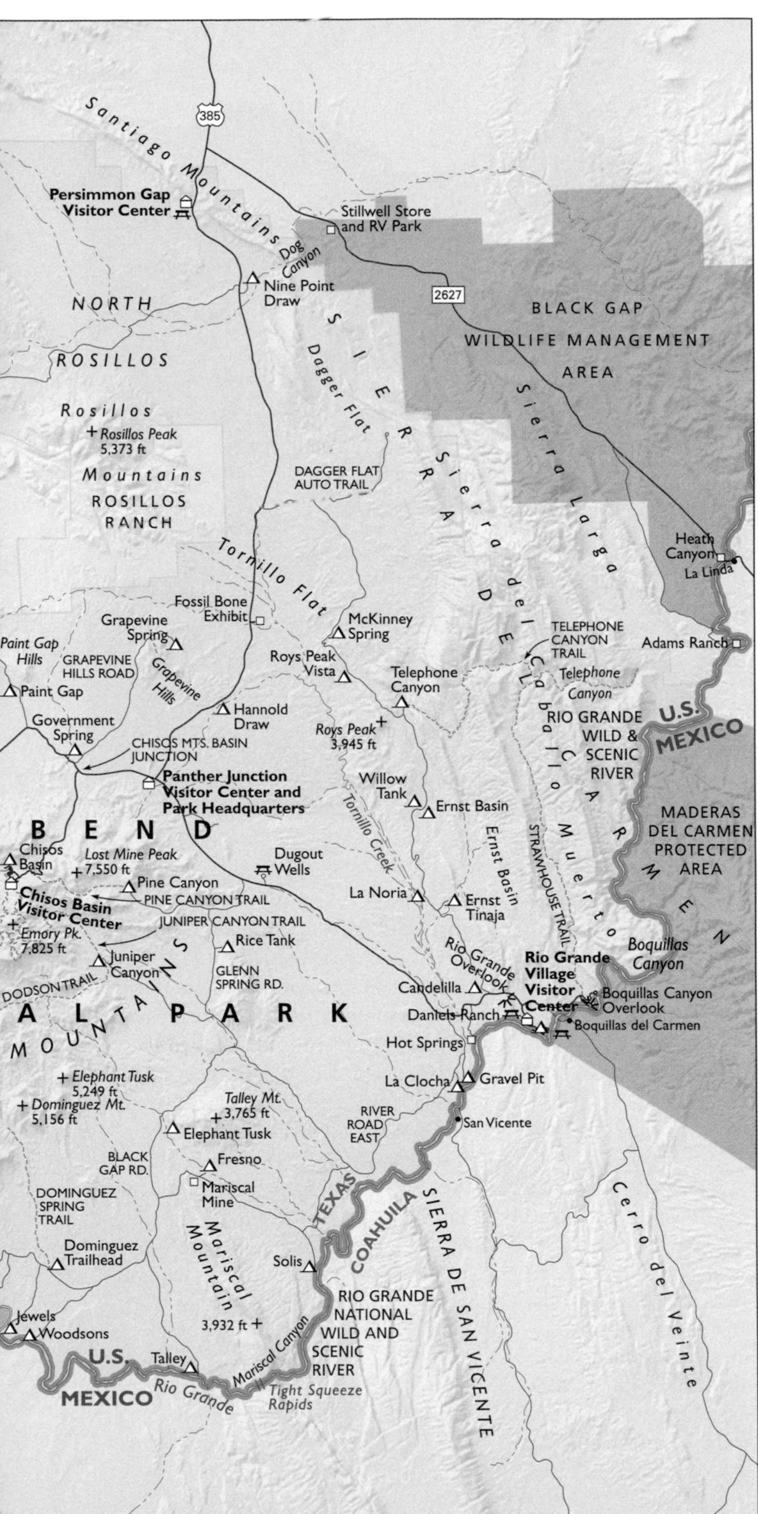
Santiago Mountains
385
Persimmon Gap Visitor Center
Stillwell Store and RV Park
Dog Canyon
Nine Point Draw
2627
NORTH ROSILLOS
BLACK GAP WILDLIFE MANAGEMENT AREA
Dagger Flat
SIERRA DEL CARMEN
Sierra Larga
Rosillos Mountains
Rosillos Peak 5,373 ft
ROSILLOS RANCH
DAGGER FLAT AUTO TRAIL
Sierra del Caballo Muerto
Tornillo Flat
Heath Canyon
La Linda
Fossil Bone Exhibit
Grapevine Spring
McKinney Spring
TELEPHONE CANYON TRAIL
Adams Ranch
Paint Gap Hills
GRAPEVINE HILLS ROAD
Grapevine Hills
Roys Peak Vista
Telephone Canyon
Paint Gap
Hannold Draw
Roys Peak 3,945 ft
RIO GRANDE WILD & SCENIC RIVER
U.S.
MEXICO
Government Spring
CHISOS MTS. BASIN JUNCTION
Panther Junction Visitor Center and Park Headquarters
Willow Tank
Ernst Basin
MADERAS DEL CARMEN PROTECTED AREA
BIG BEND NATIONAL PARK
Chisos Basin
Lost Mine Peak 7,550 ft
Dugout Wells
Ernst Basin
STRAWHOUSE TRAIL
Pine Canyon
PINE CANYON TRAIL
La Noria
Ernst Tinaja
Chisos Basin Visitor Center
JUNIPER CANYON TRAIL
Emory Pk. 7,825 ft
Rice Tank
Rio Grande Overlook
Boquillas Canyon
Juniper Canyon
GLENN SPRING RD.
Rio Grande Village Visitor Center
Candelilla
DODSON TRAIL
CHISOS MOUNTAINS
Boquillas Canyon Overlook
Daniels Ranch
Boquillas del Carmen
Hot Springs
Elephant Tusk 5,249 ft
La Clocha
Gravel Pit
Dominguez Mt. 5,156 ft
Talley Mt. 3,765 ft
RIVER ROAD EAST
San Vicente
Elephant Tusk
BLACK GAP RD.
Fresno
Mariscal Mine
DOMINGUEZ SPRING TRAIL
TEXAS
COAHUILA
SIERRA DE SAN VICENTE
Cerro del Veinte
Mariscal Mountain
Dominguez Trailhead
Solis
RIO GRANDE NATIONAL WILD AND SCENIC RIVER
Jewels
Woodsons
3,932 ft
Mariscal Canyon
U.S.
Talley
MEXICO
Rio Grande
Tight Squeeze Rapids

Chisos Mountains with prickly pear in the foreground

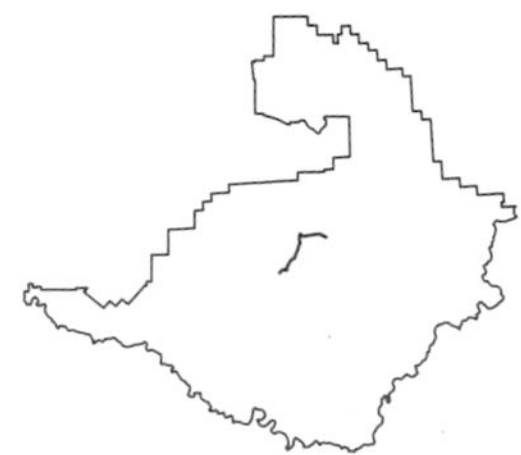

PANTHER JUNCTION TO THE CHISOS BASIN

10 miles one way; at least a half day

Start your tour at the visitor center at Panther Junction. Collect maps, information on hiking, and safety tips on avoiding encounters with rattlesnakes, mountain lions, and flash floods. Don't miss **Panther Path**—the 50-yard nature trail near the visitor center entrance whose self-guiding pamphlet provides an excellent introduction to the plants you'll see on much of your trip. Behind the visitor center lie the **Chisos Mountains,** the southernmost range in the continental United States, and your destination. When ready, return to your car and turn left out of the visitor center, then left at **Basin Junction** in 3 miles. Ahead on the right looms **Pulliam Bluff.** Look closely and you might see in the mountain the profile of a man's face, reclining. Legend relates that the man is Alsate, an important Apache chief whose ghost lives on in the high Chisos Mountains, and whose campfire can occasionally be seen at night. At 2.5 miles, the jagged summit to your left is **Lost Mine Peak.** Spanish explorers, it is told, discovered a rich silver mine near the summit and enslaved Indians to work it. The miners rebelled, killed their overlords, and sealed the entrance to the mine so that it might remain lost forever. As you drive on, the castlelike summit of **Casa Grande—** big house—will be straight ahead, a landmark for much of the park.

The road climbs higher into the mountains through a canyon called **Green Gulch:** Watch the vegetation change from desert shrub to sotol grasslands, then to pinyon pine, juniper, and oak woodland. The Chisos form a cooler, moister island in the surrounding desert. Some 10,000 years ago, pinyon-juniper forests extended down to the desert floor, but the trees withdrew to higher altitudes as the climate gradually warmed at the end of the Ice Age. In about 5 miles the road hits its highest point at **Panther Pass** (5,770 feet), named for the mountain lions that still roam these hills. Only the lucky few ever see one. If you have time, park at the nearby trailhead for the **Lost Mine Trail**, a self-guided nature trail with an informative booklet. The panorama from the top, one of the grandest in the park, makes the moderately strenuous 4.8-mile round-trip well worth the trek. But if you're short of time, just hike the 2-mile round-trip to the **Juniper Canyon Overlook,** for good vistas of wooded **Juniper Canyon** to the south and Pulliam Bluff to the northwest.

Claret cup cactus abloom in the high Chisos

After Panther Pass, the road descends in hairpin curves to the basin, a 3-mile-wide depression in the mountains, chiseled by wind and water. Many of the park's choice hikes start from the basin trailhead, west of the ranger station. At the least, make sure to stroll the easy 0.3-mile round-trip **Window View Trail.** Particularly photogenic at sunset, the Window is a v-shaped opening, or pour off, in the mountains, through which all rain and meltwater from the basin drains. A more challenging trail descends through desert and shady canyon to the **Window** itself, offering classic afternoon views of Casa Grande framed by oaks and pines. In summer, take this and other lower elevation hikes in early morning or late afternoon.

The literal high point of many visitors' trips to the park is a hike to the **South Rim** (7,400 feet), a moderately steep 13-mile round-trip that provides unforgettable vistas of much of the park. At **Boot Canyon,** 4.5 miles up the trail to the South Rim, lives an oasis of bigtooth maple, Douglas fir, and Arizona cypress. The gray-and-yellow Colima warbler nests on the canyon floor, its only home in the United States.

Before you hike, check at the **Chisos Basin Visitor Center** for maps and hiking tips, and make sure you carry plenty of water. At the visitor center, ask also about the presence of peregrine falcons. Several of these endangered birds nest in the Chisos.

Rafting the Rio Grande through Santa Elena Canyon

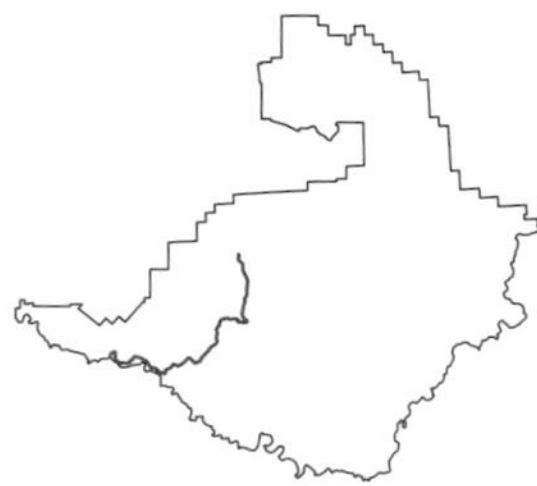

ROSS MAXWELL SCENIC DRIVE: SANTA ELENA

30 miles one way; a half to full day

Heading south from Santa Elena Junction, **Burro Mesa**—named for the burros that once grazed the top—will be to your right, and the Chisos to your left. After 2 miles, stop at the exhibit on the left for a fine view of the Window framing Casa Grande. Drive on a little over a mile, then park at the old **Sam Nail Ranch** and stroll the short path to the remains of windmills and a ranch house. The shade of the pecan and willow trees the Nails planted makes a fine resting and bird-watching spot. Walk back to your car and motor on. In about a mile, long walls of rock traverse the landscape. They are dikes, created by molten rock that squeezed up into underground cracks before hardening. The softer rock layers around them eventually eroded away, leaving the erosion-resistant dikes.

Stop next at the **Blue Creek Ranch** (Homer Wilson Ranch) **Overlook.** A century ago most of Big Bend was cloaked in grasses. But drought and ranchers grazing thousands of cattle, sheep, and goats destroyed the grass and exposed the topsoil to erosion. Creosote, mesquite, allthorn, and other spiny shrubs moved into the damaged areas. Here, and elsewhere in the park, grasses are slowly returning.

Go back to the road and take a quick left onto the **Sotol Vista** spur road, named for the ridge's rich growth of sotol, the bright green plant with sawlike teeth on the edges of the leaves. Indians roasted and ate the heart of the sotol and fermented it to yield an alcoholic drink. The parking lot at the top provides vistas of the surrounding mountains, and a plaque at the end of the loop identifies what's what.

Return to the main road; an exhibit on the left in about 6.5 miles describes how volcanism shaped this striking landscape. Take the next spur road on the left, for an excellent view of the peaks known as **Mule Ears,** a name explained at a glance. During the 1930s, Army Air Corps pilots drilled by flying planes between the twin peaks. Stop again after 4.5 miles to see **Tuff Canyon,** carved by **Blue Creek** through layers of lava flows, boulders, and compressed volcanic ash called tuff. Stroll the short trail to the right to view the canyon. The trail at the left of the parking lot provides a moderately steep hike down into the canyon, a 0.75-mile round-trip.

Back in your car, you will be approaching **Cerro Castellan,** another important landmark, rising 1,000 feet above its surroundings. Turn left into **Castolon** to stroll around the old Army post that was built after the 1914-18 border troubles with Mexico. The main building, originally the barracks, was converted to a frontier trading post around 1920. A new visitor center has exhibits and a bookstore.

After leaving Castolon, the road parallels the **Rio Grande,** passing the scattered remains of adobe houses dating back to the turn of the 20th century. The occupants once grew food crops and cotton in the Rio Grande's fertile floodplain.

Be sure to stop about 8 miles from Castolon, at the parking area for the **Santa Elena Canyon Overlook.** Laden with abrasive silt and gravel, the Rio Grande sculptured the canyon 1,500 feet deep, through the cliffs that tower above the geological trough that forms the bulk of the park.

Drive on to the end of the road, put on some old shoes, and, if the water is low, wade across **Terlingua Creek** to reach the **Santa Elena Canyon Trail.** The moderate 1.7-mile round-trip trail leads the hiker with striking views.

PANTHER JUNCTION TO RIO GRANDE VILLAGE & BOQUILLAS

24 miles one way; a half to full day

Before starting this tour, check at the visitor center for the condition of Hot Springs road. The main road, heading southeast, descends nearly 2,000 feet through desert shrub,

Eroded rock "plugs" created by volcanic eruptions

Cerro Castellan looming over an old Army post

Greater roadrunner speeding across the desert

terminating near the willows and cottonwoods on the banks of the Rio Grande.

After about 6.5 miles, turn left onto the unpaved road to see the spring at **Dugout Wells,** formerly the site of a ranch and schoolhouse, and now a fine place to picnic and look for wildlife. Return to the main road. As you continue, the peak aptly named **Elephant Tusk** will be on your right in the distance, and **Chilicotal Mountain** closer to the road. Far ahead looms the **Sierra del Carmen** in Mexico. Its striated rock formations are the same limestone and shale as in the cliffs at **Santa Elena Canyon.**

If you're up to a somewhat rough ride, be sure to take the turnoff to **Hot Springs,** whose mineral waters were valued for centuries and continue to be useable. Look for Indian pictographs on the cliffs along the trail to the springs, just beyond the old motel.

After returning to the main road, pull over at the **Rio Grande Overlook** just past the tunnel on the right and stroll a 50-yard trail for superb views of the Sierra del Carmen, the river floodplain, and part of **Boquillas del Carmen** village in Mexico. Big Bend bluebonnets bloom profusely here during a well-watered springtime.

Back on the road, continue straight for half a mile, then turn left and continue another 3 miles to the paved spur road to **Boquillas Canyon Overlook.** Turn left onto the main road, then left again to visit **Rio Grande Village,** an excellent place to watch birds. Don't miss the nature trail starting across from site No. 18 in the campground. This easy 0.75-mile loop leads through jungle-like floodplain vegetation before climbing onto a ridge that provides terrific views of the river and the Sierra del Carmen.

PANTHER JUNCTION TO PERSIMMON GAP

26 miles one way; 2 hours

This drive from park headquarters at Panther Junction to Persimmon Gap, the park's northern entrance, follows an ancient trail used by the Comanche on their annual raiding forays into Mexico, and by Army expeditions, settlers, and miners of silver and lead. The road descends gently to Tornillo Creek and Tornillo Flat, one of the park's most overgrazed and poorly recovered areas. The mountains forming the ridge to the east are the Dead Horse Mountains, the Sierra del Carmen's northernmost reach.

Highlights along the way include a view of Dog Canyon, through which camels once lumbered in a 19th-century U.S. Army experiment, and, near the north end of the Tornillo Creek bridge, an exhibit of fossil mammal bones; the fossils were found in the park in sandstone dating from 50 million years ago.

For an excellent self-guided auto tour, pick up a pamphlet at either end of the road and, if it's springtime, ask whether the giant dagger yuccas are in bloom. (If so, be sure to take the unpaved Dagger Flat Auto Trail to see stalkfuls of white blooms weighing up to 70 pounds.)

INFORMATION & ACTIVITIES

HEADQUARTERS
1 Panther Junction, Big Bend NP, TX 79834. Phone (432) 477-2251. www.nps.gov/bibe

SEASONS & ACCESSIBILITY
Open all year. Check current conditions before driving dirt roads.

VISITOR & INFORMATION CENTERS
Panther Junction and **Chisos Basin** Visitor Centers open daily all year. **Castolon** open Nov. to April.

ENTRANCE FEE
$15 per car per week.

FACILITIES FOR DISABLED
Visitor center and two nature trails are wheelchair accessible. Free brochure.

THINGS TO DO
Free naturalist-led activities: nature walks, workshops, evening programs, nature seminars. Also, hiking, fishing, river-running (permit required), cycling.

OVERNIGHT BACKPACKING
Free permits required. Obtain in person at visitor centers or ranger stations within 24 hours of trip.

CAMPGROUNDS
Three campgrounds with 14-day limit. Open all year. Fees $10-$18 per night. For mid-November through mid-April reservations: (877) 444-6777; www.reserveusa.com. Tent and RV sites. At **Rio Grande Village Trailer Park,** full hookups only available. Three group campgrounds; reservations through headquarters for groups of 10 or more.

HOTELS, MOTELS, & INNS
(unless otherwise noted, rates are for 2 persons in a double room, high season)
Big Bend Motor Inn (Tex. 118 and Rte. 170) P.O. Box 336, Terlingua, TX 79852. (800) 848-2363 or (432) 371-2218. 86 rooms, 10 with kitchenettes, 4 duplexes with kitchens, $80-$150. AC, restaurant.
Chisos Mountains Lodge National Park Concessions, Inc., Basin Rural Station, Big Bend NP, TX 79834. (432) 477-2291. 72 rooms, including 6 cottages, $89-$100. AC, restaurant.
Gage Hotel (US 90 and US 385) P.O. Box 46, Marathon, TX 79842. (800) 884-4243 or (432) 386-4205. 40 units. $76-$330. AC, restaurant.
Lajitas Resort (on Route 170) Star Rte. 70, Box 400, Lajitas, TX 79852. (877) 525-4827 or (432) 424-3471. 98 rooms. $195-$330. AC, pool, restaurant.

For a full list of accommodations contact the Alpine visitor Information Center, (432) 837-2326.

EXCURSIONS

RIO GRANDE WILD AND SCENIC RIVER
BIG BEND NATIONAL PARK, TEXAS

Don't pass up a float down the Rio Grande. Easy floats include the Mariscal and Boquillas Canyons; Santa Elena and the Lower Canyons are more difficult. 196 Wild and Scenic miles. Permits required. Main access to Lower Canyons in Mexico; most take-out points fall on private land in Texas *(permission req'd)*. Primitive camping, hiking, fishing; tubing and swimming not recommended. Information about half-day to 1-week trips at Panther Junction. (432) 477-2251.

Stalactites hang in one of the limestone caverns

CARLSBAD CAVERNS

NEW MEXICO
ESTABLISHED JUNE 12, 1944
801,163 acres

The Chihuahuan Desert, studded with spiky plants and lizards, offers little hint that what Will Rogers called the "Grand Canyon with a roof on it" waits underground. Yet, at this desert's northern reaches, underneath the Guadalupe Mountains, lies one of the deepest, largest, and most ornate caverns ever found.

Water molded this underworld 4 to 6 million years ago. Some 250 million years ago, the region lay underneath the inland arm of an ancient sea. Near the shore grew a limestone reef. By the time the sea withdrew, the reef stood hundreds of feet high, later to be buried under thousands of feet of soil. Some 15 to 20 million years ago, the ground uplifted. Naturally occurring sulfuric acid seeped into cracks in the limestone, gradually enlarging them to form a honeycomb of chambers. Millions of years passed before the cave decoration began. Then, drop by drop, limestone-laden moisture built an extraordinary variety of glistening formations—some six stories tall; others tiny and delicate.

Cave scientists have explored more than 30 miles of passageways of the main cavern of Carlsbad, and investigation continues. Visitors may tour 3 of these miles on a paved trail. Slaughter Canyon Cave provides the hardy an opportunity to play spelunker, albeit with a guide. The park has more than 100 other caves open primarily to specialists.

Some visitors think the park's most spectacular sight is the one seen at the cave's mouth. More than a quarter million Mexican free-tailed bats summer in a section of the cave, and around sunset they spiral up from the entrance to hunt for insects. The nightly exodus led to the discovery of the cave in modern times. Around the turn of the 20th century, miners began to excavate bat guano—a potent fertilizer—for shipment to the citrus groves of southern California. One of the guano miners, James Larkin White, became the first to explore and publicize the caverns beyond Bat Cave.

How to Get There

The park is off US 62/180, 20 miles southwest of Carlsbad and 164 miles east of El Paso, Texas. For the visitor center, turn west at Whites City and drive 7 miles. For Slaughter Canyon, turn west on County Road 418, 5 miles south of Whites City; drive another 11 miles, some unpaved, to the parking lot. Airports: Carlsbad, New Mexico, and El Paso, Texas.

When to Go

Year-round. The weather underground remains a constant 56°F. The main cavern gets crowded, especially in summer and on major holiday weekends. Either spring or fall, when the desert's in bloom, is an excellent time to go. You'll see the bats fly from April or early May through October.

How to Visit

One full day allows you time to tour the main cavern and take a nature walk or a drive before watching the bats fly at sunset. For a second day's activity, reserve space on a tour of "unimproved" **Slaughter Canyon Cave,** if you're ready for a more rugged caving experience.

At the visitor center, select either the **Natural Entrance Tour** or the **Big Room Tour** (both are 1-mile walks). Try the first unless you have walking, breathing, or heart problems. It starts at the natural entrance and is mostly downhill, except for one stretch where you climb 83 feet; an elevator whisks you back to ground level. The Natural Entrance Tour is more intimate and may be less crowded than the Big Room.

The Big Room Tour begins with an elevator ride directly to the Big Room, in which you can see most of the types of formations visible in areas of the cave not open to the public. If after this tour you want to see more caves, take the elevator back up to ground level and proceed with the first half of the Natural Entrance Tour.

Another option, the **Kings Palace Tour** (see **Other Trails & Sights** p. 139) visits the stunning formations in the scenic rooms.

NATURAL ENTRANCE TOUR

1 mile; about 1 hour

The visitor center rents audio guides, if you wish. Exit to the right, following the path to the cavern's natural entrance. The opening formed when part of the cave's ceiling collapsed thousands of years ago. Once in the mouth of the cave, glance right to spot 1,000-year-old

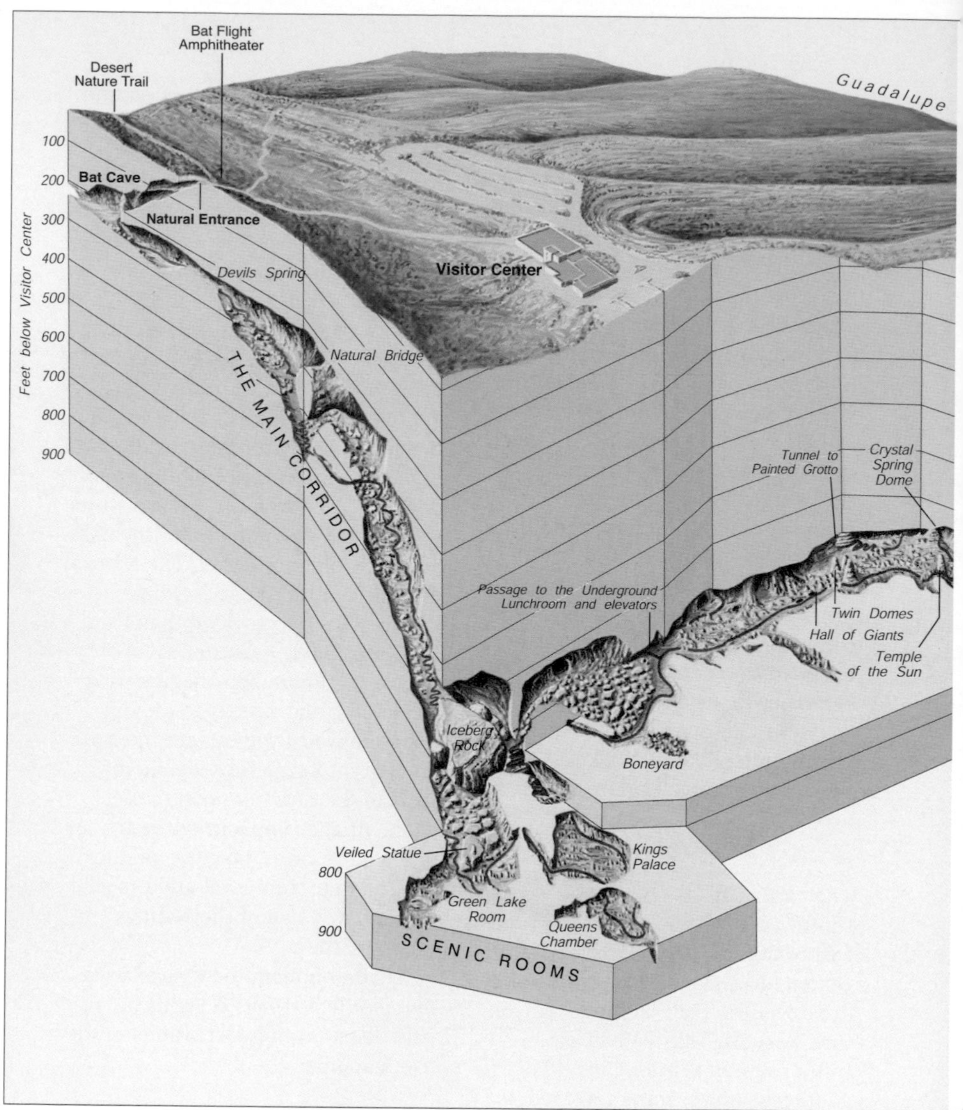

red and black pictographs high on the wall. Indians knew of the cavern and used the entrance for shelter. But without dependable lighting they could not have gone very far past the small sunlit area. You are descending the **Main Corridor,** which, if you keep looking around and up, conveys some of the cavern's enormity: The ceiling at times rises more than 200 feet above the path.

The trail soon passes **Devils Spring.** Here cave decoration continues. As water from rain and snow percolates through the ancient reef, it forms carbonic acid, which slowly dissolves the limestone. Upon reaching the cave, the water then releases calcite with each drop, splattering onto the floor

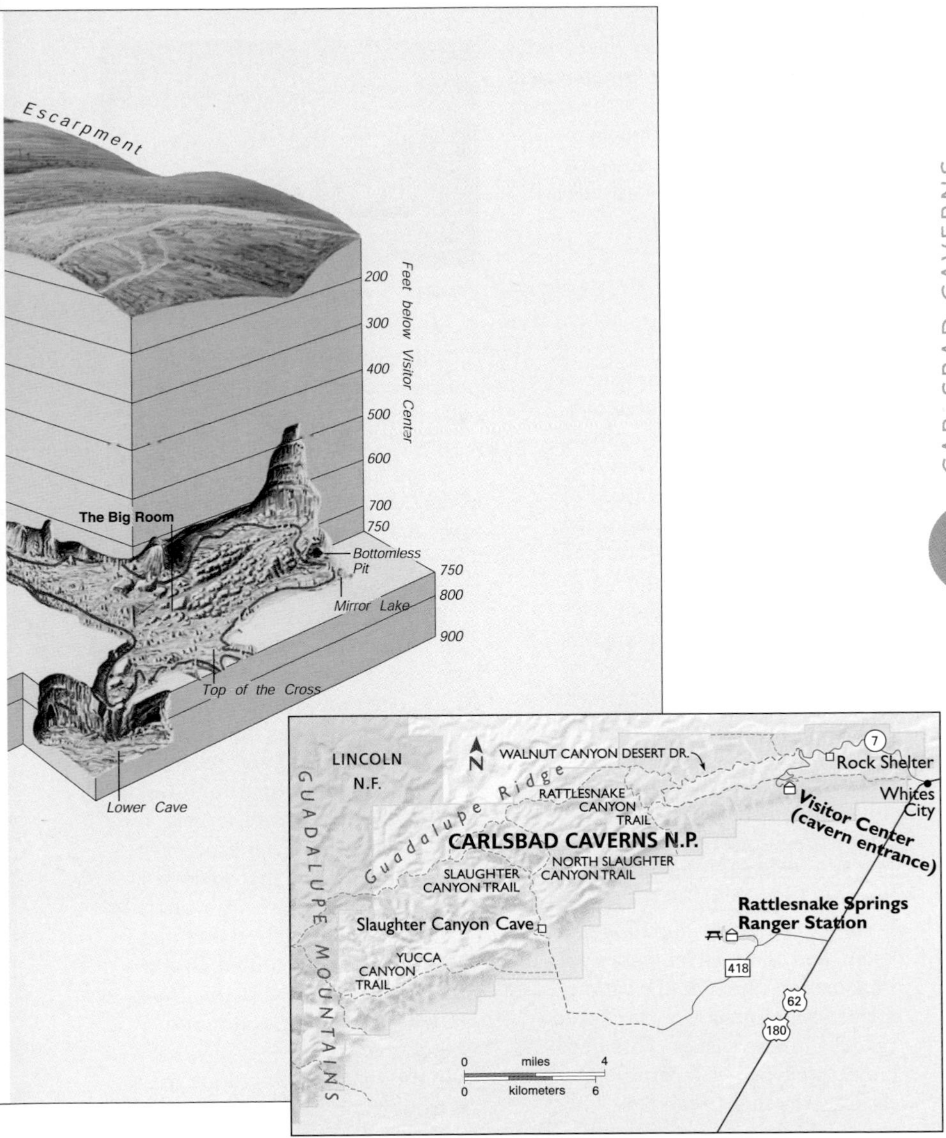

as the water drips—producing a stalagmite—or leaving the calcite on the ceiling as the water discharges carbon dioxide into the cave air—creating a stalactite. (Park rangers like to repeat the mnemonic that stalactites "hang tight" to the ceiling, while stalagmites "might touch the ceiling.") You would have heard a lot more dripping 10,000 years ago, when the climate was wetter. Now the Guadalupes receive only about 14 to 19 inches of precipitation a year, and most of the formations are no longer growing.

The trail soon skirts **Iceberg Rock,** a 200,000-ton boulder that crashed down from the ceiling thousands of years ago. After climbing **Appetite Hill,** stroll on past the **Boneyard,** which probably resembles the cavern of 4–6 million years ago, when water filled the chambers. Follow the signs to the **Underground Lunchroom** to have a meal, if you like. To reach ground level, take the nearby elevator up to the visitor center.

Mexican free-tailed bats emerge to hunt

BIG ROOM TOUR

1 mile; 1 hour

After a minute's elevator ride, you will be 755 feet, or about 75 stories, underground. (Compare your entrance to that of visitors of the early 1920s: They entered by "bucket elevator," as a pulley lowered them into the Bat Cave in a guano bucket.) Follow the signs for the Big Room: For the next hour or so, you'll be circling one gigantic chamber.

The **Big Room** is the largest single room most cave visitors will ever see (unless they go to Borneo, where there is a cave with a larger, undecorated chamber), 1,800 feet long at its longest point, and 1,100 feet at its widest. It encompasses 8.2 acres.

To best enjoy the tour, linger, look, listen, and above all let loose your imagination. What do the various formations look like to you? Layer cakes? Chinese friezes? Fossilized bonsai? Jellyfish? Draperies? In recent years the Park Service removed labels from many of the formations, so now you can enjoy naming the fantasyscape yourself.

Near the beginning of the walk, the **Hall of Giants** sports some of the largest formations in the cave, many of them about six stories tall. Look for **Giant Dome,** a 62-foot-high stalagmite, flanked by two 42-foot-high deputies. Appearances are deceptive here because of the immensity of the chamber.

The trail continues along the periphery of the room (resist the call of the shortcut) and leads past a view of **Lower Cave,** accessible by reserved tour. Farther along, at **Top of the Cross,** rangers sometimes give talks at an amphitheater. Glance up: The ceiling here soars to 255 feet, its highest point above the trail.

The footpath continues through a less ornate area that was once a bat roost. The so-called **Bottomless Pit** has been measured at about 140 feet in depth; it does not lead to other passages. As you proceed, take a good look at sparkling **Crystal Spring Dome,** the cave's largest active stalagmite: Each drop of water adds crystals that make it infinitesimally bigger. Iron carried in the water delicately stains the formations of the Painted Grotto. Just a few minutes past the grotto, you will reach the elevator and ascend to daylight.

In the visitor center, don't miss the exhibits on cave restoration. There are also historical photographs here depicting the days of guano mining and early tourism. Then climb the stairs to the **Observation Tower.** Standing high above the ancient reef, you see a striking vista of the reef's seaward side (the slope past the parking lot) and the ancient seabed, called the Delaware Basin. If it's a clear day, the panorama before you will extend 100 miles or more into Texas.

Big Room

OTHER TRAILS & SIGHTS

Desert Nature Trail: This easy half-mile loop makes an interesting diversion before the evening bat flight program. The trail's interpretive plaques describe how Indians made use of virtually every plant in sight. The trail starts to the right of the cave's natural entrance.

Walnut Canyon Desert Drive: An alternative introduction to the area's natural history. A booklet available at the start guides you along this 9.5-mile gravel loop off the main park road, just before the visitor center.

Kings Palace Tour: Led by park rangers, this 1.5-hour tour visits four highly decorative rooms, including the Kings Palace, which may be one of the world's most ornate cave rooms. Tour participants descend 830 feet to the deepest part of the cave open to the public. Look for the giant draperies, formed by tricking water down the slanted ceiling. Visitors will also find soda-straw stalactites, columns, and other interesting speleothems. Tours *(ages 4 and up)* are offered several times a day throughout the year.

Bat Flight: Don't miss the evening cyclone of bats; at its peak, more than 5,000 bats per minute speed out of the cave on their way to consume some three tons of insects. From the visitor center, walk to the amphitheater, at the natural entrance, or drive there by turning right onto the main road, then right again.

Slaughter Canyon Cave: Be prepared to slip and slide as you explore an "unimproved" cave for 2 hours by flashlight. Accompanied by rangers, you'll see several types of formations not found in the main cave, after a steep half-mile climb up to the cave's entrance from the parking lot in Slaughter Canyon. Open daily in summer; weekends only in winter.

Other guided tours include **Left Hand Tunnel** (ages 6 and up), **Spider Cave** (ages 12 and up), and **Hall of the White Giant** (ages 12 and up). For reservations call (800) 967-2283.

INFORMATION & ACTIVITIES

HEADQUARTERS
3225 National Parks Hwy., Carlsbad, NM 88220. Phone (505) 785-2232. Off-trail trip reservations (800) 967-2283. www.nps.gov/cave

SEASONS & ACCESSIBILITY
Open all year.

VISITOR & INFORMATION CENTERS
The visitor center is 7 miles from Whites City on N. Mex. 7; open daily all year. Call headquarters for information.

ENTRANCE FEES
No entrance fee for park. Fees to enter cavern and tour Natural Entrance route and Big Room: adults $6; children ages 6-15, $3; children under 6 free. To tour Kings Palace, additional $8 for adults, children under age 16, $4, children under 6 free, under 4 not permitted. To tour Slaughter Canyon Cave, additional $15 for adults, $7.50 for children under age 16; children under 6 not permitted. For off-trail caving tour, additional $12 for adults, $6 for children under age 16; children under 6 not permitted. No charge for bat flight program.

PETS
Not allowed in caves or backcountry. Kennel at the visitor center ($4 per day).

FACILITIES FOR DISABLED
The visitor center and Bat Flight Amphitheater are wheelchair accessible, as is a portion of the Big Room Tour. Picnic area and restrooms accessible at Rattlesnake Springs.

THINGS TO DO
Ranger-led activities: tours of the main cavern (call park for details), cavern talks, dusk bat flight programs (for bat flight times call 505-785-3012), flashlight trip into Slaughter Canyon Cave (see p. 139; reservations required). Also available, self-guided Desert Nature Trail, self-guided Walnut Canyon Desert Drive, backcountry trails.

SPECIAL ADVISORIES
- Wear low-heeled, nonskid shoes in the caverns, and take a jacket.
- Intense summer thunderstorms may cause floods in low-lying areas, lightning strikes in higher areas.
- Watch out for rattlesnakes when hiking the backcountry trails.
- Cactuses and other spiny desert plants can inflict painful injuries.
- Baby strollers are not permitted on cave trails.

OVERNIGHT BACKPACKING
Permits required. Available free at the visitor center.

CAMPGROUNDS
None; backcountry camping only. Food services in park. Note that campfires are not permitted in park.

HOTELS, MOTELS, & INNS
(unless otherwise noted, rates are for 2 persons in a double room, high season)

In Whites City, NM 88268:

Best Western Cavern Inn 17 Carlsbad Cavern Hwy., P.O. Box 128. (800) 228-3767 or (505) 785-2291. 42 units. $104. AC, pool, restaurant.

In Carlsbad, NM 88220:

Best Western Stevens Inn 1829 S. Canal St., P.O. Box 580. (800) 730-2851 or (505) 887-2851. 220 units, 28 with kitchenettes. $89. AC, pool, restaurant.
Carlsbad Super 8 3817 National Parks Hwy. (800) 800-8000 or (505) 887-8888. 60 units. $69, includes breakfast. AC, pool.
Continental Inn 3820 National Parks Hwy. (505) 887-0341. 60 units. $55. AC, pool.
Great Western Inn & Suites 3804 National Parks Hwy. (800) 987-5535 or (505) 887-5535. 87 units, 25 with kitchenettes. $69-$90. AC, pool.
Quality Inn 3706 National Parks Hwy. (800) 321-2861 or (505) 887-2861. 123 units. $65. AC, pool, restaurant.

Contact the Carlsbad Chamber of Commerce for a full list of accommodations: P.O. Box 910, Carlsbad, NM 88221. (505) 887-6516.

EXCURSIONS

LINCOLN NATIONAL FOREST
ALAMOGORDO, NEW MEXICO

In 1950, a game warden here rescued a black bear cub from a forest fire and named him Smokey Bear—he became a famous symbol of fire prevention. Lincoln contains life zones from desert to subalpine forest and limestone caves. 1,103,441 acres. 370 campsites. Hiking, fishing, horseback riding, hunting, picnicking, winter sports. Open all year; most campsites open seasonally. Adjoins Carlsbad Caverns NP on west. Information at Carlsbad on US 285, about 20 miles from park. (505) 434-7200.

WHITE SANDS NATIONAL MONUMENT
ALAMOGORDO, NEW MEXICO

Waves of gypsum sand, some 50 feet high, offer an ever changing vista here in the Tularosa Basin. Weathered rock from surrounding highlands settles in Lake Lucero and adjacent alkali flats; scouring southwest winds create the dunes. Features 16-mile-long Dunes Drive. 144,420 acres. Primitive camping, food services, picnic areas. Hiking. Open daily except Christmas. Visitor center on US 70, about 190 miles from Carlsbad Caverns NP. (505) 479-6124.

BOSQUE DEL APACHE NATIONAL WILDLIFE REFUGE
SOCORRO, NEW MEXICO

The Rio Grande bisects this refuge, where carefully maintained ponds and marshes shelter wintering snow geese and other waterfowl, as well as sandhill cranes and bald eagles. 57,191 acres. Hiking, fishing (in summer), biking, hunting, scenic drives. Open all year, from 1 hour before sunrise to 1 hour after sunset. Visitor center on N. Mex. 1, off I-25, about 270 miles from Carlsbad Caverns NP. (505) 835-1828.

The fossil-ladened Guadalupe Mountains

GUADALUPE MOUNTAINS

TEXAS

ESTABLISHED SEPTEMBER 30, 1972

86,416 acres

In West Texas, only about 40 miles southwest of Carlsbad Caverns, lies a gem of a park that few people outside the state have ever heard of, let alone visited. Guadalupe Mountains National Park contains the southernmost, highest part of the 50-mile-long Guadalupe range. From the highway, the mountains resemble a nearly monolithic wall through the desert. But drive into one of the park entrances, take even a short stroll, and surprises crop up: dramatically contoured canyons, shady glades surrounded by desert scrub, a profusion of wildlife and birds.

Some 80 miles of trails can lead the more energetic hiker to Guadalupe Peak, the highest point in Texas (8,749 feet), and to mountaintops with scattered but thick conifer forests typical of the Rockies hundreds of miles to the north. The range's origins may be surprising too: The Guadalupe Mountains were once a reef growing beneath the waters of an ancient inland sea. That same vanished sea spawned the honeycomb of the Carlsbad Caverns.

Pottery, baskets, and spear tips found in the mountains suggest that people first visited the Guadalupes about 12,000 years ago, hunting the camels, mammoths, and other animals that flourished in the wetter climate of the waning Ice Age. When the Spaniards arrived in the Southwest in the mid-16th century, Mescalero Apache periodically camped near the springs at the base of the mountains and climbed to the highlands to hunt and forage. Both the Apache and Europeans spun legends of fabulous caches of gold in these mountains.

As American prospectors, settlers, and cavalry pushed west, the Apache made the mountainous areas their bases and fought to ward off encroachers. By the late 1880s, however, virtually all the Indians had been killed or forced onto a reservation.

Donations of ranchlands eventually gave impetus to the park. In 1998 the park acquired 10,000 acres adjacent to its then western boundary, including some 2,000 acres of white gypsum sand dunes and dunes of brick red quartzose, both deposits left by the ancient sea.

How to Get There

The main visitor center and most visitor activities are located in the Pine Springs-Frijole area, off US 62/180, 55 miles southwest of Carlsbad and 110 miles east of El Paso. For McKittrick Canyon, turn off US 62/180 about 7 miles northeast of the main visitor center, then continue 4 miles to the parking lot. For Dog Canyon, either hike 12 miles from Pine Springs Campground or drive north on US 62/180, then west on Cty. Rd. 408, and south on N. Mex. 137, about 105 miles total from Pine Springs. Airports: Carlsbad, New Mexico; and El Paso, Texas.

When to Go

Year-round, but spring and fall are best. In spring, the foliage is fresh and, with enough rain, the blossoms abundant. In late October to mid-November, changing leaves provide splashes of red, yellow, and burgundy.

How to Visit

On a day trip, head to the visitor center and Pine Springs; take at least a short hike. On a second day, visit McKittrick Canyon for a stroll through a hidden oasis. To visit a wilder, more isolated area, where trails take you quickly into the high country, drive about 2.5 hours to reenter the park at Dog Canyon in the north.

PINE SPRINGS-FRIJOLE AREA

a half to full day

Pick up maps and trail information at the **Headquarters Visitor Center,** where you can also enjoy audiovisual programs on the park's ecology, geology, and history. Fill your water bottles before leaving. Then stroll to **The Pinery** or drive back to the highway, turn left in about a tenth of a mile, and park. The stone walls remain from the 1858 Pinery Station of the Butterfield Overland Mail Line—forerunner of the Pony Express. Buy a self-guiding leaflet, if you wish, to learn about the colorful local history. Return to your car, and go back to the highway and turn left. Go left again in about a mile onto a dirt road. Park at the end near the **Frijole Ranch,** the 1870s ranch house that now preserves artifacts and exhibits the park's cultural history.

Be sure to walk the easy 2.3-mile loop trail to **Smith** and **Manzanita Springs,** an excellent introduction to the striking contrasts the Chihuahuan Desert presents. Bear right at the trailhead. The thorny plants may seem forbidding, but the Mescalero Apache used a great majority of the plants in sight for food or fiber. Their diet consisted largely of mescal—the

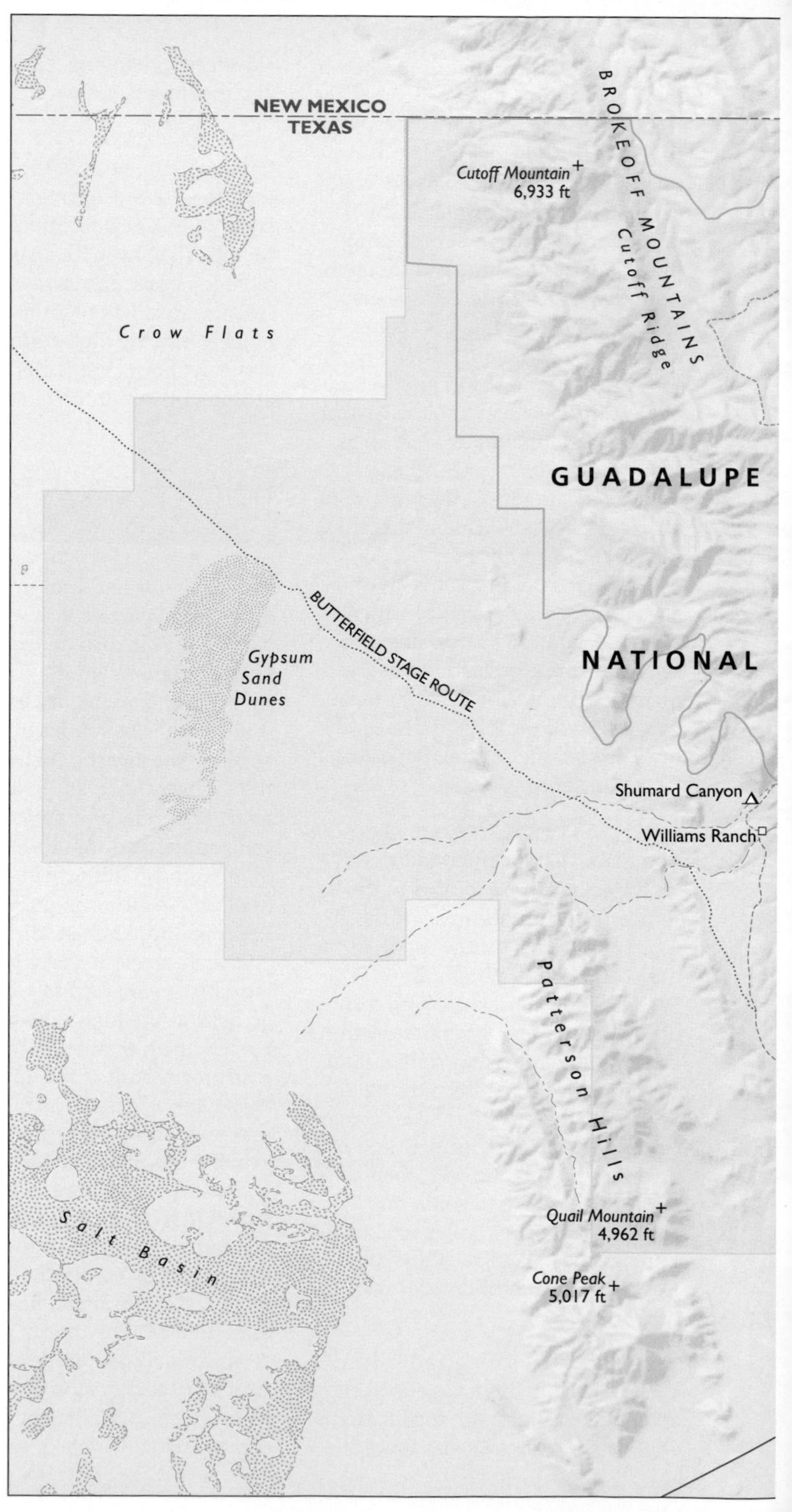
NEW MEXICO
TEXAS
BROKEOFF MOUNTAINS
Cutoff Mountain
6,933 ft
Cutoff Ridge
Crow Flats
GUADALUPE
NATIONAL
BUTTERFIELD STAGE ROUTE
Gypsum
Sand
Dunes
Shumard Canyon
Williams Ranch
Patterson Hills
Quail Mountain
4,962 ft
Cone Peak
5,017 ft
Salt Basin

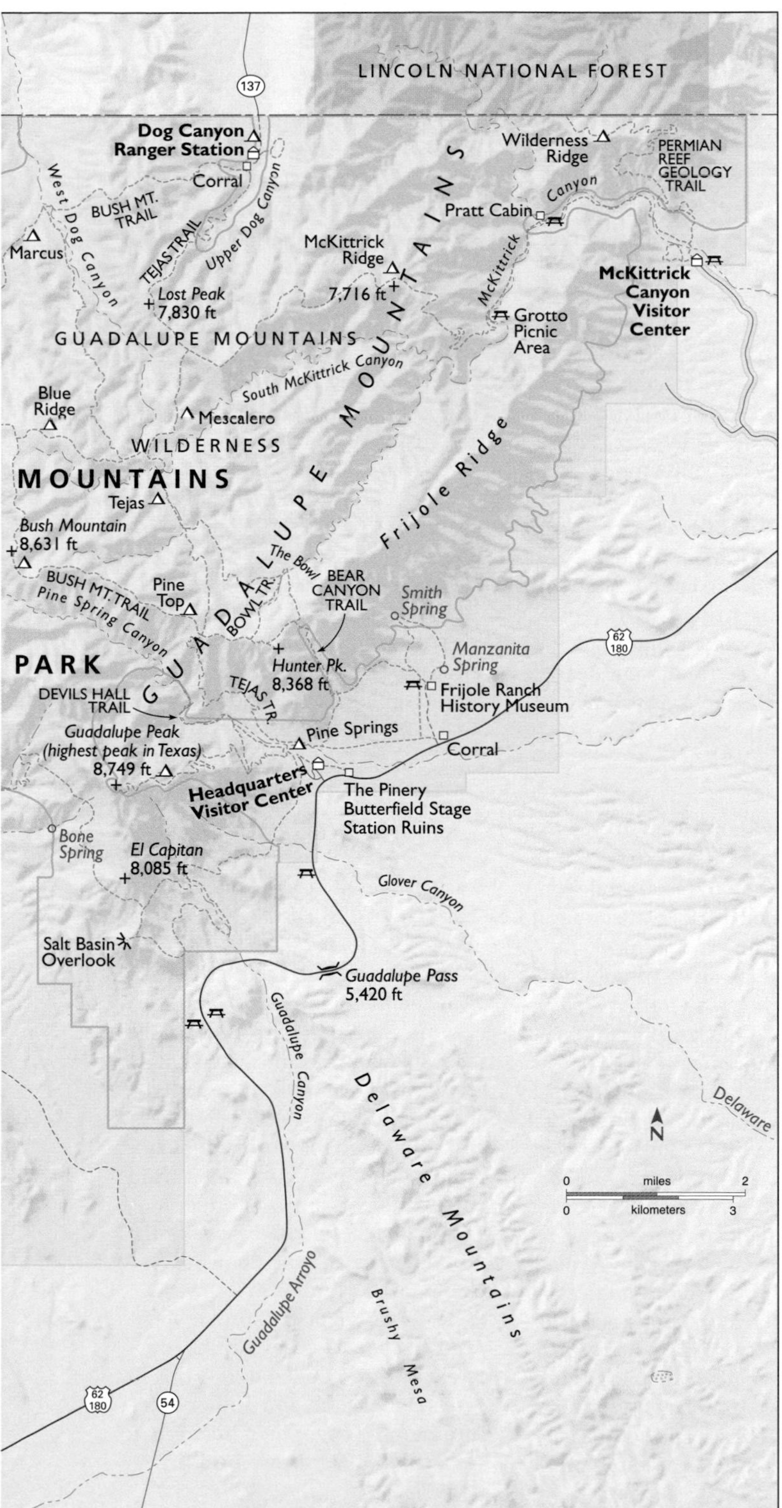

LINCOLN NATIONAL FOREST
137
Dog Canyon
Ranger Station
Corral
West Dog Canyon
BUSH MT. TRAIL
TEJAS TRAIL
Upper Dog Canyon
Marcus
Lost Peak
7,830 ft
McKittrick Ridge
7,716 ft
Wilderness Ridge
PERMIAN REEF GEOLOGY TRAIL
Canyon
Pratt Cabin
McKittrick
McKittrick Canyon Visitor Center
Grotto Picnic Area
GUADALUPE MOUNTAINS
South McKittrick Canyon
Blue Ridge
Mescalero
WILDERNESS
MOUNTAINS
Tejas
Bush Mountain
8,631 ft
GUADALUPE MOUNTAINS
Frijole Ridge
The Bowl
BEAR CANYON TRAIL
Smith Spring
BUSH MT. TRAIL
Pine Spring Canyon
Pine Top
BOWL TR.
Manzanita Spring
62
180
PARK
Hunter Pk.
8,368 ft
Frijole Ranch History Museum
DEVILS HALL TRAIL
TEJAS TR.
Guadalupe Peak
(highest peak in Texas)
8,749 ft
Pine Springs
Corral
Headquarters Visitor Center
The Pinery Butterfield Stage Station Ruins
Bone Spring
El Capitan
8,085 ft
Glover Canyon
Salt Basin Overlook
Guadalupe Pass
5,420 ft
Guadalupe Canyon
Delaware Mountains
Delaware
N
0 miles 2
0 kilometers 3
Guadalupe Arroyo
Brushy Mesa
62
180
54

heart of the agave plant, one of the succulents with spikes at the tips of the leaves—hence the culture's name. You'll soon approach **Manzanita Spring,** a place to spot wildlife.

Continue on to **Smith Spring,** a veritable garden of maidenhair ferns, Texas madrone trees (the ones shedding layers of paper-thin bark), alligator juniper (named for its distinctively textured bark), oak, and maple. As you loop back to your car, bear left at the fork.

Return to the highway and drive west-southwest about 2 miles, or at least as far as the first pullover, for a superb view of **El Capitan** (8,085 feet), the southernmost bluff of the Guadalupes. Late afternoon light shows off this imposing symbol of the region, once the beacon for conquistador, stagecoach driver, and homesteader.

MCKITTRICK CANYON

a half to full day

The walls of McKittrick Canyon shelter the only year-round stream in the park; the water creates a 3-mile-long oasis of oak and juniper, madrone and maple. The canyon itself is nearly 5 miles long. Pick up a self-guiding booklet on the area's human and natural history at the **McKittrick Canyon Visitor Center** near the trailheads. For an easy hike (although the trail is rocky and best negotiated in hiking boots), walk the 2.3 miles to the **Pratt Cabin.** If you have time, continue another mile through the woods that border the intermittent stream to the Grotto picnic area. Because the canyon plants are fragile, be sure to stay on the trail.

McKittrick Canyon exposes millions of years of geological events. During the Permian period, about 250 million years ago, an inland sea covered parts of West Texas and southeast New Mexico. Along the shore of the sea grew a reef of lime-secreting algae, sponges, other marine organisms, and calcium carbonate precipitated from the water. After millions of years, the climate changed and the ocean dried up; the Capitan Reef loomed hundreds of feet high in a horseshoe 400 miles long. Sediments and mineral salts buried both basin and reef over the next eons. Later, the region began to rise, and erosion slowly reexposed the seabed with part of the fossil reef—today's Guadalupe range—towering above.

As you walk into McKittrick Canyon, you are entering the Capitan Reef from the seaward side. To best observe the reef's varied formation and fossils, try the **Permian Reef Geology Trail.** You'll see layers of the ancient reef exposed by centuries of cutting by McKittrick Creek. The trail—4.5 miles one way—climbs the 2,000-foot ridge to a ponderosa forest on the top.

DOG CANYON

a half to full day

Accessibility to the forested high country and its spectacular scenery make Dog Canyon well worth the drive. Ask a ranger to point out Apache mescal-roasting pits, still visible among the hip-high grasses, creosote bushes, and succulents. Then picnic and hike; the trails begin past the stables. Popular hikes include the **Bush Mountain Trail,** which, in about 3 miles, leads through open pinyon-juniper woodland to splendid views of the Guadalupes and the **Cornudas Mountains,** 55 miles to the west. The **Tejas Trail** offers similar views and in about 4 miles climbs into a temperate woodland of Gambel oak, Douglas fir, and limber and ponderosa pine. This forest is a relict of the plant communities

INFORMATION & ACTIVITIES

HEADQUARTERS
HC 60, Box 400, Salt Flat, TX 79847.
Phone (915) 828-3251.
www.nps.gov/gumo

SEASONS & ACCESSIBILITY
Open all year but may be inaccessible for brief periods in winter due to snowstorms. Check with park.

VISITOR & INFORMATION CENTERS
Headquarters Visitor Center, 0.1 mile off US 62/180 near Guadalupe Pass. **McKittrick Canyon Visitor Center,** off US 62/180 on eastern edge of park. **Dog Canyon Ranger Station** to the north open intermittently. Call park for details.

ENTRANCE FEE
$3 per person (under 16 free) for a 7-day pass.

PETS
Not permitted on trails or in buildings; elsewhere must be leashed.

FACILITIES FOR DISABLED
The visitor centers, restrooms, and Pine Springs Campground and amphitheater are wheelchair accessible.

THINGS TO DO
Hikes, horseback trail rides (no rentals), evening and children's programs.

SPECIAL ADVISORIES
- Rattlesnakes and other potentially harmful desert animals live here; watch out!
- Bring maps with you if planning to hike; park is managed as wilderness, so trail signs are minimal.

OVERNIGHT BACKPACKING
Designated sites only; permits required (free, obtained at visitor centers). Backcountry use permits required to bring a horse into the park, available from main visitor center or Dog Canyon. Horses are not allowed in the backcountry overnight; they can be stabled in Frijole Ranch and Dog Canyon corrals; reserve space by calling (915) 828-3251.

CAMPGROUNDS
Two campgrounds, with 14-day limit. Open all year, first come, first served. $8 per night. No showers. Tent and RV sites; no hookups. Two group campsites; reservations required through headquarters.

HOTELS, MOTELS, & INNS
(unless otherwise noted, rates are for 2 persons in a double room, high season)
<u>In Whites City, NM 88268:</u>
Whites City Resort and Best Western, 17 Carlsbad Cavern Hwy., P.O. Box 128. (800) 228-3767 or (505) 785-2291. 105 units. $104. AC, pool, restaurant.
<u>In Van Horn, TX 79855:</u>
Best Western American Inn 1309 W. Broadway, Box 626. (800) 621-2478 or (432) 283-2030. 33 units. $65. AC, pool.

See also Carlsbad Caverns NP listings, p. 140

that cloaked the region in the last Ice Age. It still survives because of the particular, unusual combination of temperature and humidity at this high-altitude site.

OTHER HIKES

Hikers may find the following treks rewarding. They all begin from Pine Springs Campground; ask a ranger for information:

Guadalupe Peak, 8.4 miles round-trip. Lightning storms can quickly gather on hot summer afternoons—it's best to begin your ascent by 8 a.m. and your descent by 1 p.m. If you see a storm coming, start down.

The Bowl, a lush area of relict ice age conifer forest. The 8.7-mile loop comprises the Tejas, Bowl, and Bear Canyon Trails.

Devils Hall, a steep, narrow canyon; 4.2 miles round-trip, mostly level.

THE COLORADO PLATEAU

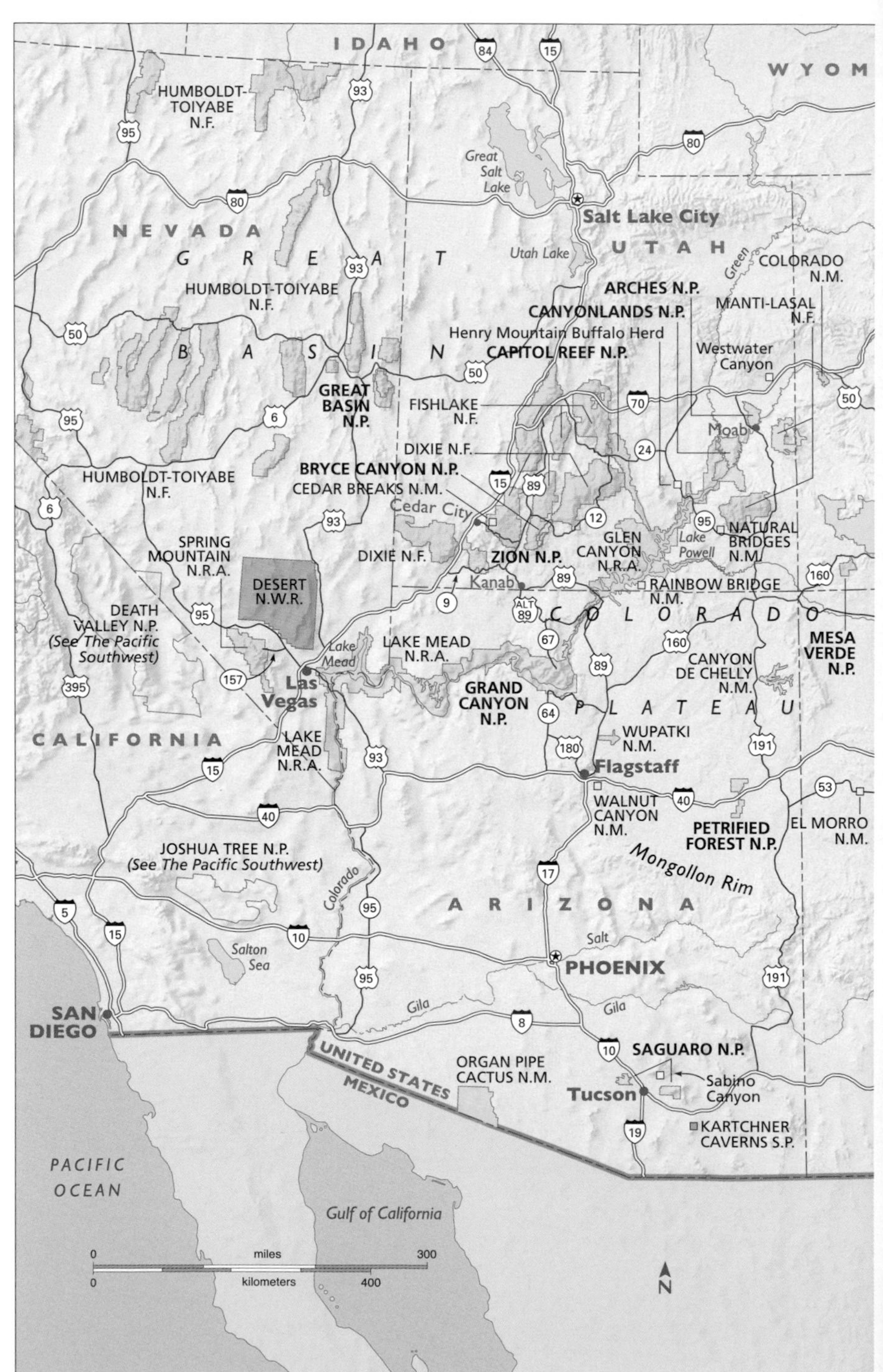
IDAHO
WYOM
NEVADA
UTAH
CALIFORNIA
ARIZONA
GREAT BASIN
COLORADO PLATEAU
HUMBOLDT-TOIYABE N.F.
Great Salt Lake
Salt Lake City
Utah Lake
COLORADO N.M.
ARCHES N.P.
CANYONLANDS N.P.
MANTI-LASAL N.F.
Henry Mountain Buffalo Herd
CAPITOL REEF N.P.
Westwater Canyon
GREAT BASIN N.P.
FISHLAKE N.F.
Moab
DIXIE N.F.
BRYCE CANYON N.P.
CEDAR BREAKS N.M.
Cedar City
SPRING MOUNTAIN N.R.A.
GLEN CANYON N.R.A.
Lake Powell
NATURAL BRIDGES N.M.
ZION N.P.
DESERT N.W.R.
Kanab
RAINBOW BRIDGE N.M.
DEATH VALLEY N.P. (See The Pacific Southwest)
LAKE MEAD N.R.A.
Lake Mead
MESA VERDE N.P.
Las Vegas
CANYON DE CHELLY N.M.
GRAND CANYON N.P.
WUPATKI N.M.
Flagstaff
WALNUT CANYON N.M.
PETRIFIED FOREST N.P.
EL MORRO N.M.
JOSHUA TREE N.P. (See The Pacific Southwest)
Mongollon Rim
Colorado
Salton Sea
Salt
PHOENIX
Gila
SAN DIEGO
UNITED STATES
MEXICO
ORGAN PIPE CACTUS N.M.
SAGUARO N.P.
Sabino Canyon
Tucson
KARTCHNER CAVERNS S.P.
PACIFIC OCEAN
Gulf of California
0 miles 300
0 kilometers 400
N

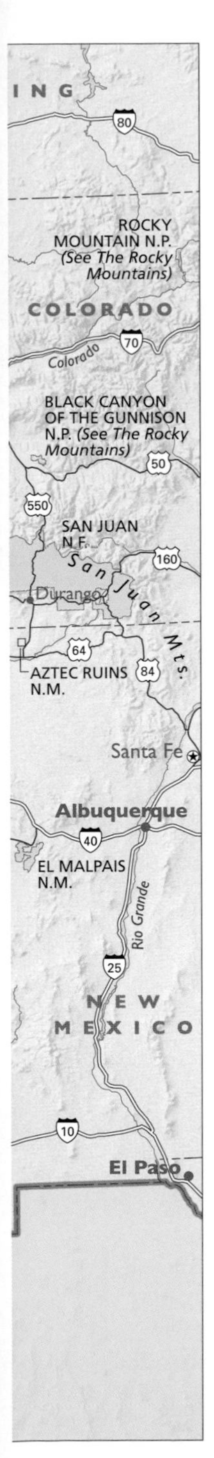

THE COLORADO PLATEAU

Theodore Roosevelt called the Grand Canyon "the one great sight ... every American should see." Although the Grand Canyon remains the most famous sight on the Colorado Plateau, this high desert drained by the Colorado River and its tributaries teems with scenic treasures. Numerous gorges slice the colorfully layered rock; stairstep terraces, buttes, and spires embellish it. The region contains the nation's largest concentration of national parks.

The striated cliffs of the canyon parks collectively encompass nearly two billion years of Earth's history, divulging tales of ancient seas and volcanoes, deserts and dinosaurs. The rush of rivers sculptured the colossal gorges and side canyons of Grand Canyon, Zion, and Canyonlands. Grit-bearing winds and the freeze and thaw of water droplets chiseled multihued rock into the hoodoos, arches, and pinnacles visible in Arches and Bryce Canyon.

Although one of the most sparsely populated regions of the United States today, the plateau features some of the country's richest remains of early Native American civilizations. Archaeological highlights range from petroglyphs in Canyonlands, Capitol Reef, and Saguaro to pueblos and solstice markers in Petrified Forest to spectacular cliff dwellings in Mesa Verde.

Thanks to abrupt changes in elevation, the canyon parks shelter a wide diversity of plants and animals. Desert or semi-desert at canyon bottom gives way to pinyon-juniper woodland and then ponderosa pine and spruce-fir forests. Lizards and deer, cottontails and bighorn sheep can coexist in the same park. The desert park Saguaro protects North America's largest cactus, as well as the many other plants and animals of the vast Sonoran Desert.

Flagstaff, Arizona, makes a convenient base for the South Rim of the Grand Canyon and for Petrified Forest. From Kanab, Utah, you can visit Grand Canyon's North Rim, Bryce, Capitol Reef, and Zion. Just west of the plateau, a 5-hour drive from Kanab, lies Great Basin. For Arches and Canyonlands, Moab, Utah, is the place to stop, and to visit Saguaro, head for Tucson, Arizona.

Red rock of Delicate Arch ablaze at sunset

ARCHES

UTAH
ESTABLISHED NOVEMBER 12, 1971
76,359 acres

This park contains more than 2,000 natural arches—the greatest concentration in the country. But numbers have no significance beside the grandeur of the landscape—the arches, the giant balanced rocks, spires, pinnacles, and slickrock domes against the enormous sky.

Perched high above the Colorado River, the park is part of southern Utah's extended canyon country, carved and shaped by eons of weathering and erosion. Some 300 million years ago, inland seas covered the large basin that formed this region. The seas refilled and evaporated—29 times in all—leaving behind salt beds thousands of feet thick. Later, sand and boulders carried down by streams from the uplands eventually buried the salt beds beneath thick layers of stone. Because the salt layer is less dense than the overlying blanket of rock, it rises up through it, forming it into domes and ridges, with valleys in between.

Most of the formations at Arches are made of soft red sandstone deposited 150 million years ago. Much later, groundwater began to dissolve the underlying salt deposits. The sandstone domes collapsed and weathered into a maze of vertical rock slabs called "fins." Sections of these slender walls eventually wore through, creating the spectacular rock sculptures that visitors to Arches see today.

The land has a timeless, indestructible look that is misleading.

More than 700,000 visitors each year threaten the fragile high desert ecosystem. One concern is a dark scale called biological soil crust composed of cyanobacteria, algae, fungi, and lichens that grow in sandy areas in the park. Footprints tracked across this living community may remain visible for years. In fact, the aridity helps preserve traces of past activity for centuries. Visitors are asked to walk only on designated trails or stay on slickrock or wash bottoms.

How to Get There

From Moab, take US 191 north 5 miles to the park entrance. From I-70, exit at Crescent Junction and follow US 191 south for 25 miles to the entrance. Airport: 15 miles north of Moab and at Grand Junction, Colorado, about 120 miles away.

When to Go

Year-round, but spring and fall are best; moderate temperatures are ideal for hiking in the high desert. Summers are hot and winters mild. Wildflowers peak in April and May.

How to Visit

Take the **Arches Scenic Drive** at least as far as The Windows Section. If possible, carry on to the historic Wolfe Ranch, Fiery Furnace, and the Devils Garden. Also allow time for hiking at least one of the park's spectacular trails, perhaps to **Delicate Arch** or even **Tower Arch,** in the park's remote Klondike Bluffs. If it's spring, summer, or fall (and you're not bothered by heights), consider joining a naturalist-led 3-hour hike through **Fiery Furnace** *(fee)*. It's strenuous, but you'll appreciate the shade in summer's heat. Contact the visitor center in person for reservations and tickets *(walks fill quickly; reserve early)*.

ARCHES SCENIC DRIVE

18 miles one way; a half to full day

The scenic drive climbs from the floor of **Moab Canyon** to **Devils Garden,** passing through the heart of the park with spur roads leading to **The Windows Section** and **Wolfe Ranch** and to the **Delicate Arch** area. Numerous pull-offs allow leisurely viewing of the park's major features.

From the visitor center the road winds up the canyon wall. Pull off after 2 miles at the **Park Avenue Viewpoint and Trailhead** for a view down an open canyon flanked by sandstone skyscrapers. If you have a willing driver (or don't mind the 320-foot return climb), walk the easy 1-mile path to the **Courthouse Towers** parking area, where you can be picked up. Here signs describe nearby rock formations that show the birth and death of an arch.

Continue your drive to the beautiful slickrock expanse known as the **Petrified Dunes.** Here you skirt

Balanced rock

knolls—ancient dunes turned to stone—as the **La Sal Mountains** rise nearly 13,000 feet in the distance. Farther along, stop at the **Balanced Rock** pull-off where a 0.4-mile trail loops past this classic hoodoo, a strangely eroded rock spire 128 feet high. Edward Abbey wrote his classic *Desert Solitaire* after living in a trailer near here as a park ranger. Just beyond, turn onto the paved road leading to The Windows.

The road to the right passes a cluster of pinnacles and monoliths called **Garden of Eden** and ends at a parking area fronted by a sandstone wall perforated by several arches. Short trails lead to closeup views of these colossal gateways. The 0.3-mile walk to **South Window,** 105 feet wide, also gives you good views of **North Window and Turret Arch.** If time allows walk the half-mile trail for a dramatic closeup look at **Double Arch.**

Return to the main road. A road leaves the scenic drive and leads 1.5 miles to historic **Wolfe Ranch,** where a Civil War veteran raised cattle around the turn of the 20th century, and the **Delicate Arch Viewpoint,** 1 mile farther. The distant view of Delicate Arch is disappointing, so if you have the stamina and at least 2 extra hours consider hiking the **Delicate Arch Trail** from Wolfe Ranch (see pp. 156). Though it is one of the most rewarding hikes in canyon country, you may be better off saving it for a second day if you plan to take the full drive and do other walks.

Return to the main road. Skip the **Salt Valley Overlook** but pull off at **Fiery Furnace,** a dense array of red fins that appear to ignite when the sun is low in the west. Here you see a world standing on end—hoodoos, spires, and slabs 200 feet high. It's easy to get lost in the maze of deeply grooved slots and dead-end passage-

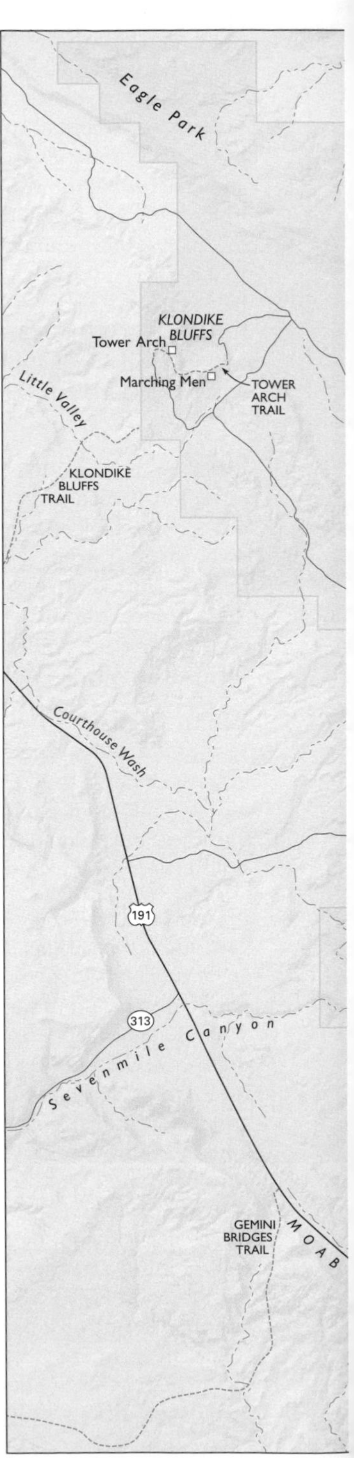

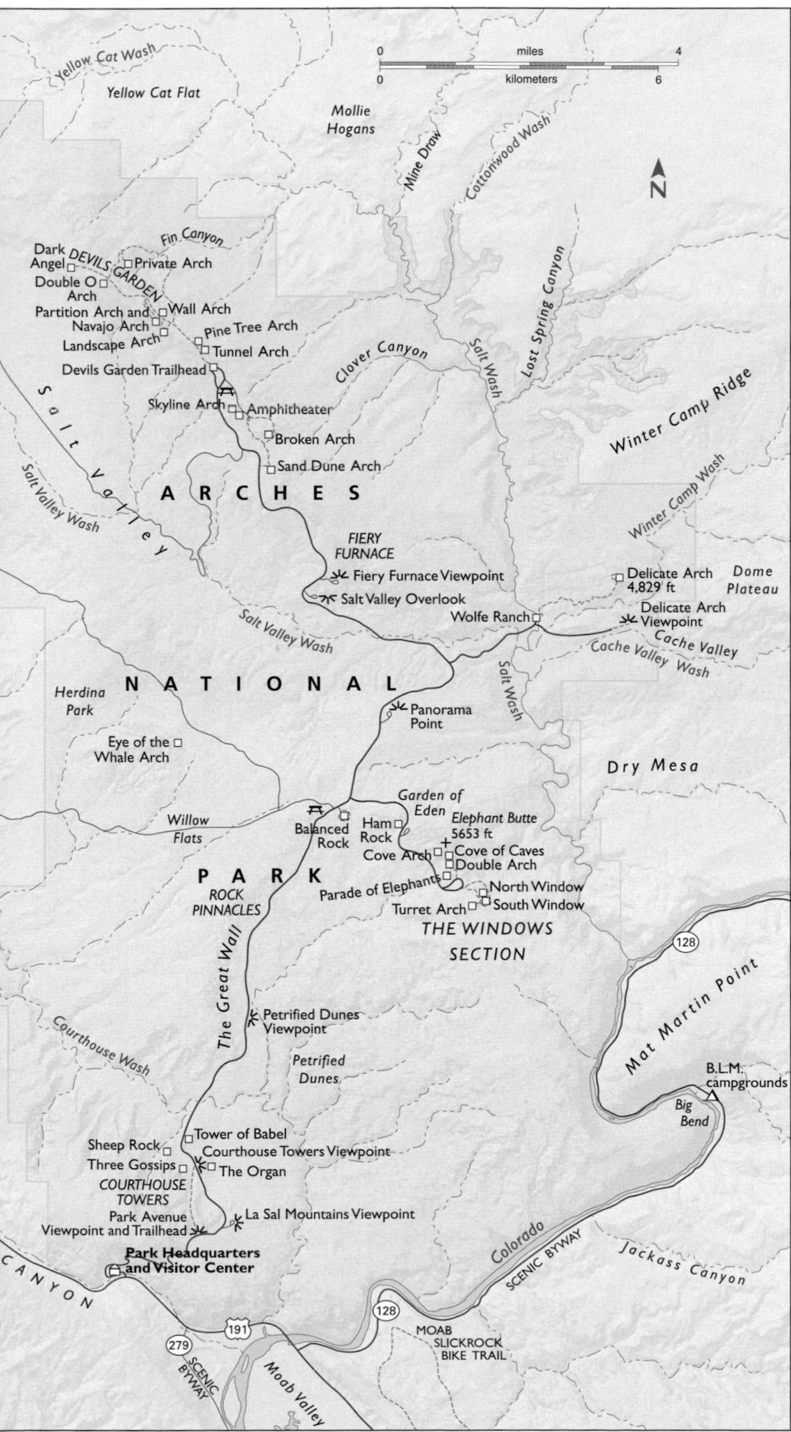

Yellow Cat Wash
Yellow Cat Flat
Mollie Hogans
Mine Draw
Cottonwood Wash
miles
kilometers
Fin Canyon
Dark Angel
DEVILS GARDEN
Private Arch
Double O Arch
Partition Arch and Navajo Arch
Wall Arch
Landscape Arch
Pine Tree Arch
Tunnel Arch
Devils Garden Trailhead
Skyline Arch
Amphitheater
Broken Arch
Sand Dune Arch
Clover Canyon
Salt Wash
Lost Spring Canyon
Winter Camp Ridge
Winter Camp Wash
Salt Valley
Salt Valley Wash
ARCHES NATIONAL PARK
FIERY FURNACE
Fiery Furnace Viewpoint
Salt Valley Overlook
Delicate Arch 4,829 ft
Dome Plateau
Wolfe Ranch
Delicate Arch Viewpoint
Cache Valley
Cache Valley Wash
Herdina Park
Panorama Point
Eye of the Whale Arch
Dry Mesa
Willow Flats
Garden of Eden
Balanced Rock
Ham Rock
Elephant Butte 5653 ft
Cove Arch
Cove of Caves
Double Arch
ROCK PINNACLES
Parade of Elephants
North Window
South Window
Turret Arch
THE WINDOWS SECTION
128
The Great Wall
Mat Martin Point
Petrified Dunes Viewpoint
Courthouse Wash
Petrified Dunes
B.L.M. campgrounds
Big Bend
Tower of Babel
Sheep Rock
Courthouse Towers Viewpoint
Three Gossips
The Organ
COURTHOUSE TOWERS
Park Avenue Viewpoint and Trailhead
La Sal Mountains Viewpoint
Park Headquarters and Visitor Center
Colorado
SCENIC BYWAY
Jackass Canyon
CANYON
191
279
MOAB SLICKROCK BIKE TRAIL
Moab Valley

Fiery Furnace fins

ways. Note that visitors who are not part of a guided walk will need a permit *(fee; available only at visitor center)* to explore Fiery Furnace.

Continue your drive. Take the 0.2-mile walk to the cool shade of **Sand Dune Arch,** tucked between two fins, but save **Broken Arch** for another time. Farther down the road **Skyline Arch** comes into view. In 1940 a great rock mass broke from the arch, doubling the size of the opening to 45 by 69 feet.

The road ends at the Devils Garden campground and trailhead beyond. The **Devils Garden Trail** meanders 7.2 miles to seven major arches, each with its own character. Be sure to save enough time to walk at least as far as **Landscape Arch,** 0.8 mile down the trail. Here a narrow ribbon of stone 306 feet long appears to defy gravity as it floats in a graceful span above a dune. It's one of the world's longest freestanding natural arches.

If you walk the trail in early morning, watch for the white evening primrose. As the sunlight grows stronger, the flowers wilt, turning the petals pink. Though primitive beyond Landscape Arch, the trail continues on another mile to **Double O Arch,** a 160-foot-wide circular arch that hangs above a smaller bore. From here you can walk about half a mile to the rock spire known as the **Dark Angel.** A primitive trail curves from Double O Arch back to Landscape for those seeking a challenge.

DELICATE ARCH HIKE

3 miles round trip; at least 2 hours

This delightful trail gains 500 feet in elevation as it traverses 1.5 miles of

Sandstone arch

slickrock as smooth and cambered as the back of a whale. It tops out, suddenly and dramatically, at the foot of Delicate Arch, a must-see.

As nature writer Edward Abbey put it in *Desert Solitaire,* "If Delicate Arch has any significance it lies, I will venture, in the power of the odd and unexpected to startle the senses and surprise the mind out their ruts of habit, to compel us into a re-awakened awareness of the wonderful—that which is full of wonder."

The hike begins on the grounds of the Wolfe Ranch, which include a weathered corral and a tattered log cabin. Follow the bridge across Salt Wash to the cliff on the left, where it is believed the Ute Indians left petroglyphs. The Ute, who once roamed from the eastern slope of the Colorado Rockies to the canyonlands of southern Utah, perhaps camped here, probably trading with Wolfe for provisions.

The trail is ingeniously designed to hide Delicate Arch from view until your very last step. From the valley floor the route threads patches of cryptobiotic soil before reaching flat slabs of sandstone, where cairns mark the way. Juniper trees grow from cracks so small the trunks seem to emerge from solid rock. The final third of a mile is a teaser. As the path climbs, it hugs a sandstone fin, then edges along a steep bowl that bars all view of the famous arch. The last few steps require some nerve, but you will be rewarded with a marvelous look at Delicate Arch straddling the edge of a slickrock basin.

Standing 45 feet tall at its highest point, Delicate Arch frames the **La Sal Mountains** some 35 miles away. Over the years other names have been attached to this famous arch—Schoolmarm's Pants, Old Maid's Bloomers, and Cowboy Chaps.

The best time to photograph Delicate Arch is near sunrise or sunset. Time your evening hike for the full moon and you may have the thrill of seeing the moon rise above the arch—though the return trip in dim light can be tricky.

TOWER ARCH TRAIL

2.4 miles round trip; 2 hours

Located in the park's remote **Klondike Bluffs** area, this 1.2-mile one-way trail to Tower Arch winds through an intricate landscape of weird sandstone formations, cresting ridge tops now and then for outstanding vistas of the Fiery Furnace, the La Sal Mountains, Book Cliffs, and clusters of towering hoodoos.

To reach the trailhead, drive 1 mile south on the main park road from the Devils Garden parking lot, then turn west on the high-clearance road just past **Skyline Arch.** *(This unpaved road may be impassable during or after storms.)* Follow the road 7.7 miles through Salt Valley to the turnoff on the left for Tower Arch Trail.

Cairns direct you from the parking lot up a steep rock ridge, and the route soon leads down through a land littered with fins and other rock outcroppings to Tower Arch, which takes its name from the pinnacle standing nearby.

INFORMATION & ACTIVITIES

HEADQUARTERS
P.O. Box 907, Moab, UT 84532. Phone (435) 719-2299. ww.nps.gov/arch

SEASONS & ACCESSIBILITY
Open year-round. Some unpaved roads may become temporarily impassable after heavy rains. Call headquarters for current weather and road information.

VISITOR & INFORMATION CENTERS
Visitor center, on US 191 at park entrance, open daily all year. Call headquarters number for visitor information.

ENTRANCE FEE
$10 per car per week allows multiple entries. Yearly fee of $25 is also good at Canyonlands NP and Natural Bridges and Hovenweep NM.

PETS
Prohibited on all hiking trails and in the backcountry.

FACILITIES FOR DISABLED
Visitor center and its restrooms are wheelchair accessible. Restroom and one campsite accessible in Devils Garden Campground. Park Avenue and Delicate Arch Viewpoints are accessible to wheelchairs.

THINGS TO DO
Naturalist-led activities: nature hikes and talks, evening programs. Reservations must be made in person at the visitor center for the Fiery Furnace Walk ($8; can be made up to 7 days in advance); not recommended for children under 6. Also available, geological and historical exhibits, self-guided auto tour, hiking, jeep tours, sight-seeing flights. Contact park headquarters for list of concessioners offering rental and guide services.

SPECIAL ADVISORIES
• Always carry water on hikes—at least a gallon a day per person is recommended in summer.
• Stay on trails to protect fragile desert soils and plant life.
• Sandstone slickrock crumbles easily and can make climbing dangerous. It is often easier to go up than down.

OVERNIGHT BACKPACKING
Permits required (free from visitor center).

CAMPGROUNDS
One campground, **Devils Garden,** 18 miles from the park entrance, has a 7-day limit. Open all year. Twenty-four sites are first come, first served; preregister at the visitor center, which opens at 7:30 a.m. (these sites fill early; plan to arrive in the morning). Fees $10 per night. No showers. Tent and RV sites; no hookups. Reservations required for the remaining 27 sites (1 wheelchair accessible) and for the **Devils Garden Group Campgrounds.** Call (435) 719-2299 or visit the website.

HOTELS, MOTELS, & INNS
(unless otherwise noted, rates are for 2 persons, double room, high season)

In Moab, UT 84532:

Best Western Green Well Motel 105 S. Main St. (800) 528-1234 or (435) 259-6151. 72 units. $69-$139. AC, pool, rest.
Big Horn Lodge 550 S. Main St. (800) 325-6171 or (435) 259-6171. 58 units. $80. AC, pool, restaurant.
Cedar Breaks Condos Center and 4th E. (800) 505-5343 or (435) 259-5125. Six 2-bedroom units with full kitchens. $98-$146. AC.
Pack Creek Ranch (15 miles southeast of Moab, off La Sal Mountain Loop Rd.) 505 N. Main St. (435) 259-5505. Cabins, houses, bunkhouses. $95-$300. Trail rides and massages for a fee. AC, pool.
Ramada Inn—Moab 182 S. Main St. (800) 272-6232 or (435) 259-7141. 82 units. $89-$139. AC, pool, restaurant.

For other accommodations in the area, contact Utah's Canyonlands Region, 805 N. Main St., Moab, UT 84532. (800) 233-8824 or (435) 259-7814.

EXCURSIONS

MANTI-LA SAL NATIONAL FOREST
MOAB, UTAH

Mountains, densely wooded with aspen, pine, fir, and spruce and rugged grassland-covered plateaus, provide cool contrast here in red-rock country. Contains Dark Canyon Wilderness. 1,265,254 acres, part in Colorado. Hiking, climbing, bicycling, fishing, horseback riding, hunting, winter sports. 25 developed campgrounds, picnic areas. Open year-round; services open late May through October. Information in Moab on US 191. The Moab District of the NF is located about 5 miles southeast of Arches NP; the Monticello District borders Canyonlands NP to the south. (435) 259-7155 or (435) 637-2817.

COLORADO NATIONAL MONUMENT
FRUITA, COLORADO

The 23-mile-long Rim Rock Drive and well-maintained trails with gentle switchbacks provide easy access to this monument's small, sheer-walled canyons and sandstone monoliths. Shelters mule deer, bighorn sheep, and mountain lions. 20,533 acres. Hiking, climbing, bicycling, horseback riding, scenic drives, winter sports. 80 campsites, picnic areas, handicapped access. Open year-round. Located on Colo. 340, about 100 miles from Arches NP. (970) 858-3617.

Bryce Amphitheater, seen from Bryce Point

BRYCE CANYON

UTAH

ESTABLISHED SEPTEMBER 15, 1928

35,835 acres

Perhaps nowhere are the forces of natural erosion more tangible than at Bryce Canyon. Its wilderness of phantom-like rock spires, or hoodoos, attracts more than one million visitors a year. Many descend on trails that give hikers and horseback riders a close look at the fluted walls and sculptured pinnacles.

The park follows the edge of the Paunsaugunt Plateau. On the west are heavily forested tablelands more than 9,000 feet high; on the east are the intricately carved breaks that drop 2,000 feet to the Paria Valley. Many ephemeral streams have eaten into the plateau, forming horseshoe-shaped bowls. The largest and most striking is Bryce Amphitheater. Encompassing 6 square miles, it is the park's scenic heart.

For millions of years water has carved, as it continues to, Bryce's rugged landscape. Water may split rock as it freezes and expands in cracks—a cyclic process that occurs some 200 times a year. In summer, runoff from cloudbursts etches into the softer limestones and sluices through the deep runnels. In about 50 years the present rim will be cut back another foot. But there is more here than spectacular erosion.

In the early morning you can stand for long moments on the rim, held by the amphitheater's mysterious blend of rock and color. Warm yellows and oranges radiate from the deeply pigmented walls as scatterings of light illuminate the pale spires.

There is a sense of place here that goes beyond rocks. Some local Paiute Indians explained it with a legend. Once there lived animal-like creatures that changed themselves into people. But they were bad, so Coyote turned them into rocks of various configurations. The spell-bound creatures still huddle together here with faces painted just as they were before being turned to stone.

How to Get There

From Zion NP (83 miles west), follow Utah 9 east, turn north on Utah 89, then continue east on Utah 12 to Utah 63, which is the park entrance road. From Capitol Reef NP (about 120 miles away), follow Utah 12 southwest to Utah 63. Airports: Salt Lake City, Utah or Las Vegas, Nevada.

When to Go

All-year park. Wildflowers peak in spring and early summer; the greatest variety of the park's 170 bird species appear between May and October. Winter lasts from November through March; snow highlights the colored cliffs and provides fine cross-country skiing and snowshoeing.

How to Visit

On a 1-day visit, tour the **Bryce Amphitheater,** beginning, if possible, with sunrise at **Bryce Point.** If limited time requires choosing between the scenic drive or a walk beneath the rim, take the walk. On a longer stay, drive to **Rainbow Point;** consider a moonlight stroll among the hoodoos.

BRYCE AMPHITHEATER

8 miles; 2 hours to a full day

Watch sunrise from **Bryce Point,** one of the highest overlooks along the rim of the amphitheater. Drive about 4 miles south of the visitor center, then walk a short distance from the parking lot to the viewpoint. Colors begin to glow just as the sun breaks over the **Aquarius Plateau,** at over 10,000 feet the highest plateau in North America. First light catches the rim of the amphitheater, then drops into the basin, igniting the crowded pillars of rock. From this vantage point you see shallow caves along the rim called the **Grottoes.** Look for the **Alligator,** a sharply incised butte that appears reptilian from above, and the **Sinking Ship,** which resembles a vanishing prow.

Drive back to **Inspiration Point,** bypassing the **Paria View** turnoff. From the parking lot walk up a short but steep trail to upper Inspiration Point. If the trail looks too ambitious, stay below at the lower viewpoint. Both look over the head of the amphitheater and place you close to the rock formations. No matter what time of day, they provide excellent all-around views.

In the valley below is the small town of **Tropic.** Scottish emigrant Ebenezer Bryce and his wife, Mary, homesteaded nearby in 1875. They grazed cattle in Bryce Canyon but moved away 5 years later, leaving

Thor's Hammer at sunrise

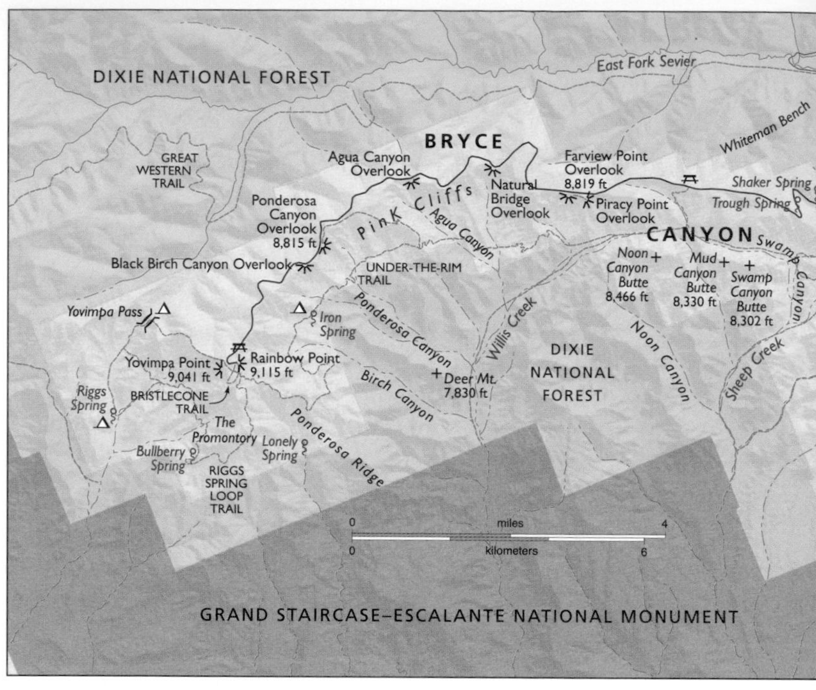

behind little more than their name.

Continue on to **Sunset Point.** The name is misleading since the viewpoint faces east, limiting sundown views. But the mix of shadows and deep-hued colors makes this an excellent vantage point in the low-angled light of later afternoon. To the left is **Thor's Hammer;** to the right is the **Silent City**—a gridwork of deep ravines that divide turreted walls suggesting the ruins of an ancient metropolis.

Those with time and stamina can follow the **Navajo Loop Trail,** a fairly strenuous 1.3-mile loop into the canyon. The trail drops steeply in a series of switchbacks before entering a narrow, steep-walled gorge called **Wall Street.** Several Douglas firs, two of them 500 years old, grow between the towering cliffs.

Continue down the trail to the junction with **Queen's Garden Trail,** the least strenuous trail below the rim. It winds along the bottom of the amphitheater to Queen's Garden, then climbs to the rim at Sunrise Point, passing weird rock formations and occasional bristlecone pines. From Sunrise Point follow the **Rim Trail** a half mile back to your car at Sunset Point.

THE DRIVE TO RAINBOW POINT

17 miles; 3 hours to a half day

Following the edge of the gently tilted plateau, this scenic drive ascends over a thousand feet to Rainbow Point, the plateau's southernmost reach.

From the **Visitor Center,** proceed South past the Sunset Point turnoff *(trailers are not allowed beyond here)* and on beyond the Bryce Point turnoff. You will leave the ponderosa pine forest behind and quickly find yourself among the high-elevation Douglas fir and blue spruce.

Pull in at **Farview Point** for a panoramic view of **Table Cliffs** and a se-

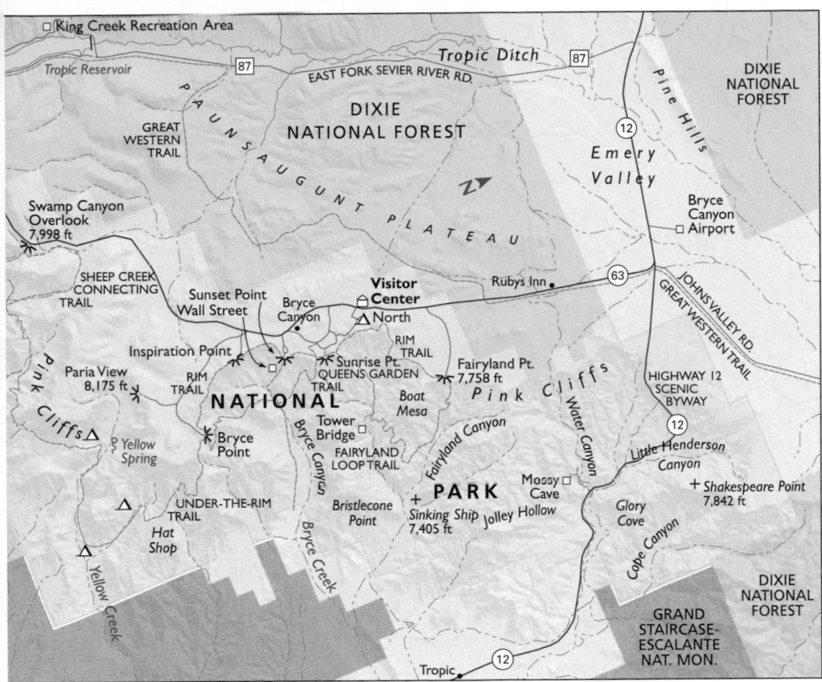

ries of broad platforms stairstepping southeast to the **Kaibab Plateau** at the North Rim of the **Grand Canyon.**

Continue south to **Natural Bridge** pull-off. Here you have a closeup view of a natural arch 85 feet long and 125 feet high. Its bright rusty red contrasts with the deep green of the trees below and the deep blue of the sky above.

The next pull-off is **Agua Canyon,** one of the finest vistas in the park. Massive hoodoos stand close to the rim; farther off are the vividly colored **Pink Cliffs;** and on the far horizon is the domed profile of **Navajo Mountain,** over 10,000 feet high.

Continue to the end of the road at **Rainbow Point.** You might choose to stop for a picnic among the thick stands of fir on the park's highest elevation, 9,115 feet. A pleasant mile walk follows the **Bristlecone Loop Trail** to expansive views. A spur trail leads to more views at **Yovimpa Point;** the cliffs that descend from there in stairsteps are named for their rock colors—pink, gray, white, vermilion, and chocolate. A stand of ancient bristlecone pines grows on the exposed edge of the plateau; the oldest bristlecone pine in the park has been alive for more than 1,500 years.

As you backtrack through the park but just before you leave, a mile-long spur road leads to the **Fairyland Point** overlook (you bypassed this on the way in). This is one of the finest vistas in the park. In colorful array, spires and

Exploring Bryce Canyon on horseback

INFORMATION & ACTIVITIES

HEADQUARTERS
Bryce Canyon, UT 84717. Phone (435) 834-5322. www.nps.gov/brca

SEASONS & ACCESSIBILITY
Park open year-round. Roads may be closed for short periods due to snowstorms. Some spur roads closed in winter for cross-country skiing. Phone headquarters for information.

VISITOR & INFORMATION CENTERS
Visitor center on main road, 1 mile inside park boundary. Open all year. Call headquarters for visitor information.

ENTRANCE FEE
$20 per car per week. From mid-May through Sept., visitors may leave their cars near the entrance. From there, a shuttle system will transport visitors to points throughout the park.

FACILITIES FOR DISABLED
Visitor center partially accessible to wheelchairs; all viewpoints and a half-mile stretch of trail between Sunset and Sunrise Points also accessible.

THINGS TO DO
Free naturalist-led activities (summer): prairie dog and other nature walks, history and geology talks, evening programs, night sky programs, moonlight walks. Also, hiking, guided trail rides (inquire at Bryce Lodge or call 435-679-8665), cross-country skiing, snowshoeing.

OVERNIGHT BACKPACKING
Allowed only on the **Under-the-Rim Trail** near Bryce Point. Purchase permits for $5 at visitor center or, in summer, at nature center.

CAMPGROUNDS
Two campgrounds; 14-day limit. Part of **North** open all year. **Sunset** open May through Sept. Both first come, first served. Fees $10 per night. Showers nearby. Tent and RV sites; no hookups. **Sunset Group Campground** reservations required; contact park. Food services in park.

HOTELS, MOTELS, & INNS
(unless otherwise noted, rates are for 2 persons, double room, high season)

Inside the park:

Bryce Canyon Lodge (south of Utah 12 on Utah 63) Xanterra Parks & Resorts, Bryce Canyon NP, UT 84717. (888) 297-2757 or (435) 834-5361. Cabins, rooms, suites. $110-$130. Rest. Open April through Oct.

Outside the park:

In Bryce, UT 84764:

Best Western Ruby's Inn (on Utah 63). (800) 528-1234 or (435) 834-5341. 368 units. $80-$130. AC, pool, rest.

Bryce Canyon Pines Motel (on Utah 12) P.O. Box 43. (435) 834-5441. 50 rooms; 4 cabins, 1 kitchenette. $75. Pool, rest.

Bryce Canyon Resorts (13500 E Utah 12. (866) 834-0043 or (435) 834-5351. 6 cabins, 3 cottages, 62 rooms. $49-$149. AC, pool, restaurant.

In Panguitch, UT 84759:

Adobe Sands Motel 390 N. Main St., P.O. Box 593. (435) 676-8874. 21 units. $59. AC. Open May through Oct.

Best Western New Western Motel 180 E. Center St., P.O. Box 73. (800) 528-1234 or (435) 676-8876. 55 units. $80. AC, pool.

Color Country Motel 526 N. Main St., P.O. Box 163. (435) 676-2386. 26 units. $48-$52. AC, pool.

monoliths rise close at hand. Some stand isolated like chess pieces; others group together like a Greek chorus. A short hike down the trail takes you right among them—a final immersion course in the effects of erosion before you depart.

An interesting note about the park: Acoustic studies have found that the natural silence in Bryce equals the quality of a sound studio. The park boasts some of the nation's best air quality as well. But naturalists worry that this purity will be threatened by development on adjacent lands.

EXCURSIONS

DIXIE NATIONAL FOREST
CEDAR CITY, UTAH

Four sections of this canyon-country forest fan out across southwestern Utah, featuring unusual rock formations, "stands" of petrified forest, and sections of the historic Spanish Trail. 1,967,129 acres. Hiking, boating, mountain biking, fishing, horseback riding, scenic drives, winter sports, water sports. 27 campgrounds, boat ramp, picnic areas. Open year-round; most campsites open May through Oct. Information in Cedar City on I-15, about 70 miles from Bryce Canyon NP. (435) 865-3700.

CEDAR BREAKS NATIONAL MONUMENT
CEDAR CITY, UTAH

Erosion carved an immense amphitheater in a 10,000-foot southern Utah plateau; in it are extraordinary rock shapes colored by iron and manganese. 6,155 acres. Hiking, scenic drives, winter sports, daily ranger-led activities. 29 campsites, picnic areas, handicapped access. Services and roads closed late fall and winter. Visitor center on Utah 148, about 60 miles from Bryce Canyon NP. (435) 586-9451.

FISHLAKE NATIONAL FOREST
RICHFIELD, UTAH

Fish Lake, hopping with splake and trout (including 35-pound Mackinaw), is only one attraction of this region of dense forests, mountains, and plateaus. The Skyline Trail winds through its 11,000-foot peaks and a large village of the prehistoric Fremont people lies within its boundaries. Over 1.7 million acres. Hiking, boating, fishing, horseback riding, hunting, scenic drives, winter sports. 40 campsites, boat ramp, handicapped access. Open year-round; most campsites open May through October. Information at Richfield, off US 89, about 80 miles from Bryce Canyon NP. (435) 896-9233.

Needles at sunset

CANYONLANDS

UTAH
ESTABLISHED SEPTEMBER 12, 1964
337,598 acres

From the rim you glimpse only segments of the Green River and the Colorado River, which flow together at the heart of Canyonlands. But everywhere you see the water's work: canyon mazes, unbroken scarps, sandstone pillars.

The paths of the merging rivers divide the park into three districts. The high mesa known as the Island in the Sky rises as a headland 2,000 feet above the confluence. South of the Island and east of the confluence is The Needles, where red- and white-banded pinnacles tower 400 feet over grassy parks and sheer-walled valleys. A confusion of clefts and spires across the river to the west marks The Maze, a remote region of pristine solitude. On every side the ground drops in great stairsteps. Flat benchlands end abruptly in rock walls on one side and sheer drops on the other. It is a right-angled country of standing rock, and only a few paved roads probe the edges of the park's 527 square miles.

Sandstone layers of varying hardness make up Canyonland's visible rock. But the character of the land is largely shaped by underlying salt deposits, which, under tremendous pressure from the rock above, push upward, forming domes that fracture the surface.

Yearly rainfall averages 8 inches but varies greatly from year to year. Trees that grow here have to be tough and resilient. In drought years, junipers survive by limiting growth to a few branches, letting the others die. Gnarled juniper and pinyon pine take root in the rimlands wherever soil collects, including slickrock cracks and potholes.

How to Get There

Island in the Sky District: From Moab (35 miles away), take US 191 north 12 miles to Utah 313 and proceed 23 miles southwest to the visitor center.

Needles District: From Moab (75 miles away), follow US 191 south to Utah 211 and then west for 34 miles to park entrance.

Maze District: From Green River, take I-70 west to Utah 24, then south to a well-marked dirt road leading 46 miles to Hans Flat Ranger Station.

Ground shuttles are available from Salt Lake City and Grand Junction, Colo. Air shuttles fly between Canyonlands Airport and Salt Lake City. The airport at Grand Junction is about 115 miles from The Island in the Sky.

When to Go

Spring and fall are ideal for exploring by foot or vehicle. Summer is hot, but humidity low. Snow and cold can make it hard to get around in winter.

How to Visit

The park's isolation and preponderance of backcountry make visiting a spectacular experience, but there are few visitor facilities and paved roads. A four-wheel-drive vehicle will let you explore. If you have only 1 day, visit **The Island in the Sky.** On another day, go to **The Needles** for a chance to explore classic canyon country. With more time, focus on the hiking trails and four-wheel-drive routes to **The Maze** and other remote areas.

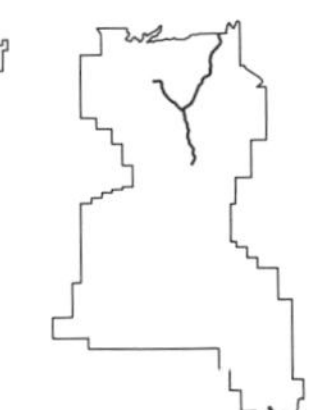

ISLAND IN THE SKY

23 miles; a half to full day

The road enters the park just before you cross **The Neck,** a rock span not much wider than the road that connects the mesa to the rimlands.

For a sweeping view of the park's narrow, interlocked canyons and its wide skies, drive right to the end of the road at **Grand View Point Overlook** (6,080 feet). Directly below in **Monument Basin,** stone columns rise more than 300 feet from the canyon floor.

Hidden in deep gorges to the south, the **Green River** joins the **Colorado River.** During his exploration of the Colorado in 1869, John Wesley Powell scaled the canyon

Snakeweed tussocks along the Colorado

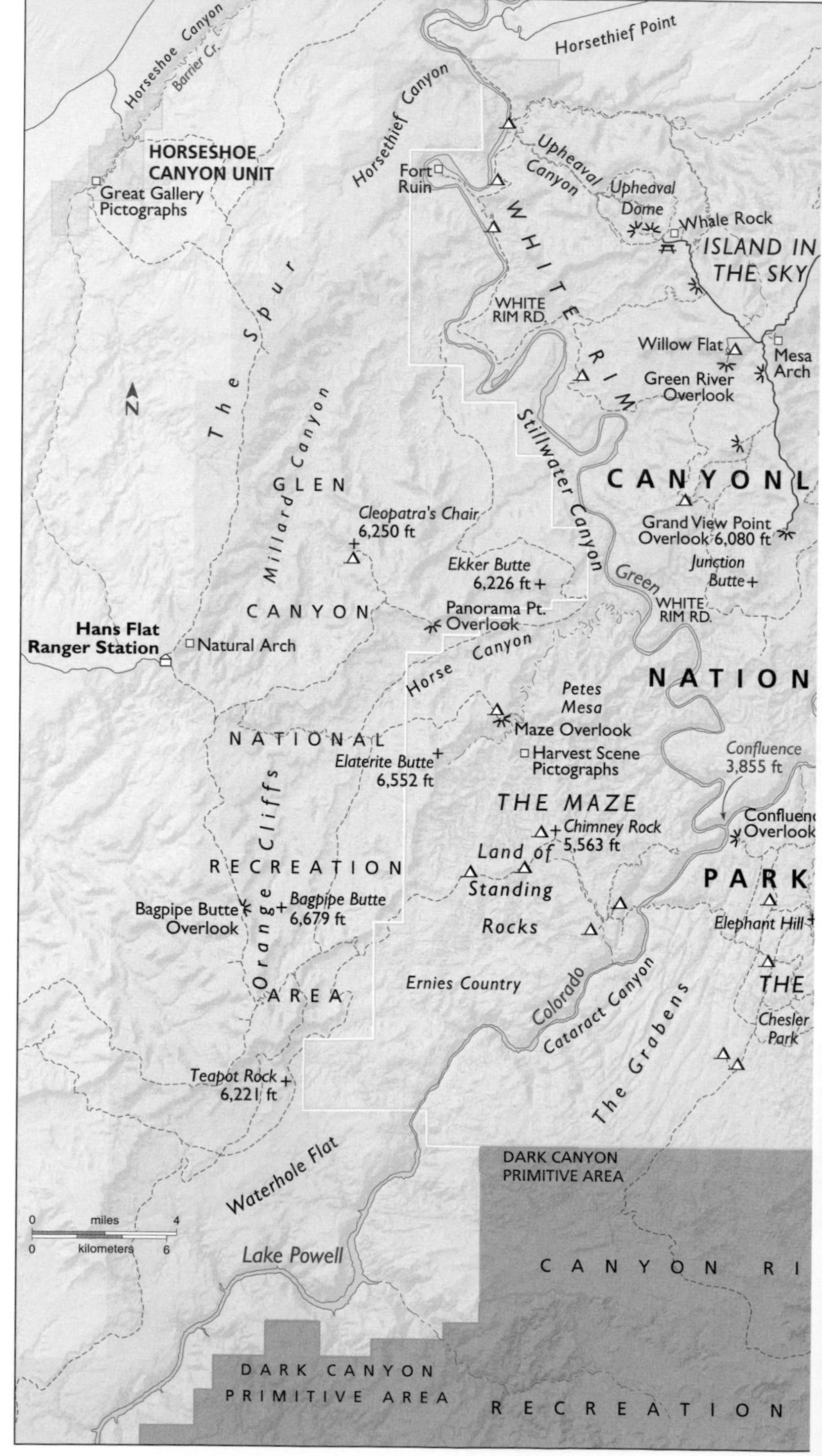
Horseshoe Canyon
Barrier Cr.
Horsethief Point
Horsethief Canyon
HORSESHOE CANYON UNIT
Great Gallery Pictographs
Fort Ruin
Upheaval Canyon
Upheaval Dome
Whale Rock
ISLAND IN THE SKY
WHITE RIM
WHITE RIM RD.
Willow Flat
Mesa Arch
Green River Overlook
The Spur
Millard Canyon
Stillwater Canyon
CANYONL
GLEN CANYON NATIONAL RECREATION AREA
Cleopatra's Chair 6,250 ft
Grand View Point Overlook 6,080 ft
Junction Butte
Ekker Butte 6,226 ft
Green
WHITE RIM RD.
Panorama Pt. Overlook
Hans Flat Ranger Station
Natural Arch
Horse Canyon
NATION
Petes Mesa
Maze Overlook
Harvest Scene Pictographs
Elaterite Butte 6,552 ft
Confluence 3,855 ft
Orange Cliffs
THE MAZE
Confluence Overlook
Chimney Rock 5,563 ft
Land of Standing Rocks
PARK
Bagpipe Butte Overlook
Bagpipe Butte 6,679 ft
Elephant Hill
THE
Ernies Country
Colorado
Cataract Canyon
The Grabens
Chesler Park
Teapot Rock 6,221 ft
Waterhole Flat
DARK CANYON PRIMITIVE AREA
0 miles 4
0 kilometers 6
Lake Powell
CANYON RI
DARK CANYON PRIMITIVE AREA
RECREATION

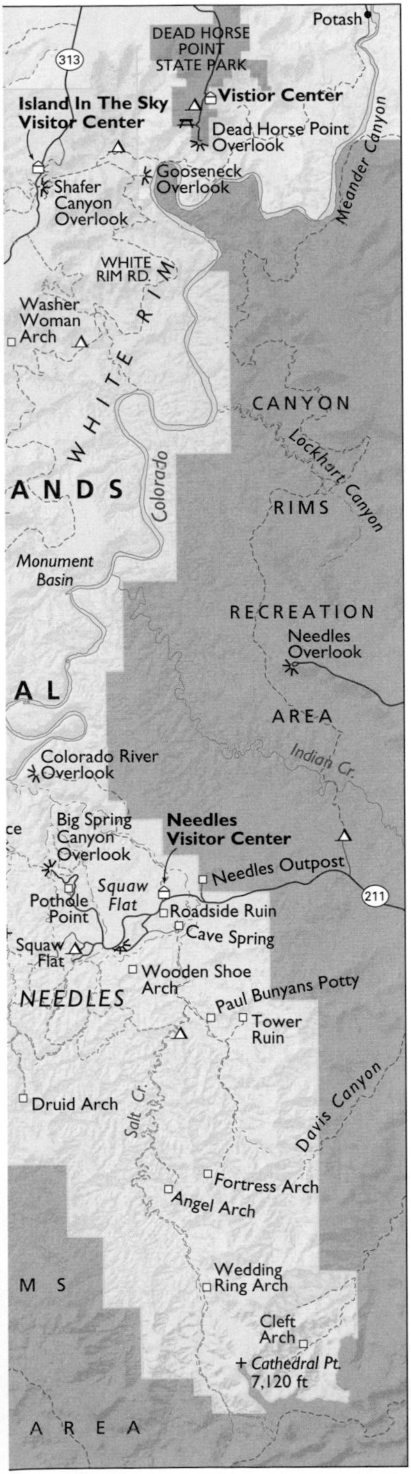

walls at the confluence and discovered a strangely carved landscape. "Wherever we looked," he wrote, "there was a wilderness of rocks."

Drive back the way you came, bypassing **Buck Canyon** and **Murphy Point Overlooks.** Turn left onto the road leading to Upheaval Dome, then follow the paved spur road past Willow Flat Campground to **Green River Overlook.** Here you view a wide expanse of canyon country: Below, a quiet stretch of the Green River runs through **Stillwater Canyon,** with **The Maze** beyond and the **Henry Mountains** topping the distant horizon.

Continue on to **Upheaval Dome,** where the road ends at a good picnic spot shaded by junipers and pinyon pines. Stretch your legs on the half-mile trail to the lip of this unusual geological feature. Here the surface drops into a mile-wide crater enclosed by rock strata upturned in concentric circles, with a center rock spire. Some geologists believe that a

Unusual pictograph called the All-American man

meteorite collided with Earth here. Retrace your path to the main road.

Be sure to pull off at the **Mesa Arch Trailhead.** An easy half-mile loop takes you through a pinyon-juniper woodland to a small natural arch carved from the rim. The curve of the arch frames a magnificent view of the **Washer Woman Arch** and the **La Sal Mountains,** snowy in winter.

Just before leaving the park, stop at the **Shafer Canyon Overlook.** The short trail leads along a promontory above canyons gouged from miles of layered stone. In late afternoon, the rocks seem to ignite in the low angle of the setting sun.

Needles rock formation

THE NEEDLES

35 miles; most of a day

Unless you have decided to camp, you'll probably be driving from Moab, 1.5 hours away, or Monticello, an hour away. The Needles area covers a lattice of canyons, flat-bottomed valleys called grabens, arches, and spectacular sandstone walls notched by rocky spires and columns. To the north, **Island in the Sky** and **Junction Butte** stand silhouetted against the horizon.

Utah 211 will take you directly to The Needles Visitor Center, where a dirt road heads north to the **Colorado River Overlook.** This road makes for rough going; don't take it unless you have a four-wheel-drive vehicle.

Continue on the paved road to the **Roadside Ruin** pull-off. Stretch your legs on a quarter-mile self-guided nature trail that leads to a small but well-preserved granary used by Indians to store corn more than 700 years ago. These ancient farmers were related to the ancestral Puebloans of Mesa Verde and Chaco Canyon. Pick up an interpretive booklet at the trailhead to learn how they used the native plants.

Your next stop will be **Pothole Point,** where a half-mile trail leads past depressions in the sandstone that fill with water after a rain. Although the water looks as still as the rock, the depressions often teem with life. Snails, fairy shrimp, and horsehair worms lay eggs that survive the heat of summer encased in dried mud. When the rains come, they hatch in days.

The road ends at **Big Spring Canyon Overlook,** where squat columns of sandstone rise from barren bedrock. Here the 5.5-mile **Confluence Overlook Trail** climbs the far side of the canyon by a ladder and ends at a point 930 feet above the junction of the rivers. This is a popular trail with most park visitors. More scenic is the 2.5-mile **Slickrock Foot Trail,** which begins just before the road ends at the overlook. If time allows, stop here on your return drive for a moderate hike across slickrock balds of Cedar Mesa sandstone.

Weathered spires of sandstone in The Needles section

Turn on the **Elephant Hill** spur, a graded dirt road that leads to the base of a notorious climb for four-wheel drivers. Along the road are great views of **The Needles.** You see tall fingers of rock arrayed along the skyline, their red- and white- bands created by the interlayering of ancient river deposits with sand dunes. A shaded area at the end of the graded road makes a good place to picnic.

HIKES & FOUR-WHEEL-DRIVE ROUTES

To really explore Canyonlands—85 percent of which is backcountry—you must leave your car and proceed on foot, mountain bike, or by four-wheel-drive vehicle.

In The Needles district, **Chesler Park Trail** leads 2.9 miles to a grassland sunk in a wide rock pocket rimmed by colorful spires. **Druid Arch Trail** branches off at **Elephant Canyon** and leads another 2.4 miles with a short ladder climb to the great arch that resembles a megalithic ceremonial site.

Elephant Hill Trail, a route only for rugged four-wheel-drive vehicles, runs 9 miles to the **Confluence Overlook.** It begins by climbing Elephant Hill's jaw-clenching switchbacks and 40 percent grade and ends with a half-mile walk to the overlook.

White Rim Road in Island in the Sky is one of the park's most popular jeep roads. Near the entrance, the **Shafer Trail** will take you to it. It follows a broad bench, lunar white along the edge where the red talus has been stripped to bedrock. For more than 80 miles it stays above the inner gorge, 1,200 feet below the Island, as it meanders through prime desert bighorn sheep country.

Northwest of The Maze lies a detached section of the park, the **Horseshoe Canyon Unit,** entered by way of a 3.5-mile trail from the boundary fence. You follow an old road into the canyon, then walk up **Barrier Creek** past some of the continent's finest prehistoric rock art. At the **Great Gallery,** ghostly figures painted in red ocher stare through eerie hollow eyes as the centuries pass. Archaeologists believe these life-size pictographs may be more than 3,000, perhaps as much as 6,000, years old.

The **Maze Overlook** can be reached by a 14-mile hike beginning at **North Trail Canyon,** 3.5 rough miles past **Hans Flat Ranger Station.** Reaching the trailhead can be an adventure, but the views from the rim of this isolated wedge of canyon country make it worth the effort. And the quiet is as expansive as the vistas. The trail passes north of **Elaterite Butte** for a tantalizing view into the twists and blind alleys of The Maze.

With a high-clearance four-wheel-drive vehicle you can drive the 34 miles from **Hans Flat** to the overlook. This is one of the park's classic jeep routes. Negotiating steep switchbacks allows the driver little chance to sightsee, and with winter snows the route becomes impassable.

La Sal Mountains through Mesa Arch

Pothole Point in The Needles

INFORMATION & ACTIVITIES

HEADQUARTERS

2282 S.W. Resource Blvd., Moab, UT 84532. Phone (435) 719-2313. www.nps.gov/cany

SEASONS & ACCESSIBILITY

Park open year-round. Flash floods from July through September can temporarily close dirt and gravel roads.

VISITOR & INFORMATION CENTERS

Moab boasts a large multiagency visitor center (805 N. Main St.; 435-259-8825 or 800-635-6622). Visitor centers by entrances to **The Island in the Sky** and **The Needles,** and at **Hans Flat Ranger Station,** just outside park near The Maze, open all year. **Headquarters** is 3 miles south of Moab.

ENTRANCE FEE

$10 per vehicle good for 7 days, multiple entries. Annual permit $25, also good at Arches National Park and Natural Bridges and Hovenweep National Monuments.

PETS

Must be leashed at all times. Not allowed on hiking trails, in river corridors, or on backcountry roads.

FACILITIES FOR DISABLED

The visitor centers and Moab headquarters are wheelchair accessible.

THINGS TO DO

Free naturalist-led activities: nature walks, interpretive exhibits. Hiking, boating, rafting (permit needed), bicycling. Contact park for list of concessioners offering four-wheel-drive (some areas require permit), mountain biking, hiking, and river-running trips.

SPECIAL ADVISORIES

- Always carry water when hiking—at least a gallon per person per day. Water available near Squaw Flat Campground and at visitor centers.
- Use care near cliff edges and on slickrock surfaces; falls often fatal.
- Do not walk on cryptobiotic crust; it is a fragile, crunchy, black soil that is composed of living plants.

OVERNIGHT BACKPACKING

Permits and reservations (fee) required for backpacking and four-wheel-drive trips. May be obtained at visitor centers or ranger stations. For information on reservations, call (435) 259-4351.
Campsites along the **White Rim Trail,** in Island in the Sky, are available to mountain bikers and campers in four-wheel-drive high-clearance vehicles.

CAMPGROUNDS

Two campgrounds, **Squaw Flat** and **Willow Flat,** both with 14-day limit. Open all year, first come, first served; March to October filled by midmorning. Fees $5-$10 per night. No showers. Tent and RV sites; no hookups. Three group campsites in **The Needles;** reservations required; contact park headquarters. No food services inside park.

HOTELS, MOTELS, & INNS

(unless otherwise noted, rates are for 2 persons, double room, high season)

In Moab, UT 84532:

Best Western Green Well Motel 105 S. Main St. (800) 528-1234 or (435) 259-6151. 72 units. $69-$139. AC, pool, rest.

Big Horn Lodge 550 S. Main St. (800) 325-6171 or (435) 259-6171. 58 units. $80. AC, pool, restaurant.

Cedar Breaks Condos Center and 4th E. (800) 505-5343 or (435) 259-5125. 6 2-bedroom units, all with full kitchens. $98-$146. AC.

Pack Creek Ranch (15 miles southeast of Moab, off La Sal Mountain Loop Rd.) 505 N. Main St. (435) 259-5505. Cabins, houses, bunkhouses. $95-$300. Trail rides for fee. AC, pool.

Ramada Inn—Moab 182 S. Main St. (800) 272-6232 or (435) 259-7141. 82 units. $89-$139. AC, pool, restaurant.

In Monticello, UT 84535:

Best Western Wayside Inn 197 E. Central Hwy. 491. (800) 633-9700 or (435) 587-2261. 38 units. $70. AC, pool.

Triangle H Motel 164 E. Central Hwy. 491. (800) 657-6622 or (435) 587-2274. 26 units. $42-$44. AC.

For other area accommodations, contact Utah's Canyonlands Region, P.O. Box 550-R9, Moab, UT 84532. (800) 635-6622 or (435) 259-8825.

EXCURSIONS

WESTWATER CANYON
MOAB, UTAH

The names of the rapids on this 17-mile section of the Colorado River tell all: Skull, Sock-it-to-Me, Last Chance. Only experienced boaters (18 and over) should attempt them; permits *(fee)* and reservations required. Sights: natural arches, mining ruins, a desperadoes' hide-out, and many bird species. Hiking, boating, fishing, picnic areas, swimming. Primitive camping (limited to 1 night), boat ramp, picnic areas. Open all year. Information at Westwater, about 80 miles northeast of Canyonlands NP. (435) 259-7012.

HENRY MOUNTAINS BUFFALO HERD
HANKSVILLE, UTAH

This herd's 375 bison roam to 11,000 feet in summer. 150,000 acres. Hiking, climbing, rockhounding, hunting, picnicking, horseback riding, scenic drives (high-clearance 4x4s only). 3 campgrounds, primitive camping. Open all year. Information Mon. through Fri. at Hanksville BLM, Utah 24 and 95, 110 miles west of Canyonlands NP. (435) 542-3461.

NATURAL BRIDGES NATIONAL MONUMENT
LAKE POWELL, UTAH

Three natural bridges here represent different states of development: youth, maturity, and old age. First discovered by white men in 1883, the three bridges bear Hopi names: Sipapu, Kachina, and Owachomo. Site also features ancestral Puebloan ruins and what was once the world's largest photovoltaic power system. 7,779 acres. 13 campsites (may fill early), primitive campsites, picnic area, scenic drive. Trails may be impassable in winter; campsites open all year. Visitor center on Utah 275, 4 miles off US 95, about 95 miles from Canyonlands NP. (435) 692-1234.

GLEN CANYON NATIONAL RECREATION AREA

PAGE, ARIZONA

The centerpiece of Glen Canyon NRA is Lake Powell, 186 miles of the Colorado River backed up behind one of the world's highest dams. The lake and the desert and canyons around it offer memorable experiences for boaters, anglers, hikers, and campers. Fishing for bass, black crappie, catfish, walleye available; trout thrive below the dam. Free dam tours. 1,217,403 acres, most in Utah. Fishing, hunting (in season with permit), boating (rentals available), water sports. Tent and RV campsites, 6 marinas, lodging, food services, picnic areas, boat ramp, handicapped access. Area and campsites open all year. Adjoins Canyonlands NP and Grand Staircase-Escalante NM to the north. (928) 608-6404.

RAINBOW BRIDGE NATIONAL MONUMENT

PAGE, ARIZONA

To the Navajo this 290-foot-high pink sandstone bridge is a sacred "rainbow of stone." Rough foot- or horse trails lead to it through the Navajo reservation (permits required)—a vigorous trip for the fit only. Most visitors to the world's largest natural bridge boat in from Lake Powell in Glen Canyon NRA (see above), via Halls Crossing, Bullfrog, Wahweap, or Hite Marinas. 160 acres.

Layers of rock uplifted and exposed on the west face of Waterpocket Fold

CAPITOL REEF

UTAH
ESTABLISHED DECEMBER 18, 1971
241,904 acres

The unifying geographic feature of Capitol Reef is the Waterpocket Fold. For a hundred miles its parallel ridges rise from the desert like the swell of giant waves rolling toward shore. Exposed edges of the uplift have eroded into a slickrock wilderness of massive domes, cliffs, and a maze of twisting canyons.

Geologists know the fold as one of the largest and best exposed monoclines on the North American continent. Travelers know it as a place of dramatic beauty and serenity so remote that the nearest traffic light is 78 miles away. And even though its 378 square miles are off the beaten track, the park still attracts nearly 750,000 visitors each year.

Capitol Reef is named for a particularly colorful section of the fold where rounded Navajo sandstone forms capitol-like domes and sheer cliffs form a barrier to travel, often referred to to as a "reef." Although a highway now crosses the "reef," travel is still challenging for those wishing to see the park's more remote regions.

The southern end of the fold offers fine wilderness backpacking in Lower Muley Twist Canyon and Halls Creek Narrows. Along the park's northern border lies Cathedral Valley, a repository of quiet solitude where jagged monoliths rise hundreds of feet.

The middle region is best known. Here the raw beauty of the towering cliffs contrasts with the green oasis that 19th-century Mormon pioneers created along the Fremont River, establishing the village of Fruita. Their irrigation ditches still water fruit trees in fields abandoned by Fremont Indians 700 years ago. Mule deer now graze on orchard grasses and alfalfa, and park visitors harvest the apples, peaches, and apricots.

The most striking reminder of the Fremont culture is the fine rock art it produced. Figures resembling bighorn sheep crowd many petroglyph panels. The last sighting in the park of a native desert bighorn, a subspecies, occurred in 1948. Their disappearance is attributed to overhunting and various diseases caught from domestic sheep. The Park Service reintroduced desert bighorn sheep in 1984, 1996, and 1997. These herds have survived.

How to Get There

From Green River (about 85 miles away), take I-70 to Utah 24, which leads to the east entrance. For a scenic approach, start at Bryce Canyon National Park. Follow Utah 12 over Boulder Mountain to Utah 24, just outside the park's west entrance. Airport: Salt Lake City.

When to Go

Year-round. Spring and fall are mild and ideal for hiking. Winter is cold but brief. Back roads can become impassable during spring thaw, summer rains, and winter snows at higher elevations.

How to Visit

On a 1-day visit, take Utah 24 along the **Fremont River** and then the **Scenic Drive** through the heart of the park. This section offers fine hiking on nearly 40 miles of developed trails. The best second-day activity is a drive along portions of the **Burr Trail Loop** with a walk to **Strike Valley Overlook.** For a longer stay, drive the **Cathedral Valley Loop** or hike in one of the more remote canyons of the **Waterpocket Fold.** Always check road, trail, and weather conditions.

FREMONT RIVER & SCENIC DRIVE

35 miles; a half to full day

Drive east on Utah 24 as you enter the park from the west. Ahead of you rises the eroded west face of the **Waterpocket Fold,** a massive line of cliffs running north and south. After the first few miles, the highway follows the course cut through the rock wilderness by the swift Fremont River, named for frontier explorer John C. Frémont.

Take the unpaved spur road to the **Goosenecks Overlook.** From the parking area an easy 0.1-mile trail ends above the deeply entrenched meanders of **Sulphur Creek.** Another short walk takes you to **Sunset Point** for a sweeping view of the **Capitol Reef** section of the Waterpocket Fold.

Imposing Chimney Rock

Take the Chimney Rock turnoff to the 3.5-mile **Chimney Rock loop trail.** The trail provides an opportunity to get up close and personal with some of Capitol Reef's most interesting geology. The trail begins with a steep climb to the rim high above Chimney Rock, a pinnacle of red Moenkopi Formation protected from erosion by a golden Shinarump cap. The trail loops back around through the gray-green and maroon Chinle Formation famous for exposures of colorful petrified wood.

Stop at the visitor center on the edge of **Fruita,** the remnants of the Mormon frontier community settled in the 1880s and now part of the national park. Be sure to see the 10-minute slide show—the view of the red sandstone cliffs from the theater window is itself worth the stop.

Take the 25-mile round-trip **Scenic Drive** along the rugged face of Capitol Reef. This paved road follows a century-old wagonway known as the Blue Dugway. The old road was used by Indians, outlaws, gypsies, and once even the devil himself, according to an early pioneer who chased him off by brandishing the *Book of Mormon.* Take the short spur road into **Grand Wash.** Look high on the cliff rim for **Cassidy Arch** named for outlaw Butch Cassidy, who reportedly used the canyon as a hideout. A 2.25-mile trail from the parking area leads down Grand Wash through spectacular narrows to the Fremont River. Another trail climbs 1.75 miles to Cassidy Arch. The Scenic Drive ends with a winding 2-mile spur road into **Capitol Gorge.** This was the main road through the reef before 1962. It now ends at a parking area where an easy 1-mile trail continues down into the canyon to historic inscriptions and a series of natural waterpockets, popular among desert denizens.

Fruita orchards along the Fremont River

Return by the same road to Fruita, then go east on Utah 24, passing well-maintained orchards. Turn in at the **Petroglyphs** pull-off. Here Fremont Indians pecked into the cliff large humanlike figures in headdresses. Since you can view this cliff art only at a distance, binoculars come in handy; spotting scopes are mounted on the main panel boardwalk.

The origin of these Indian farmers about A.D. 600 and their disappearance six centuries later are still mysteries. Early settlers found what appeared to be remnants of their irrigation ditches, granaries, and pithouses. One unusual discovery was a brick of tule sugar, grass seeds, and pulverized grasshoppers—thought to have been emergency food.

Continue down the highway a short distance to the **Hickman Bridge** parking area. Stretch your legs with a 1-mile hike up a self-guided nature trail that leads under the natural bridge, 125 feet above. For a longer and more arduous hike, take the 2.25-mile **Rim Overlook Trail** along the cliff tops. It ends at a 1,000-foot drop to the Fremont River, providing a good vantage point to view the green pocket of Fruita enclosed in a landscape of tilted rock.

Farther along the road, pull off at the **Behunin Cabin.** This one-room

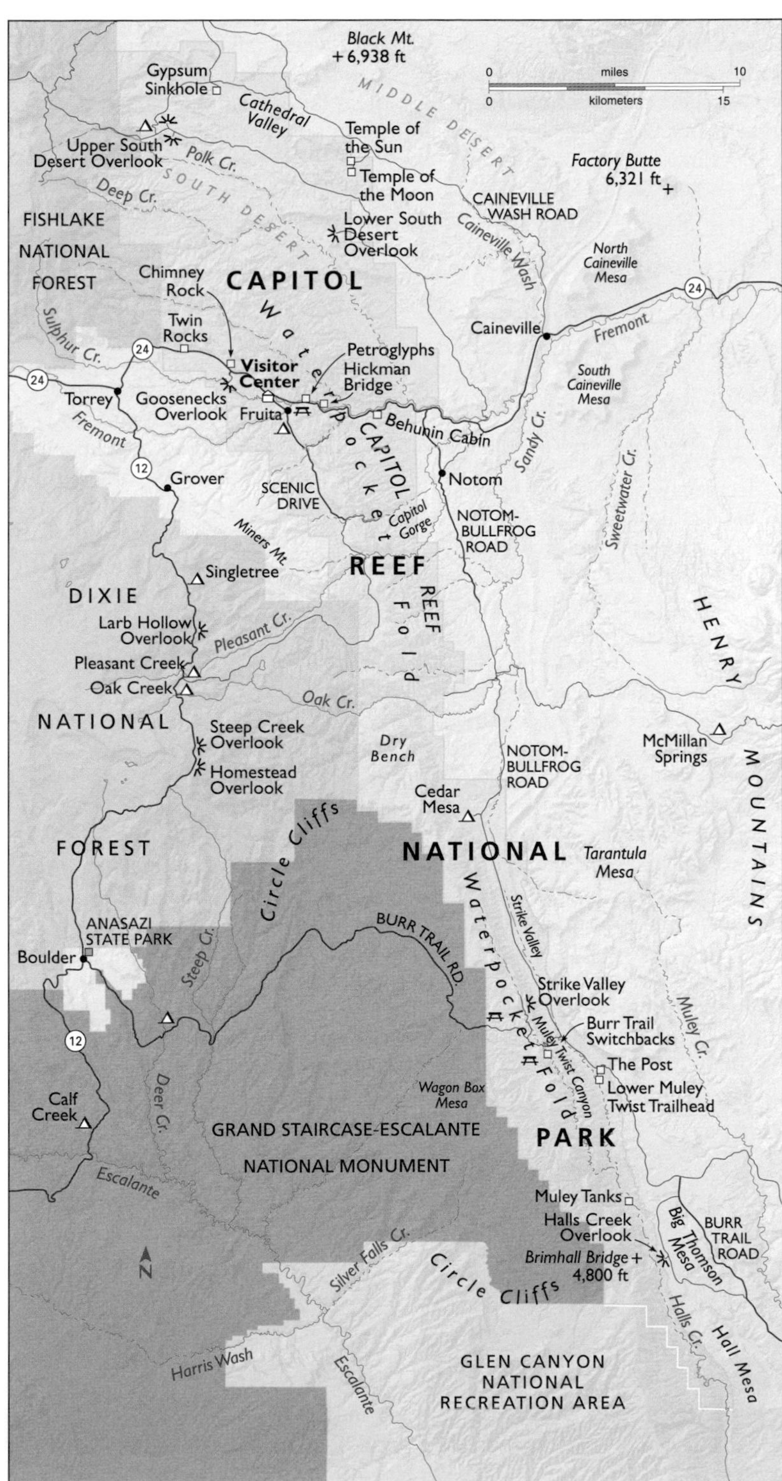
Black Mt.
6,938 ft
Gypsum Sinkhole
Cathedral Valley
MIDDLE DESERT
Temple of the Sun
Temple of the Moon
Upper South Desert Overlook
Polk Cr.
SOUTH DESERT
Deep Cr.
Factory Butte
6,321 ft
CAINEVILLE WASH ROAD
Caineville Wash
Lower South Desert Overlook
North Caineville Mesa
FISHLAKE NATIONAL FOREST
Chimney Rock
CAPITOL
Waterpocket
Twin Rocks
Sulphur Cr.
24
Petroglyphs
Hickman Bridge
Visitor Center
Caineville
Fremont
South Caineville Mesa
Torrey
Goosenecks Overlook
Fruita
Behunin Cabin
Fremont
CAPITOL
Sandy Cr.
12
Grover
Notom
SCENIC DRIVE
Capitol Gorge
NOTOM-BULLFROG ROAD
Sweetwater Cr.
Miners Mt.
Singletree
REEF
REEF Fold
DIXIE
Larb Hollow Overlook
Pleasant Cr.
HENRY
Pleasant Creek
Oak Creek
Oak Cr.
NATIONAL
Steep Creek Overlook
Homestead Overlook
Dry Bench
McMillan Springs
MOUNTAINS
NOTOM-BULLFROG ROAD
Cedar Mesa
Circle Cliffs
FOREST
NATIONAL
Tarantula Mesa
Waterpocket Fold
Strike Valley
ANASAZI STATE PARK
BURR TRAIL RD.
Boulder
Steep Cr.
Strike Valley Overlook
Burr Trail Switchbacks
Muley Twist Canyon
The Post
Lower Muley Twist Trailhead
Muley Cr.
Calf Creek
Deer Cr.
Wagon Box Mesa
GRAND STAIRCASE-ESCALANTE NATIONAL MONUMENT
PARK
Escalante
Muley Tanks
Halls Creek Overlook
Big Thomson Mesa
BURR TRAIL ROAD
Brimhall Bridge
4,800 ft
Silver Falls Cr.
Circle Cliffs
N
Halls Cr.
Hall Mesa
Harris Wash
Escalante
GLEN CANYON NATIONAL RECREATION AREA
0 miles 10
0 kilometers 15

stone cabin was once home to a family of ten. The parents and the two youngest children slept inside, the girls in a wagon box outside, and the boys in a nearby rock alcove.

BURR TRAIL LOOP

125 miles; at least a full day

The drive begins at the visitor center. Go east on Utah 24 to **Notom-Bullfrog Road.** Paved for the first several miles of its southbound route, the road becomes dirt, skirting the uplift where rock has pushed skyward at 70-degree angles. It crosses several washes that turn into slot canyons where they cut into the east flank of the Waterpocket Fold.

At the junction with **Burr Trail Road,** you must decide whether to return to the visitor center (half-day trip) or take a full day to complete the loop. If you decide to continue, turn west and climb a series of spectacular switchbacks to the high rim of the fold. Views of the **Henry Mountains** to the east, and **Burr Canyon** straight below, are dramatic.

One of the finest vistas in the park is the **Strike Valley Overlook** in the **upper Muley Twist Canyon.** Many visitors walk the 2.5 miles from the hikers' parking area to the overlook trailhead through a beautiful canyon with double arches and a large rock window on the rim. High-clearance, four-wheel-drive vehicles can follow the canyon floor to a parking area near the overlook. From the parking area the trail continues up the canyon another 6.5 miles, passing several large arches.

Those looking for solitude can backpack into **lower Muley Twist Canyon** and its miles of fine slickrock wilderness (free backcountry permits required; available at visitor center). Bends in the canyon are so tight, early teamsters said, a mule had to twist itself to get through.

Burr Trail Road becomes paved as it leaves Capitol Reef and continues west to the town of Boulder. Turn north on paved Utah 12, which winds up and over **Boulder Mountain** through a high alpine forest. Here you join Utah 24 about 10 miles west of the visitor center.

CATHEDRAL VALLEY LOOP

70 miles; a half to full day

A high-clearance, two- or four-wheel-drive vehicle is recommended for this scenic trip; check unpaved road conditions before setting out. Follow Utah 24 for 11 miles east of the visitor center. At a marked crossing, turn off Utah 24 and ford the Fremont River. If the river is too high for your vehicle, use the Caineville access to reach Cathedral Valley.

Autumn colors

Spring vegetation near Freemont River

INFORMATION & ACTIVITIES

HEADQUARTERS
HC 70 Box 15, Torrey, UT 84775. Phone (435) 425-3791. www.nps.gov/care

SEASONS & ACCESSIBILITY
Park open year-round. Many roads are unpaved. The Scenic Drive may close briefly during rainy weather and in winter. Driving dirt roads, including Cathedral Valley Loop, may require high-clearance or four-wheel-drive vehicles. Call headquarters or ask at visitor center for latest weather and road conditions.

VISITOR & INFORMATION CENTERS
The **visitor center** on Utah 24 at the north end of park is open all year. Phone headquarters for information.

ENTRANCE FEE
$5 per car per week.

FACILITIES FOR DISABLED
The visitor center, restrooms, and the Petroglyphs Trail are accessible to wheelchairs.

THINGS TO DO
Free ranger-led activities: evening programs. Also available, interpretive exhibits, auto tour, hiking, fruit picking, bird-watching. For information on horseback trips, jeep tours, and other recreational activities, contact the Wayne County Travel Council at (800) 858-7951.

SPECIAL ADVISORIES
• Always carry water, even on short hikes. Except for tap water, most water in park is not drinkable.
• Watch out for flash floods between July and September.
• Let someone know your itinerary.

OVERNIGHT BACKPACKING
Permits required. They are free and can be obtained at the visitor center or from any park ranger.

CAMPGROUNDS
Three campgrounds, all with 14-day limit. Open year-round on a first-come, first-served basis. Fees $10 per night. No showers. Tent sites at **Cathedral Valley** and **Cedar Mesa.** Tent and RV sites at **Fruita;** no hookups.

HOTELS, MOTELS, & INNS
(unless otherwise noted, rates are for 2 persons, double room, high season)

In Bicknell, UT 84715:
Aquarius Inn 240 W. Main St. (435) 425-3835. 28 units, 2 with kitchenettes. $48. AC, RV park, restaurant.
Sunglow Motel 63 E. Main St., P.O. Box 68. (435) 425-3821. 15 units, most with AC. $32. Restaurant.
In Torrey, UT 84775:
Capitol Reef Inn 360 W. Main St., P.O. Box 100. (435) 425-3271. 10 units. $44. Restaurant. Open Easter through October.
Wonderland Inn Utah 12 at Utah 24. (800) 458-0216 or (435) 425-3775. 50 units. $54-$86. AC, pool, restaurant.

For a more complete list of accommodations near the park, write or call park headquarters or visit the park website.

As the road heads north, it passes through the colorful badlands of the **Bentonite Hills** and follows a mesa called **The Hartnet** to the edge of a 400-foot escarpment overlooking **South Desert.** On the mesa's opposite side is a spectacular view into **Upper Cathedral Valley.** In this vast open space, keep a lookout for soaring golden eagles.

Eroded spires and monoliths of Entrada sandstone jut 500 feet from the valley floor like enormous weathered teeth. The road loops to the south and drops among the formations, following the valley past such landmarks as the **Walls of Jericho,** the **Gypsum Sinkhole,** and the **Temples of the Sun** and **Moon.** The drive ends at Utah 24, near Caineville.

Isis Temple from Hopi Point on the West Rim

GRAND CANYON

ARIZONA

ESTABLISHED FEBRUARY 26, 1919

1,217,403 acres

The road to the Grand Canyon from the south crosses a gently rising plateau that gives no hint at what is about to unfold. You wonder if you have made a wrong turn. All at once an immense gorge a mile deep and up to 18 miles wide opens up. The scale is so vast that even from the best vantage point only a fraction of the canyon's 277 miles can be seen.

Nearly five million people travel here each year; 90 percent first see the canyon from the South Rim with its dramatic views into the deep inner gorge of the Colorado River. So many feet have stepped cautiously to the edge of major overlooks that in places the rock has been polished smooth. But most of the park's 1,904 square miles are maintained as wilderness. You can avoid crowds by hiking the park's many trails or driving to the cool evergreen forests of the North Rim where people are fewer and viewing is more leisurely.

The Grand Canyon boasts some of the nation's cleanest air, with visibility averaging 90 to 110 miles. Increasingly, though, air pollution blurs vistas that once were sharp and rich hued. Hazy days have become more common, with visibility dropping as low as 40 miles. Haze from forest fires and pollen has always been present, but the recent increase is traced to sources outside the park, like copper smelters and urban areas in Arizona, southern California, and even Mexico.

It's hard to look at the canyon and not be curious about geology. Rock that dates back 1.8 billion years lies at the bottom. Exactly how the river formed the canyon is still unclear, but geologists generally agree that most of the cutting occurred within the last five million years.

How to Get There

South Rim: From Flagstaff, Arizona (about 80 miles away), take US 180 skirting the San Francisco Peaks to South Rim entrance, or take US 89 to Cameron, then Ariz. 64 with views of the Little Colorado River Gorge to Desert View entrance.

North Rim: Take Ariz. 67 from Jacob Lake through the Kaibab National Forest to North Rim entrance. The two rims are 10 air miles apart but 215 miles by car, a 5-hour drive. Airports: Grand Canyon near South Rim; Flagstaff; Las Vegas; Phoenix.

When to Go

South Rim is open all year; North Rim facilities are closed from mid-October to mid-May. Ariz. 67 usually closes due to deep snows late November to mid-May. Hikers and mule riders to the inner canyon, where temperatures reach 118°F, prefer spring and fall; the prime river season is April through October. During summer on the South Rim, time your visit to midweek, arriving early to avoid the crowds.

How to Visit

On a 1-day visit to the South Rim take the **Hermit Road** west of the village for classic views of the main canyon. The drive is closed to automobiles March through November, but free buses take you to the overlooks. The best second-day activity is the **Desert View Drive** tour east of Mather Point for great views of the Colorado River and eastern canyon.

On a longer stay, take the North Rim's **Cape Royal Road** for broad panoramic vistas. You may also enjoy a hike on a backcountry trail; a mule ride down the **Bright Angel Trail**; a week-long raft trip through the canyon on the **Colorado River**; and a scenic flight for a bird's-eye view of the canyon. The mule and raft trips and backcountry hikes require reservations far in advance.

SOUTH RIM: HERMIT ROAD

8 miles; at least a half day; closed to vehicles March through November

Begin at the **Canyon View Information Plaza** near Mather Point with its classic panoramic view into the heart of the Grand Canyon. Great solitary buttes rise from narrow ridges reaching out from the distant North Rim. Far below, a green cluster of Fremont cottonwood trees marks **Phantom Ranch,** a lodge and campground reached only by mule or foot. The observation station at nearby **Yavapai Point** explores the canyon's geological history and identifies major landmarks. If bad weather threatens, duck into its glass-enclosed observation room and watch as storm clouds roll in.

Board the free Hermits Rest Route bus, which travels along Hermit Road between the information center and Hermits Rest from March through November. Skirting the rim of the canyon for 8 miles, it offers superb views of the **Colorado River** and the labyrinth of side canyons and broad platforms below

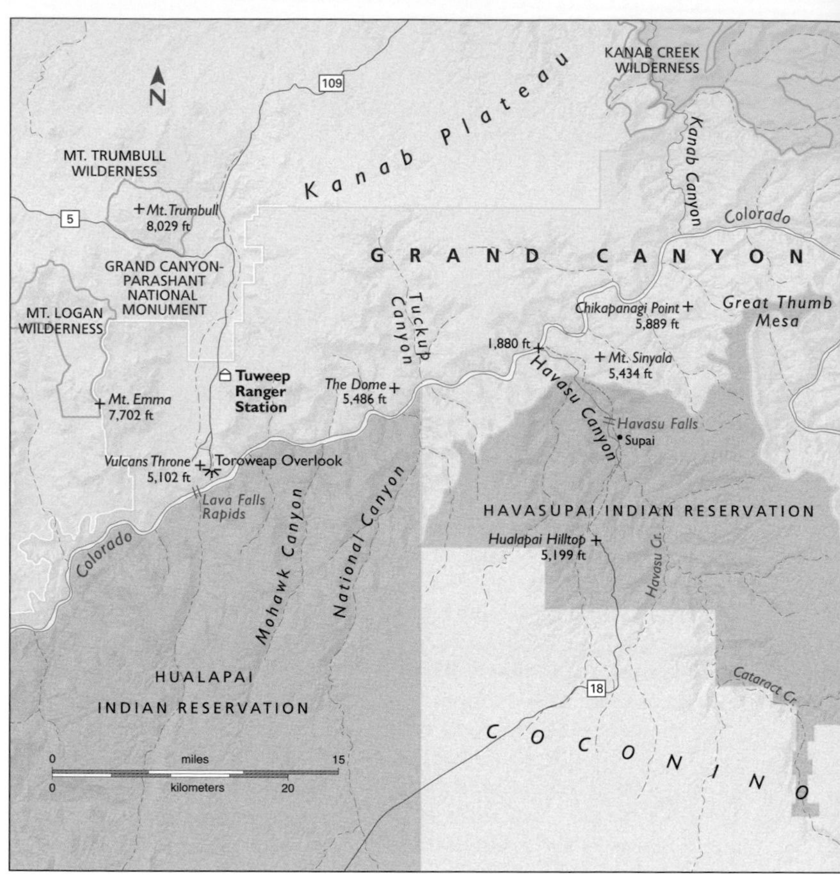

the rim. The buses can be crowded at peak times of day.

The first stop is the **Trailview Overlook.** Here you get a hint of the canyon's size. To the south, the historic **El Tovar Hotel** and **Bright Angel Lodge** look small and insignificant perched on the brink of the great precipice. Mule strings and hikers file along the **Bright Angel Trail** as it zigzags 8 miles and 4,460 feet down to the river.

Don't miss **Hopi Point,** a promontory jutting deep into the gorge. Magnificent views 45 miles both eastward and westward make this an ideal spot for watching sunset or sunrise. To avoid crowds, leave the main overlook and walk along the **Rim Trail** (see p. 185) to find your own observation point. Across the river rise the intricately carved walls of **Isis Temple** and tree-topped **Shiva Temple,** described as "the grandest of all buttes."

The bus route continues west, passing **Mohave Point** and skirting breathtakingly close to **The Abyss,** where a sheer cliff plunges 3,000 feet to a plateau below. From here the road follows the sweep of the rim out to **Pima Point,** where you see the Colorado River threading through the deep gorge. On a still day you can hear the distant rumble of **Granite Rapids** almost a mile below. What looks like a stream from above is a river 300 feet wide that, with its tributaries, drains 8 percent of the continental U.S.

The road ends at **Hermits Rest,** a limestone building that looks as if

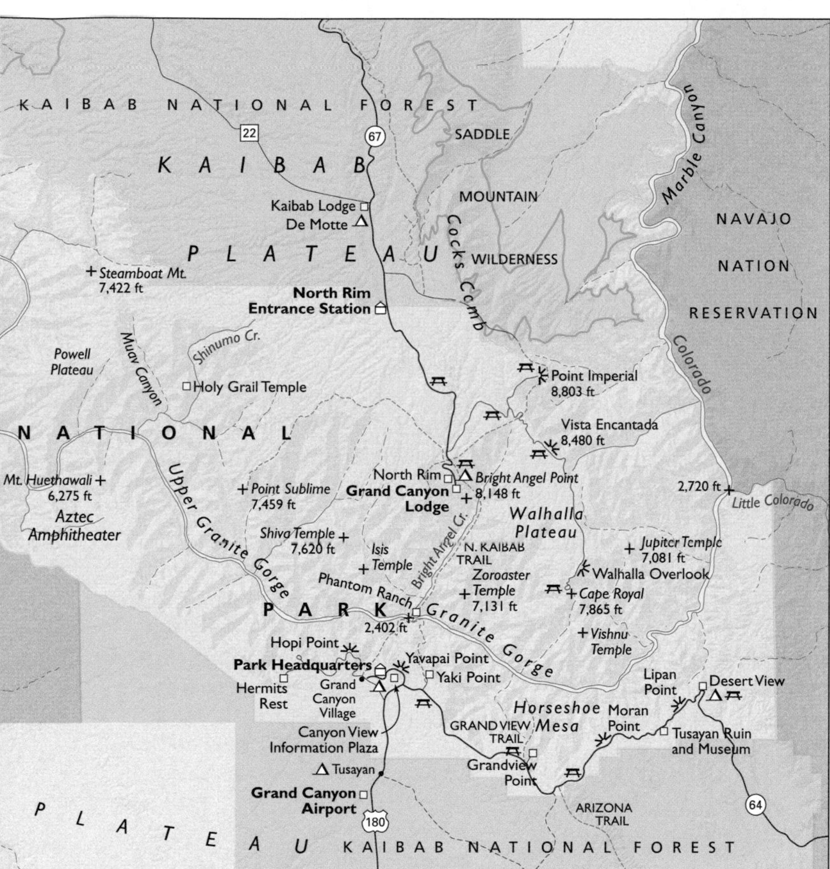

Hobbits built it on the canyon's rim; it serves as a curio shop. Those with time and stamina can hike partway down the steep **Hermit Trail** to **Dripping Springs,** 7 miles and 6 to 9 hours round-trip. Here one of the earliest guides to the Grand Canyon, Louis Boucher, raised goldfish in a watering trough at the turn of the 20th century. It's a good place to see some of the canyon's 315 species of birds. Permits are not needed for day hikes, but first ask a park ranger for conditions and advisories. On the return, buses stop only at Mohave and Hopi Points.

For the adventurous, the **Rim Trail** hugs the canyon's edge for nearly 11 miles from Mather Point to Hermits Rest, roughly paralleling Hermit Road. The path is paved to **Maricopa Point;** the rest is dirt. The trail is generally level except for a steep stretch between the village and Trailview. Short hikes can be combined with rides by catching the shuttle bus at any of the main overlooks. You can also pick up the bus at the the trail's end for an easy return.

SOUTH RIM: DESERT VIEW DRIVE

23 miles, a half to full day

Desert View Drive (Ariz. 64) begins just south of Mather Point. The drive skirts the rim eastward for 23 miles to **Desert View,** providing numerous pull-offs for long views of the main canyon. In summer, parking at the major overlooks can be a problem, so between March and November only the park shuttle is allowed on the Yaki Point/South Kaibab Trailhead road. (Board at the Canyon View Information Center.) Along the roadside are shaggy-barked Utah juniper and low clumps of Gambel oak.

Yaki Point provides a fine view of the darkly shining **Granite Gorge,** the innermost canyon. The imposing pyramid-shaped profile of **Vishnu Temple,** 7,500 feet high, dominates the eastern skyline. The practice of naming major park landforms after world deities began with Clarence Dutton, who published a classic report on the geology of the Grand Canyon in 1882.

On the way back to the main road you can leave the shuttle and hike the **South Kaibab Trail,** which switchbacks down the west side of Yaki Point. Allot a third of your time for going down and two-thirds for hiking back up. The trail eventually reaches the Colorado River at the bottom of the canyon, but a strenuous 3-mile, 2.5-hour roundtrip takes you only partway down to **Cedar Ridge.** Even though you drop 1,140 vertical feet, none of the major landforms of the canyon look any closer. Fossil ferns lie exposed in the bedrock on the west side of Cedar Ridge.

Return to your car and follow the main road as it climbs into a tall ponderosa forest. Take the turnoff to **Grandview Point,** one of the finest vistas on the South Rim. From the overlook, **Grandview Trail** (occasionally closed due to rain) drops a rugged 3 miles to **Horseshoe Mesa,** where miners once worked copper ore from the Last Chance Mine. John Hance, a prospector known for his tall tales and quick wit, led the first sightseeing parties into the canyon near here in the 1880s. On one trip a woman with a knowledge of botany described to him how trees breathe. "You know," Hance said, "that explains something that has puzzled me a long time; I used to make camp under a big mesquite tree, and night after night that thing would keep me awake with its snoring."

Drive farther east to **Moran Point** for the best view of one of the Colorado's major rapids. Here you look directly down on **Hance Rapids;** its rocky 30-foot drop is considered by river guides to be among the most difficult to run. Continue on down the road, and if you need a change of pace, stop at the small **Tusayan Museum.** It displays well-designed exhibits of Indian cultures, and the nearby ruins offer a self-guided tour of an excavated ancestral Puebloan village from A.D. 1185.

Take your time when you reach **Lipan Point,** the finest view of the eastern canyon. Here the Colorado River makes a great bend to the west, where it has carved through the **Kaibab Plateau** to form the deepest portion of the Grand Canyon. Below, the river makes an S-curve around **Unkar Delta,** which prehistoric people extensively farmed.

Bypass **Navajo Point** and continue on to **Desert View,** where you might stop at the snack bar and curio shop. While here, climb the stairs to the top of the 70-foot **Watchtower,** built in 1932. On the tower's walls Indian artist Fred Kabotie painted murals depicting Hopi legends.

NORTH RIM: CAPE ROYAL ROAD

23 miles; a half to full day

Averaging a thousand feet higher than the South Rim, the North Rim's alpine vegetation and more varied vistas appeal to many travelers. Still, you won't find the South Rim crowds here. The focus is the historic **Grand Canyon Lodge,** built in the 1920s on the lip of the canyon and rebuilt after a disastrous fire in 1932. From its Sun Room you'll get an excellent view of **Bright Angel Canyon** incised 11 miles into the plateau and overshadowed by **Deva, Brahma,** and **Zoroaster Temples.**

Pick up a self-guiding pamphlet from the box by the log shelter near the parking lot. Follow one of the paved trails to **Bright Angel Point,** which divides a side canyon called **The Transept** from **Roaring Springs Canyon.** Listen for the sound of the springs cascading from a cave 3,000 feet below the rim. This is a fine spot for watching sunrise or sunset. Those needing to stretch their legs can take the **Transept Trail,** 1.5 miles along the nearly level canyon rim, or a short hike on the **North Kaibab Trail** (1 mile down takes you 650 feet beneath the rim—and that mile back up feels like 3).

From the lodge, drive north 3 miles to the **Cape Royal Road,** one of the most scenic drives in the park. It passes through forests of spruce, fir, locust, and ponderosa pine mixed with stands of quaking aspen, and through lovely meadows of blue lupine and scarlet bugler. Long-eared mule deer often bound across the road, and you might glimpse the reclusive white-tailed Kaibab squirrel found only in the North Rim forests on the Kaibab Plateau.

Those looking for a dramatic sunrise perch can turn off onto the 3-mile road to **Point Imperial,** at 8,803 feet the highest viewpoint on either rim. Here amid tall evergreens you look across the canyon to the high plateau of the Navajo Indian Reservation. Evidence of a 2000 fire is evident in this vicinity (you probably spotted more evidence along the first portion of Cape Royal Road). Return to the main road and continue on, passing through the forested **Walhalla Plateau.** Stop at **Vista Encantada** for superb views of the northeastern canyon and the carved pinnacles of **Brady** and **Tritle Peaks.**

The road ends at a parking lot on **Cape Royal.** A paved half-mile nature trail leads along a narrow peninsula past **Angels Window,** an opening eroded through the rock spur that frames the river below. Watch your children. From the overlook **Wotans Throne** and Vishnu Temple dominate the foreground. Across the canyon rise the **Palisades of the Desert.** The unusually broad vista here provides a fine vantage point to watch the sun set and to absorb what naturalist John Burroughs described as Grand Canyon's "strange new beauty."

MULE, RIVER, & AIR TRIPS

If the extremely challenging hike to the canyon floor (8 miles down the Bright Angel Trail and 6.5 miles on the steeper South Kaibab Trail) is not for you, consider going by

North Rim aspen in fall foliage

Hikers on bridge along the North Kaibab Trail

muleback. (Though mule trips are not for everyone either—acrophobes especially!) Mules leave the South Rim for day trips and overnights at **Phantom Ranch,** which accommodates guests in rustic cabins and dormitories. The ranch lies in a deep gorge of the inner canyon near the confluence of Bright Angel Creek and the Colorado River. The creek's clear waters are known for their excellent trout fishing (license required). The lodge is the only place within the canyon where you can spend the night without camping, and it serves as a good base for hikes up Bright Angel Canyon. Advance reservations—as much as 6 months ahead for mule trips—are necessary.

Many regard a raft trip through the Grand Canyon as the experience of a lifetime. Long, quiet stretches through the scenic heart of the canyon are broken by more than 150 major rapids, three of which are consistently rated 10 on a scale of 10. Most trips stop for day hikes at waterfalls, Indian ruins, and interesting side canyons. A number of river companies offer the raft trips, which generally take 1 to 2 weeks; some companies offer partial trips. Write the park or check the park website for a list of the companies; reserve well in advance.

Companies giving helicopter and airplane tours are based at Grand Canyon Airport. Flights are no longer allowed below the rim, and because of safety and noise concerns, use of the canyon's airspace is being regulated.

CARVING THE GRAND CANYON

What looks timeless is constantly changing: The Grand Canyon's variegated layers encode two billion years of Earth's history.

Thousands of feet thick, the rock formed from sediments. About 1.8 billion years ago, cataclysmic geological forces crumpled and uplifted this rock to create a range of mountains that towered probably 5 to 6 miles high. (1)

The tremendous heat and pressure recrystallized the rock to schist; molten material from deep inside Earth oozed up, forcing itself into the rock and hardening into veins of pink granite. Over eons, wind and water gnawed the mountain range into a plain, and a primordial sea submerged it. Again, sediments wafted to the sea bottom, solidifying into rock; magma continued to well up from inside the Earth. (**2**)

About a billion years ago, Earth shuddered again, cracking its crust into giant fault blocks that tilted upward to form a second range of mountains. (**3**) The rains, frosts, and winds of millions of years wore away these mountains also.

Much of the Grand Canyon rock visible today (blue layers, **4**) accumulated over the schist in the last 600 million years. During some ages the region sank beneath advancing seas; primitive shellfish fossilized in sea bottoms that hardened to shale. During other periods the restless region rose. Topping the Grand Canyon today—about 8,000 feet above sea level—is a layer of cream-colored limestone, approximately 300 feet thick, which was formed from the remains of countless corals, sponges, and other marine animals.

In recent geological time (about six million years ago) the young, southward-flowing Colorado River—perhaps later captured by the ancestral Hualapai River encroaching from the west—began to slice into the upper layers of the canyon. Gouging inch by inch over the centuries, the river eventually reached the schist 4,000 feet below the rim and continued to cut. (**5**) Water still wears away at the massive gorge, ever widening and ever deepening the canyon's floor and walls.

INFORMATION & ACTIVITIES

HEADQUARTERS
P.O. Box 129, Grand Canyon, AZ 86023. Phone (928) 638-7888. www.nps.gov/grca

SEASONS & ACCESSIBILITY
South Rim open all year. North Rim roads often close due to snow mid-November to mid-May. For weather and road information, call (928) 638-7888.

VISITOR & INFORMATION CENTERS
Canyon View Information Plaza near Grand Canyon Village open all year. Call (928) 638-7888. **North Rim Visitor Station** open mid-May to mid-November. Call (928) 638-7864.

ENTRANCE FEE
$20 per car for 7 days; $10 per person arriving on foot, bike, or motorcycle.

PETS
Allowed, leashed, on rim trails, but not below rim. Kennels available; call (928) 638-0534.

FACILITIES FOR DISABLED
Visitor center and some shuttle buses are wheelchair accessible. Free brochures available. Hermit Road open to vehicles carrying disabled persons, with permit. Call ahead to make arrangements, (928) 638-0591.

THINGS TO DO
Free ranger-led activities: day and evening nature walks, slide shows, talks, cultural demonstrations, and campfire programs. Also, mule trips into canyon, hiking, bicycling, fishing, river rafting, air tours, cross-country skiing. For activities, call (928) 638-7888. Write headquarters for list of concessioners offering wide variety of tours. An Imax Theater featuring *Grand Canyon: The Hidden Secrets* is located a mile south of the South Rim Entrance, on Ariz. 64. (928) 638-2468.

SPECIAL ADVISORY
• Be very careful near the rim; protective barriers are intermittent.
• Due to elevation, heat, dry humidity, and steep trails, you should carry water, eat salty snacks, avoid hiking at peak temperatures, and rest often.

OVERNIGHT BACKPACKING
Permits required; $10 fee plus $5 per person per night. Backcountry Information Center, P.O. Box 129, Grand Canyon, AZ 86023. (928) 638-7875.

CAMPGROUNDS
Four campgrounds, 7-day limit, 3 on South Rim, 1 on North Rim. **Mather** open all year; reservations recommended March to December; reserve through the National Parks Reservation Service (see p. 10); other times, first come, first served. **Desert View** (first come, first served) and **North Rim** (reservations recommended) mid-May to mid-Oct. **Trailer Village** open all year; reservations recommended; contact Xanterra Parks & Resorts (303) 297-2757. Fee $24 per night. Showers at North Rim and near Mather campground. Tent and RV sites at all campgrounds; hookups only at Trailer Village. Two group campgrounds; must reserve. Food services in park.

HOTELS, MOTELS, & INNS
(unless otherwise noted, rates are for 2 persons in a double room, high season) The properties inside the park are operated by Xanterra Parks & Resorts (888) 297-2757. www.xanterra.com. Reservations recommended 6 to 9 months in advance. For same-day reservations, try (928) 638-2631.

INSIDE THE PARK (On South Rim):
Bright Angel Lodge & Cabins 89 units, some share baths. Cabins $82-$238; rooms $49-$299. Rest.
El Tovar Hotel 78 units. $129-$299. AC, rest.
Kachina Lodge 49 units. $122-$132. AC.
Maswik Lodge 278 units. Cabins $73 (June-Aug.); rooms $76-$120. Rest.
Thunderbird Lodge 55 units. $ 122-$132.
Yavapai Lodge 358 rooms. $92-$109. Rest. Open Mar.-Oct.
(On North Rim):
Grand Canyon Lodge (303) 297-2757. 209 units. $93-$124. Rest. Open mid-May–mid-Oct.
(In the canyon):
Phantom Ranch (reached by hiking, mule, or raft trips) Dorm $30 per night. Cabin $80 per night. Mule trip $366, incl. cabins and meals. AC, rest., shared showers. Reserve up to 23 months ahead.

EXCURSIONS

LAKE MEAD NATIONAL RECREATION AREA

BOULDER CITY, NEVADA

Lake Mead, water impounded from the Colorado River by Hoover Dam, is the center of this NRA, the nation's first (established in 1936). More than 2,000 bighorn sheep roam the desert canyons and plateaus surrounding the reservoir. 1,501,216 acres, part in Arizona. Boating, fishing, naturalist programs, water sports. 1,021 campsites, 191 rooms, picnic areas, food services, handicapped access. Open all year. Adjoins Grand Canyon NP on west. Visitor center at US 93 and Lakeshore Dr., about 280 miles from Grand Canyon's South Rim entrance. (702) 293-8906.

WUPATKI NATIONAL MONUMENT

FLAGSTAFF, ARIZONA

Nearly nine hundred years ago, people moved to the Wupatki area to farm the volcanic soil. Little more than a century later they left behind extensive accomplishments, including a 100-room pueblo, amphitheater, ball court, and pottery. 35,422 acres. Hiking, picnicking, scenic drives. Open all year. Off US 89, about 65 miles southeast of Grand Canyon NP. (928) 679-2365.

CANYON DE CHELLY NATIONAL MONUMENT

CHINLE, ARIZONA

These spectacular red-rock canyons, spires, and mesas rival any natural site in the Southwest. The same is true of their cultural legacy: ancient Basketmaker pithouses, the remains of ancestral Puebloan dwellings on 1,000-foot cliffs, and the many reminders of the Navajo past and present. Authorized Navajo guides offer tours into the canyons; only the White House ruin may be visited without a guide. 83,840 acres. Hiking, horseback riding, jeep tour, scenic drives. 93 campsites, food services, handicapped access. Open all year. Off US 191, about 230 miles east of Grand Canyon NP. (928) 674-5500.

Boulder field near Wheeler Peak

GREAT BASIN

NEVADA

ESTABLISHED OCTOBER 27, 1986

77,180 acres

An Ice Age landscape of glacier-carved peaks rises more than a mile from the desert floor. The park takes its name from the vast region that extends east from California's Sierra Nevada to Utah's Wasatch Range, and from southern Oregon to southern Nevada, encompassing most of Nevada and western Utah. Called Great Basin by explorer John C. Frémont in the mid-1800s, the region actually comprises not one but at least 90 basins, or valleys, and its rivers all flow inland—not to any ocean.

The park road winds up Wheeler Peak, the second highest mountain in Nevada. When the road ends at 10,000 feet, trails lead to the 13,063-foot summit and to the region's only glacier, near a stand of bristlecone pines. Great Basin is a young park compared to a Yellowstone or Yosemite, yet within its confines are some of the world's oldest trees.

The bristlecones form the rear guard of a Pleistocene forest that once covered much of the region. Now surviving in scattered stands, some trees are 3,000 years old—alive when Tutankhamun ruled Egypt.

In the flank of the mountain, at an altitude of 6,800 feet, lies Lehman Caves with 1.5 miles of underground passages. These formed when higher water tables during the Ice Age made pockets in the limestone. Park rangers guide visitors past flowstone, stalactites, and delicate white crystals that grow in darkness.

The number of visitors has reached more than 80,000 yearly since 1986, when the cave and neighboring mountains became a national park. But the park has 65 miles of trails, offering access to the hills and a chance to see glacial moraines, alpine lakes, and spectacular sweeping views of the surrounding basin and range country.

How to Get There

From Las Vegas (about 300 miles away), take I-15 to US 93, then US 50 to Nev. 487. At Baker, take Nev. 488 to the park entrance. From Salt Lake City, Utah (about 250 miles away), take I-15 to US 50, then Nev. 487 to Baker and Nev. 488 to the park entrance. Airport: Ely (about 67 miles away).

When to Go

Great Basin is open year-round, but the upper 8 miles of Wheeler Peak Scenic Drive (beyond Upper Lehman Creek Campground) are closed November to May, or as long as heavy snows makes it impassable. In summer, the most popular time, temperatures are generally mild. September and October bring cool weather and smaller crowds. Hikers must beware of sudden thunderstorms that can catch them on exposed ridges at any time of year. The best time to view Wheeler Peak is in early morning. In winter, visitors enjoy excellent cross-country skiing.

How to Visit

On a 1-day visit, take the **Wheeler Peak Scenic Drive** for dramatic views of high alpine landscapes. On your way back, stop at **Lehman Caves** for a chance to walk underground through intriguing passages.

Remember that the alpine world is fragile. At these elevations, plants grow slowly and their margin of survival is narrow. Stay on established roads and trails to avoid inadvertently damaging these areas.

WHEELER PEAK SCENIC DRIVE

12 miles; 1.5 hours to most of a day

This paved road climbs steeply from the visitor center to the Wheeler Peak Campground at 10,000 feet *(vehicles longer than 24 feet not recommended)*. Those not used to mountain driving may find both the view and the drive breathtaking. The road passes from the tough, drought-resistant pinyon-juniper woodland into the high-elevation forest of Engelmann spruce, limber pine, and aspen.

Begin the scenic drive near the visitor center. A short trail at the first pull-off takes you to the historic **Osceola Ditch,** built in the late 1880s to carry water for hydraulic gold

Ancient bristlecone pine on Mount Washington

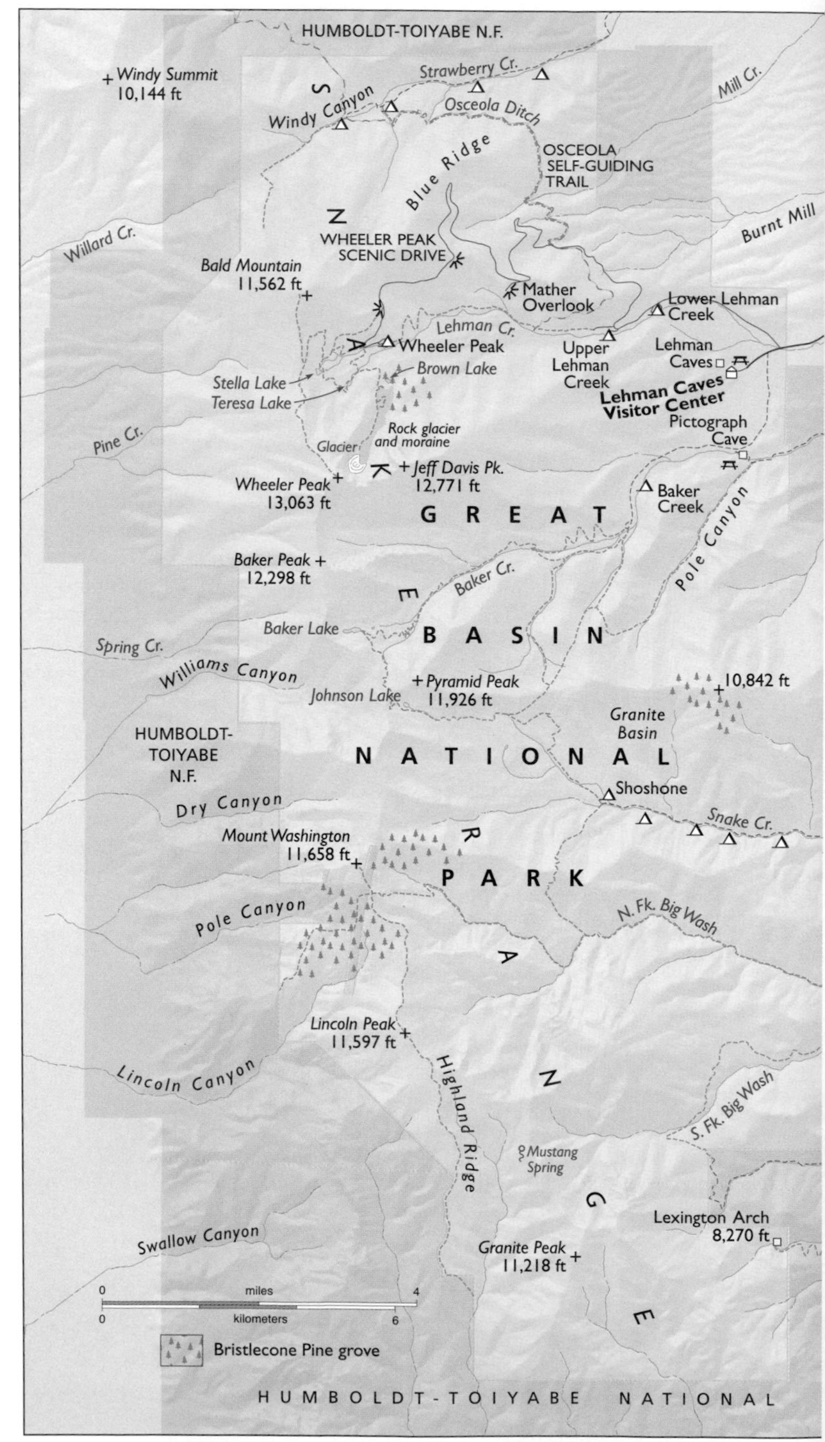
HUMBOLDT-TOIYABE N.F.
Windy Summit 10,144 ft
Strawberry Cr.
Windy Canyon
Osceola Ditch
Mill Cr.
OSCEOLA SELF-GUIDING TRAIL
Blue Ridge
Burnt Mill
Willard Cr.
WHEELER PEAK SCENIC DRIVE
Bald Mountain 11,562 ft
Mather Overlook
Lower Lehman Creek
Lehman Cr.
Wheeler Peak
Upper Lehman Creek
Lehman Caves
Brown Lake
Stella Lake
Teresa Lake
Lehman Caves Visitor Center
Pictograph Cave
Pine Cr.
Rock glacier and moraine
Glacier
Jeff Davis Pk. 12,771 ft
Wheeler Peak 13,063 ft
Baker Creek
S N A K E R A N G E
GREAT BASIN NATIONAL PARK
Pole Canyon
Baker Peak 12,298 ft
Baker Cr.
Baker Lake
Spring Cr.
Williams Canyon
Pyramid Peak 11,926 ft
Johnson Lake
10,842 ft
Granite Basin
HUMBOLDT-TOIYABE N.F.
Shoshone
Dry Canyon
Snake Cr.
Mount Washington 11,658 ft
Pole Canyon
N. Fk. Big Wash
Lincoln Peak 11,597 ft
Highland Ridge
Lincoln Canyon
S. Fk. Big Wash
Mustang Spring
Lexington Arch 8,270 ft
Swallow Canyon
Granite Peak 11,218 ft
0 miles 4
0 kilometers 6
Bristlecone Pine grove
HUMBOLDT-TOIYABE NATIONAL

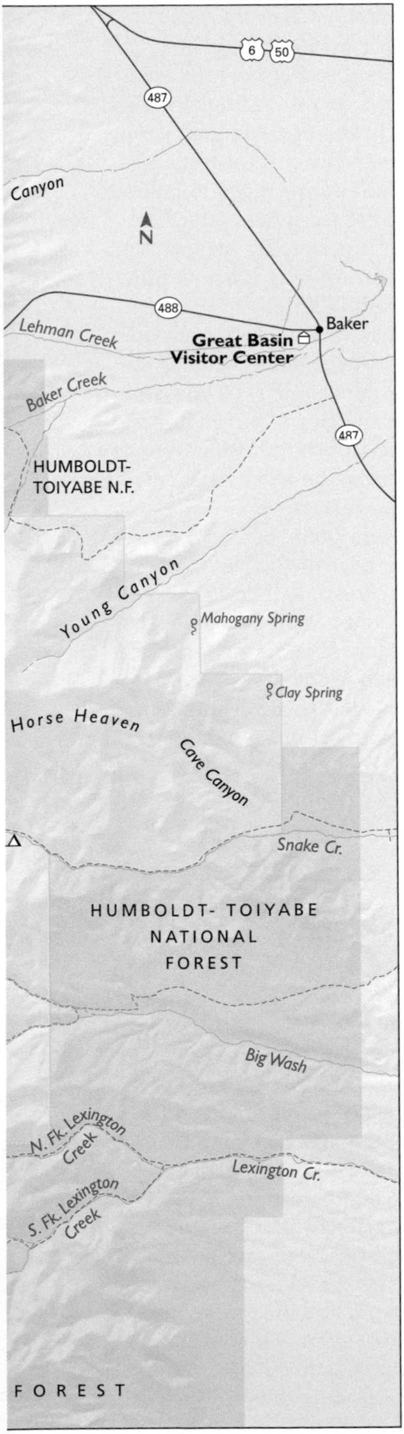

6
50
487
Canyon
N
488
Lehman Creek
Baker
Great Basin
Visitor Center
Baker Creek
487
HUMBOLDT-
TOIYABE N.F.
Young Canyon
Mahogany Spring
Clay Spring
Horse Heaven
Cave Canyon
Snake Cr.
HUMBOLDT- TOIYABE
NATIONAL
FOREST
Big Wash
N. Fk. Lexington
Creek
Lexington Cr.
S. Fk. Lexington
Creek
FOREST

Parry's primrose near alpine Stella Lake *(top)*
Blue columbine on Baker Lake Trail *(bottom)*

mining. Save this for your next trip, if pressed for time.

Skip the **Mather Overlook,** but notice the old stand of mountain mahogany. These usually grow as a shrub but here reach tree height. Pull off at **Peak Overlook** for spectacular views of **Wheeler Peak** on the right and **Jeff Davis Peak** on the left. The north face of Wheeler drops 1,800 feet to a glacier below. Snow often dusts the jagged walls of gray quartzite.

The road ends at Wheeler Peak Campground, where you have your choice of several fine walks. One of the most popular follows the 3-mile

Alpine Lakes Loop Trail past **Stella** and **Teresa Lakes.** This leads you to a dramatic alpine setting with a barren, sawtooth ridge rising above the smooth surface of the lake.

If time and stamina allow, follow the **Wheeler Summit Trail** to the ridge above the lakes for an overview of the park and sweeping views of Great Basin's seemingly endless succession of mountain ranges. The trail leaves the Alpine Lakes Loop Trail near Stella Lake and climbs another 3,000 feet to the summit. Once above tree line, watch for sturdy alpine flowers like primrose and phlox. And be prepared for harsh weather. A terse entry in the summit register reads, "Wind took no prisoners."

Just as spectacular is the 3-mile **Bristlecone/Glacier Trail.** This leaves from Teresa Lake and takes you to **Wheeler Cirque,** a glacier-hollowed valley enclosed by sheer cliffs. At the far end lies the glacier, the Great Basin's only permanent one and one of the southernmost in the country.

Before reaching the glacier be sure to take the **Bristlecone Forest Loop.** This self-guided trail passes ancient trees with twisted trunks carved and polished by wind-driven snow and ice. Nearby a tree called Prometheus lived for almost 5,000 years until it was cut down in 1964, prior to the park's creation, as part of a climate study. Even after most of its trunk and branches die, a bristlecone pine can continue to survive, sustained by very little moisture. The tree holds onto its needles for 20 to 30 years, assuring stable photosynthesis regardless of environmental stress.

LEHMAN CAVES

0.6 mile; 1.5 hours

Guided cave tours began in 1885 with Absalom Lehman, a miner turned rancher. Over the years dozens of legends have grown around his discovery of the cave. One claims he was racing along on horseback when he suddenly dropped through the entrance. He lassoed a tree and managed to hold on until rescued 4 days later. The hard part was keeping his legs wrapped around the horse to prevent it from falling.

Tour tickets must be purchased 1 day in advance (either stop by the visitor center or call 775-234-7331). You have a choice of three tours: 90 minutes ($9) 60 minutes ($6) or 30 minutes ($2), the latter visits only the Gothic Palace.

Meet your guide behind the visitor center near the cave entrance. The attraction of Lehman Caves—a single cavern despite its name—lies in the beauty of its formations, well represented in the first room you visit, the **Gothic Palace.** The cave is so filled with columns, draperies, and stalactites that the first explorers used sledgehammers to break through them. Because of the cave's manageable scale, you get closeup views of bizarre helictites and delicate aragonite crystals.

The walkway takes you past fine examples of rare cave shields. These large disks grow from cracks in the ceiling where seeping water deposits minerals in flat, circular forms. Continuing deeper, you reach two of the cave's most beautiful rooms. Rimstone pools and soda straws decorate the **Lake Room;** shields, massive columns, and bacon-rind draperies fill the **Grand Palace.**

A small variety of cave life makes its home here, including pack rats, cave crickets, and the rare pseudoscorpion—an arachnid with scorpionlike pinchers. Bats, however, stay away, finding the cave's vertical entrance too hard to negotiate.

Salactites and Stalagmites in the Gothic Palace, Lehman Caves *(top)*; Bristlecone pines worn smooth by centuries of wind, sand, and ice *(center)*; New-growth bristlecones and needles *(bottom left)*; Sage covered slopes and Spring Valley *(bottom right)*

INFORMATION & ACTIVITIES

HEADQUARTERS
100 Great Basin National Park, Baker, NV 89311. Phone (775) 234-7331. www.nps.gov/grba

SEASONS & ACCESSIBILITY
Park open year-round. Snow may cover high-elevation trails until late June or July. Some park roads require four-wheel-drive vehicles. Call headquarters about current trail and road conditions.

VISITOR & INFORMATION CENTERS
Lehman Caves Visitor Center, located at Park Headquarters; **Great Basin Visitor Center** located in Baker, NV. Open all year. Phone park headquarters number for visitor information.

ENTRANCE FEE
None for park. Fee for cave tours.

PETS
Permitted on leashes except in visitor center, caves, backcountry, and on trails.

FACILITIES FOR DISABLED
Visitor center and the first room in Lehman Caves are wheelchair accessible, as are some campsites.

THINGS TO DO
Ranger-led activities: free nature walks and talks, exhibits, movie, campfire programs. Also available: cave tours, Wheeler Peak Scenic Drive, hiking, fishing (license required), climbing, and cross-country skiing.

SPECIAL ADVISORIES
• Park's high elevation can cause altitude sickness. People who have heart or respiratory problems should take it slowly.
• Don't expect to find water sources along the trails; always carry drinking water when hiking.
• Watch out for rattlesnakes along trails.
• Summer thunderstorms are common; check weather conditions with park before setting off on a hike.

OVERNIGHT BACKPACKING
Those heading out to the backcountry should stop at the park's visitor center and complete the free permit registration form. In addition to helping to ensure visitor safety, permits allow the park to monitor how its resources are being used.

CAMPGROUNDS
Four campgrounds, all with 14-day limit, all first come, first served. **Baker Creek** and **Upper Lehman Creek** open mid-May through October. **Wheeler Peak** open mid-June through September. **Lower Lehman Creek** open all year. Snowstorms may close campgrounds occasionally. No showers. Tent and RV sites; no hookups. Food services in the park. Potable water available year-round at visitor center, and in summer at RV sanitary station, picnic areas, and developed campgrounds.

HOTELS, MOTELS, & INNS
(unless otherwise noted, rates are for 2 persons, double room, high season)

In Baker, NV 89311:
The Border Inn (on US 50) P.O. Box 30. (775) 234-7300. 28 units. $29-$39. AC, restaurant, RV park.
Silver Jack Motel (on Main St.) P.O. Box 69. (775) 234-7323. 10 units. $65. AC.

In Ely, NV 89301:
Bristlecone Motel 700 Ave. I. (800) 497-7404 or (775) 289-8838. 31 units. $46-$50. AC.
Historic Hotel Nevada and Gambling Hall 501 Aultman St. (775) 289-6665. 60 units. $25-$85. AC, restaurant.
Jailhouse Motel and Casino 5th and High Sts. (800) 841-5430 or (775) 289-3033. 61 units. $30-$85. AC, rest.
Fireside Inn Motel 2 miles north of Ely, H33 Box 33400. (800) 732-0288 or (775) 289-3765. 14 units. $45. AC.
Ramada Inn and Copper Queen Casino 805 Great Basin Blvd. (800) 851-9526 or (775) 289-4884. 65 units. $79-$92. AC, pool, restaurant.

For a complete list of accommodations contact the White Pine Chamber of Commerce. (775) 289-8877.

EXCURSIONS

HUMBOLDT-TOIYABE NATIONAL FORESTS

ELKO, NEVADA

This immense national forest is the largest in the continental United States. Contains glacier-carved Lamoille Canyon, historic mining towns, and Jarbridge Wilderness, in Nevada, one of the country's least used wilderness areas. About 6,300,000 acres. Hiking, boating, fishing, horseback riding, hunting, scenic drives, winter sports, water sports. 1,000 campsites, boat ramp, picnic areas, handicapped access. Open year-round; most campsites open late May through September. The forest's Snake Division surrounds Great Basin NP. (775) 355-5340.

DESERT NATIONAL WILDLIFE REFUGE

LAS VEGAS, NEVADA

Wildlife is the focus of this Mojave Desert refuge, just a roll of the dice from Las Vegas. Bighorn sheep, mule deer, coyotes, and some 260 species of birds are found in the refuge, the largest in the lower 48. 1,600,000 acres. Primitive camping, hiking, hunting, scenic drives (high-clearance vehicle recommended). Open year-round. Interpretive kiosk at Corn Creek Field Station entrance, off US 95, about 250 miles from Great Basin NP. (702) 879-6110

SPRING MOUNTAIN NATIONAL RECREATION AREA

LAS VEGAS, NEVADA

Many people are surprised to find a forest so close to Las Vegas: The Spring Mountains rise to almost 12,000 feet from the harsh desert of southern Nevada. The cool mountain forests are home to a wilderness of ponderosa pine, sheer limestone cliffs, and assorted wildlife. About 316,000 acres. Camping, scenic drives, hiking, wildlife viewing. Picnic areas. Take US 95 to the Kyle Canyon turnoff (Nev. 157). About 250 miles from Great Basin NP. (702) 515-5400.

Winter at Cliff Palace, a 13th-century ancestral Puebloan site

MESA VERDE

COLORADO
ESTABLISHED JUNE 29, 1906
52,074 acres

At Mesa Verde, Spanish for "green table," multistoried dwellings fill the cliff-rock alcoves that rise 2,000 feet above Montezuma Valley. Remarkably preserved, the cliff dwellings cluster in canyons that slice the mesa into narrow tablelands. Here, and on the mesa top, archaeologists have located more than 4,800 archaeological sites (including 600 cliff dwellings) dating from about A.D. 550 to 1300.

The sites, from mesa-top pithouses and multistoried dwellings to cliffside villages, document the changes in the lives of a prehistoric people once dubbed the Anasazi. They are now more accurately called the ancestral Puebloans, and modern Pueblo tribes in the Southwest consider themselves descendants of these ancestral people. Some 40 pueblos and cliff dwellings are visible from park roads and overlooks; many of these are open to the public.

Beginning about A.D. 750, the ancestral Puebloans grouped their mesa-top dwellings in pueblos, or villages. About 1200 they moved into recesses in the cliffs. So sheltered, these later villages seem to stand outside of time, aloof to the present.

In 1888 two cowboys tracking stray cattle in a snowstorm stopped on the edge of a steep-walled canyon. Through the flakes they made out traces of walls and towers of a large cliff dwelling across the canyon. Novelist Willa Cather later described the scene: "The falling snowflakes sprinkling the piñons, gave it a special kind of solemnity. It was more like sculpture than anything else ... preserved ... like a fly in amber."

Climbing down a makeshift ladder, the excited cowboys explored the honeycombed network of rooms that they named Cliff Palace. Inside, they found stone tools, pottery, and other artifacts in rooms that had been uninhabited for some 600 years.

Why the Mesa Verde people eventually left their homes may never be known. Indeed, they lived in the cliff dwellings for only about the last 75 to 100 years of their occupation of Mesa Verde. Early archaeologists guessed warfare, and the evidence for this is still being debated. Archaeologists also think they may have been victims of their own success. Their productive dry farming allowed the Mesa Verde population to grow perhaps as high as 5,000. Gradually woodlands were cut, wild game hunted out, and soils depleted. Years of drought and poor crops may have been aggravated by village squabbles. By the end of the 13th century the ancestral Puebloans had left the plateau, never to return.

How to Get There

From Cortez, take US 160 east for 8 miles to the park entrance, then follow the winding park road 15 miles to Far View Visitor Center and 5.5 miles farther to Chapin Mesa, which includes the museum and main cliff dwellings. Trailers are not allowed past Morefield Village. Airports: Cortez and Durango.

When to Go

Year-round. Wetherill Mesa, Far View Visitor Center, Cliff Palace Loop, Balcony House, and many services are closed in winter. Wildflowers bloom from April through September. In winter, cross-country skiing is allowed in Morefield and on the Cliff Palace Loop when conditions permit.

How to Visit

On a 1-day visit, begin early and stop first at the **Far View Visitor Center,** open mid-April to mid-October, to purchase tour tickets. Then go to the **Chapin Mesa Museum** for an overview; and then visit nearby **Spruce Tree House.** From there drive the **Cliff Palace Loop.** In the afternoon, follow the **Mesa Top Loop Road.** Wear sturdy shoes and be prepared for some strenuous climbing if you plan to visit the cliff dwellings. Binoculars are useful for enhancing views across the canyon.

With extra time, visit less crowded **Wetherill Mesa.**

CHAPIN MESA MUSEUM & SPRUCE TREE HOUSE

2 hours to a half day

Before descending to the sites, go through the **Chapin Mesa Museum,** located in the park headquarters area. Here you can pick up self-guiding booklets to the major sites and view a 25-minute video.

Excellent dioramas bring to life the changing world of the Mesa Verde people. Also displayed are some of the Southwest's finest artifacts and Indian arts and crafts. Also view the collection of **Mesa Verde pottery.** Decorated with black geometric designs against a white background, the pots represent the highest artistic expression of the ancestral Puebloans.

The park naturally focuses on the dramatic cliff dwellings, but they represent only the final scene in a long story. The genius of the earlier culture was best expressed not in building but in basketmaking and weaving. Look for outstanding examples in the museum, including a long sash of braided dog hair still as strong and pliable as it was when worn 1,500 years ago.

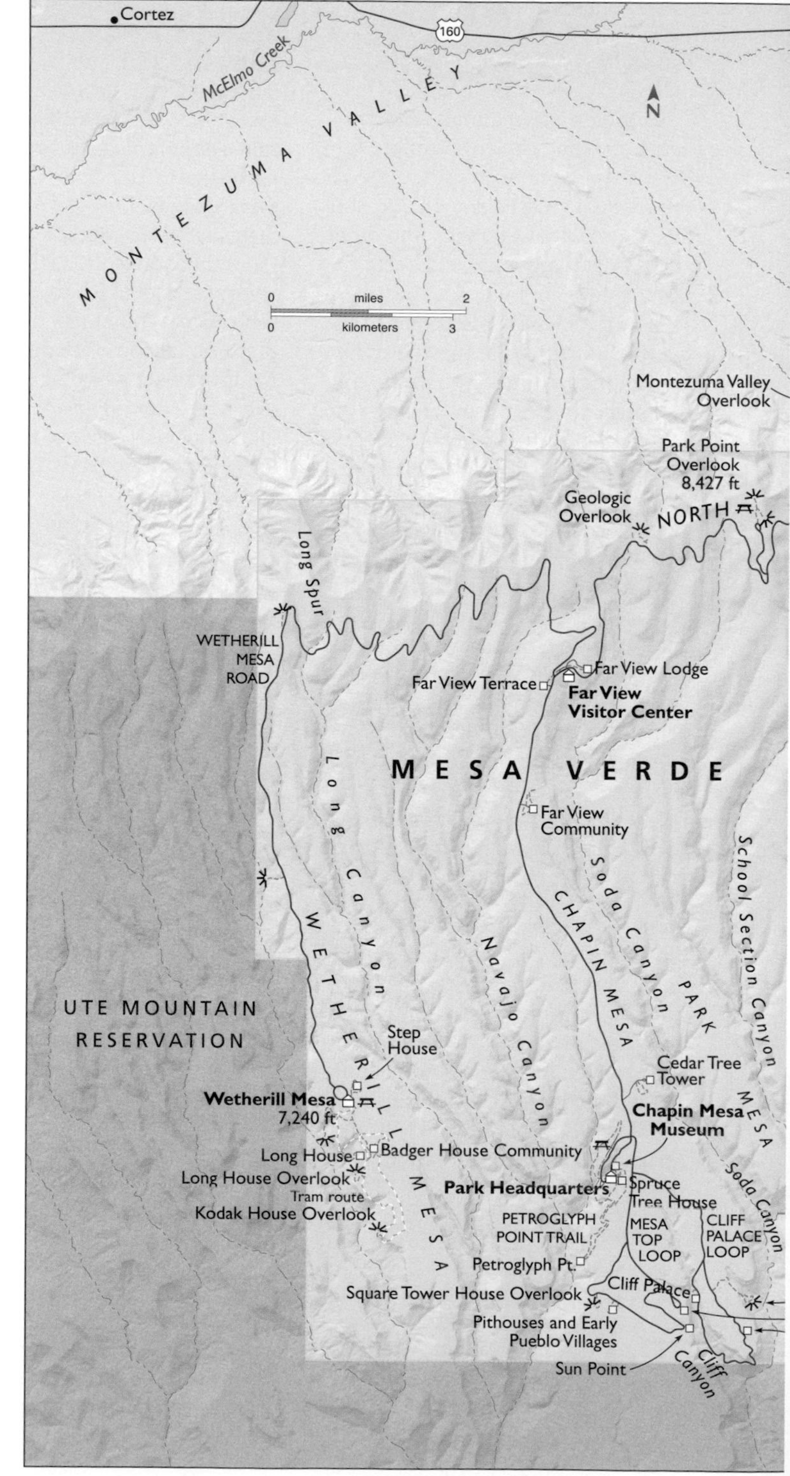
Cortez
160
McElmo Creek
MONTEZUMA VALLEY
N
0 miles 2
0 kilometers 3
Montezuma Valley Overlook
Park Point Overlook 8,427 ft
Geologic Overlook
NORTH
Long Spur
WETHERILL MESA ROAD
Far View Lodge
Far View Terrace
Far View Visitor Center
MESA VERDE
Far View Community
Long Canyon
WETHERILL MESA
Navajo Canyon
CHAPIN MESA
Soda Canyon
PARK
School Section Canyon
UTE MOUNTAIN RESERVATION
Step House
Wetherill Mesa 7,240 ft
Cedar Tree Tower
Chapin Mesa Museum
MESA
Long House
Badger House Community
Long House Overlook
Tram route
Kodak House Overlook
Park Headquarters
Spruce Tree House
Soda Canyon
PETROGLYPH POINT TRAIL
MESA TOP LOOP
CLIFF PALACE LOOP
Petroglyph Pt.
Square Tower House Overlook
Cliff Palace
Pithouses and Early Pueblo Villages
Sun Point
Cliff Canyon

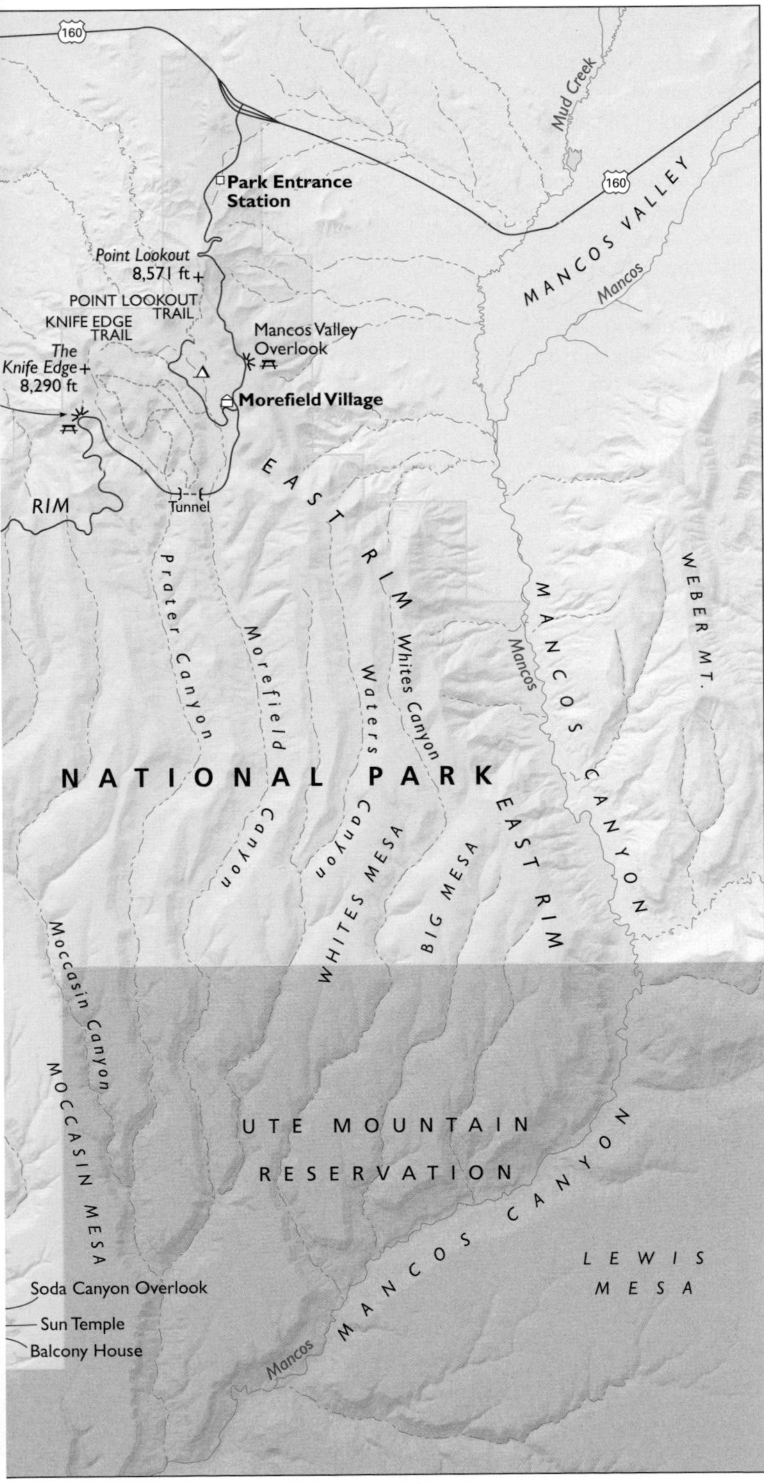
160
Mud Creek
Park Entrance Station
160
MANCOS VALLEY
Point Lookout
8,571 ft
POINT LOOKOUT TRAIL
KNIFE EDGE TRAIL
Mancos
Mancos Valley Overlook
The Knife Edge
8,290 ft
Morefield Village
RIM
Tunnel
EAST RIM
Prater Canyon
Morefield Canyon
Waters Canyon
Whites Canyon
Mancos
MANCOS CANYON
WEBER MT.
NATIONAL PARK
Canyon
Canyon
WHITES MESA
BIG MESA
EAST RIM
Moccasin Canyon
MOCCASIN MESA
UTE MOUNTAIN RESERVATION
MANCOS CANYON
LEWIS MESA
Soda Canyon Overlook
Sun Temple
Balcony House
Mancos

Pick up a self-guiding booklet to Spruce Tree House and walk the paved quarter-mile trail to the park's best preserved site. Here you will see the skillful building techniques and stonework of the ancestral Puebloans; 90 percent of the stonework is original. Rangers will be on duty to answer questions. (The rangers lead guided tours from mid-November to early March.) The trail crosses the canyon bottom, thick with Gambel oak. The site got its name from a tall Douglas fir (formerly known as a spruce) that, it is said, early explorers climbed down to reach the site.

The cliff dwelling, in an alcove more than 200 feet wide, housed 60 to 100 people. Three of its eight kivas —underground ceremonial rooms— have reconstructed roofs. You may climb down a ladder into one of them through the smoke hole.

Either now or later—if time and stamina allow—take the 2.8-mile **Petroglyph Point Trail,** a self-guided nature walk that branches off the Spruce Tree House Trail. Register and pick up a guidebook at the trailhead. The trail offers a good place to stretch your legs, familiarize yourself with plants and their prehistoric uses, and see one of the park's largest petroglyphs, a panel 12 feet across.

CHAPIN MESA

12 miles; 1.5 hours

Two 6-mile one-way loops wind through Chapin Mesa's fire-scarred pinyon-juniper woodland. Begin by turning onto the **Cliff Palace Loop** and driving to the parking area at **Cliff Palace.** A short trail takes you to a striking view of the largest cliff dwelling in North America: The 150-room site once housed more than 100 people. A park ranger will meet you at the overlook and guide you down a quarter-mile trail to tour the dwelling 120 feet below (ticket required).

The ancestral Puebloans built their dwellings in natural shelters formed by water percolating down through the sandstone. Where it reaches the denser shale layer, it seeps horizontally through the canyon wall, forming springs. These weaken the overlying rock, eroding the cliff face into eye-shaped alcoves.

Continue driving to the **Balcony House** parking area. This 40-room dwelling is one of the highlights of the park. Rangers guide adventurous groups up a 32-foot ladder to an easily defended ledge site with a panoramic view of **Soda Canyon.** To leave Balcony House, you must crawl through a tunnel on your hands and knees. Balcony House is closed in winter; you can view it at a distance from a promontory at the end of the 0.75-mile **Soda Canyon Overlook Trail.**

Keep going along the road until the junction with the **Mesa Top Loop Road,** where you turn left. At the **Square Tower House** overlook, a 500-foot trail leads to a dramatic viewpoint above the park's tallest site, the four-story remnant of a more extensive, multitiered structure. The site itself is not open to the public.

Return to your car and continue a short distance to the **pithouses and early Pueblo villages** pull-off. The squarish, sunken pithouses, earliest of Mesa Verde's permanent dwellings, were forerunners of the kivas. Farther along the trail are the excavated remains of three villages built on the same site between A.D. 900 and 1075. They show the evolution in architectural style, from post-and-adobe construction to stone masonry.

Drive to **Sun Point Overlook,** saving **Sun Point Pueblo** for your next visit. Here at the junction of **Fewkes Canyon** and **Cliff Canyon** you see a dozen cliff dwellings—among them, distant views of Cliff Palace to the northeast; **Sunset House** perched on a high rock ledge to the east; and **Mummy House**—named for the naturally desiccated mummy of a child discovered there—directly across the canyon.

The road continues past **Oak Tree House** and **Fire Temple** pull-offs to **Sun Temple.** Built by skilled masons—the stones were molded and their surfaces "dimpled"—this long, D-shaped structure with doorless chambers presents an enigma to archaeologists. Never inhabited, it may have been a ceremonial center; or perhaps it was used to record the annual movements of the sun, an attempt to predict the changeable weather. The canyon edge next to the parking area offers a superb view of Cliff Palace.

WETHERILL MESA

12 miles; a half day or more

Accessible only in summer, the **Wetherill Mesa Road** starts on the west side of **Far View Visitor Center,** where you stop to purchase tickets for the 1.5-hour tour of Long House. The steep road takes you to several sites opened to the public in 1972 after an extensive archaeological study sponsored by the National Geographic Society and the National Park Service.

Drive to the kiosk area and park. Take the 1-mile, self-guided walk to **Step House,** named for its stairway. The site is unusual, for pithouses have been uncovered next to a multistoried pueblo built in the same alcove.

Return to the kiosk area and take the mini-train to the head of **Long House Trail.** Rangers lead groups down the 0.75-mile trail to the park's second largest cliff dwelling—150 rooms with 21 kivas, an unusually high number. Gustaf Nordenskiöld, a Swedish scientist, excavated portions of **Long House** and other sites in 1891, publishing the first scientific report on Mesa Verde.

Extend your visit by taking the mini-train to the half-mile, self-guided trail that threads through the pithouses and pueblos of **Badger House Community.** These show the contrast between life on the mesa top and in the canyon alcoves below. The mini-train will return you to the kiosk area.

Cliff Palace

INFORMATION & ACTIVITIES

HEADQUARTERS
Mesa Verde National Park, CO 81330. Phone (970) 529-4465. www.nps.gov/meve

SEASONS & ACCESSIBILITY
Park open year-round, but most visitor facilities and services available mid-May to mid-October only. **Spruce Tree House** open all year; **Cliff Palace** open early April to early November; **Balcony House** open early May to mid-October; **Wetherill Mesa** open summer only. In winter, snow or ice may close Mesa Top Road. For weather and road conditions, call (970) 529-4461 or (970) 529-4465.

VISITOR & INFORMATION CENTERS
Far View Visitor Center at northwest section of park open daily mid-April to mid-October. **Chapin Mesa Museum** at southern end of park, located 20 miles from entrance, open daily year-round. Phone (970) 529-4465 for visitor information.

ENTRANCE FEE
$10 per car per week. Additional tickets required for tours of Cliff Palace, Balcony House, and Long House; purchase for small fee at Far View Visitor Center.

PETS
Permitted on leashes. Not allowed in buildings, in sites, or on trails.

FACILITIES FOR DISABLED
Visitor center, museum, overlooks, and mesa-top sites, some campsites, and most restrooms are wheelchair accessible. Site tours are not accessible, but most major cliff dwellings can be viewed from the mesa-top roads and overlooks. Free brochure.

THINGS TO DO
Ranger-led activities: archaeological walks, tours of Cliff Palace and Balcony House (spring to fall), Spruce Tree House (winter), and Long House (summer only); evening campfire programs. Also available, wayside exhibits, archaeological museum, self-guided tours; also, limited hiking (registration required for two trails), cross-country skiing, and snowshoeing.

SPECIAL ADVISORIES
• Visits to the cliff dwellings are strenuous. Wear sturdy shoes and use caution, especially if you have heart or respiratory problems.
• Hold on to your children on cliff trails and canyon rims.

OVERNIGHT BACKPACKING
Not permitted in park.

CAMPGROUNDS
One campground, **Morefield,** with a 14-day limit. Open mid-April to mid-October. First come, first served. Fees $20-$25 per night. Showers within 1 mile of campground. Tent and RV sites; 14 hookups. **Morefield Group Campsite** available first come, first served. Food services in park.

HOTELS, MOTELS, & INNS
(unless otherwise noted, rates are for 2 persons in a double room, high season)

INSIDE THE PARK:
Far View Lodge Mesa Verde Co., P.O. Box 277, Mancos, CO 81328. (800) 449-2288. 150 units. $111-$125. Restaurant. Open April-October.

OUTSIDE THE PARK:
In Cortez, CO 81321:
Anasazi Motor Inn 640 S. Broadway. (800) 972-6232 or (970) 565-3773. 85 units. $65-$71. AC, pool, restaurant.
Best Western Turquoise Inn and Suites 535 E. Main St. (800) 547-3376 or (970) 565-3778. 77 units. $80-$129. AC, pool.

In Durango, CO 81301:
Strater Hotel 699 Main Ave. (800) 247-4431 or (970) 247-4431. 93 units. $139-$205. AC, restaurant.

In Mancos, CO 81328:
Mesa Verde Motel 191 Railroad Ave., P.O. Box 552. (800) 825-6372 or (970) 533-7741. 16 units. $59. AC.

For further suggestions contact the Cortez Chamber of Commerce. (970) 565-3414; or the Durango Chamber of Commerce. (800) 525-8855.

EXCURSIONS

SAN JUAN NATIONAL FOREST
DURANGO, COLORADO

The vegetation ranges from high alpine forest to sage-and-pinyon desert in this rugged San Juan Mountains area. Contains lakes, rivers, wilderness areas, and many archaeological sites. Two million acres. Hiking, boating, climbing, bicycling, fishing, horseback riding, llama trekking, hunting, winter sports, water sports. 36 campgrounds, boat ramps, limited handicapped access. Open all year; most campsites open May through November. Information at Durango on US 550, about 50 miles east of Mesa Verde NP. (970) 247-4874.

AZTEC RUINS NATIONAL MONUMENT
AZTEC, NEW MEXICO

At Aztec, ancestral Pueblo people carefully planned and built over two centuries a large and complex settlement. Today it features the Southwest's only restored great kiva. 319 acres. Exhibits, picnic areas. Open all year. Off N. Mex. 516, on Ruins Road, about 60 miles southeast of Mesa Verde NP. (505) 334-6174.

HOVENWEEP NATIONAL MONUMENT
CORTEZ, COLORADO

Hovenweep—a Ute term meaning "deserted valley"—consists of six ancestral Puebloan sites: two in Utah and four in Colorado. They feature stone pueblos and square, circular, and D-shaped towers. Square Tower Group—located in Utah midway between Cortez, Colorado, and Blanding, Utah—is best preserved and most accessible. 785 acres. Open all year. Interpretive exhibits, hiking. 30 campsites (but not always available, so call ahead), picnic areas. Headquarters at Square Tower Group off Utah 262, about 55 miles from Mesa Verde NP. (970) 562-4282.

Fossilized logs, remnants of ancient conifers in Blue Mesa

PETRIFIED FOREST

ARIZONA

ESTABLISHED DECEMBER 9, 1962

93,533 acres

A sun-swept corner of the Painted Desert draws more than 600,000 visitors each year. While most come to see one of the world's largest concentrations of brilliantly colored petrified wood, many leave having glimpsed something more. The current 147 square miles of Petrified Forest open a window on an environment more than 200 million years old, one radically different from today's grassland.

Where you now see ravens soaring over a stark landscape, leathery-winged pterosaurs once glided over rivers teeming with armor-scaled fish and giant, spatula-headed amphibians. Nearby ran herds of some of the earliest dinosaurs. Scientists have identified several hundred species of fossil plants and animals in Petrified Forest.

The park consists of two main sections, and recent legislation has authorized doubling the land area to 218,533 acres. Located in the south are the major concentrations of the famous petrified wood; in the north rise the colorful banded badlands of the old part of the Painted Desert. Giant fossilized logs, many of them fractured into cord-wood-size segments, lie scattered throughout, like headstones bearing a deceased's likeness.

Much of the quartz that replaced the wood tissue 200 million years ago is tinted in rainbow hues. Many visitors cannot resist taking rocks, despite strict regulations and stiff fines against removing any material. To see if the petrified wood was actually disappearing at an alarming rate, resource managers established survey plots with a specific number of pieces of wood; some were nearly barren in less than a week.

The problem is not new. Military survey parties passing through the region in the 1850s filled their saddlebags with the petrified wood. As word of these remarkable deposits spread, fossil logs were hauled off by the wagonload for tabletops, lamps, and mantels. In the 1890s gem collectors began dynamiting logs searching for amethyst and quartz crystals. To prevent further destruction of its unique bounty, the area was designated a national monument in 1906 and a national park more than a half century later.

How to Get There

If you are traveling west on I-40, exit south into park. When leaving the south end of park, the road joins US 180. Follow US 180 for 19 miles to Holbrook and back to I-40. If you are traveling east on I-40, take the US 180 exit in Holbrook. The south entrance is 19 miles farther. After driving through the park, leave via I-40. Airport: Flagstaff.

When to Go

Year-round. Summer's dramatic thunderstorms enhance the beauty of the landscape. Fall, with its milder weather, also attracts many visitors. Winter on the Colorado Plateau can be cold with brief snow storms, but moderate afternoon temperatures are not uncommon. The desert blooms colorfully in spring; winds can be high.

How to Visit

Many of the features at Petrified Forest are on a scale best appreciated by leaving the car. Plan enough time to walk among the fossil logs and **Painted Desert** badlands. For a half-day visit, follow the **park road** from the **Rainbow Forest Museum** to **Pintado Point.** If you can stay longer, include a walk to **Agate House,** take the trail into the **Blue Mesa** badlands, and consider a hike in the **Painted Desert Wilderness.**

THE PARK ROAD

28 miles; a half to full day

A scenic drive connecting the south and north entrances passes through high desert grasslands broken by unexpected escarpments and bare hills banded in pastels. Begin at the south entrance with a stop at the **Rainbow Forest Museum.** (Or, from the north, begin at the **Painted Desert Visitor Center** and reverse this tour.) Be sure to see the dioramas of the late Triassic landscape and the displays of fossils and early dinosaurs.

The museum sits in the **Rainbow Forest,** one of four major concentrations of petrified logs called "forests." Behind it winds the half-mile **Giant Logs Trail** (closes 15 minutes before park); the largest fossil log is **Old Faithful** with a 9.5-foot diameter.

From the museum, a half-mile trail (closes 30 minutes before park) takes you to the trailhead for the 0.6-mile Long Logs loop and the 1-mile round-trip Agate House trail.

At **Long Logs,** you will see the largest concentration of petrified wood in the park, with logs up to 120 feet long—many crisscrossed in logjams.

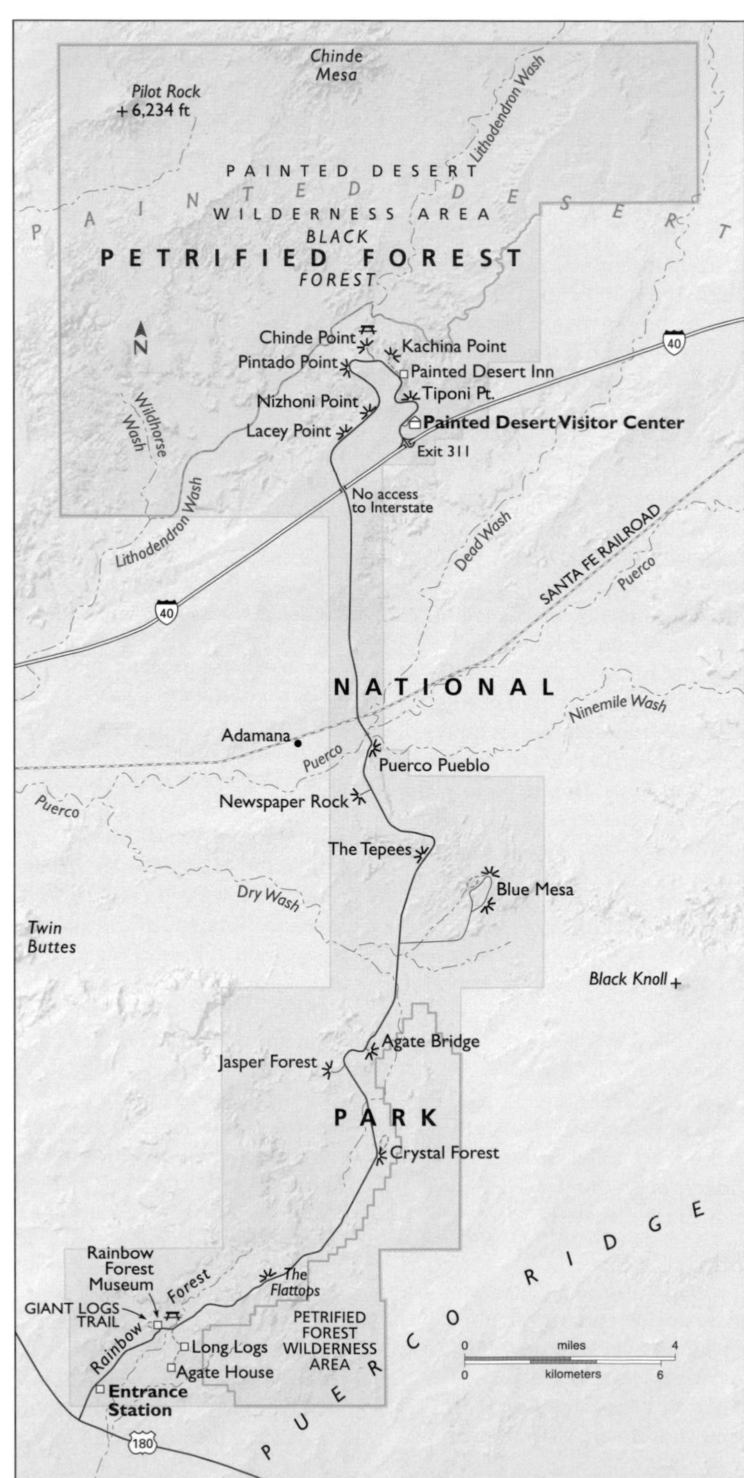
Chinde Mesa
Pilot Rock
+ 6,234 ft
Lithodendron Wash
PAINTED DESERT WILDERNESS AREA
PAINTED DESERT
BLACK FOREST
PETRIFIED FOREST
Chinde Point
Kachina Point
Pintado Point
Painted Desert Inn
Tiponi Pt.
Nizhoni Point
Painted Desert Visitor Center
Lacey Point
Exit 311
Wildhorse Wash
No access to Interstate
Lithodendron Wash
Dead Wash
SANTA FE RAILROAD
Puerco
40
NATIONAL
Ninemile Wash
Adamana
Puerco
Puerco Pueblo
Puerco
Newspaper Rock
The Tepees
Blue Mesa
Dry Wash
Twin Buttes
Black Knoll
Agate Bridge
Jasper Forest
PARK
Crystal Forest
PUERCO RIDGE
Rainbow Forest Museum
The Flattops
GIANT LOGS TRAIL
Rainbow Forest
PETRIFIED FOREST WILDERNESS AREA
Long Logs
Agate House
Entrance Station
180
0 miles 4
0 kilometers 6

The majority of the park's petrified wood, including that found here, comes from tall conifers called *Araucarioxylon*. These ancient trees grew more than 200 million years ago along waterways, where periodic flooding uprooted them. Tumbled and abraded, the fallen trees washed into logjams and were quickly buried by sediment and volcanic ash. Silica-laden water percolated through the wood, replacing organic tissue with multicolored quartz.

Next, if you have time, strike out on the paved trail to **Agate House.** During the 1930s crews restored one of the rooms in this eight-room dwelling built by ancestral Puebloans more than 800 years ago. The prehistoric structure was of mortared, petrified wood and adobe; the reconstruction uses concrete to stabilize the walls.

Continue your drive north, bypassing three turnoffs—**Crystal Forest, Jasper Forest,** and **Agate Bridge,** unless you have plenty of time. Take the 3-mile spur road that climbs **Blue Mesa.** You loop through strange badlands layered in blue, purple, and cream colors that change with weather and time of day.

Along the way, you'll spot the trailhead for the **Blue Mesa Trail,** which winds along a 1-mile, 45-minute route through the badlands. The trail is paved and nearly level except for one very steep section. Even if you can't take the full hike, park your car and walk 100 feet to where the trail begins to descend. Here are good views of the intricately eroded mesa.

Return to the main road and drive north through **The Tepees,** bare, conical hills whose reddish hues are produced by iron and other minerals.

The fabulous **Newspaper Rock,** two large boulders covered by more than 600 petroglyphs, can be viewed through scopes at the overlook. Continue driving a short distance to the **Puerco Pueblo,** one of the largest prehistoric sites in the park. Here you see the partially excavated remains of an ancestral Puebloan village abandoned about 1380 as well as many fine petroglyphs of animals and geometric designs pecked into the outcropping rock.

Scientists believe a chiseled spiral here was used by the Indians as a solar calendar. The week preceding and following the summer solstice, the sun interacts with this petroglyph. Early in the morning on the day of the summer solstice, rangers guide observers to the place where a shaft of sunlight pierces and fills the very center of the ancient symbol.

The road crosses the intermittent **Puerco River,** which divides the park in two. No permanent streams flow in Petrified Forest, and fewer than 10 inches of precipitation fall each year, mostly in summer thunderstorms.

After crossing I-40, the drive reaches the edge of a volcanic escarpment overlooking a particularly colorful section of the **Painted Desert.**

Pull off at **Lacey Point,** the first of nine overlooks. Here the bare Chinle slopes are tinted in the earthy shades of a Navajo rug. The colors are especially vivid when the sun shines on sediment still wet from a thunderstorm.

Continue on to the sweeping panoramic vista at **Pintado Point**—the highest along the Painted Desert rim. Below lies **Lithodendron Wash,** and to the northeast is the **Black Forest,** an area of dark fossilized wood. In the distance stands the dark profile of **Pilot Rock,** at 6,234 feet the park's highest point.

INFORMATION & ACTIVITIES

HEADQUARTERS
P.O. Box 2217, AZ 86028. Phone (928) 524-6228. www.nps.gov/pefo

SEASONS & ACCESSIBILITY
Open all year; extended hours May through August. Snow or icy roads may close park temporarily in winter.

VISITOR & INFORMATION CENTERS
Painted Desert Visitor Center at north entrance, just off I-40, and **Rainbow Forest Museum** near south entrance, just off US 180. **Painted Desert Inn National Historic Landmark,** 2 miles from the north entrance, also has archaeological displays and historic information.

ENTRANCE FEE
$10 per car, good for 7 days.

PETS & HORSES
Pets permitted on leashes except in public buildings, wilderness areas, and on Giant Logs Trail. Horses permitted throughout park in groups of four or less when accompanied by riders, but grazing is prohibited. No water available.

FACILITIES FOR DISABLED
Visitor centers, museum, and restrooms are wheelchair accessible.

THINGS TO DO
Free ranger-led, year-round activities: nature talks, wildlife viewing, and bird-watching. Also available, a film, interpretive exhibits, self-guided auto tours, hiking, horseback riding *(no rentals in area)*.

SPECIAL ADVISORIES
- Stay on trails to prevent damage to the fragile desert environment and personal injury from sharp edges of petrified logs.
- Take nothing from the park but memories, not even a tiny piece of petrified wood; pieces quickly add up to tons.
- Carry water when you hike; none is available outside developed areas.
- Do not approach any wildlife; as cute as they are, park animals may carry bubonic plague, Hantavirus, and rabies.

OVERNIGHT BACKPACKING
Allowed in the wilderness area. Permit required; available free at visitor center or museum up to one hour before park closing.

CAMPGROUNDS
None inside the park, but food service available.

HOTELS, MOTELS, & INNS
(unless otherwise noted, rates are for 2 persons in a double room, high season)

In Holbrook, AZ 86025:
American Best Inn 2211 E. Navajo Blvd. (800) 551-1923 or (928) 524-2654. 39 units. $46-$48. AC.
Best Western Adobe Inn 615 W. Hopi Dr. (928) 524-3948. 54 units. $74-$84. AC, pool.
Holbrook Comfort Inn 2602 E. Navajo Blvd. (800) 228-5150 or (928) 524-6131. 61 units. $75. AC, pool.

Contact the Holbrook Chamber of Commerce for additional accommodations: 100 E. Arizona St., Holbrook, AZ 86025. (928) 524-6558.

For a longer hike, walk through the rugged beauty of the **Painted Desert Wilderness.** The trail begins at **Kachina Point** behind the old **Painted Desert Inn,** originally built as a roadside inn, now open daily as a national historical landmark and museum. Once in the flats below the rim, the trail disappears, requiring you to do your own route-finding. Look for the Black Forest and **Onyx Bridge.** Finding the bridge can be an adventure since there are no landmarks to guide you.

The scenic drive ends at the **Painted Desert Visitor Center,** which is the park headquarters located at the north entrance.

EXCURSIONS

EL MORRO NATIONAL MONUMENT

RAMAH, NEW MEXICO

Here in 1605 Spaniard Juan de Oñate scratched his name at the base of a sandstone cliff. Others added inscriptions to the carvings of pre-Columbian Indians. Two ancestral Puebloan ruins sit on the cliff-top mesa. 1,279 acres. Hiking. 9 campsites (open May to mid-Oct.), picnic areas, handicapped access. Open year-round. On N. Mex. 53, off I-40, about 125 miles from Petrified Forest NP. (505) 783-4226.

EL MALPAIS NATIONAL MONUMENT AND NATIONAL CONSERVATION AREA

GRANTS, NEW MEXICO

El Malpais—"the badlands"—is located in the lava beds of western New Mexico. Featuring spatter cones, a 17-mile-long lava-tube system, and ice caves, the site also contains ancestral Puebloan ruins, a freestanding natural arch, and two wilderness areas. 376,000 acres. Primitive camping, hiking, bicycling, horseback riding, scenic drives. Open all year. Information center at N. Mex. 53 (23 miles south of Grants). About 140 miles east of Petrified Forest NP. (505) 783-4774.

WALNUT CANYON NATIONAL MONUMENT

FLAGSTAFF, ARIZONA

More than 800 years ago, Indians now known as the Sinagua lived in caves in cliff dwellings here at the edge of Flagstaff. The Sinagua's name (Spanish for "without water") is a tribute to their remarkable ability to survive in a dry region. The cliff dwellings are accessible by trail. 3,541 acres. Visitor center, picnic areas. Open daily. Located off I-40, just east of Flagstaff. About 107 miles west of the I-40 exit at Petrified Forest NP. (928) 526-3367.

Mighty Saguaro cactuses at dusk, with summer storm clouds

SAGUARO

ARIZONA
ESTABLISHED OCTOBER 14, 1994
91,445 acres

Symbol of the American Southwest and North America's largest cactus, the saguaro's imposing stature and uplifted arms give it a regal presence. Perhaps that's why this burly giant, whose only bits of exuberance are seasonal blossoms and figlike fruits at the tip of its limbs, has been dubbed the "desert monarch."

Carnegiea gigantea is the trademark of the Sonoran Desert, whose basins and ranges rumple 120,000 square miles of northwestern Mexico, southern Arizona, and southeastern California. Saguaro National Park is composed of two sections. The westerly Tucson Mountain District embraces about 24,000 acres of the hotter, drier, less-vegetated "low" Sonoran ecosystem, which occurs at an elevation around 3,000 feet. Thirty miles east, on the other side of Tucson's urban sprawl, is the 67,000-acre Rincon Mountain District, which occupies loftier ground and has a cooler, slightly wetter "high desert" environment. Most of it is inaccessible except by foot or on horseback. Here the terrain inclines from saguaro forests into nearly pristine woodlands of oak and pine. Hikers pressing on to higher elevations find Douglas fir, ponderosa pine, and solitude.

The Sonoran Desert's extreme temperatures, perennial drought, frequent lightning, banshee winds, and voracious predators keep the saguaro forever at the limit of its endurance. Odds against survival rival a lottery: Though the cactus annually produces tens of thousands of pinhead-size seeds—some 40 million over a life that may last two centuries—few ever even sprout. Even fewer seedlings achieve the grandeur of towering 50 feet and weighing up to 16,000 pounds.

Though the saguaro may be the park's centerpiece, after wet winters the spring wildflower display can be breathtaking. The brilliant gold of the Mexican poppy is often the first-noticed bloom, while penstemons, lupines, desert marigolds, brittlebushes, and globe mallows contribute their lively colors of red, lilac, blue, and yellow. Many trees, shrubs, and cactuses also bloom, including creosote bushes, paloverdes, ocotillos, chollas, and hedgehogs. Saguaros bloom in early summer.

How to Get There

Saguaro West: From Tucson take Speedway Boulevard west to Gates Pass Road, turning right on Kinney Road. *(Gates Pass not recommended for buses, rvs, and towed vehicles; instead take Ariz. 86 west from Tucson to Kinney.)*
Saguaro East: Take Broadway Boulevard east from central Tucson to Old Spanish Trail. Airport: Tucson.

When to Go

Year-round. From October through April, temperatures reach the upper 60s to mid-70s and can drop below freezing overnight. From May through September, highs routinely exceed 100°F. July through September is characterized by brief, fierce thunderstorms. Saguaros bloom nightly from late April into June.

How to Visit

On a 1-day visit, begin early and view the **Arizona-Sonora Desert Museum** before heading to **Saguaro West;** then pause at the **Red Hills Visitor Center** for an overview. Take the **Bajada Scenic Loop Drive,** stopping en route to walk the paved **Desert Discovery Nature Trail.** Return to Tucson, continuing east to Saguaro's **Rincon Mountain District.** Take the **Cactus Forest Drive** and walk the **Desert Ecology Trail.** For a scenic rest stop along the drive, visit **Mica View Picnic Area.**

SAGUARO WEST: TUCSON MOUNTAIN DISTRICT

about 25 miles; a half day

The drive west through **Tucson Mountain County Park** takes you past the excellent, zoolike **Arizona-Sonora Desert Museum** *(2021 N. Kinney Rd., 520-883-1380; fee),* whose 21 acres include every Sonoran Desert life zone and most of its animals and plants. It's worth a stop.

Continue on Kinney Road to the **Red Hills Visitor Center** with its decks and panoramic view. Here a unique slide show and desert life exhibits will enhance your understanding of what you'll encounter here and in Saguaro East. Walk the center's **Cactus Garden Trail,** a paved path through an unruly crowd of cactuses: hedgehog, barrel, fishhook, chain-fruit cholla, and prickly pear to name but a few.

Saguaros thrive in the coarse, absorbent soil of *bajadas,* long desert mountain slopes of eroded rock, gravel, sand, and clay, where a mature plant's shallow, wide-ranging roots can absorb up to 200 gallons from one rainstorm, enough to last a year. The 9-mile **Bajada Loop Drive** beginning at the visitor center explores one of these life zones. En route, about 1 mile west, look left for the **Desert Discovery Nature Trail,** a half-mile path across a bajada at the base of the Tucson Mountains.

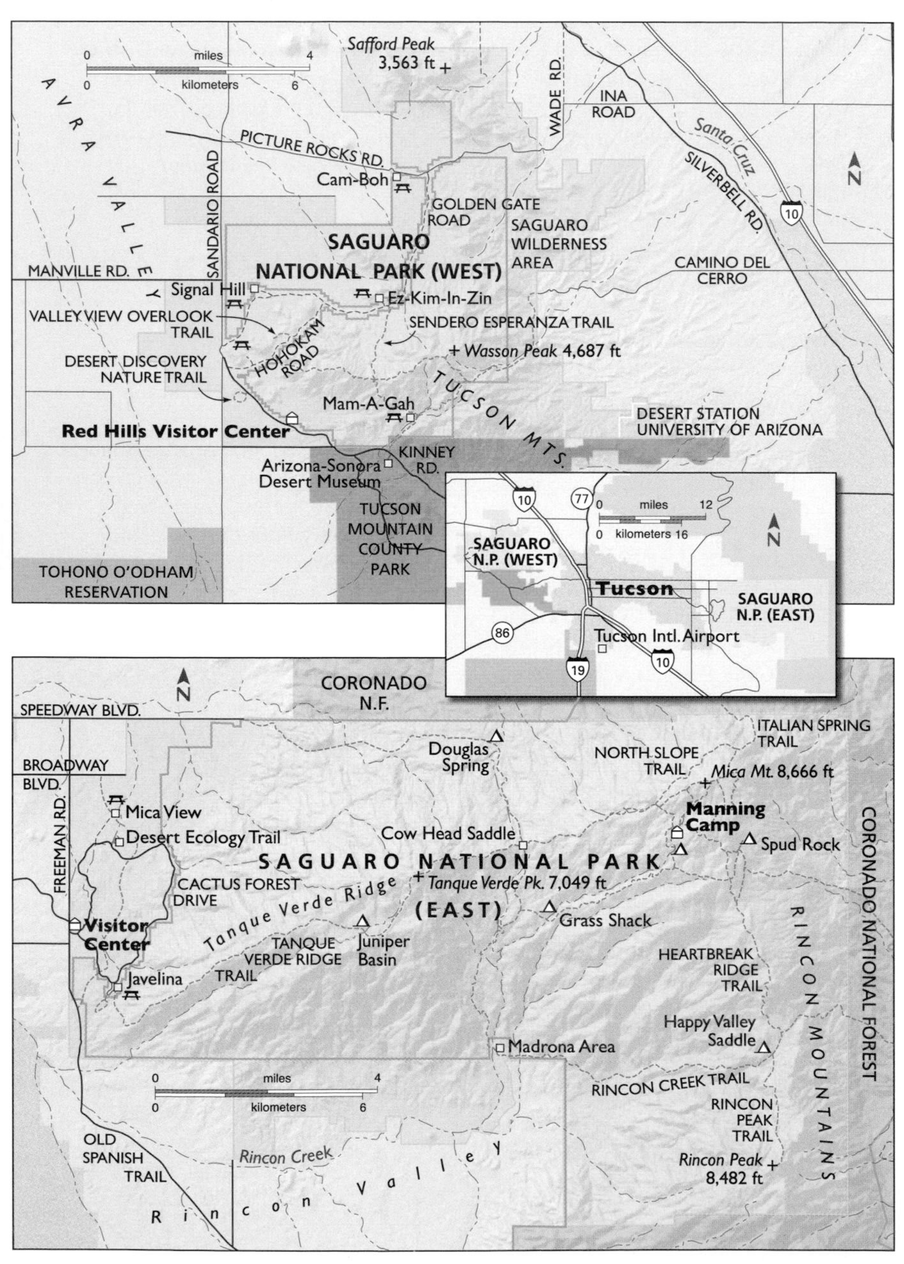
Safford Peak
3,563 ft
miles
kilometers
AVRA VALLEY
WADE RD.
INA ROAD
Santa Cruz
SILVERBELL RD.
10
PICTURE ROCKS RD.
SANDARIO ROAD
Cam-Boh
GOLDEN GATE ROAD
SAGUARO WILDERNESS AREA
SAGUARO NATIONAL PARK (WEST)
MANVILLE RD.
CAMINO DEL CERRO
Signal Hill
Ez-Kim-In-Zin
VALLEY VIEW OVERLOOK TRAIL
SENDERO ESPERANZA TRAIL
HOHOKAM ROAD
Wasson Peak 4,687 ft
DESERT DISCOVERY NATURE TRAIL
TUCSON MTS.
Mam-A-Gah
DESERT STATION UNIVERSITY OF ARIZONA
Red Hills Visitor Center
KINNEY RD.
Arizona-Sonora Desert Museum
TUCSON MOUNTAIN COUNTY PARK
TOHONO O'ODHAM RESERVATION
10
77
miles
kilometers
SAGUARO N.P. (WEST)
Tucson
SAGUARO N.P. (EAST)
86
Tucson Intl. Airport
19
10
CORONADO N.F.
SPEEDWAY BLVD.
BROADWAY BLVD.
FREEMAN RD.
Douglas Spring
ITALIAN SPRING TRAIL
NORTH SLOPE TRAIL
Mica Mt. 8,666 ft
Mica View
Manning Camp
Desert Ecology Trail
Cow Head Saddle
Spud Rock
SAGUARO NATIONAL PARK (EAST)
CACTUS FOREST DRIVE
Tanque Verde Pk. 7,049 ft
Tanque Verde Ridge
Grass Shack
Visitor Center
Juniper Basin
TANQUE VERDE RIDGE TRAIL
Javelina
HEARTBREAK RIDGE TRAIL
RINCON MOUNTAINS
CORONADO NATIONAL FOREST
Happy Valley Saddle
Madrona Area
miles
kilometers
RINCON CREEK TRAIL
RINCON PEAK TRAIL
OLD SPANISH TRAIL
Rincon Creek
Rincon Peak 8,482 ft
Rincon Valley

Hook right onto **Hohokam Road.** (Part of the loop is one way; enter here to drive it all in one direction.) About 1.5 miles from the turnoff, **Valley View Overlook Trail** winds up about half a mile to panoramas of rugged, cactus-studded landscapes. Unpaved **Golden Gate Road** turns off about a mile farther on and passes a pleasant picnic area near the head of **Sendero Esperanza Trail,** a moderately strenuous, popular half-day hike into the mountainous backcountry.

Backtrack on Golden Gate Road past Hohokam Road to **Signal Hill Picnic Area,** where rocks are etched with centuries-old Hohokam petroglyphs. Archaeologists believe the symbols, chipped through a brown patina of iron-manganese oxide called "desert varnish," signify territorial claims, clan migrations, personal accounts, visions, and pure artistic whimsy.

Continuing through ironwood and paloverde, the loop closes at **Sandario Road,** an alternative route back to Tucson via Picture Rocks, Wade, and Ina Roads to I-10.

SAGUARO EAST: RINCON MOUNTAIN DISTRICT

about 25 miles; a half day

The higher elevations here create Sonoran Desert environments different from Saguaro West's lowland desert zone. A steady, east-trending incline slants up into the roadless Rincon Mountain wilderness area, which is dotted with forests of oak, pine, and fir accessible only by foot or on horseback.

Make your first stop the **Saguaro East Visitor Center**. If you plan to hike into the backcountry, this is the place to acquire trail guides, maps, and permits. If time is limited, pick up a guide to the **Cactus Forest Drive** and take the 8-mile loop, where many of the saguaros are over 150 years old.

About 2 miles along the route, look left for a gravel road leading to scenic overlooks at **Mica View Picnic Area,** a pleasant place to stop. About a mile farther, the quarter-mile paved **Desert Ecology Trail** is designed to

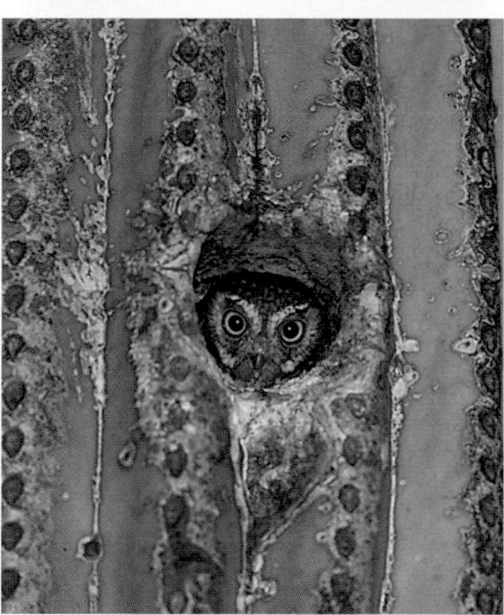

Prickly pear in bloom *(top)*
Elf owl in its saguaro nest *(bottom)*

INFORMATION & ACTIVITIES

HEADQUARTERS
3693 S. Old Spanish Trail, Tucson, AZ 85730. For information call (520) 733-5158 (Saguaro West) or (520) 733-5153 (Saguaro East). www.nps.gov/sagu

SEASONS & ACCESSIBILITY
Park open year-round.

VISITOR & INFORMATION CENTERS
Saguaro West Red Hills Visitor Center off Kinney Road.
Saguaro East Visitor Center (park headquarters) on Old Spanish Trail.

ENTRANCE FEE
$10 per vehicle.

PETS
Not permitted on trails, in backcountry, or in public buildings; elsewhere allowed on leashes.

FACILITIES FOR DISABLED
Visitor centers, nature trails, and roadside picnic areas wheelchair accessible.

THINGS TO DO
Ranger-led hikes and night walks, scenic drives, trail walks, bird- and wildlife-watching, picnicking, bicycling, backcountry hiking. Horseback riding is permitted on some trails.

SPECIAL ADVISORIES
• Avoid open and low-lying areas during thunderstorms, when lightning and flash floods pose a danger.
• Stay on trails. Abandoned mine shafts in Saguaro West make off-trail hiking and riding hazardous.
• Carry a flashlight at night to avoid encounters with rattlesnakes, scorpions, and Gila monsters.
• There is no water at picnic areas or along most trails. If hiking, carry at least one gallon of water per day.

OVERNIGHT BACKPACKING
Allowed only at designated backcountry sites. Use permits must be obtained at visitor centers in advance of trip.

CAMPGROUNDS
Six backcountry campsites in **Saguaro East,** accessible by foot, 6 miles from the nearest trailhead. $6 permit fee. Campground in **Tucson Mountain County Park,** next to Saguaro West.

HOTELS, MOTELS, & INNS
(unless otherwise noted, rates are for 2 persons in a double room, high season)

In Tucson, AZ:
Arizona Inn 2200 E. Elm St., 85719. (800) 933-1093 or (520) 325-1541. 86 units. $269-$349. AC, pool, restaurant.
Best Western 1015 N. Stone Ave., 85705. (800) 528-1234. 79 units. $79-$109. AC, pool, restaurant.
Tucson East Hilton 7600 E. Broadway, 85710. (800) 445-8667. 233 units. $145-$200. AC, pool, restaurant.

For more lodgings, contact Tucson Metropolitan Chamber of Commerce, (520) 792-1212.

illustrate the crucial role of water in desert ecosystems. While highly informative, what you are more likely to remember from this 20-minute amble is the desert stillness.

Near the south end of the Cactus Forest loop road, consider walking part of the **Tanque Verde Ridge Trail,** which heads south and then east from the Javelina picnic area. In return for 3 miles or so of fairly vigorous uphill hiking, you'll experience cactus desert, the grassland above, and a bit of oak-juniper forest on the ridge. To the east is Rincon Peak, Tucson to the west. In the grassland zone, look for sotol, which was used by Native Americans to weave mats and other objects.

EXCURSIONS

SABINO CANYON
TUCSON, ARIZONA

Just minutes from Saguaro NP, in the eastern foothills of the Santa Catalina mountains, Sabino Canyon is a world away in terms of climate, vegetation, and wildlife. It beckons with towering cliffs, waterfalls, seasonal swimming holes, and a lush riparian zone. Free from vehicular congestion; a tram *(fee)* provides access to the upper canyon, picnic areas, and trails. Located on Sabino Canyon Rd. 15 miles NW of Saguaro NP (East). (520) 749-2861 (tram information).

KARTCHNER CAVERNS STATE PARK
BENSON, ARIZONA

Discovered in 1974 but not opened to the public until 1999, Kartchner Caverns SP contains an extraordinary display of colorful speleotherms. Formations—some of the tiniest, most delicate growths, as well as the tallest column in Arizona—provide evidence of the role water plays in the creation of caves. Hiking, scenic drives, guided cave tours (call for reservations), museum, amphitheater. 62 campsites, handicapped access. Visitor center off Ariz. 90, 45 miles SE of Saguaro NP (East). (520)586-2283.

ORGAN PIPE CACTUS NATIONAL MONUMENT
WHY, ARIZONA

Located on a road leading to the Mexican border, Organ Pipe NM was designated an international biosphere reserve by the United Nations in 1976. As a protected area, the life of the Sonoran Desert, including its more than 20 species of cactuses, flourish under nearly ideal wilderness conditions. Spring bloom is the most colorful time to visit. 330,689 acres. Hiking, scenic drives. 212 campsites. 150 miles SW of Saguaro NP (West). 520-387-6849.

Morning at Court of the Patriarchs

ZION

UTAH

ESTABLISHED NOVEMBER 19, 1919

146,592 acres

Rising in Utah's high plateau country, the Virgin River carves its way to the desert below through a gorge so deep and narrow that sunlight rarely penetrates to the bottom. As the canyon widens, the river runs a gantlet of great palisade walls rimmed with slickrock peaks and hanging valleys.

The scale is immense—sheer cliffs dropping 3,000 feet, massive buttresses, deep alcoves. Nineteenth-century Mormon pioneers saw these sculptured rocks as the "natural temples of God." They called the canyon Little Zion after the celestial city.

A million years of flowing water has cut through the red and white beds of Navajo sandstone that form the sheer walls of Zion. The geologic heart of the canyon began as a vast desert millions of years ago; almost incessant winds blew one dune on top of another until the sands reached a depth of more than 2,000 feet. You can still see the track of these ancient winds in the graceful crossbedded strata of Zion's mighty cliffs.

Unlike the Grand Canyon where you stand on the rim and look out, Zion Canyon is usually viewed from the bottom looking up. The vertical topography confines most of Zion's 2.5 million yearly visitors between canyon walls.

Streamside on the canyon floor grow thick stands of Fremont cottonwood, box elder, willow, and, a short distance away, cactus and

Utah juniper. Vegetation changes rapidly as the terrain rises almost a mile in elevation. The high plateaus support Douglas fir and ponderosa pine.

Within the park's 229 square miles lies a landscape of remote terraces and narrow gorges. A number of these canyons are so hidden that early surveyors overlooked some that are 20 miles long. More than 100 miles of wilderness trails crisscross the backcountry, while 15 miles of paved trails encourage casual visits.

How to Get There

From Cedar City to the Kolob Canyons Entrance, take I-15 about 18 miles south. To Zion Canyon, take I-15 to Utah 17 then Utah 9 to the South Entrance (about 60 miles). From Kanab, take US 89 to Utah 9 (at the Mt. Carmel junction) to the East Entrance. From Las Vegas and St. George, take I-15 and Utah 9 to the South Entrance. Airports: Las Vegas, Nevada, and St. George, Utah.

When to Go

Open all year, but main season is March through October. Mild spring and fall temperatures are ideal for hiking. Summer rains can bring spectacular clouds and numerous waterfalls. Rock colors are heightened by contrast with winter snows, green summer foliage, deep blue fall skies.

How to Visit

On a 1-day visit, take the **Zion-Mt. Carmel Highway** and the **Zion Canyon Scenic Drive** (free shuttle *only* late-March to November) for the best overview of the park. For longer stays, begin with one of the classic walks in **Zion Canyon,** then take a road tour of the **Kolob Canyons** in late afternoon.

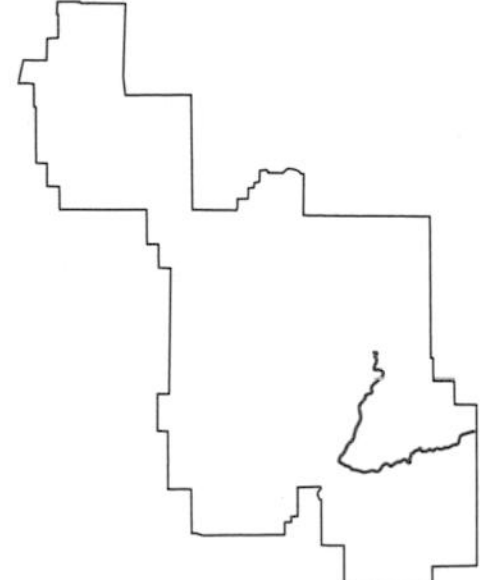

ZION-MT. CARMEL HIGHWAY & ZION CANYON

18 miles; a half to full day

The Zion-Mt. Carmel Highway (Utah 9) descends almost 2,000 feet from the high mesa country at the **East Entrance** to the **South Entrance** desert. Begin the drive on the east to see the park in the most dramatic possible way—from a tunnel on the wall of the canyon, 800 feet above the floor.

Shortly after passing through the East Entrance, stop at the **Checkerboard Mesa** pull-off. Here is a classic view of weathered sandstone beds crosshatched with vertical joints. Continue driving as the road winds along the normally dry creek bed. For the full impact of

Pinyon pine near Checkerboard Mesa

Isaac, one of the Three Patriarchs, in Winter

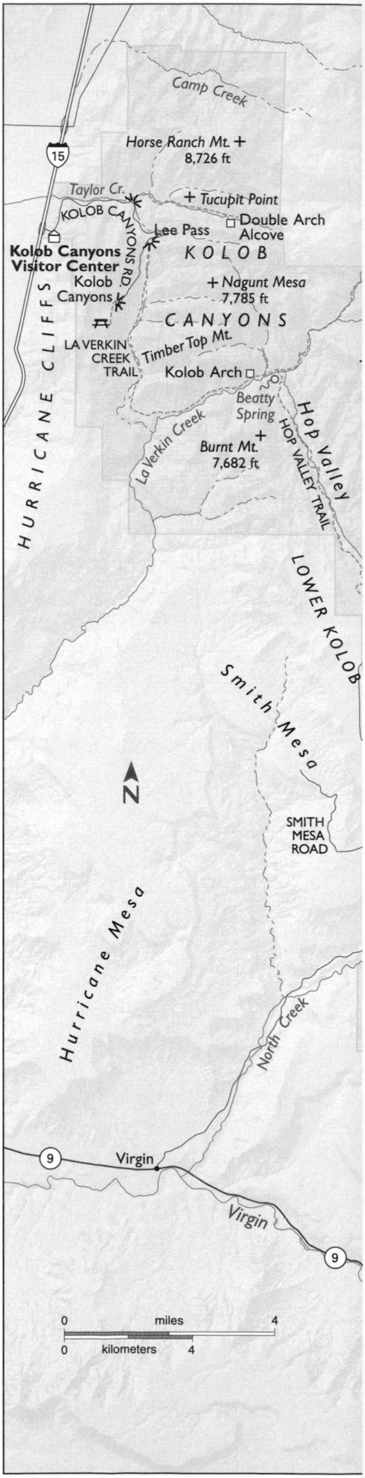

the approaching canyon, turn off at the **Canyon Overlook** parking area. If you are ready for a stop, this is a good place to stretch your legs along a 1-mile round-trip trail. You walk above the winding narrows of **Pine Creek** to an impressive view of **The West Temple** and the **Towers of the Virgin.**

The road disappears into the canyon wall at the narrow **Zion-Mt. Carmel Tunnel,** breaking into the blue sky again 1.1 miles farther. The tunnel was completed in 1930 at a cost of a half million dollars and the lives of two men. The road switchbacks down the side of **Pine Creek Canyon,** passing close to **The Great Arch,** which is 400 feet high. Geologists call it a blind arch because it is recessed into the cliff.

You next enter **Zion Canyon,** where Pine Creek meets the **North Fork Virgin River.** The canyon has an average width of half a mile, with walls 2,000 to 3,000 feet high. At Zion Canyon Visitor Center, catch a free shuttle for the 6.6-mile **Zion Canyon Scenic Drive** that follows the winding Virgin River. Get out at the **Court of the Patriarchs.** Here a short trail leads up the slope to a view of

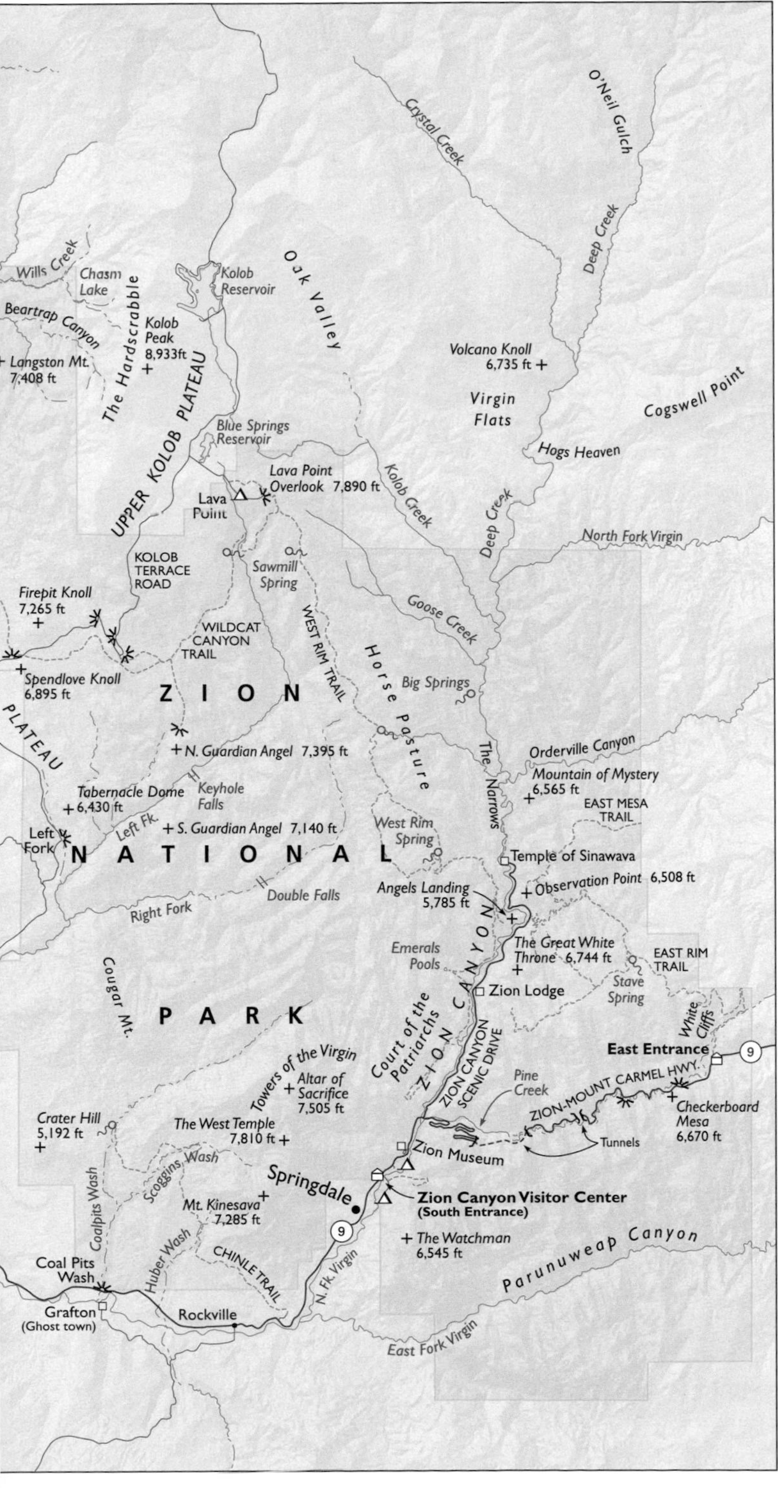
Crystal Creek
O'Neil Gulch
Deep Creek
Wills Creek
Chasm Lake
Kolob Reservoir
Oak Valley
Beartrap Canyon
The Hardscrabble
Kolob Peak 8,933ft
Langston Mt. 7,408 ft
UPPER KOLOB PLATEAU
Volcano Knoll 6,735 ft
Virgin Flats
Cogswell Point
Blue Springs Reservoir
Hogs Heaven
Lava Point Overlook 7,890 ft
Lava Point
Kolob Creek
Deep Creek
North Fork Virgin
KOLOB TERRACE ROAD
Sawmill Spring
Firepit Knoll 7,265 ft
WEST RIM TRAIL
Goose Creek
WILDCAT CANYON TRAIL
Horse Pasture
Spendlove Knoll 6,895 ft
ZION
Big Springs
PLATEAU
N. Guardian Angel 7,395 ft
The Narrows
Orderville Canyon
Mountain of Mystery 6,565 ft
Tabernacle Dome 6,430 ft
Keyhole Falls
EAST MESA TRAIL
Left Fork
Left Fk.
S. Guardian Angel 7,140 ft
West Rim Spring
NATIONAL
Temple of Sinawava
Double Falls
Angels Landing 5,785 ft
Observation Point 6,508 ft
Right Fork
The Great White Throne 6,744 ft
EAST RIM TRAIL
Emerals Pools
Stave Spring
Cougar Mt.
Zion Lodge
ZION CANYON
PARK
Court of the Patriarchs
White Cliffs
East Entrance
9
Towers of the Virgin
ZION CANYON SCENIC DRIVE
Altar of Sacrifice 7,505 ft
Pine Creek
ZION-MOUNT CARMEL HWY.
Checkerboard Mesa 6,670 ft
Crater Hill 5,192 ft
The West Temple 7,810 ft
Tunnels
Zion Museum
Scoggins Wash
Springdale
Zion Canyon Visitor Center (South Entrance)
Coalpits Wash
Mt. Kinesava 7,285 ft
9
The Watchman 6,545 ft
Parunuweap Canyon
Huber Wash
CHINLE TRAIL
Coal Pits Wash
N. Fk. Virgin
Grafton (Ghost town)
Rockville
East Fork Virgin

ZION

The Narrows *(top left)*; Virgin River *(top right)*; Left Fork North Creek *(center)*; Mountain lion *(bottom left)*; Canyon treefrog *(bottom right)*

the **Three Patriarchs,** sheer faces carved by wind and water from Navajo sandstone.

Back on the shuttle, the road continues past the **Emerald Pools** area. This is the trailhead for a popular stroll on a paved walkway to natural rock basins fed by small streams. The lowest pool on the climbing path is a tiny oasis tucked into the side of the cliff and sheltered by bigtooth maple trees.

After a sojourn at the pools, the shuttle continues past **Zion Lodge** to the Grotto picnic area, a good place to take a break. Here is the trailhead for **Angels Landing** and **West Rim Trail.**

A short distance farther, the shuttle reaches **Weeping Rock.** Here, the trailhead of a self-guided nature walk (half-mile round-trip) leads behind a curtain of water showering from the ceiling of an alcove. Water percolates through the sandstone until it hits shale and then seeps through to the surface of Weeping Rock—1,000 to 4,000 years after falling as rain on the high plateau above. The strenuous **East Rim Trail** and a branch trail that climbs to **Hidden Canyon** start here.

Just past Weeping Rock, a stop offers superb views of **The Great White Throne** rising some 2,500 feet above the river. The scenic drive ends where the canyon narrows at the **Temple of Sinawava,** named for the coyote-spirit of the Paiute Indians.

Here and elsewhere in the park, keep watch for the tiny creatures of Sinawava's realm—canyon tree frogs, pocket gophers, eastern fence lizards. There are also more than 270 species of birds, including roadrunner, Gambel's quail, and the water-skimming American dipper.

KOLOB CANYONS ROAD

5.5 miles; 1 hour to a half day or more

One of the most spectacular and most accessible regions of the park is also one of the least visited. The **Hurricane Cliffs,** forming the western boundary of the park, screen the great towers of the Kolob from I-15. Follow the Kolob Canyons Road past the **Kolob Canyons Visitor Center** as it winds into **Taylor Creek Canyon.** Here you get a hint of what's to come when the jagged face of **Tucupit Point** appears.

Continue up the road, skirting the beautiful **South Fork** of **Taylor Creek.** Each vista becomes more striking as you cross **Lee Pass,** the trailhead for routes into the hidden canyons of **La Verkin Creek.** If time and stamina allow, you can backpack (usually done as an overnight; permit required for overnight trips) the 14-mile round-trip to **Kolob Arch,** one of the world's largest freestanding natural arches, 310 feet long.

Drive to the parking area at the end of the road for a dramatic view of the **Finger Canyons.** Sheer cliffs of pale red sandstone lift more than 2,000 feet into the blue sky. Narrow canyons work deep into the sides of **Timber Top Mountain,** connecting **Shuntavi Butte** with **Nagunt Mesa.**

OTHER HIKES

The full impact of Zion's great carved landscape is best experienced from a high vantage point above the river. The park's extensive trail system gives you a wide range of choices, from walks of half an hour to backpacking trips lasting for days.

The park's most popular trail is the **Riverside Walk,** an easy, 2-mile round-trip amble. This paved path can be negotiated by strollers and assisted wheelchairs. Beginning where the Zion Canyon Scenic Drive ends at the Temple of Sinawava, the trail leads past hanging gardens of maidenhair fern and golden columbine and stands of shady cottonwood and ash. It ends where the North Fork rushes from a defile so narrow the only way to look is up. Flash floods here are a real danger; deeper in **The Narrows** the walls are 2,000 feet high but in places only 18 feet apart. In the 1960s, a sudden flood caught 26 hikers, drowning 5.

Perched midway between the river and the rim of the canyon, the high and open spire of rock called **Angels Landing** provides one of Zion's best overall views. The strenuous trail climbs 2.5 miles, at times cutting into a knife-edge ridge that joins the landing to the western wall. Sheer 1,500-foot drops surround the promontory on three sides and allow excellent cross-canyon views of The Great White Throne and down the deep cut of Zion Canyon. *Not recommended for those with a fear of heights.*

The **Observation Point Trail,** 8 miles round-trip, is not recommended for acrophobes either. One of the best routes to reach the very top of the canyon, the strenuous trail passes through a beautiful narrows and winds into the slickrock country. As it swings back to the main canyon, the trail cuts into the very edge of the cliff and opens to dramatic views. After a thunderstorm, clouds steaming up from the white sandstone of the western wall look as if the rock itself is evaporating.

Once on top, the route crosses a sandy mesa through stands of pinyon pine and juniper to **Observation Point,** with fine views of the main canyon. Stand here and listen to what Frederick Dellenbaugh called "the whisper of the wind that comes and goes, breathing with the sound of centuries."

Virgin River Valley from Observation Point

INFORMATION & ACTIVITIES

HEADQUARTERS
State Rte. 9, Springdale, UT 84767. Phone (435) 772-3256. www.nps.gov/zion

SEASONS & ACCESSIBILITY
Park open year-round. Kolob Canyons Road and main roads in Zion Canyon are plowed in winter. Dirt roads are impassable when wet. Lava Point inaccessible in winter and early spring due to snow. Call headquarters for weather conditions. Shuttle service on Zion Canyon Scenic Drive. Pick up free shuttle in Springdale or at the Zion Canyon Visitor Center. Shuttle runs April through Oct.

VISITOR & INFORMATION CENTERS
Zion Canyon Visitor Center, near the South Entrance on Utah 9, and **Kolob Canyons Visitor Center,** in the park's northwest corner off I-15, are open daily.

ENTRANCE FEE
$20 per car per week. Also, $15 charge for escorting oversize vehicles through the mile-long tunnel on East Entrance road.

PETS
Not permitted in backcountry, on shuttles, in public buildings, or on trails; elsewhere allowed on leashes.

FACILITIES FOR DISABLED
Visitor centers, museum, shuttles, some trails and restrooms are wheelchair accessible. Handicapped sites available in campgrounds.

THINGS TO DO
Free ranger-led activities: nature walks and talks, evening programs, children's programs. Zion Human History Museum. Also, hiking, horseback trail rides—inquire at Zion Lodge or call (435) 772-3810—climbing, bicycling (bicyclists must transport their bikes through the long tunnel—check at entrance or visitor center), limited cross-country skiing.

SPECIAL ADVISORIES
• Summer temperatures in park can exceed 105°F. Always carry bottled or treated water when hiking—at least a gallon a day per person in summer.

OVERNIGHT BACKPACKING
Permits required, $10 (1-2 persons), $15 (3-6 persons), $20 (7-12 persons); available at visitor centers.

CAMPGROUNDS
Three campgrounds, 14-day limit. **Watchman** open all year; **South** open May through Sept.; **Lava Point** open May through Oct., depending on weather. Reservations for Watchman through the NPRS (see p. 10). Others, first come, first served. Fees $16 per night; $18 per night for sites with hookups at Watchman; $20 per night for river sites. Showers nearby but outside park. Tent and RV sites.

HOTELS, MOTELS, & INNS
(unless otherwise noted, rates are for 2 persons in a double room, high season)

INSIDE THE PARK:

Zion Lodge (off Utah 9) Xanterra Parks & Resorts, Springdale, UT 84767. (303) 297-2757. 121 rooms, with AC; 40 cabins. $107. Rest.

OUTSIDE THE PARK:

In Springdale, UT 84767:

Bumbleberry Inn 97 Bumbleberry Ln., P.O. Box 346. (800) 828-1534 or (435) 772-3224. 47 units. $78-$88. AC, pool, rest.

Canyon Ranch Motel 668 Zion Park Blvd., P.O. Box 175. (435) 772-3357. 22 units, 4 with kitchenettes. $68-$88. AC, pool.

Cliffrose Lodge & Gardens 281 Zion Park Blvd., P.O. Box 510. (800) 243-8824 or (435) 772-3234. 39 units. $119-$145. AC, pool.

Driftwood Lodge 1515 Zion Park Blvd., P.O. Box 98. (888) 801-8811 or (435) 772-3262. 42 units. $72-$119. AC, pool, rest.

Flanigan's Inn 428 Zion Park Blvd., P.O. Box 100. (800) 765-7787 or (435) 772-3244. 35 units. $99-$119. AC, pool, rest.

O'Toole's Under the Eaves Guest House 980 Zion Park Blvd. (435) 772-3457. 6 rooms. $80-$155. AC.

In Kanab, UT 84741:

Parry Lodge 89 E. Center St. (800) 748-4104 or (435) 644-2601. 89 units. $73. AC, pool, rest.

Shilo Inn 296 W. 100 North. (800) 222-2244 or (435) 644-2562. 118 units. $55-$150. AC, pool.

For additional accommodations near Zion NP, call Kane County Travel, 78 S. 100 East, Kanab, UT 84741. (800) 733-5263 or (435) 644-5033.

THE PACIFIC SOUTHWEST

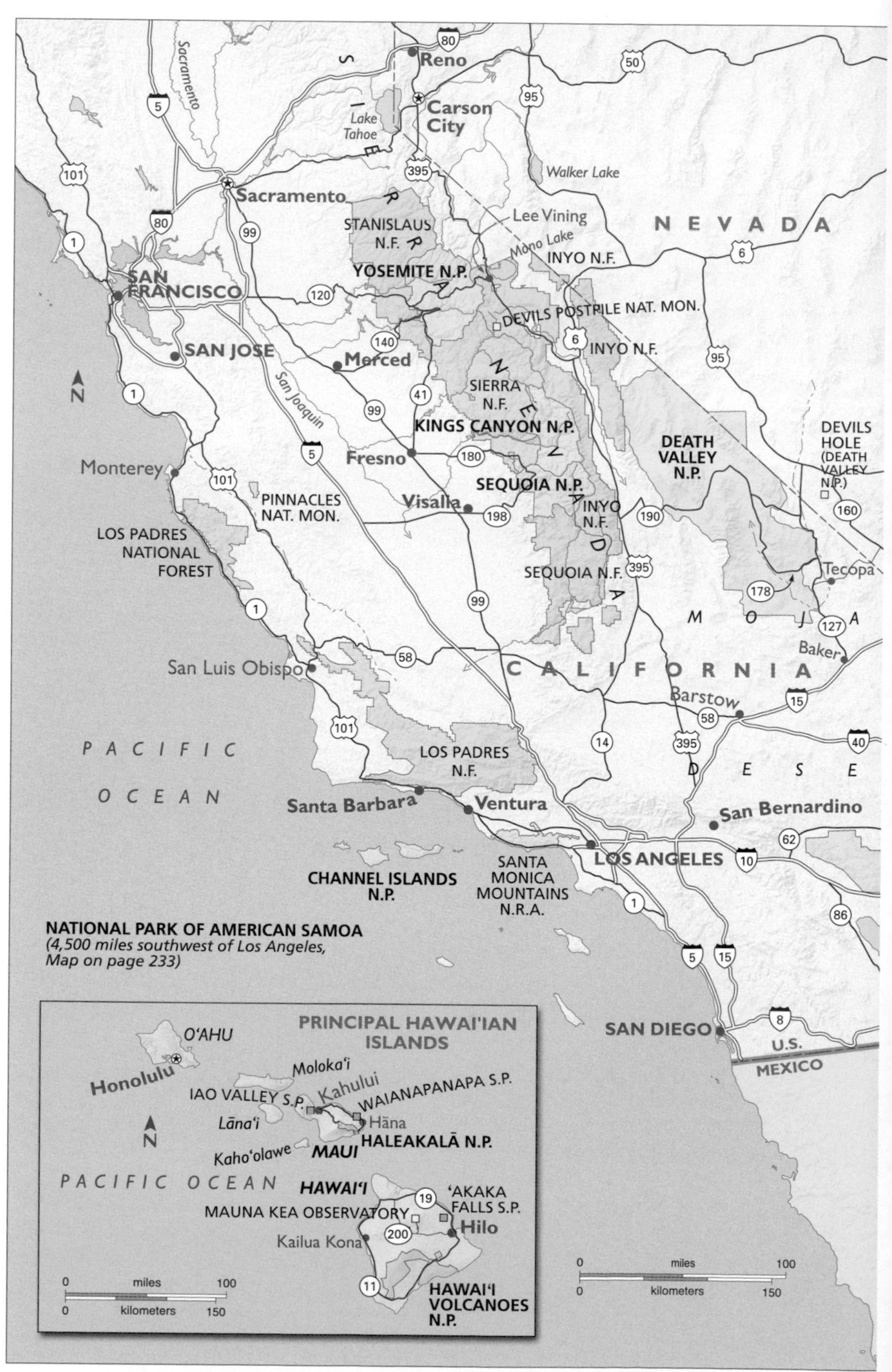
Reno
Carson City
Lake Tahoe
Walker Lake
Sacramento
Lee Vining
Mono Lake
STANISLAUS N.F.
YOSEMITE N.P.
NEVADA
INYO N.F.
SAN FRANCISCO
DEVILS POSTPILE NAT. MON.
SAN JOSE
Merced
SIERRA N.F.
KINGS CANYON N.P.
DEATH VALLEY N.P.
DEVILS HOLE (DEATH VALLEY N.P.)
Monterey
Fresno
SEQUOIA N.P.
PINNACLES NAT. MON.
Visalia
LOS PADRES NATIONAL FOREST
SEQUOIA N.F.
Tecopa
MOJAVE
Baker
San Luis Obispo
CALIFORNIA
Barstow
PACIFIC OCEAN
LOS PADRES N.F.
DESERT
Santa Barbara
Ventura
San Bernardino
LOS ANGELES
CHANNEL ISLANDS N.P.
SANTA MONICA MOUNTAINS N.R.A.
NATIONAL PARK OF AMERICAN SAMOA
(4,500 miles southwest of Los Angeles, Map on page 233)
SAN DIEGO
U.S.
MEXICO
PRINCIPAL HAWAI'IAN ISLANDS
O'AHU
Honolulu
Moloka'i
Kahului
IAO VALLEY S.P.
WAIANAPANAPA S.P.
Hāna
Lāna'i
HALEAKALĀ N.P.
Kaho'olawe
MAUI
PACIFIC OCEAN
HAWAI'I
'AKAKA FALLS S.P.
MAUNA KEA OBSERVATORY
Hilo
Kailua Kona
HAWAI'I VOLCANOES N.P.
miles
kilometers
N

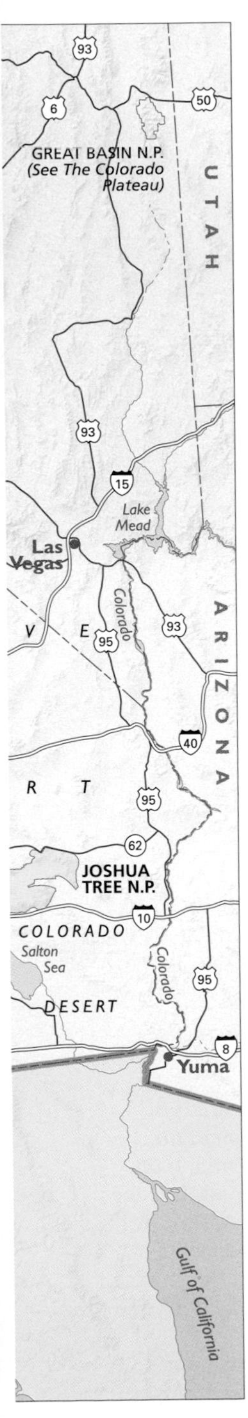

THE PACIFIC SOUTHWEST

Visitors to the national parks of the Pacific Southwest can bask on a tropical isle or climb a snow-clad peak. They can watch the vegetation change from tropical to subalpine in a single Hawai'i drive, observe plants and animals that make their home in only one place in the world, and see the Earth build itself.

The island parks, all of them on volcanoes except Channel Islands, are microcosms of evolution and laboratories of the effects of humans on the land. At Hawai'i Volcanoes and Haleakalā, preservation efforts seek to stem the damage done over centuries to the native plants, about 90 percent of which are endemic—found nowhere else. Some 2,300 miles southwest of Hawai'i, American Samoa National Park shelters fragments of tropical rain forest and coral reef as well as an endangered 3,000-year-old human culture. Off the coast of California, the Channel Islands safeguard numerous threatened seals, sea lions, and seabirds. They also harbor some 70 endemic plants.

On the mainland, Sequoia & Kings Canyon and Yosemite National Parks provide haven for a multitude of plant and animal communities in what John Muir called "the range of light"—the Sierra Nevada. Chaparral and wild oats robe the foothills; cathedral-like groves of conifers embellish slopes; wildflowers overrun alpine meadows. Marmots and pikas scurry on the glacier-carved heights, some of which soar 12,000 feet.

To the south, Joshua Tree National Park preserves the unique high Mojave Desert habitat of the giant branching yucca, while the 120-mile-long, erosion-sculptured basin that is Death Valley National Park—the continent's hottest spot—shelters more than 900 plant varieties, as well as bobcats and desert bighorn sheep.

Yosemite and Sequoia & Kings Canyon lie about 4 hours apart by car. From Sequoia, 6 road hours will get you to Death Valley, with 3.5 more to Joshua Tree. A drive from there to the Channel Islands takes 3 hours, plus a 90-minute boat ride. To reach Hawai'i from California, count on at least a 5.5-hour flight, and to American Samoa, expect an 11-hour plane trip (see p. 233) plus a Honolulu layover.

Ofu Island from Asaga Strait

AMERICAN SAMOA

AMERICAN SAMOA
ESTABLISHED 1993
10,520 acres—7,970 land, 2,550 marine

For some 3,000 years, the people of Polynesia's oldest culture have been keenly attuned to their island environment, holding it to be precious and managing it communally. The name they gave their land reflects their attitude: Samoa means "sacred earth."

Located roughly 2,300 miles southwest of Hawai'i, American Samoa, a United States territory, comprises five volcanic islands and two coral atolls. In 1988 Congress authorized the land for a national park. In 1993 Samoan chiefs agreed to sign a 50-year lease that enables the National Park Service to manage an area of rain forest, beach, and coral reef on three islands. Samoans help manage the park, and their villages offer a few guest facilities (ask the park about its unique home-stay program).

The park protects hundreds of plant species in five distinct rain forest communities: lowland, montane, coast, ridge, and cloud. It is the only such rain forest on American soil. Among the fauna visitors can see are tropical birds and the endangered flying fox—a fruit bat with the wingspan of a barn owl.

On **Tutuila,** American Samoa's largest island, lofty volcanic ridges overlook the deep blue waters of **Pago Pago Harbor.** Except for a few villages, and the scenic drive that skirts the harbor and the dramatic southern coastline, there is little level land. Atop this crumbled terrain and plunging steeply toward the sea on the island's northern side lies the park area—about 2,500 acres of land and some 1,200 acres of ocean.

Parkland on **Ta'u,** the easternmost island, encompasses about 5,400 acres—including Lata Mountain, American Samoa's highest peak—and 1,000 acres offshore. Unforgettable is the panoramic view from the cloud forest toward the rugged cliffs of the southern coast. Small, remote **Ofu Island** includes what many call American Samoa's loveliest beach. Its main attraction is the 350-acre coral reef.

How to Get There

There are flights to Pago Pago from Honolulu twice a week that take 5.5 hours. Time from California is about 14 hours, including a 3- or 4-hour Honolulu layover. From the airport, taxi or rent a car to the Rainmaker Hotel, Pago Airport Inn, Tessarea Vaitogi Inn, Tradewinds, or Motu-o-Fiafiaga Motel. From any of those accommodations you can reach the park visitor center in Pago Pago by bus or car, or by walking about 25 minutes. Accommodations are also available on Ta'u, Ofu, and Olosega. To get to Ta'u and Ofu requires about a half-hour flight each from Pago Pago. Ofu's park begins at the edge of the airport; parkland on Ta'u is about a half-hour walk from the airport.

When to Go

Any time. The islands are 14° south of the Equator, giving them a hot and rainy climate year-round. The heat and rain abate slightly from June through September.

How to Visit

Contact the park headquarters before you visit. For information, write National Park of American Samoa, Pago Pago, American Samoa 96799. Phone (684) 633-7082. www.nps.gov/npsa. Or drop in at the visitor center, located at Pago Plaza at the head of Pago Pago Harbor.

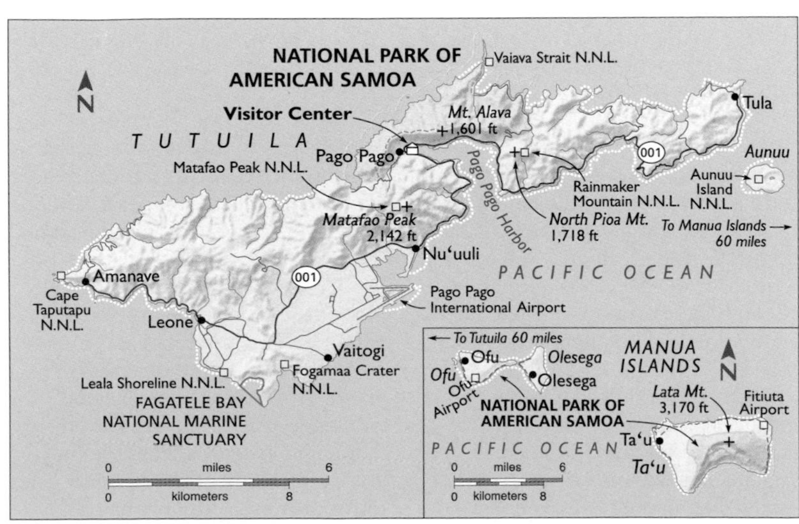

Sunrise over Anacapa Island

CHANNEL ISLANDS

CALIFORNIA
ESTABLISHED MARCH 5, 1980
249,354 acres

Strung along a stretch of California coast are five separate pieces of land surrounded by 1,252 square nautical miles of sea. Channel Islands National Park and Channel Islands National Marine Sanctuary protect these islands, the sea around them, and a dazzling array of wildlife.

Two of the islands in this unusual park, Anacapa and Santa Barbara, were earlier designated a national monument, a refuge for nesting seabirds, seals, sea lions, and other long-threatened marine animals. When those islands and three others were joined in a national park, the mission of refuge continued.

Today the park manages a long-term ecological research program that may be the best in the park system. The marine sanctuary—established in 1980—extends for 6 nautical miles around each island. Among the resources it protects are giant kelp forests with nearly a thousand kinds of fish and marine plants. The park and sanctuary also guard the area from encroachment by another kind of island—the seagoing oil rigs of the Santa Barbara Channel.

About 70 different species of plants grow only on the islands, and some plants exist on but one of them. The islands shelter the only breeding colony of northern fur seals south of Alaska. To help native animals, park managers have gotten rid of such nonnative species as black rats, burros, rabbits, and feral cats.

A permanent ranger resides on each island. Reservations are needed for camping. Fishing and diving are strictly regulated and airplanes are asked to keep their distance.

Chumash Indians lived on the Channel Islands until the early 19th century. They traveled from island to island in plank canoes caulked with tar from oil seeps. The tar from such seeps still appears on beaches, reminding strollers of the reason for the oil rigs on the horizon.

How to Get There

Take US 101 to Ventura. Northbound, exit at Victoria Avenue; southbound, at Seaward Avenue. Follow park signs to the harbor and then to the visitor center on Spinnaker Drive. Get oriented here and then go to the nearby Island Packers office and inquire about boat schedules to the islands. Airports: Camarillo, Oxnard, Santa Barbara, and Los Angeles International.

When to Go

All-year park. Boat schedules peak in spring and summer, but you should be able to book a trip in any month. Best whale-watching time: late December through March, and July and August.

How to Visit

Your exploration of this unique park depends on your time and resources. Even a short stop at the mainland visitor center will give you an understanding and appreciation of the park. For a 1-day visit, see the closest island, **Anacapa.** Take all necessities, especially food and water, and dress in layers for all types of weather. Trips to the other islands require substantial advance planning. (See **Information & Activities** p. 238.) The park cautions people from doing more than treading lightly on the islands, which are maintained for the well-being of the residents, both flora and fauna.

ANACAPA ISLAND

14 miles from Ventura; a full day

Before stepping aboard your Island Packers boat for the trip to Anacapa, take some time to explore the park's **visitor center** in Ventura. Among the attractions are an indoor marine life exhibit, a native plant garden, and Chumash artifacts. During the summer divers with cameras and microphones drop into the landing cove on East Anacapa Island to give people on the dock and in the center's auditorium a close-up of the underwater world.

Out on the water as your boat plies the **Santa Barbara Channel,** flyingfish skip through the waves and nearby pelicans skim over them. Oil rigs stand on dark stilts while gray whales may glide by during winter trips, and seals appear and disappear in the channel waters year-round.

Approaching the landing cove, the boat passes Anacapa's **Arch Rock** and sails close enough to the rocky coast for you to see resident California sea lions. At the end of the 60-minute voyage (which can be rough), you climb a ladder to the landing platform. Then you climb 154 steps up a metal-and-concrete stairway to the

Protected elephant seal

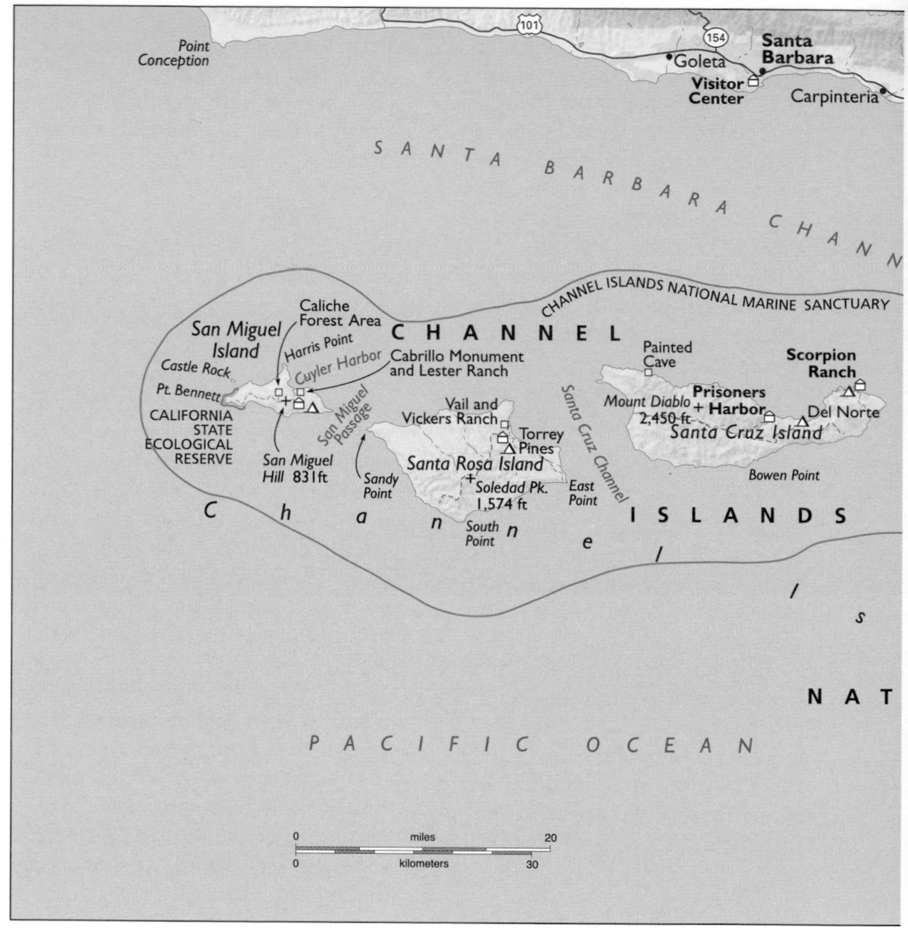

top of the cliff-girt island.

There you can walk the 1.5-mile nature trail on your own or fall in behind a ranger who dispenses island lore: That plain brown plant (giant coreopsis) is a tree sunflower; in late winter and spring it bursts into glorious gold. Those finely ground shells you are walking on are remnants of a Chumash midden. The Indians hunted on the island and used it as a stopover on trips to the mainland. The trail skirts the edge of a cliff 150 feet above the sea. Stand well back from the unstable cliff edges. You are ominously warned: *Don't risk your life for a view.*

A building that looks like a Spanish mission church is not what it seems. The structure protects two large water tanks. Vandals who in years past took potshots at the wooden tanks refrain from sniping at a "church." The few buildings date from days when the island lighthouse, now automated, had a crew. Your day ends with a descent to the boat, which picks up the passengers about 3 or 4 hours after arrival.

Anacapa consists of three islets. You visit only East Anacapa. Scuba divers, subject to strict conservation laws, plunge off Middle Anacapa to see the kelp forests or the remains of the S.S. *Winfield Scott,* which sank here in 1853 with no loss of life.

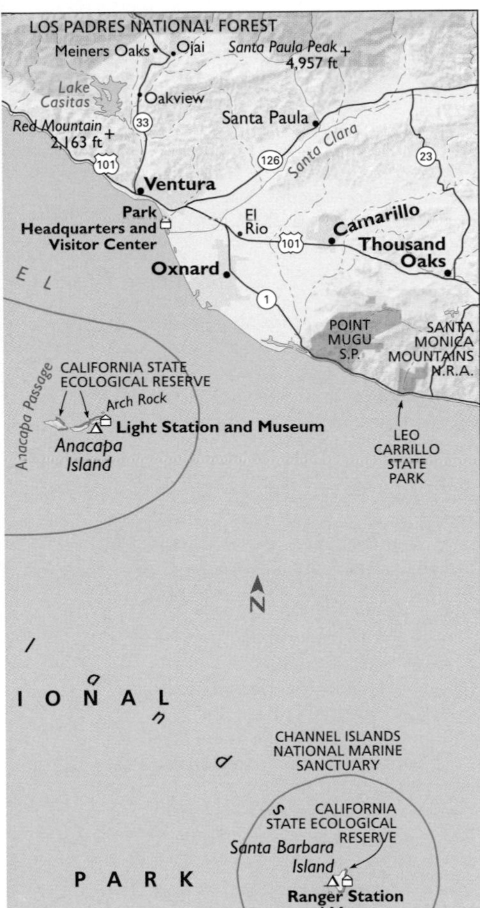

Divers can take only photographs. **West Anacapa** is closed to the public to protect the largest nesting brown pelican population on the U.S. Pacific coast.

THE OTHER ISLANDS

If you decide to go to the other islands, your visits will be controlled by weather, regulations, and boat and plane schedules.

Santa Cruz (21 miles from Ventura; 60,000 acres) is the largest of the Channel Islands. The Nature Conservancy runs the western portion of the island and strictly limits visitors. The park owns the eastern end. Among its distinctive species are the island oak, the cat-size island fox, and the island scrub jay.

Santa Rosa (45 miles from Ventura; 53,000 acres) may have been inhabited by people as long as 13,000 years. Ranchers raised sheep then cattle on the island's grasslands from the middle of the 19th century until 1997. A freshwater marsh sustains waterfowl. There are more than 195 bird species on the island and 500 plant species.

San Miguel (55 miles from Ventura; 9,325 acres), the westernmost island, is home to five seal species. Over 30,000 haul out at a time on Point Bennett (16-mile round trip hike). A bizarre caliche "forest" spikes a plateau. Caliche—a kind of limey sand—encrusted vegetation that died and decayed, leaving only the hollow, calcified sand castings.

Once used as a bombing range and missile test site, the island is owned by the United States Navy and administered by the National Park Service, which limits visitors to the beach, ranch, and campground unless they are accompanied by one of the park's rangers.

Santa Barbara (52 miles from Ventura; 640 acres), once a sheep pasturage, has 5.5 miles of nature trails. In springtime, crevices on the island's steep cliffs house the world's largest known breeding population of the remarkable Xantus's murrelet. When a chick is only two days old, it makes a bold foray into night, tumbling down to the sea where it joins its waiting parents. Except for the nesting season, the murrelet will spend the remainder of its life on the ocean. In spring and summer, you can usually see pelicans and sea lions, but don't expect to come across the rock-dwelling island night lizard. It is shy, secretive, and protected.

INFORMATION & ACTIVITIES

HEADQUARTERS

1901 Spinnaker Dr., Ventura, CA 93001. Phone (805) 658-5730. www.nps.gov/chis

ACCESSIBILITY & BOAT INFORMATION

Park open all year. Access to islands subject to unpredictable weather conditions; the channel can be rough. Call headquarters for information.

To Anacapa, Santa Rosa, San Miguel, and Santa Barbara: Boat trips offered by Island Packers and Truth Aquatics, the park's authorized concessioners (see below). Visitors using private boats must obey closed and restricted areas.

To Santa Cruz: Island Packers and Truth Aquatics offer day trips to the eastern end. Landing permits are required for Nature Conservancy property; call (805) 642-0345 ext. 510 or visit www.nature.org.

Boats from Ventura: Contact headquarters or Island Packers, 1691 Spinnaker Dr., Ste. 105B, Ventura, CA 93001. (805) 642-1393 for information and reservations or www.islandpackers.com. For weekend trips, reserve at least 3 to 5 days in advance.

Boats from Santa Barbara: Contact Truth Aquatics, 301 Cabrillo Blvd., Santa Barbara, CA 93101. (805) 963-3564, www.truthaquatics.com.

Plane information: Channel Island Aviation, 305 Durley Ave., Camarillo, CA 93010. (805) 987-1301, www.flcia.com.

VISITOR & INFORMATION CENTERS

Lagomarsino Visitor Center, 1901 Spinnaker Dr., Ventura; **Santa Barbara visitor center,** 113 Harbor Way, 4th Floor, (805) 884-1475; **East Anacapa visitor center.** Open all year.

ENTRANCE FEE

None. For boat fares to islands, inquire at headquarters, Island Packers, or Truth Aquatics (see above).

PETS

Not permitted in park headquarters or on islands.

FACILITIES FOR DISABLED

Visitor center at Ventura, restrooms, theater, exhibits, and observation tower accessible. Boats and islands are not.

THINGS TO DO

Santa Barbara Channel: whale-watching late December through March and June through September.

Anacapa: free naturalist-led walks; also, camping, bird-watching, wildlife watching, tide pools, swimming and snorkeling, scuba and skin diving, fishing (license needed; certain areas closed).

Santa Barbara: naturalist-led walks, camping, marine life observation, bird-watching, tide pools.

Santa Rosa: naturalist-led walks, camping, nature viewing, tide pools.

San Miguel: free naturalist-led walk to caliche "forest"; also, camping, seal- and sea lion-watching, tide-pools.

Santa Cruz: marine life observation, bird-watching.

SPECIAL ADVISORIES

- When hiking on islands, stay on trails and away from cliffs.
- All birds, animals, tide pools, shells, rocks, and plants are protected; do not take anything but photos.
- Avoid Hantavirus pulmonary syndrome, a potentially fatal virus carried by the deer mouse, by staying away from cabins and campsites where rodent droppings and burrows are evident.
- Fishing is prohibited.
- Sea kayaking from mainland to the islands (12 miles) is not for novices or for anyone not properly trained, conditioned, and equipped.

OVERNIGHT BACKPACKING

All five islands have campgrounds; 14-day limit. Reservations and permits required; contact the NPRS (see p. 10). $10 per night. Tent sites only. Drinking water at Scorpion on Santa Cruz and Bechers Bay on Santa Rosa. Group camping available. No food services.

HOTELS, MOTELS, & INNS

(unless otherwise noted, rates are for 2 persons in a double room, high season)

In Ventura, CA 93001:

Bella Maggiore Inn 67 S. California St. (800) 523-8479 or (805) 652-0277.

28 units. $75-$175. Rest.
Country Inn and Suites 298 S. Chestnut St. (800) 456-4000 or (805) 653-1434. 120 units. $99-$139. AC, pool.
Four Point Sheraton 1050 Schooner Dr. (800) 229-5732 or (805) 658-1212. 175 units. $119-$350. Pool, restaurant.
Inn on the Beach 1175 S. Seaward Ave. (805) 652-2000. 24 units. $129-$195.
La Mer European Bed & Breakfast 411 Poli St. 93002. (805) 643-3600. 6 units. $115-$235.

For additional lodgings, contact Ventura Visitor & Convention Bureau. (805) 648-2075.

EXCURSIONS

SANTA MONICA MOUNTAINS NATIONAL RECREATION AREA

THOUSAND OAKS, CALIFORNIA

Here southern California's rare Mediterranean climate offers habitats ranging from chaparral to oak wood lands to rocky canyons to marshes and sandy beaches. Government and private efforts preserve the area's natural and cultural resources including Paramount Ranch (a working Hollywood set), spectacular Mulholland Drive, Zuma Beach, Cold Creek Canyon Preserve, and the Will Rogers State Historic Park. 154,095-acre boundary. Hiking, mountain biking, horseback riding. More than 100 campsites. Open all year, dawn to dusk (some areas 9 a.m. to sunset or by reservation). Information at NRA headquarters in Thousand Oaks, about 30 miles west of Los Angeles. (805) 370-2301.

LOS PADRES NATIONAL FOREST

SANTA BARBARA, CALIFORNIA

This rugged forest preserves a vast area of central California coast and mountain ranges stretching over five counties. Chaparral and desert ecosystems are a short drive from Ventura. The Jacinto Reyes Scenic Byway (Calif. 33) threads through the forest north of Ojai. 1,700,000 acres. Camping, backpacking, hiking. Picnic areas. Open year-round. Information at Ojai Ranger Station, approximately 30 miles from Channel Islands NP. (805) 646-4348.

Wind-rippled sand dunes

DEATH VALLEY

CALIFORNIA & NEVADA
ESTABLISHED OCTOBER 31, 1994
About 3.4 million acres

The largest national park south of Alaska, Death Valley is known for extremes: It is North America's driest and hottest spot (with fewer than 2 inches of rainfall annually and a record high of 134°F), and has the lowest elevation on the continent—282 feet below sea level. Even with its extremes, the park still receives nearly a million visitors each year.

In 1849 emigrants bound for California's gold fields strayed into the 120-mile-long basin, enduring a two-month ordeal of "hunger and thirst and an awful silence." One of the last to leave looked down from a mountain at the narrow valley and said, "Good-bye, Death Valley."

The forbidding moniker belies the beauty in this vast graben, the geological term for a sunken fragment of the Earth's crust. Here are rocks sculptured by erosion, richly tinted mudstone hills and canyons, luminous sand dunes, lush oases, and a 200-square-mile salt pan surrounded by mountains, one of America's greatest vertical rises. In some years spring rains trigger wildflower blooms amid more than a thousand varieties of plants.

Native Americans, most recently the Shoshone, found ways to adapt to the more recent and forbidding desert conditions that exist here now. Rock art and artifacts indicate a human presence dating back at least 9,000 years.

From 1883 to 1889, wagon teams hauled powdery white borax from mines since fallen to ruin, an enterprise that spread word of Death Valley's striking landscapes, deep solitude, and crystalline air.

As night falls, Death Valley's elusive populations of bobcats, kit foxes, and rodents venture out. Far above on steep mountain slopes, desert bighorn sheep forage among Joshua trees, scrubby junipers, and pines, while hawks soar on thermals rising into vivid blue, cloudless skies.

How to Get There

No public transit services serve the park. Most visitors arrive by automobile from Los Angeles, California, or Las Vegas, Nevada.

From Los Angeles, the most scenic route crosses the eastern Mojave Desert via I-15 through Barstow. At Baker it turns north onto Calif. 127 to Shoshone, where Calif. 178 runs west and north along the valley floor to Furnace Creek.

From Las Vegas, take Nev. 160 west 42 miles to Old Spanish Trail (Tecopa Rd.), continuing through Tecopa to Calif. 127, turning north to Shoshone and picking up Calif. 178 to Furnace Creek. To include a visit to the early-20th-century Nevada gold-mining ghost town of Rhyolite, take US 95 to Beatty, picking up Nev. 374, which becomes Calif. 190 and leads west to the park.

When to Go

All-year park. Temperatures from November through February average between 25°F and 75°F. From May through September, average highs range between 100°F and 116°F; overnight lows may top 100°F.

How to Visit

Death Valley's remote location and size make an automobile essential. An overnight stay allows time for the valley's vivid sunrises and sunsets, and a visit to the **Death Valley Museum** and **Furnace Creek Visitor Center.** Plan also to visit the **Harmony Borax Works** near the Furnace Creek Campground, to walk the 1-mile **Golden Canyon Interpretive Trail,** and to drive to **Zabriskie Point** for fine views of the valley.

A second day permits exploration of the valley's northern reaches and **Scottys Castle,** the retreat of an early-20th-century millionaire, and nearby **Ubehebe Crater,** blasted out during the region's volcanic past. If you are a seasoned hiker, consider the strenuous all-day hike from **Wildrose Canyon** to sweeping views atop 11,049-foot **Telescope Peak,** Death Valley's highest point.

ENTERING FROM THE EAST: SHOSHONE TO FURNACE CREEK

130 miles (including side trips); 1 to 2 days

From the mining town of Shoshone, head west on Calif. 178 through the **Amargosa Range,** whose colorful dusky palette reflects the high mineral content in its sediments. Cresting 3,315-foot **Salsberry Pass,** you'll descend through the weathered **Black Mountains** to 1,290-foot **Jubilee Pass,** where wildflowers sometimes bloom in spring.

Approaching the ruins of gold-mining **Ashford Mill** and the **Death Valley Salt Pan**—the residue of a saline lake that existed over 20,000 years ago—you reach zero elevation. From here to Furnace Creek you travel *below* sea level, dipping to minus 282 feet at **Badwater Basin**

27 miles north, the North America's lowest point. Park at Badwater, where sunrises ignite the ridgelines. Continue north 4 miles to the turnoff onto a rough road to **Natural Bridge,** an arch spanning a richly tinted conglomerate canyon. A quarter-mile trail to the bridge passes other striking formations.

About 1.5 miles north, look left for the half-mile spur road to **Devils Golf Course,** a meringue of rock salt pinnacles that forms as water evaporates up through the salty crust.

Another 5 miles north brings you to the 9-mile one-way **Artists Drive** loop road through the **Artists Palette,** a rumpled terrain of volcanic ash whose yellows, red-oranges, greens, and muted purples challenge plein-air painters. About 4 miles north, the moderate 1-mile-long **Golden Canyon Interpretive Trail** winds through a canyon that near sunset gleams as if dusted with gold.

Continue north to the Calif. 190 junction. If you want to rest or refuel, stop at the **Furnace Creek Visitor Center.** If not, turn right onto Calif. 190 for the short drive to **Zabriskie Point,** a popular sunrise viewing spot, where rain and wind have shaped rock into dramatic contours. The promontory commands a broad view of mudstone badlands. To explore them, continue on for a mile to **Twenty Mule Team Canyon,** which is threaded by a 3-mile gravel loop road.

Return to the highway, turn right, and continue on the 13-mile spur road to 5,475-foot **Dantes View.** The mile-high panorama plunges to Badwater and sweeps across the salt pan to the forbidding Panamint Range and 11,049-foot Telescope Peak.

If you have not yet visited Furnace Creek, backtrack 24 miles to the **Furnace Creek Visitor Center,** which has exhibits and a bookstore. Check for ranger-guided walks and evening

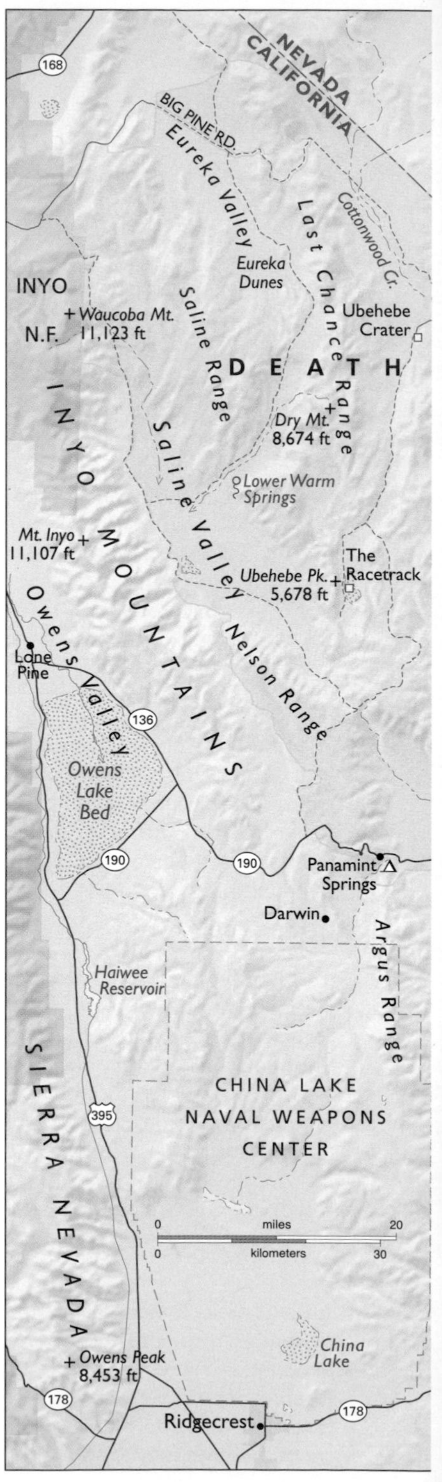

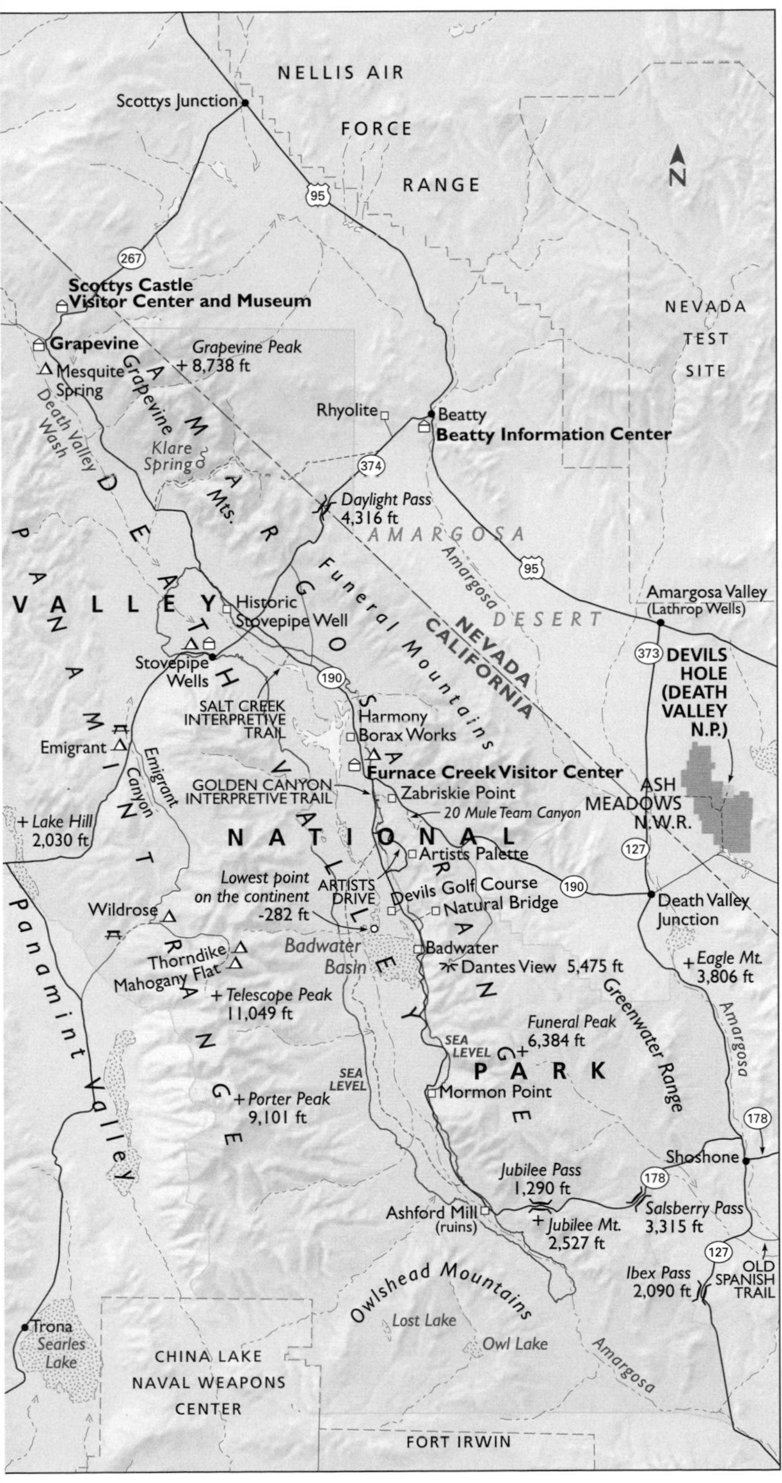

NELLIS AIR FORCE RANGE
Scottys Junction
Scottys Castle Visitor Center and Museum
Grapevine
Grapevine Peak 8,738 ft
Mesquite Spring
Death Valley Wash
Grapevine Mts.
Klare Spring
Rhyolite
Beatty
Beatty Information Center
Daylight Pass 4,316 ft
AMARGOSA DESERT
Amargosa
Funeral Mountains
AMARGOSA RANGE
NEVADA
CALIFORNIA
NEVADA TEST SITE
Amargosa Valley (Lathrop Wells)
DEVILS HOLE (DEATH VALLEY N.P.)
ASH MEADOWS N.W.R.
DEATH VALLEY NATIONAL PARK
Historic Stovepipe Well
Stovepipe Wells
SALT CREEK INTERPRETIVE TRAIL
Harmony Borax Works
Furnace Creek Visitor Center
Emigrant
Emigrant Canyon
GOLDEN CANYON INTERPRETIVE TRAIL
Zabriskie Point
20 Mule Team Canyon
Lake Hill 2,030 ft
Artists Palette
ARTISTS DRIVE
Lowest point on the continent -282 ft
Devils Golf Course
Natural Bridge
Death Valley Junction
Wildrose
Badwater Basin
Badwater
Dantes View 5,475 ft
Eagle Mt. 3,806 ft
Thorndike
Mahogany Flat
Telescope Peak 11,049 ft
PANAMINT RANGE
Panamint Valley
Greenwater Range
Funeral Peak 6,384 ft
SEA LEVEL
Mormon Point
Porter Peak 9,101 ft
Shoshone
Jubilee Pass 1,290 ft
Salsberry Pass 3,315 ft
Ashford Mill (ruins)
Jubilee Mt. 2,527 ft
Ibex Pass 2,090 ft
OLD SPANISH TRAIL
Owlshead Mountains
Lost Lake
Owl Lake
Trona
Searles Lake
CHINA LAKE NAVAL WEAPONS CENTER
FORT IRWIN
95
267
374
190
373
127
178
N

Salt crystals of Devils Golf Course

programs (Oct. through March) and visit the **Death Valley Museum.**

The springs at **Furnace Creek oasis** produce over a million gallons a day, watering oleanders, palms, and tamarisk trees, and the incongruously verdant fairways of the golf course at the **Furnace Creek Ranch** *(private)*. Guests at the Furnace Creek Inn may explore the interior and gardens of this classic Spanish mission-style structure, constructed in 1927 of adobe and native stone.

FURNACE CREEK TO SCOTTYS CASTLE

90 miles (including excursions); a half day

One mile north of the Furnace Creek Visitor Center, leave your car and walk the quarter-mile paved **Harmony Borax Works Interpretive Trail** to the ruins of Death Valley's first successful borax mining venture. Original equipment includes a borax wagon with 6-foot-high rear wheels.

Continue north on Calif. 190 past the Beatty Cutoff to the 1-mile spur road to the **Salt Creek Interpretive Trail.** Spring-fed marshy pools here are home to Death Valley's unusual desert pupfish, descendant of creatures that flourished in the basin's ancient lake at least 12,000 years ago. Like the oasis at Scottys Castle, this is a prime bird-watching area, frequented by many of the 350 species found in Death Valley, including Canada geese, peregrine falcons, hawks, and eagles.

Nearby sand dunes ripple across 14 square miles. At sunrise and sunset the wind-sculptured waves of quartz-grain sand take on a luminous rosy glow. Accessible via paved road near Stovepipe Wells Village, these dunes have no established trails; park and walk where you wish.

Back in the car, continue about 30 miles to **Grapevine Canyon** and **Scottys Castle,** a Mediterranean-style architectural gem dating from 1922. Once the retreat of a Chicago couple, the ranch is named for frequent house guest and "desert rat" Walter Scott. Daily on the hour, the Park Service conducts tours through the mansion, which holds original furnishings. In winter, be prepared to wait up to 2 hours for a tour. While waiting, consider a meal at the Castle's restaurant, a picnic outside, or an amble up **Windy Point Trail.**

INFORMATION & ACTIVITIES

HEADQUARTERS
Visitor Center, Calif. 190, P.O. Box 579, Death Valley, CA 92328. Phone (760) 786-3200. www.nps.gov/deva

SEASONS & ACCESSIBILITY
Open year-round.

VISITOR & INFORMATION CENTERS
Furnace Creek Visitor Center in Furnace Creek, off Calif. 190;
Scottys Castle Visitor Center and Museum, off Nev. 267 on north end of the park;
Beatty Information Center, US 95, Beatty, Nevada

ENTRANCE FEE
$20 per vehicle, good for one week.

PETS
Must be leashed at all times. Not allowed on trails or in backcountry.

FACILITIES FOR DISABLED
The visitor center; Scottys Castle; and Furnace Creek, Texas Spring, and Sunset Campgrounds are wheelchair accessible.

THINGS TO DO
Free ranger- and naturalist-led activities available mid-October to mid-April: nature walks and talks, evening programs, children's programs. Also, hiking, nature trails, living history tours, bicycling, bird-watching, horseback riding.

SPECIAL ADVISORIES
• Death Valley's heat can make any emergency situation life-threatening. For advice on hot weather travel, consult the *Death Valley Guide,* available at roadside kiosks, ranger stations, and the visitor center.
• Drink plenty of water; one gallon per person per day is recommended, two gallons if hiking. Emergency radiator water is available from barrels located along main park roads.
• Abandoned mineshafts and prospect holes pose dangers. Never enter an abandoned tunnel.
• Hat and sunglasses are essential.
• Desert rains, though brief, cause flash floods. Never ford washouts, even in a 4-wheel-drive vehicle.

OVERNIGHT BACKPACKING
Backcountry camping permitted in areas at least 2 miles from main roads and a quarter mile from water sources. Free voluntary permits; hikers should register at visitor center and inquire about which areas prohibit camping.

CAMPGROUNDS
Nine campgrounds, 30-day limit. **Furnace Creek, Mesquite Spring, Emigrant, Stovepipe Wells,** and **Wildrose** open all year; **Texas Spring** and **Sunset** open Oct. to April; **Thorndike** and **Mahogany Flat** open March through Oct. Reservations taken only for Furnace Creek (call NPRS; see p. 10); all others first come, first served. Fees: $10-16 at Furnace Creek; $10 at Sunset, Stovepipe Wells, and Mesquite Spring; $12 at Texas Spring; free at Thorndike, Emigrant, Mahogany Flat, and Wildrose.

HOTELS, MOTELS, & INNS
(unless otherwise noted, rates are for 2 persons in a double room, high season)

INSIDE THE PARK:
Furnace Creek Inn Furnace Creek off Calif. 190. (760) 786-2345. 66 units. $250-$375. Pool, restaurant.
Furnace Creek Ranch Furnace Creek off Calif. 190. P.O. Box 1, Death Valley 92328. (760) 786-2345. 244 units. $130-$180. Pool, restaurant.
Stovepipe Wells Village Motel Stovepipe Wells Village, P.O. Box 187, Death Valley 92328. (760) 786-2387. 83 units. $83-$103. 14 RV hookups, $23. AC, pool, restaurant.

For additional lodgings, contact the Death Valley Chamber of Commerce, P.O. Box 157, Shoshone, CA 92384, (760) 852-4524 or the Beatty Chamber of Commerce, 119 E. Main St., Beatty, NV (775) 553-2424.

Volcanic cinder slope

HALEAKALĀ

MAUI, HAWAI'I
ESTABLISHED AUGUST 1, 1916
30,183 acres

Haleakalā, a giant shield volcano, forms the eastern bulwark of the island of Maui. According to legend, it was here, in the awe-inspiring basin at the mountain's summit, that the demigod Maui snared the sun, releasing it only after it promised to move more slowly across the sky. Haleakalā means "house of the sun"; the park encompasses the basin and portions of the volcano's flanks.

A United Nations International Biosphere Reserve, the park comprises starkly contrasting worlds of mountain and coast. The road to the summit of Haleakalā rises from near sea level to 10,000 feet in 38 miles—possibly the steepest such gradient for autos in the world. Visitors ascend through several climate and vegetation zones, from humid subtropical lowlands to subalpine desert. Striking plants and animals such as the Haleakalā silversword and the nēnē may be seen in this mountain section.

The summit-area depression, misnamed Haleakalā Crater, formed as erosion ate away the mountain, joining two valleys. This 19-square-mile wilderness area, 2,720 feet deep, is the park's major draw.

From east of the rim, the great rain forest valley of Kīpahulu drops thousands of feet down to the coast. The upper Kīpahulu Valley is a biological reserve *(no public access)*, home to a vast profusion of flora and fauna, including some of the world's rarest birds, plants, and invertebrates. Some insects and plants evolved in the Kīpahulu Valley and live nowhere else.

Visitors reach the lower valley of Kīpahulu via the long winding Hāna Highway. Dominated by intense hues—azure sea, black rock, silver waterfalls, green forest and meadow—the coastal area was first farmed in early Polynesian times, more than 1,200 years ago. Mark Twain, who traveled to Hawai'i in 1866, may well have had this part of Kīpahulu in mind when he wrote: "For me its balmy airs are always blowing, its summer seas flashing in the sun; the pulsing of its surf-beat is in my ear; I can see its garlanded crags, its leaping cascades, its plumy palms drowsing by the shore."

How to Get There

Fly directly from the mainland, or from another Hawaiian island, to Kahului in central Maui. To reach the summit of Haleakalā, follow, sequentially, Hawaii 36, 37, 377, and 378. The 38-mile route is well marked, but note the last chance to buy food and gas is at Pukalani or Makawao. Continue on the switch-back road through miles of lush mountain rangeland to the park's northwest entrance. Allow up to 2 hours.

For the 62-mile drive to Kīpahulu, allow up to 3.5 hours. Take Hawaii 36 from Kahului around the northeastern side of the island to the town of Hāna. The road to Hāna, which becomes Hawaii 360, is famous for its narrow, tortuous course along 1,000-foot sea cliffs, into deep gorges. This drive affords many views of waterfalls and cascade pools, but few places to access them. Proceed past Hāna on Hawaii 31 for about 9 miles. Just beyond the Pools of 'Ohe'o, signs will point to off-road parking.

When to Go

All-year park. Most rain comes in winter, although temperatures remain fairly constant month to month. To avoid crowds, visit the summit after 3 p.m.; sunsets can be as spectacular as the famous sunrises. At Kīpahulu, avoid crowds by arriving early or camping overnight. Weather varies most at high elevations, and can change from very hot to rainy, cold, and windy in the same day. Temperatures can drop to freezing inside the wilderness area, although snow is rare. Coastal Kīpahulu stays warm but receives considerable rain all year.

How to Visit

It would be neither safe nor very enjoyable to try fitting both the **Haleakalā** summit and **Kīpahulu** coastal regions of the park into 1 day. To absorb more of the ambience of this unique sea-girt volcano, try to spend a day on the mountain, with a hike through the moonscape of the "crater," and a second day on the coast. Van and bus tours—some starting in predawn hours to take in a magical summit sunrise—can be arranged from most island hotels. Some companies will drive a group to the summit, then provide bicycles to ride down the mountain.

Consider taking a guided walk from **Hosmer Grove** into the Nature Conservancy's **Waikamoi Preserve,** home of living treasures including various species of honeycreepers, the premier family of native Hawaiian birds. Reservations required; call ahead for the schedule (see **Information & Activities** p. 252).

Air tours that fly around Maui and across the park are available from Kahului, but regulations limit them to high altitude.

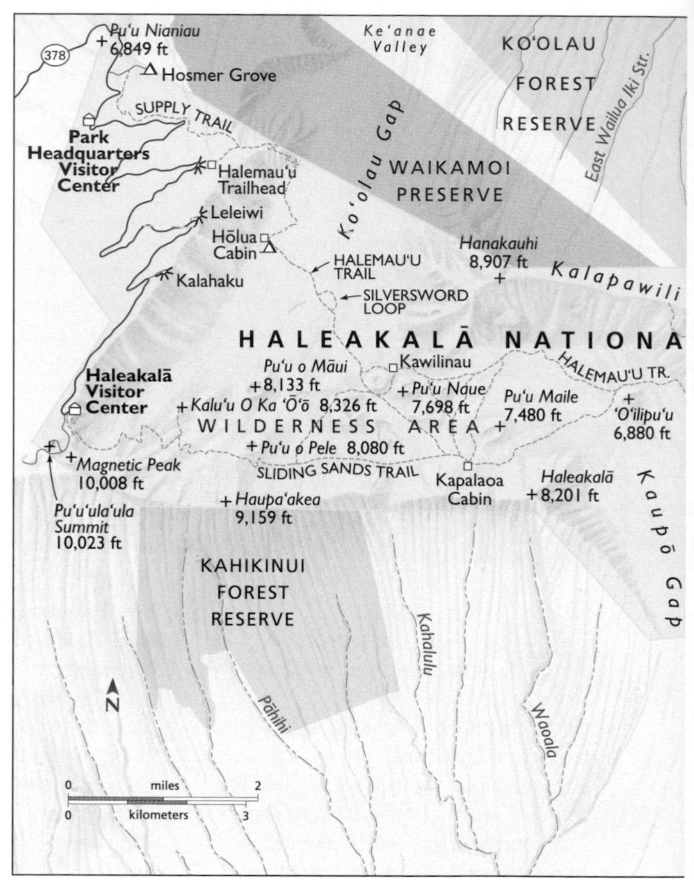

HOSMER GROVE TO HALEAKALĀ SUMMIT

11 miles; at least a half day

A short distance above the park entrance lies **Hosmer Grove,** a cool, shady spot to picnic and camp. You may recognize some of the trees, which include Douglas fir, California redwood, and eucalyptus. About 1910, forester Ralph Hosmer planted trees from all over the world to test their potential for watershed protection and timber here. A half-mile loop trail will refresh you after your drive. Back on the road, you reach **Park Headquarters Visitor Center** about a mile above the Hosmer turnoff. At this 7,000-foot elevation, you will see vegetation native to Hawai'i. In front of headquarters, plantings of Haleakalā geranium and silversword offer photo opportunities and biology lessons in adaptation and evolution. These two plants are endemic—found only on Haleakalā volcano.

Leaving headquarters, drive up the mountain through subalpine heath of soft earthy hues. In spring, māmane, a dominant shrub, brightens these slopes with sprays of

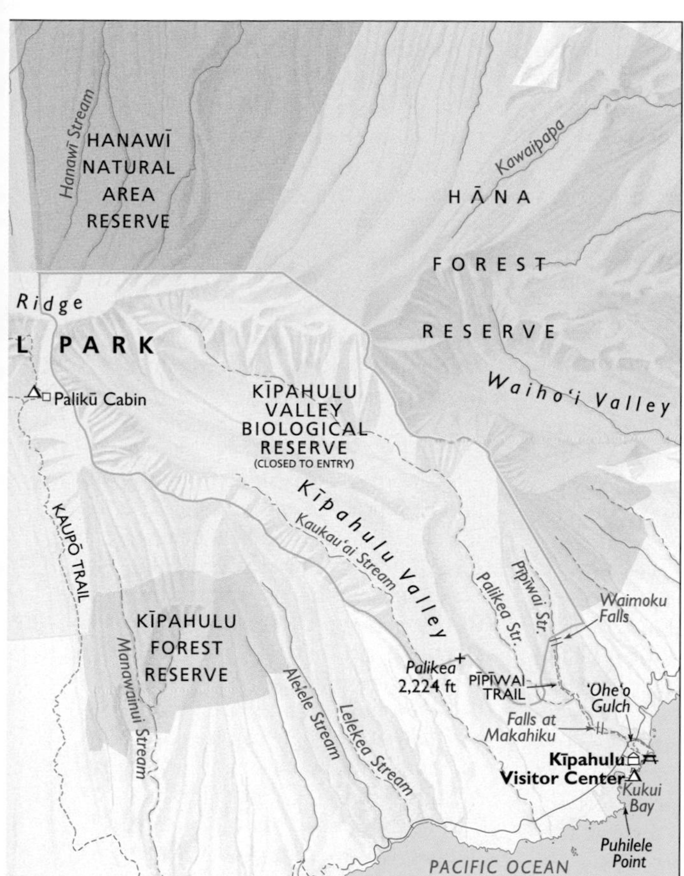

yellow blossoms. Native and invasive species frequent the area. With luck you may see some of the famous honeycreepers—brightly feathered birds that may be descendants of the first land birds to reach Hawaiʻi. From their original ancestors, the honeycreepers have evolved at least 47 species, some adapted to only one island, some spread more widely. More than half of these species have become extinct. Driven from the lowlands by habitat change and disease, others are making their last stand high on the mountain.

Summit hikers often start at the **Halemauʻu Trailhead,** 3 miles above the headquarters visitor center. This trail takes you through rolling country to the rim, then switchbacks as it steeply drops a thousand feet down the spectacular northwest wall of the wilderness area to **Hōlua Cabin** and the campground (4 miles from the trailhead). The wall is broken here by **Koʻolau Gap,** a wide, wet canyon that descends to the sea. In this corner, vegetation thrives on moisture carried by waves of clouds that slowly ebb and flow in the gap, and you will find the leathery amau fern and other unusual plants.

Drive approximately 3 more miles to the **Haleakalā Visitor Center,** where you can sign up for one of the ranger-led hikes offered throughout the park.

An exhibit shelter crowns the highest point—**Pu'u 'Ula'ula,** or "red hill." At 10,023 feet, Pu'u 'Ula'ula offers the ultimate view: Often you can see the giant volcanoes of the Big Island, as well as Maui's neighboring islands of **Lāna'i** and **Moloka'i** and sometimes, at night, far to the northwest, the lights of **O'ahu.** Nearby, but outside the park, are the Haleakalā Observatories, a cluster of buildings that are closed to the public.

The best way to experience the wilderness area is on a multiday hike, spending the night at one of the three cabins or two campgrounds inside the crater. (Reserve well in advance for cabins—see **Information & Activities** p. 252.) One popular overnight trip involves hiking the **Sliding Sands Trail** to **Kapalaoa Cabin** (5.8 miles from the visitor center). This strenuous 7- to 10-hour hike loses and gains 3,000 feet on its descent and ascent through loose cinder. Many choose to exit via **Halemau'u Trail,** an easier 8-mile hike from the cabin back to the road. You'll need to arrange a ride between the two trailheads.

Another challenging hike is to take the Sliding Sands Trail down to **Kalu'u O Ka 'Ō'ō,** the first big cinder cone; it is 5 miles round-trip.

KĪPAHULU: POOLS OF 'OHE'O

a full day

In this strip of parkland along the gorge of **Pīpīwai Stream,** visitors hike through lush rain forest and past breathtaking ocean overlooks. Perhaps the area's greatest draw, however, is the cultural past of Hawai'i. Archaeological evidence shows that large numbers of Hawaiians once lived in Kīpahulu, from precontact inhabitants (before 1778) to those who worked as cattle ranchers at the turn of the 20th century and in the sugar cane industry from 1880 to 1925. Trails reveal traces of the past: stone-walled gardens, evidence of taro and sweet potato patches, and temple and shelter sites. Please respect this legacy by staying on the trails and reporting to park rangers anyone seen damaging cultural resources.

Camping is permitted on the oceanfront meadows south of the stream at the **Kīpahulu Campground.** Bring your own drinking water, or boil stream water or treat it with halozone. No permit is required, but there is a 3-night limit per month.

If you have 2 or 3 hours, take the **Pīpīwai Trail,** one of the most memorable short hikes in the islands. This walk is easy for anyone in good health, but it is usually slippery with mud in spots; wear sturdy footgear. Don't hike if the river is swollen.

Begin about 200 yards south of the O'heo bridge, near the Kīpahulu Visitor Center. Walk up through gently sloping pasture about half a mile to overlook the **Falls at Makahiku,** 184 feet high. After another half mile, the trail enters the woods and crosses two bridges near a lovely double falls. Continue about a mile more through lush forest, including a stand of dense, 50-foot-high invasive bamboo, which on a breezy day clacks and creaks with a mysterious percussive music. Aromatic ginger and ti form the understory. Your destination looms above the forest as you get close: **Waimoku**

'Ohe'o gulch

Falls, more than 400 feet high, fills its jungle clearing with cool mists. During much of the year, non-native mango, guava, and mountain apple provide refreshment.

Swimming is a pleasant pastime in this part of the park. Those who fancy a dip congregate around the big, cool pools and waterfalls below the highway bridge in **'Ohe'o Gulch,** but less crowded spots await upstream. Some pools are deep, but beware of slippery or hidden rocks. *Jumping from the rocks is not permitted!* Always check conditions at visitor center as flash floods are dangerous and possible. There is no ocean access.

Silversword in bloom *(center)*; Iiwi, a tiny, rare honeycreeper *(bottom)*

INFORMATION & ACTIVITIES

HEADQUARTERS

P.O. Box 369, Makawao, Maui, HI 96768. Phone (808) 572-4400. www.nps.gov/hale

SEASONS & ACCESSIBILITY

All-year park. Call (808) 877-5111 for weather information from the National Weather Center.

VISITOR & INFORMATION CENTERS

Park Headquarters Visitor Center, 1 mile from park entrance, (808) 572-4400.
Haleakalā Visitor Center, near the summit, 11 miles from the park entrance, open daily all year. (808) 248-7375.

ENTRANCE FEE

$10 per car for a 7-day period; $20 for an annual pass.

PETS

Permitted on leashes in drive-in campgrounds only; not allowed on hiking trails.

FACILITIES FOR DISABLED

All visitor centers, park headquarters, and some campsites are wheelchair accessible. A free brochure about visiting Maui is available from: Disability and Communication Access Board, 919 Ala Moana Blvd., Rm. 101, Honolulu, HI 96814. (808) 586-8121. www.hawaii.gov/health/dcab.

THINGS TO DO

Free naturalist-led activities: nature walks and hikes, interpretive talks, cultural demonstrations. Also available, hiking, horseback riding, swimming in Pools of 'Ohe'o.

SPECIAL ADVISORY

• Wilderness area hikes are at high altitudes, with lower oxygen levels; take it easy. Be prepared for unpredictable weather that can change quickly from heat to cold and rain.
• Water pools in 'Ohe'o Gulch often have strong currents and submerged rocks, and they are subject to flash flooding.

OVERNIGHT BACKPACKING

Tent camping allowed only at **Hōlua** and **Palikū** campsites; free permit required; issued first come, first served at park headquarters on the day of the hike; 2-night limit at each campground; limit of 3 nights total per month.
Three small, primitive cabins at **Hōlua, Kapalaoa,** and **Palikū** contain 12 bunks, minimum equipment; can be reached by trail only. Reservation requests must be received by mail before the first of the month, 3 months prior to desired stay; give alternate dates; assignments made by lottery; limited to 3 nights per month (2 consecutive nights in one cabin); $75 per night; limit of 12 people. Send request to headquarters. Call (808) 572-4400 for recorded information on cabins, campgrounds, and vacancies.

CAMPGROUNDS

Two drive-in campgrounds, both with 3-day limit. **Hosmer Grove** and **Kīpahulu** *(no water)* open all year, first come, first served. No fees. No showers. Tent sites; no hookups.

HOTELS, MOTELS, & INNS

(unless otherwise noted, rates are for 2 persons in a double room, high season)

In Hāna, HI 96713:

Aloha Cottages 83 Keawa Pl., P.O. Box 205. (808) 248-8420. 5 small cottages, 4 with kitchens, 1 with kitchenette, in residential areas of Hāna. $65-$95.
Hāna Kai Maui Resort Condominiums 1533 Uakea Rd., P.O. Box 38. (800) 346-2772 or (808) 248-7506. 16 units, kitchenettes. $125-$195.
Heavenly Hāna Inn 4155 Hāna Hwy., P.O. Box 790. (808) 248-8442. 3 units. $210-$300.
Hotel Hāna Maui P.O. Box 9. (800) 321-4262 or (808) 248-8211. 66 units. $395. Restaurant.
Josie's Hāna Hideaway P.O. Box 265. (808) 248-7727. 14 cottages, all with kitchens, in various areas of Hāna. $100-$185.

In Kahului, HI 96732:

Maui Beach Hotel 170 Kaahumanu Ave. (888) 649-3222 or (808) 877-0051. 147 units. $110-$275. AC, pool, restaurant.

Maui Seaside Hotel 100 W. Kaahumanu Ave. (800) 367-7000 or (808) 877-3311. 186 units, 10 with kitchenettes. $140. AC, pool, restaurant.

In Kula, HI 96790:

Kula Lodge Rte. 377, 15200 Haleakalā Hwy. (800) 233-1535 or (808) 878-1535. 5 units. $185. Restaurant.

EXCURSIONS

WAIANAPANAPA STATE PARK

HĀNA, MAUI, HAWAI'I

Low volcanic cliffs and native hala (pandanus) forest line the coast in this remote, rugged park. Here, visitors can fish in the surf, explore a cave, observe an immense seabird colony, and hike the ancient coastal trail leading to Hāna. 120 acres. Hiking, fishing, swimming. Campground (permits required), 12 cabins, picnic areas. Open year-round. Off Hawaii 360 (Hāna Highway) about 80 miles from Haleakalā NP. (808) 984-8109.

IAO VALLEY STATE PARK

WAILUKU, MAUI, HAWAI'I

Velvety moss-covered cliffs surround the verdant Iao Valley and its centerpiece, the Iao Needle, a 2,250-foot basalt spire sacred to the people of Maui. Swirling waters fashioned the spire from a natural altar in an ancient volcanic caldera. Six acres. Observation pavilion, botanic gardens. Open year-round. End of Iao Valley Road, off Hawaii 32, about 40 miles from Haleakalā NP. (808) 984-8109.

Steam rising from Mauna Loa

HAWAI'I VOLCANOES

HAWAI'I
ESTABLISHED AUGUST 1, 1916
333,000 acres

Hawai'i Volcanoes National Park, on the "Big Island" of Hawai'i, offers the visitor a look at two of the world's most active volcanoes: Kīlauea and Mauna Loa.

More than 4,000 feet high and still growing, Kīlauea abuts the southeastern slope of the older and much larger Mauna Loa, or "long mountain." Mauna Loa towers some 13,679 feet above the sea: Measured from its base 18,000 feet below sea level, it exceeds Mount Everest in height. Mauna Loa's gently sloping bulk—some 19,000 cubic miles in volume—makes it the planet's most massive single mountain.

The park stretches from sea level to Mauna Loa's summit. Beyond the end of the road lies Mauna Loa's wilderness area, where backpackers encounter freezing nights and rough lava trails amid volcanic wonders: barren lava twisted into nightmarish shapes, cinder cones, gaping pits. Kīlauea, however, provides easy access to a greater variety of scenery and cultural sites.

On the slopes of Kīlauea, whose name means "spreading, much spewing," lush green rain forest borders stark, recent lava flows. This natural laboratory of ecological change displays all stages of forest regeneration—from early regrowth of lichens and ferns to dense forest. The rain forest on the windward side of Kīlauea's summit gives way to the stark, windswept Ka'ū Desert on the hot, dry southwestern slope. At the shore, waves create lines of jagged cliffs; periodic eruptions send fresh lava flows to meet the sea amid colossal clouds of steam.

Geological dynamism forms the park's primary natural theme, followed closely by evolutionary biology. Thousands of unique species have evolved on the isolated Hawaiian islands. Cultural sites abound as well, reminders of the Polynesian pioneers who steered their great double-hulled canoes to Hawai'i beginning some 1,500 years ago.

The United Nations has named the park both an international biosphere reserve and a World Heritage site. Many of the park's intriguing native plants and animals, however, are in peril, defenseless against alien species including weedy invasive plants and feral pigs.

How to Get There

Fly to the island of Hawai'i, also called the Big Island. Airlines serve the Kona airport from the mainland and from other Hawaiian islands; only inter-island flights land in Hilo. From Kona, head south around the island on Hawaii 11 past Kealakekua Bay, where Captain Cook met his death, and Ka Lae, or South Point, southernmost land in the 50 states. You'll reach the Kīlauea summit after a 95-mile drive on a good road.

From Hilo, Hawaii 11 rises 4,000 feet in 30 miles on your way past small towns, macadamia orchards, and rain forest, to reach the park at Kīlauea's summit.

When to Go

Year-round. The weather is often driest in September and October. The climate ranges from warm and breezy on the coast, to cool and frequently wet at the summit of Kīlauea, to nightly freezing with occasional snowstorms above about 10,000 feet on Mauna Loa. To avoid most tour bus crowds, plan to visit the major sights before 11 a.m. or after 3 p.m.

How to Visit

An intensive 1-day visit can encompass highlights of the Kīlauea summit via **Crater Rim Drive** and the coastal region via **Chain of Craters Road.** Regular tours by bus and small van operate daily from many Hilo and Kona hotels. Those with a botanical or ornithological bent will enjoy exploring **Mauna Loa Road** (accessible from Hawaii 11), which takes you through upland forest to the **Mauna Loa trailhead** at 6,662 feet: At **Kīpuka Puaulu,** be sure to take the 1-mile loop trail winding through 100-acre Kīpuka (an island of vegetation surrounded by a more recent lava flow) containing one of the richest concentrations of native plants and birdlife in Hawai'i.

Kīlauea eruption and lava flow

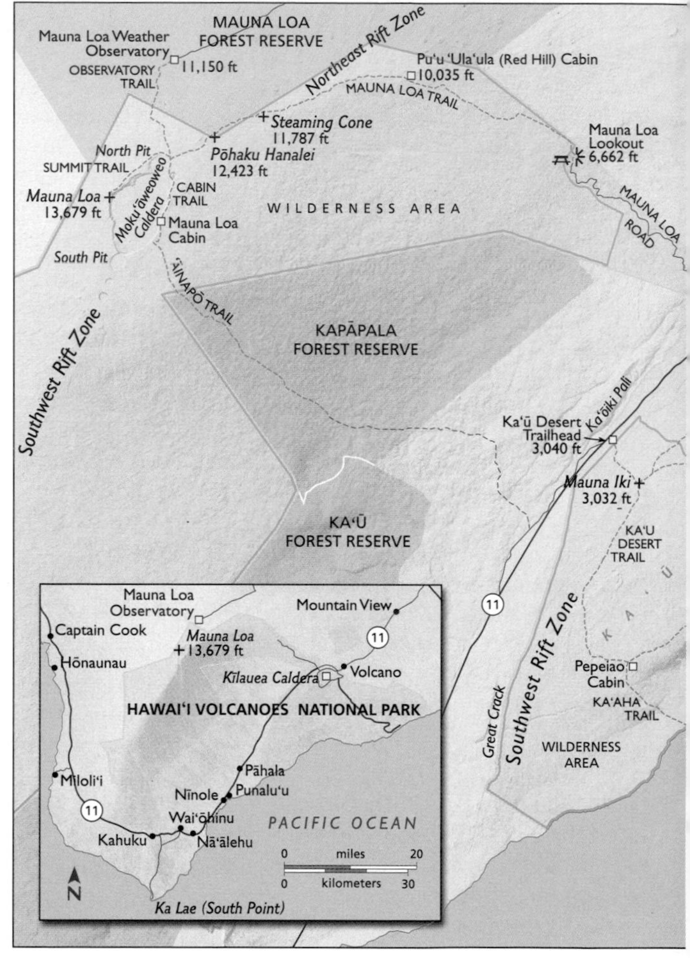

KĪLAUEA SUMMIT: CRATER RIM DRIVE

11-mile loop; about a half day

Since Kīlauea's summit areas can be rainy and chilly at any time of the year, visitors should be prepared. Bring a windbreaker or jacket and wear long pants. Begin at the **Kīlauea Visitor Center,** where you can get the latest information on park roads and safety precautions. Don't miss the stunning film of recent volcanic eruptions. The rustic **Volcano House** and the **Volcano Art Center Gallery** are just a short stroll away. Walk through the lobby of the Volcano House to the rear of the hotel for a first dramatic view across **Kīlauea Caldera,** a 3-mile-wide, 400-foot-deep depression that marks the volcanic summit.

After leaving the visitor center, proceed clockwise on **Crater Rim Drive.** For a time, the road traverses rain forest featuring Hawaiian tree ferns that lend the roadsides a prehistoric look. Scenic turnouts begin with a huge crater, **Kīlauea Iki** ("little Kīlauea") just east of the main caldera. In 1959 Kīlauea Iki erupted

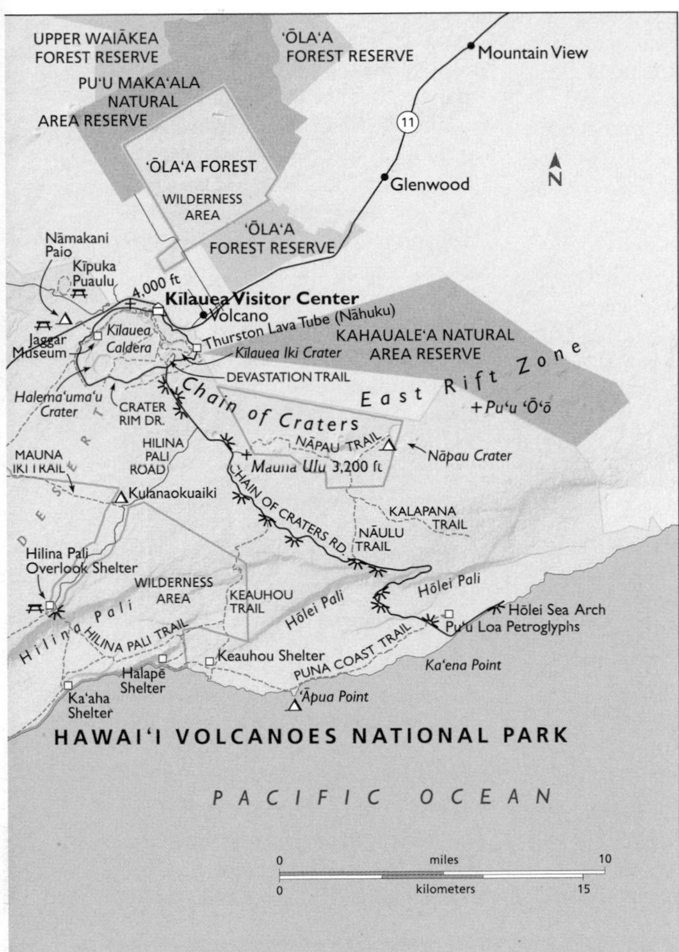

in a lava fountain 1,900 feet high, a record for Hawaiian volcanism.

Visit **Nāhuku** (Thurston Lava Tube) by taking an easy 15-minute loop trail that starts in lush tropical rain forest. The lava tube formed when the surface of a lava stream cooled to a crust while the still molten interior lava flowed out.

From the parking area, trails lead down to the floor of **Kīlauea Iki Crater** and along its rim. You can take a loop hike or walk back to Volcano House in 2 to 3 miles. Either way, you'll pass dramatic vistas of the Kīlauea Caldera, vertical lava cliffs, and verdant rain forest.

Another option is to hike the popular 4-mile **Kīlauea Iki Trail,** which winds around the rim and across the floor of a crater that last erupted in 1959. Taking about 2 hours to walk, the trail descends 400 feet, passing rain forest and steaming lava flows.

Now continuing back along Crater Rim Drive, look for koaʻe kea, white-tailed tropic birds. These ethereal-looking creatures nest on cliffside ledges, often soaring above **Kīlauea Caldera.** With luck, you may spot a nēnē, an endemic Hawaiian bird probably descended from lost

Canada geese that landed here. The state bird of Hawai'i, the nēnē are a federally protected endangered species. Do not feed or approach any nēnē and take care to avoid hitting them when driving (you'll spot "nene crossing" road signs).

Devastation Trail is a short (half-mile) but unforgettable walk through the remains of a forest killed by falling cinders during the 1959 eruption. The forest is now beginning to recover.

As the road descends along the southwestern side of Kīlauea Caldera, you will notice the landscape becoming more arid. In the rain shadow of the summit, the **Ka'ū Desert** receives about half as much rain as the 100 inches which fall annually at the Kīlauea Visitor Center. It also bears the brunt of trade winds blowing sulphuric volcanic fumes and natural acid rain—which stunt plants—down from above.

You reach the **Halema'uma'u Crater Overlook.** Walk the short path to look into the crater, a favorite abode of Pele, goddess of the volcano. Many native Hawaiians still revere her; throughout the year they privately chant and dance at the crater's edge.

The **Hawaiian Volcano Observatory** of the U.S. Geological Survey (closed to public), and the small, excellent **Jaggar Museum** of volcano lore and research are next on your route. Nearing the visitor center once more, you'll pass fumaroles, or steam vents. Some have produced the **Sulphur Banks** with crystalline deposits of pure sulphur. From here you can opt for a short hike back toward the visitor center. Alternatively, a 1- to 2-mile walk along the caldera rim provides fine views.

CHAIN OF CRATERS ROAD

20 miles one way; about 3 hours

From the Kīlauea Visitor Center follow Crater Rim Drive clockwise to the well-marked turnoff for Chain of Craters Road. For about 4 miles as you head toward the coast, your route follows the upper part of the active **East Rift Zone** of Kīlauea volcano.

Lava aglow at night

Scenic turnouts and short walks bring you to the rims of several impressive craters. If you have time, hike the **Nāpau Trail** up **Puu Huluhulu** (shaggy hill) to the overlook at the top, just over 1 mile. The overlook provides splendid views of the East Rift Zone and **Mauna Ulu,** the large, steaming domelike hill directly to the south. Look for steam from **Pu'u 'Ō'ō,** a major vent of Kīlauea's ongoing eruption, far to the east.

Back on Chain of Craters Road, you will drive over several miles of pahoehoe lava flows produced when Mauna Ulu formed in the 1970s. At the turnouts, you stand on some of the newest ground on Earth. Pahoehoe (PA-hoy-hoy) lava flows at more than 2,000°F. It begins fluid then chills to a smooth, ropy surface. This rock contrasts with aa (ah-ah)—thicker, slow-moving lava that has hardened into a chaotic jumble of rough jagged cinders.

The climate becomes drier, and patches of forest in various stages of recovery appear, as you descend toward the sea. Sulphur fumes sweep down from active volcanic vents on the rift to the east. Turnouts offer sweeping views of lava flows and white-capped waves pounding the black shoreline. About 21 miles off this coast, a huge undersea volcano is building a future Hawaiian island. Named Loihi, the volcano could breach the ocean's surface in some 100,000 years.

A steep descent of about 800 feet marks **Hōlei Pali,** a cliff formed by vertical faulting; the huge coastal shelf is breaking away from the uplands and sinking into the sea, albeit slowly on a human time scale. Reaching the lowlands, look for the **Pu'u Loa Petroglyphs** turnout; a modest hike will bring you to fine examples of ancient Hawaiian carvings, some 24,000 images and figures pecked into the lava. Visitors are asked to stay on the boardwalk to help preserve these carvings.

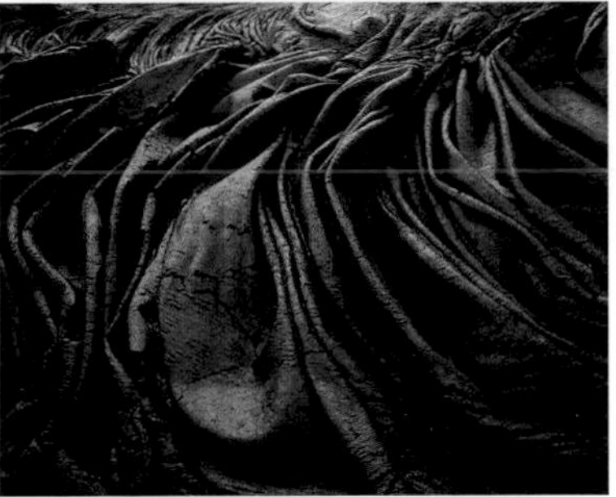

Along the Devastation Trail *(top)*
Ripples of hardened pahoehoe lava *(bottom)*

Hawaiian people lived on this dry, rocky land for centuries. Your route along the coast takes you past several of their ancient settlements, though they are difficult to discern.

The road ends abruptly at a 2003 lava flow. Since 1986, an almost continuous flow of lava from Pu'u O'o has buried several miles of the road, as well as the Kamoamoa picnic site and campground, and the Waha'ula Visitor Center. Park rangers mark a path to a viewpoint close to current flows. Lava flow viewing and access are unpredictable; obey all off-limit signs and heed the instructions of any park rangers on duty here. Ask at the visitor center for current lava flow information.

INFORMATION & ACTIVITIES

HEADQUARTERS
P.O. Box 52, Hawai'i NP, HI 96718. Phone (808) 985-6000. www.nps.gov/havo

SEASONS & ACCESSIBILITY
All-year park. Chain of Craters Road is closed by lava flow at its eastern end. For eruption bulletins call (808) 985-6000.

VISITOR & INFORMATION CENTERS
Kīlauea Visitor Center, located just off Hawaii 11 on Crater Rim Drive, a quarter mile from park entrance gate, and the **Thomas A. Jaggar Museum** on Crater Rim Drive, 3 miles from park entrance gate, are both open all year.

ENTRANCE FEE
$10 per car per week.

PETS
Not permitted on hiking trails or in backcountry; elsewhere must be leashed.

FACILITIES FOR DISABLED
Kīlauea Visitor Center, Jaggar Museum, Volcano House Hotel, Volcano Art Center Gallery all wheelchair accessible. Many paved trails and overlooks along Crater Rim Drive and Chain of Craters Road accessible with assistance. Kulanaokuaiki Campground fully wheelchair accessible. Free brochure about visiting the Big Island from Disability and Communication Access Board, 919 Ala Moana Blvd., Rm. 101, Honolulu, HI 96814. (808) 586-8121. www.hawaii.gov/health/dcab

THINGS TO DO
Free ranger-led activities: nature walks and talks, slide shows, films, museum exhibits on volcanism. Also, hiking, art center, workshops, seminars.

SPECIAL ADVISORIES
- Be prepared for intensive sunlight.
- Persons with heart or respiratory problems must beware of noxious sulphur fumes.
- Stay on marked trails; vegetation may conceal deep cracks.
- Coastline collapse can occur fast; do not go beyond barriers.
- Strong winds and unpredictable surf along the coast make swimming dangerous; it is prohibited in places.
- Do not enter any closed areas.

OVERNIGHT BACKPACKING
Registration at the visitor center is required. No fee.

CAMPGROUNDS
Two campgrounds, **Kulanaokuaiki** and **Namakanipaio;** 7-day limit. Open all year first come, first served. No fees. No showers. Tent sites only. Two patrol cabins on **Mauna Loa Trail** and one at **Kīpuka Pepeiao** may be used free, first come, first served. Must register at Kīlauea Visitor Center. Food services in park.

HOTELS, MOTELS, & INNS
(unless otherwise noted, rates are for 2 persons in a double room, high season)

INSIDE THE PARK:
The following are operated by the Volcano House, P.O. Box 53, Hawai'i Volcanoes NP, HI 96718. (808) 967-7321.
Volcano House Crater Rim Dr. 42 rooms. $95-$225. Rest.
Namakani Paio Cabins (off Hawaii 11) 10 cabins with central bath. $50.
OUTSIDE THE PARK:
In Hilo, HI 96720:
Country Club Condo Hotel 121 Banyan Dr. (808) 935-7171. 148 units, 24 with kitchenettes. $79. AC, rest.
Dolphin Bay Hotel 333 Iliahi St. (808) 935-1466. 18 units with kitchenettes. $79-$129.
Hawaii Naniloa Resorts 93 Banyan Dr. (800) 367-5360 or (808) 969-3333. 325 units. $100-$140. AC, pool, rest.
In Kailua-Kona, HI 96740:
King Kamehameha Kona Beach Hotel 75-5660 Palani Rd. (800) 367-2111 or (808) 329-2911. 460 units. $150-$250. AC, pool, rest.
In Pahala, HI 96777:
Colony One at Sea Mountain, Punaluu (on Hawaii 11) P.O. Box 70. (800) 488-8301 or (808) 928-8301. 28 condos. $95-$170. Pool, tennis, golf.

For additional lodgings contact the Chambers of Commerce of Hilo, 106 Kamehameha Ave., Ste. 208, Hilo, HI 96720, (808) 935-7178; or Kailua-Kona, 75-5737 Kuakini Hwy., Kailua-Kona, HI 96740, (808) 329-1758.

EXCURSIONS

MAUNA KEA OBSERVATORY

HILO, HAWAI'I

Mauna Kea, the world's highest island mountain, is the world's premier astronomical site. Clear, dry skies and a 13,796-foot elevation provide ideal viewing conditions; 11 countries have built state-of-the-art telescopes on the dormant volcano's summit. The visitor center at 9,300 feet has astronomical displays and evening stargazing from several telescopes, the largest being 16 inches. Saturday and Sunday tours to summit available for persons 16 and older who are not pregnant and have no heart or respiratory problems. Summit goers must provide their own vehicles equipped with four-wheel-drive. Seven-mile trail to summit from visitor center. Located off Hawaii 200 (Saddle Rd.), 34 miles from Hilo. (808) 961-2180.

'AKAKA FALLS STATE PARK

HONOMU, HAWAI'I

This park's ancient legend bears a decidedly modern ring: It says that the god 'Akaka, fleeing across the canyon after his wife returned home unexpectedly and discovered his infidelity, slipped and fell off 442-foot 'Akaka Falls. A self-guided paved path leads visitors through a lush jungle ablaze with colorful and fragrant blossoms to viewpoints over these falls and the 100-foot cascading Kahūnā Falls. 65 acres. No facilities other than the hiking trails, restrooms, scenic lookouts. Located at end of 'Akaka Falls Road, off Hawaii 220, about 15 miles north of Hilo. (808) 974-6200.

At sunset, Joshua trees etching the sky

JOSHUA TREE

CALIFORNIA
ESTABLISHED OCTOBER 31, 1994
794,000 acres

Two desert systems, the Mojave and the Colorado, abut within Joshua Tree, dividing California's southernmost national park into two arid ecosystems of profoundly contrasting appearance. The key to their differences is elevation.

The Colorado, the western reach of the vast Sonoran Desert, thrives below 3,000 feet on the park's gently declining eastern flank, where temperatures are usually higher. Considered "low desert," compared to the loftier, wetter, and more vegetated Mojave "high desert," the Colorado seems sparse and forbidding. It begins at the park's midsection, sweeping east across empty basins stubbled with creosote bushes. Occasionally decorated by "gardens" of flowering ocotillo and cholla cactus, it runs across arid Pinto Basin into a parched wilderness of broken rock in the Eagle and Coxcomb Mountains.

Many newcomers among the 1.3 million visitors who pass through each year are surprised by the abrupt transition between the Colorado and Mojave ecosystems. Above 3,000 feet, the Mojave section claims the park's western half, where giant branching yuccas thrive on sandy plains studded by massive granite monoliths and rock piles. These are among the most intriguing and photogenic geological phenomena found in California's many desert regions.

Joshua Tree's human history commenced sometime after the last ice age with the arrival of the Pinto people, hunter-gatherers who may have been part of the Southwest's earliest cultures. They lived in Pinto Basin, which though inhospitably arid today, had a wet climate and was crossed by a sluggish river some 5,000 to 7,000 years ago. Nomadic groups of Indians seasonally inhabited the region when harvests of pinyon nuts, mesquite beans, acorns, and cactus fruit offered sustenance. Bedrock mortars—holes ground into solid rock and used to pulverize seeds during food preparation—are scattered throughout the Wonderland of Rocks area south of the Indian Cove camping site.

A flurry of late 19th-century gold-mining ventures left ruins; some are accessible by hiking trails, or unmaintained roads suited only to four-wheel-drive vehicles and mountain bikes.

How to Get There

The west and north park entrances are at the towns of Joshua Tree and Twentynine Palms. From Los Angeles, take I-10 east to Calif. 62 (Twentynine Palms Hwy.) to Twentynine Palms (about 140 miles total). The south entrance is located at Cottonwood Spring, approximately 25 miles east of Indio off I-10. Call (760) 367-5500 for recorded directions. Airports: Palm Springs, Los Angeles.

When to Go

All-year park. Temperatures are most comfortable in the spring and fall, with an average high and low of 85°F and 50°F. Winter brings cooler days, around 60°F, and freezing nights. Summers are hot, with midday temperatures frequently above 100°F, and ground temperatures reaching 180°F. The Mojave Desert zone on the park's western half is on average 11 degrees cooler than the Colorado. In winter, snow may blanket the Mojave's higher elevations.

Spring blooming periods vary according to winter precipitation and spring temperatures, usually beginning in February at lower elevations and peaking park-wide in March and April, although cactuses may bloom into June. (Check with park headquarters.) For up-to-date recorded wildflower information, call (760) 367-5500.

How to Visit

The park's premier attractions, forests of giant branching yuccas known as Joshua trees, massive rock formations, fan palm oases, and seasonal gardens of cholla and ocotillo, can be enjoyed on a leisurely half-day auto tour that includes both "high" and "low" desert zones—although most of your time will be spent in your car. Scenic paved roads lead to viewpoints, all campgrounds, and trailheads. Roadside interpretive exhibits have pull-outs and parking areas, and offer insights into the region's complex desert ecology, wildlife, and human history.

If you plan to explore the park by mountain bike, you would be wise to avoid the main paved roads, which are narrow and without shoulders. You'll find far greater solitude and safety cycling the park's backcountry dirt roads, many of which, like those in **Queen Valley,** date from the area's 19th-century homestead and gold-mining era. Be sure to acquire reliable information from headquarters about your route, however, as soft sand and

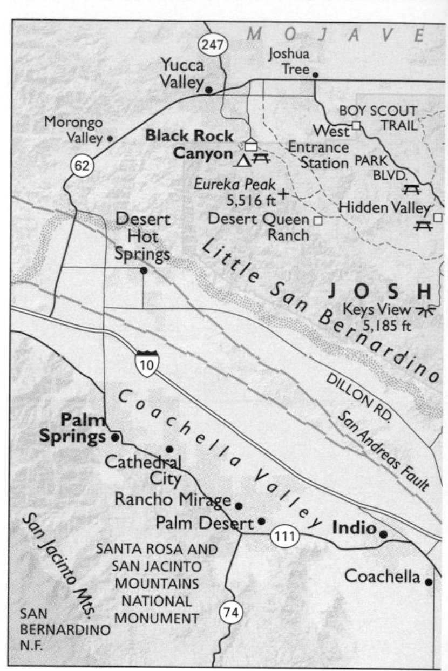

occasional steep climbs can make for arduous pedaling.

For a half-day visit starting from the park's northern boundary, take the **Park Boulevard loop** either from the town of Joshua Tree through the West Entrance Station, or from Twentynine Palms, by way of the North Entrance Station. If the air is clear (ask at the entrance about haze conditions), take the 20-minute side trip to 5,185-foot-high **Keys View,** which overlooks a vast panorama of arid desert basin and range stretching south into Mexico. If you are starting from Joshua Tree, return to Park Boulevard and continue east over **Sheep Pass** to **Jumbo Rocks,** turning right (south) onto Pinto Basin Road for the drive down into long vistas in the Colorado Desert zone. Be sure to stroll the self-guided nature trails through the **Cholla Cactus Garden** and the **Ocotillo Patch.**

Backtrack to Twentynine Palms and the **Oasis Visitor Center,** which features a small cactus garden and superb desert ecology interpretive displays. It adjoins the historic **Oasis of Mara** (one of five spring-fed oases within the park's boundaries), where Indians once found water, shade, food, and game. If you are starting from Twentynine Palms and the Oasis Visitor Center, proceed south as far as the Ocotillo Patch, then backtrack to Park Boulevard and follow it westward to Joshua Tree.

PARK BOULEVARD

64 miles (including side trips); a half to full day

A scenic drive connecting the north and west entrances skirts the sparse Colorado low desert ecosystem, then climbs into the Joshua tree forest and its surrounding plateau of mammoth rocks. Begin at the **Oasis Visitor Center** in Twentynine Palms. (Or, if entering from the south, begin at the **Cottonwood Visitor Center** and follow Pinto Basin Road north and west past the Ocotillo Patch and the Cholla Cactus Garden to the Oasis Visitor Center.) Both visitor centers provide insights into how plants and animals survive the region's withering heat and aridity, and how its unusual geology was formed, though the Oasis Visitor Center's interpretive displays are more extensive.

The Oasis Visitor Center adjoins the **Oasis of Mara,** a cluster of fan palms (the only palms native to the Southwest desert), Fremont cottonwoods, arrow weeds, and mesquite shrubs watered by a seeping spring. Take the half-mile path to this scruffy bit of green, which once sustained Indian encampments and later slaked the thirst of prospectors and homesteaders. A minute's stroll leads to a shady respite amid the chatter of birds. (Bird-watchers may

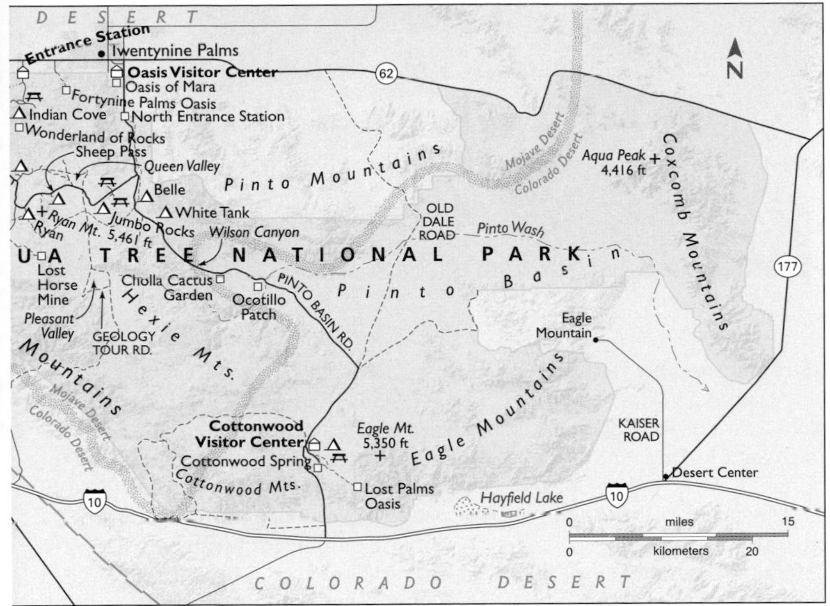

want to include a visit to **Cottonwood Springs,** an oasis sheltering many species and located about a mile from the Cottonwood Visitor Center at the south entrance.)

If your schedule allows, take time for short walks along nature trails that offer close-up looks at plant and animal life, or interesting terrain. (Park brochures describe trail highlights.) Consider starting early; sunlight playing across Joshua Tree's granite monoliths, peaks, and basins accentuates their contours and colors—especially at dawn and sunset—when rocks are aglow in warm pinks and yellows. On weekends, ask at a visitor center about ranger-led campfire talks, walks, and tours, or check campground bulletin boards.

Continue south from Twentynine Palms on Park Boulevard to the North Entrance Station. The road climbs, skirting the **Pinto Mountains** that rise to the east. Where the pavement forks (after about 5 miles), bear left onto Pinto Basin Road. You'll soon enter **Wilson Canyon** and the transition zone, where the Mojave and Colorado Desert ecosystems join. The sweep of **Pinto Basin** trending east is in fact an ancient dry lakebed, and a typical Sonoran Desert landscape dominated by the pale creosote bush.

Stroll through the **Cholla Cactus Garden,** a picturesque cluster about 6.5 miles south of the fork and threaded by a short nature trail interestingly keyed to self-guided brochures provided there. Known as "jumping" cholla for the tendency of its spiny joints to break off and cling to hapless passersby, the crooked-arm cactus appears velvety but is actually covered by tiny, sharply piercing bristles.

Continue southeast about 2 miles to the **Ocotillo Patch,** where hundreds of the spindly Sonoran Desert plants seem to languish, their rigid gray spines wobbling skyward. After rains in March and April, their tips flame with dense bouquets of bloodred flowers, a lifesaver for hummingbirds migrating north from Mexico (and a highlight of the flowering calendar).

Trailside rattlesnake

Backtrack northwest to the White Tank Campground and the **Arch Rock Nature Trail.** The easy 0.3-mile path to **Arch Rock** features interpretive information on how the surrounding geology and the natural arch were formed.

At the fork, turn left to rejoin Park Boulevard and enter the Mojave high desert. Westbound, you'll see mammoth granite formations rising from a sandy plateau. Some 800 million years in the making, worn by eons of weather into the contours of melting ice cream, the **Jumbo Rocks** are a product of this region's seismic restlessness—tectonic tumult evidenced by frequent small temblors that affect the flow of springs watering the park's oases.

Here visitors might likely see climbers scaling the monoliths, for Joshua Tree National Park contains one of America's most accessible, yet challenging, rock-climbing areas. Guidelines designed for safety and the protection of rock surfaces govern climbing within the park. Spectators gather in parking areas to watch the enthusiasts laden with equipment climb hand-over-hand up seemingly impossible routes.

Keep an eye out for aptly named **Skull Rock,** which flanks the road as you continue west toward **Hidden Valley,** a scenic garden of huge piled-up boulders resembling animals, human faces, and abstract forms. A popular picnic and camping area, this part of Joshua Tree is heavily populated by the park's trademark branching yucca. Named by early Mormon settlers who saw in its uplifted arms a symbol of the Biblical supplicant Joshua, *Yucca brevifolia* can reach 50 feet in height over a lifespan that may exceed 200 years. Some 25 bird species find protected nesting spots between its short, spiky leaves. The 1.25-mile **Hidden Valley Trail** follows a circuitous path through a stony maze to a "hidden" bowl where, according to local lore, rustlers once hid with their stolen cattle. The northern portion of this loop requires some boulder scrambling.

If you're not yet ready for a picnic, take the 6-mile scenic side trip up to **Keys View.** Just short of a mile high (5,185 feet), the mountaintop is the park's premier vantage point for motorists. Smog and natural haze from the Los Angeles Basin sometimes obscure the horizon; however, clear days afford a splendid southerly panorama of Coachella Valley farmlands, the Salton Sea, and Sonoran Desert mountains in Mexico. Across the valley looms 10,804-foot Mount Jacinto, towering above Palm Springs.

Park Boulevard continues northwest through the Joshua tree forest, descending to the West Entrance Station and the town of Joshua Tree.

INFORMATION & ACTIVITIES

HEADQUARTERS

74485 National Park Dr., Twentynine Palms, CA 92277. Phone (760) 367-5500. www.nps.gov/jotr

SEASONS & ACCESSIBILITY

Open year-round.

VISITOR & INFORMATION CENTERS

Oasis Visitor Center, off Calif. 62 near Twentynine Palms and the north entrance; **Cottonwood Visitor Center,** off I-10 at south entrance.

ENTRANCE FEE

$10 per vehicle, good for seven consecutive days; $25 for annual pass.

PETS

Permitted on leashes. Not allowed on trails or in backcountry (more than 100 yards from the road).

FACILITIES FOR DISABLED

The Oasis Visitor Center's interpretive displays, garden, and bookstore accessible, as are the 0.25- and 0.5-mile loop trails to Oasis of Mara. The Keys View wheelchair viewpoint is below the summit. The Cap Rock Nature Trail (0.5-mile loop from parking area) and the Bajada Nature Trail (0.25-mile loop) are accessible. No campsites are officially accessible, but Belle and White Tank camping areas have accessible restrooms.

THINGS TO DO

Free ranger-led activities held weekends, including tours to Keys Ranch homestead. Also, interpretive exhibits, self-guided cactus garden trails, auto touring, bicycling (on roads only), hiking, rock climbing, horseback riding on approved trails, bird-watching. ATVs and off-road motorized travel and biking prohibited.

SPECIAL ADVISORIES

• Always carry water, even on short hikes. No potable water in the park. Potable water available at the Oasis of Mara, at Black Rock and Cottonwood Campgrounds, and at the Indian Cove Ranger Station. Recommended: One gallon per person per day, two gallons if hiking.
• Campfires are not allowed in backcountry. Bring own firewood for campgrounds.
• Rock climbers should check regulations before undertaking climb.
• Use extreme caution around old mine workings—NEVER ENTER.
• Hikers should carry a compass, GPS, and topographic map. Established trails can be obscured. Landscapes have few prominent features.
• Archaeological sites and remains may not be disturbed, including rock art. Climbing within 50 feet of rock art prohibited.

OVERNIGHT BACKPACKING

Registration required at one of 12 backcountry boards. Check with rangers at entrance stations about current conditions. A permit is required for horses. Call (760) 367-5545.

CAMPGROUNDS

Nine campgrounds, all with 14-day limit from Sept. through May, and a 30-day limit rest of year. First-come, first-served basis. Fees for individuals and groups up to six: None to $10. Group camping available at **Cottonwood, Indian Cove,** and **Sheep Pass** by reservation only. Call the NPRS (see p. 10). Fees from $10 to $30. Horses permitted at **Black Rock.**

HOTELS, MOTELS, & INNS

(unless otherwise noted, rates are for 2 persons in a double room, high season)

In Twentynine Palms, CA 92277:

Best Western Gardens Motel 71487 Twentynine Palms Hwy. (800) 528-1234 or (760) 367-9141. 84 units, 12 with kitchenettes. $85. AC, pool.

Motel 6 72562 Twentynine Palms Hwy. (800) 466-8356 or (760) 367-2833. 124 units. $46. AC, pool.

In Indio, CA 92201:

Quality Inn 43-505 Monroe St. (760) 347-4044. 62 units. $69-$99. AC, pool.

Royal Plaza Inn 82-347 Hwy. 111. (800) 228-9559. 99 units. $69-$110. AC, rest.

In Yucca Valley, CA 92284:

Oasis of Eden Inn & Suites 56377 Twentnine Palms Hwy. (800) 606-6686. 40 units. $70-$199. AC, pool.

Yucca Inn 7500 Camino del Cielo. (760) 365-3311. 74 units. $69. AC, pool.

For other info contact Twentynine Palms Chamber of Commerce, (760) 367-3445.

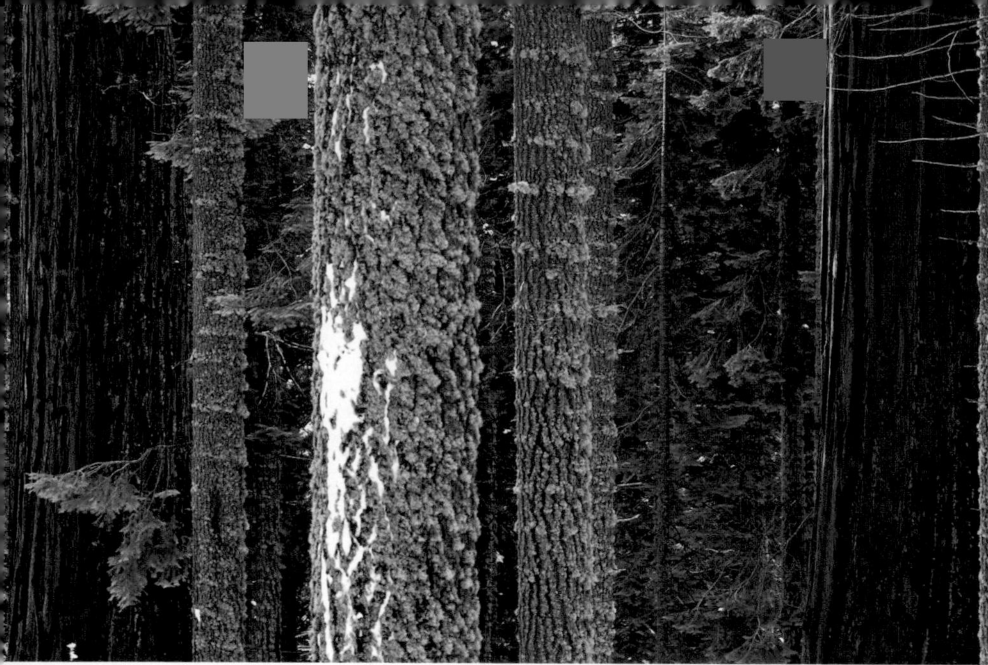

Mosaic of pines, sequoias, and mosses

SEQUOIA & KINGS CANYON

CALIFORNIA
SEQUOIA
ESTABLISHED SEPTEMBER 25, 1890;
KINGS CANYON
ESTABLISHED MARCH 4, 1940
865,257 acres

Bigness—big trees and big canyons—inspired the separate founding of each of these parks. In 1943 Sequoia and Kings Canyon National Parks began to be jointly administered. The two contiguous parks are 66 miles long and 36 miles at their widest point.

Nearly every square mile of this vast park is wilderness. A backpacker can hike to a spot that is farther from a road than any other place in the lower 48. But visitors can easily reach Sequoia's famed attraction, the Giant Forest of sequoias.

Relatively few visitors hike any of the parks' 800 miles of trails. Still, there are enough backpackers to worry officials, who protect the backcountry by regulating their numbers.

Mount Whitney, at 14,494 feet the highest peak in the United States south of Alaska, rises at the eastern border. Backpackers coming in from the east can get to Whitney in 1 or 2 days. From the park's western trailheads, they reach it by a 70-mile, 8-day trek across the park's snow-swept, glacier-dotted heights.

Visitors are startled to learn that some of the smoke they see rises from "prescribed burning"—

controlled fires deliberately set by employees to help the sequoias by removing undergrowth. In the past, when the park fought all fires, brush and deadwood built up. (Seeds cannot germinate in duff so need fires to open groundcover.) The brush fueled fires that imperiled the sequoias—which resist flames at their bases but can die if fire attacks their crowns.

How to Get There

From Visalia (about 35 miles west), take Calif. 198 to Sequoia's Ash Mountain Entrance. From Fresno, take Calif. 180 to Kings Canyon's Big Stump Entrance. The only road entrance into the main part of Kings Canyon is a dead-end, summer-only extension of Calif. 180 into Cedar Grove. Airport: Fresno.

When to Go

Spring through fall is the best time for sequoia gazing. Generals Highway, which connects the parks, is open year-round except during heavy snows. From December to April, there is cross-country skiing and snowshoeing in the Giant Forest area and at Grant Grove.

How to Visit

The two immense parks challenge anyone planning a 1-day visit. To appreciate the rugged splendor, you must hike a trail. No east-west road crosses either park. But a drive-in visitor, in a day, can see sequoias in **Giant Forest,** along the **Generals Highway,** and in **Grant Grove.** A quiet walk in a grove of sequoias will give you more than a drive to named trees, which are constantly surrounded by shutterbugs.

Stay long enough to explore both vast parks. Drive to Kings Canyon's beautiful valley, **Cedar Grove.** On another day visit **Crystal Cave** and climb **Moro Rock.** Hike in Sequoia's spectacular **Mineral King** area.

GIANT FOREST & GRANT GROVE

48 miles; a full day

From the **Ash Mountain Entrance,** on **Generals Highway,** drive 17 miles to **Giant Forest,** home of the **General Sherman Tree,** the world's largest tree. About 6 miles from the Ash Mountain Entrance, stop to see the Native American exhibit at **Hospital Rock.** Indians lived here from prehistoric times until the 1870s, when the white man's diseases killed off many of them. The Western Mono made flour from acorns—the most important staple food of early residents. They crushed the acorns in small hollows worn into streamside bedrock; you can see several such rock mortars at the exhibit.

The **Four Guardsmen,** a quartet of sequoias, stand as sentinels near the entrance to Giant Forest. Trails radiate from the star attraction, the General Sherman Tree, about 2,100 years old, 274.9 feet tall, and 102.6 feet in circumference, with a volume of 52,500 cubic feet. (In board feet, this is the equivalent of 119.3 miles of 1-by-12-inch planks.) A 13-story building would fit beneath its first large branch. The tree was named by a pioneer cattleman who had served under Gen. William Tecumseh Sherman.

The easy 2-mile **Congress Trail** (the name honors the institution that gave legal protection to the sequoias) takes 1 to 2 hours and begins at the base of the champion tree. (Buy a self-guiding pamphlet.) At stops along the way, you will see young sequoias (a mere 140 or so years old); sequoias scarred by fire but standing tall because their bark, thick and lacking resin, protects them; and fallen sequoias—not rotting because they contain tannin, which helps them resist decay.

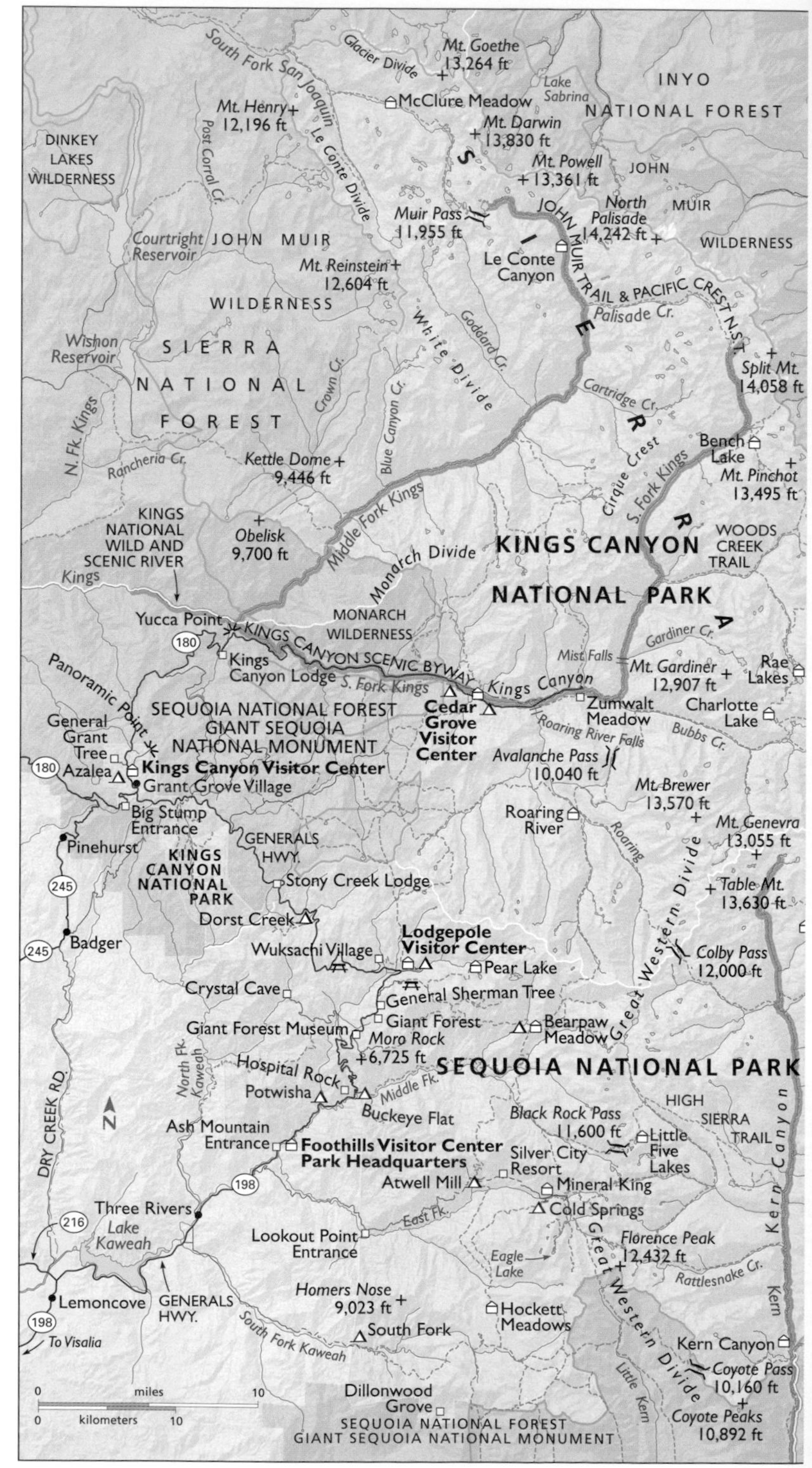

Mt. Goethe 13,264 ft
Glacier Divide
South Fork San Joaquin
Lake Sabrina
INYO NATIONAL FOREST
McClure Meadow
Mt. Henry 12,196 ft
Mt. Darwin 13,830 ft
DINKEY LAKES WILDERNESS
Post Corral Cr.
Le Conte Divide
Mt. Powell 13,361 ft
JOHN MUIR WILDERNESS
North Palisade 14,242 ft
Muir Pass 11,955 ft
Le Conte Canyon
JOHN MUIR TRAIL & PACIFIC CREST N.S.T.
Courtright Reservoir
JOHN MUIR WILDERNESS
Mt. Reinstein 12,604 ft
Palisade Cr.
White Divide
Goddard Cr.
Wishon Reservoir
SIERRA NATIONAL FOREST
Split Mt. 14,058 ft
Crown Cr.
Blue Canyon Cr.
Cartridge Cr.
N. Fk. Kings
Rancheria Cr.
Kettle Dome 9,446 ft
Cirque Crest
S. Fork Kings
Bench Lake
Mt. Pinchot 13,495 ft
SIERRA
Middle Fork Kings
KINGS NATIONAL WILD AND SCENIC RIVER
Obelisk 9,700 ft
Monarch Divide
KINGS CANYON NATIONAL PARK
WOODS CREEK TRAIL
Kings
Yucca Point
MONARCH WILDERNESS
180
KINGS CANYON SCENIC BYWAY
Gardiner Cr.
Kings Canyon Lodge
Mist Falls
Mt. Gardiner 12,907 ft
Rae Lakes
Panoramic Point
S. Fork Kings
Kings Canyon
SEQUOIA NATIONAL FOREST GIANT SEQUOIA NATIONAL MONUMENT
Cedar Grove Visitor Center
Zumwalt Meadow
Charlotte Lake
General Grant Tree
Roaring River Falls
Bubbs Cr.
Azalea
Kings Canyon Visitor Center
Avalanche Pass 10,040 ft
Grant Grove Village
Mt. Brewer 13,570 ft
Big Stump Entrance
Roaring River
Roaring
Mt. Genevra 13,055 ft
Pinehurst
GENERALS HWY.
KINGS CANYON NATIONAL PARK
245
Stony Creek Lodge
Table Mt. 13,630 ft
Dorst Creek
Great Western Divide
Badger
Lodgepole Visitor Center
Wuksachi Village
Colby Pass 12,000 ft
Pear Lake
Crystal Cave
General Sherman Tree
Giant Forest
Bearpaw Meadow
Giant Forest Museum
Moro Rock 6,725 ft
North Fk. Kaweah
Hospital Rock
SEQUOIA NATIONAL PARK
Middle Fk.
DRY CREEK RD.
Potwisha
HIGH SIERRA TRAIL
Buckeye Flat
N
Black Rock Pass 11,600 ft
Little Five Lakes
Ash Mountain Entrance
Foothills Visitor Center Park Headquarters
Silver City Resort
Kern Canyon
198
Atwell Mill
Mineral King
Three Rivers
Cold Springs
216
Lake Kaweah
East Fk.
Lookout Point Entrance
Florence Peak 12,432 ft
Eagle Lake
Rattlesnake Cr.
Homers Nose 9,023 ft
Lemoncove
GENERALS HWY.
Hockett Meadows
Kern
To Visalia
South Fork
South Fork Kaweah
Kern Canyon
Coyote Pass 10,160 ft
Little Kern
0 miles 10
Dillonwood Grove
0 kilometers 10
Coyote Peaks 10,892 ft
SEQUOIA NATIONAL FOREST GIANT SEQUOIA NATIONAL MONUMENT

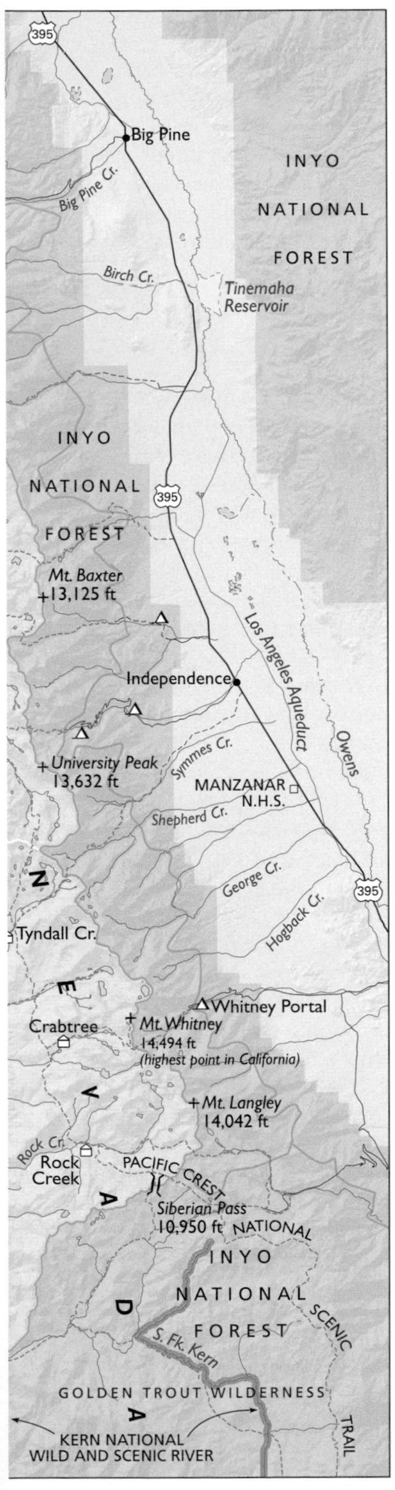

Return to Generals Highway and begin the 30-mile drive to **Grant Grove** in Kings Canyon NP by heading northwest to Calif. 180. Turn east on Calif. 180. On your right a road loops in and out of Wilsonia, a private community.

Just beyond **Kings Canyon Visitor Center,** take the road on your left to the **General Grant Tree Trail,** a half-mile loop leading to the **General Grant Tree** (267.4 feet tall, 107.6 feet in circumference). The name of the tree recalls the original 1890 name of the park, created to preserve General Grant Grove. To counteract lumbering, champions of the sequoias bought more land to expand the 4-square-mile grove. (To understand the significance of the big trees and their ecological management, visit the **Giant Forest Museum,** located in the 1928 building designed by Gilbert Stanley Underwood.)

On the trail are many of the saved giants, along with a reminder of the years of casual havoc: **Centennial Stump,** a sequoia cut down for the 1875 Centennial in Philadelphia. Near the park entrance is **Big Stump Trail** (1-mile loop), where stumps, logs, and a pile of sawdust help you imagine the sequoia logging of the past.

Return to the visitor center and head east on the steep, narrow, 2.5-mile road to **Panoramic Point** *(no trailers or large vehicles allowed)*. From the parking lot, take the 0.25-mile trail to the 7,520-foot ridge. Before you stretches the Sierra Nevada. You won't see Mount Whitney; the Great Western Divide blocks the view.

CEDAR GROVE

36 miles; a full day

Follow Calif. 180 for 30 miles north and east of Grant Grove, through Sequoia National Forest. The road winds into the canyon of the **South Fork Kings River.** Stop at **Yucca Point** to gaze down on the wild river flanked by sheer canyon walls glistening in the sun. The road continues to **Cedar Grove,** a mile-deep valley. Scouring streams began the carving of the valley, which got its U-shape from subsequent glaciers that pushed into the canyon and widened the floor.

Incense-cedar, ponderosa pine, black oak, live oak, white fir, and sugar pine grow in the valley's flats. In the 1870s the area attracted stockmen as well as gold and silver seekers. But John Muir, who explored here in 1873, would still recognize this beautiful high-country valley.

To best enjoy **Cedar Grove Village** park, get out and walk or bike, even for a short distance, to savor this hidden valley. The easy half-mile **River Trail** takes you from the South Fork Kings River to **Roaring River Falls.** From the parking lot you can hike along the curves of the river. Cross a suspension bridge and climb a slight rise for a view of the valley. Retrace your steps to the bridge and take the **Zumwalt Meadow Trail,** a 1-mile loop.

CRYSTAL CAVE

18 miles; a half day

The cave temperature is a constant 50°F, so take a jacket. Tickets must be purchased in advance at either the Lodgepole or Foothills Visitor Centers. Take the Generals Highway south from Lodgepole Visitor Center. Turn right down the rough, summer-only road *(no trailers or large vehicles)* to Crystal Cave. The twisting dusty 9-mile trip consumes about an hour. From the parking lot you walk a paved, steep path along a canyon wall, down to the entrance. Don't expect multicolored lights or tales of goblins; the 1-hour tours introduce you to a cave that got its name from an unusual geological phenomenon. The cave is formed of marble—instead of limestone—that underground water slowly dissolved and then redeposited as dazzling stalactites, stalagmites, and columns.

MORO ROCK

4.6 miles round-trip; a half day

Although you can drive to Moro Rock, a huge granite monolith, via the 2-mile **Moro Rock-Crescent Meadow Road** from Giant Forest, you get a better perception of its setting by hiking. Either way, try for sunset when the view is spectacular. The 2-mile **Moro Rock Trail** begins near Giant Forest Museum. About 1.3 miles along the trail, a short path veers off to **Hanging Rock,** a high granite stage for viewing Sierra Nevada scenery.

Continuing on to the base of Moro Rock, you start climbing a stone stairway of nearly 400 steps (with several spots for resting). Your 300-foot ascent takes you to 6,725 feet, about 4,000 feet above the canyon floor. From here you can look down on the tops of the giant sequoias. On clear days you can see the Coast Ranges, more than 100 miles west.

When you return from the summit, you can retrace your steps on the Moro Rock Trail or return to the Generals Highway via the 2.3-mile **Soldiers Trail,** named for the U.S. Cavalry troopers who patrolled the sequoias before the Park Service's rangers took over the task.

MINERAL KING

50 miles round-trip; at least a full day

Three miles north of the town of Three Rivers, near the Ash Mountain Entrance, is the sign for Mineral

Evolution Lake

King, added in 1978. It was named in the 1870s by gold prospectors who gained little more than unfulfilled dreams from it. The 1960s dreams of a ski resort failed to come true because of public opposition.

Turn off Calif. 198 onto a narrow, twisting, 25-mile road. (One driver counted 29 turns in a single mile.) To avoid driving it twice in one grueling day, plan your schedule so that you'll be able to stay at least a night. But, if you must do it in a single day, start early. Mineral King is a hiker's paradise. And the road is the secret to the paradise's solitude. "The road is terrible," one grinning hiker said. "And we hope it stays that way."

During the summer, stop at the **Mineral King Ranger Station** and check to see whether a ranger-guided walk is scheduled that day. Or take a hike on your own. Get a map at the station, find a legal parking place, and select a trail. Remember that all trails here begin at altitudes of at least 7,500 feet and climb steeply. If you are not acclimated to high elevations, you may suffer altitude sickness.

A good hike for beginners just getting their legs in shape is **Eagle Lake Trail,** which starts at the Eagle-Mosquito Parking Area. This trail starts gently, then begins to get steep near **Spring Creek,** which sprouts from the mountainside. Every switchback treats visitors to an overlook with a stunning view. If you keep your eyes open, you may catch sight of marmots (which sometimes eat car wires and tubes) standing up and watching back, and tiny pikas, which whistle and scurry around. After a 2-mile climb, you reach the **Eagle Sink Holes,** where water disappears just as suddenly as the creek appeared. Here you can turn around and start down or continue up another 1.5 miles to **Eagle Lake,** a tarn.

INFORMATION & ACTIVITIES

HEADQUARTERS
Ash Mountain, 47050 Generals Hwy., Three Rivers, CA 93271. Phone (559) 565-3341. www.nps.gov/seki

SEASONS & ACCESSIBILITY
Park open all year. Roads to Mineral King and Moro Rock (Sequoia) and to Cedar Grove (Kings Canyon) closed winter; Generals Highway from Lodgepole to Grant Grove may close due to snow and at night in winter. Call (559) 565-3341 for current weather and road information.

VISITOR & INFORMATION CENTERS
Sequoia: Lodgepole Visitor Center and **Giant Forest Museum,** Giant Forest area; **Foothills Visitor Center,** Ash Mountain, where Calif. 198 enters park; **Mineral King Ranger Station,** south of park. Foothills open daily all year; others open reduced hours in winter.
Kings Canyon Visitor Center open daily all year; **Cedar Grove Visitor Center,** on Calif. 180, open daily in summer. For visitor information call (559) 565-3341.

ENTRANCE FEE
$10 per vehicle per week, good for multiple entries. $5 per person on bus, foot, bicycle, motorcycle.

FACILITIES FOR DISABLED
Visitor centers are wheelchair accessible, as are some trails in Grant Grove and Giant Forest.

THINGS TO DO
Free naturalist-led activities (many offered in summer only): nature walks and talks, night sky watches, children's programs, evening programs, snowshoe walks. Also available, Crystal Cave tours, nature center, fishing (license needed), horseback trail rides, pack trips, cross-country skiing.

OVERNIGHT BACKPACKING
Permits required. Reservations for specific trails and dates must be made by mail or fax (559) 565-4239. ($15 fee charged for reservations.) A few permits issued on departure day, first come, first served. Information (559) 565-3766.

CAMPGROUNDS
Sequoia: seven campgrounds, 14-day limit mid-June to mid-September. **Lodgepole, Potwisha,** and **South Fork** open all year. Others open spring to fall, depending on weather. First come, first served, except Lodgepole and **Dorst Creek,** which require reservations in advance through the NPRS (see p. 10) mid-May to mid-Oct. Fees $12-$20 per night. Showers near Lodgepole, closed in winter. RV sites at Dorst Creek, Lodgepole, and Potwisha; no hookups. Food available in park.
Kings Canyon: seven campgrounds, 14-day summer limit. **Azalea** open all year, others late April to mid-Sept. First come, first served. Fees $18 per night. Showers nearby. Tent and RV sites; no hookups. Reservations required for group campsites; write Sunset/Canyon View Group Sites, P.O. Box 926, Kings Canyon National Park, CA 93633 or call (559) 565-4335. Food available in park.

HOTELS, MOTELS, & INNS
(unless otherwise noted, rates are for 2 persons in a double room, high season)

INSIDE THE PARKS:
For the following lodges in Sequoia, call (888) 252-5757 :
Bearpaw Meadow Camp Six group tent cabins, central showers. $350, includes meals. Mid-June to mid-Sept.
Wuksachi Lodge 102 units. $155-$219. Restaurant.

For the following lodges in Kings Canyon NP/Sequoia NF, call (559) 335-5500:
Cedar Grove Lodge 21 units. $109-$125. AC, restaurant. May through Oct.
Grant Grove Lodge 24 lodge rooms, $159; 8 bath cabins, $115-$125; 27 rustic cabins, $69-$80; 15 tent cabins, $58. Restaurant.
Stoney Creek Lodge 11 units. $125-$145. Restaurant. Mid-May to mid-Oct.

OUTSIDE THE PARKS:
In Three Rivers, CA 93271:
Best Western Holiday Lodge 40105 Sierra Dr. (559) 561-4119. 54 units. $106.
Lazy J Ranch Motel 39625 Sierra Dr. (888) 315-2378 or (559) 561-4449. 18 units, 7 with kitchenettes. $95-$135. AC, pool.
The River Inn 45176 Sierra Dr. (559) 561-4367. 15 units. $89-$349. AC.

EXCURSIONS

SEQUOIA NATIONAL FOREST
PORTERVILLE, CALIFORNIA

Thirty-eight groves of sequoias are only part of the attractions. Four stretches of Wild and Scenic Rivers and six wilderness areas provide recreational challenges; part of the site has been declared a national monument. 1,136,095 acres. Hiking, boating, white-water rafting, climbing, cycling, fishing, horseback riding, scenic drives, winter sports. 2,000-plus campsites, picnic areas, handicapped access. All year. Adjoins Sequoia and Kings Canyon NP on south, west, north. (559) 784-1500.

PINNACLES NATIONAL MONUMENT
PAICINES, CALIFORNIA

Rising abruptly from gentle hill country, the spires and crags of the Pinnacles formation are the remains of a volcanic mountain formed 200 miles south. Pulled north and west by the San Andreas Rift, the Pinnacles are still migrating. Hiking trails, ranging from easy to strenuous, take visitors from chaparral-covered slopes, through caves, to the high peaks. 24,154 acres. Climbing, picnic areas, handicapped access. Visitor center off Calif. 25, about 130 miles west of Sequoia and Kings Canyon NP. (831) 389-4485.

INYO NATIONAL FOREST
BISHOP, CALIFORNIA

Inyo shares, with Sequoia NP, Mount Whitney; the spectacular saline Mono Lake; and bristlecone pines, Earth's oldest living things. Also contains parts of seven wilderness areas, notably the John Muir and Ansel Adams. 2,000,000 acres. Hiking, boating, climbing, cycling, fishing, horseback riding, hunting, scenic drives, winter sports, water sports. 73 campgrounds, boat ramp, picnic areas. Most campsites open May through October. Visitor center at Mammoth Lakes on Calif. 203. (760) 873-2400.

Wintry Yosemite Valley, with El Capitan at left

YOSEMITE

CALIFORNIA

ESTABLISHED OCTOBER 1, 1890

747,956 acres

In a high-country meadow two hikers crouch near the edge of a mirroring lake and watch a pika as it harvests blades of grass for a nest deep within a huge rock pile. When they resume walking, there is no other person in sight for as far as they can see. And on this sparkling summer's day, the view seems endless.

In the valley's crowded mall, families stroll by, eating ice cream, dodging bicycles. People pile in and out of buses. Shoppers hunt for souvenirs. Kids hang around a pizza place. Rock climbers, coils of rope slung over their shoulders, swap stories over beer on a patio. On a summer's day about 14,000 people are in Yosemite Village.

Both the solitude of the alpine ridge and the throngs of the valley are part of the experience when you visit Yosemite National Park. "No temple made with human hands can compare with Yosemite," wrote John Muir, whose crusading led to the creation of the park. To this temple come 3.3 million visitors annually. And about 90 percent of them go to the valley, a mile-wide, 7-mile-long canyon cut by a river, then widened and deepened by glacial action. Walled by massive domes and soaring pinnacles, it covers about one percent of the park. In summer, the concentration of autos brings traffic jams and air pollution.

Beyond the valley, some 800 miles of marked trails offer hikers easy jaunts or grueling tests of endurance in the High Sierra wilderness. Even the casual visitor can explore this solitude without getting outfitted for a backpack expedition.

This park, roughly the size of Rhode Island, is a United Nations World Heritage site. Here, in five of the seven continental life zones, live the mule deer and chipmunks of the valley and the marmots and pikas of the heights; the brush rabbit and chaparral of the near desert; the dogwood and warblers of mid-elevation forests; the red fir and Jeffrey pine of mile-high forests; the dwarf willow and matted flowers of Yosemite's majestic mountains.

How to Get There

From Merced (about 70 miles away): Follow Calif. 140 to the Arch Rock Entrance. Merced is one of the gateway communities for the Yosemite regional bus service (www.yarts.com or 877-989-2787). Also from the west: Take Calif. 120 to the Big Oak Flat Entrance.

From the south, via Fresno: Calif. 41 takes you to the South Entrance.

From the northeast, via Lee Vining: Follow Calif. 120 to the Tioga Pass Entrance (closed mid-November to late May, depending on weather).

Trains stop at Merced; check with Amtrak about buses to Yosemite. Airports: Fresno and Merced.

When to Go

All-year park. Avoid holiday weekends. Expect filled campgrounds from June through August and some crowding in late spring and early fall. Be sure you have reserved accommodations before attempting an overnight visit. You will find skiing and other winter activities in the Badger Pass Ski Area from about Thanksgiving to mid-April.

How to Visit

When a visitor asked a Yosemite ranger what he would do if he had only a day to visit the park, the ranger answered, "I'd weep." If you must zip through this huge park in a day, begin with **Yosemite Valley.**

But even a dawn-to-dusk, 1-day visit hardly allows enough time for more than a tour of the valley plus a look at one or two of the park's other major areas, such as the vistas from **Glacier Point** (road closed in winter beyond the ski area) and the sequoias of the **Mariposa Grove.**

As an alternative take the High Sierra **Tioga Road** (closed in winter) to explore the park's alpine country. Better still, stay long enough to get beyond the crowds and discover the sense of seclusion this great park can give you along one of its trails.

YOSEMITE VALLEY

12 miles; at least a half to full day

Don't add to the traffic congestion by driving the heavily used one-way valley roads. Park at one of the lots along the shuttle bus route and take one of the free buses, which loops through the east end of the valley or elsewhere in the park. (See inset map on pp. 280-281.) You can also explore the valley on a rented bike or on foot. Or, buy a ticket for a 2-hour guided tram tour. (The open-air trams also venture out on moonlit nights and glide through the ghostly light that bathes the valley.)

If you're traveling by shuttle bus, get off at the **Valley Visitor Center** in **Yosemite Village,** where an award-winning film introduces Yosemite's history, grandeur, and geology. For an easy stroll in an oasis of quiet, look for **Cook's Meadow** just south of the visitor center. The trail begins at the west end of the mall; pick up a self-guiding brochure. Deer and humans sometimes encounter each other here. Keep your distance.

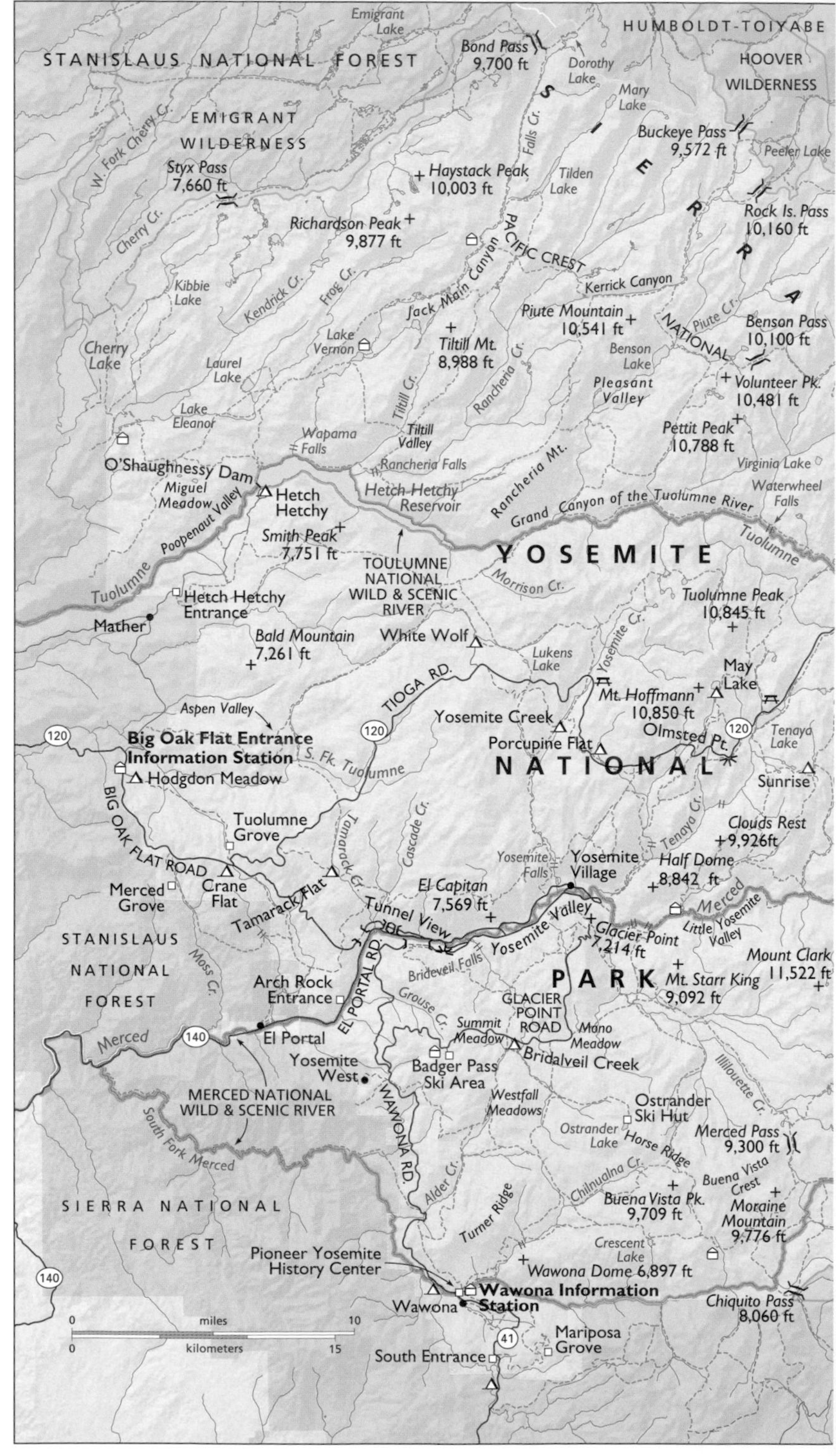
Emigrant Lake
HUMBOLDT-TOIYABE
STANISLAUS NATIONAL FOREST
Bond Pass 9,700 ft
Dorothy Lake
HOOVER WILDERNESS
Mary Lake
EMIGRANT WILDERNESS
W. Fork Cherry Cr.
Falls Cr.
Buckeye Pass 9,572 ft
Peeler Lake
Styx Pass 7,660 ft
Haystack Peak 10,003 ft
Tilden Lake
SIERRA NATIONAL
Rock Is. Pass 10,160 ft
Cherry Cr.
Richardson Peak 9,877 ft
PACIFIC CREST
Jack Main Canyon
Kerrick Canyon
Kibbie Lake
Kendrick Cr.
Frog Cr.
Piute Mountain 10,541 ft
Piute Cr.
Benson Pass 10,100 ft
Tiltill Mt. 8,988 ft
Lake Vernon
Cherry Lake
Laurel Lake
Benson Lake
Rancheria Cr.
Pleasant Valley
Volunteer Pk. 10,481 ft
Tiltill Cr.
Lake Eleanor
Wapama Falls
Tiltill Valley
Pettit Peak 10,788 ft
Rancheria Falls
Rancheria Mt.
Virginia Lake
O'Shaughnessy Dam
Miguel Meadow
Hetch Hetchy
Hetch Hetchy Reservoir
Waterwheel Falls
Grand Canyon of the Tuolumne River
Poopenaut Valley
Smith Peak 7,751 ft
Tuolumne
YOSEMITE
TOULUMNE NATIONAL WILD & SCENIC RIVER
Morrison Cr.
Tuolumne
Hetch Hetchy Entrance
Tuolumne Peak 10,845 ft
Mather
Bald Mountain 7,261 ft
White Wolf
Yosemite Cr.
Lukens Lake
May Lake
TIOGA RD.
Mt. Hoffmann 10,850 ft
Aspen Valley
Yosemite Creek
120
Big Oak Flat Entrance Information Station
Porcupine Flat
Olmsted Pt.
Tenaya Lake
S. Fk. Tuolumne
NATIONAL
Hodgdon Meadow
Sunrise
BIG OAK FLAT ROAD
Cascade Cr.
Tenaya Cr.
Tuolumne Grove
Tamarack Cr.
Clouds Rest 9,926ft
Yosemite Falls
Yosemite Village
Half Dome 8,842 ft
Crane Flat
Merced Grove
El Capitan 7,569 ft
Merced
Tamarack Flat
Tunnel View
Yosemite Valley
Little Yosemite Valley
STANISLAUS NATIONAL FOREST
Glacier Point 7,214 ft
Mount Clark 11,522 ft
Moss Cr.
Bridalveil Falls
EL PORTAL RD.
PARK
Mt. Starr King 9,092 ft
Arch Rock Entrance
Grouse Cr.
GLACIER POINT ROAD
Merced
140
El Portal
Summit Meadow
Mono Meadow
Yosemite West
Badger Pass Ski Area
Bridalveil Creek
Illilouette Cr.
MERCED NATIONAL WILD & SCENIC RIVER
WAWONA RD.
Westfall Meadows
Ostrander Ski Hut
South Fork Merced
Ostrander Lake
Horse Ridge
Merced Pass 9,300 ft
Chilnualna Cr.
Buena Vista Crest
Alder Cr.
SIERRA NATIONAL FOREST
Turner Ridge
Buena Vista Pk. 9,709 ft
Moraine Mountain 9,776 ft
Crescent Lake
Pioneer Yosemite History Center
Wawona Dome 6,897 ft
Wawona Information Station
Wawona
Chiquito Pass 8,060 ft
0 miles 10
0 kilometers 15
41
Mariposa Grove
South Entrance

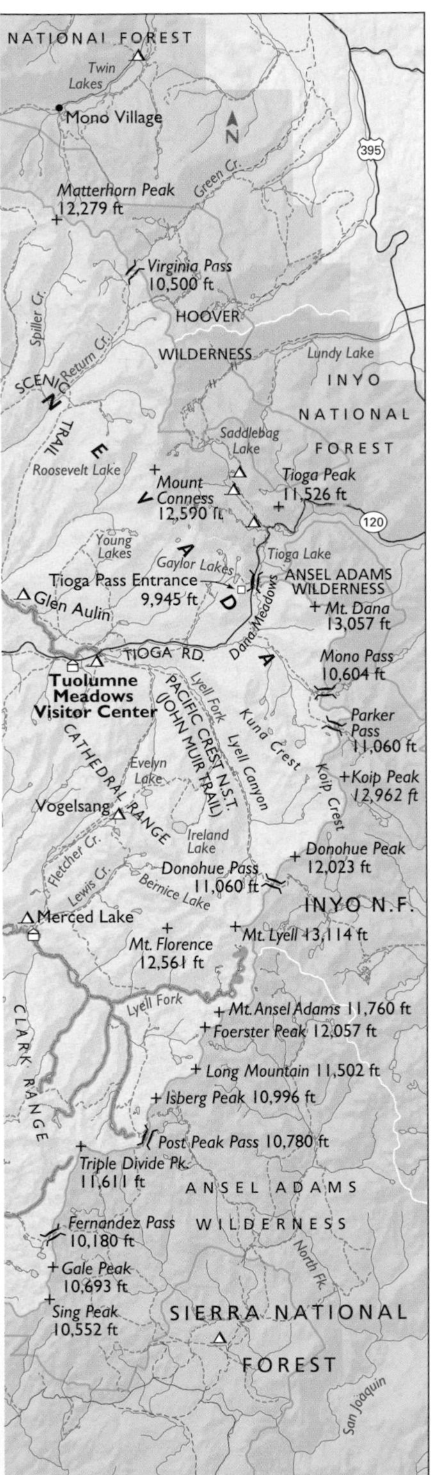

Walk around the nearby Indian village of **Ahwahnee,** where exhibits and bark houses evoke the life of the valley's earlier dwellers. Visit the **Indian Cultural Museum** to see the baskets and other works of art produced by Yosemite area tribes.

At the bustling village shops you can find just about what you would find in any resort-town mall. But if you want to see the park, don't tarry here.

Get back on the bus and travel to the **Yosemite Falls** shuttle bus stop. The upper, middle, and lower falls form the highest waterfall in North America (2,425 feet) and the second highest in the world. A quarter-mile walk takes you to the base of **Lower Yosemite Fall.** If you have the stamina and another full day, take the strenuous 3.6-mile hike to **Upper Yosemite Fall,** where you will be rewarded with spectacular valley views away from the crowds. (Look for the trailhead across from shuttle stop 7.)

Reboard the bus, and crane your neck for other scenic wonders. Get off when you want to absorb them; you will not have to wait long for another bus. Alight at the stop near the **Happy Isles Nature Center.** After a walk around these two bridge-linked river islands, consider hiking the moderately strenuous 1.5-mile trail to the top of 317-foot **Vernal Fall.** From higher up this trail, you can see **Nevada Fall** with its 594-foot cascade.

A gentle hike from the next shuttle bus stop takes you to lovely **Mirror Lake** a mile away; there a 3-mile trail loops around it and above it. In spring and early summer, the lake's serene surface reflects stunning mountain scenery; during the summer, most of its contents evaporate. Massive **Half Dome,** a cracked block of gray granite gnawed by a glacier, soars 4,788 feet above the valley

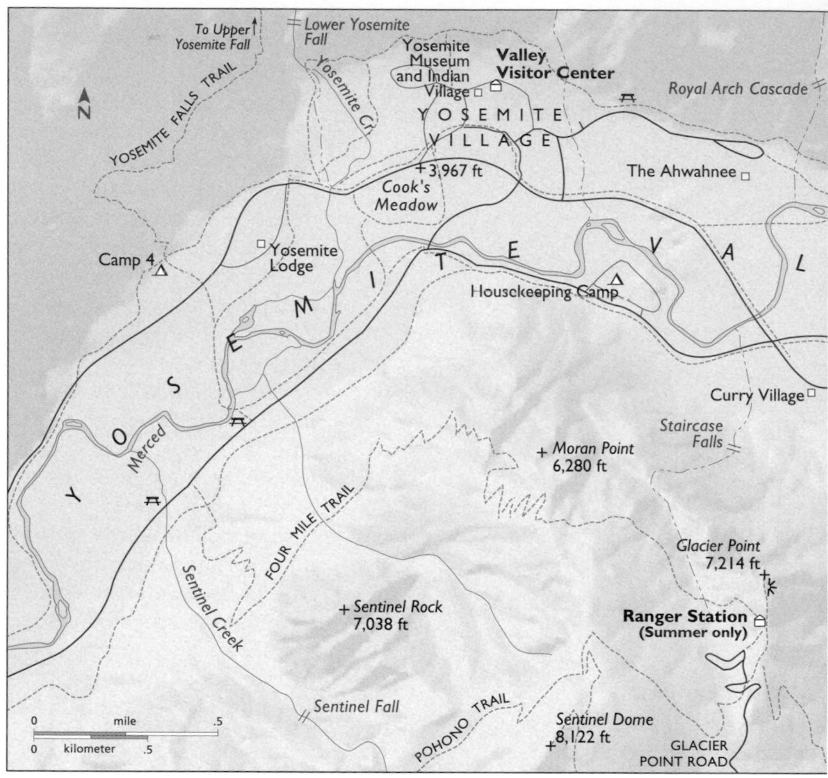

floor, its sheer face dominating this part of the valley.

As the shuttle turns back toward Yosemite Village, you'll pass the **Royal Arches,** glacier-carved granite shells. You will see the full spectrum of Yosemite accommodations along the shuttle bus route: from tents, trailer hookups, and clusters of concrete shelters to comfortable lodges, cabins, and a 1927 luxury hotel—the Ahwahnee.

GLACIER POINT & MARIPOSA GROVE

52 miles one way; a half to full day

Leave the valley by taking Calif. 41 (the Wawona Road) to the **Wawona Tunnel.** Park at the turnout at the tunnel's eastern end and walk over to the **Tunnel View Overlook** to see what has been called the most photographed vista on Earth. Spread before you is a granite panorama encompassing El Capitan, Half Dome, Sentinel Rock, **Cathedral Rocks,** and 620-foot **Bridalveil Fall,** in the late afternoon a scrim of shimmering rainbows.

On the 3,593-foot vertical wall of **El Capitan** you may spot the tiny figures of climbers. During their ascent, which may take days, they sleep in slings hanging from the cliff. (Consider catching the park's shuttle here to Mariposa Grove—see page 282—as the road is closed in winter and in peak seasons has little parking.)

About 7 miles beyond the tunnel, turn left on **Glacier Point Road**. This 16-mile road, flanked by fir-and-pine forests, ends in a small parking lot. Walk about 300 yards to the first of several overlooks on Glacier Point, which thrusts 3,214 feet above the valley, providing an enormous stage for a scenic spectacular of lights and shadows. Mirror Lake lies below; Half Dome looms across; Vernal Fall and Nevada Fall hang like white tassels in the distance. An arduous hike up **Four Mile Trail** takes you in 3 or 4 hours to Glacier Point's breathtaking vistas; for the trailhead, get off the bus at Yosemite Lodge and walk behind it to Southside Drive, then west a quarter mile to road marker V18.)

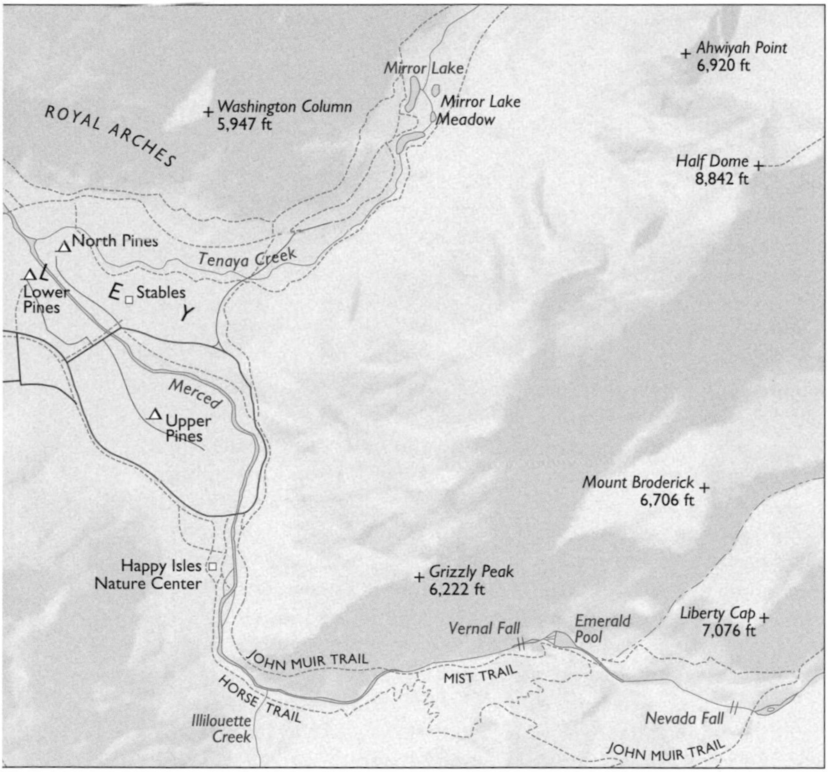

Return to the intersection of Calif. 41 and drive south 13 miles to **Wawona,** site of a hotel, golf course, and other facilities. Stop at the **Pioneer Yosemite History Center,** where, in summer, visitors can enter restored buildings and chat about the past with costumed interpreters who portray such real people as a cavalry trooper, a 19th-century homesteader, and a mountaineer. From conversations with these players you'll learn Yosemite Valley's recent history, which, according to legend, began in 1851 when members of the Mariposa Battalion were tracking down

Cathedral Peak, near Tuolumne Meadows

Indians accused of raiding nearby trading posts.

Word of the radiantly beautiful valley spread quickly, and the first tourists arrived in 1855. They were soon followed by homesteaders and hotelkeepers. Next came the nation's early conservationists, who campaigned to protect not only the valley but also a grove of giant sequoias.

On June 30, 1864, President Lincoln took time out from the Civil War to sign a bill granting both the valley and this grove to the State of California. Never before had a nation set aside land as a wilderness preserve. Yosemite became a national park in 1890, although not until 1906 did California formally give the original grants back to the federal government. More land was added in 1913, the year automobiles were again allowed in the park after a ban.

Return to Calif. 41 and continue south. Near the **South Entrance** continue straight to Yosemite's other long-cherished feature, the **Mariposa Grove** (shuttle bus recommended from Wawona). From early May to late October you can take a guided tram tour of the grove's giant sequoias *($11 adult, $5.50 child)*. Or, you can walk among them at any time of year.

The best known of the grove's more than 200 giant sequoias is the **Grizzly Giant,** whose estimated age, around 1,500 years, makes it one of the oldest living sequoias. A trail takes you past the **Fallen Monarch;** its shallow roots help explain why winds sometimes topple these giants.

Another fallen star, the **Wawona Tunnel Tree,** recalls another era. The living sequoia, gutted in 1881 to make a drive-through tree for horse-drawn wagons, became a photogenic attraction for generations of automobile travelers. The tree toppled in 1969. The decision not to cut a hole in another tree symbolized the dawning of an ecologically enlightened age.

TIOGA ROAD & TUOLUMNE MEADOWS

124 miles round-trip; at least a full day

Take the **Big Oak Flat Road,** a modern version of an old mining town road, west out of the valley for 9 miles to 6,200-foot **Crane Flat** (a local term for "meadow"). Turn right onto **Tioga Road,** which climbs into an alpine world of snowy peaks, crystal lakes, wind-tousled meadows, and relatively few people. The road (closed in winter) crosses the park. Even in July you may see snow alongside the road. Stop at the frequent turnouts for magnificent views and interpretive signs that explain the geology behind the splendor.

Gauge your time and gasoline. Beyond Crane Flat, the nearest gas station on this winding, climbing mountain road is 1 mile east of the **Tuolumne Meadows Visitor Center,** 55 miles from **Yosemite Valley.**

Millions of years ago the Tuolumne Meadows were under a sea of ice more than 2,000 feet deep. Wildflowers—among them Jeffrey shooting stars, Indian paintbrushes, monkeyflowers, and marsh marigolds—carpet this High Sierra realm in spring and summer. Trails of varying difficulty branch out here and elsewhere along the road. Some trails link five commercially run High Sierra camps with showers and dining halls. (Reservations required. See **Information & Activities** p. 284.) The camps are spaced 8 to 10 miles apart to accommodate the modest hiker.

One of the paths here is a segment of the **Pacific Crest National Scenic Trail** north of the meadows. It goes down toward the steep Grand Canyon of the Tuolumne River.

Back on Tioga Road, you'll climb to 9,945-foot **Tioga Pass,** the highest automobile pass in California. At a trailhead here you can take a half-day alpine hike that rewards you with glimpses of both beauty and history. The 2.5-mile trail climbs sharply from 9,945 feet to about 10,500, then descends to **Middle Gaylor Lake,** a gem set in a broad meadow prowled by marmots and Belding ground squirrels. The trail again winds upward, first to **Upper Gaylor Lake,** then to a surprise: the ruins of a stone cabin, rusting bits of machinery, and half-filled shafts—relics of a failed 19th-century silver mine.

Mule deer in Yosemite Valley *(top left)*; Steller's jay *(top right)*; Paintbrush and other wildflowers at Tuolumne Meadows *(bottom)*

INFORMATION & ACTIVITIES

HEADQUARTERS

P.O. Box 577, Yosemite National Park, CA 95389. Phone (209) 372-0200. www.nps.gov/yose

SEASONS & ACCESSIBILITY

Open all year. Tioga (Calif. 120 east) and Glacier Point Roads closed from about mid-Nov. to late May. Call (209) 372-0200 for recorded conditions. In winter, call (209) 372-1000 for Badger Pass ski information. Free shuttle buses operate in the valley year-round and at Wawona and Tuolumne Meadows in summer.

VISITOR & INFORMATION CENTERS

Valley Visitor Center open all year. **Tuolumne Meadows Visitor Center** near Tioga Pass Entrance open summer only. Information also available at **Happy Isles Nature Center,** in valley, and **Big Oak Flat Entrance** on Calif. 120 at western edge of park, both open spring through fall; and **Wawona Information Station,** open summer through fall.

ENTRANCE FEE

$20 per car per week.

PETS

Not permitted in buildings, backcountry, or trails, except for paved trails. Kennel available.

FACILITIES FOR DISABLED

Visitor centers, the nature and art centers, and some trails are wheelchair accessible. Free brochure.

THINGS TO DO

Free naturalist-led activities: day and evening walks, talks, hikes, children's and evening programs, living history; Indian cultural interpretation. Also, auto tape tours, bus and tram tours, plays, concerts, art and photography classes, museums, horseback riding—call (209) 372-8348—climbing, fishing, swimming, ice skating, downhill and cross-country skiing.

OVERNIGHT BACKPACKING

Free permit required; issued first come, first served; apply up to 24 hours in advance of trip to a park wilderness permit station. Advance reservations available by mail ($5 service fee); write wilderness office at park address. Call (209) 372-0200 for more information.

CAMPGROUNDS

Thirteen campgrounds; in summer, 7-day to 14-day limits; other times some have 30-day limit. Four open all year; others open mid-spring to mid-fall or summer only. Reservations through the NPRS (see p. 10) required year-round for all in the valley, except Camp 4, for **Hodgdon Meadow** spring through fall, and for **Crane Flat** and half of **Tuolumne Meadows** in summer. Fees $5-$18 per night. Most have RV sites, without hookups. Four group campgrounds; reserve through the NPRS.

HOTELS, MOTELS, & INNS

(unless otherwise noted, rates are for 2 persons in a double room, high season)

INSIDE THE PARK:

Yosemite Concession Services Corp., 5410 E. Home Ave., Fresno, CA 93727, operates the following accommodations. Reservations: (559) 252-4848 or online at http://yosemitepark.com.

The Ahwahnee (Yosemite Valley) 123 units. $380. AC, pool, restaurant.

Curry Village (Yosemite Valley) 18 rooms; 80 cabins; 427 tent-cabins. $67-$113. Pool, restaurant.

High Sierra Camps 5 camps with tent-cabins. Accessible by hiking trail only. Guided trips available. $126 per person incl. breakfast, dinner. Late June to Labor Day. Reserve by mail Sept. through Nov.

Tuolumne Meadows Lodge (8,600 feet, at Tuolumne Meadows) 69 tent-cabins, central showers. $75. Restaurant. Open summer.

Wawona Hotel (Calif. 41, 27 miles south of valley) (209) 375-6556. 104 rooms, 50 private baths. $113-$170. Pool, rest.

White Wolf Lodge (Tioga Rd.) 4 cabins, private baths; 24 tent-cabins, central bath. $75. Restaurant. Open summer.

Yosemite Lodge (Yosemite Valley) 245 rooms. $113-161. Pool, restaurant.

EXCURSIONS

STANISLAUS NATIONAL FOREST
SONORA, CALIFORNIA

This High Sierra forest offers an array of activities—from white-water rafting on the Tuolumne River to trout fishing on Alpine Lake. Contains parts of three wilderness areas. 898,322 acres. Hiking, boating, horseback riding, off-road-vehicle routes, scenic drives, winter sports. 1,450 campsites, boat ramp. Open all year; backcountry generally open June-Oct. Most campsites open May-Oct. Adjoins Yosemite NP on north and west. Information office, 19777 Greenley Rd. (off Calif. 108), Sonora. (209) 532-3671.

DEVILS POSTPILE NATIONAL MONUMENT
MAMMOTH LAKES, CALIFORNIA

Surrounded by the Inyo National Forest, this monument boasts a spectacular formation of basalt columns 60 feet high, which were born of the fire of volcanic eruptions and carved by the ice of overriding glaciers. At Rainbow Falls, water plunges 101 feet over a rhyodacite cliff. 798 acres. Hiking, fishing, shuttle bus. 21 campsites. Open mid-June to mid-Oct. Off Calif. 203 about 40 miles from Yosemite NP. (760) 934-2289. Access through Inyo NF, (shuttle fee). (760) 924-5500.

SIERRA NATIONAL FOREST
MARIPOSA, CALIFORNIA

Like the Stanislaus NF to the north, Sierra offers both rugged backcountry and developed recreational facilities. Contains parts of five wilderness areas, Kings River white water, groves of giant sequoias, and eight major reservoirs. 1,303,037 acres. Hiking, boating, bicycling, fishing, horseback riding, picnic areas, winter sports. 1,500 campsites, food services, boat ramp, handicapped access. Open all year; some areas closed in winter. Most campsites open May through Oct. Adjoins Yosemite NP. Office at 1600 Toll House Rd., Clovis. (559) 297-0706.

THE ROCKY MOUNTAINS

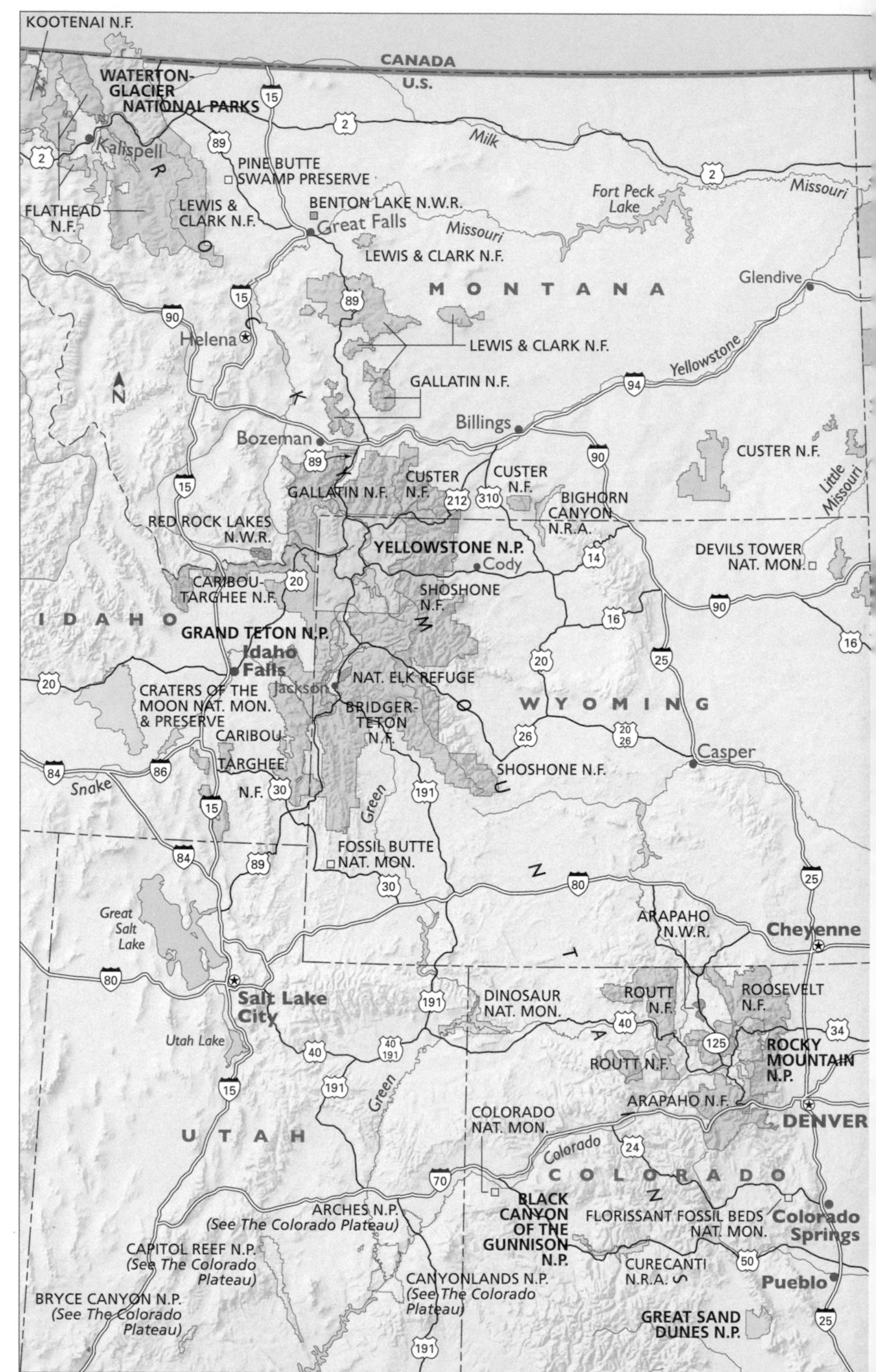
KOOTENAI N.F.
CANADA
U.S.
WATERTON-GLACIER NATIONAL PARKS
Kalispell
PINE BUTTE SWAMP PRESERVE
FLATHEAD N.F.
LEWIS & CLARK N.F.
BENTON LAKE N.W.R.
Great Falls
Milk
Missouri
Fort Peck Lake
LEWIS & CLARK N.F.
MONTANA
Glendive
Helena
LEWIS & CLARK N.F.
GALLATIN N.F.
Yellowstone
Billings
Bozeman
CUSTER N.F.
CUSTER N.F.
CUSTER N.F.
GALLATIN N.F.
BIGHORN CANYON N.R.A.
Little Missouri
RED ROCK LAKES N.W.R.
YELLOWSTONE N.P.
Cody
DEVILS TOWER NAT. MON.
CARIBOU-TARGHEE N.F.
SHOSHONE N.F.
IDAHO
GRAND TETON N.P.
Idaho Falls
Jackson
NAT. ELK REFUGE
WYOMING
CRATERS OF THE MOON NAT. MON. & PRESERVE
BRIDGER-TETON N.F.
CARIBOU-TARGHEE N.F.
Casper
SHOSHONE N.F.
Snake
Green
FOSSIL BUTTE NAT. MON.
ROCKY MOUNTAINS
Great Salt Lake
ARAPAHO N.W.R.
Cheyenne
Salt Lake City
DINOSAUR NAT. MON.
ROUTT N.F.
ROOSEVELT N.F.
Utah Lake
ROUTT N.F.
ROCKY MOUNTAIN N.P.
Green
ARAPAHO N.F.
DENVER
COLORADO NAT. MON.
UTAH
Colorado
COLORADO
ARCHES N.P. (See The Colorado Plateau)
BLACK CANYON OF THE GUNNISON N.P.
FLORISSANT FOSSIL BEDS NAT. MON.
Colorado Springs
CAPITOL REEF N.P. (See The Colorado Plateau)
CANYONLANDS N.P. (See The Colorado Plateau)
CURECANTI N.R.A.
Pueblo
BRYCE CANYON N.P. (See The Colorado Plateau)
GREAT SAND DUNES N.P.

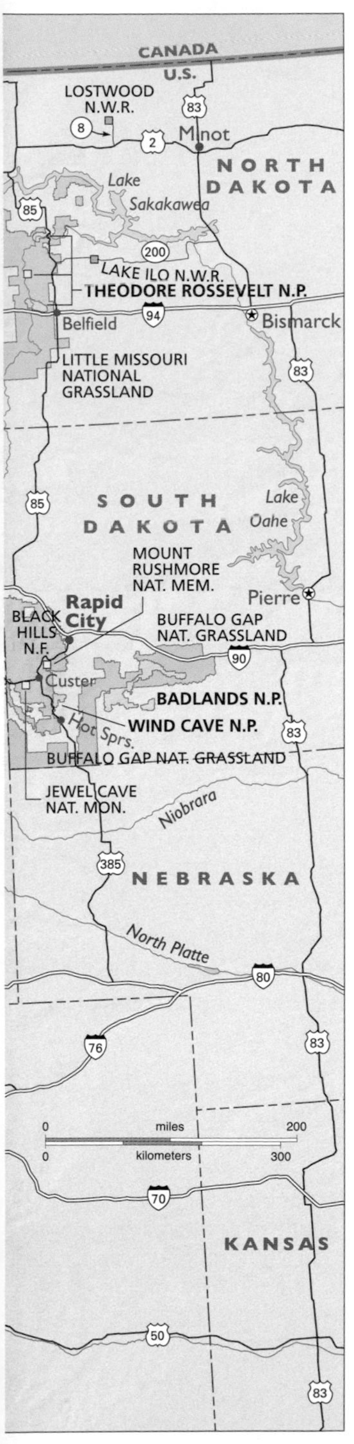

THE ROCKY MOUNTAINS

Craggy peaks capped by glimmering glaciers, fields run riot with wildflowers, lakes as smooth and blue as a summer sky—these images from the Rocky Mountains epitomize for many just what a national park should look like.

Yet this region offers more than mountains, since the forces that created the peaks contoured neighboring landscapes as well. The Black Hills of South Dakota uplifted along with the Rocky Mountains some 70 million years ago, cracking as they buckled upward. Enlarged by acidic groundwater, the cracks eventually produced the numerous underground passageways of Wind Cave. Streams flowing from the young Rockies also laid down the colorful mud that rivers would later carve into the buttes and gorges of the Dakota badlands, showcased in Badlands and Theodore Roosevelt National Parks. To the South the wind eroded the peaks and created the dunes in Great Sand Dunes National Park and Preserve, and water continues to carve the gorge in Black Canyon of the Gunnison National Park.

The Rockies' parks preserve the spirit of America's frontier in their rugged scenery and abundance of wildlife. Yellowstone and Waterton-Glacier—together with surrounding public lands—remain a stronghold of the grizzly bear. In some of the parks visitors can watch elk, bighorn sheep, mule deer, and remnants of the great bison herds that once thundered across the plains.

Rockies parks provide case studies in how wilderness manages itself. In Yellowstone, for instance, the visitor can get excellent glimpses of natural recovery in the wake of forest fires. Less encouraging are the real estate development and plans for industry on the fringes of some parks. Such activities can shrink the habitats of wide-roaming animals, endangering their future.

The Rocky Mountain region invites the visitor to experience peaks along the Continental Divide, plus geysers, prairies, caverns, badlands, sand dunes—and lots of driving. Count on a drive of 520 miles from Rocky Mountain National Park to Grand Teton and nearly 400 miles from Yellowstone to Waterton-Glacier.

Erosional formations at Cedar Pass as dawn breaks

BADLANDS

SOUTH DAKOTA
ESTABLISHED NOVEMBER 10, 1978
244,300 acres

They call it The Wall. It extends for a hundred miles through the dry plains of South Dakota—a huge natural barrier ridging the landscape, sculptured into fantastic pinnacles and tortuous gullies by the forces of water. Those who pass through the upper prairie a few miles north might not even know it exists. Those who traverse the lower prairie to the south, however, can't miss it; it rises above them like a city skyline in ruins, petrified.

The Badlands Wall, much of which is preserved within the boundaries of Badlands National Park, may not conform to everyone's idea of beauty, but nobody can deny its theatricality. It's been compared to an enormous stage set—colorful, dramatic, and not quite real. Water, the main player on this stage, has been carving away at the cliffs for the past half million years or so, and it carves away an entire inch or more in some places each year. But there have been other players, too. Beasts with names like titanothere and archaeotherium once roamed here; their fossilized bones can be found by the hundreds. And today the Badlands Wall serves as a backdrop for bison, pronghorn, and bighorn sheep, as well as the million human visitors who pass through the park every year.

A national monument since 1939, Badlands acquired the South (Stronghold) Unit in 1976, adding yet another dimension to the drama. This large stretch of land belongs to the Oglala, and one of their most sacred places is now preserved within it. It was here, on Stronghold Table, that the final Ghost Dance took place in 1890, just a few weeks before more than 150 Lakota were massacred at Wounded Knee, 25 miles south.

How to Get There

The park is about 3 miles south of I-90 at S. Dak. 240, 75 miles east of Rapid City and 27 miles west of Kadoka. Airport: Rapid City.

When to Go

All-year park. Summer is the most popular season, though daytime temperatures may top 100°F. Spring and fall are usually pleasant, with moderate temperatures and fewer crowds. Winters can be bitter cold, but snow accumulations are rarely a problem in this arid climate.

How to Visit

The 30-mile **Badlands Loop** provides a rich eyeful of classic badlands for a 1-day **North Unit** visit (a shorter loop can be devised as described below). Make sure to take advantage of the informative nature trails. For those with a second day and a pioneering spirit, a trip to the park's undeveloped **South Unit** can be rewarding; don't fail to check with rangers about road conditions before going.

BADLANDS LOOP ROAD—NORTH UNIT

32 or 89 miles; a half or full day

Enter the park at the **Northeast Entrance** off S. Dak. 240 and stop at the **Big Badlands Overlook** for your first view of **The Wall** from above. Before you are the characteristic tiered cliffs of the badlands, dropping sharply to the lower prairie, where the **White River** meanders between a fringe of cottonwoods.

Stop next at the **Windows Overlook** the trailhead for three short nature walks—each of which is highlighted by exhibits and/or wayfinding markers. While these trails may sound like the components of an architectural tour, they are actually brief forays into the Badlands Wall. The **Door Trail** (0.4-mile round-trip, boardwalk) passes through a narrow opening in The Wall into a jumble of barren, eroded hills reminiscent of the lunar surface. The **Window Trail** (0.1 -mile round-trip, paved) leads to a natural window overlooking a deeply cut canyon. And the rough **Notch Trail** (1.5 miles round-trip) leads up a ladder and along the side of a gully to a break in The Wall, where you can look out over prairie and badlands, the White River, and the Pine Ridge Reservation on the plain below.

Back in the car, a short drive brings you to the head of the **Cliff Shelf Nature Trail** (trail guide available at trailhead). This half-mile, steep loop takes you through a fascinating microenvironment in the badlands. Many years ago, a giant block of stone fell from the surrounding cliffs, creating this relatively flat shelf. The impact of the fall compacted the stone, making it less porous and allowing water to collect here. The resulting vegetation makes this place a delightful oasis in the otherwise barren wall. You can see mule deer browsing at dawn or dusk, and flamboyant magpies careening across the sky anytime.

Stop next at the recently renovated **Ben Reifel Visitor Center,** where a video and various exhibits provide a good introduction to the park's history and geology. From this point, the road descends to the lower prairie for a brief stretch and then

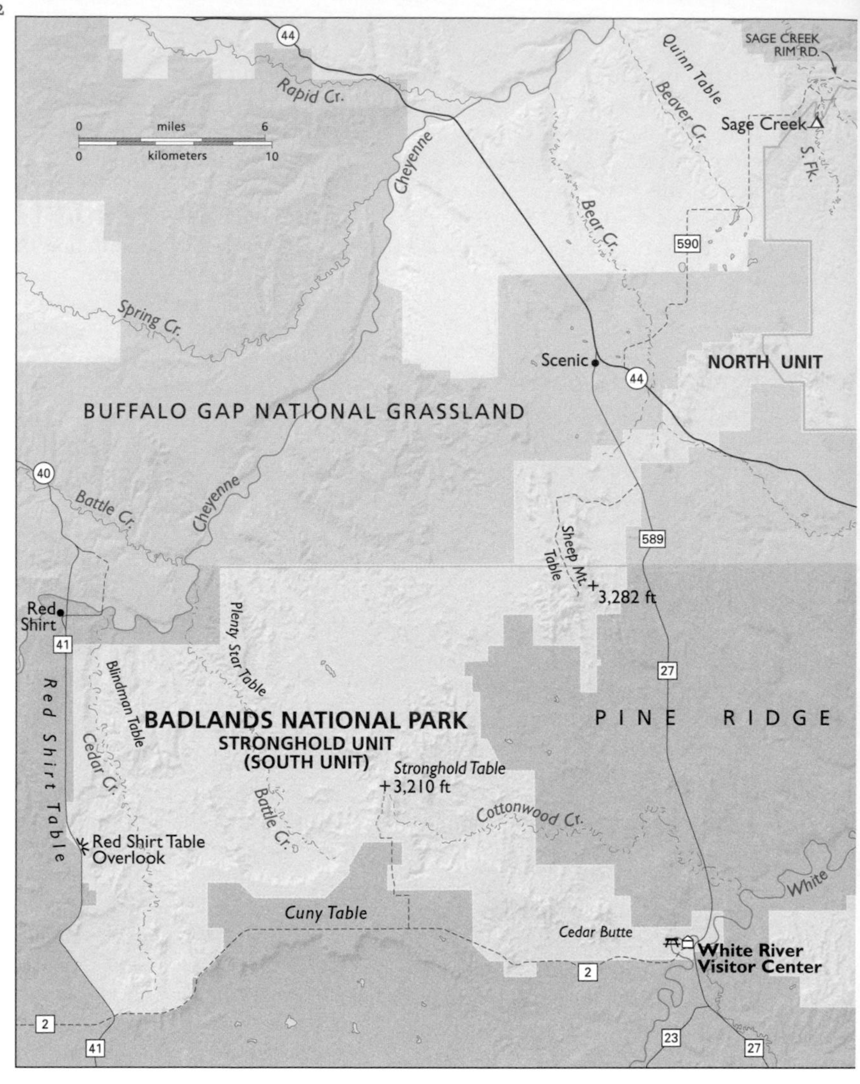

begins a gradual, stunning climb back up the Badlands Wall. The **Fossil Exhibit Trail** takes you on a quarter-mile paved walk through an area dense with fossils. Casts of some are displayed at trailside.

At mile marker 17 the accessible **Prairie Winds Trail** (150 foot, boardwalk) features a restoration of native prairie plants. The road then continues level punctuated by a dozen or so pullouts each offering a slightly different perspective on the knife-sharp ridges, twisted canyons, and multicolored hills that characterize this broken terrain. Spectacular among these are the **Yellow Mounds** and **Pinnacles Overlooks.** The later with is views into the Badlands Wilderness Area and bighorn sheep viewing (accessible by steep stairs).

If you're short of time, exit the park at this point and rejoin the interstate at the town of Wall. Otherwise make a left turn onto Sage Creek Rim Road and continue along the **Sage Creek Unit** of the **Badlands Wilderness.** This is excellent wildlife country;

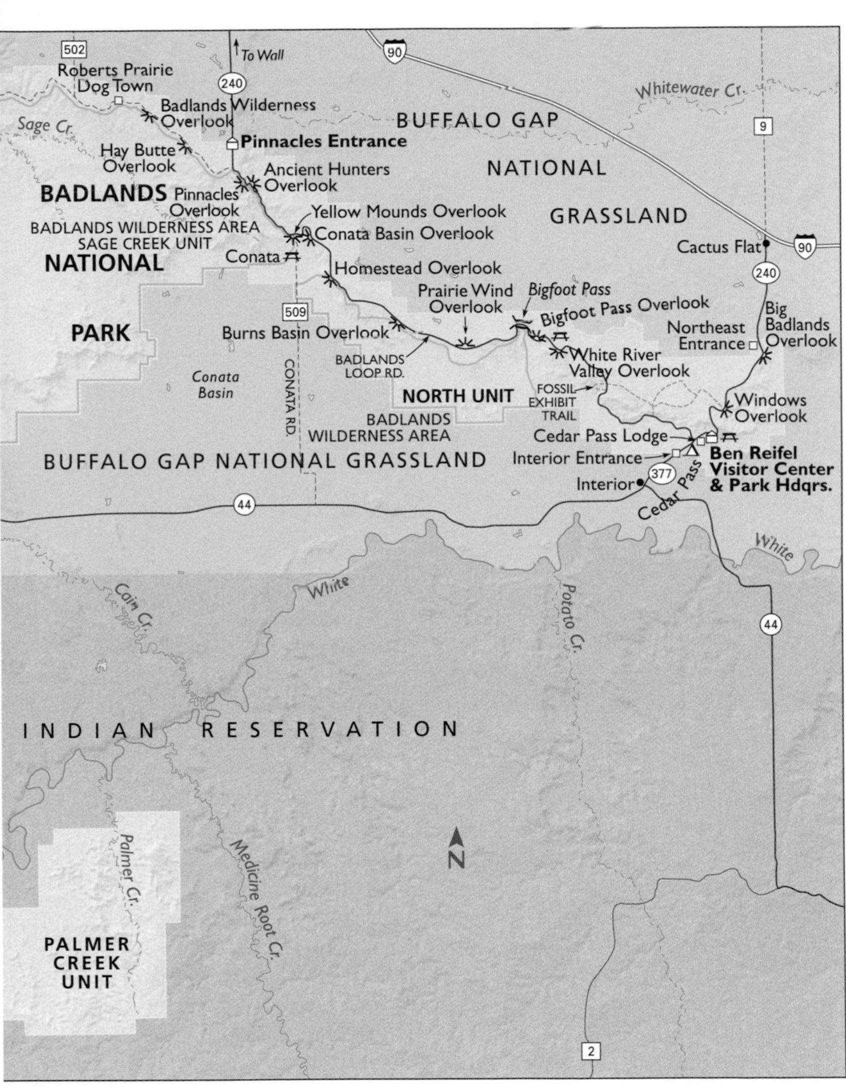

bison and pronghorn are numerous, and the road passes a town of those always entertaining prairie dogs. Longer hikes into the wilderness area start at the primitive campground about a mile off the road near the park's western boundary.

Beyond the campground turnoff, the road leaves the park. To complete the loop, continue along unpaved County Road 590 and make a left (south) onto S. Dak. 44. If you're heading toward Rapid City, turn right; this stretch takes you through beautiful **Cheyenne River Valley** prairie and gives you views of the Black Hills. The highway goes through Scenic, the turnoff for the **South Unit,** if you want to continue directly there.

SOUTH UNIT DRIVE

about 45 miles; at least a half day

The South Unit is almost entirely undeveloped, so exploring it by car will involve backtracking, driving on

Bison grazing on open prairie

rough dirt roads, and putting a lot of wear and tear on your vehicle. For your safety, be sure to check with a ranger before setting out.

Begin in the town of **Scenic,** with its automobile graveyard and shanty-like saloon, and go south on County Road 589 for 4 miles. The turnoff for **Sheep Mountain Table** is marked. Follow the road across the flats and up a seemingly impregnable cliff to a grass-topped table dotted with yuccas. If you go to the juniper grove at the road's end, you can stand on a finger of high land and be almost surrounded by a stunning assortment of rock spires and pinnacles—perhaps the park's best view.

Return to the paved road and continue south for 16 miles until you arrive at the **White River Visitor Center** (open summer). It is operated by the Oglala Tribe and offers exhibits on Indian culture and a video. Here you can also get detailed directions to the many other sites worth visiting in the South Unit.

A visit to the **Stronghold Table** will either be a disappointment or the emotional culmination of your visit, depending on your perspective and imagination. Getting there involves driving some extremely rutted tracks through lonely grasslands, where you will probably get lost (bring along a topographical map). It also involves opening and closing many gates. The reward for this effort? An unspectacular view, but the chance to stand in the place where, in December 1890, a group of Sioux danced the Ghost Dance for the last time. In this impassioned ritual, dancers fell into hypnotic trances, "died," and envisioned the paradise soon to come, sweeping the white man from the land and repopulating it with bison, elk, and pronghorn. If you go there, keep in mind that for Indians this is a sacred place.

INFORMATION & ACTIVITIES

HEADQUARTERS
Interior, SD 57750. Phone (605) 433-5361. www.nps.gov/badl

SEASONS & ACCESSIBILITY
Park open year-round. Snowstorms may block roads temporarily in winter. Call park headquarters to check on current road and weather conditions and accessibility to the undeveloped South Unit.

VISITOR & INFORMATION CENTERS
Ben Reifel Visitor Center, in the North Unit, open daily all year.
White River Visitor Center, in the South Unit, open only in summer.

ENTRANCE FEE
$15 per car.

PETS
Permitted on leashes except in the Sage Creek Unit of Badlands Wilderness and on trails.

FACILITIES FOR DISABLED
Visitor centers and some trails are wheelchair accessible. Free brochure available.

THINGS TO DO
Free naturalist-led activities during summer: nature walks and hikes, evening programs, night walks, fossil demonstrations. Also available, interpretive exhibits and audiovisual programs, hiking, wildlife watching.

SPECIAL ADVISORIES
- Prairie rattlesnakes and cactuses live here: Watch where you step when walking.
- Bison are unpredictable and can be dangerous: Keep your distance.
- Be prepared for sudden changes in weather and severe thunderstorms in summer. Check weather conditions by contacting headquarters or a visitor center before you hike.

OVERNIGHT BACKPACKING
No permit required; ask a ranger for advisories.

CAMPGROUNDS
Two campgrounds, both with a 14-day limit. **Cedar Pass** and **Sage Creek** rarely fill up and are open all year, first come, first served. (Heavy snows may close them in winter.) Cedar Pass is $10; Sage Creek is free year-round, without water. No showers. Tent and RV sites; no hookups. **Cedar Pass Group Campground,** reservations accepted Memorial Day to Labor Day; campsites $2 per person, $20 minimum; contact park headquarters. Food service in park.

HOTELS, MOTELS, & INNS
(unless otherwise noted, rates are for 2 persons in a double room, high season)

INSIDE THE PARK:
Cedar Pass Lodge (on S. Dak. 240 near visitor center) P.O. Box 5, Interior, SD 57750. (605) 433-5460. 22 cabins. $65. AC, restaurant. Open mid-April through October.

OUTSIDE THE PARK:
In Interior, SD 57750:
Badlands Inn (half mile from park entrance) P.O. Box 103. (605) 433-5401. 24 units. $70. AC. Open mid-May to Labor Day.

In Wall, SD 57790:
American Bison Inn South Blvd., P.O. Box 424. (800) 782-9402 or (605) 279-2127. 47 units. $120. AC, pool.
Best Western Plains Motel (1.5 blocks off I-90) 712 Glenn St., P.O. Box 393. (800) 528-1234 or (605) 279-2145. 74 units. $95-$120. AC, pool. Open March through November.
Kings Inn Motel 608 Main St. (800) 782-2613 or (605) 279-2179. 26 units. $65-$75. AC.
Motel 6 Tenth Ave., P.O. Box 76. (605) 279-2133. 41 units. $66. AC, pool.
Walls Econolodge 804 Glenn St., P.O. Box 426. (605) 279-2121. 49 units. $100. AC, pool. Open May through October.

For additional accommodations contact the Wall Chamber of Commerce, P.O. Box 527, Wall, SD 57790. (605) 279-2665.

Aspens above the Gunnison River, along the Oak Flat Trail

BLACK CANYON OF THE GUNNISON

COLORADO

ESTABLISHED OCTOBER 21, 1999

30,385 acres

Sheer walls of dark gray stone rise more than 2,600 feet above the swift and turbulent Gunnison River to create one of the most dramatic canyons in the country. Deeper than it is wide in some places, this great slit in the Earth is so narrow that sunlight penetrates to the bottom only at midday. The park protects the deepest, most thrilling 14 miles of the gorge, about 75 miles upstream of the Gunnison's junction with the Colorado River.

Imagine chiseling two parallel walls of hard gneiss and schist running the length of Manhattan and standing higher than two Empire State Buildings stacked atop one another, with water as your only tool. At the inconceivable rate of one inch per century, it would take all of human history just to cut through five feet of rock. What you see from the rim is the product of two million years of patient work.

The metamorphic rocks exposed at the bottom of the canyon are nearly two billion years old, dating from the Precambrian or oldest era of the Earth. Here and there swirling pink veins of igneous pegmatite shoot through the walls, livening up the canyon's somber appearance.

Indians and white explorers generally avoided the formidable canyon up through the 19th century. In 1900, five men attempted to run the river in wooden boats to survey it as a possible source of irrigation for the Uncompahgre Valley. After a month, with their boats in splinters and their supplies gone, they gave up. But the next year two men ran it in nine days on rubber air mattresses. A water diversion tunnel was soon in the works; the four-year project, completed in 1909, resulted in a 6-mile-long tunnel through rock, clay, and sand. The labor was so grueling and dangerous that the average period of employment was only two weeks. Today, three dams upstream have further tamed the Gunnison, but the canyon and its section of river remain wild.

Rim drives and hikes offer plenty of opportunities for peering into the magnificent canyon and marveling at its cliffs and towers of stone. Ravens, golden eagles, and peregrine falcons soar the great gulf of air out in front. On top grows a thick forest of Gambel oak and serviceberry, which provide cover for mule deer and black bears, while farther down the canyon Douglas firs thrive in the shade, and cottonwoods and box elders find footholds along the river.

Gnarled juniper trunk

How to Get There

The South Rim is located 15 miles northeast of Montrose, via US 50 and Colo. 347. The North Rim is 80 miles by car from the South Rim, via US 50W and Colo. 92. Turn south off Colo. 92 onto the 15-mile North Rim Road, the first half of which is paved. Airports: Montrose and Gunnison.

When to Go

Summer is the most popular time to visit. But be prepared to perspire if you hike at midday on exposed trails, and bring lots of water. Crisp days in late spring and early fall make for excellent walks. Winter affords opportunities for backcountry camping, cross-country skiing, and snowshoeing. With the rim at 8,000 feet above sea level, winter can set in as early as November and last until April. Snow closes vehicle access to the North Rim; the South Rim road stays open as far as the second overlook year-round.

How to Visit

You can spend most of the day driving the 7-mile (one-way) **South Rim** and exploring its 5 or so miles of trails. But reserve the afternoon, or a second day, for a walk down to the canyon floor. If you have more time, visit the **North Rim** and its 5-mile unpaved drive.

SOUTH RIM

Rim Drive, 7 miles one way; 2 to 3 hours

With a dozen scenic overlooks and several short trails, this dramatic drive offers plenty of topside angles on the canyon and river. The first overlook, **Tomichi Point,** allows access to the **Rim Rock Trail,** which runs north-south for about a mile between the campground and the visitor center. This trail gives you fine views of the vertiginous walls of the eastern part of the canyon and the glinting ribbon of water sluicing down its middle. You walk through a scrubby forest of Gambel oak and sagebrush, studded with pinyon pine and juniper. The latter has dark purple berries and a cedary look and smell. Breathe in the refreshing air; look for tracks of elk, bobcat, mountain lion, and other rim dwellers; and listen for the scold of Steller's jays.

Make a 2-mile loop by following the **Uplands Trail** across the road. Continue up through scrub oak forest before walking past the visitor center and rejoining the Rim Rock Trail. At the **visitor center,** exhibits on the park's geology, history, flora, and fauna will help get you started.

Just outside the visitor center you can take the invigorating **Oak Flat Trail,** which makes a loop of about 2 miles and gets you a little way below the rim. Head west, then turn right at the River Access sign and dip into a grove of aspens. At the next junction, turn left and wind through a thicket of scrub oak to an outcrop with a good view. Circle back through a forest of aspen and Douglas fir.

One of the shortest ways to the canyon floor is the **Gunnison Route,** off the Oak Flat Trail. It's a mere mile to the river, but it's a tough one—even for those in good shape, the walk down takes at least an hour. Since most of the canyon is a designated wilderness, hikers end up following drainage gullies, which plunge 1,800 vertical feet over scree slopes littered with big rocks. To

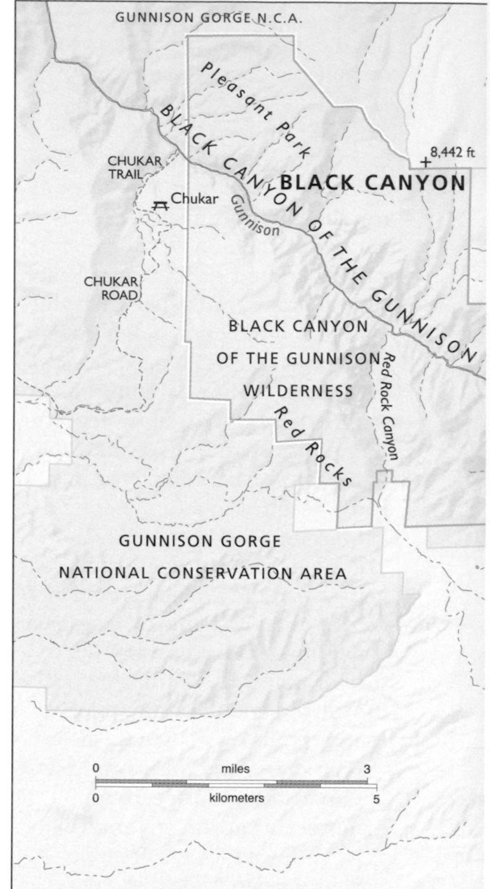

avoid ankle injuries in some places, crouch and slide; a mounted 80-foot-long chain helps out on one stretch, but the rest is a wild free-for-all. At the bottom, rest and massage your legs, staring up at the spectacular stonework all around. The walk back up—at times a hand-over-hand pull—is harder than the downhill.

Back on the road, continue driving northwest. The aptly named **Pulpit Rock** offers a terrific long view of the river knifing its way through the canyon. A walk out to **Chasm View** takes you to within about 1,100 feet of the North Rim, on the opposite side of the canyon. At this point, the canyon's 1,800-foot depth exceeds its width, and it

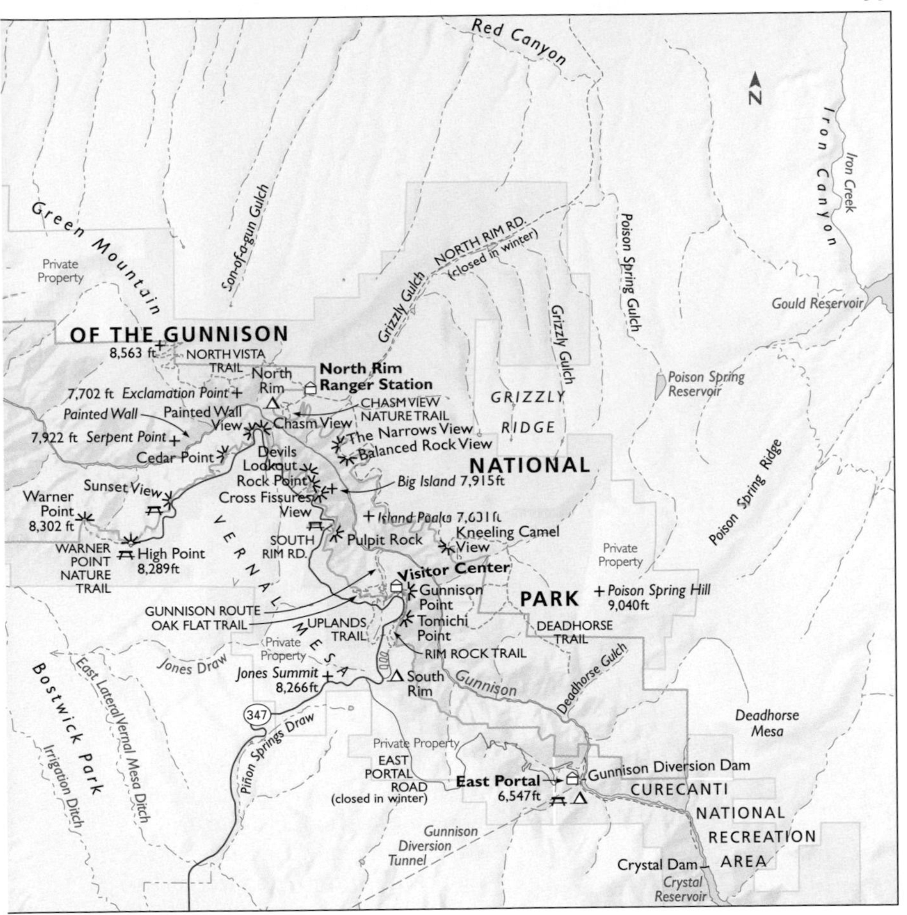

looks extremely narrow. But the narrowness is a result of the river's precipitous angle and its high volume. You're left with a sense of something newly created, which in geological terms is true.

The road now bends southwest. Several pull-offs provide views of the magnificent **Painted Wall,** a 2,250-foot sheer cliff decorated with stripes and flourishes of pink and white crystalline pegmatite, an extrusion of magma that seeped into cracks and hardened. Take the **Cedar Point Nature Trail,** an easy 0.6-mile out-and-back, to views of the wall, the river, and islands of stone rising from the canyon depths.

Drive on to **High Point,** the end of the road and, at 8,289 feet, one of the highest places on the rim. From here it is a dizzying 2,689-foot drop to the river. You can take a 1.5-mile round-trip walk out to **Warner Point** for exquisite canyon views to the north. Turning to the south you can see the verdant farmlands of the Uncompahgre Valley irrigated by water diverted from the canyon's own Gunnison River. Beyond rise the San Juan Mountains. The trail meanders among pinyon pine, juniper, mountain mahogany, and white-flowering serviceberry. Other plants scattered about include Fendler bush, mule's ear, lupine, and scarlet gilia, the last bearing lovely tubular flowers.

Precambrian-era rock flanking the Black Canyon's Gunnison River

NORTH RIM

Rim Drive (unpaved), 5 miles one way; 2 to 3 hours

While it is only 1,100 feet from one side of the canyon to the other, you must endure an 80-mile drive to reach the North Rim from the South Rim—the last several miles of it unpaved along North Rim Road. You can also reach the North Rim from the east side—a 90-mile drive on US 50 and Colo. 92 thru the Curecanti National Recreation Area. On the North Rim, you'll find yourself in a remote and awesome wilderness where the canyon walls plunge nearly vertically.

Whichever way you come, leave Colo. 92 at North Rim Road and follow it to the end. Turn right and drive to the ranger station, where one of the finest hikes in the park begins. The **North Vista Trail** wanders in and out of scrub forest along the rim for 1.5 miles. Detour at **Exclamation Point** for a jaw-dropping look into the canyon's depths. Turn around, or continue 2 more miles to trail's end on Green Mountain. This difficult section climbs from 7,702 feet to 8,563 feet. Here stirring panoramas surround —starting to the west the Uncompahgre Plateau, turning north Grand Mesa, continuing east West Elk Mountains, and finally to the south the San Juan Mountains.

Once back at the ranger station, drive about a mile south and get out for the short **Chasm View Nature Trail,** which meanders through a pinyon-juniper forest and comes out at two stunning overlooks. White-throated swifts and violet-green swallows dart from cliffside nests. The southern 4 miles of the drive zigzag along the canyon's rim. At **Balanced Rock View** and **Kneeling Camel View,** near the end of the drive, steep unmarked trails wind down side canyons to the river.

INFORMATION & ACTIVITIES

HEADQUARTERS
102 Elk Creek, Gunnison, CO 81230. Phone (970) 641-2337. www.nps.gov/blca

SEASONS & ACCESSIBILITY
South Rim open daily, limited access in winter; North Rim Road and Ranger Station closed in winter. Contact park for current information.

VISITOR & INFORMATION CENTERS
Visitor center open daily except holidays in winter. **North Rim Ranger Station** open in summer only.

ENTRANCE FEE
$7 per vehicle per week; yearly fee $15.

PETS
Pets allowed in park on leash; not allowed on trails or in backcountry.

FACILITIES FOR DISABLED
South Rim: visitor center, comfort stations, 2 camping sites; and Tomichi Point, Chasm View, and Sunset View overlooks. **North Rim:** Balanced Rock overlook accessible.

THINGS TO DO
Free naturalist-led activities. Exhibits, scenic drives, hiking, fishing, kayaking, rock climbing, winter activities. Contact park headquarters for a list of concessioners.

SPECIAL ADVISORIES
• Permits required for all inner canyon routes; available at visitor center and North Rim Ranger Station.

OVERNIGHT BACKPACKING
Backcountry permits required. Wood fires prohibited; use camp stoves only.

CAMPGROUNDS
South Rim: 102 sites; **North Rim:** 13 sites. Auto campgrounds $10 per night. All sites first come, first served, usually available. Vault toilets, limited water, no hookups.

For accommodations contact the Montrose Visitors & Convention Bureau, (800) 873-0244 or (970) 240-1414; and the Gunnison County Chamber of Commerce, (970) 641-1501.

Sightseers viewing the Black Canyon

Snake River meandering through Jackson Hole toward the Tetons

GRAND TETON

WYOMING
ESTABLISHED FEBRUARY 26, 1929
309,994 acres

The peaks of the Teton Range, regal and imposing as they stand nearly 7,000 feet above the valley floor, make one of the boldest geologic statements in the Rockies. Unencumbered by foothills, they rise through steep coniferous forest into alpine meadows strewn with wildflowers, past blue and white glaciers to naked granite pinnacles. The Grand, Middle, and South Tetons form the heart of the range. But their neighbors, especially Mount Owen, Teewinot Mountain, and Mount Moran, are no less spectacular.

A string of jewel-like lakes, fed by mountain streams, are set tightly against the steep foot of the mountains. Beyond them extends the broad valley called Jackson Hole, covered with sagebrush and punctuated by occasional forested buttes and groves of aspen trees—excellent habitats for pronghorn, deer, elk, and other animals. The Snake River, having begun its journey in southern Yellowstone National Park near the Teton Wilderness, winds leisurely past the Tetons on its way to Idaho. The braided sections of the river create wetlands that support moose, elk, deer, beavers, trumpeter swans, sandhill cranes, Canada geese, and all sorts of ducks.

The Tetons are normal fault-block mountains. About 13 million years ago, two blocks of Earth's crust began to shift along a fault line, one tilting down while the other lifted up. So far, movement has measured some 30,000 vertical feet, most of it from the subsidence of Jackson Hole.

Before Europeans arrived, the Teton area was an important plant-gathering and hunting ground for Indians of various tribes. In the early 1800s, mountain men spent time here; it was they who called this flat valley ringed by mountains Jackson's Hole after the trapper Davey Jackson. (In recent times the name has lost its apostrophe and s.) The first settlers were ranchers and farmers. Some of their buildings are historic sites today, although ranching is still practiced in the vicinity. When the park was established, it included only the mountains and the glacial lakes at their feet. Portions of the valley were added in 1950.

Today the park's 485 square miles encompass both the Teton Range and much of Jackson Hole. Park roads, all in the valley, offer an ever changing panorama of the Tetons. Most visitors never go far from the road. But the Tetons are popular with hikers; backcountry trails climb high into the mountains—and behind them. Easy trails in the valley lead around lakes and beside wetlands where visitors see moose, elk, deer, and all kinds of birds.

How to Get There

From Jackson, take US 26/89/191 north past the National Elk Refuge; the entrance station and Moose Visitor Center are at Moose. From Dubois, follow US 26/287 to Moran Junction and turn north to the Moran Entrance Station. From Yellowstone NP's South Entrance, the John D. Rockefeller, Jr., Memorial Parkway leads directly into the park. Airport: The Jackson Hole Airport is inside the park—a concern for environmentalists.

When to Go

Any time of year is a joy in the Tetons. Most people visit during July and August, when it's sunny and warm, after the snow has melted in the high country. In September and October, the days are pleasant, nights are brisk, the park is less crowded, and the animals are still active. You have a better chance of seeing elk than in summer.

Winter, although spectacular, can be very demanding; snowshoeing and cross-country skiing are popular. The main park road, US 26/89/191, remains open all year, but snow closes Teton Park Road (the "inner road") north of Cottonwood Creek from November through April. The Moose-Wilson Road is also closed. At Teton Village, just south of the park, you'll find excellent downhill skiing.

How to Visit

On a 1-day visit take the **Teton Park Road** from **Moose Junction** to **Jenny Lake** for excellent views of the **Tetons** and short walks or longer hikes. On the second day, go farther north to **Signal Mountain** and **Jackson Lake.** For a longer stay, consider floating the **Snake River,** hiking, canoeing, climbing, or attending a ranger-guided activity.

TETON PARK ROAD & JENNY LAKE LOOP

17 miles; at least a half day

From **Moose Junction,** cross the **Snake River** to the **Moose Visitor Center,** which includes a small exhibit area. The first right turn after the entrance station leads to

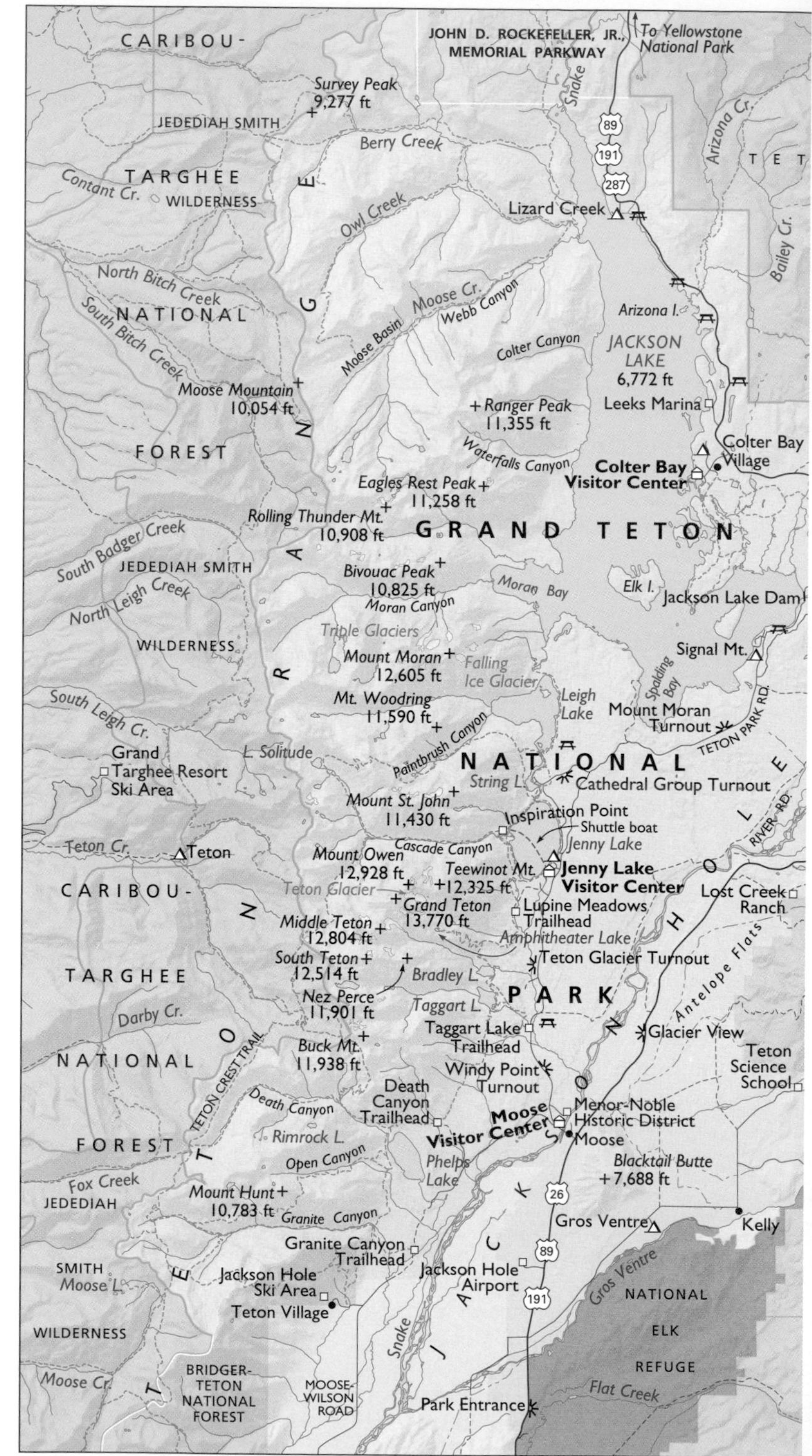

JOHN D. ROCKEFELLER, JR., MEMORIAL PARKWAY
To Yellowstone National Park
CARIBOU-TARGHEE NATIONAL FOREST
JEDEDIAH SMITH WILDERNESS
Survey Peak 9,277 ft
Berry Creek
Contant Cr.
Owl Creek
Lizard Creek
North Bitch Creek
South Bitch Creek
Moose Basin
Moose Cr.
Webb Canyon
Arizona I.
Arizona Cr.
Bailey Cr.
Colter Canyon
JACKSON LAKE 6,772 ft
Moose Mountain 10,054 ft
Ranger Peak 11,355 ft
Leeks Marina
Waterfalls Canyon
Colter Bay Village
Colter Bay Visitor Center
Eagles Rest Peak 11,258 ft
Rolling Thunder Mt. 10,908 ft
GRAND TETON NATIONAL PARK
TETON RANGE
JACKSON HOLE
South Badger Creek
North Leigh Creek
Bivouac Peak 10,825 ft
Moran Bay
Moran Canyon
Elk I.
Jackson Lake Dam
Triple Glaciers
Signal Mt.
Mount Moran 12,605 ft
Falling Ice Glacier
Spalding Bay
South Leigh Cr.
Mt. Woodring 11,590 ft
Leigh Lake
Mount Moran Turnout
TETON PARK RD.
Paintbrush Canyon
L. Solitude
Grand Targhee Resort Ski Area
String L.
Cathedral Group Turnout
Mount St. John 11,430 ft
Inspiration Point
Shuttle boat
Jenny Lake
RIVER RD.
Teton Cr.
Teton
Cascade Canyon
Mount Owen 12,928 ft
Teewinot Mt. 12,325 ft
Jenny Lake Visitor Center
Teton Glacier
Grand Teton 13,770 ft
Lupine Meadows Trailhead
Lost Creek Ranch
Middle Teton 12,804 ft
Amphitheater Lake
South Teton 12,514 ft
Teton Glacier Turnout
Antelope Flats
Bradley L.
Nez Perce 11,901 ft
Taggart L.
Darby Cr.
Taggart Lake Trailhead
Buck Mt. 11,938 ft
Glacier View
TETON CREST TRAIL
Windy Point Turnout
Teton Science School
Death Canyon
Death Canyon Trailhead
Menor-Noble Historic District
Moose Visitor Center
Moose
Rimrock L.
Open Canyon
Phelps Lake
Blacktail Butte 7,688 ft
Fox Creek
Mount Hunt 10,783 ft
Granite Canyon
Gros Ventre
Kelly
Granite Canyon Trailhead
Jackson Hole Airport
Moose L.
Jackson Hole Ski Area
Teton Village
Gros Ventre
NATIONAL ELK REFUGE
Snake
BRIDGER-TETON NATIONAL FOREST
MOOSE-WILSON ROAD
Moose Cr.
Park Entrance
Flat Creek
89
191
287
26

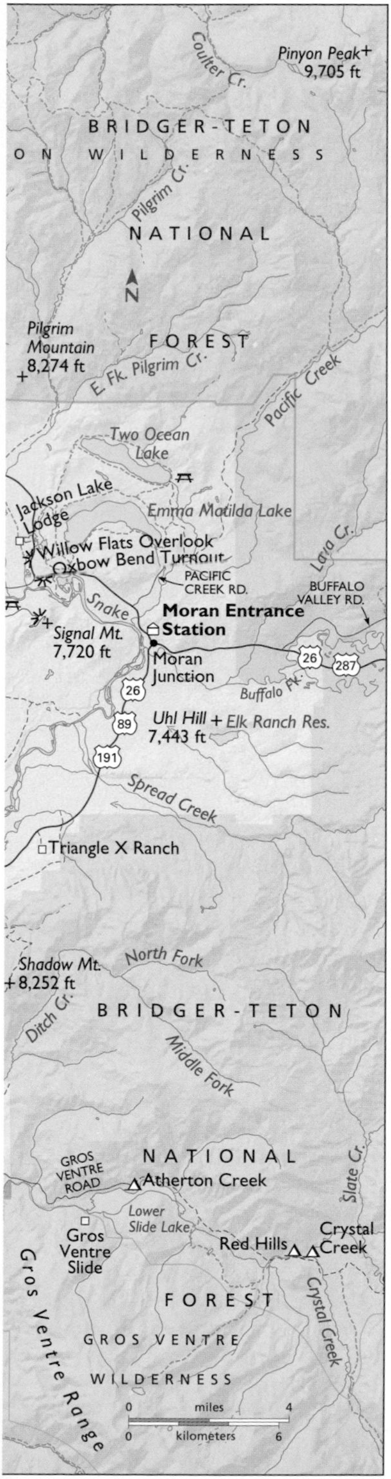

Pinyon Peak + 9,705 ft
Coulter Cr.
BRIDGER-TETON
ON WILDERNESS
Pilgrim Cr.
NATIONAL
N
Pilgrim Mountain + 8,274 ft
FOREST
E. Fk. Pilgrim Cr.
Pacific Creek
Two Ocean Lake
Jackson Lake Lodge
Emma Matilda Lake
Willow Flats Overlook
Oxbow Bend Turnout
PACIFIC CREEK RD.
Lava Cr.
BUFFALO VALLEY RD.
Snake
Moran Entrance Station
Signal Mt. 7,720 ft
Moran Junction
26
287
Buffalo Fk.
26
89
Uhl Hill + 7,443 ft
Elk Ranch Res.
191
Spread Creek
Triangle X Ranch
Shadow Mt. + 8,252 ft
North Fork
Ditch Cr.
BRIDGER-TETON
Middle Fork
NATIONAL
GROS VENTRE ROAD
Atherton Creek
Slate Cr.
Lower Slide Lake
Gros Ventre Slide
Red Hills
Crystal Creek
Gros Ventre Range
FOREST
Crystal Creek
GROS VENTRE
WILDERNESS
0 miles 4
0 kilometers 6

Menor-Noble Historic District, a pioneer homestead. Save that for another day; there are mountains ahead. The **Teton Park Road** climbs up from the river onto a sage-covered flat with the whole Teton panorama in view. You will see the mountains clearly throughout this drive from various changing angles; each viewpoint reveals striking perspectives different from the last.

If you look toward the mountains at Taggart Lake Trailhead, you can see the results of a 1985 forest fire. An easy trail offers a closeup view of forest regeneration—an especially interesting and encouraging sight if you plan to visit Yellowstone, where fires burned extensively in the summer of 1988.

Stop at Teton Glacier Turnout for a close-in view of the three Tetons. The Grand Teton, at 13,770 feet, is the highest point in the range. A major route used by climbers follows the left-hand, southern skyline; just as it appears, there is no easy way to the top. Looking to the left of the Grand, you see the **Middle** and **South Tetons.** The sharp pinnacle jutting up over the shoulder of the South Teton (actually in front of it), is the peak called **Nez Perce.** To the right of the Grand are the sharp peak of **Mount Owen** and, in the foreground, the craggy battlements of **Teewinot Mountain.**

Teton Mountains overshadow historic barn

Looking over a field of wildflowers into Targhee National Forest

Notice the steep, glacier-carved gulch coming straight down from the Grand Teton. At the head of the gulch, beneath the mountain's near-vertical northeast face, lies **Teton Glacier.** During an ancient ice age, glaciers covered Jackson Hole to a depth of 3,000 feet and carved the canyons in the Teton Range. The glaciers that exist now only at high elevations established themselves more recently.

If you can take your eyes off the mountains, scan the sage flats on both sides of the road for pronghorn, elk, deer, and coyotes, especially in the fall. Across Jackson Hole to the southeast is the **Gros Ventre Range,** where herds of elk and mule deer roam the deeply forested gorges and bighorn sheep the highest peaks.

Heading north, the **Lupine Meadows** spur road leads to a major trailhead. From here you can take a very rewarding but strenuous hike, which climbs 3,000 feet to **Amphitheater Lake** near timberline. Lupine Meadows itself is a good place to look for wildlife in the evening.

Back on the main road, the **South Jenny Lake** area is next, but unless you're planning to hike around the lake, or to take the boat across to **Cascade Canyon** at this point in your tour, you should drive past it for now.

Four miles ahead is the junction for **Jenny Lake Scenic Drive,** where a narrow 1-mile loop road provides the best approach to the area, which many consider to be the scenic heart of the Tetons. The road angles back to the southwest, offering stunning views of the central peaks. Stop at **Cathedral Group Turnout** to take it all in. The north face of the Grand is visible from here, flanked by Teewinot on the left and Owen on the right. North of them, in order, are precipitous **Cascade**

Canyon (one of the park's best hikes), **Mount Saint John, Mount Woodring,** and then the massive, flat-topped **Mount Moran.** Moran's **Falling Ice Glacier** is prominent. Notice also the obvious line of black rock rising above the glacier. Called the **Black Dike,** it was caused when molten rock intruded into a crack in the older metamorphic rock called gneiss, before the Tetons rose. The dike, now exposed by erosion of the gneiss, actually stands out from the mountain face near the summit. Similar dikes are on the Middle Teton (not visible from here) and Grand Teton.

Just ahead, a short road forks off the scenic drive and leads to tiny **String Lake.** An easy trail leaves from the end of the road to follow the shoreline through open forest to sparkling **Leigh Lake,** named after a 19th-century mountain man, Richard "Beaver Dick" Leigh, who, it was said, could "trap beaver where there warn't any." The lake has superb views of soaring Mount Moran, and, in summer, the water is sometimes warm enough for swimming.

Continuing on, the scenic drive reaches **Jenny Lake** and becomes one way. For understandable reasons, this place is highly popular; the road in summer is crowded with vehicles. Even so, if you desire solitude amid the grandeur, you can generally find it. Leave your car in a parking area and walk down to the shore. Instantly you are isolated from the world of automobiles. If you have more time, catch the boat that usually leaves three times an hour from the southeast end of the lake. Near the parking area you will find the **Jenny Lake Visitor Center,** restrooms, ranger station, a store, and a campground for tents only.

The passenger boat crosses Jenny Lake to join **Cascade Canyon Trail.** It is a half-mile walk to **Hidden Falls,** one of the park's beauties. A half-mile farther, aptly named **Inspiration Point** overlooks the lake. If you still have the energy, the trail is not steep after Inspiration Point, and the views keep getting better. You might consider walking back to the visitor center along the south shore; the easy trail is nearly 3 miles long.

JACKSON LAKE

about 30 miles; at least a half day

Start at North Jenny Lake Junction on the Teton Park Road. Drive north 2.5 miles through sage land and lodgepole pine to the **Mount Moran Turnout.** Mount Moran, at 12,605 feet, is more than a thousand feet lower than the Grand Teton, but you wouldn't know that looking up. On its summit a patch of sandstone corresponds to a sandstone layer an estimated 24,000 feet below where you stand; 13 million years of movement on the Teton fault has separated the layers by some 30,000 feet.

North of Mount Moran, **Bivouac Peak, Rolling Thunder Mountain,** and **Eagles Rest Peak** dominate the most remote section of the park, cut off from roads and easy trail access by **Jackson Lake,** just ahead. The natural lake was enlarged by a dam built before the park was established.

Before you get to the lake, take the right-hand turn to **Signal Mountain.** The road, on which trailers and RVs are not allowed, winds to the summit of a low mountain which, because it stands alone in Jackson Hole, provides a panoramic view of the region. There's no better place than here to appreciate the unusual geology of the Teton area: the abrupt meeting of valley floor and the Teton Range; the meandering course of the Snake River

Late afternoon on Jackson Lake *(top)*; Mount Moran reflection from Catholic Bay *(center left)*; Bull moose in rut *(center right)*; climbing Blacktail Butte, just east of Moose *(bottom left)*; Hidden Falls *(bottom right)*

through deposits of gravel and clay brought down by Ice Age glaciers; and the ranges to the east. From Signal Mountain, it is easy to see why the early trappers thought of mountain-ringed valleys like this one as holes.

Back on the Teton Park Road, you pass Signal Mountain Campground and cross the Snake River over the rebuilt dam. A mile farther, the road joins US 89/191/287. If you're headed north toward Yellowstone, it's worthwhile to turn right and take a short side trip (about a mile) to **Oxbow Bend,** for a classic view of the Tetons dominated by Mount Moran. Wildlife frequents this area.

Going north once again, stop at **Willow Flats Overlook.** The willows are a likely place to see moose. Failing that, watch the meadows below the bridge just to the north as you cross **Pilgrim Creek.**

A few minutes north, **Colter Bay Visitor Center** has an excellent **Indian Arts Museum.** Consider stretching your legs on the easy 3-mile **Colter Bay Nature Trail;** self-guiding booklets can be had at the trailhead or at the visitor center.

North of **Colter Bay,** the main road stays close to the lake. Just before Lizard Creek Campground, you catch one last glimpse of the Tetons and Jackson Lake, before entering dense lodgepole forest. Ten miles farther, along the John D. Rockefeller, Jr., Memorial Parkway, is the South Entrance to Yellowstone NP.

OTHER HIKES & ACTIVITIES

Grand Teton has more than 200 miles of maintained trails; many lead up canyons separating the major peaks. All trails have something to offer, but they vary in difficulty, and some are more scenic than others. Keep in mind that most trails begin at about 6,800 feet, so shortness of breath can come quickly.

Cascade Canyon is most popular. Begin at Jenny Lake and either walk along the lakeshore or take the boat across to Hidden Falls and Inspiration Point. It is a long hike to **Lake Solitude**—7 miles if you take the boat, 9.5 miles if you walk the lakeshore—but it's worthwhile to go at least partway up the canyon. (Ask when the last boat returns to the parking lot; those extra 2.5 miles around the lake can seem a lifetime after a long hike.)

From Lupine Meadows parking area, the **Amphitheater Lake Trail** climbs to 9,700 feet and rewards those who make the strenuous 9-mile round-trip with a breathtaking view of Jackson Hole. The lake nestles beneath craggy peaks; allow 8 hours minimum.

Death Canyon Trailhead, off the Moose-Wilson Road, leads to a nice view of **Phelps Lake;** from there, the trail climbs to join the **Teton Crest Trail,** a magnificent route that traverses the range and ends at **Paintbrush Canyon** near String Lake, a trip of about 40 miles and 3 days (backcountry permit required).

Consider taking a raft trip on the **Snake River** for fine Teton views and a chance to see beavers, otters, moose, eagles, ospreys, and waterfowl. Ask about outfitters at a visitor center or check the park newspaper, *Teewinot.*

You can also sign up for a mountain climbing lesson; rent a canoe and paddle on a lake; or take a summer course taught by the **Teton Science School.** The school offers 1- to 5-day seminars on ecology and the region's natural history for ages 8 and up.

INFORMATION & ACTIVITIES

HEADQUARTERS
P.O. Drawer 170, Moose, WY 83012. Phone (307) 739-3300. www.nps.gov/grte

SEASONS & ACCESSIBILITY
Main road into park (US 26/89/191) open year-round. Snow closes side roads; closed from about November to May. Call headquarters for winter road conditions.

VISITOR & INFORMATION CENTERS
Moose Visitor Center, at park's south end, open daily all year. **Colter Bay Visitor Center,** on Jackson Lake, open mid-May through September. **Jenny Lake Visitor Center** open June through Labor Day. Call (307) 739-3399.

ENTRANCE FEE
$20 per car, good for one week at both Grand Teton and Yellowstone. $40 annually for both parks.

PETS
Permitted on leashes except on trails, at ranger-led activities, in backcountry and visitor centers; not permitted on boats on the Snake River or on lakes other than Jackson Lake.

FACILITIES FOR DISABLED
Visitor centers, Indian Arts Museum, some restrooms, some ranger-led activities are accessible. Also, some trails and Menor-Noble Historic District.

THINGS TO DO
Free ranger-led activities: wildlife walks and talks, day and twilight hikes, bicycle tours, slide talks, campfire programs, children's programs, skill development programs, tepee demonstration, wildlife watches, snowshoe walks. Also, boat cruise, natural history seminars, boating (permit required), river rafting, climbing, bicycling, horseback riding (stables in park), fishing and ice fishing (license required), snowshoeing, cross-country skiing, dogsledding, snowmobiling. Ask park for list of concessioners offering variety of rental and guide services.

OVERNIGHT BACKPACKING
Permits required. Free, they can be obtained at visitor centers and Jenny Lake Ranger Station. One-third of permits can be reserved for a nonrefundable $15 fee; the rest are first come, first served. Mail requests between January and mid-May to Permits Office, in care of park.

CAMPGROUNDS
Five campgrounds, **Jenny Lake** has 7-day limit, others 14-day limit. Generally late May to Oct., except **Lizard Creek,** mid-June to early Sept. All first come, first served. $12 per night. Showers at **Colter Bay.** Only tent sites at Jenny Lake; all others have tent and trailer sites, no hookups. Two group campgrounds; reservations suggested; contact park headquarters. RV sites only at **Colter Bay RV Park,** $22 per night. Reservations required; contact Grand Teton Lodge Co. (see below). Food services in park.

HOTELS, MOTELS, & INNS
(unless otherwise noted, rates are for 2 persons in a double room, high season)

INSIDE THE PARK:
The following 3 lodges and cabins are operated by Grand Teton Lodge Co., P.O. Box 250, Moran, WY 83013. (800) 628-9988 or (307) 543-2811.
Colter Bay Village and Marina 166 cabins. $75-$140. Rest. Late May–late Sept.
Jackson Lake Lodge (1 mile north of Jackson Lake Jct.) 385 units. $141-$575. Restaurant, pool. Late May–early Oct.
Jenny Lake Lodge 37 cabins. $475-$680, incl. 2 meals. Rest. Early June–early Oct.
Signal Mountain Lodge P.O. Box 50, Moran, WY 83013. (800) 672-6012 or (307) 543-2831. 79 units. $99-$250. Restaurant. Mid-May–mid-Oct.
Triangle X Ranch Moose, WY 83012. (307) 733-2183. 22 cabins. $1,270-$1,800 per person, per week, all incl. Late May–Oct.
OUTSIDE THE PARK
Lost Creek Ranch (8 miles north of Moose) P.O. Box 95, Moose, WY 83012. (307) 733-3435. 13 rooms, 10 cabins. $5,840-$13,710 per week, all incl. June–Nov.

Contact the Jackson Hole Chamber of Commerce for a full list of accommodations: P.O. Box 550, Jackson Hole, WY 83001. (307) 733-3316. Open year-round.

EXCURSIONS

NATIONAL ELK REFUGE
JACKSON, WYOMING

In winter, visitors can ride a horse-drawn sleigh into the protected winter range of a 7,000- to 8,000-head herd of elk. The refuge offers supplemental feeding to the animals, many of which migrate south from Yellowstone NP. 24,700 acres. Fishing (Aug. through Oct.), scenic drives, visitor center. Open year-round, dawn to dusk. Adjoins Grand Teton NP on south. (307) 733-9212.

BRIDGER-TETON NATIONAL FOREST
JACKSON, WYOMING

This immense forest encompasses wildlife-rich Jackson Hole; the glaciers and lakes of the Wind River Range; and Two Ocean Creek along the Continental Divide. Contains three wilderness areas. 3.4 million acres. Hiking, boating, fishing, horseback riding, hunting, water sports, winter sports. 30 campgrounds, boat ramp. Open all year; campgrounds open spring to fall. Adjoins Grand Teton NP on east. (307) 739-5500.

CARIBOU-TARGHEE NATIONAL FOREST
IDAHO FALLS, IDAHO

Here, on the Tetons' western flank, lies a forest of lodgepole pine and fir with many rivers, streams, and lakes. Contains two wilderness areas. 1,810,000 acres, part in Wyoming. Hiking, boating, fishing, horseback riding, hunting, picnic areas, winter sports, water sports. 32 campgrounds, boat ramp. Open all year; campsites open late May through September. Adjoins Grand Teton and Yellowstone NPs. (208) 624-3151.

Sand dunes at sunset, with Sangre de Cristo Mountains in the background

GREAT SAND DUNES

COLORADO

ESTABLISHED SEPTEMBER 13, 2004

107,000 acres

Visitors to the Great Sand Dunes experience an undeniable sense of wonder, just as happens in so many of our most spectacular national parks. In contrast to the sudden shock of walking to the rim of the Grand Canyon, though, or topping a rise to view Crater Lake, the emotions evoked by this otherworldly landscape arrive in slow motion.

The dunes appear in the distance as you approach, but at first seem dwarfed by their backdrop, the 13,000-foot peaks of the Sangre de Cristo Mountains. Not until you're nearly at their border does their vast scale become apparent: dunes up to 750 feet tall, extending for mile after mile—an ocean of sand hills of breathtaking magnitude. That's just how the explorer Zebulon Pike described them in 1807: "Their appearance was exactly that of a sea in a storm (except as to color), not the least sign of vegetation existing thereon."

The dunes sprawl across part of southern Colorado's San Luis Valley, a broad, arid plain between the San Juan Mountains on the west and the Sangre de Cristos on the east. The Rio Grande flows through the valley, and in millennia of meandering has spread a deep layer of sand—eroded from the rock of the surrounding mountains—across its ancient floodplain. Strong prevailing southwesterly winds carry the tiny grains toward the Sangre de Cristos, piling them up against the foothills. The resulting dunes are the tallest in North America, covering more than 30 square miles. Adults hike across them and marvel at their beauty; children run and slide down their steep faces, enjoying a playground of fairy-tale proportions.

Winds that often top 40 miles an hour continually reshape the crests of the tall dunes, and smaller dunes may "migrate" several feet in a week. The dunes show a remarkable permanence of form, though, which geologists attribute to their unusual moisture content. The San Luis Valley receives only about ten inches of rain a year, but that amount, plus snowmelt and underground water, helps keep the Great Sand Dunes great.

The need to protect the water that protects the dunes has led to a number of changes at Great Sand Dunes. Through a cooperative effort among government agencies and private conservation groups, the purchase of private lands, identified as important to the protection of park resources, was completed on September 13, 2004. The new entity comprises the original national monument, lands west of the monument known as the Baca Ranch, and mountains east of the monument previously managed by the U.S. Forest Service. This latter realm was established as a preserve in 2000 to safeguard the small streams flowing into the area. Official designation is Great Sand Dunes National Park and Preserve.

All this means that visitors have access to a great diversity of habitats, beginning in the desert dunes, continuing up to the pinyon pines, cottonwoods, and aspens of the foothills, and arriving even higher at the spruce-fir forests and tundra of the summits of the Sangre de Cristos, with seven peaks over 14,000 feet. The region's geology and biology make it a fascinating place, unique among our national parks. It's well worth the drive across southern Colorado, even if all you do is gaze in awe at this extraordinary and lovely terrain.

How to Get There

From the east or north, take US 160 west from Walsenburg 59 miles to Colo. 150 and drive north 16 miles. From the south or west, take US 285 to Alamosa and drive 14 miles east to Colo. 150, continuing north to the monument and preserve. Airport: Colorado Springs.

When to Go

Year-round. Moderate temperatures make spring and fall best. The sand dunes can get very hot in summer, although they can be traversed comfortably early and late in the day; summer is also the park's most crowded season. Winter snow curtails trips into the high mountains, though the dunes can still be visited.

How To Visit

Stop at the **visitor center** for a quick lesson in the Great Sand Dunes environment, and to learn the schedule of ranger-led walks and programs (summer only). From there, proceed to the dunes parking lot. Then walk out into the dunes, going as far and climbing as high as time and energy permit; the **High Dune** is a popular, moderately strenuous destination.

Kids and adults alike enjoy splashing along **Medano Creek,** which meanders along the base of the dunes (when there is enough water from the spring snowmelt). The **Montville Nature Trail** and the **Mosca Pass Trail** offer additional options for exploration, from short walks to mountain hikes.

If you have a high-clearance four-wheel-drive vehicle, and are very careful, you can drive the **Medano Pass Primitive Road,** which leads 11 miles up into the Sangre de Cristo Mountains in the national preserve, exploring different habitats along the way, from foothills to coniferous forest at the 9,982-foot pass. A park concessioner offers tours along this road; ask a ranger for details.

THE DUNES & MEDANO CREEK

Short hikes; a half day

A 15-minute video at the **visitor center** offers a good introduction to the geology and history of the park. Rangers in summer present programs here, as well as at other sites and trails. Depending on when you visit, guided events might include nature walks, children's activities, or programs on wildlife, plants, hiking, geology, or the archaeology of the dunes.

Begin your exploration at the **Dunes** parking lot. The imposing dunes, like buff-brown miniatures of the surrounding Sangre de Cristo crests, rise invitingly to the west. But first take time to discover **Medano Creek.** This small stream flows along the edge of the dunes; the moisture it carries is a vital part of the dune-system environment. Kids may want to build sand castles, or just enjoy a shoes-off walk along the squishy stream bed. The wet sand is a good place to look for the tracks of coyotes, kangaroo rats, mule deer, or bobcats.

Medano Creek usually flows only in spring, carrying snowmelt down

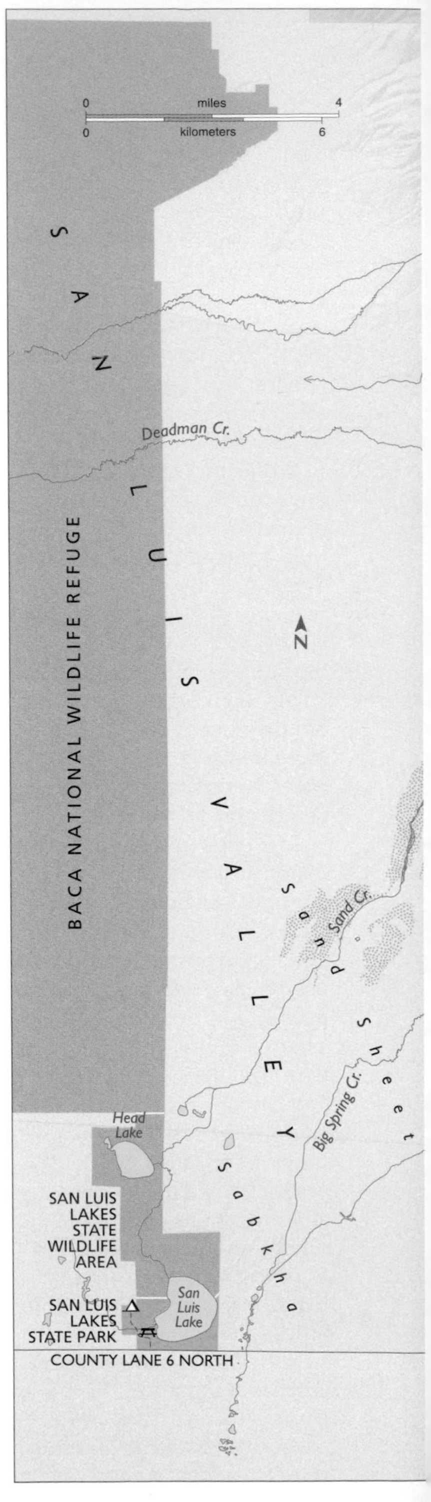

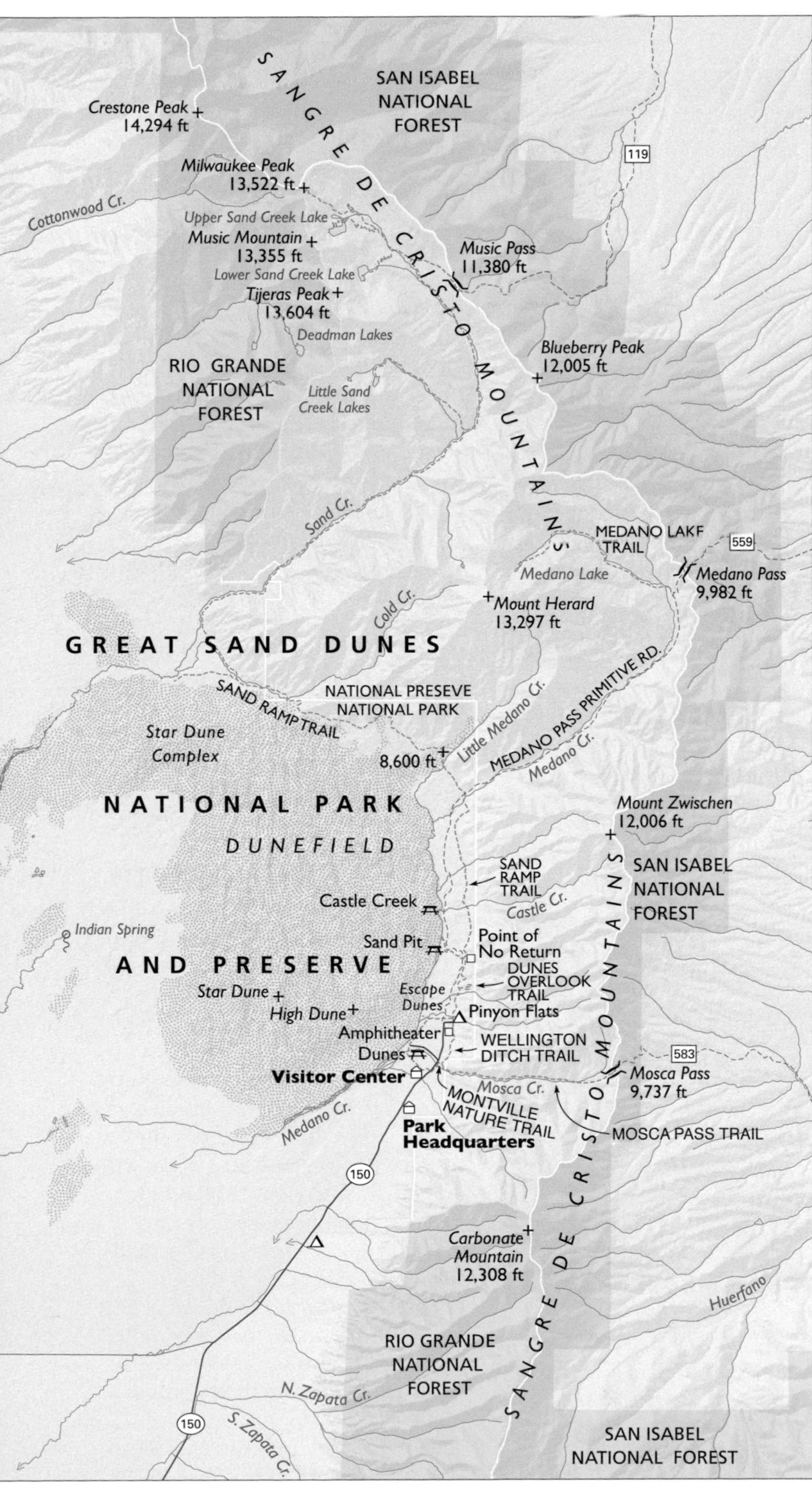
SANGRE DE CRISTO MOUNTAINS
SAN ISABEL NATIONAL FOREST
Crestone Peak 14,294 ft
119
Milwaukee Peak 13,522 ft
Cottonwood Cr.
Upper Sand Creek Lake
Music Mountain 13,355 ft
Music Pass 11,380 ft
Lower Sand Creek Lake
Tijeras Peak 13,604 ft
Deadman Lakes
Blueberry Peak 12,005 ft
RIO GRANDE NATIONAL FOREST
Little Sand Creek Lakes
Sand Cr.
MEDANO LAKE TRAIL
559
Medano Lake
Medano Pass 9,982 ft
Cold Cr.
Mount Herard 13,297 ft
GREAT SAND DUNES
SAND RAMP TRAIL
NATIONAL PRESEVE
NATIONAL PARK
MEDANO PASS PRIMITIVE RD.
Little Medano Cr.
Star Dune Complex
8,600 ft
Medano Cr.
NATIONAL PARK
Mount Zwischen 12,006 ft
DUNEFIELD
SAND RAMP TRAIL
SAN ISABEL NATIONAL FOREST
Castle Creek
Castle Cr.
Indian Spring
Sand Pit
Point of No Return
AND PRESERVE
DUNES OVERLOOK TRAIL
Escape Dunes
Star Dune
High Dune
Pinyon Flats
Amphitheater
WELLINGTON DITCH TRAIL
Dunes
583
Visitor Center
Mosca Pass 9,737 ft
Mosca Cr.
MONTVILLE NATURE TRAIL
Medano Cr.
Park Headquarters
MOSCA PASS TRAIL
150
Carbonate Mountain 12,308 ft
Huerfano
RIO GRANDE NATIONAL FOREST
N. Zapata Cr.
150
S. Zapata Cr.
SAN ISABEL NATIONAL FOREST

Bee plant on edge of the dunes *(top)*
Enjoying the view atop a high dune *(bottom)*

from the mountaintops. When it contains adequate water, watch for a phenomenon called "surge flow," which occurs when a small, temporary dam of sand upstream collapses, sending down a wave of water that can be up to a foot high.

Next, hike out into the dunes, where you'll quickly learn that walking in the soft sand is more strenuous than you might think. Take your time, and angle up the ridgelines of the dunes, rather than climbing straight up. While it might seem like fun to go barefoot, remember that in summer the sand surface can reach blistering temperatures. Wear protective shoes, as well as a hat, and apply sunscreen. Carry plenty of water if you plan on walking far. One thing you don't need to be concerned about is poisonous animals: There are no snakes or scorpions in the dunes.

You can strike out in any direction, but be sure to keep track of your location. While most people can easily orient themselves by noting the ever present peaks of the Sangre de Cristos, a compass or GPS unit isn't a bad idea for extended hikes. Many people make the 1-mile (one-way) trip to the aptly named **High Dune,** which towers 650 feet above the floor of the San Luis Valley. You'll find a great panorama at the top, taking in mountains, dunes, and valley. Another mile to the west rises the **Star Dune,** with an equally fine view. "Star" dunes are so named because they have three or more "arms," rather than the single axis of most dunes.

Photography in the dunes is best early and late in the day, when the low angle of the sun creates shadows that accentuate their contours and crests.

A night walk into the dunes can be a little eerie, but thrilling in its

Baca Ranch

sense of solitude and peace. When the moon is out, the dimly lit landscape seems even more haunting.

EAST OF THE DUNES

A full day or more

Although the dunes are fascinating and beautiful, there is a certain uniformity about them, and very few plants and animals make their homes there. The same is certainly not true for the foothills and high peaks of the Sangre de Cristo range, a large part of which is now encompassed in **Great Sand Dunes National Preserve.** (The preserve is administered similarly to the adjoining park, although hunting is allowed.) Here, you can hike or, with the proper vehicle, drive from the scrubby habitat of junipers and pinyon pines, along creeks lined with aspens and cottonwoods, up into forests of ponderosa pine and, even higher, spruce and fir. Alpine tundra tops the tallest summits above tree line, where only grasses, compact shrubs, low wildflowers, and other ground-hugging plants can survive.

East of the main road, just north of the visitor center, you'll find a parking area for three varied trails. The easy, half-mile **Montville Nature Trail** loops into the foothills, where you might spot mule deer, a least chipmunk, a desert cottontail, or a coyote. Black-billed magpies, long-tailed and conspicuous, have learned to beg for food (don't feed them or other wildlife), and friendly mountain chickadees flit from tree to tree. The **Wellington Ditch Trail** splits off the Montville trail partway around the loop, following an old irrigation ditch 1 mile north to the NPS campground.

Also beginning at the Montville trailhead, the **Mosca Pass Trail** follows an old toll road up Mosca Creek, a tributary of Medano, across the national monument boundary and into the preserve. You'll walk past cottonwoods and aspens, ascending into a forest of Engelmann spruce and subalpine fir, reaching 9,737-foot Mosca Pass after 3.5 miles; the elevation gain is just under 1,500 feet. For a moderate amount of effort, you'll get a fine overview of the way habitats change with altitude in the Rockies.

Visitors with a four-wheel-drive vehicle can take the **Medano Pass**

Primitive Road, which follows the national monument's eastern border before heading into the national preserve, climbing to reach 9,982-foot Medano Pass 11 miles from the road entrance. This trip offers a nonstrenuous way to explore the high Sangre de Cristos, although certain hazards must be taken into account. The road traverses soft sand for several miles and is not recommended for smaller SUVS lacking wide tires and high ground clearance. Even large vehicles may need to lower tire pressure to make it through the sand without bogging down. (Air to reinflate tires is available near the monument amphitheater.) The road crosses creeks several times, which can be problematic during spring high water, and it's closed in winter.

For those without the proper vehicle, a concessioner is authorized by the NPS to operate tours along the Medano Pass Primitive Road from May through September. The narrated, 2-hour trips do not climb into the preserve, but remain in the park, offering a look at areas unseen by most visitors.

Like the Mosca Pass Trail, the Medano Pass road provides a virtual natural-history lesson along with excellent scenery. Ascending from the foothills into lush montane forest is, in effect, like traveling from the southwestern desert to Canada. Ecologists call the different habitats encountered along mountain slopes "life zones"—each an altitudinal band boasting its own related set of plants and animals. Pinyon jays and mule deer, for instance, dwell among the arid-looking habitat of scattered junipers and pinyon pines, while gray jays and bighorn sheep live high on the mountain slopes.

One of the preserve's most popular hikes begins along the Medano Pass road, a half-mile west of the pass. The **Medano Lake Trail** climbs 1,900 feet in 4 miles to reach the lake, strikingly situated in a cirque under 13,297-foot Mount Herard. The trail passes through aspen groves that turn brilliant yellow in fall. The last mile of the trail is rugged, and to have a view westward over the sand dunes you must expend a little more effort, climbing the ridge above the lake. Your reward is a visit to an alpine world of flowery meadows, dense spruce-fir woodland, and wind-stunted trees at timberline, where elk bugle in fall and Clark's nutcrackers give their raucous calls. Listen for the sharp squeaks of pikas, mammals that live among rockpiles, looking like small rabbits without the long ears.

People enjoying Medano Creek

INFORMATION & ACTIVITIES

HEADQUARTERS
11500 Hwy. 150, Mosca, CO 81146. (719) 378-2312.www.nps.gov/grsa

SEASONS & ACCESSIBILITY
The park is open year-round. Sand temperatures can spike to 140°F during the summer.

VISITOR & INFORMATION CENTERS
The new expanded visitor center on Colo. 150 is open year-round with exhibits and viewing area. (719) 378-2312 ext. 220.

ENTRANCE FEE
$3 per person per week; $15 annual pass

PETS
Permitted on leashes. Be aware that mountain lions, coyotes, and foxes hunt within the park. Horses are not allowed in the dunes area.

FACILITIES FOR DISABLED
Access to the dunes is difficult for persons with traditional wheeled chairs. Check with the visitor center about borrowing a "sand wheelchair." Accessible camping sites are available at Pinyon campground as well as at the Sawmill Canyon Backcountry Campsite along Medano Pass Primitive Road. Check with park staff to answer other needs questions.

THINGS TO DO
Dunes hiking, photography, wildlife viewing, snowshoeing, nature walks, climbing, cross-country skiing, bird-watching, biking on trails away from the dunes. Summer events include sandcastle competitions and kite flying. Four-wheel-drive tours: contact Great Sand Dunes Oasis Campground, (719) 378-2222.

OVERNIGHT BACKPACKING
Free backcountry permits required for overnight camping. Primitive camping permitted without fires. Backcountry camping is allowed with horses and pack animals in most of the monument and preserve. Groups are limited to six people and animals within the monument borders and ten in the preserve. Check with park officials on specific limitations.

CAMPGROUNDS
Pinyon Flats Campground, with 88 campsites, open year-round on a first-come, first-served basis. $12 per night. Outside the park, **San Luis Lakes State Park** (13 miles on Six Mile Ln.) has 51 campsites with views of the Sangre de Cristo Mountains and the Great Sand Dunes. (719) 378-2020. $10 per night. Also see **Great Sand Dunes Lodge and Campground,** below.

SPECIAL ADVISORIES
• Shoes are necessary for walking on the dunes as sand can burn bare feet.
• Carry plenty of water—more than you normally would—for hikes of any length.
• Wear sunscreen and protective head covering.

HOTELS, MOTELS, & INNS
(unless otherwise noted, rates are for 2 persons in a double room, high season)

OUTSIDE THE PARK:
Great Sand Dunes Lodge and Campground 7900 Hwy. 150 N. Mosca, CO 81146. (719) 378-2900 (lodge). 10 rooms $89. Pool. (719) 378-2222 (campground reservations for RV and cabins). 130 tent sites. $14 first come, first serve and 20 RV ($23). Also available, four camping cabins ($35).

For other local accommodations, contact the park; the Alamosa Chamber of Commerce, (719) 589-3681 for information on locations near the main entrance; or the Custer Chamber of Commerce, (719) 783-9163 for information on the lodging near the preserve entrance.

Rocky Mountain aspen ablaze in fall

ROCKY MOUNTAIN

COLORADO
ESTABLISHED JANUARY 26, 1915
265,873 acres

Nowhere else in the United States can a visitor see so much alpine country with such ease. A mere 2-hour drive from Denver, Trail Ridge Road takes visitors into the heart of Rocky Mountain National Park, traversing a ridge above 11,000 feet for 10 miles. Along the way, tiny tundra flowers and other wild blooms contrast with sweeping vistas of towering summits; 78 of them exceed 12,000 feet. Alpine lakes reflect the grandeur.

The summits form at least the third generation of mountains to rise in this region. The first probably protruded as islands above a shallow sea more than 135 million years ago, when dinosaurs reigned. Another range grew out of a later sea some 75 million years ago. Over the eons these summits eroded to rolling hills, which rose once again, although unevenly: Some portions sank along fault lines, helping create the striking texture of the current scenery.

Rock as old as that at the bottom of the Grand Canyon—nearly two billion years—caps the Rockies' summits. Within the last million years, glaciers, grinding boulders beneath them, carved deep canyons. Erosion later scoured the more jagged summits into their present profiles.

Rocky Mountain, though only about an eighth the size of Yellowstone, accommodates as many visitors—3 million or so a year. Overcrowding worries park officials and conservationists, who cite distressed animals, trodden plants, and eroded trails. Condominium development is crowding the park's borders also, shrinking the habitats of elk and other wildlife and threatening to turn the park into an island of nature.

How to Get There

Take I-25 north from Denver (about 77 miles away) or south from Cheyenne, Wyoming (about 90 miles away), then US 34 west at Loveland. From the west, pick up US 34 at Granby. Airports: Denver, Colorado, and Cheyenne, Wyoming.

When to Go

If possible, avoid mid-June to mid-August, when the park receives about half its yearly visitors. Trail Ridge Road stays open from roughly late May to mid-October; trails thaw out by around July 4. In May, sub-alpine wildflowers bloom; in early July, the tundra flowers. September, the sunniest month, is a prime time to visit: Elk move to lower elevations, and you can hear their mating bugles. The tundra turns crimson early in the month; aspens turn golden later. In the winter there is cross-country skiing and snowshoeing.

How to Visit

On a 1-day blitz from the East Entrance, drive **Trail Ridge Road** as far as **Farview Curve** for the classic overview of the park's mountains, valleys, and tundra, then double back and take **Bear Lake Road** to see a collection of scenic lakes (which can get very congested in summer). If you wish, make a loop of the first leg by driving one-way, unpaved **Old Fall River Road** west, then Trail Ridge Road east. Old Fall River Road gives you an intimate look at a wooded mountainside, but it's usually closed by snow until early July.

With more time, drive all the way to **Grand Lake** on the west side the first day, then take your trip to **Bear Lake** the second day. Spend extra time on the excellent nature trails and day hikes.

If you go in summer and plan to backpack and hike, be sure not to be caught above timberline between about 12 and 4 p.m., when lightning storms are frequent.

TRAIL RIDGE ROAD TO GRAND LAKE, VIA FARVIEW CURVE

50 miles; at least a full day

Trail Ridge Road (US 34) roughly follows a 10,000-year-old trail; prehistoric people once hunted where you'll drive. The road climbs to a land like the vast arctic expanses of Siberia, Alaska, and northern Canada. Take warm clothing and sunscreen. From Estes Park, enter the park on US 36 and stop by the visitor center to pick up information—including a useful booklet ($1) about Trail Ridge Road—and a weather report. (If coming from the west on US 34, stop at the visitor center near Grand Lake and reverse this tour.) Continue straight on US 36 after the entrance station. The road ascends **Deer Mountain** through open ponderosa woodland.

At **Deer Ridge Junction,** either bear left onto Trail Ridge Road or, if it's summer, detour to the right, circling through **Horseshoe Park** and past **Sheep Lakes** to look for bighorn sheep, which sometimes visit the

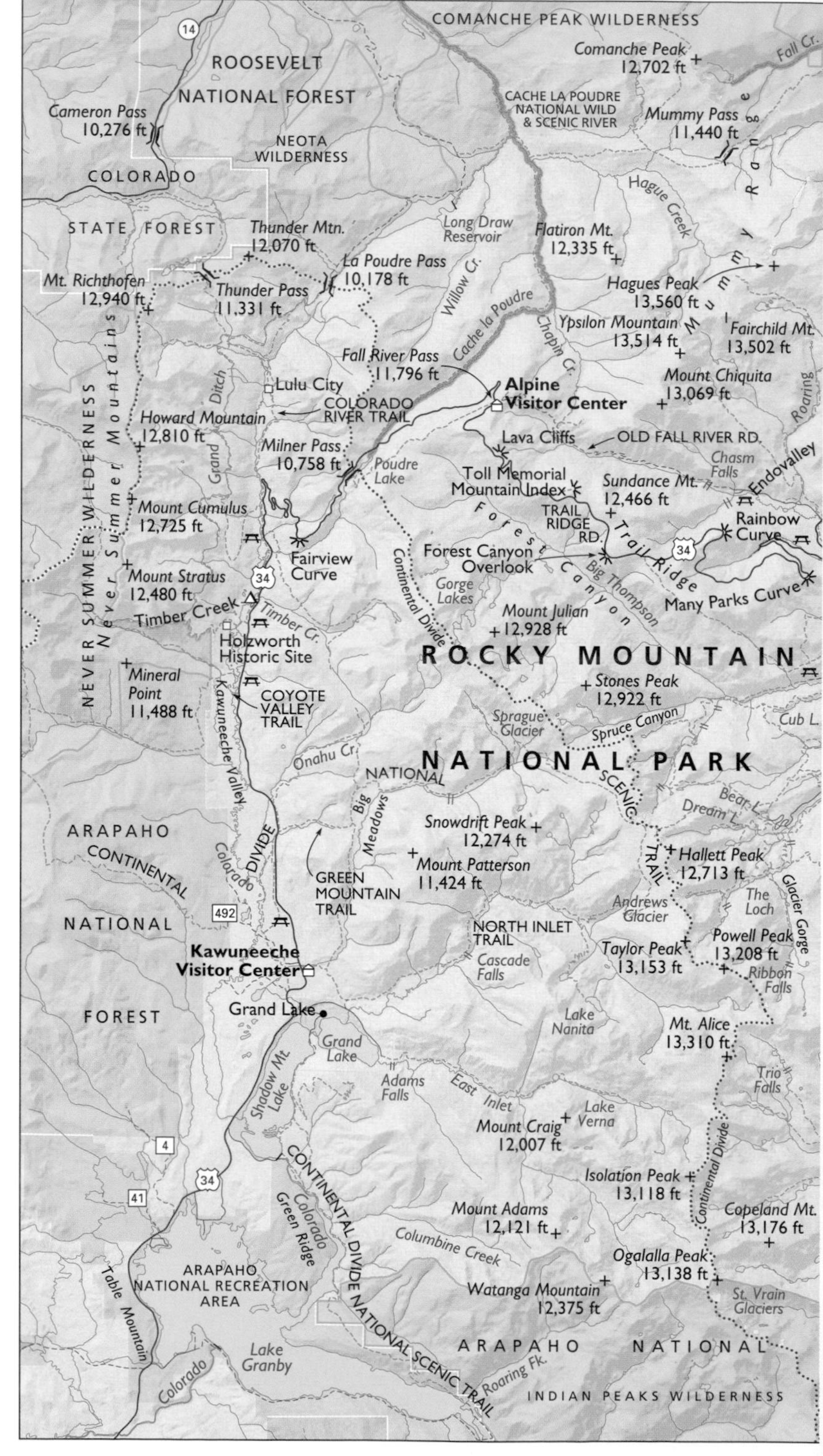
COMANCHE PEAK WILDERNESS
Comanche Peak
12,702 ft
Fall Cr.
ROOSEVELT
NATIONAL FOREST
CACHE LA POUDRE
NATIONAL WILD
& SCENIC RIVER
Mummy Pass
11,440 ft
Cameron Pass
10,276 ft
NEOTA
WILDERNESS
COLORADO
STATE FOREST
Hague Creek
Mummy Range
Thunder Mtn.
12,070 ft
Long Draw
Reservoir
Flatiron Mt.
12,335 ft
Mt. Richthofen
12,940 ft
La Poudre Pass
10,178 ft
Thunder Pass
11,331 ft
Willow Cr.
Hagues Peak
13,560 ft
Cache la Poudre
Chapin Cr.
Ypsilon Mountain
13,514 ft
Fairchild Mt.
13,502 ft
Never Summer Mountains
Fall River Pass
11,796 ft
Mount Chiquita
13,069 ft
Roaring
Lulu City
Ditch
Alpine
Visitor Center
Howard Mountain
12,810 ft
COLORADO
RIVER TRAIL
Lava Cliffs
OLD FALL RIVER RD.
Grand
Milner Pass
10,758 ft
Poudre
Lake
Chasm
Falls
Endovalley
Toll Memorial
Mountain Index
Sundance Mt.
12,466 ft
NEVER SUMMER WILDERNESS
Mount Cumulus
12,725 ft
TRAIL
RIDGE
RD.
Rainbow
Curve
Forest Canyon
Trail Ridge
Fairview
Curve
Continental Divide
Forest Canyon
Overlook
34
Mount Stratus
12,480 ft
Gorge
Lakes
Big Thompson
Many Parks Curve
Timber Creek
Timber Cr.
Mount Julian
12,928 ft
Holzworth
Historic Site
ROCKY MOUNTAIN
Mineral
Point
11,488 ft
Stones Peak
12,922 ft
COYOTE
VALLEY
TRAIL
Kawuneeche Valley
Sprague
Glacier
Spruce Canyon
Cub L.
Onahu Cr.
NATIONAL PARK
NATIONAL
SCENIC
TRAIL
Bear L.
Dream L.
Big
Meadows
ARAPAHO
CONTINENTAL
DIVIDE
Snowdrift Peak
12,274 ft
Hallett Peak
12,713 ft
Colorado
Mount Patterson
11,424 ft
GREEN
MOUNTAIN
TRAIL
The
Loch
Glacier Gorge
Andrews
Glacier
NATIONAL
492
NORTH INLET
TRAIL
Powell Peak
13,208 ft
Taylor Peak
13,153 ft
Kawuneeche
Visitor Center
Cascade
Falls
Ribbon
Falls
FOREST
Grand Lake
Lake
Nanita
Mt. Alice
13,310 ft
Grand
Lake
Shadow Mt.
Lake
Adams
Falls
East Inlet
Trio
Falls
Lake
Verna
Mount Craig
12,007 ft
4
CONTINENTAL DIVIDE NATIONAL SCENIC TRAIL
Isolation Peak
13,118 ft
41
Colorado
Green Ridge
Mount Adams
12,121 ft
Copeland Mt.
13,176 ft
Columbine Creek
ARAPAHO
NATIONAL RECREATION
AREA
Ogalalla Peak
13,138 ft
Table Mountain
Watanga Mountain
12,375 ft
St. Vrain
Glaciers
ARAPAHO NATIONAL
Lake
Granby
Roaring Fk.
Colorado
INDIAN PEAKS WILDERNESS

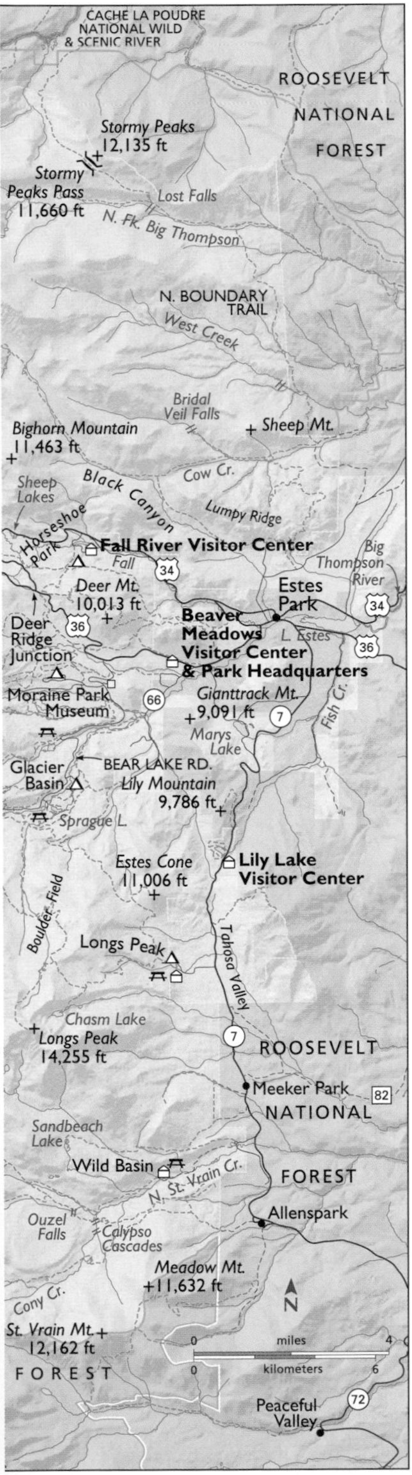

Indian paintbrush and death camas

natural mineral lick there. In fall, take time to see Horseshoe Park at dawn or dusk to view elk; bugling mating calls start soon after sunset. If you made the detour, either continue on Old Fall River Road to Fall River Pass (see next tour), or return to Deer Ridge Junction and turn west onto US 34, Trail Ridge Road.

Continue along Trail Ridge Road, which soon enters the subalpine zone, dominated by forests of Engelmann spruce and subalpine fir. Stop again on the right just past **Many Parks Curve,** and walk back to the overlook. The "parks" in the Rockies are mountain meadows: When the glaciers of the last ice age melted, they often left lakes, dammed in by debris the glaciers had pushed along their edges. The lakes eventually silted up and drained, becoming flat meadows. In another 5.8 miles, the road crosses timberline, where sub-zero winter temperatures and 100-mph winds blast trees into twisted shrubs. Higher still, the road enters tundra. Don't miss the 5-minute stroll to the overlooks of **Forest Canyon,** a glacier-carved, U-shaped valley 2,500 feet below. *Do stay on the trail*—damaged tundra plants take decades to recover.

Back in your car, drive on 2 miles, crossing smooth mountaintops that are part of a plain formed when an ancestral mountain range eroded. The plain was uplifted largely intact and remained above the ice age glaciers. Stop at Rock Cut (12,110 feet) and hike the 1-mile round-trip, paved nature trail. High altitude can cause dizziness and nausea, *so walk slowly, drink water, and don't overdo.* (If you feel ill, you'll most likely recover as soon as the road descends.) The trail leads from a parking lot to the Toll Memorial Mountain Index, a peakfinder atop a rock pile. The 360-degree views of mountain, tundra, and weird rocks are splendid.

About 4 miles farther along the road, exhibits on alpine life—and a chance to quench your thirst—await you at the Alpine Visitor Center and the Trail Ridge store and snack shop at Fall River Pass.

To continue the tour, exit the visitor center parking lot and turn right. Trail Ridge Road crosses the Continental Divide after about 4 miles, at **Milner Pass,** named for the surveyor of a never-built railway route through the Rockies. Water flowing east of the divide will eventually find its way to the Atlantic, and water wending west will flow to the Pacific. The overlook at **Farview Curve,** about 2 miles farther, provides a riveting view of the **Never Summer Mountains** and glacier-carved **Kawuneeche Valley.** Through this valley winds the infant **Colorado River,** whose headwaters lie just 5 miles north. About halfway up on the western part of the Never Summer range, you can see a horizontal scar. It is the 14-mile-long **Grand Ditch,** built between 1890 and 1932 to divert water from the wetter western side of the Continental Divide to the drier Great Plains to the east.

If short of time, turn back now. Otherwise continue the 14 miles remaining on Trail Ridge Road, descending to the beaver ponds, willows, and conifer forests of the valley floor. You might spot moose, reintroduced in 1978 after settlers eliminated them in this area. Hunters also killed off wolves, grizzly bears, and bison in the region.

In the late 19th century, smatterings of silver and gold lured miners by the hundreds to the valley. Resulting boomtowns vanished as quickly as they arose when mining claims proved unprofitable. From the **Colorado River Trailhead,** about 4 miles past Farview Curve, an easy 2-mile hike brings you to the decaying 1870s cabins of miner Joe Shipler. About 1.7 miles farther up the trail lies the site of **Lulu City,** once a bustling mining camp. Whether or not you hike, pick up an engaging leaflet on the human and natural history of this area at the visitor center.

Stop again 2 miles down the road to stroll the easy half-mile through the rippling grasses, and over the Colorado River, to **Holzworth Trout Lodge,** a dude ranch dating from the 1920s. By that time it had become clear that the real gold was in tourists' pockets. Return to your car; the road exits the park near Grand Lake.

OLD FALL RIVER ROAD TO FALL RIVER PASS

9.4 miles; a scant half day

Old Fall River Road provides an unpaved, leisurely (15 mph) drive through conifer forest and tundra. It is also a self-guided auto tour, with flyers for sale at the visitor center about 4 miles before the **Fall River Entrance Station** *(no rvs or vehicles over*

Sunrise over Sprague Lake

25 feet long). En route you'll see traces of ancient glaciers and of recent rockslides and avalanches.

You can enter the park at the entrance station on US 34 or begin the tour off US 34 shortly before Sheep Lakes. (See **Trail Ridge Road** pp. 321-24 for information on Sheep Lakes and Horseshoe Park.) Turn onto the **Endovalley** road. The huge assembly of boulders the road crosses is a reminder of the 1982 Lawn Lake flood. A dam, built prior to the creation of the park, burst one July morning, releasing a flood that turned the **Roaring River** into a tree-ripping torrent and deposited boulders, mud, and debris as far as the main street of Estes Park.

Pull over at the alluvial fan trailhead and take a few minutes to stroll the short paved pathway over the debris—up to 44 feet thick—and observe how nature recovers: Young aspens and conifers and dozens of species of willows and grasses are claiming the area, as are a wide variety of birds and other animals. Walk back to your car along the trail, not the road.

As you drive on, note the scars on the aspens: Elk and other animals gnaw the bark, which then becomes infected with the black fungus you see; given enough damage, the aspens eventually die. Research has shown that the elk herd in the park and the Estes Valley is larger, less migratory, and more concentrated than it would be under natural conditions. This lack of mobility has resulted in the decline of habitat for a wide variety of plants and animals. At Endovalley, continue on to the one-way Old Fall River Road with your self-guiding leaflet. Join Trail Ridge Road at Fall River Pass.

BEAR LAKE ROAD

10 miles; at least a half day

Popular especially for its trails, wildflowers, and fall foliage, Bear Lake Road starts off US 36 just past the **Beaver Meadows Entrance Station.** Make your first stop the **Moraine Park Museum,** near the homestead of pioneer and resort owner Abner Sprague. Buy a pamphlet for the nature trail, an easy stroll that starts in front of the building. Along the trail, be sure to smell the ponderosa pine bark; its vanilla scent is luscious.

The road is open to **Bear Lake.** Parking lots at Bear Lake and Glacier Gorge fill quickly. Take

Beaver damming a river to make a pond and home

advantage of the shuttle, which is available at the Park & Ride daily during summer. The bus comes frequently; its schedule is in the park newspaper.

The road tunnels through stands of lodgepole pine and aspen—dazzling in fall. At **Sprague Lake** awaits one of the park's wheelchair-accessible trails; as you stroll along, the forest thins out a bit to offer distant views of Flattop and Hallett.

At **Bear Lake,** buy a pamphlet and stroll the half-mile **Bear Lake Nature Walk,** enjoying this dramatic, often photographed scenery while you learn about forest ecology. The park's most popular hike climbs a mile from Bear to **Dream Lake,** over which tower the distinctive profiles of **Hallett Peak** and **Flattop Mountain.**

For a somewhat less crowded walk to another spectacular lake, start from the **Glacier Gorge Junction Trailhead,** about three-quarters of a mile back down the road. The **Loch Trail** passes **Alberta Falls** in half a mile, and reaches the rocky shoreline of **The Loch** in a moderately steep 2.7 miles.

OTHER HIKES

The park's excellent network of more than 350 miles of trails presents you with endless possibilities, just a few of which are listed below. See a ranger for details and ideas on less crowded walks.

Sprague Lake: Located off Bear Lake Road, Sprague Lake is a fishing pond created by Abner Sprague. Here's an easy, half-mile self-guided nature walk, a loop dominated by views of Continental Divide peaks.

Wild Basin: This corner of the park—14 miles south of Estes Park off Colo. 7—offers fine day hikes, including those to **Calypso Cascades** (1.8 miles) and **Ouzel Falls** (2.7 miles) through spruce-fir and mixed conifer forests along **North Saint Vrain Creek** and its tributaries. Pick up a nature booklet to learn how the forest has been making a comeback since a major fire in 1978.

Longs Peak, Chasm Lake: More than 800 people were counted climbing Longs on a summer's day. The predawn climb (8 miles one way) to the park's tallest peak requires planning—check with a ranger, especially about lightning and technical climbing. Some consider the challenging trail to Chasm Lake (4.2 miles one way) the park's most beautiful and rewarding hike. Both hikes begin at Longs Peak Ranger Station, 1 mile off Colo. 7, 10 miles south of Estes Park. *Note that parking is limited.*

Cub Lake: The less traveled **Cub Lake Trail** (an easy 4.6-mile round-trip) is known for birding and wildflowers, including the yellow water lilies afloat on Cub Lake in summer. The trail begins from a spur road off Bear Lake Road at **Moraine Park.**

Green Mountain Trail to **Big Meadows:** This easy trail (3.6 miles round-trip) passes spruce-aspen woods, lodgepole forest, marshland, beaver ponds, and meadow. It starts from Trail Ridge Road, about 3 miles north of the Grand Lake Entrance.

INFORMATION & ACTIVITIES

HEADQUARTERS
1000 Hwy. 36, Estes Park, CO 80517. Phone (970) 586-1206. www.nps.gov/romo

SEASONS & ACCESSIBILITY
Park open year-round. Trail Ridge Road closes mid-October to late May, depending on snow. Old Fall River Road closes October to early July. In summer, free shuttle bus service on Bear Lake Road.

VISITOR & INFORMATION CENTERS
Beaver Meadows Visitor Center, on US 36 at east entrance to park, and **Kawuneeche Visitor Center,** on US 34, all year. **Alpine Visitor Center**, June to mid-Oct. (weather permitting). **Fall River Visitor Center,** on US 34 west of Estes. Park at Fall River entrance, May through Oct. **Moraine Park Museum,** May to mid-Oct. Call (970) 586-1206 for information.

ENTRANCE FEE
$20 per car; $35 annual.

PETS
Not permitted on trails or in backcountry. Must be on leash and attended at all times. Allowed in parking lots, campgrounds, and picnic areas. May not be left alone in vehicles.

FACILITIES FOR DISABLED
Visitor centers and museum are wheelchair accessible, as are amphitheaters in campgrounds, but not all restrooms. Also accessible, the Lily Lake, Bear Lake, and Sprague Lake nature walks and the Coyote Valley Trail. Handicamp, at Sprague Lake, accommodates wheelchair backcountry campers—call (970) 586-1242.

THINGS TO DO
Free naturalist-led activities (most in summer only): nature and history walks, hikes, talks, slide shows, arts programs, snowshoe walks. Also, hiking, horseback trail rides, bicycling, fishing, ice fishing, rock climbing, mountain climbing, cross-country skiing, snowshoeing.

OVERNIGHT BACKPACKING
Permits required, obtainable by mail or in person from headquarters or the Kawuneeche Visitor Center. Call (970) 586-1242. Fees charged for backcountry permits in summer.

CAMPGROUNDS
Five campgrounds. 7-day limit June through September. Additional days permitted other times of year. Reservations are recommended at **Glacier Basin** and **Moraine Park** campgrounds. Reserve through the NPRS (see p. 10). **Longs Peak, Timber Creek,** and some sites at Morain Park are open year-round. $20 per night in summer; $14 per night in winter, when water is not available. No showers. RV sites at all except Longs Peak; no hookups. Reservations required at **Glacier Basin** group sites; contact NPRS. Cafeteria in Trail Ridge Store (summer only).

HOTELS, MOTELS, & INNS
(unless otherwise noted, rates are for 2 persons in a double room, high season)

In Estes Park, CO 80517:

Aspen Lodge Ranch Resort 6120 Hwy. 7. (800) 332-6867 or (970) 586-8133. 56 units. $549 per person, all inclusive. 3-day minimum. April–Dec. Pool.

Romantic RiverSong Bed & Breakfast Inn P.O. Box 1910. (970) 586-4666. 10 units. $150-$295, includes breakfast.

The Stanley Hotel 333 Wonderview Ave. (970) 586-3371. 140 units. $179-$249. Pool, restaurant.

Wind River Ranch 5770 Hwy. 7. (970) 586-4212. 28 units. $1,400-$1,600 per person per week, includes meals. Pool. June–Sept.

In Grand Lake, CO 80447:

Bighorn Lodge 613 Grand Ave. (800) 341-8000 or (970) 627-8101. 20 units. $85-$150.

Black Bear Lodge 12255 Hwy. 34. (970) 627-3654. 17 units, 9 with kitchenettes. $84-$107. Pool.

Western Riviera Motel 419 Garfield. (970) 627-3580. 16 rooms, 12 cabins, 3-bedroom house with dock. $75-$275.

For additional accommodations, contact the Chambers of Commerce of Estes Park, (800) 378-3708; and Grand Lake, (970) 627-3372.

EXCURSIONS

ROOSEVELT NATIONAL FOREST

FORT COLLINS, COLORADO

This high mountain forest in the Front Range offers craggy peaks with canyons and passes and clear alpine lakes. Contains five wilderness areas. 650,022 acres. Hiking, boating, fishing, horseback riding, scenic drives, water sports, winter sports. More than 800 campsites, boat ramp, picnic areas. Four campgrounds open all year; others May through Sept. Backcountry accessible July through Oct. Jointly administered with Arapaho NP. Adjoins Rocky Mountain NP on east. Information at Fort Collins off I-25, 45 miles from Rocky Mountain NP. (970) 295-6700.

ROUTT NATIONAL FOREST

STEAMBOAT SPRINGS, COLORADO

High grasslands, forests, and jagged peaks along the Continental Divide. Alpine lakes brim with trout. Also contains waterfalls and parts of three wilderness areas. 1,124,774 acres. Hiking, boating, fishing, horseback riding, winter sports, water sports. 450 campsites, boat ramp, picnic areas, handicapped access. Most campsites open June through Sept. Information at Steamboat Springs, off US 40, about 75 miles from Rocky Mountain NP. (970) 879-1870.

ARAPAHO NATIONAL WILDLIFE REFUGE

WALDEN, COLORADO

Ringed by mountains, Arapaho's carefully maintained irrigated meadows provide essential nesting habitat for waterfowl such as gadwall, lesser scaup, mallard, and wigeon. Black-crowned night herons breed on the property and sage grouse winter in upland hills. Features 6-mile-long auto tour (closed in winter). 24,804 acres. Fishing, hunting, scenic drives, nature trails. Open year-round, dawn to dusk. Headquarters on Colo. 125 south of Walden, about 60 miles from Rocky Mountain NP. (970) 723-8202.

EXCURSIONS

ARAPAHO NATIONAL FOREST
FORT COLLINS, COLORADO

The nation's highest paved highway traverses the steep mountains of this ski-country forest. Five wilderness areas, virgin timber, alpine lakes, and streams. 718,149 acres. Hiking, boating, climbing, bicycling, fishing, horseback riding, hunting, scenic drives, winter sports, water sports. 633 campsites, boat ramp, picnic areas. Open year-round, most campsites open June through September. Visitor center at Idaho Springs on I-70, about 50 miles south of Rocky Mountain NP. (970) 295-6700.

FLORISSANT FOSSIL BEDS NATIONAL MONUMENT
FLORISSANT, COLORADO

Some 34 million years ago a nearby volcanic field erupted, trapping wildlife in the ash that fell on ancient Lake Florissant. More than 1,000 species of fossil insects, 140 plants, and numerous fish, bird, and small mammal species have been excavated. 5,998 acres. Hiking, horseback riding. Picnic areas, handicapped access. Open all year, 9 a.m. to 5 p.m. Visitor center on Teller County Road 1, off US 24, about 150 miles south of Rocky Mountain NP. (719) 748-3253.

DINOSAUR NATIONAL MONUMENT
DINOSAUR, COLORADO

Apatosaurus, Diplodocus, Stegosaurus—these Jurassic period giants once roamed here. Now their bones lie exposed in a fossil-filled cliff in the Dinosaur Quarry building. White-water rafting on Green and Yampa Rivers and Fremont pictographs and petroglyphs are also featured. 210,278 acres, part in Utah. Hiking, swimming, boating, fishing. 125 campsites, picnic areas, handicapped access. Open all year; most campsites open May through October. Dinosaur Quarry on Utah 149, off US 40, about 220 miles west of Rocky Mountain NP. (435) 789-2115.

Bison wading in park stream

THEODORE ROOSEVELT

NORTH DAKOTA
ESTABLISHED NOVEMBER 10, 1978
70,447 acres

Theodore Roosevelt is unique among the scenic parks in that it preserves not only an extraordinary landscape but also the memory of an extraordinary man. It honors the president who probably did more for the National Park System than anyone before or since.

Theodore Roosevelt, who would later establish five national parks and help found the U.S. Forest Service, first came to Dakota Territory as a young man in 1883 to "bag a buffalo." He tried cattle ranching with no luck, but returned many times over the next 13 years, developing into a confirmed conservationist. It was the rugged badlands that taught him a healthy respect for nature while toughening him physically and mentally. "I would not have been President," he would later say, "had it not been for my experience in North Dakota."

The history of the North Dakota badlands, however, goes back long before Roosevelt—65 million years, to be exact. It was then that streams flowing from the newly arisen Rockies began depositing sediments here that would later be carved by the Little Missouri River and its tributaries. The results of this ongoing process of deposition and erosion are spectacular: wildly corrugated cliffs; steep, convoluted gullies; and dome-shaped hills, their layers of rock and sediment forming multicolored horizontal stripes that run for miles.

This austere landscape is home to a surprisingly dense population of wildlife. Bison, pronghorn, elk, white-tailed and mule deer, wild horses, and bighorn sheep inhabit the three units of the park, as do numerous smaller mammals, amphibians, and reptiles. After a rainy spring, a wealth of wildflowers colors the river bottomlands and prairie flats. And perhaps best of all is the shortage of one particular mammal—human beings. This relatively isolated park is hardly ever crowded, so you can experience the gorgeous loneliness of the badlands much the way Roosevelt did more than a hundred years ago.

How to Get There

South Unit: From Bismarck, 130 miles east, take I-94 west across the prairie to the entrance near Medora. From points south, use US 85 north to Belfield, then I-94 west 17 miles to Medora. **North Unit:** US 85 north from Belfield will bring you to the North Unit entrance. Airports: Dickinson and Bismarck, North Dakota, and Billings, Montana (280 miles).

When to Go

Although this is an all-year park, portions of the park road may close in winter, and services are quite limited from October to May. Summer is the most popular time to visit; the days are very long.

Late spring and early autumn are best for wildflower enthusiasts.

How to Visit

If you have only 1 day, take the **Scenic Loop Drive** in the **South Unit,** allowing yourself time for nature trails and longer hikes. A second day can be devoted to the **Scenic Drive** in the **North Unit,** 70 miles away. A visit to the undeveloped site of Roosevelt's **Elkhorn Ranch** or an overnight horse-packing trip from the **Peaceful Valley Ranch** in the South Unit can fill out a longer stay.

SOUTH UNIT: SCENIC LOOP DRIVE

36 miles; a half to full day

Start at the **visitor center** near Medora, where you can visit the relocated **Maltese Cross Cabin.** The rustic headquarters of Roosevelt's first ranch, it contains period furnishings, ranching equipment, and some of Roosevelt's personal belongings. Then follow the road up the side of the eroded cliff to the **Medora Overlook.** Here you get a good view of the rough little town that epitomized the Wild West back in Roosevelt's day.

Continue on, making sure to stop at the roadside prairie dog town (they bark warnings to each other as you approach). A little farther along is the **Skyline Vista.** Here you are on a high plateau, looking over the

Cabin from Roosevelt's Maltese Cross Ranch

broken badlands. Actually, you are not so much "up" as the badlands are "down." The plateau is just a remnant of the original prairie before erosion took its toll, scooping out the bewildering landscape below.

The road descends again to the **River Woodland Overlook.** Beyond the row of cottonwood trees on the left lies an agent of the visual feast around you—the **Little Missouri River.** Notice how, in this arid environment, the vegetation is rigidly stratified according to the availability of water. There are tall cottonwoods near the river, and dark green junipers on the relatively moist northern hillsides and in places where water-bearing layers are exposed. On the dry southern slopes, where the sun quickly evaporates rainwater, little grows except grasses.

Continue right past East River Road to begin the **Scenic Loop Drive.** When you reach **Scoria Point,** you are deep into classic badlands territory. The bricklike material around you, which provides the brightest color in the badlands palette, was formed when a layer of black coal ignited. It baked the gray clay above, turning it into the reddish material known locally (but inaccurately) as scoria.

Along the next 6 miles of road, you will encounter two self-guided nature trails that are well worth taking. The **Ridgeline Nature Trail,** while only 0.6 mile long, involves some strenuous climbing; a pamphlet at the trailhead introduces the complex interaction of wind, fire, water, and vegetation in this harsh environment. The **Coal Vein Trail,** at the end of the short unpaved road branching off at mile 15.6 (there's a sign), is a full mile but less difficult; look for the manifold effects of a lignite bed that burned here from 1951 until early 1977. Between these two trails, pull off at the **North Dakota**

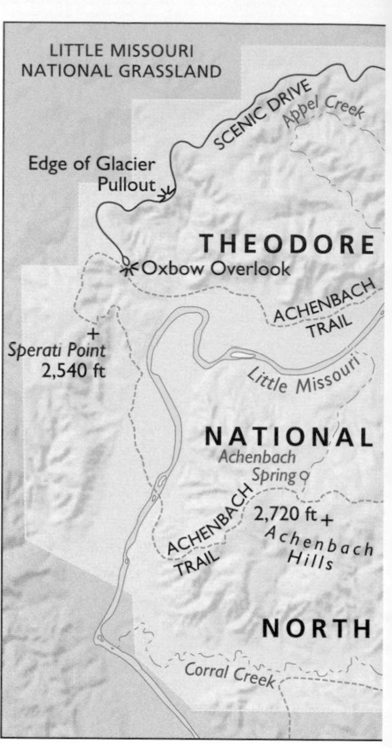

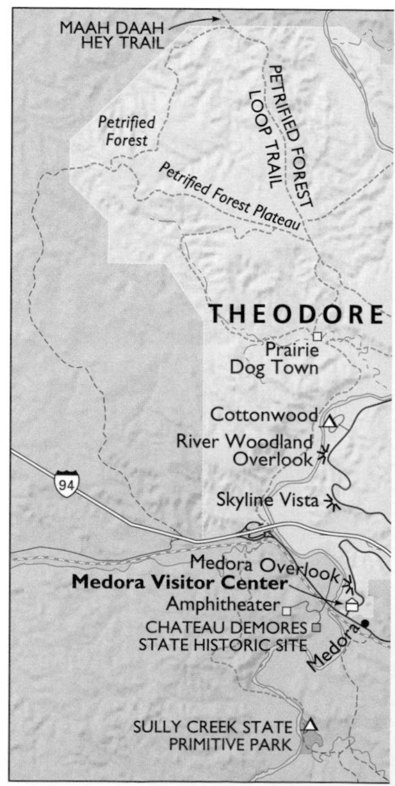

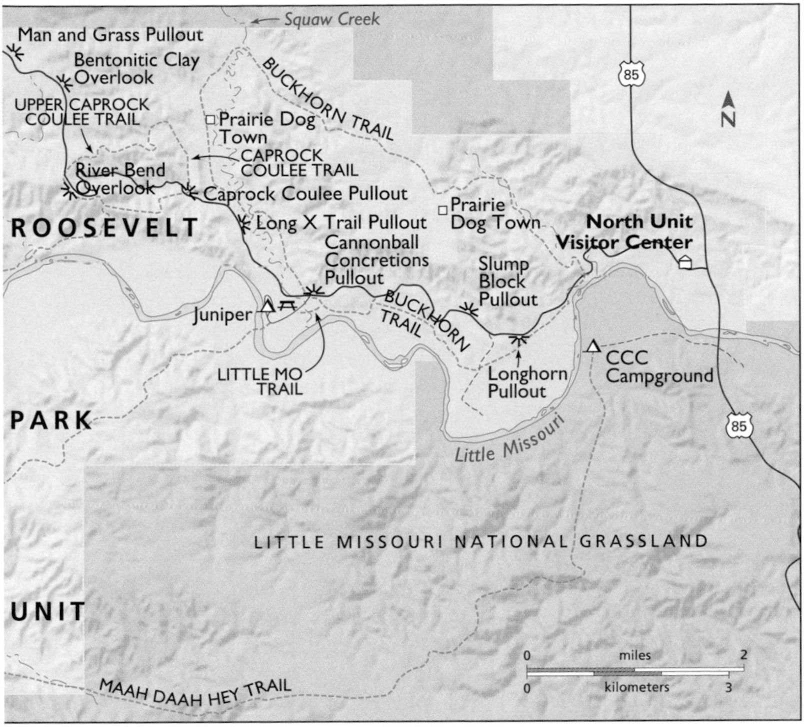

Squaw Creek
Man and Grass Pullout
Bentonitic Clay Overlook
BUCKHORN TRAIL
85
N
UPPER CAPROCK COULEE TRAIL
Prairie Dog Town
CAPROCK COULEE TRAIL
River Bend Overlook
Caprock Coulee Pullout
Prairie Dog Town
ROOSEVELT
Long X Trail Pullout
North Unit Visitor Center
Cannonball Concretions Pullout
Slump Block Pullout
Juniper
BUCKHORN TRAIL
Longhorn Pullout
CCC Campground
LITTLE MO TRAIL
PARK
85
Little Missouri
LITTLE MISSOURI NATIONAL GRASSLAND
UNIT
0 miles 2
0 kilometers 3
MAAH DAAH HEY TRAIL

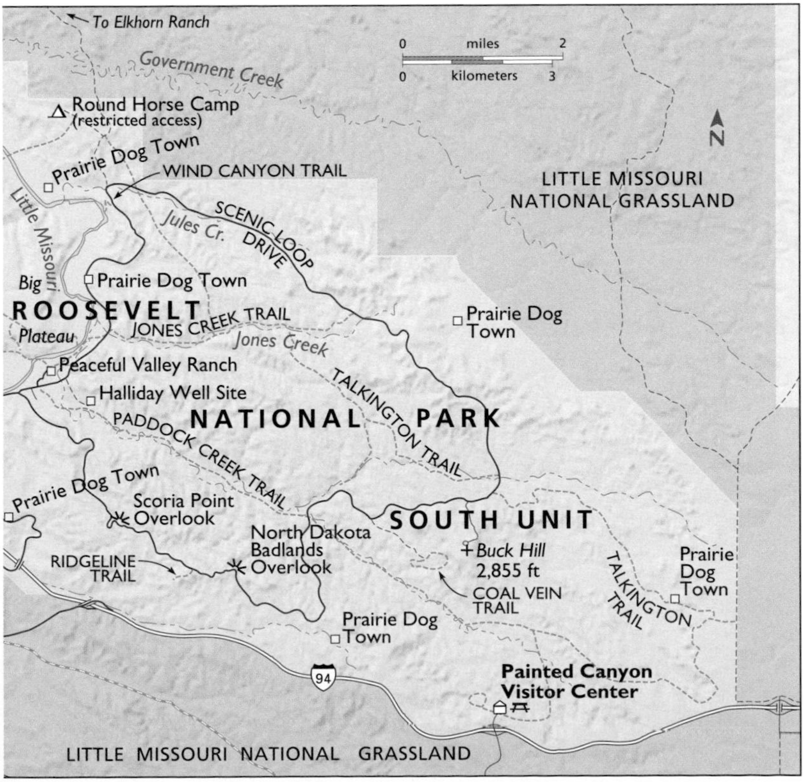

To Elkhorn Ranch
Government Creek
0 miles 2
0 kilometers 3
Round Horse Camp (restricted access)
N
Prairie Dog Town
WIND CANYON TRAIL
LITTLE MISSOURI NATIONAL GRASSLAND
Little Missouri
SCENIC LOOP DRIVE
Jules Cr.
Big
Prairie Dog Town
ROOSEVELT
Prairie Dog Town
Plateau
JONES CREEK TRAIL
Jones Creek
Peaceful Valley Ranch
TALKINGTON TRAIL
Halliday Well Site
NATIONAL PARK
PADDOCK CREEK TRAIL
Prairie Dog Town
Scoria Point Overlook
SOUTH UNIT
North Dakota Badlands Overlook
Buck Hill 2,855 ft
RIDGELINE TRAIL
COAL VEIN TRAIL
TALKINGTON TRAIL
Prairie Dog Town
Prairie Dog Town
94
Painted Canyon Visitor Center
LITTLE MISSOURI NATIONAL GRASSLAND

Caprock formations Petrified Forest Plateau *(top)*; prairie dog eyeing a rattler *(center)*; calf from the South Unit's bison herd *(bottom)*

Badlands Overlook for an exceptional view of the surroundings.

One-and-a-half miles past the turnoff for Coal Vein is the short road to **Buck Hill.** Take the 100-yard path to the summit for a 360-degree panorama of the eastern end of the park and beyond. Those oil wells on the horizon remind you that, although the badlands stretch for hundreds of miles, the park does not.

Return to the main road and turn right. The backstretch of the loop, running from Buck Hill to **Wind Canyon,** offers several possibilities for longer hikes. The **Talkington Trail** can be followed to the east or to the west, but even better is the **Jones Creek Trail** at mile 21. This trail follows a deeply eroded creek bed for about 3.5 miles, bisecting the loop road and offering good opportunities to see wildlife (including prairie rattlesnakes, *so be careful*). Since this trail is not a loop, you'll want to turn back at the half-way point or arrange to be picked up at the other end.

Back in the car, continue to the **Wind Canyon Trail.** This short but steep path offers a double treat: Not only do you get a magnificent vista of a long oxbow curve in the Little Missouri River, you also get a glimpse of how wind plays a part in shaping this unique landscape. The prevailing winds pick up sand from the riverbed and elsewhere and blow it into the northwest-facing canyon to your left, sandblasting the rock into smooth, bizarre shapes.

Back on the road, you pass another prairie dog town and then the **Peaceful Valley Ranch** on your right. These historic buildings have had a number of incarnations over the years, from working cattle ranch to park headquarters. These days the ranch is a private saddle horse concession, so you can stop for a ride (May to September) before rejoining the entrance road back to the visitor center.

NORTH UNIT: SCENIC DRIVE

28 miles round-trip; a half to full day

Many people regard the North Unit as the more attractive of the two major portions of the park. Certainly the canyons seem steeper here, the river bottomlands lusher, and the blue, black, red, and beige stripes on every butte more pronounced. Located about 52 miles north of I-94, the North Unit is also more isolated, and consequently less visited. According to one ranger, there are times off-season when visitors can be almost alone in the North Unit.

Starting at the visitor center, take the **Scenic Drive** west into the park. Stop at the **Longhorn Pullout** to catch a glimpse of the park's demonstration herd of longhorn steers, kept here to commemorate the historic Long-X Trail, the major conduit for longhorns traveling from Texas to the Long-X Ranch just north of the park. If you hike the 11-mile **Buckhorn Trail Loop,** you'll travel along a part of this Old West "highway."

Stop at the **Slump Block Pullout** to see badlands erosion in action. The small hill to your right was once part of the higher cliff beyond—until unstable underlying sediments caused this piece to slump away. Try matching the diagonal layers of the slump block to the horizontal layers on the cliff to see how the block once fit in.

Pull off at the **Cannonball Concretions Pullout** to see how weathering agents have eroded out sandstone spheres formed by groundwater minerals cementing. Opposite the pullout, look for the **Little Mo Nature Trail.** This easy half-mile loop takes you through typical river woodlands, and a guide leaflet (available at the trailhead) allows you to identify many native plants the Plains Indians used for medicine, food, and raw materials. Be on the lookout for beaver and white-tailed deer.

Returning to the car, follow the road to the **Caprock Coulee Pullout,** where you can pick up the nature trail of the same name. Take this easy trail 0.75 mile up a dry canyon (a "coulee") to a grove of pedestal rocks ("caprocks"). The harder caprocks protect the sediments below while the surrounding sediments erode away, leaving the mushroom-shaped formations around you. At the end of the nature trail, you can either turn back or make a 5-mile loop by continuing to the **Upper Caprock Coulee Trail,** a choice which involves some steeper climbing but lots of opportunities to view wildlife.

Beyond the Caprock parking lot, the road climbs steeply to the level of the original prairie. At the top, the **River Bend Overlook** offers an absolutely stunning vista of the deep Little Missouri Valley and the extensive badlands on either side. The **Bentonitic Clay Overlook** a little farther on offers a less dramatic but perhaps more instructive view. The blue-colored bentonite layer visible for miles is composed of an extremely absorbent volcanic ash that flows when wet. The plasticity of this layer accounts for much of the dynamism of the badlands landscape.

The road now traces the edge of a grassy plateau. This is prime bison territory; you may even have to wait while a herd crosses the road in front of you. At the **Man and Grass Pullout** you can get some idea of the extensive grasslands that made this part of Dakota worth the trip up the Long-X Trail. Finally, the road ends—spectacularly—at the **Oxbow Overlook.** After enjoying the visual banquet of badlands, return along the same road to the visitor center.

INFORMATION & ACTIVITIES

HEADQUARTERS
P.O. Box 7, Medora, ND 58645. Phone (701) 623-4466. www.nps.gov/thro

SEASONS & ACCESSIBILITY
Park open all year, but access may be limited in winter due to snow. The South Unit road from Medora Visitor Center through Wind Canyon to the north boundary is kept plowed, but not the Scenic Loop Drive. The North Unit road is plowed from the entrance to the Caprock Coulee Trailhead. Call headquarters for weather and road information.

VISITOR & INFORMATION CENTERS
Medora Visitor Center and the **Maltese Cross Cabin,** at the entrance to the South Unit, open daily all year. **Painted Canyon Visitor Center,** in the southeastern part of the South Unit off I-94, open from April to mid-November. **North Unit Visitor Center,** open daily April through September, and weekends in winter. Call headquarters for visitor information.

ENTRANCE FEE
$5 per person, maximum of $10 per vehicle per week; $20 annually.

PETS & HORSES
Pets are permitted on leashes except on trails and in buildings. Horses are prohibited in campgrounds, picnic areas, and on self-guided trails.

FACILITIES FOR DISABLED
Visitor centers, restrooms, campground sites, and some trails are wheelchair accessible.

THINGS TO DO
Free naturalist-led activities: nature walks and talks, tours of Roosevelt's Maltese Cross Cabin (mid-June to mid-Sept.), evening campfire programs. Also available, hiking, horseback riding (contact the Peaceful Valley Ranch in South Unit, 701-623-4568), interpretive exhibits, auto tours, limited canoeing and float trips, fishing (license required), and cross-country skiing.

SPECIAL ADVISORIES
• View bison from a distance; they are known to attack if provoked.
• Rattlesnakes and black widow spiders often live in prairie dog burrows; be alert for them when hiking.
• Do not feed the prairie dogs; they bite and may carry disease.
• Be prepared for extremes of temperatures and sudden violent thunderstorms.

OVERNIGHT BACKPACKING
Permits required. They are free and can be obtained at visitor centers.

CAMPGROUNDS
Two campgrounds, both with 15-consecutive-day limit (30 days per year). **Cottonwood** and **Juniper** open all year, first come, first served. Fees $10 per night. No showers. Tent and RV sites; no hookups. Three group campgrounds, **Cottonwood, Juniper,** and **Roundup** (horses); reservations required; contact park headquarters.

HOTELS, MOTELS, & INNS
(unless otherwise noted, rates are for 2 persons in a double room, high season)

In Dickinson, ND 58601:
Comfort Inn 493 Elk Dr. (800) 228-5150 or (701) 264-7300. 115 units. $80. AC, pool.
Days Inn 532 15th St. W. (800) 422-0949 or (701) 227-1853. 149 units. $69. AC, pool, restaurant.
Oasis Motel 1000 W. Villerd St. (701) 225-6703. 35 units, 6 with kitchenettes. $49-$54. AC.

In Medora, ND 58645:
Badlands Motel 501 Pacific Ave. (800) 633-6721 or (701) 623-4444. 115 units. $99-$109. AC, pool. Mid-April–Oct.
Medora Motel 1 Main St., P.O. Box 198. (800) 633-6721 or (701) 623-4444. Bunkhouse: 150 units, 3 cabins, 2 houses. $69-$109. AC, pool. June–Labor Day.
Rough Riders Hotel 301 3rd Ave. (800) 633-6721 or (701) 623-4444. 10 units. $85. AC, restaurant. June–Labor Day.

In Watford City, ND 58854:
Roosevelt Inn 600 2nd Ave. S.W., P.O. Box 1003. (800) 887-9170 or (701) 842-3686. 42 units. $54. AC, pool.

EXCURSIONS

LITTLE MISSOURI NATIONAL GRASSLAND

DICKINSON & WATFORD CITY, NORTH DAKOTA

Bighorn sheep, elk, pronghorn, eagles, hawks, and grouse live in the prairie and badlands around Theodore Roosevelt NP. 1.1 million acres. Hiking, horseback riding, hunting. 5 campgrounds. Open all year; campgrounds late May to Labor Day. Information in Dickinson, off I-94. (701) 225-5151 or (701) 250-4443.

LAKE ILO NATIONAL WILDLIFE REFUGE

DUNN CENTER, NORTH DAKOTA

Waterfowl nest in the grasslands surrounding 1,240-acre Lake Ilo, offering recreation not found on all refuges. 3,903 acres. Boating, fishing, picnic areas, nature trail, archaeological exhibits, scenic drives. Open year-round. Located on N. Dak. 200, about 50 miles east of Theodore Roosevelt NP's North Unit. (701) 548-8110.

LOSTWOOD NATIONAL WILDLIFE REFUGE

KENMARE, NORTH DAKOTA

Ducks, marsh birds, grouse, hawks, Baird's sparrows, and Sprague's pipits inhabit this stretch of prairie dotted with shallow glacial lakes, attracting bird-watchers from near and far. 26,900 acres. Hiking, hunting, scenic drives. Open May through September, dawn to dusk. Located off N. Dak. 8, about 135 miles northeast of Theodore Roosevelt NP's North Unit. (701) 848-2722.

Prince of Wales Hotel on Waterton Lakes

WATERTON-GLACIER

ALBERTA, CANADA, & MONTANA
ESTABLISHED JUNE 18, 1932
Waterton Lakes, 129,700 acres
Glacier, 1,013,572 acres

Waterton-Glacier International Peace Park World Heritage site contains 1,800 square miles of what naturalist John Muir called "the best care-killing scenery on the continent." Multi-hued summits—whittled by ancient glaciers into walls and horns—rise abruptly from gently rolling plains. Some 650 lakes, dozens of glaciers, and innumerable waterfalls glisten in forested valleys. A scenic highway crosses the park, making much of its beauty accessible to the casual visitor. More than 700 miles of trails await hikers and horseback riders.

In 1932 Canada and the United States declared Waterton Lakes National Park (founded in 1895) and neighboring Glacier National Park (founded in 1910) the world's first International Peace Park. While administered separately, the park's two sections cooperate in wildlife management, scientific research, and some visitor services.

The tremendous range of topography in Waterton-Glacier supports a rich variety of plants and wildlife. More than 1,800 plant species provide food and haven for 64 native species of mammals and more than

275 species of birds. In the 1980s the gray wolf settled into Glacier for the first time since the 1950s.

But now strip-mining and oil, gas, housing, and logging projects proposed or underway near the park's respective borders endanger the habitats of both water and land animals, including elk, bighorn sheep, and the threatened grizzly. Park officials and conservation groups are working with the U.S. Forest Service, the Canadian government, the Blackfeet Tribe, and private companies to try to protect critical habitats.

Sheltered valleys and bountiful food have lured people here for nearly 10,000 years. Ancient cultures tracked bison across the plains, fished the lakes, and traversed the mountain passes. The Blackfeet controlled this land during the 18th and much of the 19th centuries.

How to Get There

Approach West Glacier (from Kalispell, Montana, about 35 miles) and East Glacier Park from US 2. US 89 leads to Many Glacier and St. Mary in the east; US 89 and Mont. 17 (Chief Mountain International Hwy.) form the shortest connection between Glacier and Waterton Lakes. Coming from Canada, follow Alberta 2, 5, or 6. Amtrak trains from Chicago and Seattle stop year-round just outside the park at West Glacier (Belton), Essex, Browning, and East Glacier Park; by prior arrangement, buses take travelers into the park. Nearest airports: Kalispell and Great Falls, Montana; and Lethbridge, Alberta.

When to Go

Summer. Starting in 2006, road rehabilitation may occur on portions of the Going to the Sun Road before and after the core summer season with possible closures. (June 15-Sept. 15 delays will be limited to a maximum of 30 minutes during a one-way trip across Logan Pass.) Otherwise, all of Going-to-the-Sun Road is open about mid-June to mid-September; Chief Mountain International Highway, mid-May to late September. Trails at lower elevations are usually clear of snow by mid-June; higher trails can remain snowed-in until mid-July. Cross-country is skiing popular late from December to April in many areas of the park.

How to Visit

Spend your first day on and around **Going-to-the-Sun Road,** considered by many one of the world's most spectacular highways. On a second day, travel the **Chief Mountain International Highway** north to Waterton Lakes, enjoying the contrast of peak and prairie. Drive Waterton's **Akamina Parkway** and **Red Rock Parkway.** Stay at least another day to visit Glacier's **Many Glacier.** For a longer visit, drive to **Two Medicine** for a boat ride and walk to an exquisite lake, then continue on to the Walton **Goat Lick Overlook,** both also in Glacier. If you have the stamina and overnight reservations, hike or ride horseback to one of the two remaining chalets built in Glacier early in the 20th century by the Great Northern Railway.

GOING-TO-THE-SUN ROAD

50 miles; a full day

Note: Vehicles longer than 21 feet and wider than 8 feet prohibited on this road.

Begin early at **Apgar** on Glacier's west side. At the visitor center pick up details about trails and, since this is grizzly and black bear country,

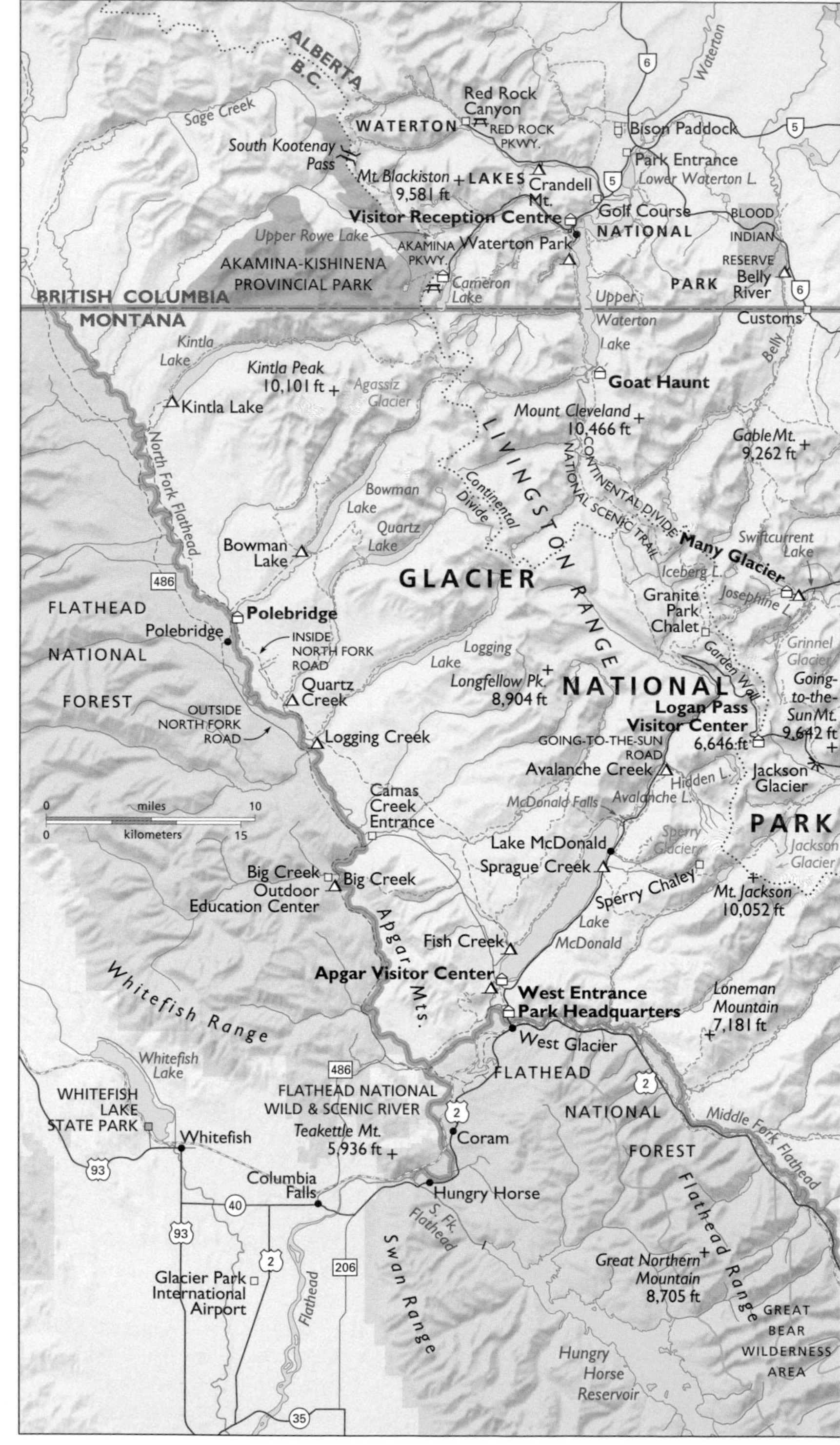
ALBERTA
B.C.
Sage Creek
WATERTON
LAKES
NATIONAL
PARK
Red Rock Canyon
RED ROCK PKWY.
Bison Paddock
Park Entrance
Lower Waterton L.
South Kootenay Pass
Mt. Blackiston 9,581 ft
Crandell Mt.
Visitor Reception Centre
Golf Course
BLOOD INDIAN RESERVE
Upper Rowe Lake
AKAMINA PKWY.
Waterton Park
AKAMINA-KISHINENA PROVINCIAL PARK
Cameron Lake
Belly River
BRITISH COLUMBIA
MONTANA
Upper Waterton Lake
Customs
Belly
Kintla Lake
Kintla Peak 10,101 ft
Agassiz Glacier
Goat Haunt
Kintla Lake
Mount Cleveland 10,466 ft
Gable Mt. 9,262 ft
LIVINGSTON RANGE
CONTINENTAL DIVIDE NATIONAL SCENIC TRAIL
Continental Divide
North Fork Flathead
Bowman Lake
Quartz Lake
Swiftcurrent Lake
Bowman Lake
Many Glacier
Iceberg L.
GLACIER
NATIONAL
PARK
Granite Park Chalet
Josephine L.
486
FLATHEAD NATIONAL FOREST
Polebridge
Polebridge
INSIDE NORTH FORK ROAD
Logging Lake
Garden Wall
Grinnel Glacier
Longfellow Pk. 8,904 ft
Going-to-the-Sun Mt. 9,642 ft
Quartz Creek
OUTSIDE NORTH FORK ROAD
Logan Pass Visitor Center 6,646 ft
Logging Creek
GOING-TO-THE-SUN ROAD
Avalanche Creek
Jackson Glacier
Hidden L.
Camas Creek Entrance
McDonald Falls
Avalanche L.
0 miles 10
0 kilometers 15
Lake McDonald
Sperry Glacier
Jackson Glacier
Sprague Creek
Big Creek Outdoor Education Center
Big Creek
Sperry Chalet
Mt. Jackson 10,052 ft
Apgar Mts.
Lake McDonald
Fish Creek
Apgar Visitor Center
West Entrance
Park Headquarters
Loneman Mountain 7,181 ft
Whitefish Range
West Glacier
Whitefish Lake
486
FLATHEAD NATIONAL FOREST
2
WHITEFISH LAKE STATE PARK
FLATHEAD NATIONAL WILD & SCENIC RIVER
Middle Fork Flathead
2
Whitefish
Coram
Teakettle Mt. 5,936 ft
93
Columbia Falls
Hungry Horse
40
S. Fk. Flathead
Flathead Range
93
2
Great Northern Mountain 8,705 ft
Glacier Park International Airport
206
Flathead
Swan Range
GREAT BEAR WILDERNESS AREA
Hungry Horse Reservoir
35

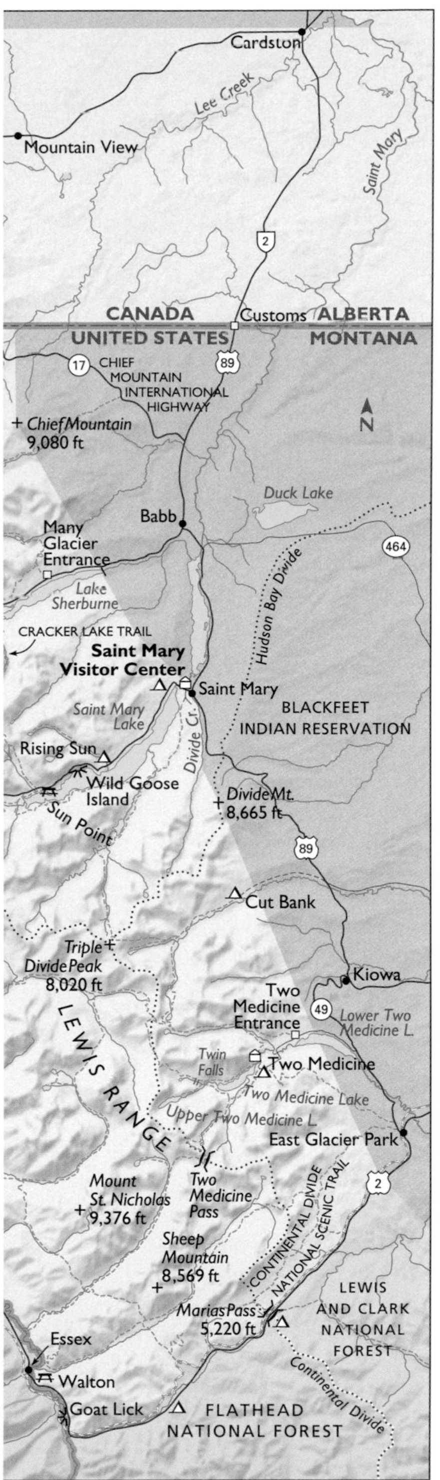

cautionary advice on avoiding bear encounters. Take time to admire **Lake McDonald** from the vantage point a little farther down the road. The park's largest lake, McDonald is 10 miles long and 472 feet deep; a glacier more than 2,000 feet thick gouged out its basin. Kootenai Indians, who performed lakeshore ceremonies, called the waters Sacred Dancing Lake.

Continue driving the Apgar loop and turn left at Going-to-the-Sun Road. Then pull over at **McDonald Falls,** on your left after about 10 miles. Stroll down to the viewpoint and note the layered rock. Waterton-Glacier's mountains are built mainly of sedimentary rock formed from mud and sand at the bottom of a sea that existed here for nearly a billion years. Over the eons, pressures in the Earth uplifted, thrusted, and folded the seabed into mountains. The rock exposed at McDonald Falls is among the oldest in the park.

Pull over near the campground at **Avalanche Creek** and start the self-guided **Trail of the Cedars** on the right side of the road. This wheelchair- accessible trail is on a boardwalk.The easy, quite popular, a 0.75-mile nature stroll acquaints you with the cedar-hemlock forest through which you've been driving. Along the trail, Avalanche Creek tumbles through contoured walls of surprisingly red stone, formed during a period when the sea here retreated. In contact with oxygen, iron-bearing minerals in the mud formed the bright red mineral hematite that colors the rock. Extend your walk, if you wish, by taking the **Avalanche Lake Trail** from near the gorge up to glacier-fed **Avalanche Lake.** The gently climbing trail, about 4 miles round-trip, offers fine views of creek, lake, and waterfalls.

Massive Grinnell Glacier

Return to your car. Ahead, in about 2 miles, you'll see the **Garden Wall,** part of the Continental Divide. West of the divide, waters flow to the Pacific; east of it, to the Arctic or Atlantic. Two glaciers ground down opposite sides of a ridge to form the knife-edged Garden Wall. At the **Bird Woman Falls** viewpoint (some 10 miles from the campground at Avalanche Creek), an exhibit illustrates how glaciers also carved this spectacular U-shaped valley. Glacier National Park takes its name from the huge rivers of ice that sculptured the landscape during ice ages of the last two million years.

At **Logan Pass,** atop the Continental Divide, the peaks crowd around as if close enough to touch. Park and walk up the hill past the visitor center to take the **Hidden Lake Overlook Nature Trail.** Be sure to buy or borrow a self-guiding pamphlet at the trailhead. The 3-mile round-trip begins on the boardwalk and offers vast displays of wildflowers framed by dramatic peaks. A breathtaking vista of **Hidden Lake** awaits you at the end. Watch for mountain goats grazing, marmots sunning, and golden eagles scanning for rodents. *Always stay on the trail:* Alpine plants, growing for short seasons in thin soil, are extremely fragile.

Return to your car and turn right onto the main road. Soon you'll be approaching **Going-to-the-Sun Mountain**—at 9,642 feet, the highest in this area of the park. The name comes, depending on which story you believe, from a Blackfeet legend or an early explorer. The legend says that Napi, the creator, came to help the Blackfeet, then climbed this mountain to return to the sun.

Pull over again to view **Jackson Glacier,** one of the few glaciers visible from the road, about 4.5 miles after Logan Pass. The turnoff for **Sun Point** leads to picnic tables, fine vistas of **St. Mary Lake,** and a nature trail that introduces the ecology of the drier eastern portion of the park. Next, stop at the **Wild Goose Island Overlook,** 1.5 miles down the road, and again at the display about **Triple Divide Peak,** less than 3 miles beyond. Crossing grasslands punctuated by groves of aspen and conifers, the Going-to-the-

Sun Road ends at **Divide Creek,** the border of the Blackfeet Reservation.

CHIEF MOUNTAIN HIGHWAY TO WATERTON LAKES

75 miles; at least a full day

Chief Mountain International Highway begins north of Babb off US 89. **Chief Mountain** (9,080 feet) dominates the horizon to your left, a solitary peak that commands awe. Blackfeet seeking spiritual guidance still tie a traditional offering of colored cloth to trees at its base.

Chief Mountain also represents the easternmost extension of the Lewis Overthrust, a major geological feature. About 8.5 miles after the U.S.-Canada customs station, an exhibit explains the overthrust. Pull over again in 1.5 miles for a superb view of **Waterton Valley** and a display that identifies the summits.

Follow the signs for Waterton Lakes National Park. The park's main information center will be on your right, about 4 miles beyond the park entrance, just before Waterton Park townsite. On your left stands the **Prince of Wales Hotel,** which commands a first-rate view of **Upper Waterton Lake** from its lobby. For a loftier panorama, climb the steep but gratifying **Bears Hump Trail,** 2 miles round-trip. The path starts from the information center.

At road's end awaits **Waterton Park** townsite, a village of about a hundred year-round residents. It blossoms in summer with eateries and gift shops. Wildlife is often on hand: Bighorn sheep and deer may be hiding in the shadows; you'll less likely spot the rare mountain lion or bear. On the lakeshore, near the end of the road, a pavilion reviews the park's history.

Back in your car, turn onto **Akamina Parkway,** which traces **Cameron Valley** 10 miles to **Cameron Lake.** At the lake, which lies in a large glacier-carved basin, rent a boat, fish for trout, or stroll the 2-mile round-trip **Cameron Lakeshore Trail** through the forest of Englemann spruce and subalpine fir. *Do not continue past the end of the trail—grizzlies are often sighted there.*

Back in your car, return to Alberta 5; turn left, then left again onto 10-mile-long **Red Rock Parkway.** The prairie here brims with flowers in May, June, and early July. Indians hunted bison along **Blakiston Creek,** driving them over the cliff to your left. In about 3 miles, near Crandell Mountain Campground, stop at the exhibit on ancient Indian life. Drive on to the road's end at **Red Rock Canyon,** where archaeologists found a camp dating from 8,400 years ago. Don't miss the half-mile **Red Rock Canyon Loop Trail.**

MANY GLACIER & SWIFTCURRENT VALLEY

13 miles from Babb; at least a half day

Many Glacier, named for the glaciers on surrounding mountains, is a hiker's Eden and a good place to see bighorn sheep and other wildlife. A dam a few miles outside the park created **Lake Sherburne,** on your left as you enter the park. The lake submerged much of Altyn, a boomtown built during the mining frenzy that started and fizzled out here at the turn of the 20th century.

Just beyond the lake, to your left, is the **Many Glacier Hotel.** The Great Northern Railway built it in 1915 to help promote tourism along its tracks. The company also built more than a dozen backcountry tent camps and chalets in Waterton-Glacier. Park at the hotel and, for an easy walk and fine introduction to the area's plants, animals, peaks, and glaciers, take the **Swiftcurrent Nature Trail.** This 2.5-mile loop around the lake starts at the shore south of the hotel. The trail traverses both 400-year-old spruce-fir forest and 60-year-old lodgepole pine forest, planted in the aftermath of a great fire in 1936.

For an easy 2.5-mile stroll through old-growth forest, go on the **Swiftcurrent and Josephine Lakes** boat tour and hike. With more time and plenty of stamina, join a naturalist-led hike (8 miles) and boat ride (fee) to the edge of **Grinnell Glacier,** one of the largest in the park. Check departure times in the park newspaper.

OTHER SIGHTS & TRAILS

Before hiking, be sure to stop by a visitor center or ranger station to pick up maps and schedules—and check for trail closings due to bears.

Drive to **Two Medicine,** inside the park's southeastern border off Mont. 49, and take the boat across **Two Medicine Lake.** Then walk past **Twin Falls** through huckleberry meadows to **Upper Two Medicine Lake,** which is surrounded by brightly colored cliffs (4.4 miles round-trip). Back in your car, head south on Mont. 49 and west on US 2 to the **Goat Lick Overlook.** A natural salt lick attracts mountain goats from miles around, usually in spring and early summer.

From Logan Pass, the **Highline Trail** offers splendid panoramic views as it crosses Glacier's high country to Waterton townsite (43.6 miles). The trail following the slopes of the Garden Wall, a razor-backed arête, between McDonald Valley and the Many Glacier area. Consider a stop along the way at **Granite Park Chalet** (7.6 miles one way), one of the Great Northern's two remaining chalets. (The other chalet, **Sperry,** was recently restored. Sperry can be reached by horse or on foot from **Jackson Glacier Overlook** or Lake McDonald.) Part of the trail is cut into the cliff face, so it is not for the fainthearted.

From Many Glacier, **Iceberg Lake Trail** leads you among wide panoramas to an iceberg-studded turquoise lake, a 10-mile round-trip. **Cracker Lake Trail,** 12.3 miles round-trip, parallels boulder-strewn **Canyon Creek** part way to this glacier-fed lake. Nearby lie remains of **Cracker Mine.**

From Akamina Parkway, **Rowe Meadow** (a moderately strenuous, 6.5-mile round-trip) offers a rainbow of wildflowers in early summer. Climb another 0.7-mile to **Upper Rowe Lake** through an alpine larch forest. The **International Peace Park Hike,** held on Wednesday and Saturday mornings (reservations required), leads 8.4 miles from Waterton Park to **Goat Haunt** in the United States. Return by boat.

Pedaling the Going-to-the-Sun Road

INFORMATION & ACTIVITIES

HEADQUARTERS
Waterton: Waterton Park, Alberta, TOK 2MO, Canada. (403) 859-2224.
Glacier: West Glacier, MT 59936. (406) 888-7800. www.nps.gov/glac

SEASONS & ACCESSIBILITY
Parks open year-round; winter snows limit access and services.

VISITOR & INFORMATION CENTERS
Waterton: Waterton Information Centre in Waterton Park; (403) 859-5133. Usually open mid-May through Sept. call ahead.
Glacier: Apgar Visitor Center, West Entrance, open late May through Oct., weekends in winter. **Logan Pass Visitor Center,** open mid-June to Oct. **St. Mary Visitor Center** at East Entrance open mid-May to mid-Oct.

ENTRANCE FEES
Waterton: Canadian $6 per adult/$3 per child.
Glacier: $20 per car valid for 7 days; $25 one-year pass.

FACILITIES FOR DISABLED
Waterton: International Peace Park Pavilion, Heritage Centre, Cameron Lake exhibit building wheelchair accessible. Also, several camping facilities, Lake Linnet Trail, drive through the Bison Paddock, and most restrooms.
Glacier: Most visitor center facilities accessible; also, Trail of the Cedars, Running Eagle Falls Trail, Oberlin Bend Trail, and Apgar Bike Path.

THINGS TO DO
Waterton: Free naturalist-led activities: walks and hikes, slide shows, campfire programs. Also, swimming, fishing (license needed), boating, launch tours, nature courses, horseback rides, golf, cross-country skiing.
Glacier: Free naturalist-led activities: walks and hikes, slide talks, campfire programs. Also, hiking, horseback rides, boating, fishing (no license required), bicycling, launch tours, nature courses, cross-country skiing.

OVERNIGHT BACKPACKING
Permits required. Call in advance about reservations and fees. Waterton back-country: (403) 859-5133; Glacier back-country: (406) 888-7857.

BACKCOUNTRY CHALETS
Granite Park Chalet ($66 plus $10 for linen) and **Sperry Chalet** ($155 per room plus $100 per additional person, incl. meals) offer lodgings. (888) 345-2649.

CAMPGROUNDS
Waterton: Three campgrounds, 14-day limit. Open mid-May to early Sept. (**Townsite** open to mid-Oct.). First come, first served. Fees Can. $13-$33. Must reserve at **Belly River Group Campgrounds;** contact park. Food in park.
Glacier: 13 campgrounds, limit 7 days July & August, otherwise 14 days. **Apgar** and **St. Mary** open all year, others late spring to mid-fall. Reservations for Fish Creek and St. Mary through the NPRS (see p. 10). Others, first come, first served. Fees $12-$17 per night. **Apgar Group Campground** first come, first served. Food in park.

HOTELS, MOTELS, & INNS
(unless otherwise noted, rates are for 2 persons in a double room, high season)

INSIDE WATERTON, Alberta TOK 2MO:
Aspen Village Inn P.O. Box 100. (403) 859-2255. 50 units. Can. $139-$245.
Bayshore Inn 111 Waterton Ave. (403) 859-2211 or (403) 238-4847. 70 units. Can. $139. Restaurant. April to Oct.
Crandell Mt. Lodge 1 Waterton Park. (403) 859-2288. 17 units. Can. $129-$149. March to Oct.
Prince of Wales Hotel (near Waterton Townsite) Reservations: Glacier Park, Inc. (see below). (406) 756-2444. 86 units. Can. $259-$799. Rest.
INSIDE GLACIER:
The following are open from June to mid-Sept. Contact Glacier Park, Inc., P.O. Box 2025, 774 Railroad St., Columbia Falls, MT 59912. (406) 756-2444.
Glacier Park Lodge 161 units. $135-$500.
Lake McDonald Lodge 131 units. $96-$147. Restaurant.
Many Glacier Hotel 216 units. $111-$219.
Rising Sun Motor Inn 72 units. $92-$110.
Swiftcurrent Motor Inn 88 units. Cabins $43-$73; rooms $94-110.
The Village Inn 36 units. $100-$165.

EXCURSIONS

FLATHEAD NATIONAL FOREST
KALISPELL, MONTANA

Recreation opportunities abound here amid mountains, lakes, Wild and Scenic Rivers, and more than 2,000 miles of trails. Contains parts of three wilderness areas, notably the Bob Marshall. 2.3 million acres. Hiking, boating, climbing, fishing, horseback riding, hunting, scenic drives, winter sports, water sports. 400 campsites, boat ramp, picnic areas. Open all year; campsites open June to mid-September. Visitor center off US 2 at Hungry Horse Dam, about 7 miles from Waterton-Glacier NP. (406) 758-5200.

LEWIS & CLARK NATIONAL FOREST
GREAT FALLS, MONTANA

This forest has two sections separated by plains: The Rocky Mountain front section boasts steep terrain with parts of two wilderness areas; the Jefferson section contains gentler peaks and rolling hills with broad plateaus. Large bighorn herd. 1.8 million acres. Hiking, boating, climbing, fishing, horseback riding, winter sports, water sports. 24 campsites, 5 winter cabins (reservations required), boat ramp, handicapped access. Campsites open late spring to fall. Adjoins Waterton-Glacier NP on south. (406) 791-7700

KOOTENAI NATIONAL FOREST
LIBBY, MONTANA

With a climate closer to that of the Pacific coast than to Montana, Kootenai features virgin stands of western red cedar. Lake Koocanusa, 90 miles long, and many other streams and reservoirs offer abundant recreation. Contains Cabinet Mountains Wilderness. 2,250,000 acres. Hiking, boating, climbing, bicycling, fishing, scenic drives, winter sports. 509 campsites, most open late spring to fall. Information at Libby on US 2. 120 miles from Waterton-Glacier NP. (406) 293-6211.

PINE BUTTE SWAMP PRESERVE

CHOTEAU, MONTANA

Pine Butte, a 500-foot promontory, overlooks this Nature Conservancy refuge dedicated to maintaining the essential habitat of the grizzly. Also contains many other wildlife species, including lynx, mountain lion, sandhill crane, golden eagle, mink, and bighorn sheep. Features the Egg Mountain duckbill dinosaur nesting site; daily paleontological tours during summer. Permission required to explore. 18,000 acres, along the Teton River. Hiking. The Pine Butte Guest Ranch offers horseback riding, natural history tours (open May through Oct.). Preserve open all year. Off US 89, about 60 miles southeast of Waterton-Glacier NP. (406) 466-5526.

BENTON LAKE NATIONAL WILDLIFE REFUGE

BLACK EAGLE, MONTANA

More than 200 species of birds find food, protection, and carefully maintained nesting areas on this prairie marsh in the midst of wheat fields and grasslands. Northern pintail, gadwall, Canada goose and white-faced ibis are among the species that nest in the ancient glacial lakebed that holds the marsh. 12,383 acres. Hunting, bird-watching, self-guided auto tour. Open when accessible (snow drifts often cover road Nov. to March), dawn to dusk. Headquarters off US 87, 100 miles from Waterton-Glacier NP. (406) 727-7400.

Bison Flats tall-grass prairie

WIND CAVE

SOUTH DAKOTA
ESTABLISHED JANUARY 9, 1903
28,295 acres

Too many visitors leave Wind Cave National Park knowing only half of its charms. Ironically, the half they know is the half that's not visible from the surface.

Above the spectacular underground labyrinth for which the park is named lies an unusual ecosystem, one that marks the boundary between the mixed-grass prairie of the western Great Plains and the ponderosa pine forests of the Black Hills. Thus, the park plays host to plant and animal species from several distinct geographical areas—prairie falcons and meadowlarks from the grasslands coexist here with nuthatches and wild turkeys from the forests.

Wildlife could be the major draw here. Because of the park's small size and relatively large bison population, the chances of seeing bison—the so-called American buffalo—are probably better at this park than at almost any other; indeed it's often difficult to avoid the great beasts. The park's bison are decendents of 14 bison reintroduced to the area in 1913 from the New York Zoological Society.

Pronghorn, mule deer, and prairie dogs are present in large numbers—and highly visible since 75 percent of the park is open grassland. Elk live in the forest fringes; you probably won't see many, but if you have the good luck to come in the autumn you'll hear their eerie bugling.

Below ground lies Wind Cave. The first recorded discovery of the cave occurred in 1881, when two brothers named Bingham heard a loud whistling noise coming from the cave's only natural entrance.

Today, more than 116 miles of explored passages make it one of the world's longest caves. Because the cave is relatively dry, it contains few of the stalactites and stalagmites you see in other caves. But it has many unusual mineral formations, including perhaps the world's best collection of boxwork, a calcite formation resembling irregular honeycombs. Perhaps it's most distinctive feature may be the strong winds that alternately rush in and out of its mouth, equalizing air pressure between the passages inside and the atmosphere outside, and causing the noise the Binghams heard.

How to Get There

For the scenic route from Rapid City (74 miles away), take US 16 to US 16A south, detouring for a glimpse of Mount Rushmore, to S. Dak. 87 south. This route—*not open to RVs and trailers*—takes you along the Needles Highway and through Custer State Park to Wind Cave's north entrance.

The faster route is to follow S. Dak. 79 south from Rapid City to Hot Springs and then turn north onto US 385 to the south entrance. From the west, take US 16 east to Custer and US 385 south from there. Airport: Rapid City.

When to Go

All-year park. Although the cave and visitor center are open every day except Thanksgiving and Christmas and New Year's Day, the park offers far fewer cave tours off-season (late September to May). Late spring to midsummer is best for wildflowers. Saturdays and Sundays in summer are the days least likely to be crowded. The campground is rarely, if ever, full.

How to Visit

A good plan of action for a single-day visit would be to spend the morning in **Wind Cave** on one of the shorter introductory tours and the afternoon exploring the park's prairies and forests on the **Scenic Drive.** A second day would be the time for one of the longer **Candlelight** or **Cave Tours.**

People with physical limitations will want to stick to the shorter, less strenuous tours, although even the shortest involves climbing up and down about 150 steps. (If claustrophobia is a problem for you, you might think twice about entering the cave at all.)

Wear good walking shoes, and, since the cave temperature is a constant 53°F, take a jacket even on hot summer days. Reservations for Candlelight and Wild Cave Tours are recommended. You must be 8 years old for the Candlelight Tour and 16 years old for the Wild Cave Tour.

WIND CAVE: GUIDED TOURS

1 hour to a half day

All tours begin at the historic 1936 **visitor center,** where exhibits provide important background information. A video explains the connection between the park's subsurface world and the aboveground prairie. The same forces that lifted the nearby Black Hills created cracks in the limestone layers beneath the present-day park. Water seeped into these cracks and, over millions of years, gradually dissolved the rock, creating the maze of passages and tunnels we see today.

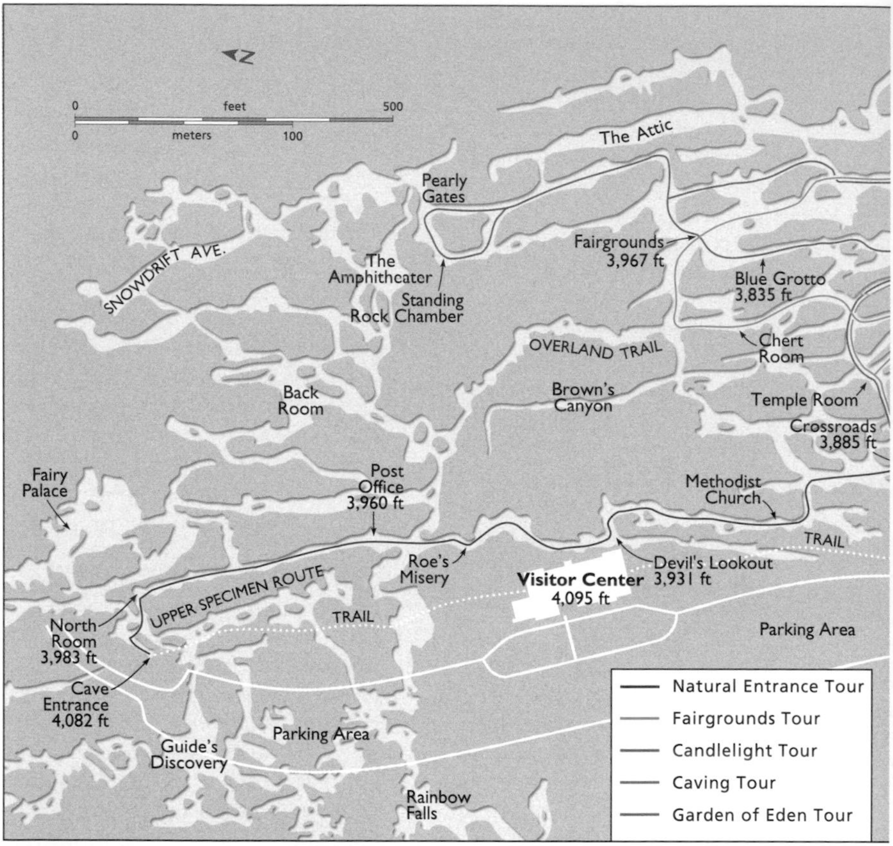

N
0 feet 500
0 meters 100
The Attic
Pearly Gates
SNOWDRIFT AVE.
The Amphitheater
Standing Rock Chamber
Fairgrounds 3,967 ft
Blue Grotto 3,835 ft
Chert Room
OVERLAND TRAIL
Back Room
Brown's Canyon
Temple Room
Crossroads 3,885 ft
Fairy Palace
Post Office 3,960 ft
Methodist Church
TRAIL
Roe's Misery
Devil's Lookout 3,931 ft
Visitor Center 4,095 ft
UPPER SPECIMEN ROUTE
TRAIL
North Room 3,983 ft
Parking Area
Cave Entrance 4,082 ft
Guide's Discovery
Parking Area
Rainbow Falls
Natural Entrance Tour
Fairgrounds Tour
Candlelight Tour
Caving Tour
Garden of Eden Tour

The cave's famous boxwork, a calcite formation

Most first-timers will choose to take either the **Natural Entrance Tour,** which lasts about an hour and 15 minutes, or the **Fairgrounds Tour,** which is 15 minutes longer. These tours introduce you to the underground world, stressing basic information about caves and cave formations; they take you through such colorfully named places as the **Post Office** (named for the extensive boxwork on the walls), the **Devil's Lookout,** and the **Blue Grotto.**

The **Garden of Eden Tour** is an easy loop around from the elevator to the **Garden of Eden** lasting one hour; it is the best choice for people with time or physical limitations.

If you are a history buff, by all

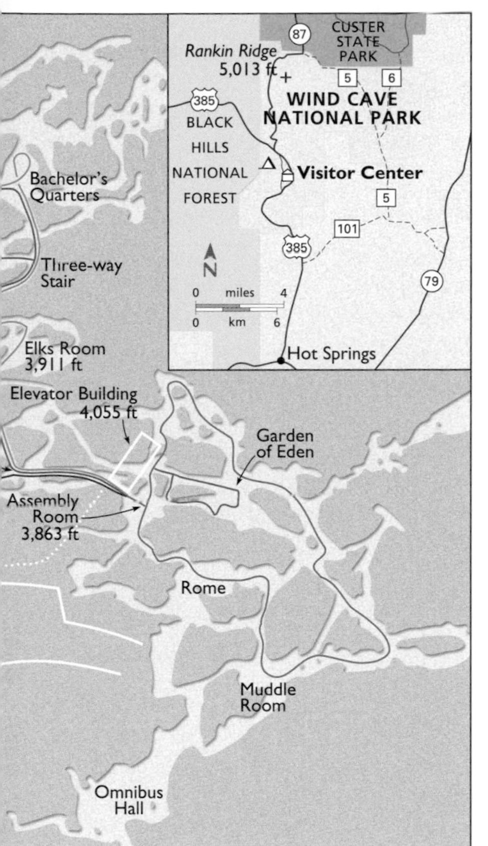

means take the **Candlelight Tour** (summer only). Conducted by the light of candle lanterns, this 2-hour tour harks back to the 1890s, when Wind Cave was owned by the Wonderful Wind Cave Improvement Company and tours were measured by the number of candles needed to complete them. The tour goes past the **Blue Grotto** to the **Pearly Gates** and beyond; it stresses the cave's ambience and exploration. The tour involves some stooping and stairclimbing.

For those in good condition with a keen interest in caves, the park offers the 4-hour **Wild Cave Tour,** designed to simulate a cave exploration trip. Park staff lead participants into the ghostly far reaches of the cave. You crawl through narrow openings, squeeze into tight passages, and make a glorious mess of yourself (take a change of clothes). The guide's commentary focuses on recreational caving and its impact on cave ecology.

SCENIC DRIVE

13 miles; at least a half day

Begin on US 385 at the southern boundary of the park, about 11 miles north of Hot Springs. At the **Bison Pullout** you get the first of many excellent views of the prairie, much as it existed before the plows of the white man drastically changed it. You may see bison and pronghorn grazing side by side on the grassy hillsides. The **Mineral Lick Pullout** a little farther on overlooks a site where bison lick salt from the soil.

From the visitor center, drive out to the campground for the self-guided **Elk Mountain Nature Trail.** This easy 1-mile hike takes you through a transitional prairie-and-pine-forest environment, where you'll see the grasses and trees encroaching on each other's domain. An accompanying trail guide points out some of the plant life around you, including prickly pear cactus and yucca.

Back on the road, continue to the junction with S. Dak. 87 and turn right, stopping at the **Prairie Dog Pullout** just after the turn. This is a good place to observe these once abundant rodents, who survive the predation of many natural enemies by their system of scanning territory and warning their fellows of imminent danger. Your approach will probably set off a cacophony of barks. If you stay in the car, you'll

INFORMATION & ACTIVITIES

HEADQUARTERS
Hot Springs, SD 57747. Phone (605) 745-4600. www.nps.gov/wica

SEASONS & ACCESSIBILITY
Open year-round.

VISITOR & INFORMATION CENTERS
Visitor center located 11 miles from Hot Springs on US 385; both it and the cave open all year. A variety of tours offered daily Memorial Day to Labor Day.

ENTRANCE FEES
None. Fees for cave tours: **Garden of Eden** $7, **Natural Entrance Cave** $9, **Fairgrounds Cave** $9, **Historic Candlelight Cave** $9, **Wind Cave** $23; children ages 6 to 16 fees range from $3.50-$4.50.

FACILITIES FOR DISABLED
The visitor center and a cave tour are wheelchair accessible.

THINGS TO DO
Naturalist-led activities: a variety of cave tours, nature walks, campfire talks. Also, interpretive exhibits, scenic drive, nature trails, hiking, bicycling, wildlife watching.

OVERNIGHT BACKPACKING
Permits required; free at visitor center.

CAMPGROUNDS
One campground; 14-day limit. Fees $12 per night mid-May to mid-September; $6 per night rest of year, with reduced services. First come, first served. Tent and RV sites; no hookups or showers.

HOTELS, MOTELS, & INNS
(unless otherwise noted, rates are for 2 persons in a double room, high season)

In Custer, SD 57730:
Bavarian Inn Motel P.O. Box 152. (800) 657-4312 or (605) 673-2802. 64 units, 1 condo. $99. AC, pool, rest.
Dakota Cowboy Inn 208 W. Mt. Rushmore Rd. (800) 279-5079 or (605) 673-4659. 48 units. $98. AC, pool, restaurant. May–early Oct.

In Hot Springs, SD 57747:
Best Value Inn by the River 602 W. River St. (888) 605-4292 or (605) 745-4292. 31 rooms $110; 3 cabins $125. $104. AC, pool.
Historic Braun Hotel 902 N. River St. (605) 745-3187. 11 units. $100. AC, rest.

Also, write or phone adjacent Custer State Park for information about its lodges: HC 83 Box 70, Custer, SD 57730. Phone (800) 710-2267 or (605) 255-4515.

have more to watch; cars don't spook the prairie dogs but people do. At dawn or dusk, watch the outskirts of the prairie dog town for patrolling coyotes.

The road now climbs from the prairie into the higher ponderosa pine forests that cover much of the Black Hills. Stop at the **Ancient Foundations Pullout** to learn about the granite core of the Black Hills. Other pullouts show how various kinds of plants and animals coexist in this dynamic prairie-forest border area.

Turn right at the **Rankin Ridge Pullout** and follow the half-mile road to the trailhead. The Rankin Ridge Trail, a 1-mile loop, climbs up among the pines to a fire tower. In summer, you can climb part way up the tower for a great view.

Back in the car, return to the main road and continue to the north entrance of the park to complete the tour. Those with high clearance vehicles may wish to make a loop by turning right on unpaved Park Road 5. This road connects with Park Road 6 and then County Road 101; it takes you through pronghorn and bison territory. Turn right on County Road 101 to return to US 385 south of the park.

EXCURSIONS

BUFFALO GAP NATIONAL GRASSLAND

WALL, SOUTH DAKOTA

These mixed grasslands and badlands dotted with prairie dog towns offer superb rock hunting. 591,727 acres. Hiking, fishing, horseback riding, hunting, mountain biking, camping. Open year-round. National Grassland Visitor Center at Wall, off I-90, about 75 miles from Wind Cave NP. Surrounds Badlands NP. (605) 279-2125.

MOUNT RUSHMORE NATIONAL MEMORIAL

KEYSTONE, SOUTH DAKOTA

Colossal visages of Washington, Jefferson, Theodore Roosevelt, and Lincoln gaze out over the Black Hills NF. From June through September the sculptor's studio is open; an evening program ends in the dramatic lighting of the memorial (mid-May through early October). 1,278 acres. Food services, handicapped access. Located on S. Dak. 244, about 25 miles north of Wind Cave NP. (605) 574-2523.

JEWEL CAVE NATIONAL MONUMENT

CUSTER, SOUTH DAKOTA

Sparkling crystals of calcite are the "jewels" of this 133-mile-long cave. 12,776 acres. Spelunking, hiking, picnic areas, visitor center. Open all year (cave tours year-round). In Black Hills NF on US 16, about 35 miles northwest of Wind Cave NP. (605) 673-2288.

Travertine hot springs

YELLOWSTONE

WYOMING, IDAHO, & MONTANA
ESTABLISHED MARCH 1, 1872
2,221,766 acres

Yellowstone is a geological smoking gun that illustrates how violent the Earth can be. One event overshadows all others: Some 600,000 years ago, an area many miles square at what is now the center of the park suddenly exploded. In minutes the landscape was devastated. Fast-moving ash flows covered thousands of square miles. At the center only a smoldering caldera remained, a collapsed crater 45 by 30 miles. At least two other cataclysmic events preceded this one. Boiling hot springs, fumaroles, mud spots, and geysers serve as reminders that another could occur.

Yellowstone, however, is much more than hot ground and gushing steam. Located astride the Continental Divide, most of the park occupies a high plateau surrounded by mountains and drained by several rivers. Park boundaries enclose craggy peaks, alpine lakes, deep canyons, and vast forests. In 1872, Yellowstone became the world's first national park, the result of great foresight on the part of many people about our eventual need for the solace and beauty of wild places.

In early years, what made Yellowstone stand out was the extravaganza of geysers and hot springs. The wild landscape and the bison, elk, and bears were nice but, after all, America was still a pioneer country filled with scenic beauty and animals.

As the West was settled, however, Yellowstone's importance as a wildlife sanctuary grew. The list of park animals is a compendium of Rocky Mountain fauna: elk, bison, mule deer, bighorn sheep, grizzly bears, black bears, wolves, moose, pronghorn, coyotes, mountain lions, beaver, trumpeter swans, eagles, ospreys, white pelicans, and more.

During the summer of 1988, fire touched many sections of the park, in some areas dramatically changing the appearance of the landscape. Yet not one major feature was destroyed. The geysers, waterfalls, and herds of wildlife are still here. Many places show no impact at all, while those that are regenerating benefit both vegetation and animal life. Side by side, burned areas and nonburned areas provide an intriguing study in the causes and effects of fire in wild places. Yellowstone has witnessed bigger natural events than this and may well again.

Of far greater concern to environmentalists than the fires are the impact of the increasing numbers of visitors, the threatened grizzly bear population, and, on nearby lands, the planned development of natural resource projects. Cooperative management between the park and the six forests that make up the greater Yellowstone ecosystem is essential if wildlife and thermal features are to survive.

How to Get There

There are five entrances: from the west, West Yellowstone (Montana); from the north and northeast, Gardiner and Cooke City (Montana); from the east, on US 14/16/20 from Cody (Wyoming); and from the south, at Flagg Ranch (Wyoming), which is north of Grand Teton National Park and Jackson (64 miles away). Airports: West Yellowstone (summer only), Bozeman, and Billings in Montana; Cody and Jackson in Wyoming.

When to Go

More than half of the 3 million annual visitors come in July and August. In September and early October, the weather is good, the visitors few, and the wildlife abundant. In May and June, you can see newborn animals, but the weather may be cold, wet, and even snowy. Between about November through April most park roads are closed to vehicles.

During the winter season, mid-December to mid-March, Yellowstone becomes a fantasy of steam and ice; facilities are limited but sufficient. Only the road between the North and Northeast Entrances stays open to cars, but snowmobiling is permitted on unplowed roads.

Bull moose wading in the Yellowstone River

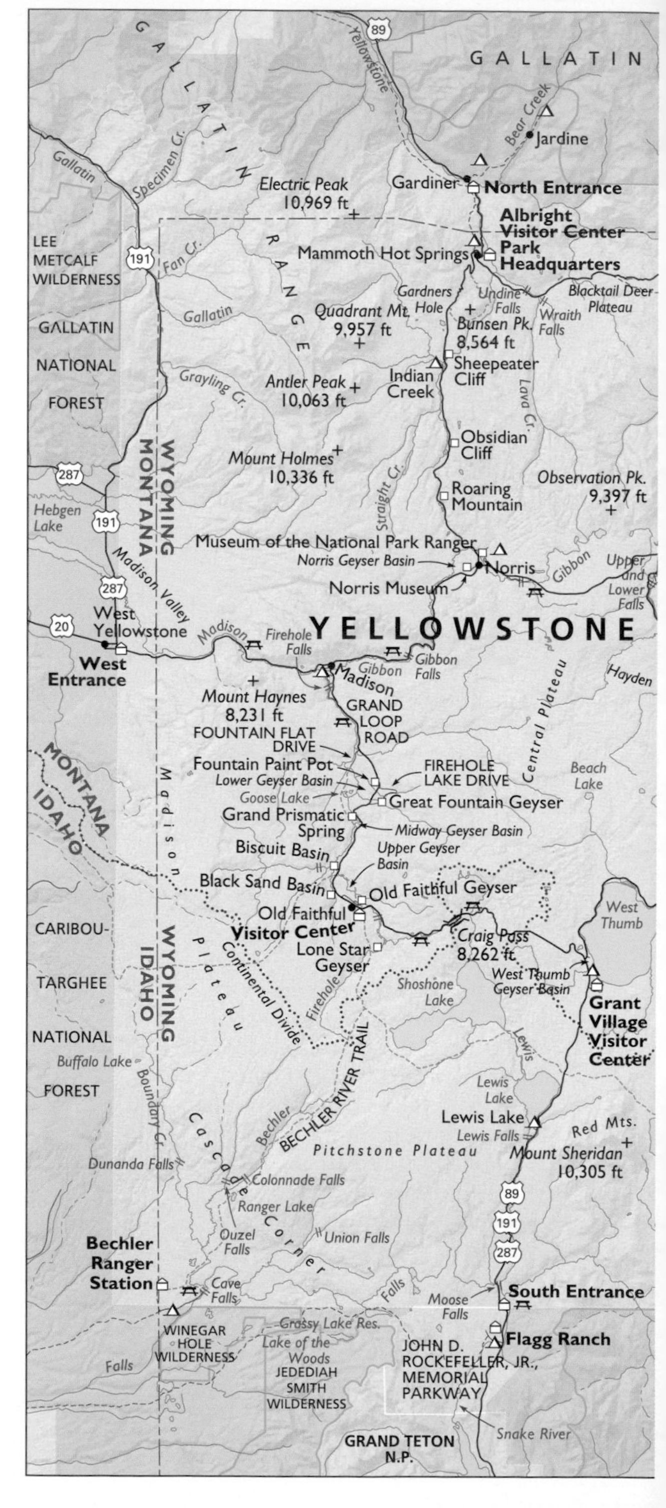
GALLATIN RANGE
GALLATIN
Jardine
Bear Creek
Yellowstone
Gallatin
Specimen Cr.
Electric Peak
10,969 ft
Gardiner
North Entrance
Albright
Visitor Center
Park
Headquarters
Mammoth Hot Springs
LEE
METCALF
WILDERNESS
Fan Cr.
GALLATIN
NATIONAL
FOREST
Gallatin
Quadrant Mt.
9,957 ft
Gardners
Hole
Undine
Falls
Bunsen Pk.
8,564 ft
Wraith
Falls
Blacktail Deer
Plateau
Sheepeater
Cliff
Indian
Creek
Grayling Cr.
Antler Peak
10,063 ft
Lava Cr.
Obsidian
Cliff
WYOMING
MONTANA
Mount Holmes
10,336 ft
Observation Pk.
9,397 ft
Roaring
Mountain
Straight Cr.
Hebgen
Lake
Museum of the National Park Ranger
Norris Geyser Basin
Norris
Gibbon
Upper
and
Lower
Falls
Norris Museum
Madison Valley
West
Yellowstone
Madison
Firehole
Falls
YELLOWSTONE
Gibbon
Falls
Gibbon
Madison
West
Entrance
Central Plateau
Hayden
Mount Haynes
8,231 ft
GRAND
LOOP
ROAD
FOUNTAIN FLAT
DRIVE
Fountain Paint Pot
Lower Geyser Basin
FIREHOLE
LAKE DRIVE
Beach
Lake
MONTANA
IDAHO
Goose Lake
Great Fountain Geyser
Grand Prismatic
Spring
Midway Geyser Basin
Madison
Biscuit Basin
Upper Geyser
Basin
Black Sand Basin
Old Faithful Geyser
Old Faithful
Visitor Center
West
Thumb
CARIBOU-
TARGHEE
NATIONAL
FOREST
Plateau
Continental Divide
Lone Star
Geyser
Craig Pass
8,262 ft
West Thumb
Geyser Basin
Grant
Village
Visitor
Center
WYOMING
IDAHO
Firehole
Shoshone
Lake
BECHLER RIVER TRAIL
Lewis
Buffalo Lake
Boundary Cr.
Lewis
Lake
Lewis Lake
Lewis Falls
Red Mts.
Mount Sheridan
10,305 ft
Bechler
Pitchstone Plateau
Cascade Corner
Dunanda Falls
Colonnade Falls
Ranger Lake
Ouzel
Falls
Union Falls
Bechler
Ranger
Station
Cave
Falls
Falls
Moose
Falls
South Entrance
Flagg Ranch
WINEGAR
HOLE
WILDERNESS
Grassy Lake Res.
Lake of the
Woods
JEDEDIAH
SMITH
WILDERNESS
Falls
JOHN D.
ROCKEFELLER, JR.,
MEMORIAL
PARKWAY
Snake River
GRAND TETON
N.P.
89
191
287
20

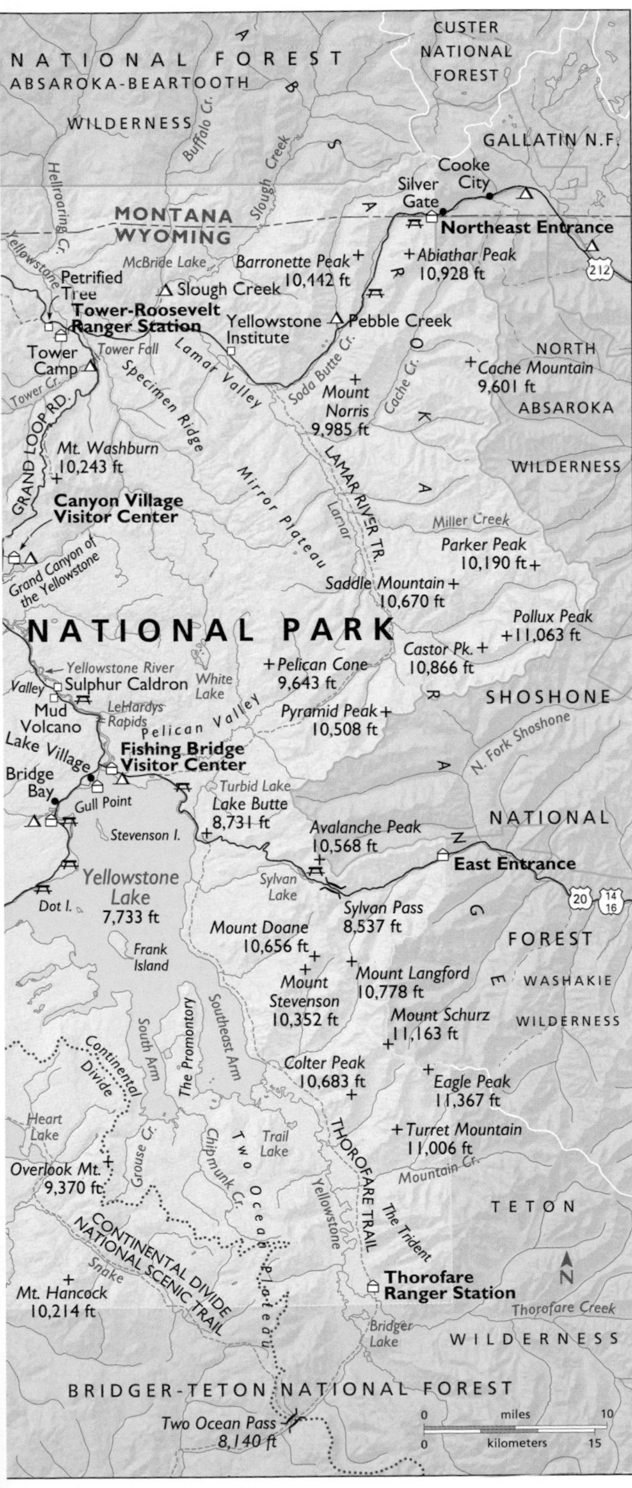

ABSAROKA-BEARTOOTH
WILDERNESS
NATIONAL FOREST
CUSTER NATIONAL FOREST
GALLATIN N.F.
Cooke City
Silver Gate
Northeast Entrance
212
MONTANA
WYOMING
Buffalo Cr.
Slough Creek
Hellroaring Cr.
Yellowstone
McBride Lake
Barronette Peak 10,142 ft
Abiathar Peak 10,928 ft
Petrified Tree
Slough Creek
Tower-Roosevelt Ranger Station
Yellowstone Institute
Pebble Creek
Tower Camp
Tower Fall
Tower Cr.
Lamar Valley
Specimen Ridge
Soda Butte Cr.
Cache Cr.
Mount Norris 9,985 ft
NORTH
Cache Mountain 9,601 ft
ABSAROKA
WILDERNESS
GRAND LOOP RD.
Mt. Washburn 10,243 ft
Canyon Village Visitor Center
Mirror Plateau
LAMAR RIVER TR.
Lamar
Miller Creek
Parker Peak 10,190 ft
Grand Canyon of the Yellowstone
Saddle Mountain 10,670 ft
NATIONAL PARK
Pollux Peak 11,063 ft
Castor Pk. 10,866 ft
Yellowstone River
Pelican Cone 9,643 ft
Valley
Sulphur Caldron
White Lake
Mud Volcano
LeHardys Rapids
Pelican Valley
Pyramid Peak 10,508 ft
SHOSHONE
N. Fork Shoshone
Lake Village
Fishing Bridge Visitor Center
Bridge Bay
Gull Point
Turbid Lake
Lake Butte 8,731 ft
NATIONAL
Stevenson I.
Avalanche Peak 10,568 ft
East Entrance
Yellowstone Lake 7,733 ft
Sylvan Lake
Sylvan Pass 8,537 ft
20
14 16
Dot I.
Mount Doane 10,656 ft
FOREST
Frank Island
Mount Stevenson 10,352 ft
Mount Langford 10,778 ft
WASHAKIE
Mount Schurz 11,163 ft
WILDERNESS
Continental Divide
South Arm
The Promontory
Southeast Arm
Colter Peak 10,683 ft
Eagle Peak 11,367 ft
Heart Lake
Trail Lake
Turret Mountain 11,006 ft
Grouse Cr.
Chipmunk Cr.
Two Ocean Plateau
THOROFARE TRAIL
Mountain Cr.
Overlook Mt. 9,370 ft
Yellowstone
TETON
The Trident
CONTINENTAL DIVIDE NATIONAL SCENIC TRAIL
Snake
Thorofare Ranger Station
N
Mt. Hancock 10,214 ft
Thorofare Creek
Bridger Lake
WILDERNESS
BRIDGER-TETON NATIONAL FOREST
Two Ocean Pass 8,140 ft
0 miles 10
0 kilometers 15

Heated snow coaches offer tours and give cross-country skiers access to about 50 miles of groomed trails.

How to Visit

The 142-mile **Grand Loop Road** forms a figure eight, with connecting spurs to the five entrances. In early years, visitors took a week going around the loop—still a good idea. On any visit, start with the geyser basins and **Mammoth Hot Springs** to see wildlife and thermal features *(caution: both can be hazardous if approached too closely)*. On the second day, travel to the **Grand Canyon of the Yellowstone, Hayden Valley,** and **Yellowstone Lake.**

On a longer stay, visit the **northern range,** or consider a boating or fishing trip on Yellowstone Lake; a backcountry excursion on foot or horse; or any of the numerous easy nature trails throughout the park.

Your best chance of seeing wildlife is in early morning or evening.

Mud pot near the Grand Canyon

GEYSER BASINS: OLD FAITHFUL TO MAMMOTH

51 miles; a full day

Begin by leaving your car in the parking lot at **Old Faithful.** Check at the visitor center for predicted eruption times of the major geysers. While there, pick up an **Upper Geyser Basin** map (also available from area dispensers). Wait on benches near the visitor center for the eruption of Old Faithful (named and celebrated for its steadiness rather than a predictable schedule of eruptions) or walk the path that circles it. Almost any point along the path offers a good view of the eruption, so don't worry if you're not at the benches when it happens. You can see from here that Old Faithful is not alone. The mile-long Upper Geyser Basin contains the world's greatest concentration of hot springs and geysers.

Try to allow a minimum of two hours to see more of it. This must be done on foot, but trails are easy and diversions many. The best choice is to start from the back side of Old Faithful, on the trail that crosses the **Firehole River** to **Geyser Hill,** and follow the map (or your nose; you can't get lost here). You can cross the river at several points and return on the other side, making the walk as long or short as you like. You'll pass dozens of colorful boiling springs and delicate formations of geyserite, a silicate mineral deposited by hot

Morning Glory Pool, named for the flower

water. Chances are good to see one or more geysers erupt at short range. Keep an eye out for elk and bison. **Morning Glory Pool,** named for its resemblance to the flower, marks the far end of the basin.

Back in your car, drive north. **Black Sand Basin** is worth a quick stop, but bypass **Biscuit Basin.** The road follows the Firehole River several miles to **Midway Geyser Basin,** where a 20-minute stroll on the boardwalk takes you past the enormous crater of **Excelsior Geyser.** It erupted for two days in 1985. A huge boiling vat, it produces about 4,000 gallons of scalding water each minute. The boardwalk continues across the delicate terraces of **Grand Prismatic Spring,** 370 feet wide, the largest and most beautiful hot spring in the park. The bright colors are caused by algae and bacteria, different types of which thrive in different water temperatures.

Two miles farther, turn right on the one-way **Firehole Lake Drive** to **Great Fountain Geyser.** Check the prediction board for the estimated time of eruption. Great Fountain goes off every 11 hours or so. If you have the time, wait. This eruption is one of the best. A bit farther along is **White Dome Geyser.** Its cone may be massive, but its eruption is a thin spray. Perhaps centuries ago it had more power. Yellowstone is always changing.

Rejoin the main road at **Fountain Paint Pot,** a cauldron of hot reddish-pinkish mud, blooping and spitting—always entertaining. Any hot spring could become a mud pot with the right balance of acidity, moisture, and clay; however, a constant flow of water keeps most springs clear.

For the next few miles, rest your eyes on meadows and forest. Look for bison on **Fountain Flat;** also for purple-colored western fringed gentian, the park flower. **Fountain Flat Drive** is closed to vehicles 1 mile from the main road. But it's open to visitors walking to **Goose Lake,** a peaceful picnic site. The Firehole River, warmed by hot water from springs and geysers along its course, flows through the meadows and along the main road before dropping into a canyon with nice waterfalls; to see them, turn left on **Firehole Canyon Drive** just before **Madison Junction.**

At Madison Junction, a left turn follows the Madison River to the West Entrance, but stay on the road to Norris. In this area, the fires of 1988 burned extensively. Their effects—the jagged sweeps of charred lodgepole pine forest—will be visible for a long time. However, millions of new lodgepole pines have since grown back (the fires' heat released seedlings from cones on the forest floor). And, because the fires moved erratically, the burned areas are not far from unburned areas, another source of seeds for regrowth.

The road climbs beside the **Gibbon River** to **Gibbon Falls** and continues through the **Gibbon Canyon** and large meadows, where elk are commonly seen, to Norris.

Norris Geyser Basin contains the hottest ground in the park, as well as the world's tallest geyser, **Steamboat.** The geyser's eruptions are infrequent and unpredictable; it may stay quiet for years at a time. Steamboat last erupted on May 23, 2005 the third time since October 2, 1991. Contrast its sleepy behavior with that of **Echinus,** which goes off about every 40 to 80 minutes, an easy show to witness.

Highlights of the drive north include the steamy fumaroles of **Roaring Mountain** that snore rather than roar and **Obsidian Cliff,** an outcrop containing black volcanic glass that was valued for arrow points by Indians throughout the area. The road crosses **Gardners Hole,** with nice views of the **Gallatin Range** to the west, and drops toward Mammoth through **Golden Gate,** cliffs gilded with the bright yellow lichen that grows on them.

At **Mammoth Hot Springs** you can drive or walk around the dozens of colorful steaming terraces. They are

Minerva Terrace at Mammoth Hot Springs

made of travertine—calcium carbonate—which the hot water brings to the surface from beds of limestone. The formations look quite different from the silica-based geyserite deposits seen elsewhere in the park. The park's headquarters and largest visitor center are at Mammoth. The **North Entrance** is located 5 miles down the **Gardner River Canyon.**

YELLOWSTONE LAKE & RIVER: CANYON TO WEST THUMB

37 miles; at least a half day

From the **Canyon Village Visitor Center,** follow the one-way **Canyon Rim Drive** to lookout points for great views of the canyon and the **Yellowstone River's** 308-foot **Lower Falls,** nearly twice as high as Niagara. The bright yellow, orange, and red of the canyon walls are caused by heat and chemical action on gray or brown rhyolite rock.

Walk the rim trail from **Inspiration Point** to **Grandview Point** for the best look at the canyon's natural grandeur. Also consider the paved but strenuous **Brink of the Lower Falls Trail,** which descends several hundred feet through steep forest. Standing beside the green river where it suddenly drops into space is one of the most exciting experiences in the park.

Continue south on the main road. The **Upper Falls** are, at 109 feet high, almost as impressive as the Lower Falls and easier to reach. A short trail leads to **Upper Falls View.** Half a

Storm Creek fire 1988 *(top)*
Fumaroles in Norris Geyser Basin *(bottom)*

mile farther south, a side road crosses the river to **Artist Point,** the best overall view of the canyon.

Upriver, the Yellowstone flows gently through the sage-covered hills of **Hayden Valley.** Go slowly and stop often in the roadside parking areas; this is prime wildlife country. American white pelicans and trumpeter swans share the river with Canada geese, gulls, and ducks. Bison are visible most of the year. *Keep your distance.* Use binoculars to check meadows across the river for grizzlies digging for roots or rodents. Grizzlies are often seen in the open; black bears, their smaller, shier relations, rarely. But be careful not to surprise one; both are dangerous.

Well-named **Mud Volcano** and **Black Dragon's Caldron** are not pretty to look at, but they are impressive. Springs in this area have been known to hurl football-sized blobs of mud tens of feet. From here to the lake, the **Yellowstone River** provides excellent catch-and-release fishing for cutthroat trout. At **Le Hardys Rapids** in June you can watch cutthroat jumping on their way to spawning grounds (no fishing).

Look for trout also at **Fishing Bridge** (no fishing allowed) where the river flows out of the lake. Two miles farther east is **Pelican Valley,** a lush lakeside meadow where you might find moose or white pelicans.

Return to the loop road, following the shore of **Yellowstone Lake** most of the next 21 miles. This is the largest lake in North America above 7,000 feet. The **Absaroka Range,** visible across the blue waters, was named for the Absaroka, or Crow Indians. The volcanic peaks define the park's eastern boundary.

Bison frequent the meadows near **Bridge Bay,** while moose favor ponds along the **Gull Point Road. Gull Point** is a good picnic site.

West Thumb, almost a separate lake, is a water-filled caldera created by an eruption about 150,000 years ago, a smaller version of the great Yellowstone caldera. A boardwalk leads around the **West Thumb Geyser Basin,** a modest group of thermal features made charming by its location beside the lake.

NORTHERN RANGE

Between Mammoth Hot Springs and Cooke City, Yellowstone is warmer and drier than the interior. Called the Northern Range for its importance as wintering ground for large animals, this area is characterized by sagebrush and grassy valleys. Open all year, the road from Mammoth stays high above the Yellowstone River, crosses it near **Tower-Roosevelt,** and follows the **Lamar River** and **Soda Butte Creek** to the **Northeast Entrance,** a magnificent little-used gateway. A few miles past Tower, **Specimen Ridge** contains the world's largest fossil forest. More than a hundred plant species, including redwoods, are found in 27 layers of volcanic ash from repeated eruptions 50 million years ago.

HIKING, FISHING, & BOATING

More than a thousand miles of trails lead to wilderness valleys, mountaintops, lakes, and thermal basins. Take horses and a guide for a week-long trip, or go on foot for an hour or two. Even a short walk can put you in a wilderness setting beyond roads and crowds. Ask for recommended hikes at any visitor center.

Yellowstone offers fine trout fishing, especially for the fly-fisherman. A permit is required ($15 for 3 days; $20 for 7 days; $35 for the season), available at visitor centers and ranger stations. Regulations are complicated, and often different for sections of any given stream, so read them carefully. Guide services are available at fishing shops in surrounding communities.

Motorboating is permitted on most of **Yellowstone Lake** and **Lewis Lake;** passenger boats operate from **Bridge Bay Marina** for sight-seeing and fishing. Other lakes are limited to hand-propelled craft. Rivers and streams are closed to all boating to avoid disturbing wildlife; an exception is the channel between Lewis and **Shoshone Lakes,** where paddlers are permitted.

Bison grazing near Firehole River *(top)*; Landing a cutthroat trout on Slough Creek *(center)*
Male elk during mating season *(bottom left)*; Rust-colored cones that release seeds after fire *(bottom right)*

INFORMATION & ACTIVITIES

HEADQUARTERS
P.O. Box 168, WY 82190. Phone (307) 344-7381. www.nps.gov/yell

SEASONS & ACCESSIBILITY
Park open year-round. Road from North Entrance to Northeast Entrance open all year; most other roads closed to cars Nov. through April. Call headquarters for latest weather and road conditions.

VISITOR & INFORMATION CENTERS
Mammoth Hot Springs/Albright Visitor Center open all year. **Old Faithful Visitor Center** open May through October and mid-December to mid-March, depending on weather. **Canyon Village Visitor Center,** near center of park, and **Fishing Bridge and Grant Village Visitor Centers,** on Yellowstone Lake, open May through September (reduced hours in Sept.).

ENTRANCE FEES
$20 per vehicle, good for one week at both Yellowstone and Grand Teton. $40 annual.

FACILITIES FOR DISABLED
Visitor centers; exhibits; Madison; Bridge Bay; Grant, Lewis Lake, and Fishing Bridge Campgrounds; most restrooms; amphitheaters; and many ranger-led activities and walks are wheelchair accessible. Brochure available.

THINGS TO DO
Free naturalist-led activities: nature walks, camera walks, evening programs. Also available, hiking, boating, fishing (permit required), horseback riding (stables at Roosevelt, Canyon, and Mammoth), bicycling, stagecoach rides, courses in natural history and photography, art exhibits, children's activities, bus and boat tours, snow-coach tours, cross-country skiing, ice-skating, snowshoeing, and snowmobiling.

OVERNIGHT BACKPACKING
Permits required. They are free and available at visitor centers and ranger stations; apply in person not more than 48 hours in advance of use. Advance reservations $15.

CAMPGROUNDS
Twelve campgrounds, all with 14-day limit (except Fishing Bridge RV Park) from May through October; other times 30-day limit. **Mammoth** open all year, others open late spring to mid-fall. Reservations accepted for **Fishing Bridge RV Park, Madison, Grant Village, Canyon Village,** and **Bridge Bay;** contact Xanterra Parks & Resorts, P.O. Box 165, Yellowstone NP, WY 82190. (307) 344-7311. All others first come, first served. Fees $10-$15 per night; Fishing Bridge RV Park $29. Pay showers near several campgrounds. Both tent and RV sites at most campgrounds; at Fishing Bridge RV Park hard-sided units only. Hookups at Fishing Bridge RV Park only. For group campgrounds, reserve through Xanterra Parks & Resorts. Food services in park.

HOTELS, MOTELS, & INNS
(unless otherwise noted, rates are for 2 persons in a double room, high season)

INSIDE THE PARK:
The following are operated by Xanterra Parks & Resorts, Yellowstone NP, P.O. Box 165, WY 82190. For reservations call (307) 344-7311.

Canyon Lodge 527 cabins, 81 rooms. $45-$142. Restaurant.

Grant Village 300 units. $116. Restaurant. Open May through Sept.

Lake Lodge & Cabins 186 units. $61-$121. Restaurant. Open June to mid-Sept.

Lake Yellowstone Hotel & Cabins 194 rooms, 102 cabins. $101-$192. Restaurant. Open mid-May to early Oct.

Mammoth Hot Springs Hotel & Cabins 97 rooms, 116 cabins. $65-$164. Restaurant. Open May to Oct. and late Dec. to early March.

Old Faithful Inn 327 units. $81-$192. Rest. Open early May to late Oct.

Old Faithful Lodge & Cabins 97 cabins. $57-$85. Open mid-May to early Oct.

Old Faithful Snow Lodge & Cabins 100 rooms, 34 cabins. $83-$161. Restaurant. Open mid-May to late Oct. and mid-Dec. to mid-March.

Roosevelt Lodge & Cabins 80 cabins. $57-$94. Restaurant. Open mid-June to early Sept.

See also Grand Teton NP listings, p. 310.

EXCURSIONS

SHOSHONE NATIONAL FOREST

CODY, WYOMING

Theodore Roosevelt dubbed this forest's North Fork the "most scenic 52 miles in the United States." Elk (wapiti) find a year-round home here in the lee of the Absaroka and Beartooth Ranges, as do bighorn sheep, grizzlies, moose, and deer. Contains parts or all of five wilderness areas. 2,433,000 acres. Hiking, boating, fishing, horseback riding, hunting, winter sports. 374 campsites, food services, boat ramp, picnic areas. Campsites open June through September. Adjoins Yellowstone NP on the east. (307) 527-6241.

RED ROCK LAKES NATIONAL WILDLIFE REFUGE

LAKEVIEW, MONTANA

In this Centennial Valley refuge, trumpeter swans and nesting sandhill cranes find shelter among grasslands, lakes, and marshes. Large mammals include moose, mule deer, pronghorn, and coyotes. 45,000 acres. 10 campsites, hiking, canoeing, fishing, hunting, scenic drives. Snow closes roads in winter. Off US 20/191, about 45 miles from Yellowstone NP. (406) 276-3536.

BIGHORN CANYON NATIONAL RECREATION AREA

FORT SMITH, MONTANA

Water-based recreation is the focus of this 71-mile-long reservoir impounded from the Bighorn River by the Yellowtail Dam. Fossils exposed in steep canyon walls, wildlife from four life zones, and historic and archaeological sites also featured. Surrounded by Crow Reservation. 120,284 acres. Hiking, boating, bicycling, fishing (and ice fishing), hunting, scenic drives, water sports. 125 campsites, boat ramps, picnic areas, handicapped access. Visitor center at Lovell on US 14A, about 100 miles east of Yellowstone NP. (307) 548-2251.

THE PACIFIC NORTHWEST

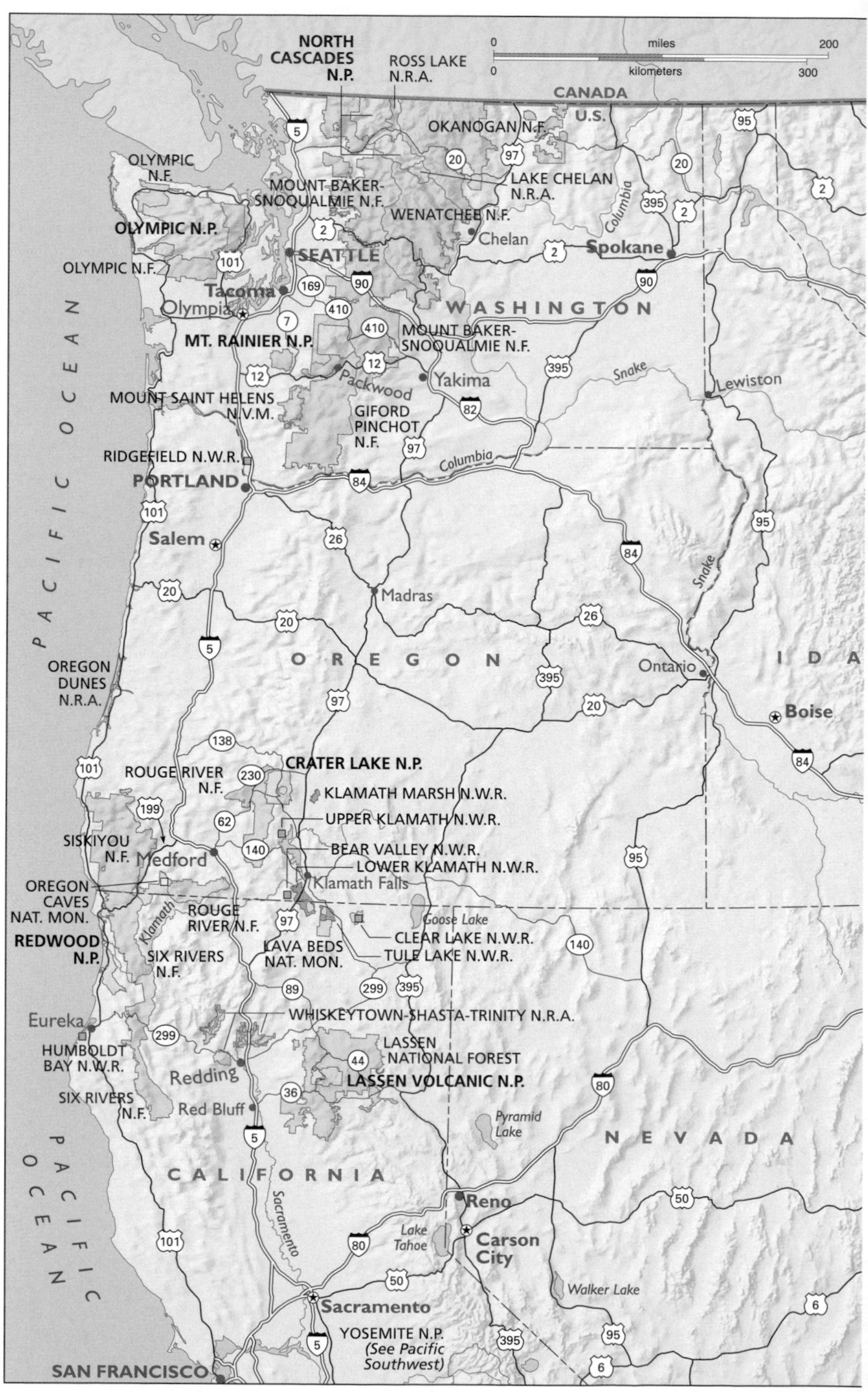
NORTH CASCADES N.P.
ROSS LAKE N.R.A.
0 miles 200
0 kilometers 300
CANADA
U.S.
OKANOGAN N.F.
OLYMPIC N.F.
MOUNT BAKER-SNOQUALMIE N.F.
LAKE CHELAN N.R.A.
WENATCHEE N.F.
Chelan
OLYMPIC N.P.
SEATTLE
Spokane
Columbia
OLYMPIC N.F.
Tacoma
Olympia
WASHINGTON
MOUNT BAKER-SNOQUALMIE N.F.
MT. RAINIER N.P.
Packwood
Yakima
Snake
Lewiston
MOUNT SAINT HELENS N.V.M.
GIFORD PINCHOT N.F.
RIDGEFIELD N.W.R.
Columbia
PORTLAND
PACIFIC OCEAN
Salem
Madras
Snake
OREGON
Ontario
IDA
OREGON DUNES N.R.A.
Boise
CRATER LAKE N.P.
ROUGE RIVER N.F.
KLAMATH MARSH N.W.R.
UPPER KLAMATH N.W.R.
SISKIYOU N.F.
BEAR VALLEY N.W.R.
Medford
LOWER KLAMATH N.W.R.
OREGON CAVES NAT. MON.
Klamath Falls
ROUGE RIVER N.F.
Goose Lake
Klamath
REDWOOD N.P.
CLEAR LAKE N.W.R.
LAVA BEDS NAT. MON.
TULE LAKE N.W.R.
SIX RIVERS N.F.
WHISKEYTOWN-SHASTA-TRINITY N.R.A.
Eureka
LASSEN NATIONAL FOREST
HUMBOLDT BAY N.W.R.
Redding
LASSEN VOLCANIC N.P.
SIX RIVERS N.F.
Red Bluff
Pyramid Lake
NEVADA
PACIFIC OCEAN
CALIFORNIA
Sacramento
Reno
Lake Tahoe
Carson City
Walker Lake
Sacramento
YOSEMITE N.P. (See Pacific Southwest)
SAN FRANCISCO
5
95
20
97
20
2
395
2
2
101
169
90
90
410
7
410
12
12
395
82
97
84
101
26
84
95
20
20
26
5
395
97
20
138
84
230
101
199
62
140
95
97
140
89
299
395
299
44
80
36
5
50
101
80
50
6
95
5
395
6

THE PACIFIC NORTHWEST

In the late 19th and early 20th centuries, East Coast loggers pushed west, downing mile after mile of the continent's primeval forests. Today, almost all of the large ancient forests left in the lower 48 states grow in the Pacific Northwest, most of them in national forests and parks.

Visitors to Mount Rainier, Olympic, and North Cascades can hike cathedral-like glades of Douglas fir, western red cedar, and other conifers. The redwoods in the park named for them include trees in their second millennium, some of the tallest on Earth. In Olympic, temperate rain forests soar near some of the nation's wildest coastline; in the United States, only there and at Mount Rainier do such forests still exist. All these ancient forests knit together the lives of hundreds of species of plants, animals, and microbes in a web we don't fully understand. Yet that web is increasingly threatened as trees in private, state, and national forests are cut down.

The Northwest is also known for its volcanoes, many of which, including Mount Rainier and Mount St. Helens, lie in the Pacific Ring of Fire, the great belt of crustal instability responsible for three-quarters of the world's active volcanoes. Visitors to Lassen Volcanic National Park can see evidence of the planet's violence in broken mountains and boiling mud pots. At Crater Lake, they can imagine the titanic forces that collapsed a mountaintop, turning it into a lake 6 miles wide and the deepest in the nation. They can marvel at the majesty of cloud-swathed Mount Rainier, which grew on a foundation of lava flows from extinct volcanoes, and now shoulders breathtaking wildflowers and more glaciers than any other U.S. peak south of Alaska.

Each of the region's northernmost national parks is less than half a day's drive from Seattle. This group merits at least a week of touring, more if you want to visit other natural areas nearby. The more southern peaks can each be seen in a day, but allow plenty of time for travel between them. Beautiful but winding Calif. 299 that connects the Lassen Volcanic and Redwood areas can wash out in spring, so check conditions if that's when you plan to go.

Wizard Island rising out of Crater Lake

CRATER LAKE

OREGON
ESTABLISHED MAY 22, 1902
183,224 acres

Few forget their first glimpse of Crater Lake on a clear summer's day—21 square miles of water so intensely blue it looks like ink, ringed by cliffs towering up to 2,000 feet above. The mountain bluebird, Indian legend says, was gray before dipping into the waters.

The tranquil Gem of the Cascades is set in a dormant volcano called Mount Mazama, one in the chain of volcanoes that includes Mount St. Helens. Mount Mazama's eruption about 5700 B.C. catapulted volcanic ash miles into the sky and expelled so much pumice and ash that the summit soon collapsed, creating a huge, smoldering caldera.

Eventually, rain and snowmelt accumulated in the caldera, forming a lake more than 1,900 feet deep, the deepest lake in the United States. Wildflowers, along with hemlock, fir, and pine, recolonized surroundings. Black bears and bobcats, deer and marmots, eagles and hawks returned.

Scientists have yet to understand completely Crater Lake's ecology. In 1988 and 1989, using a manned submarine, they discovered evidence that proves hydrothermal venting exists on the lake's bottom and may play a role in the lake's character.

Crater Lake forms a superb setting for day hikes. Thanks to some of the cleanest air in the nation, you can see more than 100 miles from points along many of the park's 100 miles of trails. Forests of mountain hemlock and Shasta red fir predominate near the caldera rim. At the rim twisted whitebark pine testify to the harshness of the long winter. Ponderosa pine, the park's largest tree, and lodgepole pine are common farther down from the rim.

How to Get There

Enter the park from the west (Medford, about 85 miles away) or the south (Klamath Falls, about 65 miles away) on Oreg. 62, or from the north on Oreg. 138. Airports: Medford and Klamath Falls.

When to Go

The lake best displays its dazzling color in summer. Oreg. 62 and the access road leading to Rim Village remain open during daylight in winter, and cross-country skiing is becoming increasingly popular. The drive around the lake usually closes in October because of snow; in some years, the drive may not reopen completely until mid-July. Peak wildflower viewing is late July/early August.

How to Visit

Spend at least a half day touring the 33-mile **Rim Drive,** enjoying its many overlooks and several hiking trails. On a second day, consider a hike down to the shore for the hour-and-45-minute, narrated **boat tour of the lake.** The boat stops at **Wizard Island;** if time and weather permit, climb to the top of it and catch a later boat back.

RIM DRIVE & GODFREY GLEN TRAIL

33 to 38 miles; a half to full day

Rim Drive circles Crater Lake, providing more than 25 scenic overlooks and some good picnic areas. *(Trailers and other oversize vehicles not recommended on east Rim Drive.)* Begin by parking in **Rim Village** and strolling to the **Sinnott Memorial Overlook,** a prime vantage point directly over the lake. Crater Lake's vivid color is a sign of purity and depth. The lake contains few minerals and impurities. Its only fish—rainbow trout and kokanee salmon—were introduced. As sunlight penetrates the deep, pure lake, water molecules absorb the colors of the spectrum except for blue, which is scattered back to the surface. Scientists have found green moss growing at a record 725 feet below the surface, indicating that sunlight may penetrate deeper here than in any other body of water in the world.

To begin your lake tour, set your car's odometer at zero (or note the setting) as you leave Rim Village parking lot. Head west or clockwise around the lake, and be careful: The road is narrow and has sharp curves. Watch out for bikers and pedestrians. Turn right at 0.1 mile for Rim Drive. The first stop (mile 1.3) brings you near **Discovery Point,** where, on June 12, 1853, a group of prospectors searching for a gold mine happened upon the lake, which they named Deep Blue Lake. Indians, believing the lake sacred, had told no outsiders about it. **Hillman Peak,** to the far left on the rim, is named for one of the prospectors. The peak is a 70,000-year-old volcano—one of the compact cluster of overlapping volcanic cones that formed Mount Mazama. It was cleaved in half when the summit collapsed. At 1,978 feet above the water, it forms the highest point on the rim.

The overlook at mile 4 offers a good view of **Wizard Island,** named for its resemblance to a sorcerer's hat. Rising 767 feet above the surface of the lake, Wizard Island is a classic cinder cone—built of red-hot cinders ejected from the caldera floor sometime after Mount Mazama collapsed. An Indian legend portrays

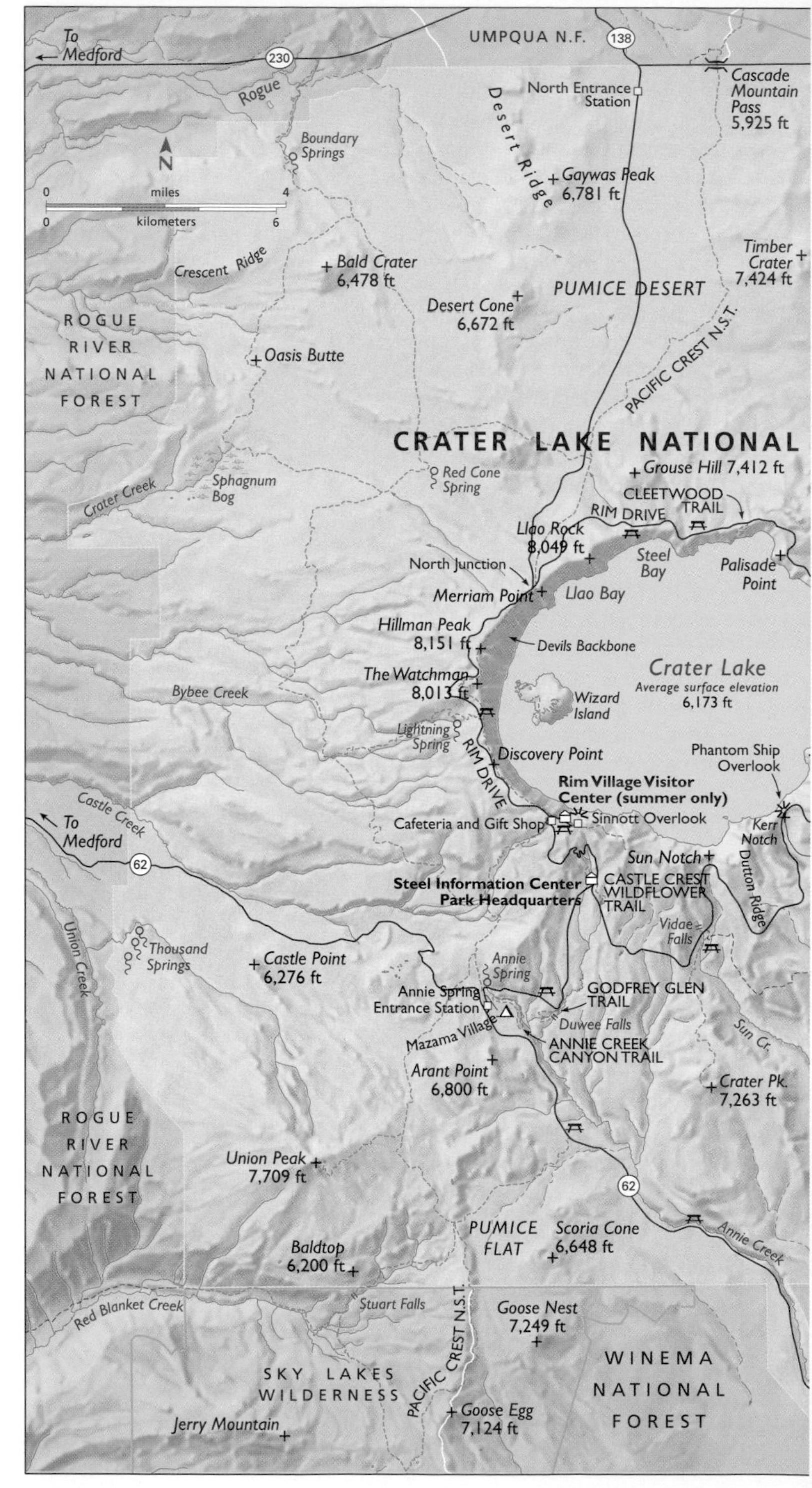

To Medford
230
UMPQUA N.F.
138
North Entrance Station
Cascade Mountain Pass 5,925 ft
Rogue
Desert Ridge
Boundary Springs
N
0 miles 4
0 kilometers 6
Gaywas Peak 6,781 ft
Timber Crater 7,424 ft
Crescent Ridge
Bald Crater 6,478 ft
Desert Cone 6,672 ft
PUMICE DESERT
ROGUE RIVER NATIONAL FOREST
Oasis Butte
PACIFIC CREST N.S.T.
CRATER LAKE NATIONAL
Grouse Hill 7,412 ft
Red Cone Spring
Sphagnum Bog
Crater Creek
CLEETWOOD TRAIL
RIM DRIVE
Llao Rock 8,049 ft
Steel Bay
Palisade Point
North Junction
Merriam Point
Llao Bay
Hillman Peak 8,151 ft
Devils Backbone
Crater Lake
Average surface elevation 6,173 ft
The Watchman 8,013 ft
Bybee Creek
Wizard Island
Lightning Spring
RIM DRIVE
Discovery Point
Phantom Ship Overlook
Rim Village Visitor Center (summer only)
Castle Creek
To Medford
Cafeteria and Gift Shop
Sinnott Overlook
Kerr Notch
62
Sun Notch
Steel Information Center
Park Headquarters
CASTLE CREST WILDFLOWER TRAIL
Dutton Ridge
Union Creek
Vidae Falls
Thousand Springs
Castle Point 6,276 ft
Annie Spring
Annie Spring Entrance Station
GODFREY GLEN TRAIL
Duwee Falls
Mazama Village
ANNIE CREEK CANYON TRAIL
Sun Cr.
Arant Point 6,800 ft
Crater Pk. 7,263 ft
ROGUE RIVER NATIONAL FOREST
Union Peak 7,709 ft
62
PUMICE FLAT
Scoria Cone 6,648 ft
Annie Creek
Baldtop 6,200 ft
Red Blanket Creek
Stuart Falls
PACIFIC CREST N.S.T.
Goose Nest 7,249 ft
WINEMA NATIONAL FOREST
SKY LAKES WILDERNESS
Goose Egg 7,124 ft
Jerry Mountain

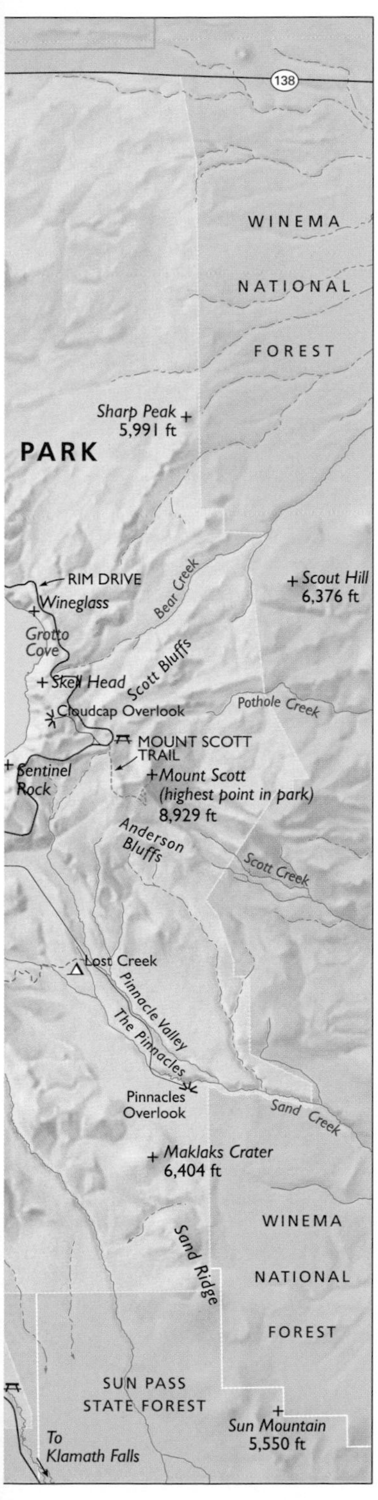

the island as the head of Llao, Chief of the Below World. Skell, Chief of the Above World, killed and dismembered Llao in the final, literally earth-shattering battle waged on the mountain. Time and weather permitting, you'll enjoy superb views in every direction if you take the moderately steep, 0.8-mile trail that leads to the fire tower on **The Watchman** (8,013 feet) south of the overlook.

Back in your car, turn away from the lake at the **Mount Thielsen Overlook** on the left. A plaque identifies the major landmarks of the countryside. When the road forks at North Junction (mile 6.1), bear right to remain on Rim Drive. (Straight, the road leads to the **North Entrance.**)

Steel Bay (mile 8.8) commemorates William Gladstone Steel, who dedicated his fortune and career to making Crater Lake a national park. Steel became fascinated by the lake when he read about it in a newspaper used to wrap his school lunch. Seventeen years of lobbying, culminating in a personal appeal to President Theodore Roosevelt, succeeded in making it the country's sixth national park in 1902. The tireless Steel stocked the lake with fish and led the efforts to build Rim Drive and the Crater Lake Lodge.

Six miles farther on, pull off the road at **Skell Head** for another excellent view of the entire lake. **Mount Scott,** highest point in the park, looms ahead as you drive on toward Cloudcap; it may have been the oldest of Mount Mazama's volcanic cones. Bear right (mile 17.4) for the short spur road to **Cloudcap,** Rim Drive's highest overlook (7,960 feet). **Phantom Ship,** an island to the southwest, consists of 400,000-year-old lava flows from the extinct Phantom cone. Dwarfed by the surrounding cliffs, it nevertheless stands 160 feet above the water.

Circle back to Rim Drive and then turn right. For a closer look at Phantom Ship, which in some lights seems to vanish and reappear, stop at **Kerr Notch** (mile 23.2), one of the U-shaped valleys carved by a glacier before Mount Mazama exploded. A road here leads to **The Pinnacles,** spires of hardened volcanic ash. Just after Kerr Notch, bear right to stay on Rim Drive.

At mile 31.2 you can stretch your legs on the **Castle Crest Wildflower Trail.** This fragrant half-mile loop begins in a forest of mountain hemlock and red fir, then enters a meadow run riot with flowers, many of them identified by plaques. Watch your step—the wet rocks can be slippery.

From here you can either proceed back to Rim Village or, if time permits, turn left toward Oreg. 62 and, after 2.3 miles, park on the left for a final stroll on the **Godfrey Glen Trail,** an easy, 1-mile-loop accessible nature trail. The path leads through forest that developed on a flow of pumice and ash 250 feet thick. The fluted pinnacles on the walls of the gorges began as the same material, but hot gases seeped up from within the Earth and hardened these areas. They defied erosion as the creeks formed canyons.

Rabbitbrush at Cleetwood Cove

BOAT TOUR & HIKES

The mile-long **Cleetwood Trail,** which begins at the visitor center (mile 10.7), leads down to the water and the landing for the boat tour *(fee)*. The hike back up is strenuous (and there's no other way); only attempt the trail if you are in good physical condition, and take it slowly. Wear sturdy shoes and bring water, a snack, and a jacket.

The boat tour shows you the lake from a different perspective. You will see waterfalls and geological features invisible from the rim, and a ranger-guide offers a detailed account of the lake and its environs. The tour leaves every hour between 10 a.m. and 4 p.m. (July–mid-Sept., weather permitting).

If you have taken a morning boat tour, explore the island on your own. The relatively steep **Wizard Island Summit Trail** (0.9 mile one way) begins at the island's dock and winds through mountain hemlock, Shasta red fir, and wildflowers to the crater at the top. Awaiting you are superb views of bleached, contorted white-bark pines against the blue water, as well as a wonderful panorama of the inside of the 90-foot-deep caldera.

Another good park hike on which to stretch your legs is the **Annie Creek Canyon Trail,** a 1.7-mile self-guided loop that winds through beds of wildflowers to the bottom of a deep, stream-cut canyon and back. It begins behind the amphitheater at the Mazama Campground.

The **Mount Scott Trail,** considered by many to be the park's most spectacular, starts on the left side of Rim Drive just after mile 17, 14 miles east of park headquarters. It ascends 2.5 miles to the park's highest point, offering panoramic views of Crater Lake, as well as over the east side of the park and Klamath Basin. On this trail you might see falcons, hawks, and eagles, particularly in fall.

INFORMATION & ACTIVITIES

HEADQUARTERS
P.O. Box 7, Crater Lake, OR 97604. Phone (541) 594-3000. www.nps.gov/crla

SEASONS & ACCESSIBILITY
South Entrance open year-round. North Entrance open mid-June to mid-October, weather permitting. East side of Rim Drive, from Cleetwood Cove to park headquarters, may remain closed by snow until mid-July. Call (541) 594-3000 for weather information.

VISITOR & INFORMATION CENTERS
Rim Village Visitor Center, on rim overlooking the lake, 7 miles off Oreg. 62, open daily from early June to mid-Sept. Closed rest of year.
Steel Center, located at park headquarters, open daily all year.

ENTRANCE FEE
$10 per car per week; $20 annual.

PETS
Pets must be leashed at all times and are not permitted on the trails.

FACILITIES FOR DISABLED
Most viewpoints are accessible to wheelchairs, as are the visitor centers, Mazama Campground, the cafeteria and gift shop at Rim Village, the Crater Lake Lodge, and the 1-mile Godfrey Glen Trail.

THINGS TO DO
Free naturalist-led activities: nature walks, children's programs, campfire programs. Fees for the ranger-narrated boat tours (adults $23.50, children $14). Also available, hiking, bicycling, fishing, snowshoeing, and cross-country skiing.

SPECIAL ADVISORY
• Hiking inside the caldera rim permitted only on the Cleetwood Trail. Volcanic rock and soil are unstable and dangerous to climb on.

OVERNIGHT BACKPACKING
Permits required. They are free and can be obtained at the Steel Information Center, the Rim Village Visitor Center, and on the Pacific Crest Trail where it enters the park.

CAMPGROUNDS
Two campgrounds, both with 14-day limit. **Lost Creek** open mid-July to late September. **Mazama** open late-June to mid-October. Both first come, first served. Fees $10-$18 per night. Showers at Mazama Village. Both tent and RV sites at Mazama; some hookups available. Tent sites only at Lost Creek. Food services at Rim Village.

HOTELS, MOTELS, & INNS
(unless otherwise noted, rates are for 2 persons in a double room, high season)

INSIDE THE PARK:

Rim Village/Crater Lake Lodge 1211 Ave. C, White City, OR 97503. (541) 830-8700. 71 units. $129-$248. Restaurant. Late May to mid-Oct.
Mazama Village Motor Inn (541) 830-8700. 40 units. $110. Early June to mid-Oct.

OUTSIDE THE PARK:

In Chiloquin, OR 97624:

Melita's Motel 39500 Hwy. 97. (541) 783-2401. 14 units. $42-$58. 20 RV hookups. $21.50. AC, restaurant.
Spring Creek Ranch Motel 47600 Hwy. 97 N. (541) 783-2775. 10 units, 7 with kitchens. $50-$75.
Rapids Motel 33551 Hwy. 97 N. (541) 783-2271. 10 units. $47-$52. Rest.

In Diamond Lake, OR 97731:

Diamond Lake Resort 350 Resort Dr. (541) 793-3333. 92 units, 42 with kitchenettes. Rooms $80; cabins $165-$195; studios $90.

In Prospect, OR 97536:

Union Creek Resort 56484 Hwy. 62. (541) 560-3565. 21 cabins, 17 with kitchenettes; 9 rooms with shared baths. Cabins $65-$180; rooms $45-$55. Restaurant.

Ask the park for a complete list of accommodations within a 1-hour drive, or contact the Klamath County Great Basin Visitor Association, 507 Main St., Klamath Falls, OR. (800) 445-6728 or (541) 882-1501. Or visit www.greatbasinvisitor.info.

EXCURSIONS

ROGUE RIVER NATIONAL FOREST

MEDFORD, OREGON

Sugar pines and Douglas firs cloak the western Cascades where the Rogue River emerges from underground lava tubes. The forest contains six wilderness areas, numerous lakes, and a stretch of the Pacific Crest Trail. 1.8 million acres, part in California. Hiking, boating, fishing, horseback riding, hunting, scenic drives, winter and water sports. 815 campsites, food services, boat ramp, picnic areas. Open all year; most campsites open May through September. In two sections; one adjoins Crater Lake NP on west and south, with entrance at Prospect on Oreg. 62. Reach other section by following I-5 south of Ashland, about 85 miles from Crater Lake NP. (541) 858-2200.

OREGON CAVES NATIONAL MONUMENT

CAVE JUNCTION, OREGON

Guided tours take visitors through the "Marble Halls of Oregon," chambers and corridors formed by groundwater dissolving marble bedrock. 480 acres. Hiking. National Historic Landmark chateau (23 rooms, May–Oct.), food services, picnic areas. Open mid-March through November. East on Oreg. 46 from Cave Junction, about 150 miles from Crater Lake NP. (541) 592-2100.

LAVA BEDS NATIONAL MONUMENT

TULELAKE, CALIFORNIA

Myriad lava-tube caves and cinder cones mark this rugged terrain where prehistoric Indians left glyphs on the soft rock. Excellent spring and fall bird-watching. 46,560 acres. Hiking, summer tours, battle sites. 41 campsites, picnic areas. Open year-round. Headquarters 30 miles south of Tulelake (26 miles off Calif. 139), about 120 miles south of Crater Lake NP. (530) 667-2282.

OREGON DUNES NATIONAL RECREATION AREA
REEDSPORT, OREGON

Forty-seven miles of towering dunes—some as high as 400 feet—stretch along the Pacific coast, inviting visitors to explore. Half of area open to off-road vehicles. The 426 wildlife species include black bear, black-tailed deer, and tundra swan. 32,000 acres. 13 hiking trails, boating, fishing, horseback riding, swimming. 13 campgrounds, picnic areas, handicapped access. Open all year. Headquarters at Reedsport on US 101, about 200 miles west of Crater Lake NP. (541) 271-3611.

KLAMATH BASIN NATIONAL WILDLIFE REFUGES
TULELAKE, CALIFORNIA

These six refuges protect diverse habitats—marsh, open water, meadows, croplands, coniferous forest, sagebrush and juniper uplands, rocky slopes—and numerous waterfowl. The basin also provides a home for the largest wintering bald eagle population in the lower 48 states. Bicycling, hiking, boating, fishing, hunting. Open all year, dawn to dusk, except Bear Valley (closed Nov. through April to protect eagles) and Clear Lake (closed spring and summer). In Oregon: Klamath Marsh, 40,885 acres; Upper Klamath, 14,966 acres; Bear Valley, 4,120 acres; Lower Klamath, 50,912 acres (part in Calif.). In California: Tule Lake, 39,116 acres; Clear Lake, 24,123 acres. Visitor Center near Tule Lake off Calif. 139, about 100 miles from Crater Lake NP. (530) 667-2231.

Dersch Meadows, Lassen Volcanic National Park

LASSEN VOLCANIC

CALIFORNIA

ESTABLISHED AUGUST 9, 1916

106,372 acres

On June 14, 1914, three men climbed Lassen Peak to see why a seemingly dormant volcano had started rumbling 16 days before. Now, peering into a newborn crater, they felt the ground tremble. As they turned and ran down the steep slope, the mountain erupted. Rocks hurtled through the ash-filled air. One struck a man, knocking him out. Ashes rained down on the men. They seemed doomed. But the eruption stopped as suddenly as it had begun, and the three men survived.

From 1914 to early 1915, Lassen spewed steam and ashes in more than 150 eruptions. Finally, on May 19, 1915, the mountaintop exploded. Lava crashed through the 1914 crater. A 20-foot-high wall of mud, ash, and melted snow roared down the mountain, snapping tree trunks. Three days later, a huge mass of ashes and gases shot out of the volcano, devastating a swath a mile wide and 3 miles long. Above the havoc a cloud of volcanic steam and ash rose 30,000 feet.

Eruptions of steam, ash, and tephra continued until June 1917, when the volcano resumed its quiet profile, with minor steam clouds occasionally reported. Since 1921 Lassen Peak has remained quiet.

But it is still considered an active volcano, the centerpiece of a vast panorama, where volcanism displays its spectaculars—wrecked mountains, devastated land, bubbling cauldrons of mud. Until Mount St. Helens blew in 1980, Lassen's eruption was the most recent volcanic explosion in the lower 48 states. Ecologists now study Lassen's landscape to see what the future may bring to the terrain around St. Helens.

How to Get There

From Redding (about 45 miles away), take Calif. 44 east then Calif. 89 south to Manzanita Lake Entrance; from Red Bluff, follow Calif. 36 east to Mineral, turn north on Calif. 89 to Southwest Entrance. The three other entrances—at Warner Valley, Butte Lake, and Juniper Lake—are reached via unpaved roads. Airports: Redding and Chico, California; Reno, Nevada.

When to Go

The volcanic areas are best visited in summer and fall. Heavy snows close most of the main road in winter. But small sections at the southern and northern ends remain open for snowshoe hikes and cross-country skiing.

How to Visit

On a 1-day visit, drive the **main park road,** linking Calif. 89. The road, snaking across the western side of the park between the Southwest and Manzanita Lake Entrances, takes you near the major volcanic features. Explore **Bumpass Hell** and other sites along the way. If you can stay longer, climb **Cinder Cone,** an outstanding example of the results of volcanism, and, if you have the stamina for a more demanding trek, try **Lassen Peak.**

PARK ROAD & BUMPASS HELL TRAIL

30 miles; a half to full day

If you start at the Southwest Entrance, your first stop on this twisting, climbing road will be the **Sulphur Works.** You walk through sulphur fumes and see hissing fumaroles, sputtering mud, and gurgling clay tinted in pastels by minerals. Here was the heart of ancestral Mount Tehama. The peaks around you once formed part of Tehama's rim, created by lava oozing from the inner Earth 600,000 to 200,000 years ago. Layer by layer, the lava built a mountain 11,500 feet high and 11 miles across.

Tehama gave birth to small volcanoes that emerged on its flanks. Repeated eruptions weakened the structure of the volcano, which collapsed, leaving behind a bowl-like caldera. Glaciers later scoured the caldera, wiping out the last remains of Tehama. **Lassen Peak,** born at least 27,000 years ago, was one of Tehama's offspring.

At **Bumpass Hell,** the road's next major stop, note a large balanced rock at the edge of the parking lot; it's a glacial erratic—a polished, glacier-borne boulder. The fairly easy 3-mile **Bumpass Hell Trail** takes about 3 hours. Go on it if you have time. The place is named after K.V. Bumpass, a local guide and promoter who, in the 1860s, plunged a leg through the thin crust covering a seething mud pot. Though badly burned, he wisecracked about his easy descent into hell.

As you walk along, you'll note (and smell) sulphurous vapors drifting over parts of the trail, which leads down to a railed boardwalk that winds past roiling mud pots, rumbling fumaroles, and hissing boiling springs. At the springs' steamy pools

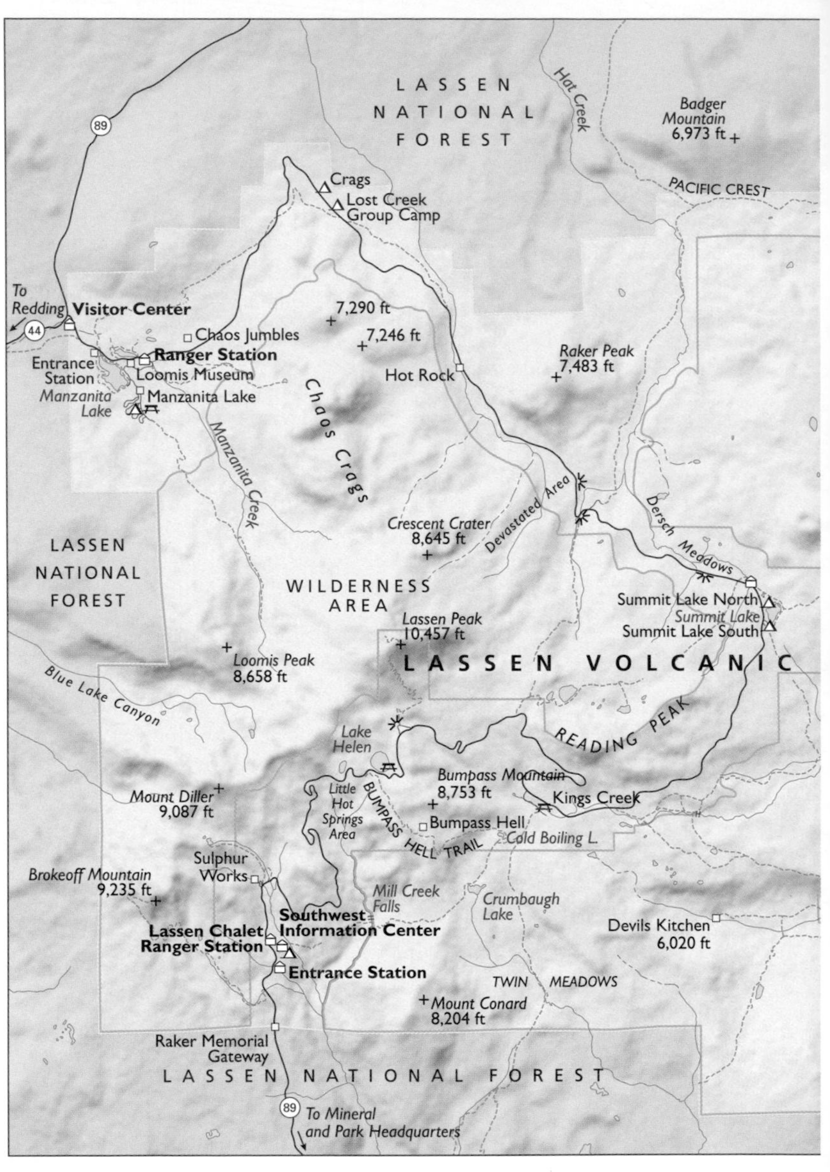

look for floating golden flakes. They are crystals of iron pyrite—fool's gold—carried along in the superheated steam.

Resume driving on the road, which curves around Lassen Peak. Continue to the **Devastated Area,** wrecked by the massive May 1915 eruption. Amid the scarred and fallen trees you will notice the signs of renewal: Young trees and stubborn grasses are growing in a slow, natural comeback unaided by human hand. The road offers many turnoffs for viewing the crags and canyons that are Lassen's volcanic heritage.

You'll pass churned-up landscape dubbed **Chaos Crags** and **Chaos Jumbles;** if space along the road permits, stop and walk around it. Here, about 300 years ago, a nearby

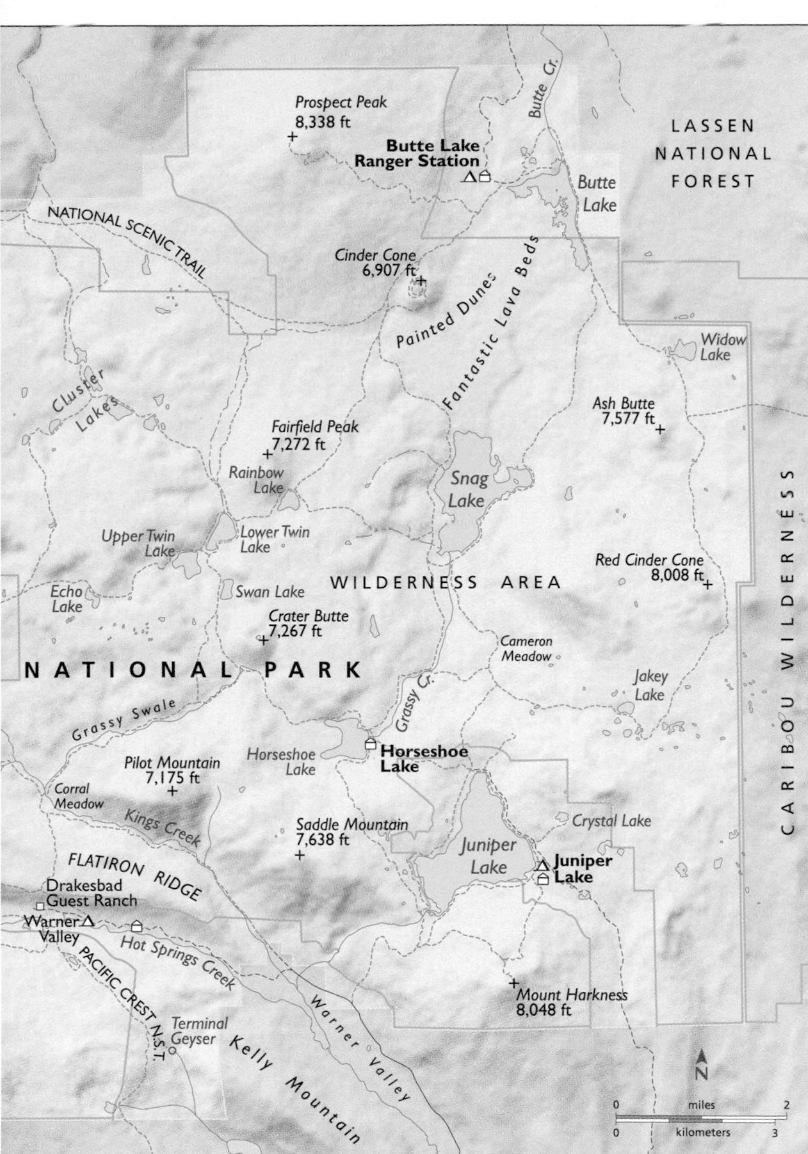

volcanic dome suddenly collapsed, perhaps because of an earth tremor. Millions of tons of rock, riding a cushion of trapped air, sped across 2 miles of flat land. The horizontal avalanche smashed into a mountain and veered into a creek, damming it and forming **Manzanita Lake.**

Just beyond, the road ends its course through the park and enters Lassen National Forest.

CINDER CONE NATURE TRAIL

31-mile drive, 5-mile hike; a full day

The trail begins at the Butte Lake Campground, reached via Calif. 44 and a marked dirt road. **Cinder Cone,** a nearly symmetrical, 755-foot-high mound of lava surrounded by multi-colored cinders—light lava that

INFORMATION & ACTIVITIES

HEADQUARTERS

P.O. Box 100, Mineral, CA 96063. Phone (530) 595-4444. www.nps.gov/lavo

SEASONS & ACCESSIBILITY

Park and both its entrances open year-round. The main park road can be closed by snow from late October to late June. For road conditions in the park, phone (530) 595-4444 or check the park website.

VISITOR & INFORMATION CENTERS

Loomis Museum at **Manzanita Lake** is open daily from mid-June to about Labor Day. Contact the park headquarters for current information.

ENTRANCE FEE

$10 per car; good for 7 days. Those entering on foot or by bicycle pay $5 for 7 days.

FACILITIES FOR DISABLED

Park headquarters, Loomis Museum, some restrooms, the Devastated Area Interpretive Trail, and some picnic areas are wheelchair accessible.

THINGS TO DO

Among the free ranger-led activities are nature walks and hikes, talks, nature and geology demonstrations, children's programs, evening programs, and snowshoe walks. Other activities include hiking, swimming, fishing, boating (no motors), and cross-country skiing.

OVERNIGHT BACKPACKING

Wilderness permits required. They are free and can be obtained at headquarters, visitor center and Butte Lake, Warner Valley, and Juniper Lake trailheads. No wood fires permitted.

CAMPGROUNDS

Eight campgrounds, **Summit Lake-North** and **Summit Lake-South** have a 7-day limit; all others have a 14-day limit. Most sites open late May through Sept., weather permitting. First come, first served. Fees $10-$14 per night. Showers are available at **Manzanita Lake.** Roads to Warner Valley and Juniper Lake not recommended for RVs. Three group campgrounds; reservations required (go to www.ReserveUSA.com or call 877-444-6777). Food services in park.

HOTELS, MOTELS, & INNS

(unless otherwise noted, rates are for 2 persons in a double room, high season)

INSIDE THE PARK:

Drakesbad Guest Ranch (47 miles southeast of headquarters) Chester, CA 96020. Call (530) 529-1512 and leave a

shattered in the air and fell back down—stands black and solitary above a pine forest. Don't expect to hurry on the trail, a round-trip of about 5 miles. Walking on loose cinders is like walking through sand: Your feet sink with every step. At the top (6,907 feet), you will see the craters of recent eruptions; the last was in the mid-1600s.

LASSEN PEAK TRAIL

5 miles round-trip; a half to full day

This steep, zigzagging trail begins at 8,463 feet, near the park road, and takes you to the 10,457-foot summit. The going can get tough for people used to breathing at sea level. Before you try the climb, acclimatize to the park's high elevations. Carry water, wear a hat, and take a jacket. Turn back if a storm threatens; the peak is a lightning attractor. Lassen has scant vegetation. But you can almost always spot a ground squirrel. And sometimes thousands of tortoiseshell butterflies suddenly flit by, their shadows cascading along the grayish volcanic rocks. At the summit, you can see the hardened vestige of the 1915 lava flow. And visible on a clear day, 75 miles away, is Mount Shasta.

message; or call long-distance operator and ask for Drakesbad #2 in the 530 area code. 6 lodge rooms, 4 cabins. $134. 6 bungalows. $153. All meals included. Pool. Open June to early Oct.

OUTSIDE THE PARK:
In Mineral, CA 96063:
Lassen Mineral Lodge (on Calif. 36E, 8 miles from park gate) P.O. Box 160. (530) 595-4422. 20 units, 2 with kitchenettes. $75. Restaurant.
In Redding, CA 96002:
Best Western Hilltop Inn 2300 Hilltop Dr. (800) 336-4880 or (530) 221-6100. 115 units. $149. AC, pool, restaurant.
Comfort Inn 2059 Hilltop Dr. (800) 228-5150 or (530) 221-6530. 90 units. $85-$95. AC, pool.
Red Lion Hotel 1830 Hilltop Dr. (800) 547-8010 or (530) 221-8700. 192 units. $104-$134. AC, pool, restaurant.
Vagabond Inn 536 E. Cypress Ave. (800) 522-1555 or (530) 223-1600. 71 units. $80. AC, pool, restaurant.

For more information on area accommodations, contact the park or the Redding Chamber of Commerce, 747 Auditorium Dr., Redding, CA 96001. (530) 225-4433.

EXCURSIONS

LASSEN NATIONAL FOREST
SUSANVILLE, CALIFORNIA

Volcanic features dot this mountain forest surrounding Lassen Volcanic National Park. Also contains many lakes and streams. One million acres. Hiking, boating, fishing, horseback riding, hunting, winter sports, water sports.More than 40 campgrounds, boat ramp, picnic areas, handicapped access. Open year-round; most campsites open from mid-May to mid-October. Information at Chester on Calif. 36, about 40 miles from Lassen Volcanic NP. (530) 258-2141.

WHISKEYTOWN-SHASTA-TRINITY NATIONAL RECREATION AREA
WHISKEYTOWN, CALIFORNIA

Here in Gold Rush country, three impounded lakes provide unlimited opportunities for recreation on, in, and around water. Backcountry hiking and recreational gold panning also featured. 217,823 acres. Hiking, boating, fishing, horseback riding, mountain biking, scenic drives, water sports. 693 campsites, cabins, boat ramp, food services, handicapped access. Open year-round. Whiskeytown headquarters on Calif. 299, off I-5, about 60 miles west of Lassen Volcanic NP. (530) 242-3400. For Shasta and Trinity units call (530) 226-2500.

Mount Rainier, known to Indians as Tahoma—"the great mountain"

MOUNT RAINIER

WASHINGTON
ESTABLISHED MARCH 2, 1899
235,625 acres

One of the world's most massive volcanoes, Mount Rainier can dominate the skyline for 100 miles before you reach the park named after it. At nearly 3 miles in height, Mount Rainier is the tallest peak in the Cascade Range; it dwarfs 6,000-foot surrounding summits, appearing to float alone among the clouds.

Mount Rainier may be the centerpiece of the national park, but it is hardly the only attraction. Here, less than 3 hours' drive from Seattle, you can stroll through seemingly endless fields of wildflowers, listen for cracking glacier debris, wander among trees nearly a thousand years old. The park's convenient location, however, also leads to weekend traffic jams, both summer and winter, and guarantees you company on popular trails.

Mount Rainier is the offspring of fire and ice. Still active, it was probably born more than a half million years ago, on a base of lava spewed out by previous volcanoes. Lava and ash surged out of the young volcano's vent thousands of times, filling the neighboring canyons and building up a summit cone, layer by layer, to a height of some 16,000 feet.

Even while Mount Rainier was growing, glaciers carved valleys on and around the mountain. The 25 major glaciers here form the largest collection of permanent ice on a single U.S. peak south of Alaska.

Mount Rainier's summit deteriorated over time, but eruptions in the last 2,000 years rebuilt it to its current height of 14,411 feet. The mountain last erupted about a century ago.

How to Get There

From Seattle (95 miles) or Tacoma (70 miles) to the Nisqually Entrance (open year-round), take I-5 to Wash. 7, then follow Wash. 706. From Yakima, take Wash. 12 west to Wash. 123 or Wash. 410, and enter from the park's east side (Stevens Canyon or White River Entrances closed in winter). For the northwest entrances (Carbon River and Mowich Lake), take Wash. 410 to Wash. 169 to Wash. 165, then follow the signs. Carbon River Road is subject to flooding in all seasons and may close at any time. Contact the park. Airports: Seattle, Washington, and Portland, Oregon.

When to Go

Year-round. Wildflowers are at their best in July and August. High trails may remain snow covered until mid-July. Cross-country skiing and snowshoeing are popular in winter. Summer and winter, to miss the crowds, time your visit to midweek.

How to Visit (Summer)

If you have only a day, drive from the **Nisqually Entrance** in the southwest to the flowered fields of **Paradise,** then on to **Sunrise,** the highest point accessible by car, open early July to early October. If you have 2 days, take the same route but do it more leisurely: Plan to explore as far as Paradise the first day, then tour **Stevens Canyon Road** and the route to Sunrise the next; arrive before 10 a.m. to catch the early light and wend your way back.

For a longer stay, drive out and re-enter the less known northwest corner at **Carbon River** for a look at a rain forest and a hike to a dark, shiny glacier. Because Mount Rainier creates its own clouds and can hide for days or weeks at a time, come prepared to focus on delights close at hand: waterfalls, woods, and wildflowers.

NISQUALLY TO PARADISE

19 miles; a half to full day

The pilgrimage to Paradise has been a classic for nearly a century. The first miles of your tour wind through a forest of giant Douglas fir, western red cedar, and western hemlock. As you cross **Kautz Creek,** about 3 miles from the Nisqually Entrance, look for flood debris and dead trees amid the recovering forest. In 1947 the **Kautz Glacier** disgorged a flash flood of meltwater. The flood raged down the creek valley, carrying volcanic debris, trees, and boulders, and burying the road under 50 feet of mud. Similar, though mostly smaller, mudflows occur at least every few years at Mount Rainier.

Park at **Longmire Museum,** 7 miles from the entrance. Pioneer James Longmire discovered mineral springs here in 1883 and built Mount Rainier's first hotel; his ads for miraculous water cures helped generate early tourism and a constituency for the creation of the park. Take time for the easy half-mile **Trail of the Shadows** that starts on the opposite side of the main road. While in Longmire, also visit the **Wilderness Information Center,**

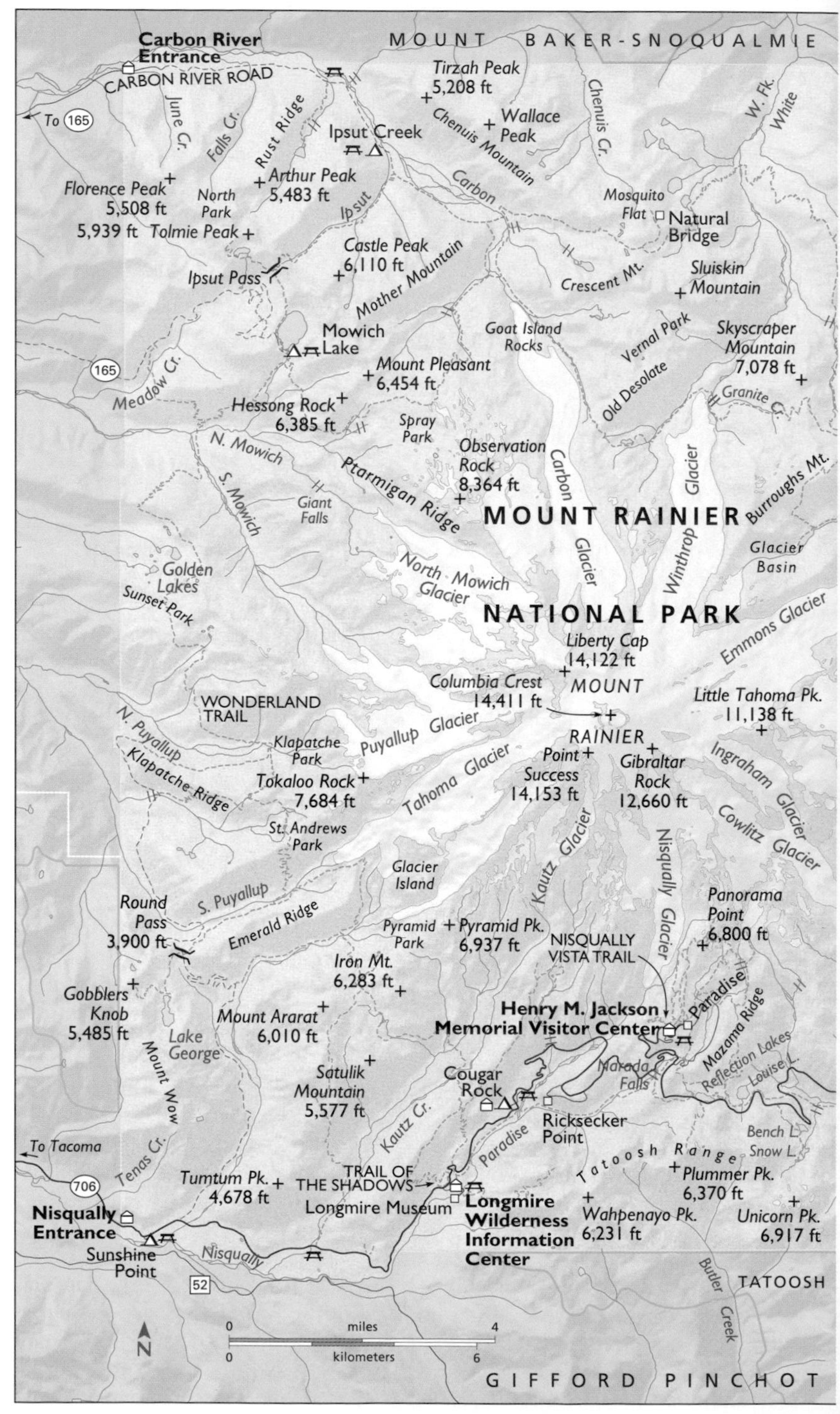
MOUNT BAKER-SNOQUALMIE
Carbon River Entrance
CARBON RIVER ROAD
To 165
Tirzah Peak 5,208 ft
Wallace Peak
Chenuis Mountain
Ipsut Creek
Florence Peak 5,508 ft
Arthur Peak 5,483 ft
North Park
5,939 ft Tolmie Peak
Mosquito Flat
Natural Bridge
Castle Peak 6,110 ft
Ipsut Pass
Mother Mountain
Crescent Mt.
Sluiskin Mountain
Mowich Lake
Goat Island Rocks
Vernal Park
Skyscraper Mountain 7,078 ft
165
Mount Pleasant 6,454 ft
Old Desolate
Hessong Rock 6,385 ft
Spray Park
Observation Rock 8,364 ft
Giant Falls
Ptarmigan Ridge
MOUNT RAINIER
NATIONAL PARK
Golden Lakes
Sunset Park
North Mowich Glacier
Carbon Glacier
Winthrop Glacier
Glacier Basin
Emmons Glacier
Liberty Cap 14,122 ft
Columbia Crest 14,411 ft
MOUNT RAINIER
Little Tahoma Pk. 11,138 ft
WONDERLAND TRAIL
Klapatche Park
Puyallup Glacier
Tahoma Glacier
Point Success 14,153 ft
Gibraltar Rock 12,660 ft
Ingraham Glacier
Cowlitz Glacier
Klapatche Ridge
Tokaloo Rock 7,684 ft
St. Andrews Park
Kautz Glacier
Nisqually Glacier
Glacier Island
Round Pass 3,900 ft
Emerald Ridge
Pyramid Park
Pyramid Pk. 6,937 ft
NISQUALLY VISTA TRAIL
Panorama Point 6,800 ft
Iron Mt. 6,283 ft
Gobblers Knob 5,485 ft
Mount Ararat 6,010 ft
Henry M. Jackson Memorial Visitor Center
Paradise
Mazama Ridge
Lake George
Mount Wow
Satulik Mountain 5,577 ft
Cougar Rock
Narada Falls
Reflection Lakes
Louise L.
Ricksecker Point
To Tacoma
Tenas Cr.
Kautz Cr.
Tatoosh Range
Bench L.
Snow L.
706
Tumtum Pk. 4,678 ft
TRAIL OF THE SHADOWS
Longmire Museum
Longmire Wilderness Information Center
Plummer Pk. 6,370 ft
Wahpenayo Pk. 6,231 ft
Unicorn Pk. 6,917 ft
Nisqually Entrance
Sunshine Point
Nisqually
52
Butler Creek
TATOOSH
N
0 miles 4
0 kilometers 6
GIFFORD PINCHOT

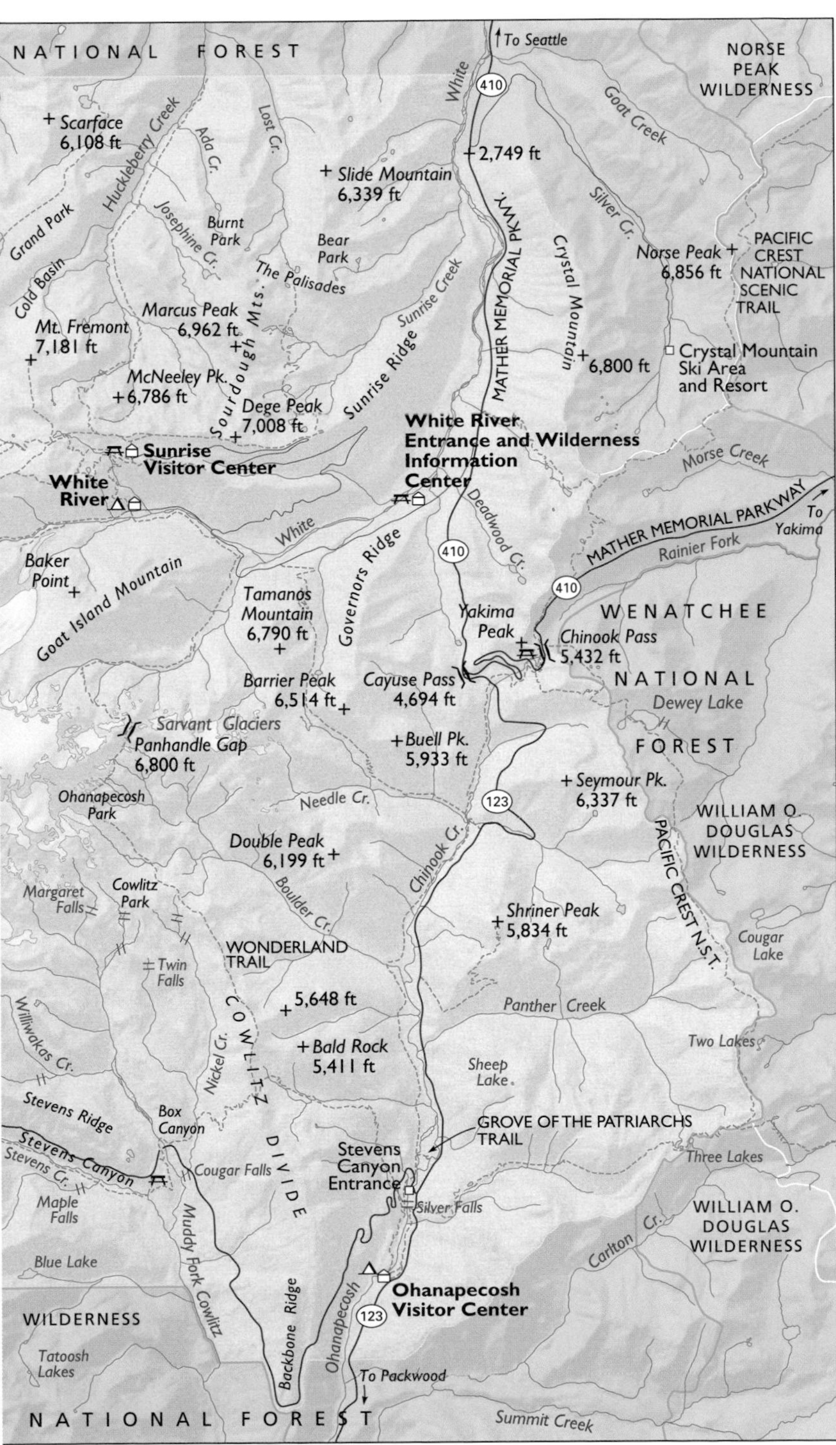

MOUNT RAINIER

Camping on 4-mile-long Nisqually Glacier

closed between October and late April, for trail and weather information and backcountry permits.

Back in your car, continue east for about 6.5 miles, then take the spur road to the right to **Ricksecker Point.** To the south loom the saw-toothed peaks of the **Tatoosh Range,** dramatic remains of lava flows that predated Mount Rainier by some 25 to 35 million years. Glaciers that developed and receded during the last million years carved the sharp pinnacles and the steep-sided mountainside hollows called cirques. Below meanders the **Nisqually River,** which originates at the snout of the **Nisqually Glacier,** which faces you on Mount Rainier. This glacier is about 4 miles long and flows downhill 6 to 12 inches every summer's day.

Rejoin the highway. Another 1.5 miles brings you to the **Narada Falls** parking area. The shimmering, 168-foot plunge of the **Paradise River** is well worth the steep but short walk down to the viewing area below the bridge. Climb back up to your car and proceed; in less than 3 miles you'll reach the most popular part of the park.

"It looks just like paradise!" exclaimed Martha Longmire in 1885 on first sighting the rolling hills swathed in wildflowers and framed by Mount Rainier's white dome. An average of 140 inches of precipitation falls here each year; as many as 40 species of flowers bloom on the thin, volcanic soil during July and August. Park near the **Henry M. Jackson Memorial Visitor Center,** or the **Paradise Inn,** built in 1916.

Begin your exploration of Paradise meadows on the **Nisqually Vista Trail** (1.2 miles), especially if time is short. This easy, self-guided nature walk starts at the staircase to the west of the visitor center. Its booklet acquaints you with the geology and meadow life of Mount Rainier.

Make sure you stay on the path, no matter how tempting a meadow stroll. Trampling by just a few people can kill these fragile plants. The park is still at work replanting old trails and other damaged areas. Only recently have the meadows recovered from the Camp of the Clouds, a tent city in operation here from 1898 to 1915.

If you're up to tackling some steep hills, try the 5-mile **Skyline Trail.** Start from the staircase west of the visitor center. The trail will take you to **Panorama Point** for some spectacular views.

PARADISE TO SUNRISE

45 miles; a half to full day

Leaving Paradise, turn left at the sign for **Sunrise** and Yakima. You'll soon pass the glacier-carved **Reflection Lakes** on your left; on a calm morning, the reflection looks as solid as the mountain. Continue a mile past the lakes' pullover and park on the right for a 2.5-mile, hilly, round-trip walk to **Snow** and **Bench Lakes,** gems surrounded by the steep headwalls of the Tatoosh Range.

Drive on and stop after about 3 miles at an overlook of **Stevens Canyon.** Huge glaciers grating through this river gorge deepened and widened it into a classic U-shaped valley. Tributaries of **Stevens Creek** spill from the canyon's rim as waterfalls. Drive on another 3 miles, to **Box Canyon** (just past the picnic area). Park and cross the street for the nearly level half-mile **Canyon Stroll** and you'll see a 100-foot-deep gorge whose straight walls were carved by the **Muddy Fork** of the **Cowlitz River.**

Continue another 9.5 miles, then park to walk the **Grove of the Patriarchs** nature trail. This easy 1.3-mile loop leads to an island in the **Ohanapecosh River** dominated by grand Douglas firs, western red cedars, and western hemlocks, many of them 500 to 1,000 years old. After rejoining the road, turn left on Wash. 123 for Sunrise. If time allows, take a short detour south on Wash. 123 to visit the **Ohanapecosh Visitor Center.**

At **Cayuse Pass,** continue north on Wash. 410, then make a sharp left toward the **White River Entrance.** The road ends at **Sunrise.** Spire-shaped subalpine fir and whitebark pine grow here. Near tree line, harsh temperatures and winds stunt the trees into twisted shrubs called krummholz, or elfin timber; trees only inches in diameter may be 250 years old. Fragile wildflowers bloom among grass and sedge in terrain inhospitable to trees.

Marmot dining on lupine *(top)*
Northern saw-whet owl *(bottom)*

Narada Falls in summer

At the visitor center, ask about snow conditions on the higher trails. If time is short, take the self-guided **Sourdough Ridge Nature Trail** for 1.5 miles, then the **Emmons Vista Trail** for half a mile. The Sourdough Ridge trail, which starts with a climb, introduces you to the plants and animals of the subalpine region. The former flourish in this fertile but fragile volcanic soil. The Emmons Vista Trail offers an easy way to view **Emmons Glacier,** Mount Rainier's largest, covering more than 4 square miles.

If you have more time and energy, and the snow has melted *(snow on the slopes can be dangerous if you're not equipped with an ice ax and trained to use it),* take the **Burroughs Mountain Trail** (5 miles to **First Burroughs,** or 6 miles to **Second Burroughs**). Begin as you did for the Sourdough Ridge Nature Trail, but turn left about half way up the hill and follow the signs. The trail soon enters tundra. Compact little plants sport exquisite lilliputian blossoms and leaves that are a dull gray from the tiny hairs that protect them against drying winds. *It is most important that you stay on the trail:* If trod on, these delicate plants can take decades to heal.

At Second Burroughs it feels as if you could almost touch Mount Rainier's imposing peak. Return to your car by way of the **Sunrise Rim Trail.**

THE NORTHWEST CORNER: CARBON RIVER

5 miles inside park boundary; a half day

Note: The Carbon River is subject to flooding. Call the park's visitor center for status before attempting this drive.

To get a feel for a rare inland temperate rain forest and for the opportunity to peer at a glacier, take the **Carbon River Road** (it forks left off Wash. 165 about 6 miles past Wilkeson). Unpaved inside the park, the road may be passable for ordinary cars. Stop at the entrance to take the quarter-mile self-guided **Carbon River Rain Forest Trail** loop among colossal Sitka spruces, Douglas firs, and western red cedars. If the road is passable, drive to the parking lot at Ipsut Creek Campground. If you are game for a 6-mile round-trip hike with a short, moderately steep climb, take the **Carbon Glacier Trail.** Bear right at the first fork, left at the second, then cross the swinging bridge over Carbon River and continue on to the glistening glacier. *Don't get close:* Boulders continually tumble off the glacier's snout.

Clockwise from top: Giant red paintbrush and daisies along Tatoosh Range, western pasqueflowers, pink mountain heather, fireweed, phlox, shooting stars, glacier lilies.

INFORMATION & ACTIVITIES

HEADQUARTERS

Tahoma Woods, Star Route, Ashford, WA 98304. Phone (360) 569-2211. www.nps.gov/mora

SEASONS & ACCESSIBILITY

Park open year-round. Many roads closed by snow from late November through May or June. Call (360) 569-2211 for recorded weather, road, and trail information, or in the Nisqually area tune in to 1610 AM.

VISITOR & INFORMATION CENTERS

Longmire Wilderness Information Center open daily mid-May through Sept.
Longmire Museum open all year.
Henry M. Jackson Memorial Visitor Center, at Paradise, open daily from early May to mid-Oct., weekends and holidays in winter.
Ohanapecosh Visitor Center, at park's southeast entrance, open daily Memorial Day to mid-Oct.
Sunrise Visitor Center open daily, mid-July to early Oct., weather dependent.

ENTRANCE FEE

$10 per car per week; $30 annual.

PETS

Permitted leashed on roads. Pets not allowed on trails or in the backcountry.

FACILITIES FOR DISABLED

Most public buildings and some restrooms are wheelchair accessible. Portions of some trails may be accessible (assistance may be needed). Inquire at park for details.

THINGS TO DO

Free naturalist-led activities: nature and history walks, hikes, campfire and children's programs, talks, films, slide shows. Also available, hiking, mountain climbing, fishing (license not needed), cross-country skiing, snowshoeing.

SPECIAL ADVISORIES

- Mount Rainier is an active volcano. While eruptions are usually preceded by an increase in earthquake activity, other hazards, such as mudflows, glacial outburst floods, or rockfalls can occur without warning.
- Watch out for falling rocks, debris, and avalanches. Look up!
- Some areas may be subject to flash floods, especially in late summer and fall. Inquire about current conditions before hiking.
- Stop by a visitor center for additional safety information.

OVERNIGHT BACKPACKING

Permit required; available from visitor centers, ranger stations, and wilderness centers, where you can also get help with your trip planning. Contact the Wilderness Information Center in care of park headquarters, or call (360) 569-2211. Make reservations through the NPRS (see p. 10).

CAMPGROUNDS

Five campgrounds, all with 14-day limit. **Sunshine Point** open all year. Others open late spring to early fall. Fees $8-$15 per night. Showers available in the visitor center at Paradise. Both tent and RV sites; no hookups. Advance reservations required at **Cougar Rock** and **Ohanapecosh** from late June to Labor Day. Call NPRS (see p. 10). All others, first come, first served. Food services in park.

HOTELS, MOTELS, & INNS

(unless otherwise noted, rates are for 2 persons in a double room, high season)

INSIDE THE PARK:

The following are operated by Mt. Rainier Guest Services, P.O. Box 108, Ashford, WA 98304. (360) 569-2275.
National Park Inn (at 2,700-foot level of Mount Rainier) 25 units, 18 with private baths. $98-$132. Restaurant.
Paradise Inn (at 5,400-foot level of Mount Rainier) 118 units, 86 with private baths. $92-$137. Restaurant. Open late May to early October.

For more information on area accommodations, contact the park's Guest Services (see above) or refer to the website.

EXCURSIONS

GIFFORD PINCHOT NATIONAL FOREST
VANCOUVER, WASHINGTON

Dense coniferous forest offers superb views of Mount St. Helens. Contains glaciers and seven wilderness areas. 1.3 million acres. Hiking, boating, climbing, fishing, horseback riding, hunting, winter sports, water sports. 65 campgrounds (30 primitive), 3 group campgrounds, picnic areas, handicapped access. Open all year; most campsites open June through October. Adjoins Mount Rainier NP on the south. Information at Randle on Wash. 12, about 10 miles from the park. (360) 891-5001.

MOUNT ST. HELENS NATIONAL VOLCANIC MONUMENT
AMBOY, WASHINGTON

This monument owes its existence to the day in May 1980 when Mount St. Helens erupted, laying waste the surrounding forest. Witness the rebirth of a forest through interpretive programs and tours. 110,000 acres. Hiking, bicycling, climbing (reservations required), fishing, scenic drives, winter sports. Picnic areas, handicapped access. Open year-round, but winter snows close many roads. Within Gifford Pinchot NF. Five visitor centers east of Castle Rock on Wash. 504. Many viewpoints and trails accessed from the north via Wash. 12 at Randle and from the south via Wash. 503 at Woodland. (360) 274-2100.

RIDGEFIELD NATIONAL WILDLIFE REFUGE
RIDGEFIELD, WASHINGTON

Established to protect the winter habitat of the dusky Canada goose, this site on the floodplain of the Columbia River provides a winter haven for many waterfowl species. It also serves as a year-round home for great blue herons and a resting spot for migrating sandhill cranes. 5,150 acres. Hiking, hunting, scenic drives. Open all year, dawn to dusk (winter best time). Off I-5, about 90 miles from Mount Rainier NP. (360) 887-4106.

Glacier-carved peaks of the North Cascades

NORTH CASCADES

WASHINGTON
ESTABLISHED OCTOBER 2, 1968
684,000 acres, includes two recreation areas

With glacier-clad peaks rising almost vertically from thickly forested valleys, the North Cascades are often called the American Alps. The national park forms two units, North and South, of the North Cascades National Park Service Complex. The two other units—Ross Lake National Recreation Area and Lake Chelan National Recreation Area—contain most visitor facilities and permit private land ownership and certain commercial activities.

The park complex preserves virgin forests, fragile subalpine meadows, and hundreds of glaciers. Mule deer and black-tailed deer graze the high meadows, where black bears gorge on berries and hoary marmots sunbathe. Mountain goats clamber on rock faces. Mountain lions and bobcats, seldom seen, help keep other wildlife populations in balance.

The wildness and ruggedness of the park especially lure hikers, backpackers, and mountaineers. “A more difficult route to travel never fell to man’s lot,” complained trapper Alexander Ross, who came here in 1814. But today the main road (through Ross Lake NRA) and easy access into the park—on some of its 360 miles of trails—also allow more casual visitors to experience the peaceful forests and the drama of the mountains.

The region forms part of the Cascade Range, named for its innumerable waterfalls. The range extends from British Columbia to northern California. A geological theory proposes that the mountains began as a micro-continent several hundred miles out in the Pacific Ocean. Over the eons a series of islands floated on their plate toward North America. About a hundred million years ago, the plate smashed into the North American continent, folding and crumpling into a mountain range as it lodged against the landmass. Those mountains eroded; the Cascades you see today rose only five or six million years ago.

The western part of the park differs markedly from the east. Moisture blows in from Puget Sound and the Strait of Juan de Fuca. It hits the western slopes and rises, condensing to rain and snow. Western red cedars, hemlocks, and Douglas firs luxuriate on slopes that receive 110 inches of precipitation a year. When the winds reach the east, they are mostly wrung dry: Only 35 inches of precipitation fall in Stehekin at the head of Lake Chelan. Arid-dwelling sagebrush and ponderosa pine grow in the peaks' rain shadow.

How to Get There

From Seattle (about 115 miles from the park), take I-5 to Wash. 20, also called the North Cascades Highway. From the east, get on Wash. 20 at Winthrop. To reach Stehekin Valley, either hike over Cascade Pass from the Cascade River Road (2-day hike) or take a 1-hour, high-speed catamaran, a slower ferry, or a chartered floatplane from Chelan, at the southern tip of Lake Chelan. Chelan is on US 97. Airports: Seattle and Bellingham.

When to Go

Summer gives the best access, though snow can block high trails into July. The North Cascades Highway, from Ross Dam to beyond Washington Pass, closes in winter. Stehekin, a year-round community, offers winter cross-country skiing.

How to Visit

On a day trip, take the **North Cascades Highway** through the **Ross Lake National Recreation Area** for an overview of the recreation area's lakes and dams, the park's mountains, and the glacier-fed **Skagit River.** If you have 2 days, drive up the unpaved **Cascade River Road** and picnic and hike among the park's peaks and alpine meadows. On a longer stay, drive south to **Chelan,** and take the ferry or fly to **Stehekin** to overnight in a serene, isolated community or in the backcountry.

CASCADES HIGHWAY: MARBLEMOUNT TO WASHINGTON PASS

60 miles; a half to full day

The ease of driving the North Cascades Highway belies the terrain's ruggedness, although names supplied by explorers and climbers attest to it: Mount Terror, Mount Despair, Damnation Peak, Mount Fury, Mount Challenger. This transmountain road was completed only in 1972.

Enter the **Ross Lake National Recreation Area** after crossing **Bacon Creek,** 6.5 miles beyond the Wilderness Information Center at Marblemount. Parallel to the road, the **Skagit River** appears emerald in summer—evidence of the park's

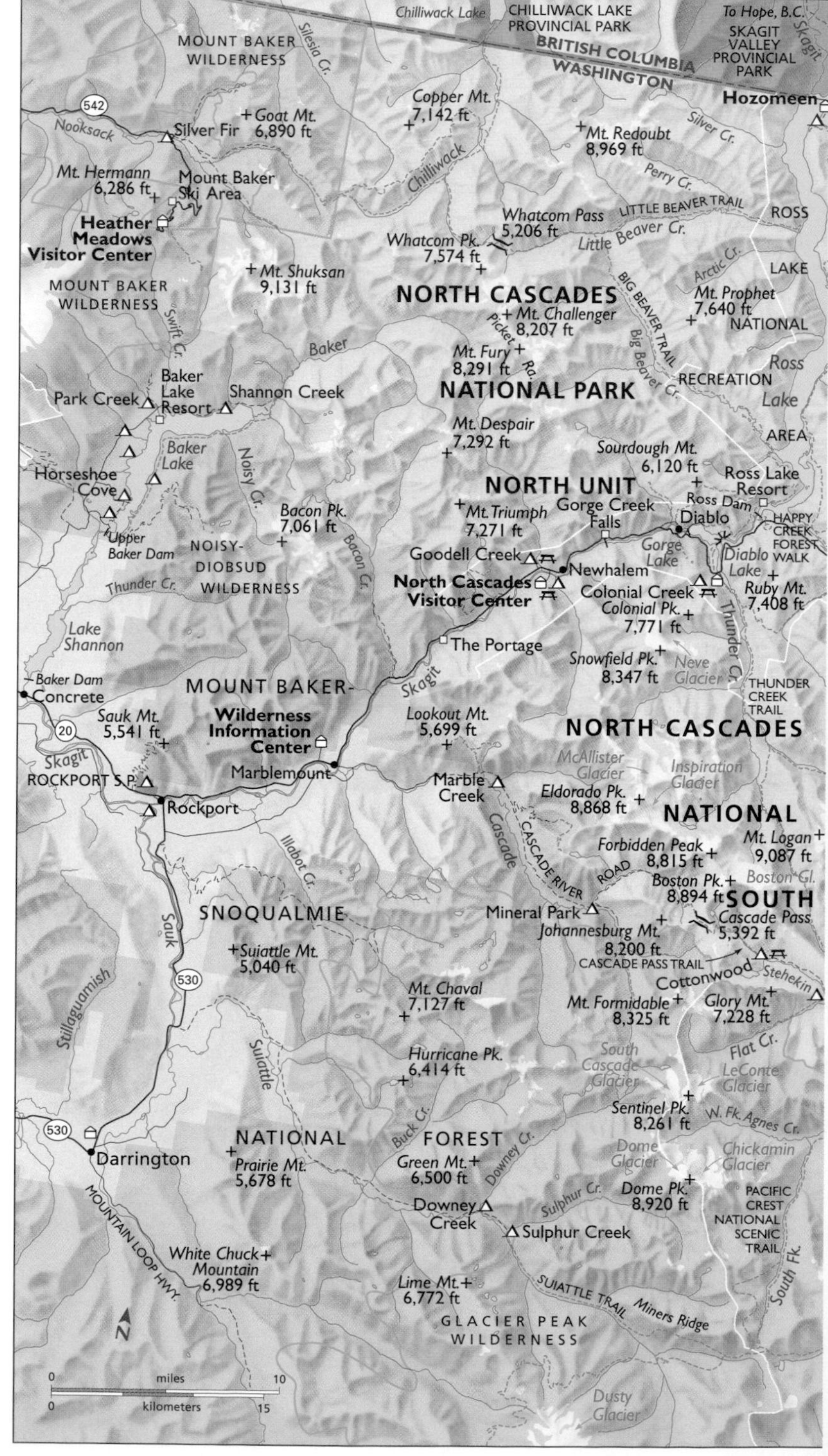

Chilliwack Lake
CHILLIWACK LAKE PROVINCIAL PARK
To Hope, B.C.
SKAGIT VALLEY PROVINCIAL PARK
BRITISH COLUMBIA
WASHINGTON
MOUNT BAKER WILDERNESS
Hozomeen
Copper Mt. 7,142 ft
Goat Mt. 6,890 ft
Silver Fir
Mt. Redoubt 8,969 ft
Mt. Hermann 6,286 ft
Mount Baker Ski Area
Heather Meadows Visitor Center
Whatcom Pass 5,206 ft
LITTLE BEAVER TRAIL
Whatcom Pk. 7,574 ft
Mt. Shuksan 9,131 ft
NORTH CASCADES
Mt. Challenger 8,207 ft
Mt. Prophet 7,640 ft
ROSS LAKE NATIONAL RECREATION AREA
BIG BEAVER TRAIL
Mt. Fury 8,291 ft
NATIONAL PARK
Baker Lake Resort
Park Creek
Shannon Creek
Horseshoe Cove
Upper Baker Dam
Mt. Despair 7,292 ft
Sourdough Mt. 6,120 ft
NORTH UNIT
Ross Lake Resort
Ross Dam
Diablo
Mt. Triumph 7,271 ft
Gorge Creek Falls
HAPPY CREEK FOREST WALK
Bacon Pk. 7,061 ft
NOISY-DIOBSUD WILDERNESS
Goodell Creek
Newhalem
North Cascades Visitor Center
Colonial Creek
Ruby Mt. 7,408 ft
Colonial Pk. 7,771 ft
Lake Shannon
The Portage
Snowfield Pk. 8,347 ft
Baker Dam
Concrete
MOUNT BAKER-
Wilderness Information Center
THUNDER CREEK TRAIL
Sauk Mt. 5,541 ft
Lookout Mt. 5,699 ft
NORTH CASCADES
ROCKPORT S.P.
Marblemount
Marble Creek
Eldorado Pk. 8,868 ft
NATIONAL
Rockport
CASCADE RIVER ROAD
Forbidden Peak 8,815 ft
Mt. Logan 9,087 ft
Boston Pk. 8,894 ft
SOUTH
SNOQUALMIE
Mineral Park
Johannesburg Mt. 8,200 ft
Cascade Pass 5,392 ft
CASCADE PASS TRAIL
Suiattle Mt. 5,040 ft
Cottonwood
Mt. Chaval 7,127 ft
Mt. Formidable 8,325 ft
Glory Mt. 7,228 ft
Hurricane Pk. 6,414 ft
Sentinel Pk. 8,261 ft
NATIONAL
FOREST
Darrington
Prairie Mt. 5,678 ft
Green Mt. 6,500 ft
Dome Pk. 8,920 ft
PACIFIC CREST NATIONAL SCENIC TRAIL
Downey Creek
Sulphur Creek
White Chuck Mountain 6,989 ft
MOUNTAIN LOOP HWY.
Lime Mt. 6,772 ft
SUIATTLE TRAIL
Miners Ridge
GLACIER PEAK WILDERNESS
Dusty Glacier
miles
kilometers

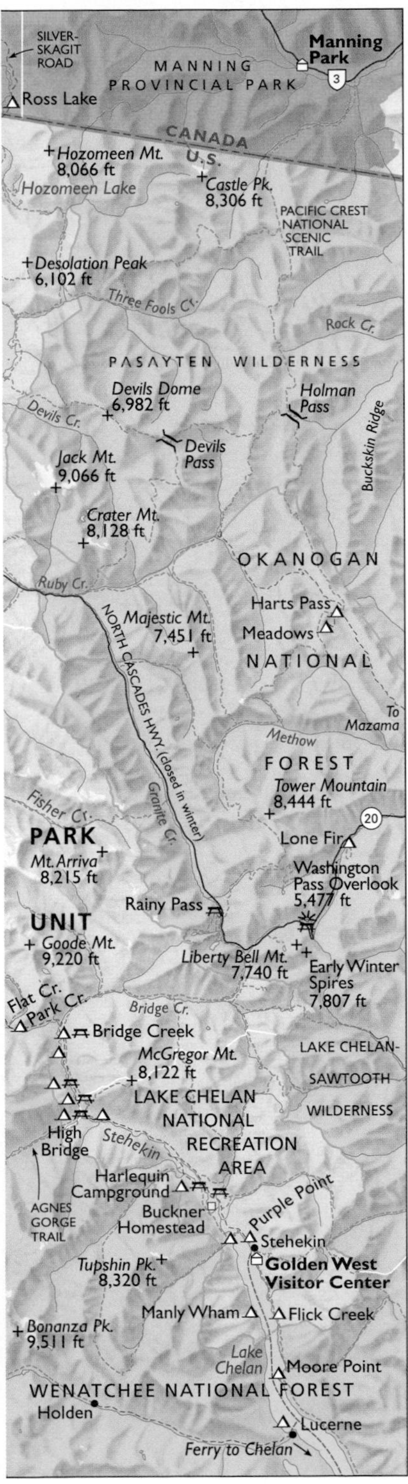

many glaciers. As they move, glaciers grind bedrock into a fine "flour." Water carrying a high concentration of glacial flour reflects the green and blue part of the light spectrum. In winter bald eagles feast on salmon running the Skagit.

At **Goodell Creek Bridge** (milepost 119), look left to catch a rare glimpse of the high, sawtoothed peaks of the **Picket Range.** Discover the natural and human history of these mountains along trails or at the **North Cascades Visitor Center.** The visitor center features slide and film programs about the North Cascade Wilderness. Nearby is an accessible viewpoint trail.

Farther east on Wash. 20, turn right onto Main Street at **Newhalem,** a town of Seattle City Light (milepost 121). The company's dams—Gorge, Diablo, and Ross—generate about a quarter of Seattle's peak-time electricity. The dams created **Diablo, Ross,** and **Gorge Lakes.** To haul men and materials for construction, the company built a railway from Rockport to Diablo in the 1920s.

Drive on to **Diablo,** another City Light settlement, by turning left at milepost 126. Near here in 1901, pioneer Lucinda Davis and her three children cleared land and put up a roadhouse to feed and house the miners who still trudged the mountains in the wake of two abortive gold rushes. The Davis family built the first hydroelectric project on the Skagit—a waterwheel that generated enough electricity to light three light bulbs. A replica of the waterwheel stands next to the modern Diablo powerhouse; the **Davis Museum** preserves mementoes of the era (open during dinner tour only).

Call the Seattle City Light information center to see if there is

Lake Chelan, ringed by the snowcapped Chelan Mountains

room on City Light's 2.5-hour tour of Diablo Lake. If you are without a boat, this is the only way to actually get on the water. (Or board a City Light ferry traveling between **Diablo** and **Ross.** This enjoyable 1-hour round-trip begins across Diablo Dam Road, near the parking for the Ross Lake Resort.)

Drive back to the highway and, if you are looking for an invigorating climb, turn right after about 4 miles at Colonial Creek Campground. Behind the amphitheater the **Thunder Woods Nature Trail** begins. This moderately steep 1-mile loop rises among giant, fragrant cedar trees, some of them more than three centuries old. The red cedar—characterized by ropy, cinnamon-colored bark and flat, fernlike foliage—provided Indians with wood for canoes and houses and fiber for mats, clothing, and baskets. To extend your walk, continue along the 19-mile **Thunder Creek Trail** for a while; the views are good and the hiking relatively easy at first. (Eventually it ascends 6,100 feet.)

When you're back in the car, don't miss the **Diablo Lake Overlook** (1,600 feet), milepost 132. Amid the splendid scenery are exhibits that honor Senator Henry M. Jackson, who helped create the park and to whom Congress dedicated it in 1987. The highest mountain visible here is **Colonial Peak** (7,771 feet) to the southwest; note the glacial cirque, or bowl-shaped depression, carved out of its side. North is **Sourdough Mountain,** site of a fire lookout.

Near milepost 134 you'll find an informative 0.3-mile boardwalk nature trail, the **Happy Creek Forest Walk.** A few miles farther on, the highway leaves the park complex and enters the **Okanogan National Forest** (milepost 139). For a superb view of Cascade peaks, follow the road about 20 miles to **Washington Pass Overlook** (5,477 feet), the highest point on the North Cascades Highway. Exit to the left at milepost 162, and walk to the overlook. Directly to the south is massive **Liberty Bell Mountain** (7,740 feet), south of that the **Early Winter Spires** (7,807 feet). With binoculars you might spot climbers and mountain goats on the solid granite faces.

CASCADE RIVER ROAD

45 miles round-trip; a half day

The Cascade River Road, the only road to enter the park proper from the west, passes through national forest for most of its length. The road starts in front of the Buffalo Run Inn in Marblemount. Before departing, pick up maps and check road conditions at Marblemount's

Wilderness Information Center. The road becomes progressively narrower, steeper, and bumpier, though high-clearance cars can travel it in an hour without difficulty *(trailers should not attempt the last few miles)*. The drive ends at a parking lot and picnic area (3,660 feet) between the glacier-studded summits of **Johannesburg Mountain** (8,200 feet) to the west and **Boston Peak** (8,894 feet) to the east.

Hikers will enjoy the 3.75-mile trail to **Cascade Pass** (5,392 feet). The Skagit and Chelan Indians used the pass to and from **Lake Chelan** for hunting and trading. The trail leaves the lowland forest to enter woods of silver fir, mountain hemlock, and Alaska yellow cedar, then flower-strewn subalpine meadows. Stay on the path; previous visitors have damaged the fragile meadow flora.

Park employees grow native plants in a greenhouse in Marblemount, then backpack or airlift them in for planting in summer to revegetate the pass. The greenhouse (near the Wilderness Information Center in Marblemount) is open for visits.

STEHEKIN VALLEY

an overnight or 2

Stehekin has been a tourist hideaway since hotels first opened here at the turn of the 20th century and miners spread tales of magical scenery. On the northern shores of glacier-carved Lake Chelan and inaccessible by road, Stehekin is a community of hardy contemporary homesteaders, complete with a one-room schoolhouse in use from 1921 to 1988.

The valley offers many lodging alternatives as well as backcountry camping without backpacking: Simply fill out a backcountry permit after you get there, take a shuttle bus and stake your claim.

Even if you don't plan to camp, head for the **Golden West Visitor Center** when you arrive at Stehekin Landing to pick up hiking maps and schedules of tours and buses. Be sure to ask about trail conditions; high trails can be closed by snow or flood damage. In addition, a 2003 flood damaged the park road so access is limited.

After lunch, tour the **Buckner Homestead.** Home of the Buckner family from 1911 to 1970, it offers a look at the challenges of frontier life.

Next morning follow the nature trails near the landing. The informative 0.75-mile **Imus Creek Nature Trail** starts near the visitor center, and the **McKellar Cabin Historical Trail** begins just past the post office. Or catch the early shuttle bus (fee) upvalley; it currently can access a number of trailheads. Ask a ranger for the latest bus schedule.

For an easy hike try the **Agnes Gorge Trail,** 5 miles round-trip and level. Get off the bus at **High Bridge** near the intersection with the Pacific Crest Trail and walk across the bridge, past the sign for **Agnes Creek,** to the trailhead for **Agnes Gorge.** The trail provides excellent views of the 210-foot gorge and **Agnes Mountain** (8,115 feet). Be sure to keep a bus schedule with you at all times to avoid being stranded.

If you like to hike and backcountry camp, a good bet is the **Horseshoe Basin Trail** (off the **Cascade Pass Trail**), a moderately steep 3.9-mile trail that passes more than 15 waterfalls among spectacular glacier and mountain views. Though the trail itself is short, the 14.4 miles to the trailhead are no longer accessible by bus and take several days to hike.

INFORMATION & ACTIVITIES

HEADQUARTERS

810 State Rte. 20, Sedro-Woolley, WA 98284. Phone (360) 856-5700. www.nps.gov/noca

SEASONS & ACCESSIBILITY

Park open year-round; snow prevents access to much of it from mid-October to April.

VISITOR & INFORMATION CENTERS

North Cascades Visitor Center (near Newhalem) open mid-April to mid-Nov., weekends only rest of year. Call (206) 386-4495.
Information center on Wash. 20 (North Cascades Hwy.), Sedro Woolley, open late May to mid-Oct., weekdays rest of year.
Wilderness Information Center in Marblemount (just west of park boundary off North Cascades Hwy.) open daily summer only.
Lake Chelan NRA: Golden West Visitor Center (Stehekin), access by ferry, floatplane, or foot, open mid-May to mid-Oct. Limited hours in winter; call headquarters for information.

ENTRANCE FEE

No entrance fee, but $5 for one-day vehicle pass to park at some trailheads. $30 for annual pass.

PETS

Prohibited in national park except in front country and on Pacific Crest Trail, if leashed. Permitted on leashes in NRA.

FACILITIES FOR DISABLED

Information facilities and numerous short trails near North Cascades Highway are wheelchair accessible.

THINGS TO DO

Free naturalist-led activities: **Ross Lake NRA:** guided nature walks, evening campfire programs. **Lake Chelan NRA:** nature and Buckner Orchard walks, evening programs. Also available, hiking, boating, fishing, hunting (NRA only, in season), horseback riding, rafting on Skagit River, cross-country skiing. In summer, tours of Diablo Lake and Ross Lake. Reserve at least a month in advance through Seattle City Light's Skagit Tour Desk, 500 Newhalem St., Rockport, WA 98283. Phone (206) 684-3030.

OVERNIGHT BACKPACKING

Permits required; available free at Wilderness Information Center in Marblemount and Golden West Visitor Center.

CAMPGROUNDS

Ross Lake NRA: Three campgrounds, 14-day limit. **Colonial Creek** open mid-spring to mid-fall. **Newhalem Creek** open mid-May to early Oct. **Goodell Creek** open all year. All first come, first served. Fees: None to $12 per night. No showers. Tent and RV sites; no hookups. Goodell Creek and Newhalem Creek Group Campground, reservations required; call (877) 444-6777 or visit www.ReserveUSA.com.
Lake Chelan NRA: Three campgrounds, **Harlequin, Bullion,** and **Purple Point,** 14-day limit. Open mid-spring to mid-fall. First come, first served. No fees. Showers are located near Purple Point. Tent sites only. Reservations required at **Harlequin Group Campground** (contact 360-856-5700). Limited food service is available in Lake Chelan NRA.

HOTELS, MOTELS, & INNS

(unless otherwise noted, rates are for 2 persons in a double room, high season)

In Ross Lake NRA:
Ross Lake Resort (Access by boat or foot) 503 Diablo St., Rockport, WA 98283. (206) 386-4437. 15 units floating on lake, kitchens. $100-$288. Mid-June–late Oct.
In Lake Chelan NRA:
North Cascades Stehekin Lodge P.O. Box 457, Chelan, WA 98816. (509) 682-4494. 28 units. $98-$128. Rest.
Silver Bay Inn P.O. Box 85, Stehekin, WA 98852. (800) 555-7781 or (509) 687-3142. 4 cabins, $145-$295. April–Oct.
Stehekin Valley Ranch P.O. Box 36, Stehekin, WA 98852. (509) 682-4677. 12 cabins, some with showers. $65-$85 per person, meals. June–Sept.
In Birdsview-Concrete, WA 98237:
Cascade Mountain Inn 40418 Pioneer Ln. (360) 826-4333. 6 units. $135, incl. breakfast.

For accommodations in Chelan, contact the Chamber of Commerce, P.O. Box 216, Chelan, WA 98816. (800) 424-3526 or (509) 682-3503.

EXCURSIONS

MT. BAKER- SNOQUALMIE NATIONAL FOREST
MOUNTLAKE TERRACE, WASHINGTON

The Cascades' evergreen-covered western slopes feature active and dormant volcanoes, glaciers, lakes, streams, and waterfalls. Eight wilderness areas. Long winter sports season. Over 1.7 million acres. Hiking, boating, swimming, climbing, fishing, horseback riding, scenic drives, winter sports. More than 700 campsites, boat ramp, picnic areas. Open all year; campsites open May through Sept. Roads often impassable in winter. Located between North Cascades NP to the north and Mount Rainier NP to the south. (206) 470-4060.

SKAGIT RIVER BALD EAGLE NATURAL AREA
ROCKPORT, WASHINGTON

This refuge, partially controlled by the Nature Conservancy, is the favored wintering ground of several hundred bald eagles that feed on chum salmon carcasses along the upper Skagit River. Population peaks in mid-Jan. 10,000 acres. No visitor facilities. Marked viewing vistas with handicapped access located off Wash. 20 about 10 miles from North Cascades NP. (425) 775-1311.

OKANOGAN NATIONAL FOREST
OKANOGAN, WASHINGTON

In a remote, rugged mountain area, this national forest features high peaks, mountain lakes, meadows, evergreens, and open woodlands. Contains the Pasayten and Lake Chelan-Sawtooth Wildernesses. 1,790,633 acres. Hiking, boating, climbing, fishing, horseback riding, hunting, scenic drives, winter sports. 38 campgrounds, boat ramp, picnic areas. Open year-round; most campsites open May through October. Adjoins North Cascades NP on east. (509) 826-3275.

Club moss on vine maple and bigleaf maple in the Hoh Rain Forest

OLYMPIC

WASHINGTON
ESTABLISHED JUNE 29, 1938
922,000 acres

Encompassing 1,441 square miles of the Olympic Peninsula, Olympic National Park invites visitors to explore three distinct ecosystems: subalpine forest and wildflower meadow; temperate forest; and the rugged Pacific shore. Because of the park's relatively unspoiled condition and outstanding scenery, the United Nations has declared Olympic both an international biosphere reserve and a World Heritage site.

Inside the park, the Olympic mountain range is nearly circular, contoured by 13 rivers that radiate out like the spokes of a wheel. No road traverses the park, but a dozen spur roads lead into it from US 101, making it easily accessible from outside the park.

Residents of the Olympic Peninsula refer to it as a gift from the sea, and its features were indeed shaped by water and ice. The rock of the Olympics developed under the ocean—marine fossils are embedded in the mountain summits. Another component, basalt, originated from undersea lava vents. About 30 million years ago, the plate carrying the Pacific Ocean floor collided with the plate supporting the North American continent. As the heavy oceanic plate slid beneath the lighter continental plate, the upper layers of seabed jammed against the coastline, crumpling into what would become the Olympic Mountains. Glaciers and streams sculptured the mountains into their current profiles.

Glaciers nearly 1-mile thick also gouged out Puget Sound and Hood Canal to the east, and the Strait of Juan de Fuca to the north, isolating the peninsula from the mainland.

Ice Age isolation led to the 15 animals and 8 plants that evolved nowhere else on Earth, including the Olympic mountain milkvetch, Olympic marmot, Olympic Mazama pocket gopher, and Olympic mud minnow.

There are also the 11 mammals common in the nearby Cascades and Rockies that either died out in the Olympics or never found their way into the peninsula. The missing include the grizzly bear, lynx, and mountain sheep.

The mountain goats found here are non-native. They were introduced in the 1920s before the park was established. The goats so damaged Olympic's alpine meadows in 1988 the park staff began efforts to manage the population that had grown to over 1,000.

Moist winds from the Pacific condense in the cool air of the Olympics and drop rain or snow, bestowing on the mountains' western slopes the wettest climate in the lower 48 states. Mount Olympus, which crowns the park at 7,980 feet, receives 200 inches of precipitation a year.

How to Get There

Approach the park from US 101, which skirts three sides of the Olympic Peninsula. The main visitor center and entrance are in Port Angeles. From Seattle, take the Washington State Ferry to Bainbridge Island, then drive north to Wash. 104 to join US 101 west to Port Angeles, a drive of about 60 miles. Airports: Port Angeles, Seattle, Sequim, and Olympia.

When to Go

All-year park. Summer is the "dry" season, but be prepared for cool temperatures, fog, and rain at any time. Hurricane Ridge opens for skiing on winter weekends and holidays, weather permitting.

How to Visit

Plan to spend at least 2 days. On the first day, stroll subalpine meadows at **Hurricane Ridge** while admiring the peaks and glaciers in the distance. Savor the **Lake Crescent** area and, if you're feeling energetic, wind up with a dip at **Sol Duc Hot Springs.**

On the second day, drive to the **Hoh Rain Forest** and sample its nature trails before heading west for the Pacific Ocean beaches and tide pools. If you have more time, consider a trip to **Ozette** along the coast, or visit less known **Quinault.**

OLYMPIC

DRIVE TO HURRICANE RIDGE, LAKE CRESCENT & SOL DUC

76 miles; a very full day

Plan to spend the night in the area to get an early start. At the **visitor center** in Port Angeles, inquire about the weather on Hurricane Ridge and pick up a tide table for the next day.

On a clear day, the ridge offers spectacular views of the **Olympic Mountains** and northward as far as the Strait of Juan de Fuca and Canada's Vancouver Island. The

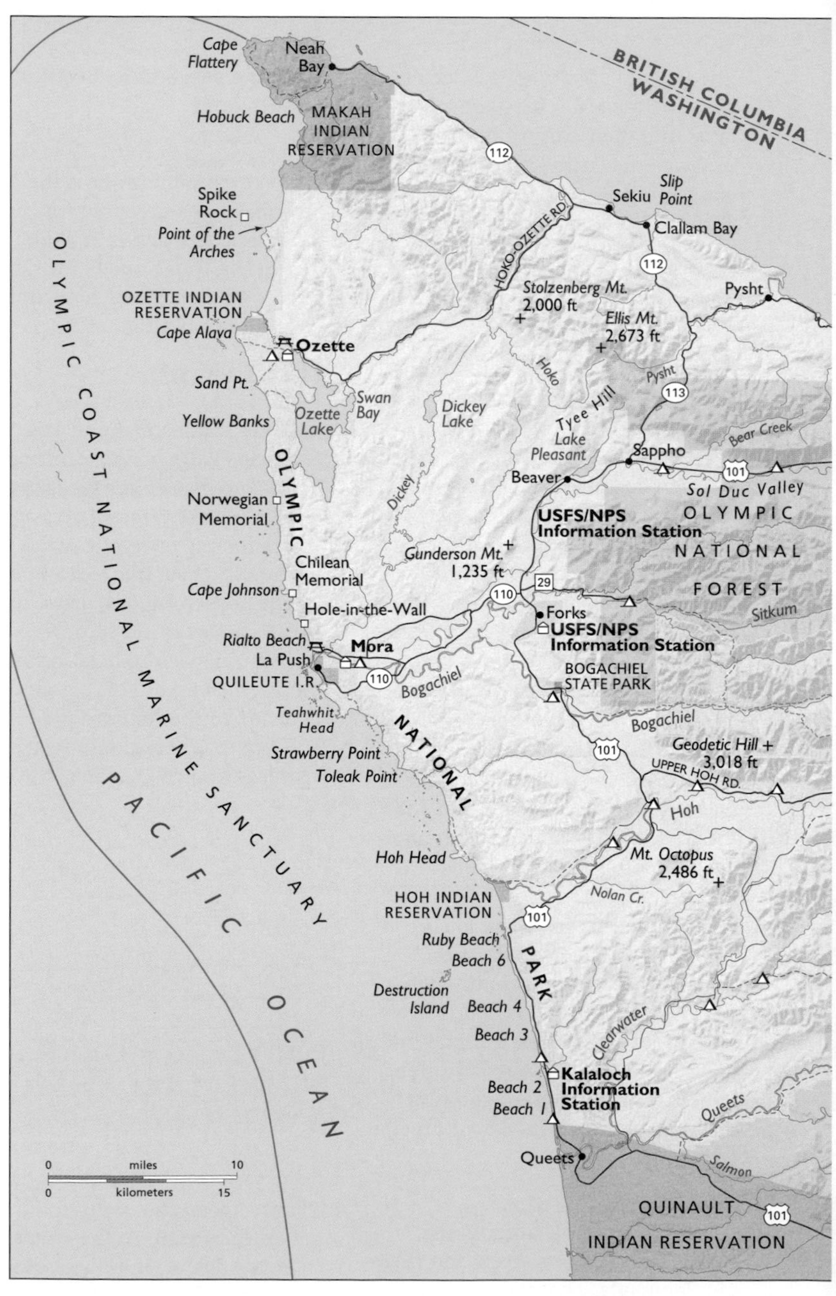

17-mile drive to Hurricane Ridge—so named for the force of its winter winds—takes you from lowland forest to tree line, nearly a mile above sea level, and reveals some of the remarkable geology of the peninsula.

After the tunnels, 9 miles in, stop at a pullover and look at the rock faces above the road. The bubbles of rock, called pillow basalt, are a clue that these mountains began under the ocean; when hot lava

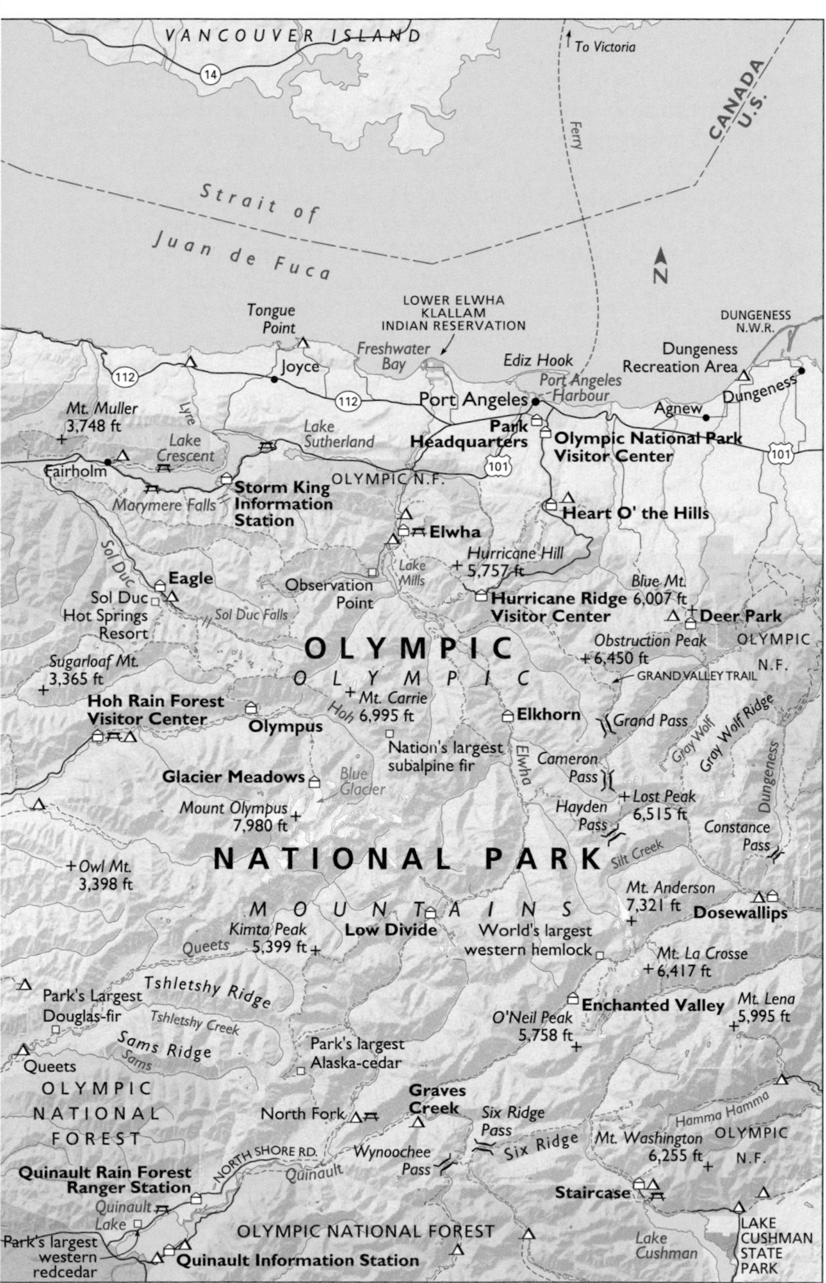

oozes into seawater, its surface cools and hardens quickly, often forming the globules you see here.

Drive on toward **Hurricane Ridge Visitor Center.** Plaques identify the peaks and glaciers of the inner Olympics. **Mount Olympus** carries 7 of Olympic's 60 named glaciers. Its **Blue Glacier** can receive up to 100 feet of snow a year and flows downhill as much as 5 inches a day.

You will probably see black-tailed

deer here, and possibly Olympic marmots that whistle when approached. Most of the trees are subalpine fir. Their distinctive steeple shape helps shed snow. Near tree line, a 3-foot-tall tree may be 100 years old; summer wildflowers thrive where no tree can take hold.

Fine picnic sites lie near the road's end, about a mile beyond Hurricane Ridge. Try the partly-paved **Hurricane Hill Trail,** starting where the road ends, for 3 miles (round-trip; 700 foot elevation change) of wildflowers and stunning mountain views. Layers of sedimentary rock along the trail stand folded and tilted on end from the continental collision.

If you prefer to continue driving —some of it is tricky—take the 8-mile, unpaved road to **Obstruction Peak,** from the east end of the Hurricane Ridge parking lot, for the park's best windshield view of Mount Olympus and some of Olympic's most diverse wildflower displays. (The road generally opens by July 4.) **Grand Valley Trail** (3.5 miles one way) starts at the parking lot at road's end. Take at least a short stroll on it for grand ridgetop views.

Back in your car double back to Port Angeles and pick up US 101 west. Here, the highway passes **Lake Sutherland** before tracing the southern shore of **Lake Crescent.** Carved by a glacier, the two lakes began as one, but a great landslide created the dam that now divides them. Indian legend says that Mount Storm King, angered at the fighting between the Quileute and Clallam Indians, threw down a boulder, killing the combatants and splitting the lake in two. Lake Crescent, 600 feet deep, is known for its azure waters and trout.

Turn off at the **Storm King Information Station** to walk the **Marymere Falls Trail**, a 1.75-mile round-trip through lowland forest to a graceful, 90-foot waterfall. Fifty cents buys a booklet that identifies the trees—mostly Douglas fir and western hemlock, with a few western red cedar. Back in the car, time permitting, turn left 1.5 miles west of Fairholm to take the 14-mile road to **Sol Duc**. Indians may have used the hot springs for medicinal treatments. Travelers have soothed tired muscles in pools here since a resort was first established in 1912. In case you want to stroll before you soak, the **Sol Duc Falls Trail**, starting at the end of the road, leads through three-quarters of a mile of dense forest to a waterfall.

HOH RAIN FOREST TO THE PACIFIC BEACHES

45 miles; a full day

The Hoh Rain Forest is located 2.5 hours from Port Angeles. To see it and the coast, continue skirting the park as you drive west and south on US 101. Check the schedule of guided tide-pool walks in your park newspaper and then decide whether to go first to the rain forest or to the beaches.

For the rain forest, take the **Upper Hoh Road** inland 19 miles to the visitor center. You'll pass large recently reforested areas on private, state, and national forest lands, once entirely clear-cut. Logging is prohibited in the park, yet environmentalists cite evidence of damage done to park wildlife—some of whose living area extends outside the park—by shrinking habitat.

Two nature trails start behind the

Glacier-carved Lake Crescent

visitor center and are well worth taking: the **Hall of Mosses Trail** (0.75 mile) and the **Spruce Nature Trail** (1.25 miles). This is an enchanted land. Sitka spruce, western hemlock, and western red cedar, measuring up to 25 feet in circumference, tower 300 feet in the air. Club moss and licorice ferns drape the conifers and bigleaf maples, suffusing the air with green. Seedlings, unable to compete on the crowded forest floor, sprout luxuriantly on fallen trees, called nurse logs. Aged giants, lined up in colonnades, stand on huge roots called stilts where their nurse log rotted away. You may see or hear the eerie bugle of the Roosevelt elk, named for Theodore Roosevelt. (He so loved them, the park was almost named Elk Park.) The elk are members of the largest unmanaged herd in the nation.

To see how the forest develops, take the Spruce Nature Trail. Where the **Hoh River** has shifted course in the last few decades, the first trees to move in needed full sunlight to grow—red alder, willow, and Douglas fir. Later, shade-tolerant spruce and hemlock will succeed these pioneers to dominate the forest. As you stroll, note how the downed trees provide nutrients for the emerging seedlings.

After your forest sojourn, rejoin US 101 south, stopping at **Ruby Beach.** Walk the trail down to the sand—and keep track of where you came out of the woods. It might be hard to find the trail again, and the tough, oval-leaved shrubs off the trail are virtually impenetrable.

Olympic preserves over 60 miles of coastal wilderness: To the north, the beaches tend to have more pebbles and rocks; to the south, the beaches are broader and sandier. Rock outcroppings called sea stacks, isolated from the shoreline by erosion, have caused many a shipwreck.

The driftwood you might have to climb over once grew where you just were: upriver in the forest. Toppled by a winter storm or undercut by a flooding creek, trees tumbled downstream to the sea. *Beware: Picturesque at low tide, drift logs can suddenly roll with lethal force at high tide.*

You may see harbor seals, the most common marine mammal on this coast, swimming or lounging on the rocks. In the spring and fall,

California gray whales dive and spout near land on their migration between Alaska and Baja California. Gulls and crows drop clams from 50 feet in the air to crack them open on the rocks. Bald eagles soar from their forest perches to nab fish.

Continue south on US 101 and turn left at the sign for the big cedar tree, one of the world's largest. Standing at the end of a short spur road, the tree looks like something conjured up from the land of Oz. Monstrous in scale, its girth exceeds 66 feet.

The stretch of road from here to the park's southwest border is dotted with overlooks and short access trails to the beaches. If it's low tide—and you missed the guided tide-pool walk—try the trail at **Beach 4,** just north of milepost 160. A short, steep hike brings you to the shoreline and the rocky tide pools. Alternately battered by waves and dried out by the sun, tide pools nevertheless teem with life. An area 1 foot square may support 4,000 individual creatures belonging to more than 20 species. Look closely to spot gooseneck and acorn barnacles, periwinkle snails, and rocks with holes drilled by piddock clams. Brightly colored sea stars, or starfish, prowl the rocky pools, preying on the mussels and other mollusks. Green sea anemones stun their tiny prey with stinging cells on their tentacles. Purple sea urchins dine on bits of kelp and other algae.

To view a third mood of Olympic beach, park near **Beach 1,** a stroller's delight, at milepost 155. Follow the sign to the **Spruce Burl Trail** for a brief detour before descending to the sand. Near the ocean, Sitka spruce commonly develop large, nobby growths that may be triggered by a virus, a bacterium, or some substance carried in the ocean spray.

For a remote and peaceful visit to the rain forest, drive south to **Quinault** (32 miles from Kalaloch) and take the North Shore spur road. Walk the half-mile **Maple Glades Nature Trail** from near the **Quinault Rain Forest Ranger Station** or the 2.2-mile round-trip **Irely Lake Trail,** which begins a quarter mile before the North Fork Campground. Look for beaver dams, herons, and ospreys, which often nest at the lake.

OZETTE

Remote Ozette, a town near the northernmost realm of the park, offers a good departure point for supreme coastal hiking. To get there, take US 101 to Sappho, then head north to Wash. 112; follow this into Sekiu. From here, head southwest to the town.

For a level 9.3-mile loop, take the triangular route shaped by the **Ozette Lake-Cape Alava-Sand Point Trail.** The jaunt begins at the ranger station on the north end of **Ozette Lake** *(where you must register),* off Hoko-Ozette Road. The 3-mile trail goes southwest to Sand Point, tunneling through coastal forest, taking you over marshes and bogs on wooden walkways.

You emerge at the Pacific at **Sand Point.** Here head north along the rocky beach to **Capa Alava,** the westernmost point of the contiguous United States. Along the way, you are treated to stunning seacoast scenery, tide pools filled with sea critters, and rock etchings left by Indians who lived by whaling and fishing. Watch for rhinoceros auklets, tufted puffins, oyster catchers, and perhaps even a black bear.

INFORMATION & ACTIVITIES

HEADQUARTERS
600 E. Park Ave., Port Angeles, WA 98362. Phone (360) 565-3000. www.nps.gov/olym

SEASONS & ACCESSIBILITY
Park open year-round. Some roads closed in winter. For weather and road information, call (360) 565-3131.

VISITOR & INFORMATION CENTERS
In Port Angeles, the **Olympic National Park Visitor Center,** 3002 Mt. Angeles Road; call (360) 565-3132.
The **Hoh Rain Forest Visitor Center** off US 101 at western edge of park, (360) 374-6925.
Hurricane Ridge Visitor Center open all year, weather permitting.
In summer, information stations open at **Storm King** on Lake Crescent, **Kalaloch,** and other locations.
For park information, tune in to 530 AM in the Port Angeles and Lake Crescent areas.

ENTRANCE FEE
$10 per vehicle for 7-day pass May to Sept. Some areas charge an entrance fee in winter.

FACILITIES FOR DISABLED
Visitor centers and some campsites are accessible to wheelchairs. Also accessible are Hurricane Ridge's paved trails; a short loop trail into the Hoh Rain Forest; the Madison Falls Trail in the Elwha Valley, and the Moments in Time Trail at Lake Crescent.

THINGS TO DO
Free naturalist-led activities: meadow, forest, beach, and tide-pool walks; campfire programs. Also available, hiking, boating, fishing (no license needed), climbing, swimming, windsurfing, waterskiing, river rafting, cross-country and alpine skiing, snowshoeing.

SPECIAL ADVISORY
• Be careful when hiking along the coast; rocks and logs can be slippery and unstable.
• Be aware of incoming tides (current tables posted at trailheads).
• Surf logs can roll and kill.

OVERNIGHT BACKPACKING
Call ahead for reservations. Permits required; obtain at Wilderness Information Center (directly behind Olympic National Park Visitor Center, 360-565-3131), visitor centers, ranger stations, or trailheads.

CAMPGROUNDS
Fifteen campgrounds, all with a 14-day limit. **Deer Park, Dosewallips, North Fork,** and **Queets** campgrounds do not allow RVs. All first come, first serve except for **Kalaloch** that requires reservations in summer—contact NPRS (see p.10). Fees: None to $16 per night. No showers. Three group campgrounds; reservations required; contact headquarters. Food services in park.

HOTELS, MOTELS, & INNS
(unless otherwise noted, rates are for 2 persons in a double room, high season)

INSIDE THE PARK:
Kalaloch Lodge (on US 101, 36 miles south of Forks) 157151 Hwy. 101, Forks, WA 98331. (360) 962-2271. 20 rooms; 44 cabins, 38 with kitchenettes. $143-$275. Restaurant.
Lake Crescent Lodge (on US 101) 416 Lake Crescent Rd., Port Angeles, WA 98363. (360) 928-3211. 45 units, 40 with private bath. $106-$211. Restaurant. Open late April through Oct.
Log Cabin Resort (on Lake Crescent) 3183 E. Beach Rd., Port Angeles, WA 98363. (360) 928-3325 or (360) 928-3245. 28 units, 3 with kitchenettes; $61-$154. 10 tent sites; $23. 32 RV hookups; $35. Restaurant. Open May through Sept.
Sol Duc Hot Springs Resort (12 miles off US 101) P.O. Box 2169, Port Angeles, WA 98362. (360) 327-3583. 32 cabins, 6 kitchens. $119-$139. Pool, restaurant. Open mid-May through Sept.

For other lodgings, contact the Chambers of Commerce in Port Angeles, 121 E. Railroad, 98362. (360) 452-2363; and Forks, P.O. Box 1249, Port Angeles, WA 98331. (800) 443-6757 or (360) 374-2531.

Coast redwoods, a grove of giants

REDWOOD

CALIFORNIA
ESTABLISHED OCTOBER 2, 1968
108,400 acres, including 3 state parks

Sometimes, when the morning fog caresses the great trees, you can imagine the past flowing through the long, misty shadows ... Vast redwood forests flourishing across a lush and humid North America ... After the final ice age, a last stand here in the sustaining climate along the Pacific coast ... Tree after tree falling to the loggers. Then, in a windswept moment, the past vanishes and you stand beside other visitors, gazing up at the Earth's tallest living things. That is the essence of Redwood National and State Parks.

The park, near the northern limit of the coast redwood's narrow range, preserves the remnants of a forest that once covered two million acres and, at the turn of the 20th century, was badly threatened by logging. The state of California and the Save-the-Redwoods League came to the rescue by acquiring hundreds of groves and protecting them within 26 state parks. Three redwood state parks—**Jedediah Smith, Del Norte Coast,** and **Prairie Creek**—were encompassed by the national park when it was created in 1968.

Logging on surrounding private land, however, threatened the parks' protected redwoods. Soil and sediments from the logged-over tracts washed into the rivers and creeks, settling to the bottom downstream. Silt deposits can smother redwoods—for the giants are amazingly vulnerable. And the waterlogged soil weakens the trees' resistance to wind. Their roots are shallow, often only 10 feet deep.

In 1978 Congress added 48,000 acres to the national park's 58,000 acres, including about 36,000 that had been logged. The raw, clear-cut land, a park official wrote, had "the look of an active war zone." Today, in an epic earthmoving project—a redwood renaissance—crews are beginning to reclaim vast stretches of logged-over lands. Hillsides, carved away for logging roads, are being restored. Most of the 400 miles of roads are being erased. It will take at least 50 years for the scars of logging to disappear and another 250 or so years for the replanted redwood seedlings to grow to modest size.

The renaissance has added a new dimension to the traditional rite of staring up at redwoods. Today's visitor can look at hillsides shorn of giants and know that generations from now the trees will grow there again.

How to Get There

Tree-lined US 101, the Redwood Highway, runs the length of the park. From the south, take US 101 to the information center near Orick, about 40 miles north of Eureka. From the north, enter through Crescent City, also an information center site. From the east, take US 199, another redwood-flanked highway, to Hiouchi. Airports: Arcata and Crescent City.

When to Go

Year-round. Summer draws highway-clogging crowds, so think about a visit in spring or fall. In both seasons, bird migrations enhance the redwood groves. Rhododendrons burst forth in spring; deciduous trees add color in fall. Rains, welcome to the redwoods but not to visitors, drench the park in winter.

How to Visit

US 101, with its many redwood sentinels, gives you a windshield-framed panorama of the trees. But to appreciate the redwoods, you must walk among them. If you have only a day to visit this 50-mile-long park, stop and see the **Lady Bird Johnson Grove** and **Big Tree.** Hike or just stretch your legs (depending on your time) along the **Coastal Trail** and savor the Pacific prospect of the park. For a longer stay, visit the **Tall Trees Grove,** drive **Howland Hill Road,** and end your visit with a splash in a kayak on the **Klamath River** or a jouncy drive to **Fern Canyon** and **Gold Bluffs Beach.** If you are driving an RV or towing a trailer, some stretches of road may be closed to you; check at information centers.

LADY BIRD JOHNSON GROVE & BIG TREE

13 miles; 2 hours

Just before Orick, stop at the **Kuchel Visitor Center** (once the site of a redwood-slicing lumber mill) to see the exhibits, and then continue north on US 101 to the Bald Hills Road sign. Turn right and drive 2 miles to **Lady Bird Johnson Grove,** a jewel that gives you an understanding of the entire park treasure. On the grove's mile-long trail you feel the cool, moist air that redwoods need. You see a hollowed-out tree that still lives. Such redwoods—"goose-pen" trees—once sheltered settlers' fowl and livestock. You smell and touch the many plants that share the redwoods' domain. Most of all, you feel the peace; visitors speak quietly in this pillared place.

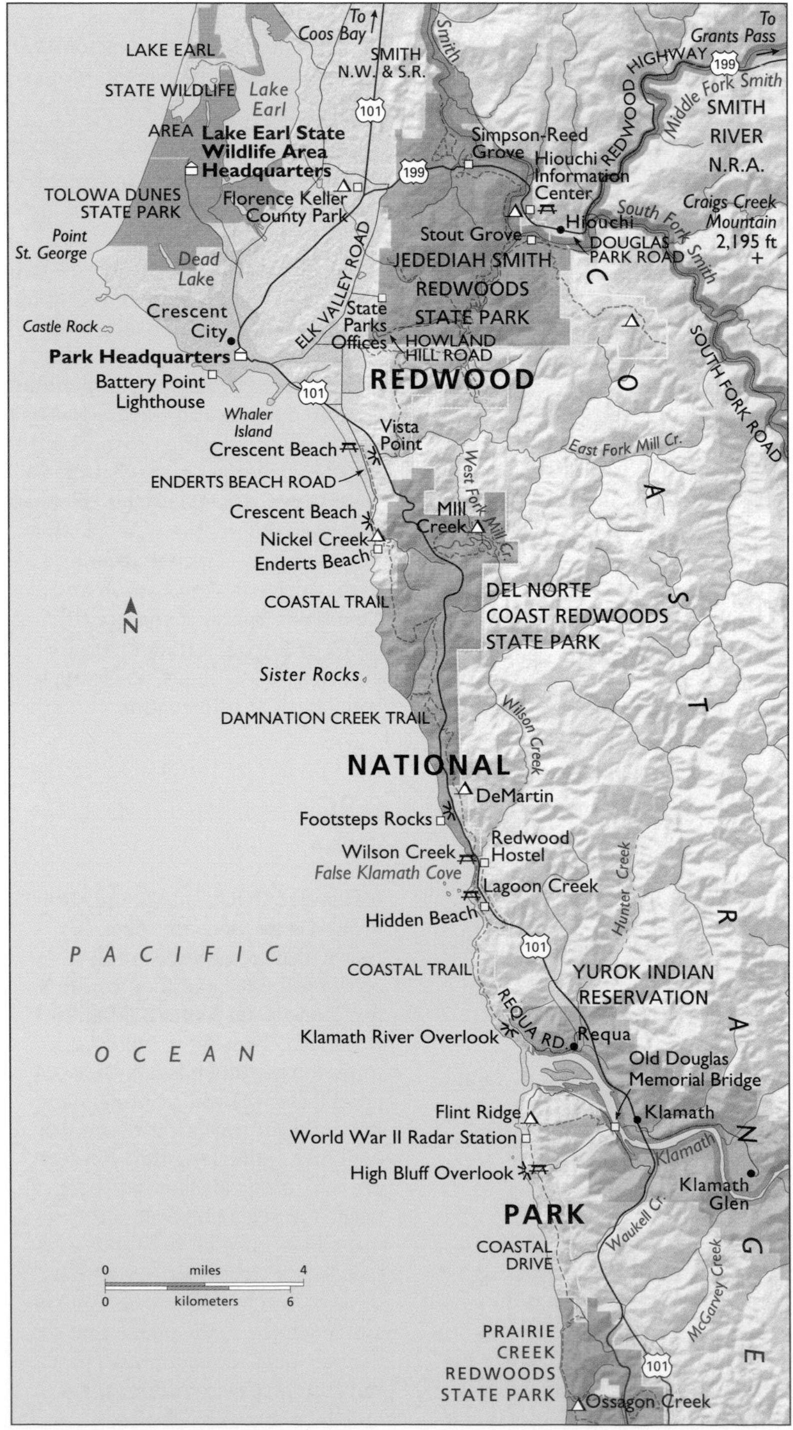

To Coos Bay
LAKE EARL
STATE WILDLIFE
AREA
Lake Earl
SMITH N.W. & S.R.
Smith
To Grants Pass
REDWOOD HIGHWAY
199
Middle Fork Smith
SMITH RIVER N.R.A.
101
Lake Earl State Wildlife Area Headquarters
Simpson-Reed Grove
Hiouchi Information Center
TOLOWA DUNES STATE PARK
Florence Keller County Park
Craigs Creek Mountain 2,195 ft
South Fork Smith
Hiouchi
Point St. George
Stout Grove
DOUGLAS PARK ROAD
Dead Lake
JEDEDIAH SMITH REDWOODS STATE PARK
ELK VALLEY ROAD
Crescent City
State Parks Offices
HOWLAND HILL ROAD
SOUTH FORK ROAD
Castle Rock
Park Headquarters
REDWOOD
Battery Point Lighthouse
Whaler Island
Vista Point
Crescent Beach
East Fork Mill Cr.
ENDERTS BEACH ROAD
West Fork Mill Cr.
Crescent Beach
Mill Creek
Nickel Creek
Enderts Beach
COASTAL TRAIL
DEL NORTE COAST REDWOODS STATE PARK
N
Sister Rocks
Wilson Creek
DAMNATION CREEK TRAIL
NATIONAL
DeMartin
Footsteps Rocks
Redwood Hostel
Wilson Creek
False Klamath Cove
Lagoon Creek
Hunter Creek
Hidden Beach
PACIFIC
OCEAN
COASTAL TRAIL
YUROK INDIAN RESERVATION
REQUA RD.
Requa
Klamath River Overlook
Old Douglas Memorial Bridge
Flint Ridge
Klamath
World War II Radar Station
Klamath
High Bluff Overlook
Klamath Glen
PARK
Waukell Cr.
COASTAL DRIVE
McGarvey Creek
COAST RANGE
0 miles 4
0 kilometers 6
PRAIRIE CREEK REDWOODS STATE PARK
Ossagon Creek

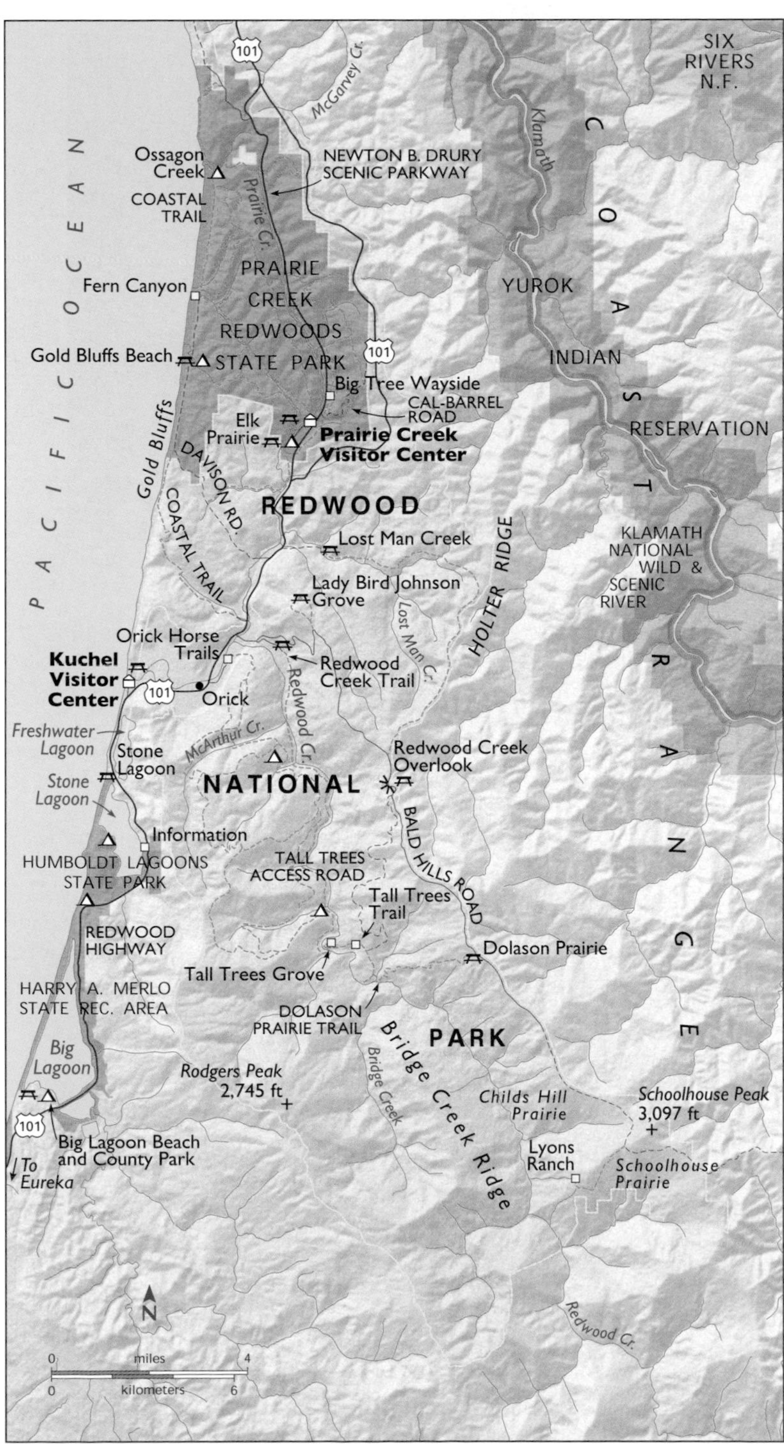
SIX RIVERS N.F.
PACIFIC OCEAN
Ossagon Creek
COASTAL TRAIL
NEWTON B. DRURY SCENIC PARKWAY
McGarvey Cr.
Prairie Cr.
Klamath
COAST RANGE
PRAIRIE CREEK REDWOODS STATE PARK
Fern Canyon
Gold Bluffs Beach
YUROK INDIAN RESERVATION
Big Tree Wayside
CAL-BARREL ROAD
Elk Prairie
Prairie Creek Visitor Center
Gold Bluffs
DAVISON RD.
COASTAL TRAIL
REDWOOD NATIONAL PARK
Lost Man Creek
HOLTER RIDGE
KLAMATH NATIONAL WILD & SCENIC RIVER
Lady Bird Johnson Grove
Lost Man Cr.
Orick Horse Trails
Kuchel Visitor Center
Redwood Creek Trail
Redwood Cr.
Orick
Freshwater Lagoon
Stone Lagoon
Stone Lagoon
McArthur Cr.
Redwood Creek Overlook
Information
BALD HILLS ROAD
HUMBOLDT LAGOONS STATE PARK
TALL TREES ACCESS ROAD
Tall Trees Trail
REDWOOD HIGHWAY
Dolason Prairie
Tall Trees Grove
HARRY A. MERLO STATE REC. AREA
DOLASON PRAIRIE TRAIL
Bridge Creek Ridge
Bridge Creek
Big Lagoon
Rodgers Peak 2,745 ft
Childs Hill Prairie
Schoolhouse Peak 3,097 ft
Big Lagoon Beach and County Park
Lyons Ranch
Schoolhouse Prairie
To Eureka
101
Redwood Cr.
N
miles
kilometers
0
4
0
6

Wildflowers blooming above Enderts Beach

Return to US 101 and continue north about 4 miles. Near the entrance to **Prairie Creek Redwoods State Park,** pull into the turnout to watch the free-roaming Roosevelt elk that live in the park. A mile ahead on the right is a wayside sign for **Big Tree.** A short trail from the parking lot leads to the aptly named tree. It's 304 feet tall, 21.6 feet in diameter, 66 feet in circumference, and about 1,500 years old. Here the experience is singular: you and one great tree.

COASTAL TRAIL

4 miles one way; at least 2 hours

From Orick, drive north 20 miles on US 101, passing Klamath, and turn left onto Requa Road. Park and picnic at **Klamath River Overlook,** a high hill. On a clear day you can see 65 miles down the bluff-guarded coast. **The Hidden Beach Section** of the Coastal Trail begins here, heads west, and then veers north along the wild, driftwood-decorated shore. Yurok Indians walked these shores, as did Jedediah Smith, the first white man to reach California's northern coast by land.

The trail, often bowered by branches of spruce and alder, sometimes seals you from the sight—though not the sounds—of the ocean. But there are many spots where you can sit and gaze out to sea. In spring and fall you may see migrating gray whales. Almost any time you will see gulls, cormorants, and ospreys.

A short side path leads down to **Hidden Beach.** Even on a day when the park is crowded yours may be the only footprints on the sand. Look at the ocean but don't swim: The undertow is dangerous all along the park's coast. The beach walk ends at a wall of gnarled black rocks. Follow your footprints back to the path and return to the trail, which heads north along the wild shore, then veers inland.

The north trailhead is at **Lagoon Creek,** where fresh water and forest meet ocean and high bluff. If you don't want to trudge the 4 miles back, have someone drive up to meet you at the parking lot.

TALL TREES GROVE

2.6 miles; a half day

Obtain a permit to drive your vehicle to the Tall Trees Grove parking area, off Bald Hills Road. (Permits can be obtained at any of the information centers.) From the parking area, the trail is a very steep 2.6-miles round-trip. The hike down to the grove, replete with ferns and rhododendrons, takes at least 30 minutes. Plan on another 30 to 45 minutes in the grove among the giant coast redwoods. The star is the **Nugget Tree,** which was measured at 365.5 feet in 1995. This is one of the world's tallest known trees. It's estimated to be between 900 and 1,500 years old.

HOWLAND HILL ROAD

8 miles; about 2 hours

Just south of Crescent City, take Elk Valley Road northeast. Keep a sharp watch on your right for the turnoff to Howland Hill Road, once a miners' supply road partially redwood-planked for oxcarts and horse-drawn wagons. The 6-mile road winds between redwoods that loom much closer than the ones along the highways. Mostly unpaved and often one lane, motor homes and trailers are not recommended. Stop at **Stout Grove,** where you can see one of many preserves set aside, this one donated by the wife of a logging company owner. Take time to enjoy the 1-mile trail among the redwoods. (In summer you can also reach the grove from the **Hiouchi Information Center** via a footbridge across the crystal-clear **Smith River.**)

Continue past the grove to Douglas Park Road, which ends at South Fork Road. Turn left to US 199 and drive west about 2.5 miles to the Hiouchi Information Center. Park here and sign up for an interpretive walk with a ranger. Or, continue west on US 199 to **Simpson-Reed Grove,** where you'll find a short pleasant self-guided trail.

GOLD BLUFFS BEACH & FERN CANYON

20 miles; a half day

From the Kuchel Visitor Center, head north for 4.5 miles to Davison Road, on your left. Elk are often spotted along the first few hundred yards on this road. Its rough dirt surface bounces you for about 4 miles down to **Gold Bluffs,** named for the gold found here. The road continues for 4 miles along the beach, ending near **Fern Canyon,** where a 0.75-mile loop trail climbs to a prairie—site of a vanished mining camp. Back down the canyon, walk through elk-roamed grass to a beautiful, desolate beach sprinkled with driftwood and often shrouded in fog.

Return the way you came, pausing to admire the fern-covered, 30-foot-high walls. The more adventurous can make a longer hike by climbing to **Prairie Creek** and walking along its banks before heading back toward the ocean. Return to the parking area at Fern Canyon via the windswept southern stretch of the **Coastal Trail.** Be on the lookout for a variety of birds, including pelicans, terns, gulls, and wading birds. In the fall or spring scan the horizon for the telltale spouts of migrating gray whales, en route to or from their winter retreat in Baja California.

INFORMATION & ACTIVITIES

HEADQUARTERS
1111 2nd St., Crescent City, CA 95531. Phone (707) 464-6101. www.nps.gov/redw

SEASONS & ACCESSIBILITY
Open year-round.

VISITOR & INFORMATION CENTERS
Crescent City Park Headquarters Information Center, at north end of park, open daily all year.
Kuchel Visitor Center, at south end of park near Orick, also open all year.
Hiouchi Information Center, at north end of park, open spring through summer.

ENTRANCE FEE
No admission fee. $6 day-use fee for Jedediah Smith, Del Norte Coast, and Prairie Creek State Parks.

PETS
Permitted on leashes except on trails and in backcountry.

FACILITIES FOR DISABLED
Information centers, Crescent Beach, Lagoon Creek picnic area, Klamath Overlook, and some trails are accessible to wheelchairs.

THINGS TO DO
Free naturalist-led activities: tide-pool and seashore walks, evening programs. Also available, hiking, canoeing, guided kayak trips, horseback riding, freshwater and ocean fishing (need license), swimming (inland only), whale watching.

SPECIAL ADVISORIES
• Be aware that ticks may transmit Lyme disease.
• Ocean swimming is not advised due to extremely cold water and treacherous undertow.

OVERNIGHT BACKPACKING
Permit required; can be obtained free at trailheads and at the National Park Information Centers and State Park Visitor Centers. The National Park lands offer three backcountry campsites—**DeMartin, Flint Ridge,** and **Nickel Creek;** 14-day limit. Open all year, first come, first served. No fees. Tent sites only. No showers.
Ossagon Creek campsite in Prairie Creek State Park is available to bikers and hikers only ($3 per night). Reserve at Prairie Creek Visitor Center.

CAMPGROUNDS
There are four state-run campgrounds inside the park—**Gold Bluffs Beach, Jedediah Smith, Mill Creek,** and **Elk Prairie;** 15-day limit. Mill Creek open April to October; others open all year; Gold Bluffs Beach may close in bad weather. Showers available nearby. Tent and RV sites; no hookups; large RVs not recommended and trailers prohibited at Gold Bluffs Beach. Fees $20 per night. Reservations recommended from mid-May through August and available at www.parks.ca.gov. The reservations number for these state-run campgrounds is (800) 444-7275. No food services inside park.

HOTELS, MOTELS, & INNS
(unless otherwise noted, rates are for 2 persons in a double room, high season)

In Crescent City, CA 95531:
Best Value Inn 440 Hwy. 101N. (707) 464-4141. 61 units. $62.
Curly Redwood Lodge 701 Hwy. 101S. (707) 464-2137. 36 units. $62-$67.
Econo Lodge Crescent City 725 Hwy. 101N. (707) 464-6106. 52 units. $59-$80.
Front Street Inn 102 L St. (707) 464-4113. 35 units. $45-$65.

In Eureka, CA 95501:
Carter House Inns 301 L St. (800) 404-1390 or (707) 444-8062. 31 units. $155-$595, incl. breakfast. Restaurant.

In Klamath, CA 95548:
Historic Requa Inn 451 Requa Rd. (866) 800-8777 or (707) 482-1425. 12 units. $85-$135, incl. breakfast. Restaurant.
Motel Trees 15495 Hwy. 101. (800) 848-2982 or (707) 482-3152. 23 units. $61. Restaurant.

EXCURSIONS

HUMBOLDT BAY NATIONAL WILDLIFE REFUGE

LOLETA, CALIFORNIA

The islands and wetlands of Humboldt Bay provide critical habitat for the brant, a small, stocky sea goose. From late winter to early spring, thousands of brants use the refuge as a staging area en route to northern nesting grounds. Other waterfowl and peregrine falcons are also present. 3,500 acres. Excellent bird-watching from the Hookton Slough Trail and Salmon Creek. Off US 101, about 40 miles south of Redwood NP. (707) 733-5406

SIX RIVERS NATIONAL FOREST

EUREKA, CALIFORNIA

Six major rivers cross this mountain forest of pine, fir, spruce, and cedar, providing nearly 10 percent of the state's runoff. Recreational opportunities include white-water rafting, kayaking, and excellent steelhead and salmon fishing. Contains parts of four wilderness areas. 957,590 acres. Hiking, boating, fishing, horseback riding, hunting, scenic drives, winter sports, water sports. 355 campsites, boat ramp, picnic areas, handicapped access. Open all year, though most off-highway routes close in winter. Most campsites open May through November, weather permitting. Composed of four ranger districts. For information contact the superintendent's office in Eureka on US 101, about 30 miles from Redwood NP. (707) 457-3131.

ALASKA

ALASKA

In 1867 Secretary of State William Seward bought Alaska from Russia for two cents an acre—and the public labeled the vast empty land Seward's Folly. Today, more than 14 billion barrels of oil have gushed through the Prudhoe Bay pipeline, and Alaska's wilderness and wildlife attract visitors by the thousands.

Eight national parks protect 42.1 million acres of these natural treasures. Katmai and Lake Clark lie along the Pacific Ring of Fire—a region of active volcanoes, earthquakes, giant brown bears, and salmon. Whales, sea lions, and flocks of seabirds seek out the cold, food-laden waters of Glacier Bay and Kenai Fjords. Wrangell-St. Elias is a jumble of mountains and glaciers so rugged that many remain unnamed and untrodden by humans. Above the Arctic Circle, Gates of the Arctic and Kobuk Valley protect the tundra and migrant herds of caribou. By comparison, Denali seems civilized with its nearby railroad and hotels; yet here the wildlife is so abundant and visible, the park is called a "subarctic Serengeti."

Alaska parks include national preserves that allow hunting, vast wilderness areas that prohibit buildings and roads, and native-owned lands still used for subsistence in a tradition thousands of years old.

In 1989 the *Exxon Valdez* ran aground in Prince William Sound, spilling nearly 11 million gallons of oil, the largest such spill in U.S. history. The slick spread into the Gulf of Alaska and onto the beaches of Katmai and Kenai Fjords. It killed more than 3,500 sea otters and 350,000 seabirds, as well as unknown numbers of scavenging mammals. Although the long term consequences for the habitat are still unknown, years of winter storms and massive environmental cleanup efforts have made the effects of the oil spill invisible to the naked eye.

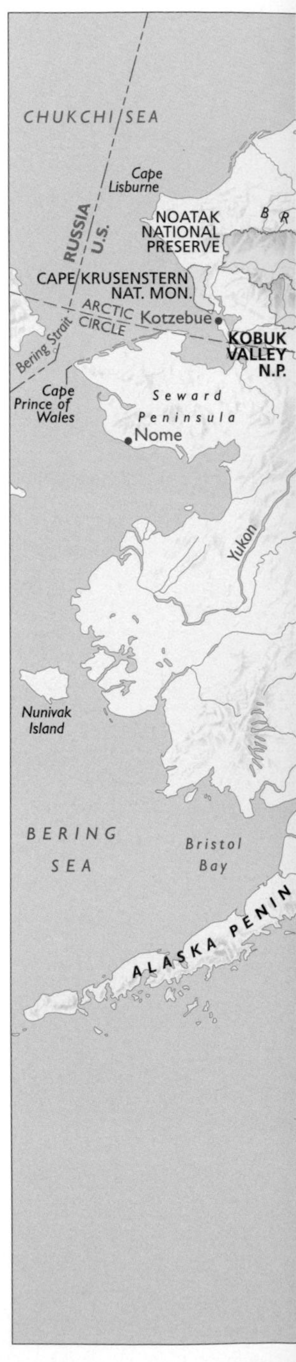

Most of Alaska's national parks are accessible only by plane or boat, but you can drive to Denali and Wrangell-St. Elias and to the edges of Kenai Fjords and Gates of the Arctic. The loop connecting Anchorage to Denali to Fairbanks to Wrangell-St. Elias, with a side trip to Kenai Fjords, is 1,100 miles. It's a 600-mile round-trip from Fairbanks to Gates of the Arctic on the unpaved Dalton Highway. Alaska parks are rugged, yet fragile; tread lightly.

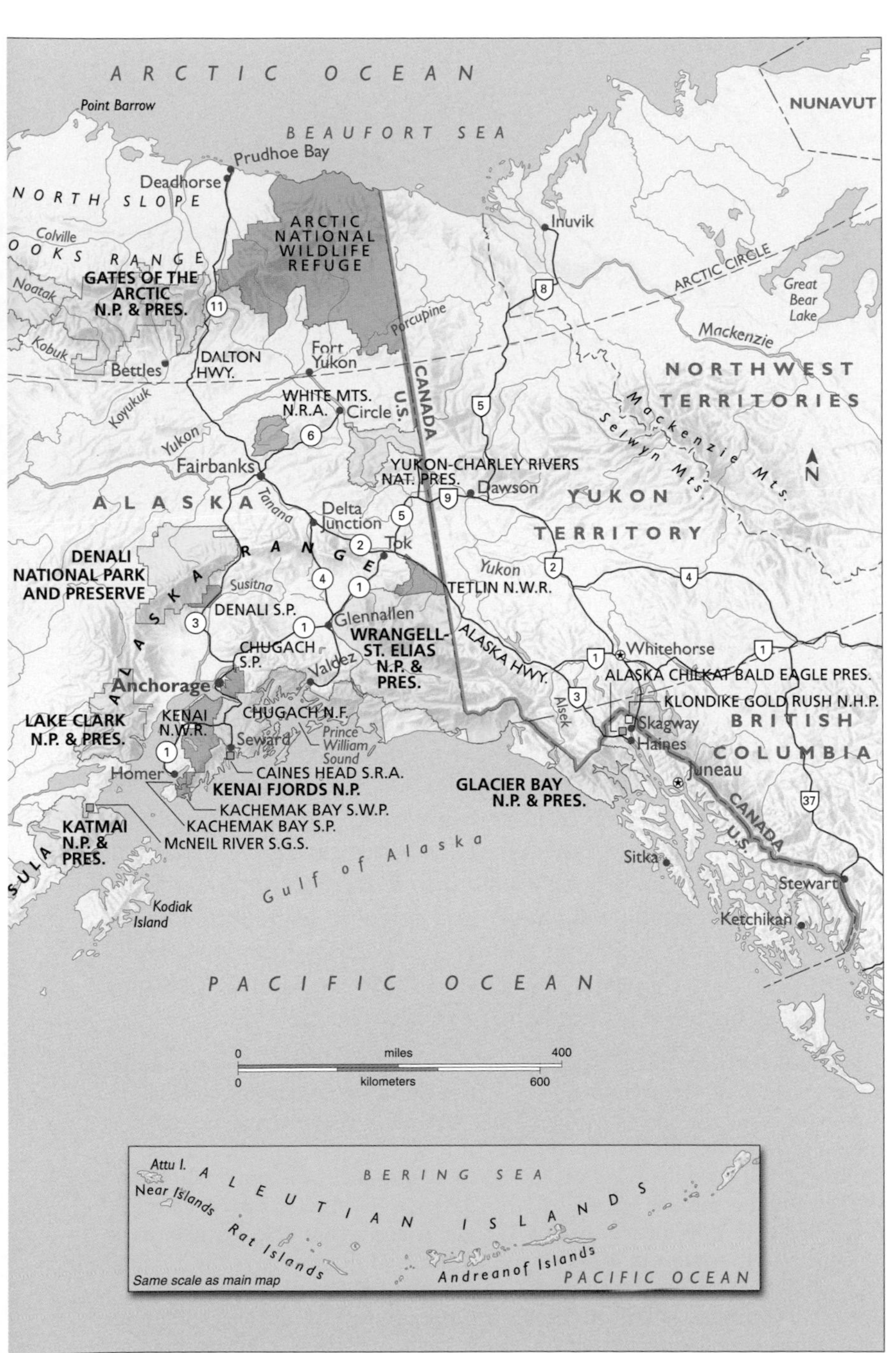
ARCTIC OCEAN
Point Barrow
BEAUFORT SEA
NUNAVUT
Prudhoe Bay
Deadhorse
NORTH SLOPE
ARCTIC NATIONAL WILDLIFE REFUGE
Inuvik
Colville
BROOKS RANGE
GATES OF THE ARCTIC N.P. & PRES.
Noatak
ARCTIC CIRCLE
Great Bear Lake
Porcupine
Mackenzie
Kobuk
Bettles
DALTON HWY.
Fort Yukon
NORTHWEST TERRITORIES
Koyukuk
WHITE MTS. N.R.A.
Circle
U.S.
CANADA
Mackenzie Mts.
Selwyn Mts.
Yukon
Fairbanks
YUKON-CHARLEY RIVERS NAT. PRES.
Dawson
N
ALASKA
Tanana
Delta Junction
YUKON TERRITORY
ALASKA RANGE
Tok
DENALI NATIONAL PARK AND PRESERVE
Susitna
Yukon
TETLIN N.W.R.
DENALI S.P.
Glennallen
WRANGELL-ST. ELIAS N.P. & PRES.
ALASKA HWY.
CHUGACH S.P.
Valdez
Whitehorse
Anchorage
ALASKA CHILKAT BALD EAGLE PRES.
KLONDIKE GOLD RUSH N.H.P.
Alsek
LAKE CLARK N.P. & PRES.
KENAI N.W.R.
CHUGACH N.F.
Prince William Sound
Skagway
Haines
BRITISH COLUMBIA
Seward
Homer
CAINES HEAD S.R.A.
KENAI FJORDS N.P.
GLACIER BAY N.P. & PRES.
Juneau
KACHEMAK BAY S.W.P.
KACHEMAK BAY S.P.
KATMAI N.P. & PRES.
McNEIL RIVER S.G.S.
Gulf of Alaska
Sitka
Stewart
Kodiak Island
Ketchikan
PACIFIC OCEAN
0 miles 400
0 kilometers 600
Attu I.
ALEUTIAN ISLANDS
BERING SEA
Near Islands
Rat Islands
Andreanof Islands
PACIFIC OCEAN
Same scale as main map
ALASKA

Autumn tundra near Savage River

DENALI

ALASKA
ESTABLISHED FEBRUARY 26, 1917
6,028,203 acres

On any summer day in Denali, Alaska's most well-known national park, hundreds of people see sights that will stay with them the rest of their lives. Perhaps a golden eagle will soar off the cliffs at Polychrome Pass, or 20 Dall's sheep will rest on a green shoulder of Primrose Ridge, or a grizzly will ramble over the tundra at Sable Pass. Maybe a caribou will pause on a ridgetop, silhouetted by the warm light of day's end, or a loon will call across Wonder Lake, or clouds will part to reveal the great massif of Mount McKinley, 20,320 feet high, the roof of North America.

The drama is always there. To see it, all you need to do is travel the 92-mile park road. The farther you go, the more you'll see, for the subarctic landscape will open up as big as the sky and the animals will move through it with wild, ancient poetry.

Other North American parks have their wildlife, but none has animals so visible or diverse as Denali. And other parks have their mountains, but none with a stature so stunning, a summit so towering as McKinley.

Denali's visitors have increased 1,000 percent in 30 years. Accommodating them without eroding the park's wilderness has been a struggle. A bus system that permits maximum wildlife viewing while holding down traffic has been designed. Campgrounds are modest and unobtrusive. And the wilderness areas have strict visitation ceilings to prevent overcrowding and damage to the flora and fauna. Unless you plan ahead by using the parks easy-to-use reservation system, you may have to wait a day or two to get your preferred campsite or bus reservation.

How to Get There

From Anchorage, take Alas. 1 (Glenn Hwy.) 35 miles north to Alas. 3 (George Parks Hwy.). Go north 205 miles. From Fairbanks, take Alas. 3 west and south 120 miles. In summer, the Alaska Railroad runs between Anchorage and Fairbanks and stops daily at the Denali railroad station. In winter, the train runs on weekends only. Air service available in summer to nearby airstrips from Anchorage, Fairbanks, and Talkeetna.

When to Go

In summer, there are up to 21 hours of daylight. Buses carry visitors into the park late May to mid-September. June is usually less crowded than July and August. In late August or early September, the tundra turns rich tones of red, orange, and yellow. In winter, visitors can take the road 3 miles to park headquarters and cross-country ski, snowshoe, or dogsled from there.

May and early June are the best times to climb Mount McKinley; after June, avalanches and crevasses threaten. Most mountaineers fly from Talkeetna and land at 7,200 feet on the Kahiltna Glacier to begin a climb that will take 15 to 30 days.

How to Visit

The more time the better, but plan on at least 2 days. The park is undergoing significant changes to handle the increased visitors; check ahead for road and trail changes.

Any private vehicle can travel the park road for 15 miles to **Savage River Check Station;** after that only those with camping permits for Teklanika Campground may continue. For everyone else, shuttle buses and tour buses operate on the road by day and into evening, late May to mid-September; schedules vary.

The 85-mile shuttle bus trip along the park road to **Wonder Lake** takes 11 hours round-trip but stops at destinations along the way. Visitors can take other buses as far as Kantishna, the end of the road, a 13-hour trip. Take a jacket, binoculars, and lunch (available near the **Denali Visitor Center** or outside the park; no food along the way). In the park, consider getting off the bus for a hike; buses will stop almost anywhere. To get on another bus, just wave one down. In busy times, you may have to wait a while for one with space.

Park campgrounds and buses fill quickly, so plan for the possibility of staying a night or two in a hotel or private campground if you must wait for a campsite or bus ticket.

Mount McKinley is often covered with clouds; you may be more likely to get a clear view of it early or late in the long day.

PARK ROAD BY BUS

92 miles one way; 13 hours round-trip

Although the complete trip takes a full day, shorter bus rides into the park can provide an equally enjoyable visit. Your bus journey begins at the **Wilderness Access Center** (mile 0.6), surrounded by the spruce forest and taiga.

Within minutes you'll see the railroad station used by the Alaska Railroad, and the new **Denali Visitor Center** campus. After a mile you'll pass park headquarters, where sled dogs are kept for winter patrols and summer demonstrations.

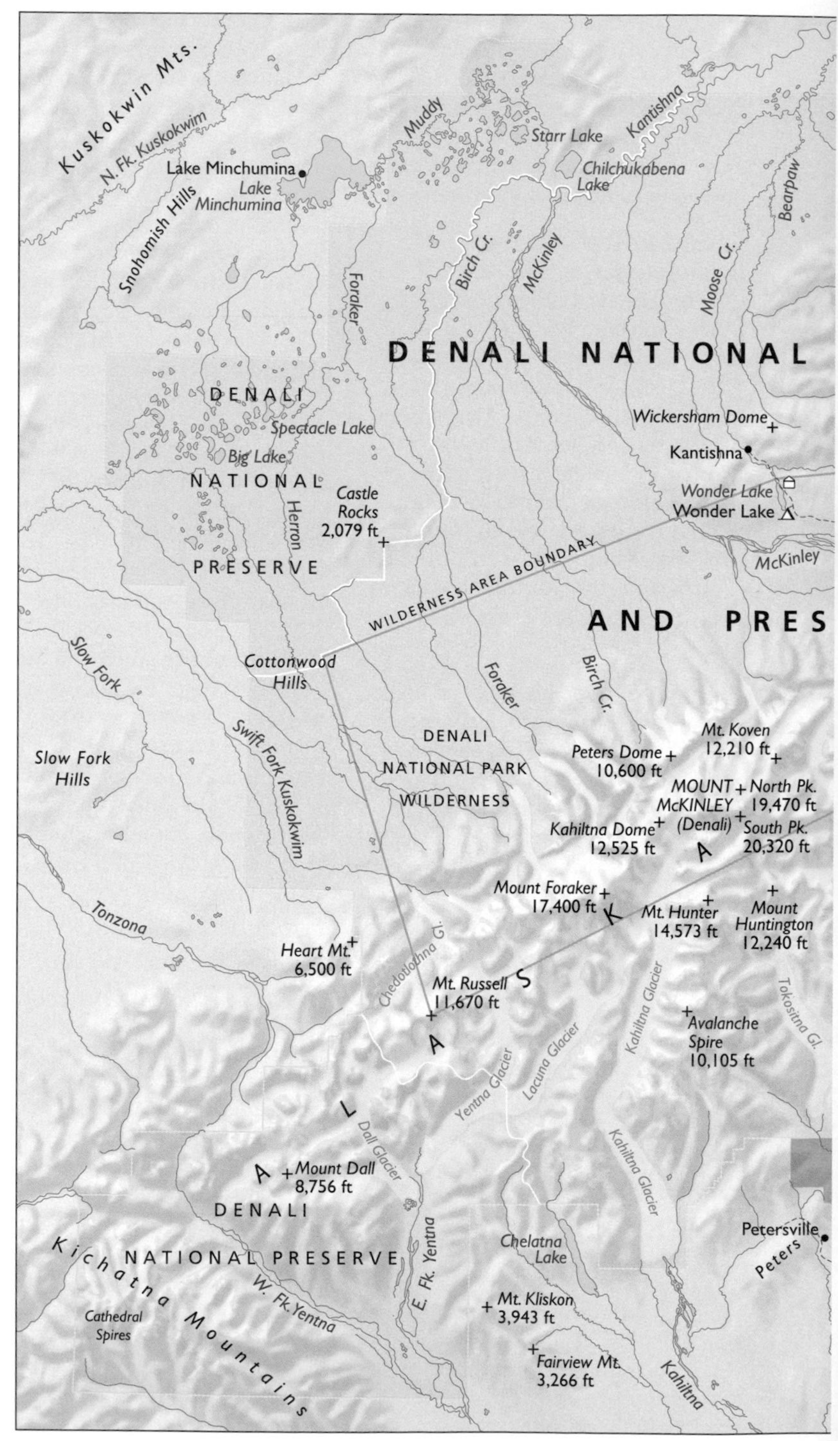

Kuskokwin Mts.
N. Fk. Kuskokwim
Lake Minchumina
Lake Minchumina
Snohomish Hills
Muddy
Starr Lake
Kantishna
Chilchukabena Lake
Bearpaw
Birch Cr.
McKinley
Moose Cr.
Foraker
DENALI NATIONAL
DENALI
Spectacle Lake
Big Lake
NATIONAL
PRESERVE
Castle Rocks 2,079 ft
Herron
Wickersham Dome
Kantishna
Wonder Lake
Wonder Lake
McKinley
WILDERNESS AREA BOUNDARY
AND PRES
Slow Fork
Cottonwood Hills
Foraker
Birch Cr.
Swift Fork Kuskokwim
Slow Fork Hills
DENALI
NATIONAL PARK
WILDERNESS
Peters Dome 10,600 ft
Mt. Koven 12,210 ft
MOUNT McKINLEY (Denali)
North Pk. 19,470 ft
South Pk. 20,320 ft
Kahiltna Dome 12,525 ft
Mount Foraker 17,400 ft
Mt. Hunter 14,573 ft
Mount Huntington 12,240 ft
Tonzona
Heart Mt. 6,500 ft
Chedotlothna Gl.
Mt. Russell 11,670 ft
Kahiltna Glacier
Tokositna Gl.
Avalanche Spire 10,105 ft
Lacuna Glacier
Yentna Glacier
A L A S K A
Dall Glacier
Kahiltna Glacier
Mount Dall 8,756 ft
DENALI
NATIONAL PRESERVE
Kichatna Mountains
E. Fk. Yentna
Chelatna Lake
Petersville
Peters
W. Fk. Yentna
Cathedral Spires
Mt. Kliskon 3,943 ft
Fairview Mt. 3,266 ft
Kahiltna

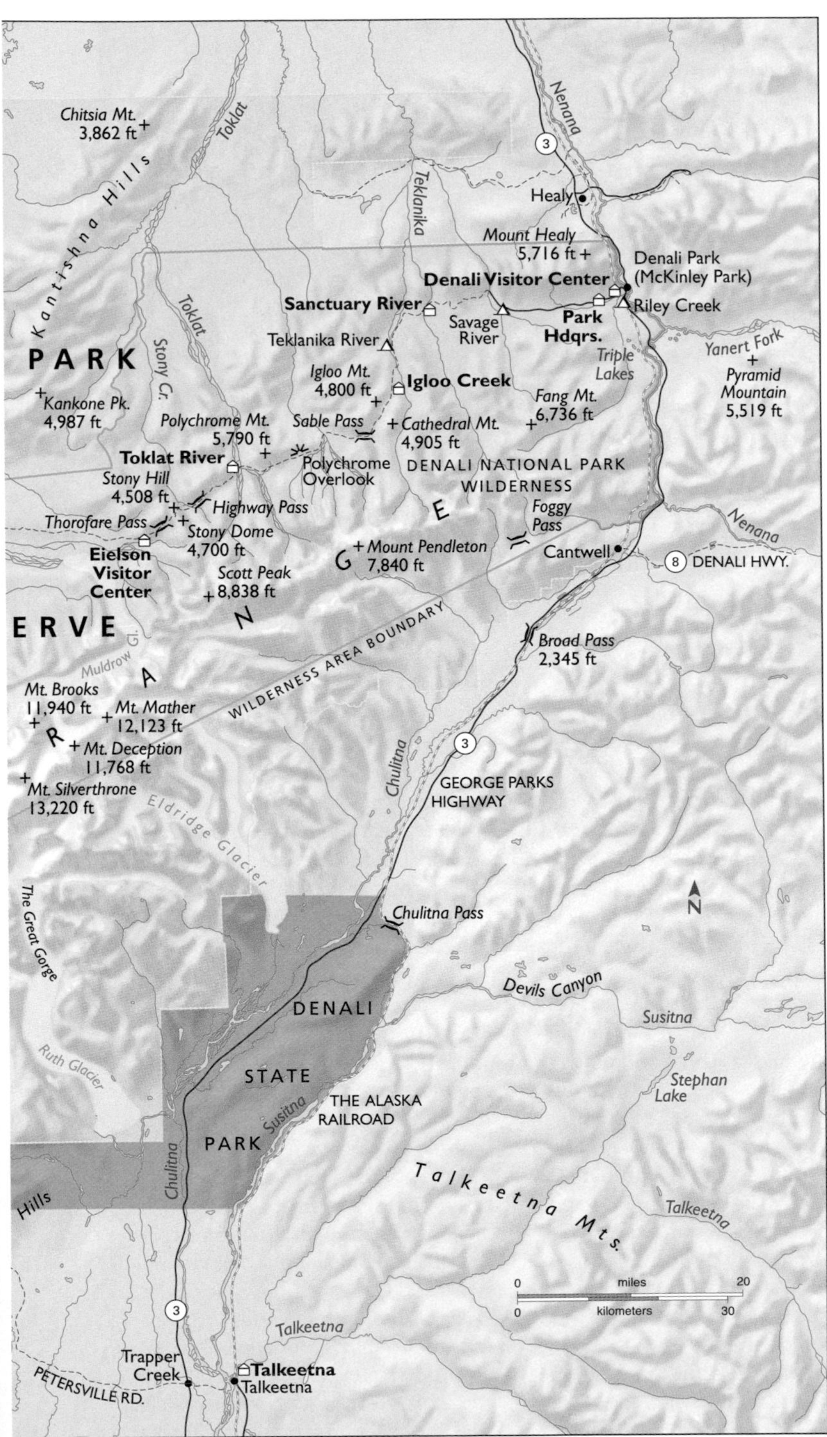
Chitsia Mt.
3,862 ft
Toklat
Kantishna Hills
Teklanika
Nenana
Healy
Mount Healy
5,716 ft
Denali Park
(McKinley Park)
Denali Visitor Center
Sanctuary River
Riley Creek
Savage River
Park Hdqrs.
Toklat
Teklanika River
PARK
Stony Cr.
Triple Lakes
Yanert Fork
Pyramid Mountain
5,519 ft
Igloo Mt.
4,800 ft
Igloo Creek
Kankone Pk.
4,987 ft
Fang Mt.
6,736 ft
Polychrome Mt.
5,790 ft
Sable Pass
Cathedral Mt.
4,905 ft
Toklat River
Polychrome Overlook
DENALI NATIONAL PARK
WILDERNESS
Stony Hill
4,508 ft
Highway Pass
Thorofare Pass
Stony Dome
4,700 ft
Foggy Pass
Nenana
Eielson Visitor Center
Mount Pendleton
7,840 ft
Cantwell
8
DENALI HWY.
Scott Peak
8,838 ft
ERVE
WILDERNESS AREA BOUNDARY
Broad Pass
2,345 ft
Muldrow Gl.
Mt. Brooks
11,940 ft
Mt. Mather
12,123 ft
Mt. Deception
11,768 ft
Mt. Silverthrone
13,220 ft
Chulitna
GEORGE PARKS
HIGHWAY
Eldridge Glacier
The Great Gorge
Chulitna Pass
Devils Canyon
Susitna
DENALI
STATE
PARK
Ruth Glacier
Stephan Lake
THE ALASKA
RAILROAD
Susitna
Chulitna
Hills
Talkeetna Mts.
Talkeetna
0
miles
20
kilometers
30
Talkeetna
Trapper Creek
Talkeetna
Talkeetna
PETERSVILLE RD.

DENALI

North Face of Mount Hunter

Soon the road begins climbing out of the taiga and into the treeless expanse of the tundra. Magnificent vistas open up; on clear days **Mount McKinley** can be seen 70 miles to the southwest. As the bus crosses the **Savage River Bridge** (mile 14.8), note how the gentle, glacier-sculptured topography to the south meets the rugged river-cut canyon to the north; this spot marks the farthest advance of a glacier that flowed north out of the **Alaska Range** and across the valley thousands of years ago.

The road winds below **Primrose Ridge** before dropping into a marshy flat where spruce trees lean haphazardly. This "drunken forest" forms as permafrost thaws and the land slumps gradually downhill, tilting the trees. Watch for moose here and in other spruce forests, especially in areas with willow.

Just beyond Teklanika River Campground (mile 29) is the **Teklanika River Bridge.** Like other rivers in Denali, the Teklanika is braided by channels. Its Athabaskan name means "middle water." The road passes Igloo Creek Campground and cuts between **Igloo** and **Cathedral Mountains,** favorite haunts of Dall's sheep, the world's only species of wild white sheep. Watch for them on the upper slopes.

If you want to see grizzly bears, a good place is up the road at **Sable Pass** (3,895 feet). Grizzlies feed primarily on roots, berries, and other plant materials, and occasionally on arctic ground squirrels, moose calves, injured caribou, and carrion. To protect the bears' habitat, this area is closed to off-road foot traffic.

About 5 miles farther, the road climbs a steep slope to **Polychrome Pass** and a spectacular view of the Alaska Range to the south. Below see the **Plains of Murie,** where fast running water has created alluvial terraces. At mile 53.1 the **Toklat River** has special significance, for it was here (5 miles north of where the bridge crosses the river today) that naturalist Charles Sheldon built a cabin and wintered in 1907-08. The area so inspired him that he moved back East and spent 9 years lobbying for legislation to create Alaska's first national park. Originally called Mount McKinley, the park in 1980 was renamed Denali—an Athabaskan name for the mountain meaning "the great one."

The road reaches its highest elevation at **Highway Pass** (3,980 feet) before descending to cross **Stony Creek** and climbing again to the **Stony Hill Overlook,** where, weather permitting, Mount McKinley looms into view 40 miles away. Watch for caribou as they funnel through the Stony Hill area. Although the total Denali herd numbers about 1,800, caribou usually move in small groups. They can appear almost any time of day anywhere in the lowlands between the park road and the Alaska Range.

While the **Eielson Visitor Center** (mile 66) is under construction during the 2006 and 2007 seasons, visitor services will be provided in temporary facilities at the **Toklat Rest Stop** (mile 53) where park naturalists will lead interpretive walks.

Continuing west, the road cuts along a steep cliff, then enters gentler terrain as it comes within a mile of the dark, gravel-covered snout of the **Muldrow Glacier** to the south. Beginning just below the summit of Mount McKinley, the Muldrow flows 35 miles through a granite gorge and across the tundra to its terminus. Twice in the last hundred years (and for reasons not fully understood) the Muldrow has surged forward, most recently in the winter of 1956-57, when it advanced 5 miles.

The road passes several ponds where chances improve for sighting beaver, moose, and waterfowl, and finally arrives at Wonder Lake Campground. Here the shuttle bus will either turn around for the 5.5-hour trip back or continue on to **Kantishna.**

Twenty-seven miles to the south looms Mount McKinley, its north face—the **Wickersham Wall**—rising more than 14,000 feet in a single precipice, one of the greatest mountain walls in the world. And just north of the campground lies **Wonder Lake,** 2.6 miles long, 280 feet deep, and home to lake trout, burbot, and moose that occasionally wade in belly-deep to feed on aquatic vegetation near the shore. Loons, grebes, and mergansers also visit.

HIKES

In a park larger than New Hampshire, the hiking opportunities are endless. Most of the maintained trails are near the Denali Visitor Center. Maps are available at the nearby Denali bookstore or other locations near the park entrance.

The **Horseshoe Lake Trail** winds gently through a handsome forest of aspen and spruce 1.25 miles to **Horseshoe Lake,** an old oxbow of the **Nenana River.** It takes about 1 hour round-trip. Branching off this trail is a more strenuous one, the **Mount Healy Overlook Trail.** Climbing 1,700 feet in less than 3 miles (one way), it breaks above timberline and arrives at the overlook among wildflowers, rock outcrops, arctic ground squirrels, and pikas. And, if the weather is clear, Mount McKinley is visible more than 80 miles to the southwest. A new accessible quarter-mile trail begins at the Savage Cabin Campground and leads to **Savage Cabin,** where summer living history

Prairie dog surveying the action *(top left)*; red fox *(top right)*
Observant Dall's sheep *(bottom)*

demonstrations are held.

For those seeking a moderate hike, the 3-mile **Triple Lakes Trail** is a good choice with its excellent views of **Mount Fellows, Pyramid Mountain,** and other peaks in the Alaska Range at its beginning.

In the backcountry, hiking is a matter of taking whatever route you wish—down a drainage, up a ridge, across a valley. The object is to spread out and tread lightly, and leave no evidence of your visit.

Popular backcountry hiking areas (without trails) include Primrose Ridge, Mount Wright, Igloo Mountain, Cathedral Mountain, Calico Creek, Tattler Creek, the Polychrome Cliffs, Stony Dome and Stony Hill, the Stony Creek, the Sunrise Glacier, Sunset Glacier, Thoroughfare Ridge, and around Wonder Lake. Some of these hikes take an hour or more, some take several days.

Since a backcountry management unit might be closed or full, those wishing to camp are required to check at the Backcountry Information Center before choosing an overnight hike. Some areas may be restricted in order to protect critical wildlife habitats, and animal activity may temporarily close backcountry sections.

INFORMATION & ACTIVITIES

HEADQUARTERS
P.O. Box 9, Denali, AK 99755. Phone (907) 683-2294. www.nps.gov/dena

SEASONS & ACCESSIBILITY
Park open all year. Entire park road open, weather permitting, late-May to mid-Sept. to buses. Car travel to Savage River, 15 miles into the park, permitted. Those with camping reservations are permitted to drive to the Teklanika Campground (mile 29). If the road is passable, private vehicles are allowed to drive the first 31 miles when the buses are not running. During snow season, park road is not plowed beyond headquarters (mile 3.1), which limits access to skiers, snowshoers, and dogsledders.

VISITOR & INFORMATION CENTERS
Denali Visitor Center (mile 1.6) open mid-May to mid-Sept.
Murie Science and Learning Center (mile 1.7) serves as winter visitor center.
Talkeetna Ranger Station open mid-April to Labor Day; weekdays rest of year. Off-season information available at headquarters, open all year.

ENTRANCE FEE
$10 fee per person per week; $20 per family; $40 annual.

SHUTTLE BUSES
From the Wilderness Access Center, buses depart regularly from 5:00 a.m. to 3:00 p.m. between late May and mid-Sept. Reserve in advance. Fees range from $18.50 to $33 for adults, depending on destination. To make reservations, call (800) 622-7275 or (907) 272-7275. Trips not narrated, but buses stop for wildlife watching. Twice daily campers bus. Also, Tundra Wilderness tour ($74) and Natural History tour ($40). (800) 276-7234 or (907) 276-7234 for required reservations.

FACILITIES FOR DISABLED
Most buildings accessible to wheelchairs, as are some tour and shuttle buses. Please advise staff of need when making reservations.

THINGS TO DO
Free ranger-led activities: nature walks and hikes, children's programs, sled-dog demonstrations, talks, slide shows, and films. Also, narrated bus tours, hiking, limited fishing, mountain climbing, rafting, horseback riding, cross-country skiing, dogsledding.

OVERNIGHT BACKPACKING
Backcountry divided into units with limits (2-12) on the number of campers. Permits required; available free at Backcountry Information Center, first come, first served. Must carry bear-proof containers. Backpacker shuttle fee $23.75.

CAMPGROUNDS
Five campgrounds (294 sites), 14-day limit from mid-May to mid-Sept.; other times, 30-day limit. **Riley Creek** open all year. Others open late spring to early fall. In summer, reservations strongly recommended (800) 622-7275 or (907) 272-7275. Fees $6-$16 per night. RV sites except at **Sanctuary** and **Wonder Lake;** no hookups. Buses transport campers to Sanctuary, **Igloo Creek,** Wonder Lake, and farther. Must reserve for **Savage River Group Campground;** contact headquarters.

HOTELS, MOTELS, & INNS
(unless otherwise noted, rates are for 2 persons in a double room, high season)

INSIDE THE PARK:
Camp Denali and **North Face Lodge** P.O. Box 67, Denali NP, 99775. (907) 683-2290. Camp Denali: 17 cabins, central showers. North Face Lodge: 15 rooms. $425 per person, all inclusive. Early June to mid-Sept.
Denali Backcountry Lodge Denali NP, 99775 (800) 841-0692. 30 units. $325-$560 per person per night, all inclusive. June to Sept.
Kantishna Roadhouse, Denali NP, 99775. (800) 942-7420. $360 per person, all inclusive, 2 day min. June to mid-Sept.
OUTSIDE THE PARK:
Denali Cabins P.O. Box 229, Denali NP, 99755. (907) 683-2643. 45 units. $139-$219. Rest. Mid-May to mid-Sept.
Denali Princess Lodge P.O. Box 110, Denali NP, 99755. (907) 683-2282. 352 units. $219. Restaurant. Mid-May to mid-Sept.

ALASKA EXCURSIONS

DENALI STATE PARK
TALKEETNA, ALASKA

Wedged between the Talkeetna Mountains and the Alaska Range, 325,240-acre Denali State Park abuts the larger national park. The state park contains terrain and animals similar to its neighbor, but provides additional accessibility and camping when the neighboring NP is full. There are 4 developed campgrounds with more than 120 campsites and 2 year-round cabins (reservations required). Located on Parks Hwy. Mileposts 131.7–169.2. (907) 745-3975.

CHUGACH NATIONAL FOREST
ANCHORAGE, ALASKA

The Chugach includes 3,550 miles of coastline, more than 200 bird species, and numerous glaciers, including one, the Portage, that is easily accessible from Anchorage. 5,936,000 acres. 400 campsites, 36 cabins. Activities: hiking, boating, boat ramp, climbing, bicycling, fishing, horseback riding, hunting, picnic areas, scenic drives, winter sports, water sports. Handicapped access. Open all year; most campsites open late May to early September. Visitor center at Portage on Seward-Anchorage Hwy., about 35 miles SE of Anchorage. (907) 271-2500.

KENAI NATIONAL WILDLIFE REFUGE
SOLDOTNA, ALASKA

Large numbers of moose share this refuge with bears, mountain goats, Dall's sheep, loons, eagles, and salmon, rainbow trout, and arctic char. Nearly 2,000,000 acres including two large glacier carved lakes—Skilak and Tustumena. Activities: camping, hiking, boating, fishing, hunting, picnicking, scenic drives, water sports. Handicapped access. Adjacent to Kenai Fjords NP. Visitor center at Soldotna on Sterling Hwy., about 110 miles SW of Anchorage. (907) 262-7021.

TETLIN NATIONAL WILDLIFE REFUGE
TOK, ALASKA

Bounded by the Alaska Highway on the north and Wrangell-St. Elias National Park on the south, Tetlin's 930,000 acres offer a wilderness experience among marshes, lakes, ponds, rivers, forests, and hills abundant with waterfowl and fish. Facilities include 23 campsites, picnic areas, boat ramp. Activities include hiking, boating, fishing, and hunting. Open all year. Visitor center on Alaska Hwy. (milepost 1229) about 300 miles SE of Fairbanks. (907) 883-5312.

YUKON-CHARLEY RIVERS NATIONAL PRESERVE
EAGLE, ALASKA

For millennia, the Yukon corridor has seen passing boats and sleds and migrating herds of caribou, but humans have made little imprint. Breeding ground for a large population of peregrine falcons. With its tributary, the Yukon offers superb boating and floating. 2,527,000 acres. Activities include primitive camping, climbing, fishing, hunting. Open all year. Gateway towns of Circle and Eagle reached by Steese and Taylor Hwys. respectively. Access by boat or air charter. Info. at Eagle headquarters. (907) 547-2233.

WHITE MOUNTAINS NATIONAL RECREATION AREA
FAIRBANKS, ALASKA

The jagged White Mountains preside over wild Beaver Creek and an extensive winter cabin/trail system, inviting a closeup look by skiers, dog mushers, and snowmobile riders. Summer hiking trail traverses spruce forests and alpine ridges for 22 miles to reach the creek. 1,000,000 acres. Activities include primitive camping, 10 cabins (reservations required), boating, climbing, fishing, horseback riding. Open all year. Trailheads located off Steese and Elliot Hwys. 30 to 70 miles N of Fairbanks. (907) 474-2351.

Meandering Alatna River

GATES OF THE ARCTIC

ALASKA

ESTABLISHED DECEMBER 2, 1980

8,500,000 acres

"The view from the top gave us an excellent idea of the jagged country toward which we were heading. The main Brooks Range divide was entirely covered with snow. Close at hand, only about ten miles to the north, was a precipitous pair of mountains, one on each side of the North Fork. I bestowed the name Gates of the Arctic on them."

It was the early 1930s, and Robert Marshall had found his wilderness home, an unpeopled, uncluttered source of inspiration that would make him one of America's greatest conservationists. Gates of the Arctic was the ultimate North American wilderness. Congress created the park to keep it that way.

Climb practically any ridge in the heart of the park and you'll see a dozen glacial cirques side by side; serrated mountains that scythe the sky; and storms that snap out of dark, brooding clouds. Six National Wild and Scenic Rivers—Alatna, John, Kobuk, Noatak, North Fork Koyukuk, and Tinayguk—tumble out of high alpine valleys into forested lowlands. The park lies entirely above the Arctic Circle, straddling the Brooks Range, one of the world's northernmost mountain chains.

Along with Kobuk Valley National Park and Noatak National Preserve, Gates of the Arctic protects much of the habitat of the western arctic caribou. Grizzlies, wolves, wolverines, and foxes also roam over the severe land in search of food. Ptarmigan nibble on willow, and gyrfalcons dive for ptarmigan.

Shafts of cinnabar sunlight pour through the mountains at 2 a.m. in June, setting the wild land ablaze. In this mammoth mountain kingdom—the northernmost reach of the Rockies—the summer sun does not set for 30 straight days.

"No sight or sound or smell or feeling even remotely hinted of men or their creations," wrote Marshall. "It seemed as if time had dropped away a million years and we were back in a primordial world."

How to Get There

Bush pilots say that where the road ends, the real Alaska begins. And so it is in Gates of the Arctic. You can fly or walk in; most people fly. From Fairbanks (about 250 miles away), scheduled flights serve Anaktuvuk Pass, an Eskimo village within the park borders; Bettles/ Evansville; and Ambler, to the west.

Arrigetch Creek

From those points or from Fairbanks or Coldfoot, you can air taxi into the park. Allow time for bad weather and delayed flights. From Anaktuvuk Pass, you can also hike into the park along the John River.

Or, you can drive up from Fairbanks on the unpaved Dalton Highway (a pipeline haul road that's also open to the public) and hike to the park from Wiseman or other points. But it's a long, hard walk into the interior.

When to Go

Summer. It is short, but days are very long and for a while temperatures may be relatively mild. Weather is highly unpredictable. Expect snow or rain in any month. August can be very wet, with freezing temperatures by mid-month. Mosquitoes and gnats are bad in late June and July. Fall colors peak in mid-August at high elevations, late August to early September at low elevations.

How to Visit

Allow enough time to savor the subtle beauty of this vast wilderness. A combination river-hiking trip offers the best of both. Air taxis are equipped to land on lakes and gravel bars for drop-offs and pickups.

Plan carefully and bring everything you need; there are no visitor facilities in the park. This spare, harsh land is so fragile that a hiker's step can kill lichens that take 150 years to reach full growth. Certain areas were badly damaged by the increase in visitors after Gates of the Arctic became a park.

Write or call Bettles Ranger Station before planning a trip. There are no trails in the park, but you can ask for suggestions about areas to visit, along with names of air taxis, guides, and outfitters who operate in the park.

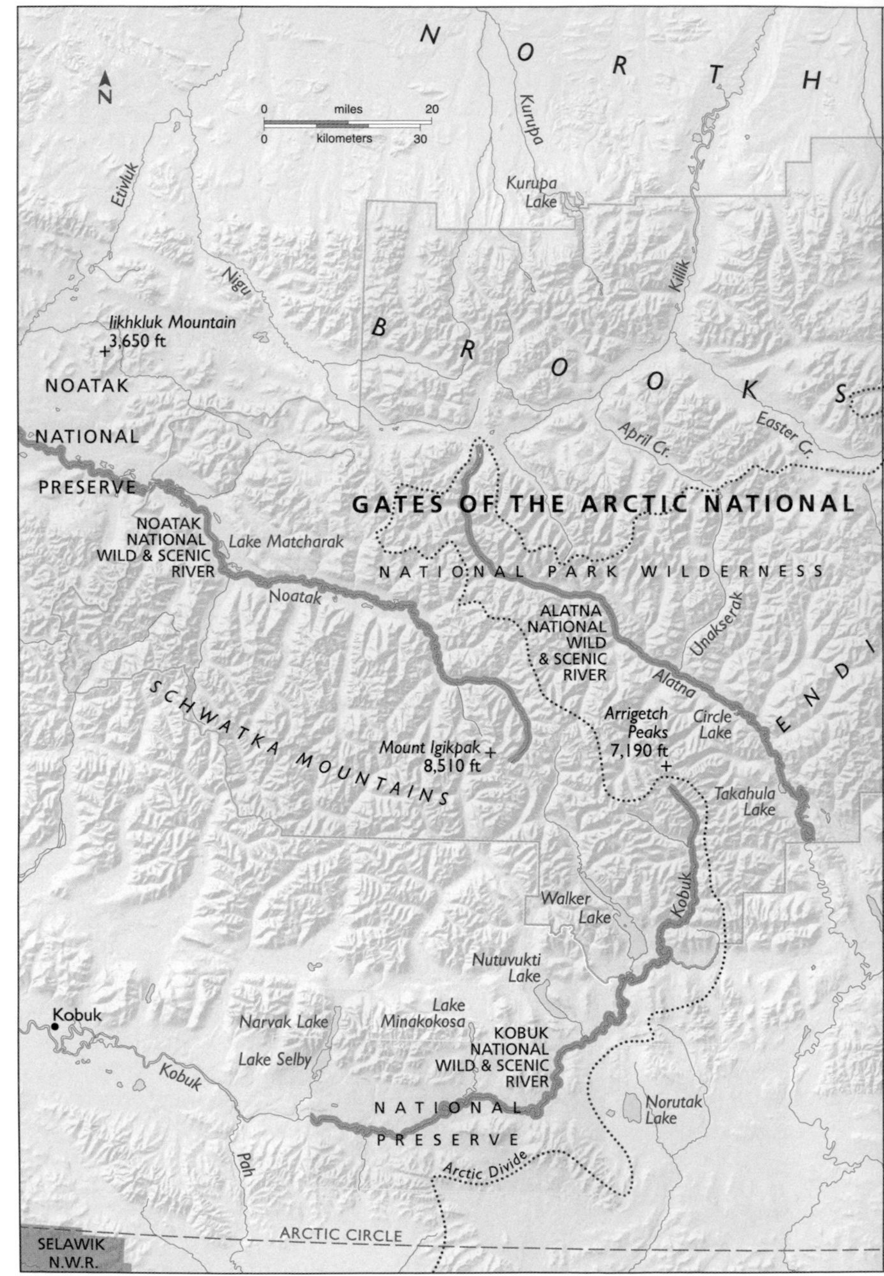

RIVER TRIPS

Rivers are the main travel routes through the park. Alaskan natives and caribou have followed them for centuries. Near some are lakes on which aircraft can land. Camping is good on the gravel bars, but be aware that summer rainstorms can quickly raise water levels. Most rivers are at their highest in May and June. Hiking is difficult but rewarding,

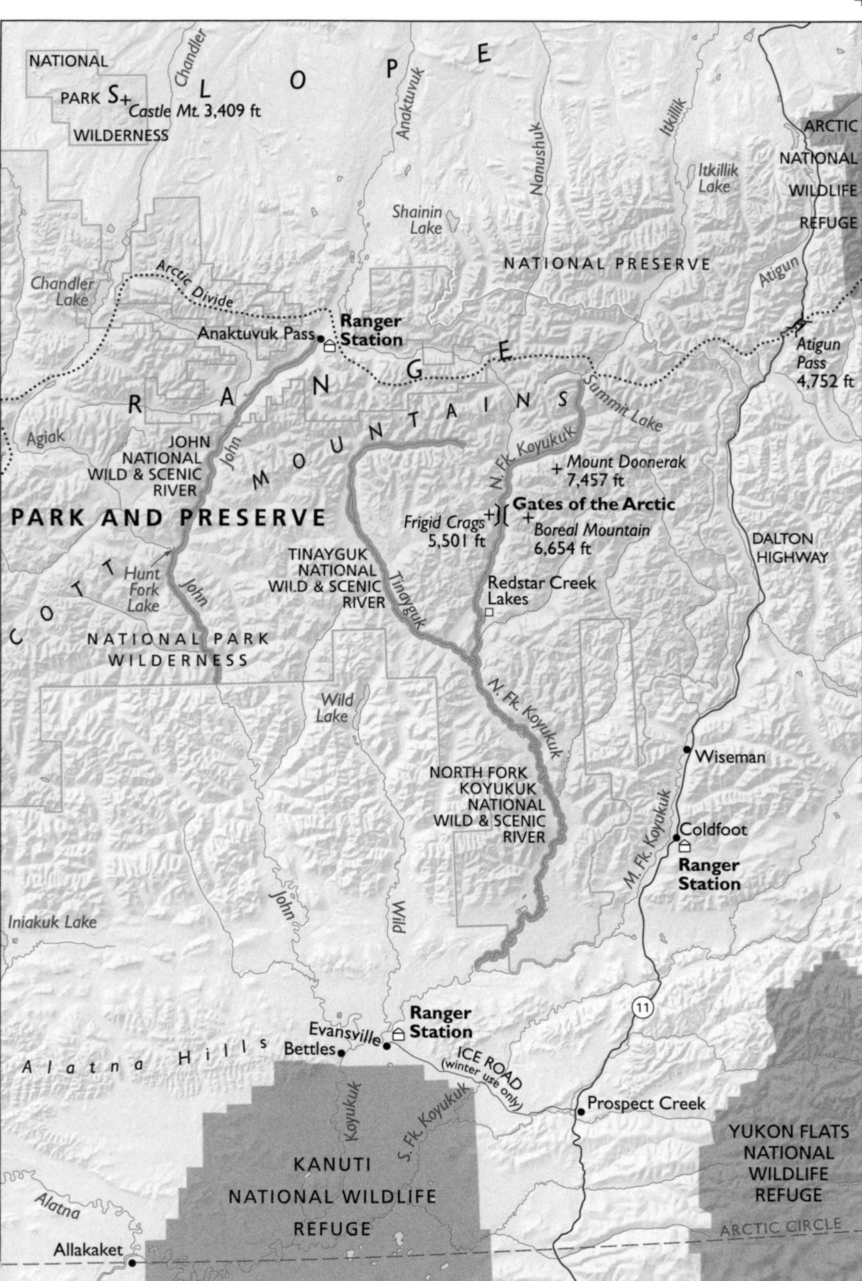

especially in alpine areas. The following rivers are a sampling of what the park has to offer:

Alatna River is ideal for a first wilderness float trip. It takes 4 to 7 days, running gently down from the treeless Arctic Divide through beautiful tundra to the forested **Koyukuk River** lowlands. There are put-ins at **Takahula Lake, Circle Lake,** or the unnamed lakes upstream. Most boaters take-out at the village of

Alatna River Valley near Circle Lake *(top)*; purple saxifrage *(bottom)*

Allakaket (75 and 85 miles from Takahula and Circle Lakes, respectively), where the Alatna meets the Koyukuk River.

John River is a mere stream at its headwaters, Anaktuvuk Pass (the permanent settlement of the inland Nunamiut Eskimo), but it gains power and momentum as it flows through the heart of the park. **Hunt Fork Lake** is the best put-in; water levels above this point are usually too low. The John River drops into lowland forest and joins the Koyukuk River just downstream of Bettles, a journey of a hundred miles.

Kobuk River begins at **Walker Lake** (with a portage) and runs south and west through mountains, canyons, foothills, and lowlands. Kobuk village, 140 river miles from Walker Lake, serves as a take-out. Or you can continue downriver to Ambler and on through Kobuk Valley NP to Kiana.

North Fork Koyukuk begins at **Summit Lake** and cuts between **Boreal Mountain** and **Frigid Crags**—the **Gates of the Arctic**—then flows past **Redstar Creek Lakes** (a good put-in) and continues south 100 miles to Bettles.

Creating one of the largest wilderness river basins on the continent, the **Noatak** flows 450 miles from Gates of the Arctic through Noatak preserve into the Chukchi Sea. The trip from a put-in at **Lake Matcharak** to Noatak village is 350 miles. The river, a major thoroughfare in a trackless realm, demands minimal boating skills but maximal planning. Allow a month for the trip.

The seldom visited **Tinayguk** flows through a broad glacier-cut valley and joins the Koyukuk below Boreal Mountain and Frigid Crags. Put in along the Tinayguk 35 miles north of where it joins the Koyukuk. (Consult local maps and outfitters for the exact location.) Float down to the Koyukuk, then continue on for another 80 miles to Bettles.

INFORMATION & ACTIVITIES

HEADQUARTERS
Bettles Ranger Station, P.O. Box 26030, Bettles, AK 99726. Phone (907) 692-5494. www.nps .gov/gaar

SEASONS & ACCESSIBILITY
Park open year-round. Access by air or foot; there are no roads to the park (except Dalton Highway, an unpaved pipeline haul road that's parallel to park's east boundary). There are no roads in the park. Contact park headquarters before planning a visit.

VISITOR & INFORMATION CENTERS
There are no visitor centers or facilities of any kind within the park. The only ranger stations are located in Bettles and Anaktuvuk Pass. An interagency visitor center is staffed in Coldfoot during the summer.

PETS
Only pack dogs allowed.

FACILITIES FOR DISABLED
Bettles and Anaktuvuk Pass Ranger Stations and Coldfoot Visitor Center.

THINGS TO DO
Hiking (no established trails), backpacking, canoeing, kayaking and rafting, fishing (license required), hunting (in preserve only, with license), rock- and mountain climbing, wildlife watching. In winter: cross-country skiing, snowshoeing, dogmushing, skiing. Ask park for list of licensed guides and outfitters (www.nps.gov/gaar/com mops.htm.)

SPECIAL ADVISORIES
• Bring all supplies with you—Fairbanks has a full selection, few available in communities of Bettles and Anaktuvuk Pass.
• Gas stations are on the Dalton Highway at milepost 56 and at Coldfoot, milepost 173.6.
• All visitors should be well skilled in the outdoors; firearms may be carried for protection.
• Grizzly and black bears are unpredictable and dangerous. Visit ranger station in Bettles or Coldfoot for advice on preventing an encounter.
• Eskimos and other Native Alaskans use the park for subsistence fishing and hunting; respect them and their property.
• From mid-June through July, be prepared for plenty of mosquitoes and gnats; bring insect repellent, a head net, and an insect-proof tent.
• Swift currents and freezing water can make river crossings particularly hazardous. Hypothermia is possible in 24-hour sunlight.

OVERNIGHT BACKPACKING
No permit required, but get up-to-date bear information from ranger station. An orientation is available at ranger stations. Food, stoves, and all equipment must be carried. Camp on gravel bars to avoid damaging fragile tundra. Bear barrels required; purchase or rent beforehand.

CAMPGROUNDS
None; backcountry camping only.

HOTELS, MOTELS, & INNS
(unless otherwise noted, rates are for 2 persons in a double room, high season)

INSIDE THE PARK:

Alatna Lodge (on headwaters of the Alatna River) Alatna Guide Service, P.O. Box 80424, Fairbanks, AK 99708. (907) 479-6354. 1 cabin, 6 beds. $4,150 per person for 3 days, including airfare from Fairbanks and activities. Open July to early Sept.

Nahtuk Wilderness Cabins (on Alatna River near Arrigetch Peaks) P.O. Box 80424, Fairbanks, AK 99708. (907) 479-6354. 1 cabin, 4 beds. $2,950 per person for 3 nights, including airfare. Open mid-June to early Sept.

OUTSIDE THE PARK:

Slate Creek Inn Mile 175, Dalton Hwy., Coldfoot, AK 99701. (907) 474-3500. 52 units. $145. Restaurant.

Coldfoot Services Motel Mile 175, Dalton Hwy., Coldfoot, AK 99701. (800) 474-3500. 50 units. $145. Restaurant.

Iniakuk Lake Wilderness Lodge (on Iniakuk Lake) P.O. Box 80424, Fairbanks, AK 99708. (907) 479-6354. 6 rooms, central bath. $3,750 per person for 3 nights, including airfare. Mid-June to mid-Sept.

Sunset view of Adams Inlet, from Muir Inlet

GLACIER BAY

ALASKA
ESTABLISHED DECEMBER 2, 1980
3,280,198 acres

When Capt. George Vancouver sailed the Alaska coast in 1794, Glacier Bay did not exist. It lay beneath a sheet of glacial ice several miles wide and thousands of feet thick. Since then, in one of the fastest glacial retreats on record, the ice has shrunk back 65 miles to unveil new land and a new bay, now returning to life after a long winter's sleep.

Scientists call Glacier Bay a living laboratory for the grand processes of glacial retreat, plant succession, and animal dynamics. It is an open book on the last ice age. At the southern end, where the ice departed 200 years ago, a spruce-hemlock rain forest has taken root. Farther north, the more recently deglaciated land becomes rugged and thinly vegetated.

The bay branches into two major arms, the west arm and Muir Inlet, which themselves branch into smaller inlets. There, on slopes deglaciated 50 to 100 years ago, alder and willow grow, while mosses, mountain avens, and dwarf fireweed pioneer areas exposed within 30 years.

The new vegetation creates habitats for wolves, moose, mountain goats, black bears, brown bears, ptarmigan, and other wildlife, and the sea supports a food chain that includes salmon, bald eagles, harbor seals, harbor porpoises, humpback whales, and killer whales—all in an environment less than 200 years old.

Glacier Bay is home to nine tidewater glaciers that calve. In part because of variations in snow accumulations, most glaciers in the eastern and southwestern areas of the bay are receding, while several on its west side are advancing.

The glaciers calve icebergs that hit the water with a sound like cannon shot. "White thunder," the Tlingit called it, the awesome voice of glacial ice. An iceberg's color often reveals its makeup; dense bergs are blue, while those filled with trapped air bubbles are white.

How to Get There

By boat or plane only. From Juneau, take a scheduled flight 53 miles to Gustavus. Catch the bus to Glacier Bay Lodge and Bartlett Cove Campground, 10 miles away at the park's southern end. Charter flights also service Gustavus from Juneau, Skagway, Haines, and Hoonah. Express ferries depart Thursday through Tuesday from Juneau to Bartlett Cove. Also the Alaska Marine Highway System began limited service in 2005. Private boats can enter the bay with permits (required June to August) obtained by phone, by mail from headquarters at Bartlett Cove, or online (www.nps.gov/glba).

When to Go

Late May to mid-September. Summer days are long and temperatures cool. May and June have the most sunshine, but the upper inlets can be thick with icebergs then and the tidewater glaciers less approachable. September is often rainy and windy.

How to Visit

Glacier Bay is a marine highway. Most visitors experience the park from the deck of a cruise ship, or a tour boat, or from waterline in a sea kayak. Many of the large cruise ships that travel southeastern Alaska's Inside Passage go into Glacier Bay. Other tours offer accommodations at **Glacier Bay Lodge** (the park's center of activity) and a 1-day trip to the glaciers and back. Campers and kayakers can take the boat and be dropped off at one of three sites up the bay, either to be picked up at a later date or to paddle back to Bartlett Cove.

THE LOWER BAY

The lower bay reaches from **Bartlett Cove** north to **Tlingit Point,** where it separates into its two arms and continues north. Bartlett Cove has the only three maintained trails in the park. Beginning at the **Glacier Bay Lodge,** the **Forest Loop Trail** is a 1-mile, 1-hour round-trip through the young spruce-hemlock rain forest. A wheelchair-accessible boardwalk covers the first part of the trail out to **Blackwater Pond.**

For a half-day more rugged trip, the **Bartlett River Trail** begins at the roadside, a half mile from the lodge, and winds another 1.5 miles through the rain forest to the **Bartlett River,** ending in a quiet meadow. It's not unusual to see red squirrels, blue grouse, and black bears along either of these trails. Finally, the **Beach Trail** runs one-half mile from the lodge area to park headquarters along the beachline. It is especially popular among walkers and cyclists.

If you want to kayak, the **Beardslee Islands** just north of Bartlett Cove offer a maze of shorelines and waterways—a quiet counterpoint to the buses and boats coming and going at the cove.

Reaching across the lower bay, **Sitakaday Narrows** is a shoal that creates strong and dangerous whirlpools and currents as the tides (rising and falling an average of 15 feet in 6 hours) rush over it. Check the tide before venturing into the Narrows.

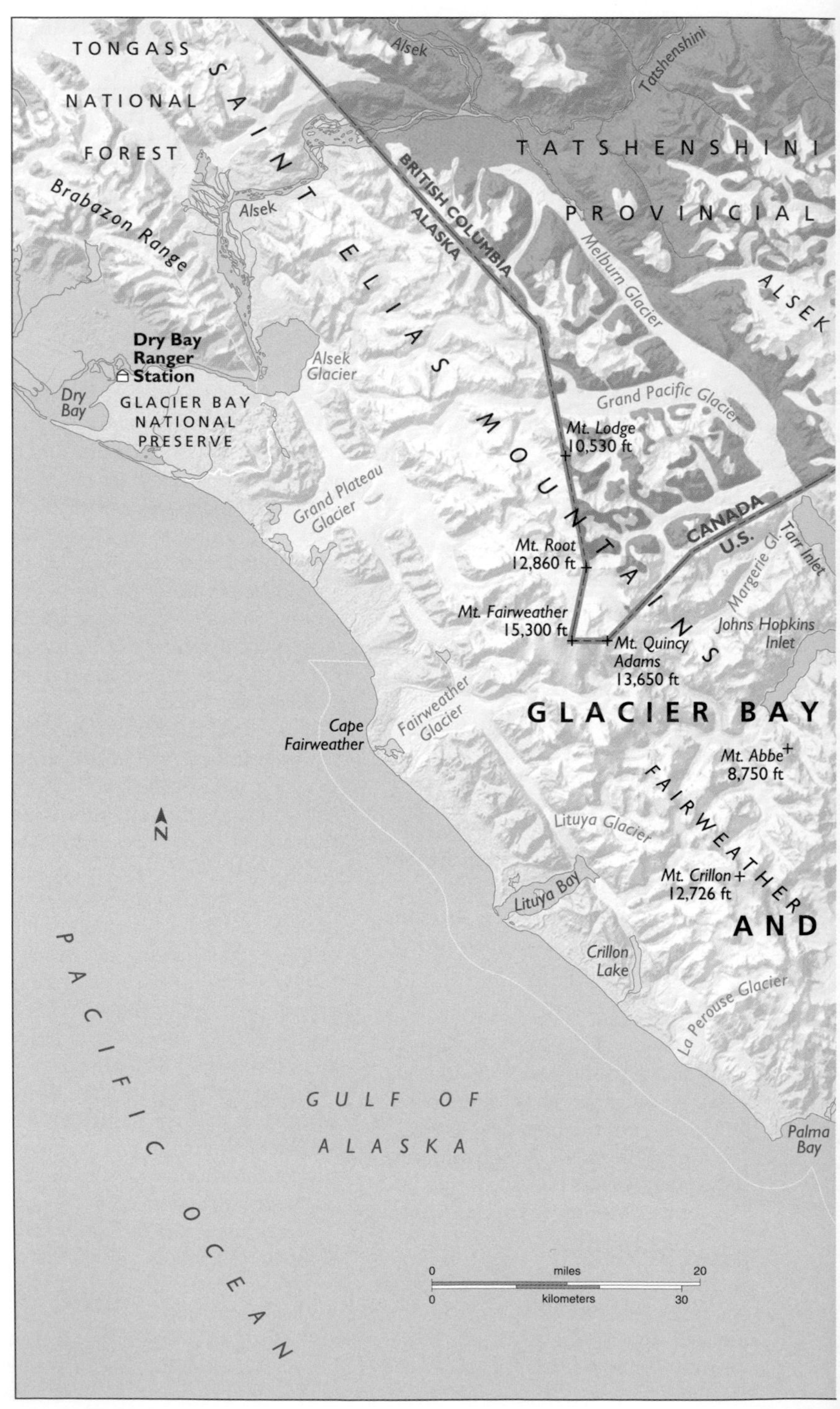
TONGASS NATIONAL FOREST
SAINT ELIAS MOUNTAINS
TATSHENSHINI PROVINCIAL
ALSEK
Alsek
Tatshenshini
BRITISH COLUMBIA
ALASKA
Brabazon Range
Alsek
Melburn Glacier
Dry Bay Ranger Station
Alsek Glacier
Dry Bay
GLACIER BAY NATIONAL PRESERVE
Grand Pacific Glacier
Mt. Lodge 10,530 ft
Grand Plateau Glacier
CANADA
U.S.
Tarr Inlet
Margerie Gl.
Mt. Root 12,860 ft
Mt. Fairweather 15,300 ft
Mt. Quincy Adams 13,650 ft
Johns Hopkins Inlet
GLACIER BAY
Cape Fairweather
Fairweather Glacier
Mt. Abbe 8,750 ft
FAIRWEATHER
Lituya Glacier
Mt. Crillon 12,726 ft
Lituya Bay
AND
Crillon Lake
La Perouse Glacier
N
PACIFIC OCEAN
GULF OF ALASKA
Palma Bay
0 miles 20
0 kilometers 30

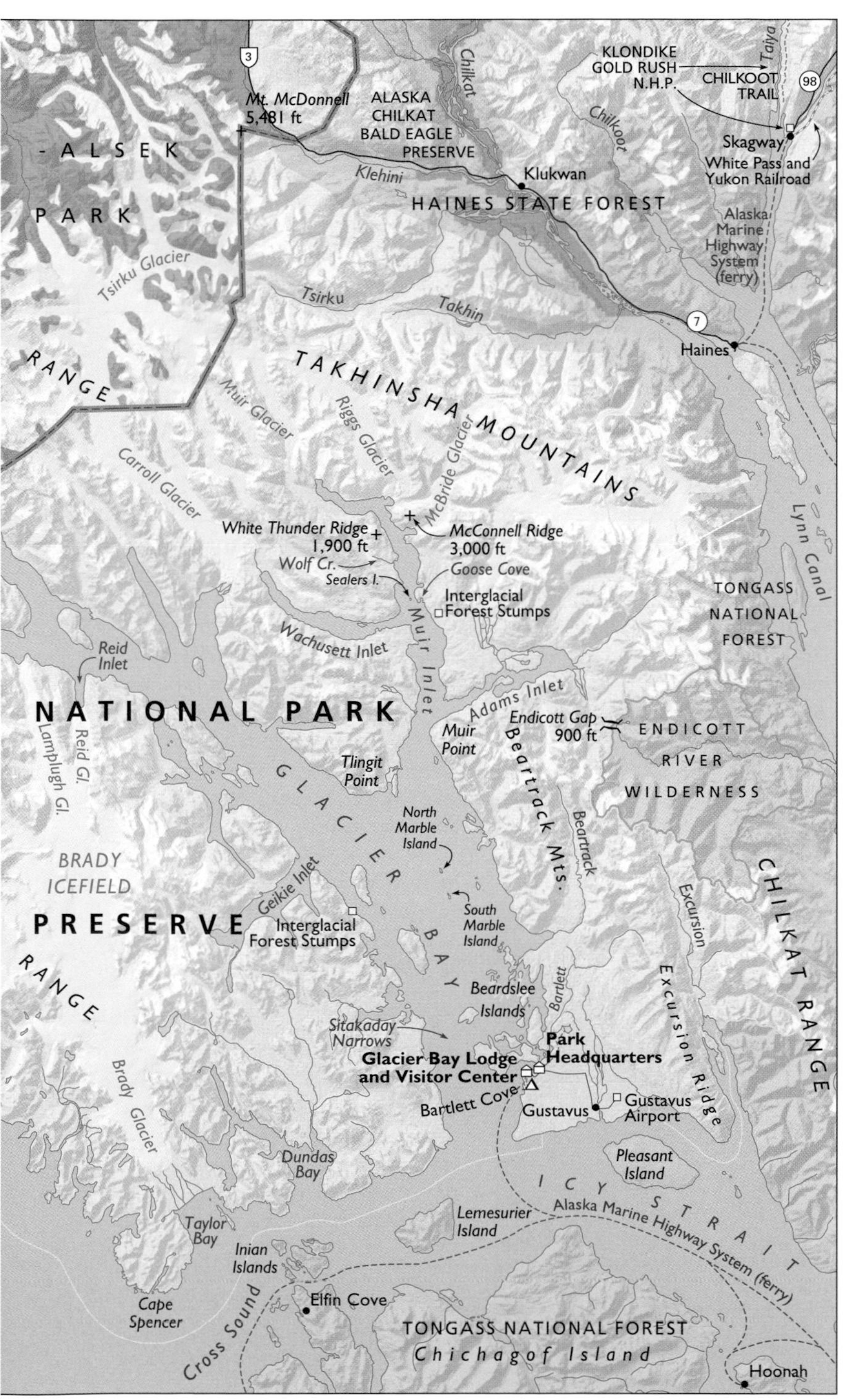

-ALSEK
PARK
RANGE
Tsirku Glacier
Mt. McDonnell 5,481 ft
3
ALASKA CHILKAT BALD EAGLE PRESERVE
Chilkat
Klehini
Klukwan
HAINES STATE FOREST
Chilkoot
KLONDIKE GOLD RUSH N.H.P.
CHILKOOT TRAIL
Taiya
98
Skagway
White Pass and Yukon Railroad
Alaska Marine Highway System (ferry)
Tsirku
Takhin
7
Haines
TAKHINSHA MOUNTAINS
Muir Glacier
Riggs Glacier
McBride Glacier
Carroll Glacier
White Thunder Ridge 1,900 ft
McConnell Ridge 3,000 ft
Wolf Cr.
Sealers I.
Goose Cove
Interglacial Forest Stumps
Lynn Canal
TONGASS NATIONAL FOREST
Wachusett Inlet
Muir Inlet
Reid Inlet
Adams Inlet
Endicott Gap 900 ft
ENDICOTT RIVER WILDERNESS
NATIONAL PARK
Reid Gl.
Lamplugh Gl.
Muir Point
Beartrack Mts.
Beartrack
Tlingit Point
GLACIER BAY
North Marble Island
BRADY ICEFIELD
PRESERVE
Geikie Inlet
Interglacial Forest Stumps
South Marble Island
Excursion
CHILKAT RANGE
RANGE
Beardslee Islands
Bartlett
Excursion Ridge
Sitakaday Narrows
Park Headquarters
Glacier Bay Lodge and Visitor Center
Bartlett Cove
Gustavus
Gustavus Airport
Brady Glacier
Dundas Bay
Pleasant Island
ICY STRAIT
Alaska Marine Highway System (ferry)
Lemesurier Island
Taylor Bay
Inian Islands
Cape Spencer
Cross Sound
Elfin Cove
TONGASS NATIONAL FOREST
Chichagof Island
Hoonah

GLACIER BAY

Watch for phalaropes, gulls, terns, and other birds feeding here as the swirling water flushes small fish to the surface. To the north, the **Marble Islands** rise out of the middle of the bay. The deglaciated islands support breeding colonies of gulls, cormorants, puffins, and murres (and are off-limits to visitors during the summer). Watch for Steller's sea lions on **South Marble Island.**

THE WEST ARM

The bay's west arm contains the park's highest mountains and most active tidewater glaciers. Clear days afford stunning views of the **Fairweather Range,** crowned by **Mount Fairweather** at 15,300 feet; cloudy days lend a moody, rich blue cast to the tidewater faces of the **Margerie, Grand Pacific, Lamplugh,** and **Reid Glaciers.**

In the wildest inlet—**Johns Hopkins**—seven glaciers tumble down 8,000 foot mountain peaks. Each June thousands of harbor seals give birth to their pups on icebergs in Johns Hopkins Inlet (to protect the seals, the inlet closes seasonally).

Steller's sea lions

Blue Mouse Cove and the northwest corner of **Reid Inlet** are the best anchorages. Good camping can be found almost anywhere (except in Johns Hopkins Inlet with its steep terrain). Hiking is a matter of going where the spirit and the topography take you. Brown bears are common. This is their home, and you are the visitor. *Be careful.*

MUIR INLET

Reaching 25 miles into the park's northeast corner, **Muir Inlet** is a mecca for kayakers. Tour and fishing boats seldom come here (and the waters north of McBride Glacier are closed to motor boats June to mid-July). The camping is good, and so is the hiking, if you avoid thickets of alder.

Adams Inlet branches east off lower Muir Inlet and is a favorite among kayakers. You can time your entry and exit by the strong tides that flow in and out through the narrow opening. To the north, **Sealers Island** was once a breeding site for arctic terns and black oystercatchers.

Nearby is **Goose Cove**. In contrast to the tidewater glaciers that are advancing in the west arm, most in Muir Inlet are in retreat. The **McBride** and **Riggs Glaciers** separated from the retreating **Muir Glacier** in 1941 and 1960 respectively; since then, all three continue to retreat.

A journey up **White Thunder Ridge** or **McConnell Ridge** rewards hikers with spectacular views of upper Muir Inlet. Both hikes are strenuous. Be prepared to struggle through alder. Each hike takes a full day and climbs about 1,500 feet. Also rewarding is a hike along **Wolf Creek** (beginning at the south end of White Thunder Ridge), where running water has exposed a forest buried by a glacier 4,000 to 7,000 years ago.

INFORMATION & ACTIVITIES

HEADQUARTERS
P.O. Box 140, Gustavus, AK 99826. Phone (907) 697-2230. www.nps.gov/glba

SEASONS & ACCESSIBILITY
Park open year-round, but late May to mid-September is visitor season; transportation and facilities limited rest of year. Call the park before going in the off-season.

There are no roads to the park; access by airplane, boat, or ferry only. Allen Marine Tours (888-289-0081) offers ferry service between Auke Bay (north of Juneau) and Bartlett Cove. The Alaska Marine Highway System (800-642-0066) offers limited ferry service from Juneau to Bartlett Cove. Visitors with private boats need a permit from June through August; phone (907) 697-2627.

VISITOR & INFORMATION CENTERS
Information centers are located on the dock at **Bartlett Cove** and at **Glacier Bay Lodge.** Call (907) 697-2627 for visitor information.

ENTRANCE FEE
None.

PETS
Permitted on leashes on Bartlett Cove roads only. Prohibited in backcountry; boaters must keep pets aboard vessels.

FACILITIES FOR DISABLED
Glacier Bay Lodge is accessible to wheelchairs. One trail, with a stretch of boardwalk, is also accessible.

THINGS TO DO
Free ranger-led activities (from Glacier Bay Lodge): nature walks, films, slide presentations, and evening programs. Also available, kayaking, fishing (license required), scheduled boat tours, glacier viewing, whale-watching and bird-watching, crabbing (license required), hiking, berry picking, mountain and glacier climbing (for the experienced only), aerial sight-seeing, cross-country skiing.

For information and reservations for ranger-guided boat tours from Bartlett Cove, contact Glacier Bay Lodge, Inc., (888) 299-8687. Ask the park for a list of other concessioners offering a variety of rental and guide services. Or visit www.visitglacierbay.com.

SPECIAL ADVISORIES
- Do not get close to icebergs when boating, and do not climb on the glaciers without a guide or plenty of experience.
- Load up on insect repellent.
- Be aware of bears. Obtain safety guidelines from information centers or rangers.

OVERNIGHT BACKPACKING
Permit required. Backcountry users must receive orientation from rangers before setting out. Use of Park Service food storage canisters required.

CAMPGROUNDS
One campground only; **Bartlett Cove** has 14-day limit. Open all year; first come, first served. No fees. Showers at lodge (within a mile) available only seasonally. Warming hut provided. Tent sites only. **Bartlett Cove Group Campground;** open all year; first come, first served.

HOTELS, MOTELS, & INNS
(unless otherwise noted, rates are for 2 persons in a double room, high season)

<u>INSIDE THE PARK:</u>

Glacier Bay Lodge P.O. Box 199, Gustavus, AK 99826. (888) 229-8687 or (907) 697-4000. 55 units. $185. Packages that include airfare available. Restaurant. Open mid-May to early Sept.

<u>OUTSIDE THE PARK:</u>

<u>*In Gustavus, AK 99826*</u>

Annie Mae Lodge P.O. Box 55. (800) 478-2346 or (907) 697-2346. 11 units. $115-$140, includes meals and ground transportation.

Glacier Bay Country Inn P.O. Box 5. (800) 628-0912 or (907) 697-2288. 10 units. $370, includes meals. Open mid-May to mid-Sept.

Gustavus Inn P.O. Box 60. (907) 697-2254. 13 units, 11 with private baths. $165 per person, includes meals and some activities. Open May to early Sept.

Alaskan brown bears—the frightful grizzly—fishing for salmon at Brooks Falls

KATMAI

ALASKA
ESTABLISHED DECEMBER 2, 1980
4,725,188 acres

Volcanoes and bears—powerful, unpredictable, and awe inspiring—embody the wild heart of Katmai. Within the borders of the national park and preserve are 15 volcanoes, some of them still steaming, and North America's largest population of protected brown bears—about 2,000 of them.

You can hike, kayak, and canoe here. You can fish waist-deep in rivers as clear as glass. And you can watch the best fish catcher of all, the great Alaskan brown bear, sometimes diving completely under the water for its prey, sometimes catching fish in midair. At the end of the day you can relax in a rustic yet sumptuous lodge on the shore of a sapphire lake and recount the day's enchantments.

In 1912 a volcano here erupted with a force ten times that of Mount St. Helens in 1980. Suddenly news of Katmai, a place hardly anyone had heard of, was on front pages around the world. Ash filled the air, global temperatures cooled, acid rain burned clothing off lines in Vancouver, British Columbia, and on Kodiak Island, just across Shelikof Strait from Katmai, day became night.

Leading a 1916 expedition sponsored by the National Geographic Society, botanist Robert Griggs ascended Katmai Pass from Shelikof Strait. "The whole valley as far as the eye could reach was full of hundreds, no thousands—literally, tens of thousands—of smokes curling up from its fissured floor," he wrote. The smokes were fumaroles steaming 500 to 1,000 feet into the air. Griggs, who named the Valley of Ten Thousand Smokes, spearheaded the campaign to include Katmai in the National Park System.

Today, the smokes are gone from the valley. But steam vents still appear elsewhere in the park.

How to Get There

From Anchorage, scheduled jets fly the 290 miles to King Salmon, park headquarters; from there, June to mid-September, daily floatplanes fly the last 33 miles to Brooks Camp, site of a summer visitor center and the center of activity. Air charters can be arranged into other areas. You can drive the 9 miles from King Salmon to Lake Camp, at the western end of the park on the Naknek River, then go by boat to Brooks Camp, the Bay of Islands, and other areas of Naknek Lake.

When to Go

June to early September. Only then, with transportation from between Brooks Camp and the Valley of Ten Thousand Smokes, are the lodges, cabins, and Brooks Camp Campground open. Bear watching, an increasingly popular pastime, is best in July when the sockeye salmon spawn (bear watching suffers a brief lull in June and again in August). Fishing and hiking are good throughout summer, but come prepared for rain. Heavy snowpack may remain in the upper elevations into July. Summer daytime temperatures range from the mid-50s to mid-60s; the average low is 44°F.

How to Visit

If your time is short, get to **Brooks Camp.** People, fish, bears, boats, and planes concentrate here. Compared to the rest of the park, it's crowded. But the lodge and campground are comfortable (reservations required) and the bear viewing unforgettable. You'll find good hiking and fishing.

If at all possible, take the bus or van tour 23 miles out from Brooks Camp to the **Valley of Ten Thousand Smokes.** Return the same day or hike into the valley and camp. You can extend your stay by boating or flying to the many other lakes, streams, rivers, and lodges in the park. Pick your area, make a safe plan, and go.

BROOKS CAMP & VALLEY OF TEN THOUSAND SMOKES

Some very pleasant hikes begin near Brooks Camp. The trail you'll first want to take goes to the bear-viewing platform. The 1-mile trail starts at Brooks Camp and winds gently through the forest to **Brooks Falls,** ending at the viewing platform. Wooden steps ascend a balcony overlooking the fascinating spectacle of jumping fish and feeding bears. Averaging a thousand pounds and measuring up to ten feet long, these Alaskan brown bears are the largest land carnivores on the continent of North America.

The hike up **Dumpling Mountain** is a good day trip. The trail begins at the campground and climbs to an 800-foot overlook in 1.5 miles. From there you can continue another 2 miles over alpine tundra to the summit, elevation 2,440 feet. Both the overlook and summit afford tremendous views of **Naknek Lake** and the surrounding mountains.

The most popular and spectacular hiking in the park is in the **Valley of Ten Thousand Smokes.** There's no other landscape like it in the world. Daily tours connect Brooks Camp with the **Three Forks Overlook** and a

Kukaklek Lake
Alagnak
Battle Lake Cabins
Battle Lake
ALAGNAK NATIONAL WILD & SCENIC RIVER
Nonvianuk Camp
Nonvianuk Lake
Kulik Lodge
Kulik Lake
Enchanted Lake Lodge
Sugarloaf Mountain 2,085 ft
Oakley Peak 4,625 ft
American Cr.
Hammersly Lake
Idayain Lake
Lake Coville
KATMAI
PORTAGE TRAIL
Lake Camp
Grosvenor Lake Lodge
Lake Grosvenor
Naknek Lake
Naknek
North Arm
Bay of Islands
Dumpling Mountain 2,440 ft
Brooks Camp
Brooks Falls
Visitor Center
Iliuk Arm
Brooks Lake
Mount Kelez 3,250 ft
Margot Falls
Ukak
Granite Peak 1,683 ft
Three Forks Overlook
Valley of Ten Thousand Smokes
Buttress Ra.
Mount Griggs 7,600 ft
Yori Pass
Windy Cr.
Knife Creek Glaciers
Crater Lake
Katmai Pass
Mount Katmai 6,715 ft
Red Mountain 1,721 ft
King Salmon
Gertrude Peak 1,141 ft
Mount Megeik 7,250 ft
KEJULIK MTS.
Katmai
BECHAROF NATIONAL WILDLIFE REFUGE
Katmai Bay
Becharof Lake
Kejulik
Cape Kubugakli

COOK INLET
McNeil Cove
MCNEIL RIVER STATE GAME SANCTUARY
Kamishak
Douglas
Mt. Douglas 7,063 ft
Cape Douglas
NATIONAL PARK
Fourpeaked Glacier
Kiukpalik Island
Savonoski
Kaguyak Crater
Swikshak Bay
Wolverine Falls
Rainbow
Hook Glacier
Ninagiak I.
Mount Denison 7,606 ft
Hallo Bay
Hallo Glacier
Serpent Tongue Glacier
SHELIKOF STRAIT
Kukak Bay
Kaflia Bay
Kinak Bay
Takli Island
Dakavak Bay
KODIAK ISLAND
0 miles 20
0 kilometers 30
N

Valley of Ten Thousand Smokes

cabin at the north end of the valley, where you can camp or picnic. A short trail descends 200 feet to where the **Ukak River** roars through a bedrock canyon crowned by cliffs of volcanic ash.

To hike into the valley, take the trail that begins a half mile back from the end of the road and plan to camp overnight. The trail crosses **Windy Creek,** passes the north end of the **Buttress Range,** crosses the **River Lethe,** and finally climbs a thousand feet to the Baked Mountain Cabin, a shelter available for overnights. The challenging 12-mile trip takes a full day; *drinking water is scarce.* The river crossing can be extremely dangerous; be sure to be briefed at the visitor center before you hike.

Due south 5.5 miles from the cabin is **Katmai Pass,** where Robert Griggs first beheld the valley in 1916. Strong winds often funnel through here.

A fascinating side trip between **Baked Mountain** and Katmai Pass is to **Novarupta,** a 200-foot-high dome of volcanic rock that was the extrusion plug of the great eruption. Scientists believe most of the 1912 lava and ash spewed out through a fissure here, drawing magma from nearby **Mount Katmai** and causing its summit to collapse into a caldera.

To reach the caldera (a strenuous 1- to 2-day trip), head east from Novarupta or Baked Mountain to the stagnant, ash-covered **Knife Creek Glaciers,** then climb 3,800 feet up ash and ice to the caldera rim, where, if you peer over the edge, you'll see what Robert Griggs saw: "a wonderful lake, of a weird vitriolic robin's-egg blue."

WATER & AIR TRIPS

Boaters, kayakers, and canoeists find no shortage of places to explore in Katmai. Guides and equipment are available for hire through Brooks Lodge or one of the other, smaller lodges catering mostly to fishermen. An especially popular and picturesque spot is the **Bay of Islands** in the **North Arm** of Naknek Lake, 22 miles from Brooks Camp.

For serious paddlers looking for the wild side of Katmai, the **Savonoski Loop** is an 85-mile round-trip from Brooks Camp that takes 4 to 8 days, depending on weather. You paddle through the Bay of Islands, portage to **Lake Grosvenor,** and float the **Grosvenor** and **Savonoski Rivers** into the **Iliuk Arm** of Naknek Lake for the return to Brooks Camp. (Follow the shorelines, for wind can suddenly transform lakes from tranquil to tempestuous.)

If you'd like to take a river trip, inquire about the **Alagnak River,** a designated Wild and Scenic River, and the **Ukak River,** which, with class v rapids, is for the very experienced only.

Like Alaska's other national parks, Katmai is spectacular from the air. Flight-seeing trips can be arranged in **King Salmon** or Brooks Camp. Swing over the Valley of Ten Thousand Smokes, through Katmai Pass, up the coast from **Katmai Bay** to **Swikshak Bay,** over **Kaguyak Crater,** and down the Savonoski River back to Brooks Camp. Take plenty of film and a calm stomach.

INFORMATION & ACTIVITIES

HEADQUARTERS

P.O. Box 7, King Salmon, AK 99613. Phone (907) 246-3305. www.nps.gov/katm

SEASONS & ACCESSIBILITY

Park open year-round. Scheduled flights from Anchorage to King Salmon with connecting seaplane flights to Brooks Camp in the park available June to mid-Sept only. Reserve well in advance. Accessible by private or charter plane all year; the park has a list of licensed air charter companies.

VISITOR & INFORMATION CENTERS

Brooks Camp Visitor Center and the concessions are open from June to mid-Sept. All visitors to Brooks Camp are required to attend the 15-minute orientation on bear etiquette. For visitor information contact park or Katmailand, Inc., the park's main concessioner, at 4125 Aircraft Dr., Anchorage, AK 99502; or call (800) 544-0551 or (907) 243-5448.
King Salmon Interagency Visitor Center is open year-round (907-246-4250).

ENTRANCE FEE

None.

FACILITIES FOR DISABLED

Brooks Lodge is accessible, but with assistance.

THINGS TO DO

Free ranger-led activities: daily interpretive programs, evening programs, nature walks. Also, bus trips to the Valley of Ten Thousand Smokes, bear watching, hiking, kayaking, canoeing, boating, mountain climbing, aerial sight-seeing, fishing (license required; available in park), float trips. Katmailand, Inc., has guides, boating, and fishing equipment available at Brooks Lodge. Reserve ahead. Ask the park for a list of other approved outfitters and guides within its borders.

SPECIAL ADVISORIES

- Alaskan brown bears, or grizzlies, are unpredictable and dangerous; stay far away from them unless at the bear-viewing platforms.
- Be very careful when crossing glacial streams.
- When hiking into the valley to Baked Mountain Cabin, be sure to carry sufficient water.
- Take a guide when kayaking unless extremely experienced; check with visitor center before leaving on skills needed and weather conditions.

OVERNIGHT BACKPACKING

Camping allowed anywhere in park without reservations, except at Brooks Camp (see below). Bear-resistant food canisters required for overnight stays, available free at Brooks Camp or King Salmon visitor centers.

CAMPGROUNDS

One backcountry campground, **Brooks Camp** (with 7-day limit in July and Sept.). Open June to mid-Sept.; reservations required. Call the NPRS (see p. 10) for reservations. Campground fee $8 per night per person. Showers at Brooks Lodge. Tent sites only. Three-sided shelters for cooking. Limited food services in park.

HOTELS, MOTELS, & INNS

(unless otherwise noted, rates are for 2 persons, double room, high season)

INSIDE THE PARK:

Katmailand, Inc., offers multiday package tours from Anchorage that can include airfare; lodging at Brooks Lodge, Grosvenor Lake Lodge, or Kulik Lodge; meals; guides; fishing tackle; rafts; licenses; and boats or planes to fishing spots. For information, write Katmailand, Inc., 4125 Aircraft Dr., Anchorage, AK 99502; or call (800) 544-0551 or (907) 243-5448.

Brooks Lodge 16 cabins. Packages starting from $519 per person. Open June to mid-Sept.
Grosvenor Lake Lodge 3 cabins. Packages starting from $2,275 per person. Open June to late Sept.
Kulik Lodge 12 cabins. Packages starting from $2,350 per person. Open mid-June to late Sept.

Late Afternoon at Tern Lake

KENAI FJORDS

ALASKA
ESTABLISHED DECEMBER 2, 1980
607,000 acres

Distill the essence of coastal Alaska into one place—wild, dynamic, and scenic, rich with the signatures of glaciers, light with the marks of people, unforgiving in stormy seas, unforgettable in warm sunshine—and you have Kenai Fjords, the smallest national park in Alaska. Here the south-central part of the state tumbles into the Gulf of Alaska; here the land challenges the sea with talon-like peninsulas and rocky headlands, while the sea itself reaches inland with long fjords and hundreds of quiet bays and coves.

The Harding Icefield is the park's crown jewel, almost 700 square miles of ice up to a mile thick. It feeds nearly three dozen glaciers flowing out of the mountains, 6 of them to tidewater. The Harding Icefield is a vestige of the massive ice sheet that covered much of Alaska in the Pleistocene era.

The ancient ice gouged out Kenai's fjords, creating habitats for throngs of sea animals. About 20 species of seabirds nest along the rocky coastline; most of the birds are clown-faced puffins. Bald eagles swoop along the towering cliffs, and peregrine falcons hunt over the outer islands. Seabirds, by the tens of thousands, migrate or congregate here.

Approximately 23 species of mammals, including harbor seals, northern sea lions, and sea otters, live here. Moose, black bears, wolverines, lynx, and marten roam narrow bands of forest between the coast and icefield. And just above them, on the treeless slopes, climb surefooted mountain goats.

How to Get There

Seward is the gateway to Kenai Fjords. To get to Seward, take the Seward Highway (Alas. 9) south from Anchorage. The 130-mile drive is spectacular. Buses and small commuter planes also connect Anchorage and Seward, and the Alaska Marine Highway (ferry) links Seward with Homer, Seldovia, Kodiak, Valdez, and Cordova.

You can also charter a flight from Seward or Homer directly to the park. In summer, the Alaska Railroad serves Seward from Anchorage (with connections to Fairbanks and Whittier).

When to Go

Usually summer. The days lengthen; the seas calm down. The road to Exit Glacier generally opens in May and closes with the first snowfall, usually in October. Many winter visitors ski the road into Exit Glacier, or snowmobile in. Flight-seeing trips can be arranged in Seward any time of the year, subject to weather.

How to Visit

The most popular and accessible area in the park is **Exit Glacier,** 13 miles northwest of Seward. You can drive to it or take a tour bus. Trails offer half-hour hikes to the glacier and a half-day hike to the **Harding Icefield.**

Otherwise, hiking is a matter of exploring wilderness shores and ridges accessible only by boat and plane. From mid-May to late September, daily tour boats from Seward offer round-trip half-day and full-day excursions to the fjords and outlying islands. Charter boats take kayakers and campers to any fjord they wish (most often **Aialik Bay**) and pick them up the same day or days later. Kayaking, fishing, and backpacking guides are available. Ask the park for a list.

From Seward or Homer you can book a breathtaking 1-hour flight over the Harding Icefield and Kenai coast. For extended adventures, skiplanes drop off and pick up skiers on the icefield, and floatplanes do the same for kayakers in the fjords, weather permitting.

EXIT GLACIER & HARDING ICEFIELD

Exit Glacier is one of many rivers of ice that flow off the Harding Icefield. From Seward, follow the highway north to mile 3.7, where a paved road leads 9 miles to a parking lot. There are three trails: The **Main Trail** is paved for a third of a mile to a viewing area. The trail then separates into two loops. The lower loop continues to the outwash plain for a close view of the glacier terminus; the upper loop climbs a third of a mile for a view of deep crevasses and towering seracs along the glacier's flank.

A half-mile **nature trail** begins at the glacier and winds over old moraines and through cottonwoods, alders, and willows before following **Exit Creek** to connect with the Main Trail. The **Harding Icefield Trail** branches off the Main Trail and climbs 3,000 feet in 3.5 miles, ending on the icefield. The upper section of the trail is usually snow covered; the lower portion is slippery and muddy after rain. Ask a

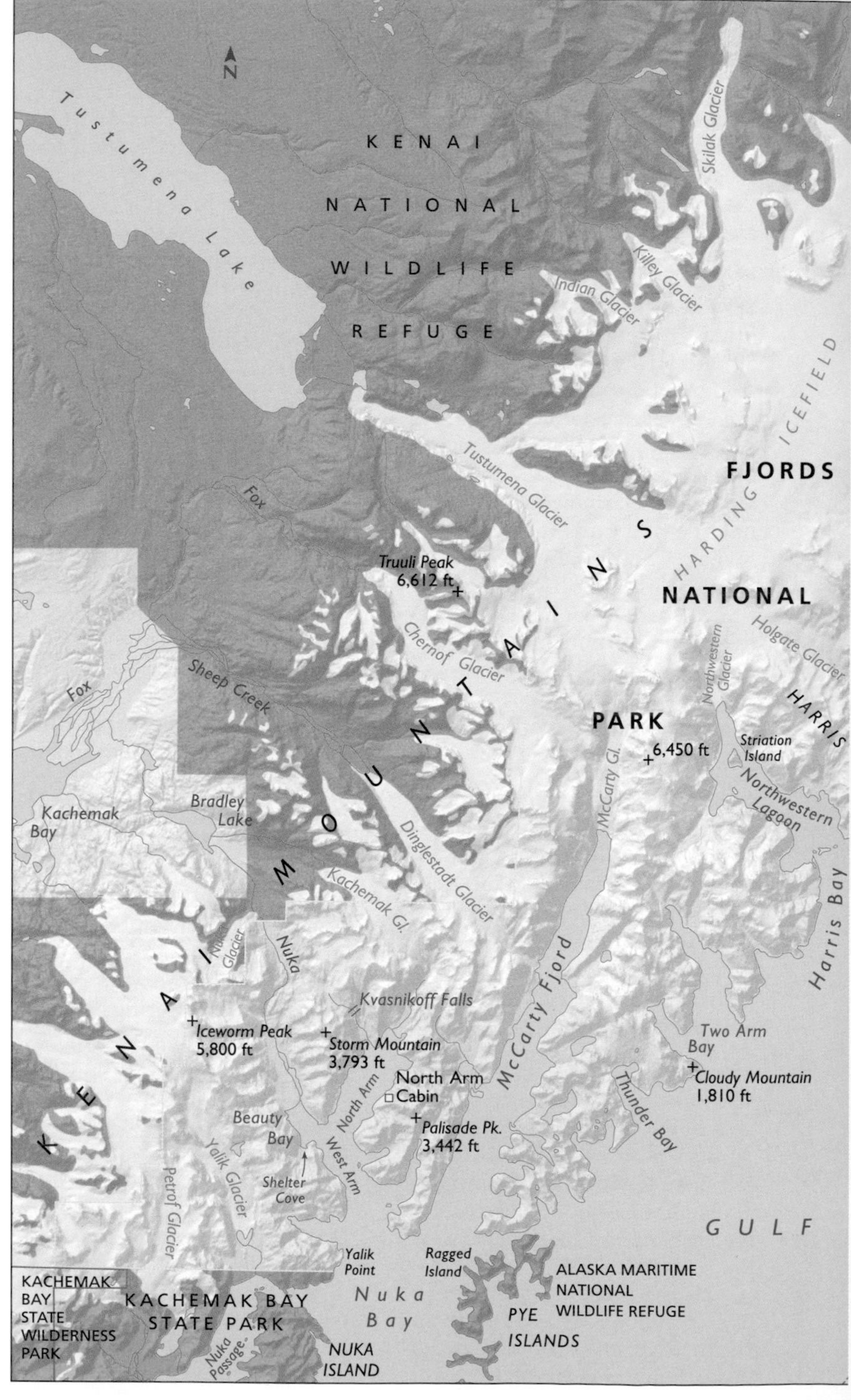
N
Tustumena Lake
KENAI
NATIONAL
WILDLIFE
REFUGE
Skilak Glacier
Killey Glacier
Indian Glacier
HARDING ICEFIELD
Tustumena Glacier
FJORDS
NATIONAL
PARK
Fox
Truuli Peak
6,612 ft
Chernof Glacier
Holgate Glacier
Northwestern Glacier
HARRIS
Sheep Creek
Fox
6,450 ft
Striation Island
Northwestern Lagoon
McCarty Gl.
Kachemak Bay
Bradley Lake
Dinglestadt Glacier
Kachemak Gl.
Harris Bay
KENAI MOUNTAINS
Nuka Glacier
Nuka
Kvasnikoff Falls
McCarty Fjord
Iceworm Peak
5,800 ft
Storm Mountain
3,793 ft
Two Arm Bay
Cloudy Mountain
1,810 ft
North Arm Cabin
North Arm
Thunder Bay
Beauty Bay
Palisade Pk.
3,442 ft
West Arm
Yalik Glacier
Petrof Glacier
Shelter Cove
GULF
Yalik Point
Ragged Island
ALASKA MARITIME
NATIONAL
WILDLIFE REFUGE
KACHEMAK BAY STATE WILDERNESS PARK
KACHEMAK BAY STATE PARK
Nuka Bay
PYE ISLANDS
Nuka Passage
NUKA ISLAND

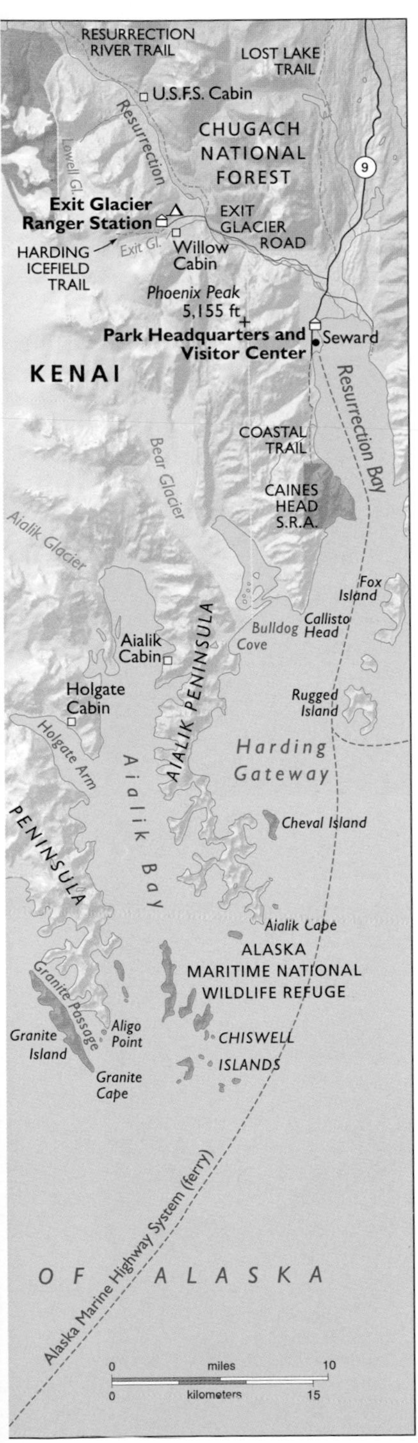

ranger about current conditions and sign in at the trail register. On the slopes you may see mountain goats and black bears.

THE FJORDS

Daily tour boats travel down **Resurrection Bay,** pass picturesque **Caines Head** and **Callisto Head,** then round rugged **Aialik Cape** and enter **Aialik Bay,** the most visited fjord in the park. The **Holgate** and **Aialik Glaciers** flow into this fjord. Tour boats usually visit the Holgate, then return to Seward via the **Chiswell Islands** (part of the Alaska Maritime NWR), an excellent place to see sea lions resting on rocks and nesting seabirds.

Endless exploring awaits boaters and hikers on the shores of Kenai Fjords. If you are without a guide, be sure to inquire at the visitor center about weather, landing sites, tides, and hazards. The farther down the coast to the southwest, the fewer the people. Narrow **Granite Passage** is an exciting entrance into **Harris Bay.** From 1910 to 1960, **Northwestern Glacier** retreated 9.5 miles and opened up **Northwestern Lagoon** at the head of Harris Bay. The lagoon should be entered on calm water (preferably in a kayak) and at high tide only. Once you are inside and on the shore, you will find excellent hiking, especially to **Northeastern, Southwestern,** and **Sunlight Glaciers.**

Down the coast, **Thunder Bay** is a welcome anchorage during inclement weather. A narrow waterway cuts between the mainland and the **Pye Islands.** From here, **McCarty Fjord** slices 23 miles into the coast, its steep walls rising more than 4,000 feet overhead on either side of **McCarty Glacier.** The **West** and **North Arms** of **Nuka Bay** offer a variety of terrain and wildlife. Watch for the craggy profile of **Palisade Peak,** a 900-foot waterfall, historic gold mine sites, and for black bears, moose, and river otters near the **Nuka River,** for shorebirds along the mud flats at **Shelter Cove,** and for black-sand beaches around **Yalik Point,** at the park's southern end. Few people come here; travel to Nuka Bay and you might have it all to yourself.

Horned puffins *(top)*, Red Fox *(center left)*, Northern sea lions *(center right)*
Humpback whale in Aialik Bay *(bottom)*

INFORMATION & ACTIVITIES

HEADQUARTERS

P.O. Box 1727, Seward, AK 99664. Phone (907) 224-7500. www.nps.gov/kefj

SEASONS & ACCESSIBILITY

Park open year-round, but, from about mid-Oct. to May, snow may close the road to Exit Glacier. Access then is by ski, snowmobile, dog team, or snowshoe only. Call headquarters for information about weather and road conditions.

VISITOR & INFORMATION CENTERS

Information center in Seward, on Alas. 9 just outside the eastern border of the park, open daily from Memorial Day to Labor Day; weekdays only Fall and Spring.
Ranger Station at Exit Glacier open summer only. Phone (907) 224-2132 for visitor information.

ENTRANCE FEE

None.

PETS

Permitted leashed on the Exit Glacier Road and in parking areas. Prohibited on all trails.

FACILITIES FOR DISABLED

Exit Glacier is the most accessible area. From the Ranger Station, wheelchairs can maneuver the glacier trail for the first third of a mile, to an interpretive shelter offering exhibits and views of the glacier. Visitor center is also wheelchair accessible.

THINGS TO DO

Free ranger-led activities: In summer (from the Ranger Station at Exit Glacier), walks to the glacier's base, and all-day hikes to the icefield. Also available, advanced mountain climbing, sailing, fishing (license required), wildlife watching, cross-country skiing, dogsledding, snowshoeing.
Authorized commercial guides offer camping, fishing, kayaking, flight-seeing, and boat trips for exploring the fjords and watching seabirds, whales, porpoises, and other wildlife. Call park headquarters or visit the park's website for a list of companies that do business in the park.

SPECIAL ADVISORIES

- If planning a backcountry trip without a guide, first check conditions with park staff.
- Hypothermia is a danger on the icefield, even in summer.
- Do not venture out in a boat unless well experienced in rough water.
- Remember glaciers are moving bodies of ice, they can pose a danger when portions break off; crevasses should not be crossed by the inexperienced.

OVERNIGHT BACKPACKING

Permits, free at the visitor center, are required; voluntary registration is requested for Harding Icefield.

CAMPGROUNDS

One walk-in campground at **Exit Glacier.** Three cabins in the fjords available May through Sept. for overnight use by permit. Access by boat or plane only. In winter, a public-use cabin is available at Exit Glacier. Write or phone the visitor center.

HOTELS, MOTELS, & INNS

(unless otherwise noted, rates are for 2 persons in a double room, high season)

<u>In Seward, AK 99664:</u>
Breeze Inn 1306 Seward Hwy., P.O. Box 2147. (907) 224-5237. 86 units, 1 with a kitchenette. $139-$199. Restaurant.
Hotel Seward (on 5th Ave.) P.O. Box 670. (907) 224-2378. 38 units. $139-$224. AC.
Marina Motel (on Alas. 9) P.O. Box 1134. (907) 224-5518. 18 units, 1 with a kitchenette. $105-$130.
Murphy's Motel 911 4th Ave., P.O. Box 736. (907) 224-8090. 24 units. $99-$154.
Van Gilder Hotel 308 Adams St., P.O. Box 609. (800) 204-6835, (907) 224-3525, or (907) 224-3079. 24 units shared baths; $109. 21 with private baths; $216.

Great Kobuk Sand Dunes, encroaching on a spruce forest

KOBUK VALLEY

ALASKA
ESTABLISHED DECEMBER 2, 1980
1,750,000 acres

"Now we were alone between fringes of spruce by a clear stream where tundra went up the sides of mountains," wrote John McPhee in *Coming into the Country*. The Kobuk Valley, said McPhee, "was, in all likelihood, the most isolated wilderness I would ever see." Located entirely above the Arctic Circle, Kobuk Valley has fewer tourist visits than any other national park. Float a river here in late August and the only other humans you're likely to encounter are Inupiat hunting the caribou that migrate through each year.

Twelve thousand years ago, when continental glaciers covered much of North America and a land bridge connected Alaska and Asia, Kobuk Valley was an ice-free refuge with grassy tundra similar to that found in Siberia today. Bison, mastodons, and mammoths roamed the valley, along with the humans who hunted them. Since then, the climate has shifted, and sea level has risen to flood the land bridge; many of the early mammals have disappeared. But today's shrubby flora harbors relicts of the preglacial steppe, and in the cold, hard ground lie the legacies of ancient animals and peoples.

Here the Kobuk Valley, cordoned off by the Baird and Waring Mountains, protects the midsection of the Kobuk River, the drainage of the wild and scenic Salmon River, and an array of wildlife. This is where the boreal forest reaches its northern limit, and the North American and Asiatic flyways cross. Pockets of tundra blend into birch and spruce, dwarfed by blasts of freezing air. And along the Kobuk River stretch 25 square miles of active sand dunes, where summer temperatures can climb to 100°F.

Kobuk Valley National Park's management plan encourages traditional native subsistence practices over tourism, so no facilities or trails lie within the park.

How to Get There

Commercial planes fly daily from Anchorage to Kotzebue, where the park's information center is located. From Kotzebue or the neighboring villages planes or boats can be chartered to explore the park.

When to Go

Summer. Days are long (from about June 3 to July 9 the sun doesn't set), and temperatures in many places can reach into the 80s or higher. Ice breaks up on the Kobuk River in May and begins to reform by mid-October. Mid-June to late July is best for wildflowers. August can bring rain and September snow. In late August, the aspens begin to turn yellow and the tundra red, and the caribou migration begins. The ranger station at Onion Portage is staffed periodically from June to September.

How to Visit

Take a combination river-hiking trip that alternates between days out on the open water with days exploring the surrounding land. That way you can paddle to different landing points, leave your gear in the canoe, and hike unencumbered. Bring everything you need; no visitor facilities exist within the park. The **Kobuk River,** wide and placid, is a pleasant river to travel by canoe, kayak, or motorboat. Most people put in at Ambler and take out at Kiana, both outside the park. You can also float or paddle the **Salmon,** a Wild and Scenic River, but it has rougher water and is harder to reach. Hiking in most places is excellent, but the park maintains no trails or river crossings. So be sure to plan your trip carefully.

While in the park, be respectful of private lands, most of which are along the Kobuk River.

KOBUK RIVER

Beginning in the central Brooks Range, the Kobuk River flows west 200 miles, winds slowly through the park for 50 miles, dropping only 2 to 3 inches per mile, and then continues west to drain into **Hotham Inlet,** off **Kotzebue Sound.** At times its placid aspect makes it seem more like a lake than a river, with a current that's hardly detectable.

Although steep bluffs sometimes rise above the riverbanks, hiking opportunities from the Kobuk are limitless. Both shores have forest, lakes, and tundra; the south shore has sand dunes also. Hike high ground to avoid swamps. In late August and early September you can sit on a bluff and watch caribou in striking autumn pelage as they swim across the river. Huge antlers and white ruffs mark the bulls.

A river trip through the park from Ambler to Kiana, with plenty of time for hiking, takes about a week. Or, if you want a more ambitious trip (2 to 3 weeks, depending on weather and river conditions), begin 5 miles

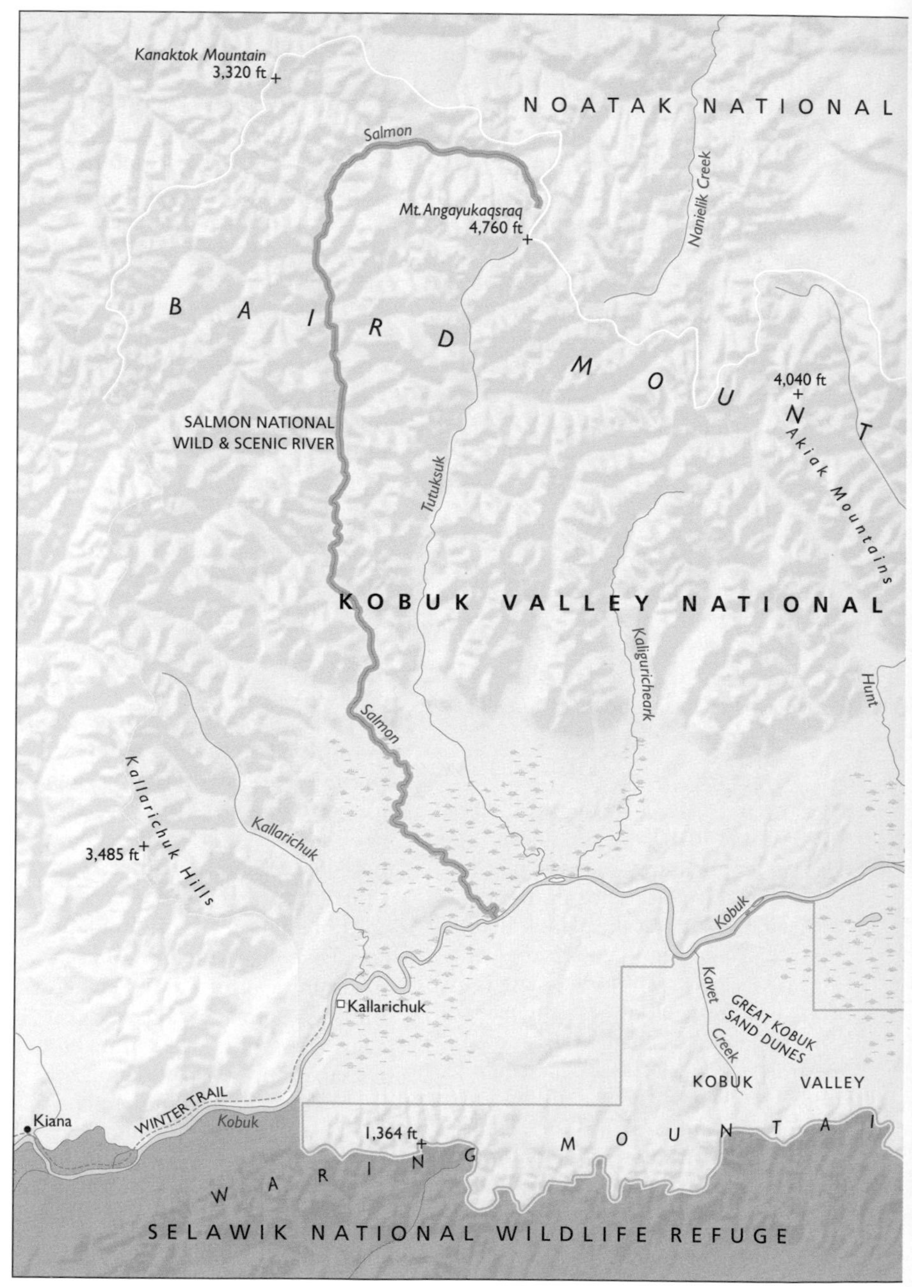

below **Walker Lake,** in Gates of the Arctic National Park (see p. 432), and paddle or motor all the way to Kiana.

On either trip you'll pass **Onion Portage,** a river bend, where for thousands of years migrating caribou have crossed the Kobuk. Here, in 1961, archaeologist J. Louis Giddings dug into the earth and could hardly believe his eyes. He

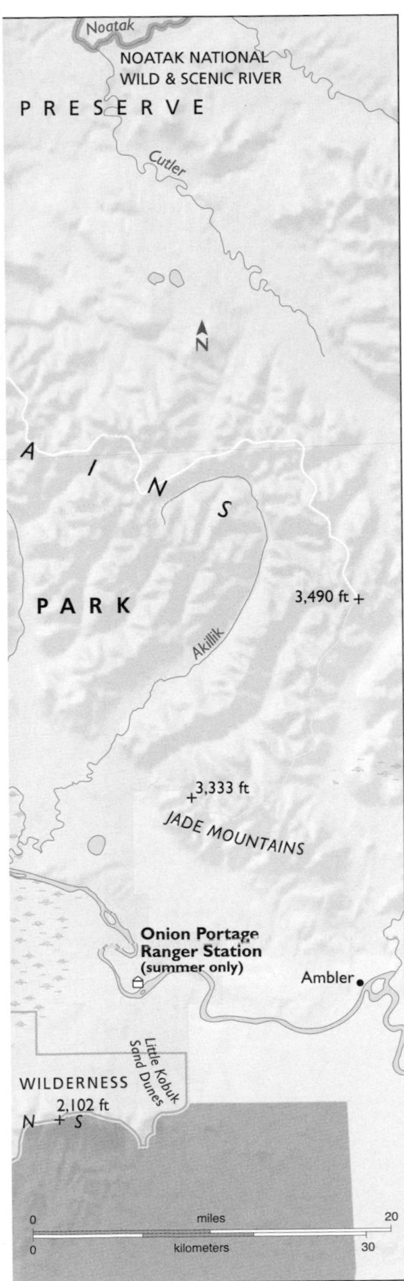

had discovered what a Smithsonian Institution ethnologist would later call "the most important archaeological site ever found in the Arctic." Giddings' 2-acre plot yielded 30 artifact-bearing layers, reflecting seven cultural traditions of flint-working technology, the oldest dating back nearly 10,000 years.

Today, the archaeological site is inactive and overgrown. But in late summer and fall, Inuit hunt caribou here as they've done for millennia. During the summer, a backcountry ranger is sometimes stationed at Giddings' old cabin. Hiking is good at Onion Portage. The name comes from the wild chives growing here.

GREAT KOBUK SAND DUNES

Farther downstream sprawl the Great Kobuk Sand Dunes, a 25-square-mile mini-Sahara. Visitors arrive by the river and leave their boats on shore for the short, but arduous, hike to the adventure of scaling the dunes. An Ice Age relic, the dunes formed from the windblown outwash of melting glaciers. A special combination of topography and eastern and northern winds keeps the dunes moving and inhospitable to vegetation. Some dunes measure 200 hundred feet high. Older, thinly vegetated dunes surround this ever changing landscape located 35 miles above the Arctic Circle.

Brown bear

Caribou migrating across the Kobuk River *(top)*
Easily stowed inflatable craft for river runners *(center)*
Cranberries, club moss, and sphagnum in the tundra *(bottom)*

INFORMATION & ACTIVITIES

HEADQUARTERS

P.O. Box 1029, Kotzebue, AK 99752. Phone (907) 442-3890. www.nps.gov/kova

SEASONS & ACCESSIBILITY

Open year-round but access—by boat or charter aircraft from Kotzebue—generally June through Sept. (The Kobuk River usually thaws by June 1 and freezes by mid-Oct.) There are no roads to or in the park.

• Be prepared for severe arctic weather at any time. Contact park headquarters before visiting. If you plan to fly in, ask the park for a list of licensed companies.

INFORMATION CENTERS

Located 80 miles from the park, the **Kotzebue Headquarters and Information Center** is open daily, call for hours.

ENTRANCE FEE

None.

PETS

Strongly discouraged.

FACILITIES FOR DISABLED

Kotzebue Headquarters and Information Center accessible to wheelchairs; otherwise none.

THINGS TO DO

Films at Kotzebue information center. The park organizes no activities, but rafting, kayaking, canoeing, hiking, sportfishing (license required), and aerial sight-seeing are available. Commercial outfitters offer a variety of private guide services for floating, fishing, trekking trips. Call or write headquarters for a list of those licensed to work in the park.

SPECIAL ADVISORIES

• Take a guide along unless you are well experienced in the wilderness.

• Mosquitoes and gnats can be brutal; bring plenty of repellent, a head net, and an insect-proof tent.

• Inuit own much of the land along the river and engage in subsistence hunting and fishing. Respect their activities and property.

OVERNIGHT BACKPACKING

No permit required, but call park for current information on weather, river conditions, bears, and resident subsistence activities before venturing out.

CAMPGROUNDS

None; backcountry camping only.

HOTELS, MOTELS, & INNS

(unless otherwise noted, rates are for 2 persons in a double room, high season)

In Kotzebue, AK 99752:

Bayside Inn 303 Shore Ave., P.O. Box 336. (907) 442-3600. 12 units. $125. Restaurant.

EXCURSION

CAPE KRUSENSTERN NATIONAL MONUMENT

KOTZEBUE, ALASKA

For more than 6,000 years, Eskimos have forged a living on this stretch of gravel projecting into the Chukchi Sea; its 114 beach ridges, rich in artifacts, reveal their archaeological benchmarks. Today, the large land and sea mammals are crucial to local subsistence. 560,000 acres. Primitive camping, boating, fishing. Access by charter boat or plane from Kotzebue. (907) 442-3890.

Turquoise Lake, tinted by glacial silt

LAKE CLARK

ALASKA
ESTABLISHED DECEMBER 2, 1980
4,045,000 acres

"Think of all the splendors that bespeak Alaska," conservationist John Kauffmann has written. "Glaciers, volcanoes, alpine spires, wild rivers, lakes with grayling on the rise. Picture coasts feathered with countless seabirds. Imagine dense forests and far-sweeping tundra, herds of caribou, great roving bears. Now concentrate all these and more into less than one percent of the state—and behold the Lake Clark region, Alaska's epitome."

Diversity is Lake Clark's hallmark. The Turquoise-Telaquana Plateau has tundra similar to Alaska's North Slope, while the coast has forests similar to the southeast panhandle. Black bears and Dall's sheep reach their southern limits here, and Sitka spruce, Alaska's state tree, reaches its northern limit. Three rivers—the Mulchatna, Chilikadrotna, and Tlikakila—have been officially designated part of the Wild and Scenic system.

The Chigmit Mountains, spine of the park, are as rugged as mountains get. They lie on the edge of the North American plate where the oceanic plate slides under it, and their jumbled contours reflect centuries of geological violence. Two volcanoes here, Iliamna and Redoubt, are still active and vent gases regularly. Redoubt erupted in 1966, spewing clouds of ash 40,000 feet into the air—and it erupted dramatically again in late 1989 and early 1990. The area averages one to two earthquakes per year that register at least a 5 on the Richter scale.

Archaeological finds show that humans, most recently Dena'ina Indians, have lived in the area for centuries. The abundant salmon and game made their settled existence possible.

How to Get There

Take a plane into the heart of the park, or travel by boat or plane to the coast. Bush pilots in Anchorage say, "Lake Clark is just out the back door"—a 1-hour flight. From Anchorage you can charter a plane to Port Alsworth, a small community on the southeast shore of Lake Clark. The flight through Lake Clark Pass takes you over immense blue glaciers, winding rivers, and snowcapped mountains. Planes also land on the coast for salmon fishing.

Another alternative is to take a scheduled flight from Anchorage to Iliamna, 30 miles outside the park, and an air taxi from there into the park. Air taxis fly in from Homer and Kenai, too. To reach the park by boat, you must travel down Cook Inlet from Anchorage or across the inlet from the Kenai Peninsula.

When to Go

Summer. Wildflowers are best in late June. Autumn colors peak in early September at upper elevations, in mid-September lower down. June through August, daytime temperatures usually hover in the 50s and low 60s in the eastern part of the park and are somewhat higher in the western part and the interior.

How to Visit

Most visitors fly into the interior lake region of the park. Air taxis can make drop-offs and pickups at prearranged places—depending on weather conditions. The smaller lakes offer excellent kayaking, and several rivers give kayakers and rafters great white-water experiences.

Hiking is good around the lakes and from lake to lake. Fishing is usually first class. Contact park headquarters in Anchorage for information on approved guide services and lodges. Remember to make your reservations early. If you don't plan to be completely self-sufficient, be sure to make thorough arrangements before going and plan for the possibility of delays due to weather changes.

ON THE LAKES & RIVERS

Fishing is superb on the lakes and rivers of this fly-in park. Rainbow trout, arctic grayling, northern pike, and five kinds of salmon—king, chum, coho, humpback, and sockeye—lure anglers, many of whom take off from Port Alsworth, site of the park's field headquarters.

As in many Alaska parks, a kayak in Lake Clark is an invitation to freedom. You can explore large areas, carry a lot of gear, and take intermittent hikes as the mood strikes you. Keep in mind that sudden winds can stir up large waves in a matter of minutes. Good lakes for paddling are **Telaquana, Turquoise, Twin, Lake Clark, Kontrashibuna,** and **Tazimina.**

Another way to see the country is to let a river take you through it. Your options are long trips (averaging three to four days) on the Wild and Scenic **Mulchatna, Chilikadrotna,** and **Tlikakila,** or short trips (generally one to two days) on the **Tanalian** and the **Tazimina.** Hire a guide or check with rangers on water conditions, places to put in and take out, and what to look out for along the way.

quakes per year that register at least a 5 on the Richter scale.

Archaeological finds show that humans, most recently Dena'ina Indians, have lived in the area for centuries. The abundant salmon and game made their settled existence possible.

How to Get There

Take a plane into the heart of the park, or travel by boat or plane to the coast. Bush pilots in Anchorage say, "Lake Clark is just out the back door"—a 1-hour flight. From Anchorage you can charter a plane to Port Alsworth, a small community on the southeast shore of Lake Clark. The flight through Lake Clark Pass takes you over immense blue glaciers, winding rivers, and snowcapped mountains. Planes also land on the coast for salmon fishing.

Another alternative is to take a scheduled flight from Anchorage to Iliamna, 30 miles outside the park, and an air taxi from there into the park. Air taxis fly in from Homer and Kenai, too. To reach the park by boat, you must travel down Cook Inlet from Anchorage or across the inlet from the Kenai Peninsula.

When to Go

Summer. Wildflowers are best in late June. Autumn colors peak in early September at upper elevations, in mid-September lower down. June through August, daytime temperatures usually hover in the 50s and low 60s in the eastern part of the park and are somewhat higher in the western part and the interior.

How to Visit

Most visitors fly into the interior lake region of the park. Air taxis can make drop-offs and pickups at prearranged places—depending on weather conditions. The smaller lakes offer excellent kayaking, and several rivers give kayakers and rafters great white-water experiences.

Hiking is good around the lakes and from lake to lake. Fishing is usually first class. Contact park headquarters in Anchorage for information on approved guide services and lodges. Remember to make your reservations early. If you don't plan to be completely self-sufficient, be sure to make thorough arrangements before going and plan for the possibility of delays due to weather changes.

ON THE LAKES & RIVERS

Fishing is superb on the lakes and rivers of this fly-in park. Rainbow trout, arctic grayling, northern pike, and five kinds of salmon—king, chum, coho, humpback, and sockeye—lure anglers, many of whom take off from Port Alsworth, site of the park's field headquarters.

As in many Alaska parks, a kayak in Lake Clark is an invitation to freedom. You can explore large areas, carry a lot of gear, and take intermittent hikes as the mood strikes you. Keep in mind that sudden winds can stir up large waves in a matter of minutes. Good lakes for paddling are **Telaquana, Turquoise, Twin, Lake Clark, Kontrashibuna,** and **Tazimina.**

Another way to see the country is to let a river take you through it. Your options are long trips (averaging three to four days) on the Wild and Scenic **Mulchatna, Chilikadrotna,** and **Tlikakila,** or short trips (generally one to two days) on the **Tanalian** and the **Tazimina.** Hire a guide or check with rangers on water conditions, places to put in and take out, and what to look out for along the way.

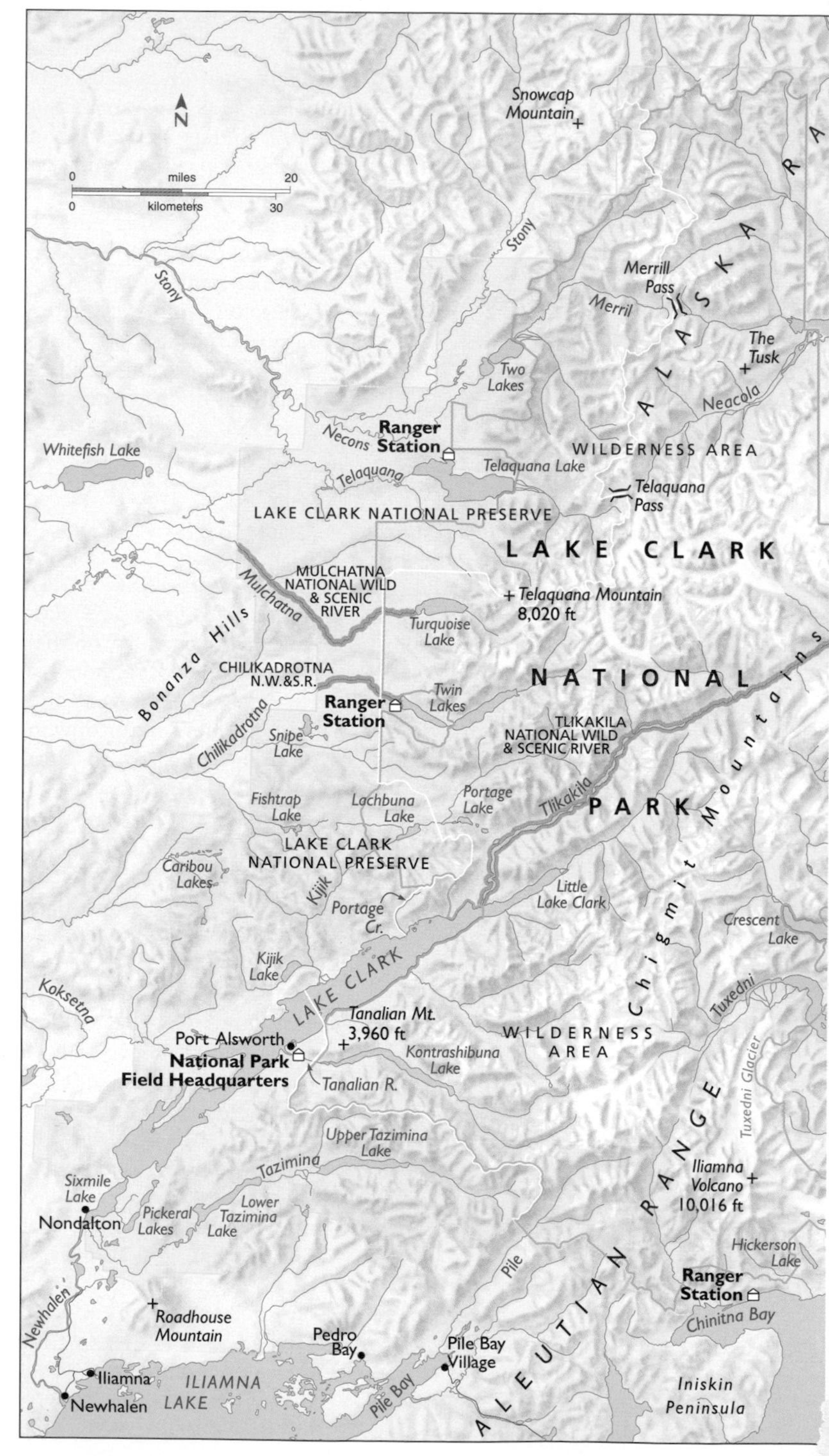

Snowcap Mountain
N
0 miles 20
0 kilometers 30
Stony
Stony
Merrill Pass
Merril
The Tusk
Two Lakes
Neacola
ALASKA RA
Necons
Ranger Station
WILDERNESS AREA
Whitefish Lake
Telaquana Lake
Telaquana
Telaquana Pass
LAKE CLARK NATIONAL PRESERVE
LAKE CLARK
MULCHATNA NATIONAL WILD & SCENIC RIVER
Mulchatna
Telaquana Mountain 8,020 ft
Bonanza Hills
Turquoise Lake
CHILIKADROTNA N.W.&S.R.
NATIONAL
Ranger Station
Twin Lakes
TLIKAKILA NATIONAL WILD & SCENIC RIVER
Chilikadrotna
Snipe Lake
Chigmit Mountains
Fishtrap Lake
Lachbuna Lake
Portage Lake
Tlikakila
PARK
LAKE CLARK NATIONAL PRESERVE
Caribou Lakes
Kijik
Portage Cr.
Little Lake Clark
Crescent Lake
Kijik Lake
LAKE CLARK
Koksetna
Tanalian Mt. 3,960 ft
Tuxedni
Port Alsworth
National Park Field Headquarters
WILDERNESS AREA
Kontrashibuna Lake
Tanalian R.
Tuxedni Glacier
Upper Tazimina Lake
Tazimina
Sixmile Lake
Iliamna Volcano 10,016 ft
Nondalton
Pickeral Lakes
Lower Tazimina Lake
Hickerson Lake
Pile
Newhalen
Roadhouse Mountain
Ranger Station
Chinitna Bay
Pedro Bay
Pile Bay Village
Iliamna
ILIAMNA LAKE
Newhalen
Pile Bay
Iniskin Peninsula
ALEUTIAN RANGE

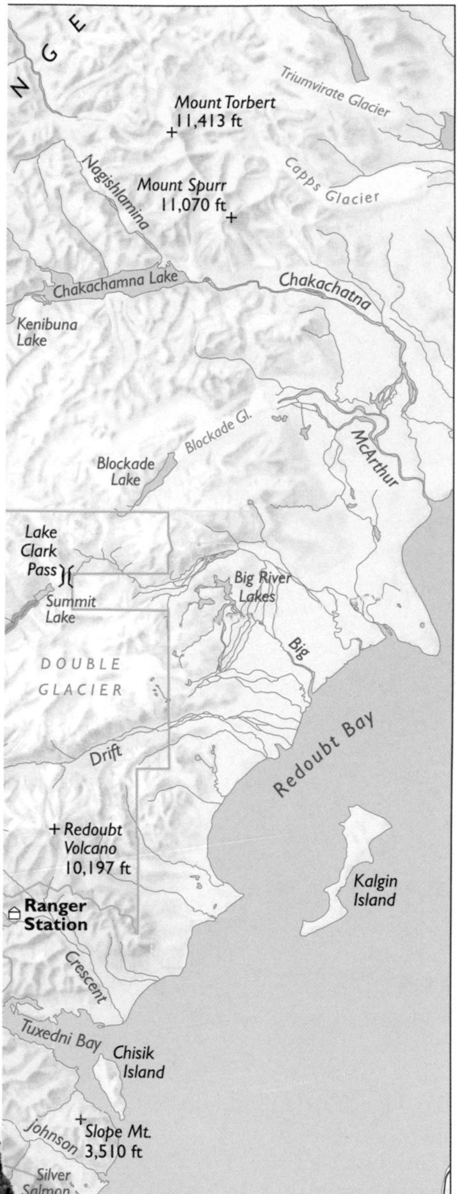

N G E
Triumvirate Glacier
Mount Torbert
11,413 ft
Nagishlamina
Capps Glacier
Mount Spurr
11,070 ft
Chakachamna Lake
Chakachatna
Kenibuna
Lake
Blockade Gl.
McArthur
Blockade
Lake
Lake
Clark
Pass
Big River
Lakes
Summit
Lake
Big
DOUBLE
GLACIER
Drift
Redoubt Bay
Redoubt
Volcano
10,197 ft
Kalgin
Island
Ranger
Station
Crescent
Tuxedni Bay
Chisik
Island
Johnson
Slope Mt.
3,510 ft
Silver
Salmon
Lakes
COOK
INLET
Anchor Point
KENAI PENINSULA

Autumn rainbow over Stony River

HIKING

When in a park with no trail system and only one maintained hiking trail, planning and route selection are critical. So is being prepared: wind and rain gear for swift changes in the weather and repellent for mosquitoes. If you intend to hike without a guide, consult with a park ranger before starting out and take a good map with you. Some general rules for hikers are: Stay as long as possible on dry tundra where footing is good, avoid heavy brush, and choose your river crossings carefully. Hiking is generally best above 2,000 feet in the interior (where the dry tundra begins), or along the coast on the numerous gravel river bars. Below tree line the vegetation can be thick and nearly impenetrable, especially the alder.

The 2.5-mile **Tanalian Falls Trail** is the only developed trail in the park. Beginning in Port Alsworth, this easy hike takes you through a forest of black spruce and birch, past bogs and ponds, up along the tumbling

Tanalian Mountain rising from Lake Clark shores *(top)*, Alpine bearberry and lichens *(bottom left)*, Arctic ground squirrel nibbling a fireweed flower *(bottom right)*

Tanalian River, to **Kontrashibuna Lake,** and on to the falls, a half mile beyond. Watch for moose in the ponds, arctic grayling in the river, Dall's sheep on **Tanalian Mountain,** and bears everywhere.

Another hike from Port Alsworth is the strenuous 3,600-foot climb up **Tanalian Mountain.** You can begin the climb off the Tanalian Falls Trail, or by hiking the shore of Lake Clark and heading up a ridge where the walking is easier, a round-trip of about 7 miles.

North of Lake Clark, several lakes offer excellent hiking. You can take an air taxi to one and hike to another, or stay at one lake—a world in itself—and go on day hikes along the shore and up the ridges. If a lake-to-lake trek appeals to you, try the 16 miles from **Telaquana Lake** south to **Turquoise Lake,** or from Turquoise Lake 13 miles south to **Twin Lakes.**

INFORMATION & ACTIVITIES

HEADQUARTERS
4230 University Dr. #311, Anchorage, AK 99508. (907) 271-3751. www.nps.gov/lacl

SEASONS & ACCESSIBILITY
Park open and accessible by small aircraft from Anchorage, Kenai, Homer, and Iliamna year-round. There are no roads to or in the park.
Weather changes rapidly. Call Port Alsworth at (907) 781-2218 for up-to-date conditions.

VISITOR & INFORMATION CENTERS
Field headquarters and a visitor center are located in **Port Alsworth,** on the south shore of Lake Clark (1 Park Pl., Port Alsworth, AK 99653). Call Anchorage headquarters at (907) 271-3751, or Port Alsworth field headquarters at (907) 781-2218 for visitor information.

ENTRANCE FEE
None.

PETS
Park recommends that you leave your pets at home because they can attract bears.

FACILITIES FOR DISABLED
All park buildings and lodges are accessible.

THINGS TO DO
Minimal interpretive programs (June through Sept.). Also, hiking, backpacking, climbing, rafting, kayaking, fishing (license required), boating, bird-watching and wildlife watching, aerial sight-seeing, hunting (in preserve).Call or write headquarters for a list of concessioners offering a variety of guide services in the park, or visit the website at www.nps.gov/lacl/visiting_the_park.htm

SPECIAL ADVISORIES
- You must possess good wilderness skills if you intend to hike, camp, or fish without a guide.
- Do not trespass on or in any way disturb the property of local residents.
- Be sure to bring insect repellent. A head net and insect-proof tent are also desirable.

OVERNIGHT BACKPACKING
No permit required, but campers are encouraged to contact field station before setting out. (907) 781-2218.

CAMPGROUNDS
None. Backcountry camping only. No showers or other visitor amenities except in lodges. Restrooms at the field headquarters at Port Alsworth.

HOTELS, MOTELS, & INNS
(unless otherwise noted, rates are for 2 persons in a double room, high season)

INSIDE THE PARK:

Alaska's Wilderness Lodge (on southern shore of Lake Clark) P.O. Box 90748, Anchorage, AK 99519. (907) 781-2223. 7 cabins. $5,950 per person, per week. 7-day sportfishing packages available. All inclusive as well as airfare. Open mid-June to early Oct.

OUTSIDE THE PARK:

Newhalen Lodge (On Six Mile Lake near Nondalton). (907) 294-2233 (lodge) or (907) 522-3355 (all year). 9 rooms. Sportfishing packages. $6,000 per person, per week all inclusive. Open June to Oct.

Contact park headquarters for additional lodgings in and near the park.

From Twin Lakes you can hike 17 miles to **Portage Lake,** a beautiful tarn in an alpine valley, and from there 11 miles to **Lachbuna Lake,** over a ridge and down the arduous **Portage Creek** drainage to Lake Clark.

For a longer, wilder, and more demanding hike through truly spectacular country, try taking the 50-mile trek from **Telaquana Lake** east over **Telaquana Pass,** along the **Neacola River** to **Kenibuna Lake.** From there, continue your hike to the huge rock spire called **The Tusk.**

Flowing Kennicott Glacier, with Mount Blackburn at left

WRANGELL-ST. ELIAS

ALASKA
ESTABLISHED DECEMBER 2, 1980
13,188,000 acres

Even in a state famous for its size, Wrangell-St. Elias stands out. It is by far the largest of our national parks—almost six times the size of Yellowstone. You fly over it and see mountains beyond mountains, glaciers after glaciers, rivers upon rivers. You float a river and watch the moods and mountains change by the minute. As you walk the tundra, you find Dall's sheep and mountain goats grazing.

Four major mountain ranges converge here: the volcanic Wrangells, the Alaska, the Chugach, and the St. Elias—tallest coastal mountains in the world. Together they contain 9 of the 16 highest peaks in the United States, 4 of them above 16,000 feet. There are more than 150 glaciers; one, the Malaspina, is larger than Rhode Island. In 1980 Wrangell-St. Elias and adjoining Kluane National Park Reserve in Canada, along with Glacier Bay NP and Tatshenshini in British Columbia, were designated a United Nations World Heritage site.

Vast and rugged as it is, the park is not a fortress. Two roads lead into small communities, remnants of the gold- and copper-mining towns that thrived in the early days of the 20th century. Today not mining but the nearly limitless hiking, rafting, kayaking, and climbing opportunities beckon.

How to Get There

Drive, take a bus, or charter a plane. By car from Anchorage, take Alas. 1 (Glenn Hwy.) 189 miles northeast to Glennallen. Continue northeast 74 miles along the Copper River and the park's western boundary to Slana, where an unpaved road branches 42 miles into the park, ending at the town of Nabesna.

Or, head toward McCarthy on the Richardson Hwy. from Glennallen 32 miles southeast to the Edgerton cutoff (Alas. 10), then turning left and continuing 33 miles to Chitina. There the pavement ends but a road follows an old railroad bed about 60 miles into the park. Buses run regularly in summer from Anchorage to Valdez with stops in Glennallen.

Air charters into the park operate out of Anchorage, Fairbanks, Yakutat, Cordova, Glennallen, Gulkana, Tok, Chitina, McCarthy, Nabesna, and Northway. Commercial jets service Yakutat and Cordova. In summer, the Alaska State Ferry serves Valdez.

When to Go

Summer. Lodges and guide services operate in the park from mid-May to the end of September. June is best for wildflowers; July has the warmest days; berries ripen in August. Be prepared for cloudy skies, but September can be beautiful with clear skies, autumn colors, no mosquitoes, and a dusting of new snow on the mountain peaks. March and April offer excellent cross-country skiing for those of strong will.

How to Visit

Take one of the two unpaved roads into the park. The **McCarthy Road** is maintained and usually passable in summer, though a four-wheel drive may be needed in other seasons. Stop at park headquarters in Copper Center for latest road conditions. The **Slana-Nabesna Road** is also maintained, including some river crossings, but can require four-wheel drive in high water. Both roads end at trailheads for many backcountry hikes.

Or, charter a plane into a remote part of the park and hike or run a river. Several commercial companies offer guided rafting or kayaking trips on the rivers and in the spectacular coastal bays. You can get a full listing of them from the park.

McCARTHY ROAD TO KENNECOTT

61 miles one way; a half day

From the town of Chitina and the confluence of the **Chitina** and **Copper Rivers,** the road follows the abandoned Copper River and Northwest Railroad bed. At mile 17 the road crosses the **Kuskulana River Bridge.** It spans 525 feet, crossing 238 feet above the river. Another abandoned railroad trestle spans the **Gilahina River** at mile 28.5. Near the end of the road are parking spots and the **Kennicott River.** To reach the old mining town of **McCarthy** on the other side of the river, walk across a footbridge and catch a shuttle bus. Today a tiny community of hardy individualists, McCarthy had a population near 2,000 in mining days.

From McCarthy, a dirt road climbs 500 feet in 5 miles to the former town and millsite of **Kennecott.** You can take a bus or rent a bike in McCarthy if you prefer not to walk. Kennecott was once the site of the world's richest copper mine. From 1906 to its closing in 1938, it yielded 591,000 tons of copper and 900,000 ounces of silver. Today, the silent 13-story mill and other Kennecott buildings are still dressed in mineral oxide red with white trim. Currently being renovated, they form one of

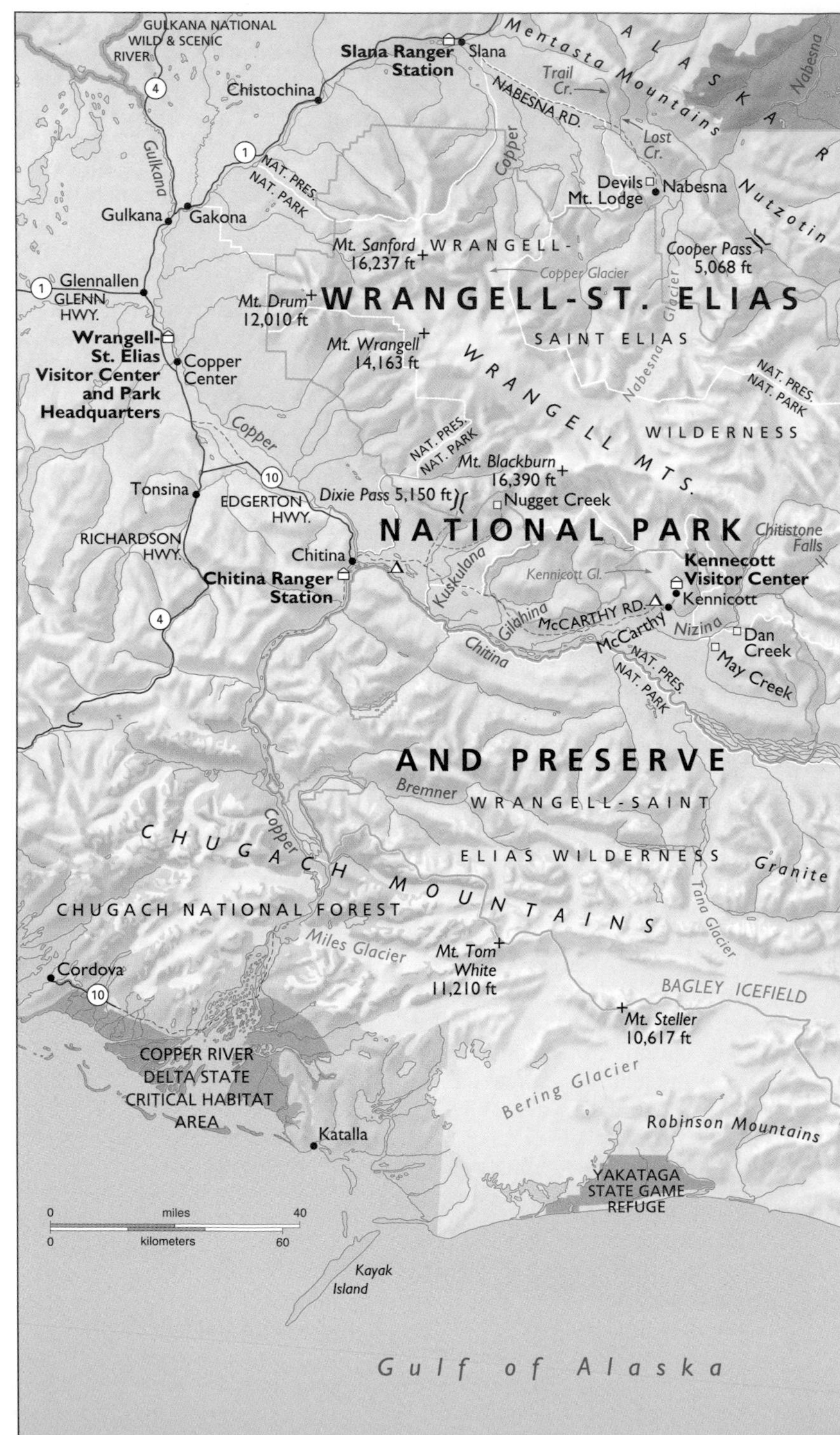
GULKANA NATIONAL WILD & SCENIC RIVER
Slana Ranger Station
Slana
Mentasta Mountains
ALASKA R
Nabesna
Trail Cr.
NABESNA RD.
Lost Cr.
Chistochina
Gulkana
Copper
NAT. PRES.
NAT. PARK
Devils Mt. Lodge
Nabesna
Nutzotin
Gulkana
Gakona
Mt. Sanford 16,237 ft
WRANGELL-
Cooper Pass 5,068 ft
Copper Glacier
Glennallen
GLENN HWY.
Mt. Drum 12,010 ft
WRANGELL-ST. ELIAS
SAINT ELIAS
Wrangell-St. Elias Visitor Center and Park Headquarters
Copper Center
Mt. Wrangell 14,163 ft
WRANGELL MTS.
Nabesna Glacier
WILDERNESS
Copper
Mt. Blackburn 16,390 ft
Tonsina
EDGERTON HWY.
Dixie Pass 5,150 ft
Nugget Creek
NATIONAL PARK
Chitistone Falls
RICHARDSON HWY.
Chitina
Kennecott Visitor Center
Kennicott Gl.
Kuskulana
Chitina Ranger Station
Kennicott
McCARTHY RD.
Gilahina
McCarthy
Nizina
Dan Creek
May Creek
Chitina
AND PRESERVE
Bremner
WRANGELL-SAINT ELIAS WILDERNESS
CHUGACH MOUNTAINS
Copper
Granite
CHUGACH NATIONAL FOREST
Tana Glacier
Miles Glacier
Mt. Tom White 11,210 ft
Cordova
BAGLEY ICEFIELD
Mt. Steller 10,617 ft
COPPER RIVER DELTA STATE CRITICAL HABITAT AREA
Bering Glacier
Robinson Mountains
Katalla
YAKATAGA STATE GAME REFUGE
0 miles 40
0 kilometers 60
Kayak Island
Gulf of Alaska
1
4
10

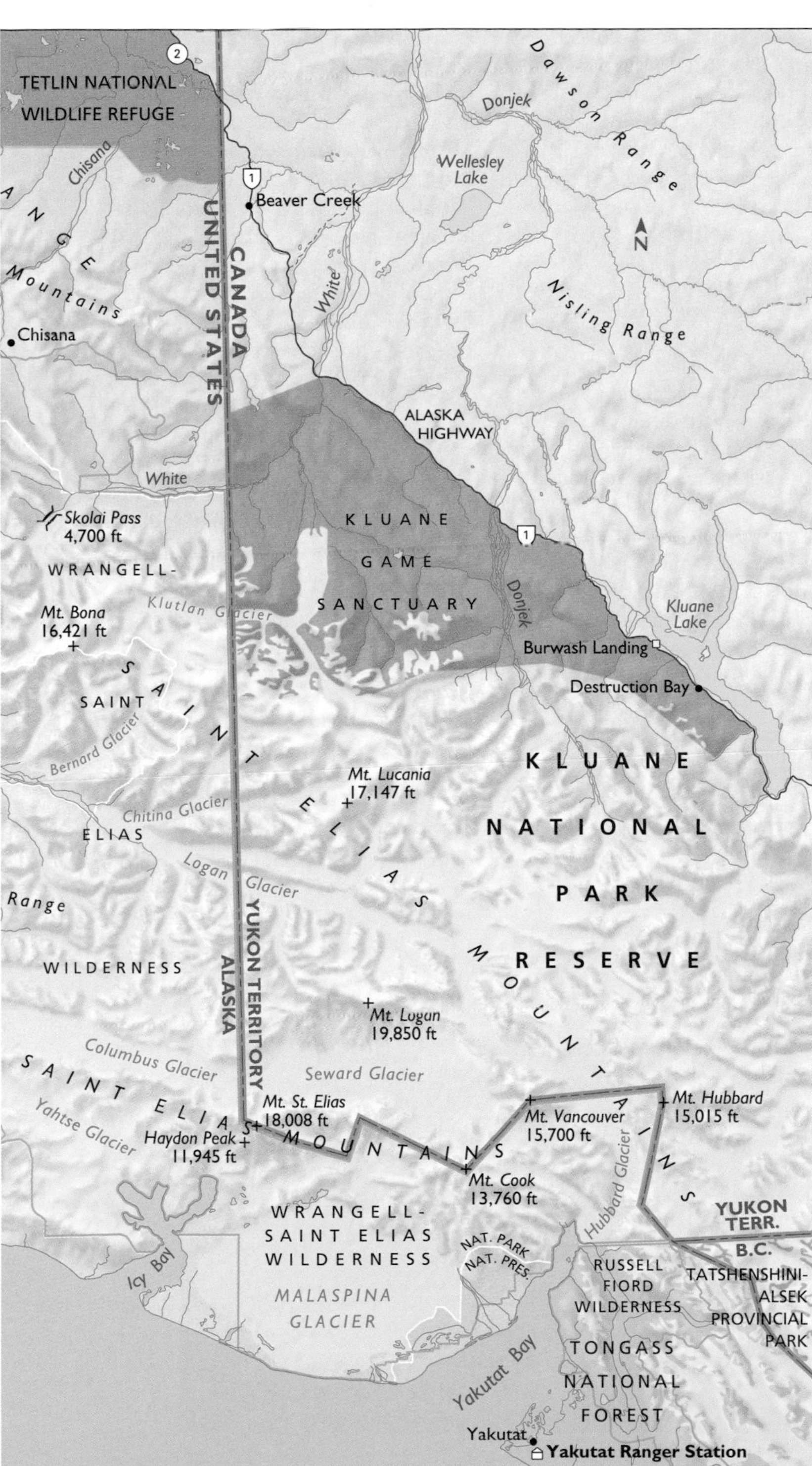
TETLIN NATIONAL
WILDLIFE REFUGE
Chisana
Beaver Creek
UNITED STATES
CANADA
Dawson Range
Donjek
Wellesley Lake
White
Mountains
Chisana
Nisling Range
ALASKA HIGHWAY
White
Skolai Pass
4,700 ft
KLUANE
GAME
SANCTUARY
WRANGELL-
Klutlan Glacier
Mt. Bona
16,421 ft
Donjek
Kluane Lake
Burwash Landing
Destruction Bay
SAINT
Bernard Glacier
KLUANE
Mt. Lucania
17,147 ft
Chitina Glacier
NATIONAL
ELIAS
Logan Glacier
PARK
Range
YUKON TERRITORY
ALASKA
RESERVE
WILDERNESS
SAINT ELIAS MOUNTAINS
Mt. Logan
19,850 ft
Columbus Glacier
Seward Glacier
Yahtse Glacier
Mt. St. Elias
18,008 ft
Haydon Peak
11,945 ft
Mt. Vancouver
15,700 ft
Mt. Hubbard
15,015 ft
Mt. Cook
13,760 ft
Hubbard Glacier
YUKON TERR.
B.C.
WRANGELL-
SAINT ELIAS
WILDERNESS
NAT. PARK
NAT. PRES.
RUSSELL
FIORD
WILDERNESS
TATSHENSHINI-
ALSEK
PROVINCIAL
PARK
Icy Bay
MALASPINA
GLACIER
Yakutat Bay
TONGASS
NATIONAL
FOREST
Yakutat
Yakutat Ranger Station
N

Alaska's most photogenic collections of historic structures and are on the National Register of Historic Places. After exploring the town of Kennecott, you can hike the trail north of town for spectacular views of the Kennicott and Root Glaciers.

NABESNA ROAD

42 miles one way; a half day

Since parts of this road into the **Wrangell Mountains** are subject to washouts, check conditions with the park before you set out. Beginning in **Slana,** the road passes homesteads and fishing camps on privately owned land and then climbs over the watershed divide (mile 25) between the **Copper River,** which drains into the Gulf of Alaska, and the **Nabesna River,** which drains into the **Tanana,** the Yukon, and finally the Bering Sea. There are excellent views of **Mount Sanford** and the **Copper Glacier** to the southwest. The final 4 miles, from **Devil's Mountain Lodge** to **Nabesna,** are the most rugged.

OTHER HIKES & WATER TRIPS

At mile 13.5 on the McCarthy Road, the **Nugget Creek-Kotsina Road** branches northeast 2.5 miles to the **Nugget Creek Trail.** A thousand feet higher and 16 miles later, the trail arrives at a public-use cabin beneath Mount Blackburn, where you can picnic and camp. A dozen day hikes can be taken from here. Watch for Dall's sheep. A little more than a mile past the Nugget Creek trailhead begins the **Dixie Pass Trail.** Climbing 3,600 feet in 10 miles, it's a strenuous hike, but worth it if the weather is clear.

Off the Nabesna Road, **Trail Creek** at mile 30 and **Lost Creek** at mile 30.8 offer good hiking routes. Little of the route's trails are defined; simply follow the creek beds northward as far as you like. Though the hiking is not generally difficult, you will run into rocky patches and may have to hop or wade the creeks. But you will be rewarded with excellent views of the upper Copper River basin. Talk to a ranger and fill out a backcountry itinerary before any overnight stays.

Commercial outfitters offer rafting trips down the **Nabesna, Copper, Kennicott, Chitina,** and **Nizina Rivers.** Short trips last 3 hours; extended ones two weeks. There are all classes of water. It's an adventuresome way to see Wrangell-St. Elias. Contact the park for a full listing of the outfitters that operate there.

Kennecott Mine, silent since 1938

INFORMATION & ACTIVITIES

HEADQUARTERS
P.O. Box 439, Copper Center, AK 99573. Phone (907) 822-5234. www.nps.gov/wrst

SEASONS & ACCESSIBILITY
Park open year-round, but best time is mid-May through Sept. Snow limits winter access. Call headquarters for road conditions before attempting to drive to the park.

VISITOR & INFORMATION CENTERS
Park headquarters at mile 106.8 on Old Richardson Highway at western edge of park. Open daily Memorial Day through Labor Day, weekdays the rest of year. Information also available at **Yakutat, Slana,** and **Chitina Ranger Stations,** all outside park boundaries. Chitina closed Oct. through May.

ENTRANCE FEE
None.

PETS
Permitted on leashes except in public buildings; permitted off leashes in the backcountry.

FACILITIES FOR DISABLED
None.

THINGS TO DO
No park-organized activities, but the following are available: hiking, horseback riding (rentals in McCarthy), pack trips, river running, kayaking, jet-boat rentals, lake fishing, mountain climbing, air tours, cross-country skiing. Ask park for list of companies that offer guide and outfitting services, or visit the park website at www.nps.gov/wrst/wrstcommercialservices.htm.

SPECIAL ADVISORIES
- This is a wilderness park; hikers and backpackers must be wholly self-sufficient; do not attempt the backcountry without a guide unless you're experienced and equipped.
- Choose your river crossings carefully; many rivers are impassable.
- Be respectful of native camps, fishnets, and other private property.
- Mosquitoes can be brutal in June, July, and August; bring repellent, a head net, and an insect-proof tent.

OVERNIGHT BACKPACKING
Permit not required, but best to register before going into backcountry.

CAMPGROUNDS & CABINS
Two private campgrounds within park: **Silver Lake Campground** (milepost 9.3 on McCarthy Road) offers camping and limited services. **Tram Station Campground** and **Glacier View Campground** at end of McCarthy Road. Camping also available at several roadside pull-outs along Nabesna Road. First come, first served. No fee. The park also maintains 12 public-use cabins. Fees $15 per night. Contact headquarters for information.

HOTELS, MOTELS, & INNS
(unless otherwise noted, rates are for 2 persons in a double room, high season)

INSIDE THE PARK:

Kennicott Glacier Lodge (in Kennecott) P.O. Box 103940, Anchorage, AK 99510. (800) 582-5128 or (907) 258-2350. 25 rooms shared baths;$189.10 rooms private baths; $249. Per person, includes meals.

OUTSIDE THE PARK:

Copper Center Lodge (mile 101.5 on Old Richardson Hwy.) Drawer J, Copper Center, AK 99573. (907) 822-3245. 21 rooms, 11 with private baths. $119-$139. Restaurant.

Gakona Lodge (on Alas. 1, north of Glennallen) P.O. Box 285, Gakona, AK 99586. (907) 822-3482. 8 rooms, shared baths $95. Open May through Sept. Restaurant.

Contact headquarters for additional accommodations in and near the park.

ACKNOWLEDGMENTS

We are indebted to the many individuals and the federal, state, and private agencies that helped prepare this guide, especially to the National Park Service and the superintendents and chiefs of interpretation and their staffs at each park.

ILLUSTRATIONS CREDITS

Abbreviations for terms appearing below: (t)-top; (b)-bottom; (l)-left; (r)-right; (c)-center; PBS-Biological Photo Service; NGS-National Geographic Society Image Collection; NPS-National Park Service PR-Photo Researchers, Inc.; TGP-Terra Galleria Photography.

Cover, Ron Watts/CORBIS; 2-3, QT Luong/TGP; 4, QT Luong/TGP; 6-7, Galen Rowell/CORBIS; 8, QT Luong/TGP.

The East

12 (t), Tom Jones; (c), Stephen J. Krasemann/Peter Arnold, Inc.; (b), David Muench; 13, QT Luong/TGP; 18, Adam Jones/Getty Images; 20, Angelo Lomeo; 24, Raymond Gehman/CORBIS; 25, Alan Nyiri; 27 (t), Bill Silliker, Jr.; (c), Joel Sartore/www.joelsartore.com; (b), Jeff Lepore/PR; 28, QT Luong/TGP; 29, QT Luong/TGP; 31, QT Luong/TGP; 32, Brian Skerry/NGS; 33 (t), QT Luong/TGP; (cl), Charles V. Angelo/PR; (cr)&(bl)&(br), Stephen Frink; 35 (t), James Valentine; (c), C.C. Lockwood; (b), Caulion Singletary; 36, Raymond Gehman; 37, Raymond Gehman; 40, QT Luong/TGP; 41, Michael S. Quinton/NGS; 43 (t), Arthur Morris/CORBIS; (b), David Muench/CORBIS; 44, Tom Jones; 47, Tom Jones; 48, Tom Jones; 50, Matt Bradley; 52, Matt Bradley; 54, James P. Blair; 58, QT Luong/TGP; 59, Stephen J. Krasemann/Peter Arnold, Inc.; 61 (tl), Bianca Lavies; (tr), NPS; (cl), Jim Kern Expeditions; (cr), Fred Hirschmann; (b), Raymond Gehman/CORBIS; 63 (t), James Valentine; (c), Farrell Grehan; (b), QT Luong/TGP; 64, Marc Muench/CORBIS; 68, Dennis Flaherty; 69 (t), NPS; (b), Raymond Gehman/CORBIS; 70, Raymond Gehman; 72 (t), Larry Ulrich; (c), David Muench/CORBIS; (b), Dick Durrance II; 73 (t), James Randklev/CORBIS; (c), David Muench/CORBIS; (b), James Valentine; 74, QT Luong/TGP; 75, Matt Bradley; 78, Matt Bradley; 79 (t), Richard Hamilton Smith/CORBIS; (c)&(b), Matt Bradley; 80, Tom Bean/CORBIS; 83, John & Ann Mahan; 84, Jim Brandenburg/Minden Pictures; 86 (t), John & Ann Mahan; (c), Richard Hamilton Smith/CORBIS; (b), John & Ann Mahan; 87 (t), John & Ann Mahan; (c), Carl R. Sams; (b), Photographer/PR; 88, Chip Clark; 90-91, Richard Schlecht; 91 (l) & (r), Chip Clark; 92, Laurence Parent; 92-93, Richard Schlecht; 95 (t), Dan J. Dry; (b), David Muench/CORBIS; 96, NPS; 100, NPS; 101, George Grall/NGS; 103 (t), Carr Clifton; (c), David Muench/CORBIS; (b), Jeff Lepore/PR; 104, M. Dillon/CORBIS; 108, Jodi Cobb/NGS; 111, Stephen Frink; 112, John & Ann Mahan; 113, Erwin & Peggy Bauer; 116, Richard Olsenius; 117 (t), Erwin & Peggy Bauer; (b), Terraphotographics/BPS; 119 (t), John & Ann Mahan; (c), Jim Zipp/PR; (b), Richard Hamilton Smith/CORBIS.

The Southwest

120 (t), Larry Ulrich; (c), George F. Mobley, NGS; (b), David Muench; 121, QT Luong/TGP; 124, QT Luong/TGP; 125, Matt Bradley; 128, William Manning/CORBIS; 129, Larry Ulrich; 130, George F. Mobley, NGS; 131 (l), Jim Steinberg/PR; (r), Tom Bean; 132, Bruce Dale/NGS; 133, David Muench/CORBIS; 134, Adam Woolfitt/CORBIS; 138, Walter Meayers Edwards/NGS; 139, QT Luong/TGP; 141 (t), Wendy Shattil/Bob Rozinski; (c), Lewis Kemper; (b), Wendy Shattil/Bob Rozinski; 142, Jonathan Blair/CORBIS.

The Colorado Plateau

148 (t), Farrell Grehan; (c)& (b), Larry Ulrich; 149, Tom & Pat Leeson; 152, Tom & Pat Leeson; 153, NPS; 156, QT Luong/TGP; 157, NPS; 159 (t), Farrell Grehan; (b), Larry Ulrich; 160, Larry Ulrich; 161, Fred Hirschmann; 163, Grant Haist; 165 (t), Fred Hirschmann; (c), Raymond Gehman/CORBIS; (b), Pat O'Hara; 166, QT Luong/TGP; 167, David Muench; 169, Gary Vestal; 170, NPS; 171, Walter M. Edwards/NGS; 172 (t), Gary Vestal; (b), Pat O'Hara; 174 (t), Tom Till Photography; (c), Farrell Grehan; (b), Donna Ikenberry/Animals Animals; 175 (t), Larry Ulrich; (b), Neil Rabinowitz/CORBIS; 176, Gordon Anderson; 177, Larry Ulrich; 178, Charlie Borland/Wild Vision Photo; 180 (l), David Muench/CORBIS; (r), QT Luong/TGP; 182, Larry Ulrich; 187, Jack Dykinga; 188, George H. H. Huey; 189, Ned Seidler/NGS; 191 (t), Jeff Gnass; (c), Larry Ulrich; (b), Jeff Gnass; 192, David Muench/CORBIS; 193, David Muench; 195 (t), Larry Ulrich; (b), Larry Ulrich; 197 (t), QT Luong/TGP; (c)& (bl), Richard Olsenius; (br), QT Luong/TGP; 199 (t), Jack Olson; (c), Joe McDonald/CORBIS; (b), Jan Nachlinger; 200, David Muench; 205, NPS; 207 (t), Larry Ulrich; 207 (c)&(b), Tom Till Photography; 208, Tom Algire; 213 (t)& (c), Fred Hirschmann; (b), George H. H. Huey; 214, George H. H. Huey; 217 (t), QT Luong/TGP; (b), George H. H. Huey; 219 (t), David Muench/CORBIS; (c), AP/Wide World Photos; (b), Joe Raedle/Getty Images; 220, QT Luong/TGP; 221, James Randklev; 222, Fred Hirschmann; 224 (tl), David Muench; (tr)&(c), QT Luong/TGP; (bl), Jeff Lepore/PR; (br), Fred Hirschmann; 226, Pat O'Hara.

The Pacific Southwest

228 (t), Steve Raymer/NGS; (c), Harald Sund; (b), QT Luong/TGP; 229, Jeff Gnass; 232, QT Luong/TGP; 234, Jeff Gnass; 235, Roy Toft/NGS; 239 (t), Caroline Sheen; (b), David Muench; 240, Carr Clifton; 244, David Muench; 246, Larry Dale Gordon/CORBIS; 251 (t), David Muench; (c), NPS; (b), Robert J. Western/NPS; 253 (t), Jeff Gnass; (b), Douglas Peebles/CORBIS; 254, CORBIS; 255, Douglas Peebles/CORBIS; 258, Paul A. Souders/CORBIS; 259 (t), Darodents/PacificStock.com; (b), Jeff Gnass; 261 (t), Roger Ressmeyer/Starlight Collection/CORBIS; (b), Joseph Sohm; ChromoSohm Inc/CORBIS; 262, Harald Sund; 266, NPS; 268, QT Luong/TGP; 273, Galen Rowell/CORBIS; 275 (t)& (b), Pat O'Hara; (c), NPS; 276, Dewitt Jones; 281, Pat O'Hara; 283 (tl), Steve Raymer/NGS; (tr), Jim Brandenburg/Minden Pictures; (b), QT Luong/TGP; 285 (t), Pat O'Hara; (c), Lewis Kemper; (b), QT Luong/TGP.

The Rocky Mountains

286 (t), Joel W. Rogers/CORBIS; (c), Pat O'Hara; (b), Larry Ulrich; 287, Jim Brandenburg/Minden Pictures; 290, QT Luong/TGP; 294, Thomas J. Abercrombie/NGS; 296, Larry Ulrich; 297, David Muench/CORBIS; 300, George H. H. Huey; 301, Michael Lewis/CORBIS; 302, Tom Danielsen; 305, QT Luong/TGP; 306, Pat O'Hara; 308 (t), NPS; (cl)&(br), QT Luong/TGP; (cr), K.D. McGraw; (bl), Scott Rutherford; 311 (t), Raymond Gehman; (c), Pat O'Hara; (b), Charles Gurche; 312, George H. H. Huey; 316 (t), George H. H. Huey; (b), Taylor S. Kennedy/NGS; 317, Wendy Shattil/Bob Rozinski; 318, Wendy Shattil/Bob Rozinski; 320, QT Luong/TGP; 323, Linde Waidhofer; 325, Wendy Shattil/Bob Rozinski; 326, Leonard Lee Rue III; 328 (t), CORBIS; (c), Tom Bean/CORBIS; (b), Wendy Shattil/Bob Rozinski; 329 (t), John Fielder; 329 (c), Wendy Shattil/Bob Rozinski; (b), Tom Bean/CORBIS; 330, Layne Kennedy/CORBIS; 331, Steven C. Kaufman; 334 (t), QT Luong/TGP; (c), Jim Brandenburg/Minden Pictures; (b), Steven C. Kaufman; 337 (t), David Muench; (c), Herbert Kehrer/zefa/CORBIS; (b), Bates Littlehales/NGS; 338, Lowell Georgia/NGS; 342, Steven C. Kaufman; 344, Buddy Mays/CORBIS; 346 (t), Lowell Georgia /NGS; (c), Brian A. Vikander/CORBIS; (b), George Wuerthner; 347 (t), Joel W. Rogers/CORBIS; (b), Rod Planck/PR; 348, QT Luong/TGP; 350, Francois Gohier/PR; 353 (t), Rod Planck/PR; (c), NPS; (b), Joel Strasser; 354, NPS; 355, Dean Krakel II; 358, Steven Fuller; 359, Jim Brandenburg/Minden Pictures; 360, Jim Brandenburg/Minden Pictures; 361 (t), Craig Fujii/The Seattle Times; (b), Tom Danielsen; 363 (t), Pat O'Hara; (c), Laurance B. Aiuppy; (bl), Farrell Grehan; (br), Jeff Vanuga; 365 (t), Pat O'Hara; (c), Wayne Lankinen; (b), Randy Ury.

The Pacific Northwest

366 (t), Charles Mauzy/CORBIS; (c), Steve Terrill; (b), Jeff Gnass; 367, Pat O'Hara; 370, James A. Sugar/BLACK STAR; 374, Steve Terrill; 376 (t), Raymond Gehman/CORBIS; (c), Larry Ulrich; (b), Jeff Gnass; 377 (t), Steve Terrill; (b), Farrell Grehan; 378, Ron Watts/CORBIS; 383 (t), Pat O'Hara; (b), Jeff Gnass; 384, Art Wolfe/ArtWolfe.com; 388, Galen Rowell/CORBIS; 389 (t), Darrell Gulin/CORBIS; (b), Art Wolfe/ArtWolfe.com; 390, Steve Terrill; 391 (tl)&(cr), Pat O'Hara; (tr)&(cl), Farrell Grehan; (bl), Charles Mauzy/CORBIS; (br), George F. Mobley; 393 (t), Pat O'Hara; (c), Layne Kennedy/CORBIS; (b), Darrell Gulin/CORBIS; 394, Pat O'Hara; 398, Pat O'Hara/CORBIS; 401 (t)&(b), Pat O'Hara; (c), Art Wolfe/ArtWolfe.com; 402, Pat O'Hara; 407, David M. Seager; 410, David Muench; 414, QT Luong/TGP; 417 (t), Richard R. Hansen/PR; (b), Jean Hawthorne/Six Rivers National Forest.

Alaska

418 (t), Michio Hoshino/Minden Pictures; (c), Tom Bean; (b), Fred Hirschmann; 419, George Herben; 422, QT Luong/TGP; 426, QT Luong/TGP; 428 (tl), John Eastcott and Yva Momatiuk/NGS; (tr), Joel Sartore/www.joelsartore.com; (b), QT Luong/TGP; 430 (t), NPS; (c), Marc Muench/Getty Images; (b), Paul Souders/Getty Images; 431 (t), Len Rue, Jr.; (c), Michael Melford; (b), Kennan Ward/CORBIS; 432, QT Luong/TGP; 433, QT Luong/TGP; 436 (t), QT Luong/TGP; (b), Fred Hirschmann, 438, Tom Bean; 442, Joel Sartore/NGS; 444, Fred Hirschmann; 448, QT Luong/TGP; 450, QT Luong/TGP; 454 (t), Momatiuk & Eastcott/Animals Animals; (cl), Art Wolfe/PR; (cr), Boyd Norton; (b), George Herben; 456, QT Luong/TGP; 459, Len Rue, Jr.; 460 (t), Michio Hoshino/Minden Pictures; (c), Tim Thompson; (b), Michael Melford; 461, Pat O'Hara; 462, Will Troyer; 465, Fred Hirschmann; 466 (t)&(bl), Fred Hirschmann; (br), Victoria McCormick/Animals Animals; 468, Kim Heacox; 472, Dicon Joseph/AccentAlaska.com.

Back cover: (t) Tom Jones; (cl) George F. Mobley, NGS; (cr) Harald Sund; (b) Lowell Georgia/NGS.

INDEX

Index Abbreviations

Bureau of Land Management = BLM
National Forest = NF
National Historic Park = NHP
National Marine Sanctuary = NMS
National Monument = NM
National Park = NP
National Recreation Area = NRA
National Recreation Trail = NRT
National Wildlife Refuge = NWR
State Park = SP

A

B

Printed and bound by Print Plus, China. Color separations by Quad Graphics, Alexandria, Virginia.

MAP KEY and ABBREVIATIONS

- National Park .... N.P.
- National Park and Preserve .... N.P. & Pres.
- National Preserve .... Nat. Pres.
- National Conservation Area .... N.C.A.
- National Historical Park .... N.H.P.
- National Memorial .... Nat. Mem.
- National Monument .... Nat. Mon.
- National Natural Landmark .... N.N.L.
- National Recreation Area .... N.R.A.

- National Forest .... N.F., Nat. For.
- National Recreation Area .... N.R.A.
- National Volcanic Monument .... N.V.M.
- State Forest .... S.F.

- National Wildlife Refuge .... N.W.R.
- National Wildlife Range
- State Game Refuge
- State Game Sanctuary .... S.G.S.
- State Wildlife Area
- Habitat Area

- National Grassland

- Bureau of Land Management .... B.L.M.
- National Monument (B.L.M.) .... Nat. Mon.
- National Recreation Area (B.L.M.) .... N.R.A.

- State Park .... S.P.
- State Historic Site .... S.H.S.
- State Primitive Park
- State Recreation Area .... S.R.A.
- State Wilderness Park .... S.W.P.
- Provincial Park .... P.P.
- County Park

- Indian Reservation .... I.R.
- Reserve (Canada)

- Built-up Area

U.S. Interstate 5
U.S. Federal, State or Provincial Highway 50 33 1
Other Road J59
Unpaved Road
Trail
Ferry
Railroad / Tram
Continental Divide
Fault Line
Wilderness Area
National Marine Sanctuary
National Wild & Scenic River
Military Reservation
National boundary
State boundary

- State capital / Provincial capital
- Ranger Station / Visitor Center / Park Headquarters
- Point of interest
- Campground
- Picnic area
- Overlook / Viewpoint
- Elevation
- Pass
- Tunnel
- Dam
- Intermittent river
- Intermittent lake
- Dry lake
- Sand dunes
- Falls
- Spring
- Geyser
- Glacier
- Swamp
- Reef
- Shipwreck

POPULATION

DENVER	above 500,000
Sacramento	50,000 to 500,000
Helena	10,000 to 50,000
Morton	under 10,000

OTHER ABBREVIATIONS

Admin.	Administrative
AVE.	Avenue
Cr.	Creek
DR.	Drive
E.	East
Fk.	Fork
ft.	feet
Gl.	Glacier
Hdqrs.	Headquarters
HWY.	Highway
I.-s.	Island-s
L.	Lake
M.	Middle
Mt.-s.	Mount-ain-s
N.	North
NAT.	National
N.M.S.	National Marine Sanctuary
N.S.T.	National Scenic Trail
Pk.	Peak
PKWY.	Parkway
P.P.	Provincial Park
PRES.	Preserve
Pt.	Point
R.	River
Ra.	Range
RD.	Road
Rec.	Recreation
Res.	Reservoir
S.	South
ST.	Street
TERR.	Territory
TR.	Trail
U.S.F.S.	United States Forest Service
W.	West
WILD.	Wilderness

Published by
The National Geographic Society

Staff for 2006 Edition

Caroline Hickey, *Project Manager*
Jane Sunderland, *Editor*
Cinda Rose, *Art Director*
Melanie Doherty Design, *Designer*
Jennifer Davis, *Illustrations Editor*
Thomas B. Allen, John L. Culliney, Carole Douglis, Kim Heacox, Catherine Herbert Howell, Gary Krist, Mark Miller, Jeremy Schmidt, Gene S. Stuart, John M. Thompson, Scott Thybony, Mel White,
Writers
Marty Christian, *Copy Editor*
Janet Dustin, *Illustrations Manager*
Matt Chwastyk, Steven Gardner, Thomas L. Gray, Nicholas P. Rosenbach, Gregory Ugiansky, Mapping Specialists, and XNR Productions
Map Edit, Research, & Production
Amy Jicha, *Researcher*
Dianne Hosmer, *Indexer*
R. Gary Colbert, *Production Director*
Richard S. Wain, *Production Project Manager*
John Dunn, *Technical Director*
Barbara Noe, *Contributor*

Founded in 1888, the National Geographic Society is one of the largest nonprofit scientific and educational organizations in the world. It reaches more than 285 million people worldwide each month through its official journal, *National Geographic*, and its four other magazines; the National Geographic Channel; television documentaries; radio programs; films; books; videos and DVDs; maps; and interactive media. National Geographic has funded more than 8,000 scientific research projects and supports an education program combating geographic illiteracy.

For more information, please call 1-800-NGS LINE (647-5463) or write to the following address:

National Geographic Society
1145 17th Street N.W.
Washington, D.C. 20036-4688 U.S.A.

Log on to nationalgeographic.com;
AOL Keyword:NatGeo.

This 2007 edition printed for Barnes & Noble, Inc, by National Geographic.
Fifth Edition:
ISBN: 978-1-4351-2950-4

Printed in China

12/PPS/3